Praise for **WIGMORE ON ALCOHOL**

"It will certainly be the new Alcohol Bible for decades to come, and be of great value to active practitioners and researchers."

— Dr. Kurt M. Dubowski,
George Lynn Cross Distinguished Professor Emeritus of Medicine,
University of Oklahoma

"This book is a must for anyone who is working on medicolegal issues involving alcohol. It will be appreciated by lay persons interested in this topic as well as scientific and legal experts involved in alcohol-related medicolegal issues."

— Thomas L. Pazdernik, PhD, University of Kansas Medical Center

"In short, *Wigmore on Alcohol* is a wonderful research tool that will prove a valuable resource in both legal and scientific libraries."

— Justice Rick Libman, Judge, Ontario Court of Justice

"I regret that *Wigmore on Alcohol* was not available to me during my years of active practice in forensic science."

— Doug Lucas, MSc, PhD (Hons),
Retired Director of the Centre of Forensic Sciences, Toronto

"In summary, this work provides scientist and non-scientist, student and expert alike with a source of relevant articles to assist them in learning about, understand or deepening their knowledge of alcohol toxicology."

— Canadian Society of Forensic Science Journal

"I worked in the insurance industry for many, many years and I have attended mediations, discoveries and trials. I have also published articles and presented at seminars. Your book would have been of such a help as a reference had it been available .... It's certainly one that could and should be used by the Insurance Industry, the Law Society and Police Departments across the country."

— *Carolan Shannon, RN, Claims Consultant*

WIGMORE ON CANNABIS

WIGMORE ON CANNABIS

The Forensic Toxicology of Marijuana for Lawyers and Other Medicolegal Professionals

JAMES G. WIGMORE

IRWIN LAW

Wigmore on Cannabis: The Forensic Toxicology of Marijuana for Lawyers and Other Medicolegal Professionals

James G. Wigmore
Forensic Alcohol Toxicologist
283 Danforth Ave., Suite 517
Toronto, ON M4K 1N2
james.wigmore@rogers.com
www.wigmoreonalcohol.com

Published in 2018 by
Irwin Law Inc.
14 Duncan Street, Suite 206
Toronto, ON M5H 3G8
www.irwinlaw.com

ISBN 978-1-55221-484-8
e-book ISBN 978-1-55221-485-5

Cataloguing in Publication available from Library and Archives Canada

Ontario Media Development Corporation
Société de développement de l'industrie des médias de l'Ontario

Printed and bound by CPI Group (UK) Ltd, Croydon, CR0 4YY

1 2 3 4 5 22 21 20 19 18

This book is dedicated to Dr. Natalie Marmur of the Toronto East General Hospital (now the Michael Garron Hospital); Dr. Mark Petersen, Nurse Practitioner Marnee Wilson, and Dr. Howard Leong-Poi of St. Michael's Hospital; and Yvonne Dover and the staff of the Toronto Rehabilitation Institute (University Health Network), whose knowledge, skill, expertise, and passion have improved, enriched, and saved the lives of many.

Summary Table of Contents

Detailed Table of Contents

CHAPTER 2
BLOOD CANNABINOIDS 37

CHAPTER 3
ORAL FLUID CANNABINOIDS 46

CHAPTER 4
CANNABINOIDS IN BREATH, URINE, HAIR, SWEAT, AND BIOMARKERS OF CANNABIS USE 74

CHAPTER 5

EFFECTS OF CANNABINOIDS ON DRIVING ABILITY *106*

CHAPTER 6

EFFECTS OF CANNABIS ON HEALTH AND OTHER BEHAVIOURS *194*

List of Tables

(Reference number in bold parentheses)

- Mean Day of Urine First Negative THCCOOH Test and Time of Last Positive THCCOOH Test in Three Groups with Initial Urine THCCOOH of 0-50 ng/mL, 51 to 150 ng/mL, and >150 ng/mL **(40217)**
- Percent Positive Hair Cannabinoids Detected in Non-, Light, and Heavy Users of Marijuana **(40306)**
- Concentrations of THCCOOH Found in the Hair of 6 Cannabis Users and 3 Non-Users **(40309)**
- THC Concentrations in Hair Samples without and with Washing (Three times with 5 mL of Methanol) [Note ND = not detected] **(40310)**
- Neonatal Growth Comparisons Independent of Tobacco Results, According to Meconium Cannabinoid Results **(40508)**
- Tracking Test (Percent of Time-Simulated Car in the Lane) at 2.5, 4, 5.5, and 10 Hours after Drug Administration **(50205)**
- Mean Distance (Metres) from the Traffic Sign at which the Correct Recognition Was Made after Placebo, Alcohol, and/or Cannabis Use **(50301)**
- Standard Deviation of Lane Position (SDLP) and Time to Speed Adaptation (TSA) in a Car-Following Task **(50404)**
- Percentage of Cases for Non-RTC (comparison) and RTC Cases at Each THC Concentration Group **(50503)**
- Index of Responsibility (Percent Responsible/Percent Not Responsible) According to the Presence of Alcohol and/or Cannabis **(50509)**
- Odds Ratio (OR) of an Injured Driver with a BAC > 0.08 g/100 mL or Blood THC > 3 ng/mL **(50511)**
- Culpability Ratio (Drivers Responsible/Drivers Not Responsible) for Alcohol, THC, Benzodiazepines, and Opioids **(50515)**
- Comparison of the Odds Ratio for Alcohol and Cannabis Using the Standard Case Control and QIE Models **(50523)**
- Odds Ratio of Driving Error/Violation with Cannabis, Alcohol, or Combination **(50524)**
- Percent of Injured Drivers with a Positive BAC or Positive Blood THC with Age **(50526)**
- Alcohol and Cannabis Detected in Drivers of Single or Multi-Vehicle Fatal Motor Vehicle Collisions (FMVC) **(50527)**

- Percentage of Reported Conditions of Colorado Medical Marijuana Registrants (Note: Some patients registered for multiple conditions) **(61117)**
- Mean Age of Onset of Psychosis by Degree of Exposure to Cannabis **(61402)**
- Odds Ratio of Psychosis with Increasing Use of Skunk **(61403)**
- Odds Ratio of Relapse of Psychosis with Cannabis Use **(61407)**
- Adjusted Odds Ratio of Psychosis According to Drug **(61410)**
- Adjusted Odds Ratio for Panic Attack and Disorder after Lifetime or 12-Month Cannabis Use **(61411)**
- Mean Global Assessment of Functioning (GAF) Score by Cannabis Use Group [Note: The higher the GAF score, the better the recovery] **(61419)**
- Odds Ratio of Various Respiratory Symptoms in Current Cannabis Use Compared to Non-Users **(61604)**
- Cannabis and Tobacco Use as Continuous Variables and Risk of Lung Cancer **(61611)**
- Drugs Found in the Blood and Urine of Female Sexual Assault Victims **(61702)**
- Some Responses after Smoking Placebo, One-half of 1.77%, 1.77%, and 3.58% THC joints **(61704)**
- Twenty-Three Sexual Assault Cases in which Three or More Illicit Drugs Were Detected **(61709)**
- Teens' Perceptions of Pros and Cons of Edible Cannabis **(61710)**
- Percent of Male Alcohol/Drug Users Who Intentionally Employ Them for Sexual Purposes **(61713)**
- Frequency of Past-Year Marijuana Use in Male and Female Athletes and Non-Athletes Who Smoked Cannabis **(61803)**
- Global Odds Ratio of Using Doping Agents and Recreational Drug Use in Pre-Adolescent Athletes **(61804)**
- The Odds Ratio (OR) of Participants in Contact, Semi-Contact, and Non-Contact Sports of Substance Use, Compared to Non-Participants of Sports **(61807)**
- Adjusted Odds Ratio According to Suicide Method and Use of Alcohol, Cannabis, or Central Stimulants **(61901)**
- Percentage of Cases in which a Drug Was Detected in Male and Female Suicide Victims and the Odds Ratio According to Gender of Using that Drug **(61903)**

Foreword

In the current "Information Age," with so much information available on the internet, it is becoming harder to separate the wheat from the chaff, validated information from anecdotal, subjective, speculative, or even unfounded information. Into this era, for those interested in forensic toxicology, we have, among others, James Wigmore. For over thirty years, Jim has been compiling a database of papers in forensic alcohol toxicology in order to provide an objective record of how alcohol affects the body and behaviour, but also, more importantly, to debunk those opinions not supported by the scientific literature. He initially provided this information to his colleagues in the toxicology section at the Centre of Forensic Sciences in Toronto, Ontario, to members of the Canadian Society of Forensic Science's Alcohol Test Committee (a national committee in Canada that provides advice on alcohol and alcohol testing to Canada's federal minister of justice), and to students of the Borkenstein Breath Course in the United States. Following his retirement, he consolidated his alcohol database to the essential papers and published them in *Wigmore on Alcohol: Courtroom Alcohol Toxicology for the Medicolegal Professional* in 2011.

Following that publication, Jim realized that the medicolegal community needed similar databases on other drugs. The obvious first choice is cannabis. From our perspectives in Canada and the United States, this is the drug of the moment, given that a number of states have legalized its sale and use, and Canada is poised to do the same, country-wide, sometime in 2018.

The need for this publication now is due to a number issues, including the complexity of this drug, which is in fact a combination of related, but not necessarily similar-acting drug compounds, termed cannabinoids, and the limits of information on these compounds. Furthermore, many popular misconceptions, such as that individuals drive better on cannabis than alcohol, so it must be safer to drive after use, need to be countered fully by the scientific realities of the behavioural and impairing effects that cannabis produces.

Unlike alcohol, most blood drug concentrations cannot be determined from the dose. This is particularly true for cannabinoids for several reasons, chief among them that cannabinoids, especially tetrahydrocannabinol (THC), are more fat soluble than water-soluble. Thus, the absorption, distribution, and elimination of cannabis compounds is very different from most other drugs, as you will see from the papers in Chapter 1, and provides distinct limits on the usefulness of other bodily fluids, as described in Chapters 2 to 4. Perhaps one of the most difficult issues is the disconnect between blood THC concentrations and THC behavioural effects. Blood THC concentrations peak very rapidly after smoking marijuana and then drop rapidly as well, while brain concentrations remain high for hours after blood concentrations have greatly diminished, and thus impairment is correlated with recency of use and dose rather than blood concentrations.

With all drugs, dosage is key, and as Paracelsus wrote in the sixteenth century, "all things are poisons, for there is nothing without poisonous qualities. It is only the dose which makes a thing poison." The scientific literature of the 1960s and 1970s certainly detailed dose-related responses for THC, the principal psychopharmacological compound in cannabis. However, most cannabis products, such as marijuana, contained no more than approximately 5 percent THC during those decades, and very few, if any, poisonous effects of THC were noted. As cannabis plant cultivars were bred to produce higher THC yields, US research could not initially keep pace, as American researchers were limited to National Institutes of Health (NIH) cannabis, which had been restricted to a maximum of 3.55 percent THC. European studies with higher THC content proved more useful but incomplete as the search for a greater (or more "pure") high was sought by methods to extract even higher concentrations of THC and other cannabinoids in "wax," "shatter," and "oil." Research labs in a number of countries, including the US, now have some access to these high potency forms of THC but reproducing thirty to forty years of studies that used lower concentrations of THC will take some time, and time is of the essence as cannabis use in daily life, including school, workplace, and driving will be more widespread once the drug becomes legal, just as occurred with alcohol.

Behavioural, physical, and psychological effects are covered in Chapters 5 and 6. Without belabouring the point, impairment of the ability to operate a motor vehicle is impaired by cannabis use, as can be readily seen in the various laboratory studies of specific faculties and skills affected by cannabis to the epidemiological studies of driver populations. You will notice that Jim also categorizes this data in interesting ways, such as different conveyances, including motorcycles (section 6.12), trucks and trains (section 6.15), and even pedestrians (section 6.13). This is a product of his years as a forensic toxicologist, having to provide evidence on alcohol impairment during the operation of a wide range of vehicles, including trains, boats, and construction equipment. The depth of his review of the literature is perhaps best illustrated in section 5.03 on the paradoxical hyperemetic effects that can occur with chronic use.

As indicated above, toxic effects of substances depend upon dose, so given the increasing THC concentrations in cannabis products now available, with legalization it is tempting to suggest that toxic effects, such as cardiac (section 6.04) and psycho-inductive effects (section 6.14), of cannabis will rise as health concerns for a predisposed subset of cannabis users. The use of edible cannabis products (now including gummy bears and other candy) presents a further problem, not just due to the accidental ingestion by children (section 6.06), but also due to overdoses in adults used to the rapid onset of effects following smoking who fail to realize that effects take longer following oral consumption and falsely assume they need to consume more of the product than they should have.

The book is rounded out by the two final chapters. Chapter 7, on cannabinoids in postmortem toxicology, is the most modest chapter, yet still displays surprising depth, including a paper (reference 70109) on the possible use of ear wax as a specimen to confirm cannabis use! The final chapter summarizes the literature on naturally occurring cannabinoids, medicinal cannabinoids, and synthetic cannabinoids, the latter of which are not necessarily cannabinoids, but act through cannabinoid receptors.

In summary, I believe the reader will find this a very useful book for the breadth and depth of the studies and areas covered, and also for the many tables that elegantly summarize and provide an easier way to understand the take-away messages for a range of studies Jim has categorized in his second “Wigmore On” book.

Robert M. Langille, PhD

Forensic Toxicologist
roblangille@rogers.com

Centre of Forensic Sciences, Toxicology Section,
Toronto (1997–2018; Retired)

Member/past Board Member,
Canadian Society of Forensic Science

Member/past Chair,
Canadian Society of Forensic Science Alcohol Test Committee, 2006–2018

Member, Society of Forensic Toxicologists

Member, International Association of Chemical Testers

Member, International Association of Forensic Toxicologists

Preface

can·na·bis, *noun.* 1. A tall plant with a stiff upright stem, divided serrated leaves, and glandular hairs. It is used to produce hemp fibre and as a psychotropic drug. **2.** A dried preparation of the flowering tops or other parts of this plant, or a resinous extract of it (cannabis resin), used (generally illegally) as a psychotropic drug, chiefly in cigarette form.

— *Google search of "what is cannabis?": over 93 million results*

I am delighted by the response to my first book, *Wigmore on Alcohol: Courtroom Alcohol Toxicology for the Medicolegal Professional*, and the wide praise it has received from not only prosecutors, but criminal defence lawyers, personal injury lawyers, forensic toxicologists, coroners, medicolegal examiners, and the police as well. The book made my dream of having the voluminous forensic alcohol literature available in one well-organized and -summarized book come to fruition. *Wigmore on Alcohol* contained 711 studies on such wide topics as alcoholic blackouts, the effect of blood in the mouth on breath alcohol testing, the effect of alcohol swabs on blood alcohol tests, and the effect of alcohol ingestion on snoring. My well-thumbed copy of the book has a place of honour next to my computer. Since it was published, I have referred to it numerous times to clarify the nitty-gritty of issues that arise from time to time in medicolegal cases. In fact, one criminal defence lawyer told me that he only requires two books to go to court, Dean John Henry Wigmore's book, *Wigmore on Evidence*, and mine on alcohol. Hopefully now, with the publication of *Wigmore on Cannabis*, he will increase that number of essential books to three.

I have been asked many times to publish a book about the second most common drug found in medicolegal cases — cannabis, especially in regard to its increasing use, with more and more jurisdictions legalizing both medical and recreational marijuana. Canada will be the first G7 country to legalize this drug and is scheduled to do so in summer 2018.

After much research, I have found many similarities and interesting contrasts between alcohol and the main psychoactive drug found in marijuana — tetrahydrocannabinol or THC. One similarity is that the active psychoactive drug (THC) is an "alcohol," identified as such by its suffix, ol, just the same as in ethanol, the main psychoactive drug of alcoholic beverages. THC, however, has twenty-one carbons in its structure compared to a mere two carbons for alcohol. Both active drugs, THC in marijuana and ethanol in alcoholic beverages, have little or no odour. The distinctive odour of marijuana is due mainly to the terpenes and other cannabinoids. The main differing odours of alcoholic beverages are based on other chemicals, or congeners, such as hops and not ethanol.

Both active drugs are eliminated mainly by the liver, as shown in the two equations below. THC is metabolized into active 11- hydroxy-tetrahydrocannabinol (11-OH-THC), which is at least as psychoactive as the original drug, and some studies have even suggested it is even more potent than THC. The active metabolite 11-OH-THC is converted into inactive 11-nor-9-carboxy-delta 9-tetrahydrocannabinol (THCCOOH) and is eliminated via the urine. Urine THCCOOH is used as a screening test for cannabis use, as little THC or 11-OH-THC appears in the urine due to their fat solubility.

THC → 11-OH-THC (active) → THCCOOH (inactive)

Alcohol has a similar metabolism by the liver and is converted to an active metabolite, acetaldehyde, which causes facial flushing, and then to acetate. Unlike THC, alcohol appears in the urine as it is water soluble.

Ethanol → Acetaldehyde (active) → Acetate (inactive)

Both THC and alcohol have also been restricted and made illegal by their respective prohibitions, as a result of exaggerated side effects and heightened fears of this drug use in immigrant groups, such as beer drinking in German immigrants, wine drinking in Italian immigrants, and marijuana use in Mexican workers. In both drugs, prohibition was eroded by alleged or potential medical use.

Comparison of THC and alcohol:

- Both alcohol and THC are classified as "alcohols."
- Both drugs cause impairment of driving ability, affect memory, and can cause unconsciousness.
- Both alcohol and cannabis have been known for thousands of years, initially as a food source (beer from barley) and as nutritious (cannabis or hemp seeds).
- Both alcohol and THC do not have strong odours by themselves. It is the congeners (hops, etc.) that provide the odour for alcoholic beverages and mainly terpenes that provide the strong odour of marijuana, especially when it is smoked.
- Both drugs underwent prohibition and exaggerated fears of their risks to society. Prohibition was ended in part due to the alleged medical benefits of these drugs.
- Both alcohol and THC are converted by the liver into active metabolites, acetaldehyde and 11-hydroxy-tetrahydrocannabinol, respectively.
- Alcohol is water soluble and is eliminated from the body within hours of consumption, whereas THC is fat soluble and is slowly removed from the body over a period of days or weeks. THC is eliminated mainly in the feces, whereas insignificant amounts of alcohol are eliminated by that route. THC is eliminated in a biphasic manner, whereas alcohol is eliminated at a fixed constant rate.
- Alcohol is measured in units of grams of alcohol in 100 millilitres of blood (g/100mL), whereas THC is measured in nanograms (one-billionth of a gram) per millilitre of blood (ng/mL). And so THC is more potent than alcohol at much lower concentrations.

The physical effects of the main psychoactive drug of marijuana, THC, have been known for many centuries, just like the typical physical effects of alcohol. According to Patrick Mathews, writing in *Cannabis Culture: A Journey through Disputed Territory* (Bloomsbury Publishing, London, 1999), the following two quotes were written by medieval Arab hashish poets.

> Stoned people pounce on sweets as much as a lover on the mouth of his beloved
>
> — *Ibn al Afif al Tilimsani, (1262–89)*

and

> Our friend is clutching half a pill
> Gleaning as green as a pomegranate tree
> We kept him company after he swallowed it
> And an hour later it blossomed in his eye
>
> — *Ibn al Kharrat, (1375–1436)*

The first poem describes the well-known effect of marijuana on the "munchies," especially in male users. The second describes the reddening of the eyes after eating a hashish pill. At that time hashish was eaten, as smoking was not known of until Columbus returned from the New World in 1492.

The second poem accurately describes the reddening of the eye, which occurs within minutes after smoking cannabis, but much slower (one to two hours) after eating cannabis. Red eyes are currently used as an indicator of cannabis ingestion by the police in their screening of drivers.

I extensively assessed the peer-reviewed, published, scientific literature of approximately 5,000 studies for *Wigmore on Cannabis.* From these numerous studies I have chosen nearly 600 for this book.

The set-up of *Wigmore on Cannabis* is similar to my earlier book on alcohol. Each peer-reviewed, published reference or study has a unique five-digit number assigned to it. The first digit indicates the chapter, the next two digits indicate the section, and the last two digits show where the reference appears in that section.

For example, reference number 50511 refers to the fifth chapter of the book (Effects of Cannabis on Driving Ability); the next two digits refer to the section in that chapter (or the fifth, 05), which is "Field (Epidemiological Studies)"; and the last two digits (11) indicate that this study is the eleventh paper cited in that section. If you look up that reference, you will find the following:

Reference Number: 50511

BRUBACHER, J.R., H. CHAN, W. MARTZ, W. SCHREIBER, M. ASBRIDGE, J. EPPLER, A. LUND, S. MACDONALD, O. DRUMMER, R. PURSSELL, G. ANDOLFATTO, R. MANN, AND R. BRANT. "Prevalence of Alcohol and Drug Use in Injured

British Columbia Drivers." *British Medical Journal Open*, 6: 9 pp, March 10, 2016 (2 tables, 3 figures, 48 references)

Abstract: Blood samples were collected from 1,097 drivers attending seven trauma centres in British Columbia between 2010 and 2012, and were analyzed for alcohol (GC), cannabis, or other drugs (LC/MS or GC). The blood was collected a median of 87.2 minutes after the MVC. The majority of drivers were male (64 percent) and 61 percent were between twenty and fifty years of age. Alcohol was detected in 17.8 percent of the drivers and 15.4 percent of the BACs were 0.080 g/100mL or greater. A positive blood THC concentration (> 0.2 ng/mL) was detected in 7.3 percent of the drivers, of whom 3 percent had a blood THC > 3 ng/mL. A total of 12.6 percent of the drivers were cannabis users (THCCOOH was positive). Overall, alcohol, or at least one impairing drug, was detected in 40.1 percent of drivers and alcohol and cannabis were detected in 1.6 percent of the drivers. Approximately 15 percent of THC-positive drivers had consumed alcohol. Drivers with a blood THC > 3 ng/mL were less likely to be male, less than thirty years of age, less likely to be involved in SMVCs during the night and on weekends than drivers with BAC > 0.080 g/100mL.

Table: Odds Ratio (OR) of an Injured Driver with a BAC > 0.08 g/100mL or Blood THC > 3 ng/mL

	BAC > 0.08 g/100mL	Blood THC > 3 ng/mL
Gender (male vs female)	3.4 X	2.1 X
Age (<30 vs >30 years)	3.8 X	2.7 X
Crash Type (single vs multi-vehicle)	6.9 X	0.7 X
Night vs Day	15.3 X	1.4 X
Weekend vs Weekday	3.9 X	0.8 X
Admitted vs Discharged	1.8 X	1.2 X

Adapted from Brubacher et al, 2016

After alcohol, cannabis was the next most commonly detected recreational drug. Like alcohol, cannabis impairs driving ability and increases the risk of crashes, although to a lesser extent than alcohol.

This is the format for all the references in the book. The reference number is followed by a citation of the article, including authors' names, title of the study, the journal, volume, pages, and year it was published.

In brackets is the number of tables, figures, and references that are found in the article.

Next, a short abstract of the article appears, which I wrote. The abstract is generally shorter than the equivalent of one handwritten page, as I handwrote all abstracts initially while reading the reference. In the abstract, I have attempted to avoid as much scientific jargon as possible and to obtain the essential point of the article, and so I may not have included some obscure points or subtleties. It is therefore important that for any medicolegal proceedings that the *original published article* be referred to, not just my short abstract.

Most of the references can be obtained at the US National Library of Medicine at PubMed, www.ncbi.nim.nih.gov/pubmed.

A table appears after the abstract for 127 of the articles, in which I have summarized and simplified some of the data to make it easier to understand. I find that tables are more useful than figures for medicolegal cases, which typically rely on oral testimony. In fact, I find them so useful that I have increased the number of tables from the eighty-seven that appeared in *Wigmore on Alcohol*.

Finally, at the end of the reference, I have included (in italics) the author(s) own words, in order to retain the flavour and gist of the study.

Both alcohol and cannabis have an interesting and fascinating history. Cannabis has been used for thousands of years by the Chinese for medicine (mainly the low THC seeds), paper and fibre, and food, but not for its hallucinogenic effects. The cannabis grown in China and northern Europe typically had low THC concentrations (hemp) and were used to make sails and ropes, which were important for equipping sailing ships, especially warships for the navy. As such, growing hemp was a strategic crop and many governments and leaders (including Henry VIII and George Washington) encouraged its farming, not because they smoked cannabis, but for military power.

Hemp however was replaced on ships by cotton, which, after the invention of the cotton gin in 1793, was much more economical to use, and the farming of hemp declined dramatically. Non-psychoactive hemp (usually less than 0.03% THC) has been grown legally in Canada for many years and its high cannabidiol (CBD) appears to have more effective medical uses than psychoactive THC.

The THC content in marijuana has increased dramatically since the 1960s, '70s, and '80s from about 1 to 3 percent to the nearly 30 percent found today in skunk or sinsemilla (Spanish for "without seeds"), buds, or flowers, and even up to nearly 90 percent in cannabis concentrates or dabs.

The cannabis plant produces cannabinoids (including THC) and other compounds such as terpenes to protect the flowers and seeds of the next generation from insects and animals and perhaps from drying out in the hot sun.

Marijuana is one of only 5 percent of the world's plants that have separate male and female plants. It has been found that if only female plants are grown, they will produce higher and higher concentrations of THC as long as they are not fertilized by the pollen of the male plant. Hence the name sinsemilla, indicating high potency cannabis. The THC concentration in marijuana has also been increased by careful breeding and highly controlled growing conditions indoors.

Thus, a lot of the early research showing limited risks and impairment of driving ability using the 1 to 3 percent THC marijuana has to be updated to the marijuana currently available (15 to 30 percent THC), an issue that this book addresses. The fond memories some people have of marijuana use from the 1960s to the 1980s with low THC joints containing low THC seeds and stems cannot be applied to the current generation. It is like someone who only consumed bottles of beer (5 percent alcohol) saying there is no problem consuming the same number of bottles of liquor (40 percent alcohol). Obviously the greater the dose of the drug (either alcohol or THC), the greater the risks and greater impairment causing traffic crashes. There is an even greater risk of driving impairment, addiction, and other health problems when alcohol is consumed together with cannabis.

I have been able to lecture on numerous occasions at one of the best and largest library systems in the world, the Toronto Public Library, which has over 100 branches and great, helpful staff, on "Not Your Granddad's Weed: The Forensic Science of Cannabis." I was able to summarize some of the differences in the following table.

1970s – 1990s	Today
Headshops Mimeographs Illegal	Dispensaries Social network (e.g. YouTube shows how to make concentrates and dabs) Home delivery Legal
Marijuana had low THC and high CBD	Marijuana now has high THC and low CBD (e.g. skunk)

1970s – 1990s	Today
Hash, hash oil	Dabs, shatter, BHO, concentrates, edibles
Botanical cannabis	Synthetic cannabinoids

It has been a very interesting experience, learning all the ins and outs of this fascinating drug, and I hope this book will help others understand and appreciate some of its risks as Canada and other countries begin legalization.

Acknowledgements

Since my retirement from the Centre of Forensic Sciences in Toronto over ten years ago, I have encountered many people who contributed to the eventual publication of this book. My colleagues from the Toxicology Section, including Dr Rob Langille and Dr Daryl Mayers, have provided valuable insights, as did the former director of the CFS and my mentor, Dr Doug Lucas.

Rob Langille recently retired from the Centre of Forensic Sciences and kindly volunteered to write the Foreword to this book. Hopefully we will see more of each other and have more joint projects now that he is retired.

I have not seen much of my other valued colleagues and forensic toxicologists at the Centre of Forensic Sciences, such as Betty Chow, Karen Woodall, Teri Martin, and J-P Palmentier, since it moved from its downtown location at Yonge and Wellesley to its new location at Keele and Wilson in the northwest part of Toronto.

Another former colleague at the Centre of Forensic Sciences, Chris House, who is now in Ottawa with the RCMP forensic laboratory system, has assisted greatly in obtaining cannabis studies to include in this book.

Senior crown attorneys James Palangio and Phil Perlmutter have been great at advising me of the new changes to Canada's law on cannabis and impaired driving, and we have had many good lunches together.

Jeff Teitelbaum, MLIS, of the Forensic Laboratory Services Bureau of the Washington State Patrol, has been a constant over my many years of retirement and provided an invaluable service to me and numerous forensic scientists, keeping us up to date with the latest research and delving into the long-forgotten history of the science.

Andrew Bell, who used to work with me at the Centre of Forensic Sciences in the Breathalyzer section and is now retired, has been a wonderful walking companion and friend. He has been an able assistant for my cannabis lecture series, which I continue to present at the Toronto Public Library system. I think of him as being a bit of a Boswell to my Johnson and I have always considered Boswell the smarter and wittier of the two.

Over the years, I have maintained a lively, provocative, and enjoyable correspondence with Dr Wayne Jones of Sweden, who is probably the top forensic alcohol toxicologist in the world.

I would also acknowledge Sherry Colbourne, currently the President and CEO of the Spark Centre, who has been a constant and supportive friend and lunch companion (even when she went to Oman), as well as a wonderful webmistress and all-around media guru.

I am also extremely thankful to my publisher, Irwin Law, and its wonderful editors and designer, Alisa Posesorski, Marg Anne Morrison, and Carmen Siu, for their support over the years.

Finally, I would like to acknowledge and express my profound gratitude to my amazing wife, Penelope, and our wonderful children, Alexander (and spouse Ginny), and Kathleen (and spouse Kris), and especially our terrific and enthusiastic grandchildren, Chloe, Calvin, Simon, and Alice, who continue to inspire and encourage me.

CHAPTER 1

Absorption, Distribution, and Elimination of Cannabis

The absorption, distribution, and elimination of a drug such as tetrahydrocannabinol (THC) is commonly referred to as the pharmacokinetics of the drug, and it is what the body does to the drug: how THC is absorbed into the body, mainly by smoking or vaping of cannabis, but also by oral ingestion; how it is distributed via the blood to the various fat tissues of the body; and finally, elimination (metabolized mainly by the liver) and it is eliminated in a large proportion by the feces. In comparison, alcohol is water soluble and little is excreted via the feces.

Due to its fat solubility, initially THC is eliminated very rapidly as it is redistributed throughout the body to the various fat tissues, and then, after several hours, THC is eliminated at a slow rate, which may take several days. As alcohol is water soluble, it does not have a biphasic elimination and is removed from the body at a fixed, constant rate in a matter of hours.

1.01 ABSORPTION

Absorption is how the drug gets into the body. THC is most rapidly absorbed by smoking or vaping the cannabis plant material, concentrates, or dabs. The peak blood THC concentrations are reached within minutes after smoking, whereas after oral ingestion, peak blood THC concentrations usually occur in sixty to ninety minutes after ingestion, but it may take longer (10111).

Oral ingestion of cannabis results in a three to four times greater concentration of the active metabolite 11-OH-THC in the blood than occurs after smoking (10113), which may explain the more severe reactions that occur with oral ingestion.

Significant blood THC concentrations cannot be obtained by passive inhalation of cannabis smoke unless there is no ventilation in the room and a large amount of cannabis is smoked (10101). Under such extreme conditions, it may be argued that absorption is no longer passive, but may be deliberate. The higher the blood THC concentration the shorter the time lapse has occurred since smoking (10107). Vaporization of cannabis has less respiratory symptoms (such as coughing) and is the most popular method of cannabis administration in medical marijuana users (10114, 10115).

CBD does not affect the pharmacokinetics of THC (10110).

Reference Number: 10101

CONE, E.J., G.E. BIGELOW, E.S. HERMANN, J.M. MITCHELL, C. LODICO, R. FLEGEL, AND R. VANDREY. "Non-Smoker Exposure to Secondhand Smoke. I Urine Screening and Confirmation Results." *Journal of Analytical Toxicology*, 39: 1–12, 2015 (3 tables, 3 figures, 27 references)

Abstract: Six experienced marijuana smokers smoked cannabis cigarettes (5.3 percent and 11.3 percent THC) in a sealed room beside six non-smokers, with and without ventilation. The subjects wore goggles to prevent eye irritation, as a considerable amount of smoke was generated. The subjects were exposed to the smoke for one hour. At a 50 ng/mL THCCOOH cutoff, all screening tests were negative for non-smokers except for one, which was a presumptive result. The mean THCCOOH urine concentration was much lower with ventilation.

Cannabis potency and room ventilation were demonstrated to be two major factors in determining the extent of cannabis smoke exposure to non-smokers residing in close proximity to smokers. Short term exposure to high intensity smoke from combusted cannabis resulted in non-smoker inhalation of sufficient amounts of THC to produce positive presumptive urine tests by immunoassay with a 20 ng/mL cutoff concentration, but only a single positive occurred at higher cutoff concentrations (50 ng/mL). GC-MS analysis of presumptive positives confirmed the presence of THCCOOH at > 15 ng/mL in some specimens.

Reference Number: 10102

CONE, E.J., G.E. BIGELOW, E.S. HERMANN, J.M. MITCHELL, C. LODICO, R. FLEGEL, AND R. VANDREY. "Nonsmoker Exposure to Secondhand Cannabis Smoke. III Oral Fluid and Blood Drug Concentrations and Corresponding Subjective Effects." *Journal of Analytical Toxicology*, 39: 497–509, 2015 (7 tables, 4 figures, 31 references)

Abstract: Six experienced cannabis users smoked marijuana cigarettes (5.3 percent and 11.3 percent THC) for one hour with or without ventilation in the same sealed room as six non-smokers. Oral fluid, whole blood, and subjective effects were determined at various points in time after exposure to secondhand smoke. OF was analyzed by ELISA (4 ng/mL cutoff) and LC/MS/MS (LOQ 1 ng/mL THC). Blood was analyzed by LC/MS/MS. There was a subjective report of pleasant drug effect at the session of high THC with no ventilation in the six non-smokers.

This study demonstrated that extreme exposure to environmental cannabis smoke by non-smokers situated in close proximity to smokers led to deposition of THC in oral fluid. Oral fluid specimens for non-smokers in the two sessions conducted without ventilation tested positive by IA (4 ng/mL cutoff) and were confirmed for THC by LC-MS-MS (2 ng/mL) for up to three hours following cessation of exposure. In the third session of this study, conducted with ventilation that simulated a r conditioning, some initial positive tests occurred but the number was substantially diminished. Importantly, no THCCOOH was detectable in oral fluid by LC-MS-MS at the LOQ (0.02 ng/mL) in any exposure sessions for non-smokers.

Reference Number: 10103

MORLAND, J., A. BUGGE, B. SKUTERUD, A. STEEN, G.H. WETHE, AND T.C. KJELDSEN. "Cannabinoids in Blood and Urine after Passive Inhalation of Cannabis Smoke." *Journal of Forensic Sciences*, 30: 997–1002, 1985 (2 tables, 1 figure, 12 references)

Abstract: Three female and seven male control subjects (ages 35 to 50 years) were divided into two groups. One group was exposed to passive inhalation of hashish by three subjects who smoked two hashish cigarettes over thirty minutes. The other group was exposed to the passive inhalation by two subjects who smoked six marijuana cigarettes each for thirty minutes. In both groups, the exposure took place in a small car with an air volume of 1,650 L. The cannabis smokers were instructed not to inhale too much of the smoke but to let most of it escape into the ambient air to increase the THC concentration for the nonsmokers to inhale. All participants complained about the amount of smoke in the car and complained that it was very adverse. Blood and urine samples were collected from both the smokers and nonsmokers before and after exposure and analyzed for cannabinoids by RIA and GC-MS. The maximum peak blood THC concentration was 6.3 ng/mL immediately after passive exposure. No subjects experienced any euphoria.

> The main conclusion is presently that the demonstration of cannabinoids in blood or urine is not unequivocal proof of active cannabis smoking. Therefore, the results of laboratory tests in this field, which might have both legal and other important consequences, should be interpreted with great caution.

Reference Number: 10104

ROHRICHM, J., I. SCHIMMEL, S. ZORNTLEIN, J. BECKER, S. DROBNIK, T. KAUFMAN, V. KUNTZ, AND R. URBAN. "Concentrations of Delta 9 Tetrahydrocannabinol and 11-Nor-9-Carboxytetrahydrocannabinol in Blood and Urine after Passive Exposure to Cannabis Smoke in a Coffee Shop." *Journal of Analytical Toxicology*, 34: 196–203, 2010 (5 tables, 6 figures, 16 references)

Abstract: Four male and four female subjects (ages 27 to 59 years) were exposed to passive inhalation of cannabis smoke in a Netherlands coffee shop. Coffee shops in The Netherlands are places where cannabis can be consumed legally. Blood and urine samples were collected and analyzed by immunoassay screening and by GC/MS for THC, 11-OH-THC, and THCCOOH. It could be demonstrated that all subjects absorbed some THC. The urine IA screening reached a maximum of 16 ng/mL six to fourteen hours after the start of exposure. No urine result was greater than the 25 ng/mL cut-off. The GC/MS results for serum THC and THCCOOH were all less than 1 ng/mL and 2 ng/mL respectively.

> Furthermore, the results of this study indicate that passive exposure to cannabis smoke may only lead to trace amounts of THC in serum. Apparently, the THC serum concentrations are considerably below 1 ng/mL

during or for a short time after exposure and the concentrations of TH-CCOOH in serum do not exceed levels of about 2 ng/mL.

Reference Number: 10105

HAYDEN, J.W. "Passive Inhalation of Marijuana Smoke: A Critical Review." *Journal of Substance Abuse*, 3: 85–90, 1991 (1 table, 7 references)

Abstract: Five studies were conducted, involving passive inhalation of marijuana smoke and its effect on urine cannabinoid tests for THC-COOH using the EMIT method. There was a 20 ng/mL cutoff and a 100 ng/mL cutoff.

Obviously, the inhalation of high concentrations of marijuana smoke, whether from a marijuana cigarette or from a closed compartment, will cause cannabinoids to appear in the urine. As the Cone and Johnson study shows, the presence of significant amounts of urinary cannabinoids is accompanied by subjective effects of intoxication. Individuals, particularly Medical Review Officers reviewing the results of urine drug tests, should realize that drug intoxication is a function of how much THC is absorbed, irrespective of whether the THC was eaten, injected intravenously, actively smoked, or inhaled at high concentrations from a closed container. If passive inhalation is defined as the act of a non-smoker inhaling room air that contains smoke produced by other individuals smoking marijuana in a social situation, it is readily apparent that passive inhalation will not cause spurious positive EMIT drug tests for cannabinoids.

Reference Number: 10106

HERMANN, E.S., E.J. CONE, J.M. MITCHELL, G.E. BIGELOW, C. LODICO, R. FLEGEL, AND R. VANDREY. "Non-Smoker Exposure to Secondhand Cannabis Smoke II: Effect of Room Ventilation on the Psychological, Subjective, and Behavioral/Cognitive Effects." *Drug and Alcohol Dependence*, 151: 194–202, 2015 (2 tables, 1 figure, 32 references)

Abstract: Six cannabis smokers smoked 11.3 percent THC cigarettes for one hour, in the same sealed chamber as six non-smokers. The chamber was either ventilated (eleven air exchanges per hour) or non-ventilated. Blood, urine, OF, and hair samples were collected for up to six hours post-exposure from smokers and thirty-four hours from non-smokers. Blood THC, 11-OH-THC, and THCCOOH were determined by LC/MS/

MS. Urine analysis of THCCOOH was measured by IA and LC/MS/MS. Non-smokers in a ventilated room did not have detectable cannabinoids in the blood beyond thirty minutes post-exposure and did not screen positive.

> Room ventilation has a pronounced effect on exposure to secondhand smoke. Under extreme unventilated conditions, secondhand smoke exposure can produce detectable levels of THC in blood and urine, minor physiological and subjective drug effect, and minor impairment on a task requiring psychomotor ability and working memory.

Reference Number: 10107

HUESTIS, M.A., A. BARNES, AND M.L. SMITH. "Estimating the Time of Last Cannabis Use from Plasma delta 9-Tetrahydrocannabinol and 11-nor-9-Carboxy-delta9 Tetrahydrocannabinol Concentrations." *Clinical Chemistry*, 51: 2289–95, 2005 (3 tables, 36 references)

Abstract: Two models (using the plasma THC and the plasma THC-COOH: THC ratio) were applied to multiple doses at low plasma THC concentrations (0.5 to 2 ng/mL). Thirty-eight male cannabis users smoked 2.64 percent THC in the morning and thirty smoked a second joint in the afternoon. Plasma THC and THCCOOH concentrations were determined by GC/MS in 717 blood samples collected throughout the dosing.

Table: Measured Plasma THC Concentration and Mean Estimated Time Since Smoking (Model 1) and Measured THCCOOH/THC Ratio and Mean Estimated Time Since Smoking (Model 2).*

Plasma (Blood) THC Concentration (ng/mL)	Mean Estimated Time Since Smoking (hrs)	THCCOOH/THC ratio	Mean Estimated Time Since Smoking (hrs)
50 (25)	0.32 (19 min)	0.1	0.2 (12 min)
26 (13)	0.50 (30 min)	1.0	0.7 (42 min)
10 (5)	1.0	2.0	1.0
5 (2.5)	1.6	5.0	1.7
4 (2)	1.9	10.0	2.5
3 (1.5)	2.3	20.0	3.7
2 (1)	3.0	40.0	5.6
1 (0.5)	4.9	80.0	8.3

* To convert the plasma THC concentration into a blood THC concentration divide by approximately two.

Source: Adapted from Huestis Barnes and Smith, 2005

In conclusion, in this study we extend the validation of two previously described models for predicting the time of last cannabis use from plasma THC and THCCOOH concentrations to samples collected after multiple cannabis exposures and those with low THC concentrations. The predictive models provide an objective and validated method for assessing the contribution of cannabis to accidents or clinical symptoms based on cannabinoid concentrations in a single plasma sample.

Reference Number: 10108

HUESTIS, M.A., H. SAMPSON, B.J. HOLICKY, J.E. HENNINGFIELD, AND E.J. CONE. "Characterization of the Absorption Phase of Marijuana Smoking." *Clinical Pharmacology and Therapeutics*, 52: 31–43, 1992 (2 tables, 5 figures, 21 references)

Abstract: Six healthy male subjects smoked marijuana cigarettes (placebo, 1.75 percent or 3.55 percent THC) in eight puffs inhaled over 11.2 minutes. Continuous blood samples were collected via an indwelling catheter and plasma THC concentrations were determined by GC/MS. Various other measures were determined such as BP, pupil size, and skin temperature. Active THC was found in plasma after the first puff and were 7.0 and 18.1 ng/mL respectively for the low and higher THC joints. At 9.8 minutes, the plasma THC concentrations were 79.0 and 152.0 ng/mL respectively. Within two hours, the plasma THC concentrations were < 5 ng/mL. HR increased by 46 and 56 bpm shortly after smoking and skin temperatures decreased.

Significant increases in heart rate and diastolic blood pressure occurred shortly after peak blood levels. Previous studies have indicated that there is a substantial delay between peak plasma levels of delta 9 tetrahydrocannabinol and drug-induced effects. This study showed that behavioural and physiological effects appear concurrently or within minutes after the rapid appearance of delta 9 tetrahydrocannabinol in blood during marijuana smoking.

Reference Number: 10109

EARLEYWINE, M. AND N.T. VAN DAM. "Case Studies in Cannabis Vaporization." *Addiction Research and Theory*, 18: 243–49, 2010 (2 tables, 12 references)

Abstract: Two female and two male cannabis smokers with respiratory symptoms agreed to consume cannabis using a vaporizer for one month. A glass whip that holds the cannabis is placed over the heating element and the cannabis releases the cannabinoids as a fine mist at a lower temperature than smoking. The cannabis is not burned or combusted in a vaporizer. After one month of use, the FEV1 increased from 7 to 10 percent and FVCs from 2 to 7 percent, which showed an improvement of lung function. All four participants refused to go back to smoking and had fewer respiratory symptoms with the vaporizer.

Despite these outcomes, the vaporizer is not a panacea for all cannabis-related troubles. Other negative consequences of use, particularly legal problems and dependence, are unlikely to improve with the vaporizer.

Reference Number: 10110

KARSCHNER, E.L., W.D. DARWIN, R.S. GOODWIN, S. WRIGHT, AND M.A. HUESTIS. "Plasma Cannabinoid Pharmacokinetics following Controlled Oral delta 9 Tetrahydrocannabinol and Oromucosal Cannabis Extraction Administration." *Clinical Chemistry*, 57: 66–75, 2011 (2 tables, 4 figures, 29 references)

Abstract: Sativex is a cannabis extract oromucosal spray containing THC and CBD. Three female and six male cannabis smokers (ages 19 to 43 years) were administered low and high dose Sativex (5 and 15 mg THC and CBD respectively), oral synthetic THC (5 and 15 mg THC only), and placebo on five occasions. Frequent blood samples were collected and plasma THC, 11-OH-THC, THCCOOH, and CBD were measured by GC/MS. The mean peak plasma THC concentrations were 5.1 ng/mL and 4.7 ng/mL for the low dose sativex and oral dose respectively and increased to 15.3 ng/mL and 14.3 ng/mL for the high dose. The mean peak plasma 11-OH-THC concentrations were 4.2 ng/mL (sativex) and 3.0 (oral) at the low dose and increased to 8.4 ng/mL (sativex) and 11.1 ng/mL (oral) at the high dose respectively. The maximum THCCOOH concentrations were obtained 1.2 to 7.5 hours post dose. The time to first detection of CBD was 2.5 hours for the low dose and 2.0 hours for the high dose sativex. CBD did not affect the pharmacokinetics of THC.

Several advantages exist for oromucosal cannabis plant extracts over single oral synthetic cannabinoids. A combination of cannabinoids and other plant compounds probably provide additional therapeutic possibilities for treating a variety of medical conditions. Oromucosal administration is also more desirable than the oral route for treating nausea and increasing appetite. In addition, self-titration often is necessary in this population to control pain and spasticity and to reduce unwanted subjective effects.

Reference Number: 10111

KARSCHNER, E.L., D.M. SCHWOPE, E.W. SCHWILKE, R.S. GOODWIN, D.L. KELLY, D.A. GORELICK, AND M.A. HUESTIS. "Predictive Model Accuracy in Estimating Last delta-9-Tetrahydrocannabinol (THC) Intake from Plasma and Whole Blood Cannabinoid Concentrations in Chronic, Daily Cannabis Smokers Administered Subchronic Oral THC." *Drug and Alcohol Dependence*, 125: 313–19, 2012 (2 tables, 4 figures, 19 references)

Abstract: Ten male chronic cannabis smokers (mean age 23.9 years) were administered orally 20 mg capsules of synthetic THC (Dronabinol, Marinol) as an escalating, round-the-clock dose (40 to 120 mg daily) for up to eight days. Blood and plasma THC, 11-OH-THC, and THCCOOH concentrations were determined after solid-phase extraction (SPE) by 2D GC/MS. The maximum whole blood THC concentrations occurred at 3.0 hours after the first oral dose and 103.5 hours (4.3 days) during multiple dosing. The median whole blood/plasma ratio across all time points was THC (0.63), 11-OH-THC (0.60), and THCCOOH (0.55).

Table: Whole Blood Pharmacokinetics for THC, 11-OH-THC, and THCCOOH After a Single Oral 20 mg THC Dose and 37 Multiple Oral THC Doses for 8 days.

Cannabinoid	Single Dose	Multiple Doses
Mean Maximum Blood THC Concentration	8.7 ng/mL	22.4 ng/mL
Mean Time to Obtain Maximum Blood THC Concentration	3.0 hours	101 hours
Mean Maximum Blood 11-OH-THC Concentration	4.0 ng/mL	11.0 ng/mL
Mean Time to Obtain Maximum Blood 11-OH-THC Concentration	2.8 hours	106 hours

Cannabinoid	Single Dose	Multiple Doses
Mean Maximum Blood THCCOOH Concentration	38.4 ng/mL	142.2 ng/mL
Mean Time to Obtain Maximum Blood THCCOOH Concentration	3.1 hours	144.0 hours

Source: Adapted from Karschner et al, 2012

Maximum cannabinoid concentrations for all analytes after multiple THC doses were almost three-fold higher than following a single 20 mg oral THC dose. When daily THC doses increased from 100 to 120 mg/day on day five, THC and 11-OH-THC concentrations decreased. As proposed by Schwilke et al (2009), repeated oral THC dosing in daily cannabis smokers may induce gastrointestinal THC metabolism, resulting in lower concentrations later in the dosing regimen. Although these individuals were chronic, daily cannabis smokers at the time of study initiation and hepatic metabolism was expected to be at a steady state, oral ingestion was uncommon, suggesting that gastrointestinal metabolism might be inducible with chronic oral THC exposure.

Reference Number: 10112

ROMERO-SANDOVAL, E.A., S. ASBILL, C.A. PAIGE, AND K. BYRD-GLOVER. "Peripherally Restricted Cannabinoids for the Treatment of Pain." *Pharmacotherapy*, 35: 917–25, 2015 (3 tables, 57 references)

Abstract: One strategy to avoid the psychotropic and CNS-related undesired effects of medicinal cannabis is to target the peripheral endocannabinoid system, such as using transdermal patches. The transdermal administration of THC increased fentanyl levels.

The endocannabinoid system modulates nociceptive pathways and inflammation processes. In general, activation of the endocannabinoid system has been shown to reduce inflammation and pain (or nociceptive responses) through CB1 and CB2 receptors (or, in some cases, other non-cannabinoid receptors). Due to the lipophilic nature of cannabinoids, the therapeutic effects of these compounds are generally associated with acute to long-term related neurologic undesirable effects mostly dependent on CNS CB1 receptors. Some advances have been made in the development of novel chemically modified cannabinoid molecules that are restricted to the periphery, to avoid CNS-related side effects.

Reference Number: 10113

NADULSKI, T., F. SPORKERT, M. SCHNELLE, A.M. STADELMANN, P. ROSER, T. SCHEFTER, AND F. PRAGST. "Simultaneous and Sensitive Analysis of THC, 11-OH-THC, THC-COOH, CBD and CBN by GC-MS in Plasma after Oral Application of Small Doses of THC and Cannabis Extract." *Journal of Analytical Toxicology*, 29: 2005 (4 tables, 4 figures, 50 references)

Abstract: Blood (plasma) samples were collected from volunteers who consumed a placebo, 10 mg THC, or 10 mg THC and 5.4 mg CBD (cannabis extract) before and at eight different times. Altogether, 648 samples were analyzed for THC, 11-OH-THC, and THCCOOH by GC/MS. CBN was not detected in any samples. The 11-OH-THC ratio was three to four times greater after oral ingestion than after smoking. At six hours, the ratio was approximately 1.2:1 after smoking and 4.5:1 after oral ingestion. In general, CBD was detected three to four hours after administration.

> The rapid increase of the metabolite concentrations is caused by the extensive first-pass metabolism of THC, which is specific for oral intake. This is particularly the case for the primary metabolite 11-OH-THC. Therefore, the concentration ratio of 11-OH-THC/THC could be a criterion for distinguishing between oral and inhalative drug consumption.

Reference Number: 10114

SHIPLO, S., M. ASBRIDGE, S.T. LEATHERDALE, AND D. HAMMOND. "Medical Cannabis Use in Canada: Vapourization and Modes of Delivery." *Harm Reduction Journal*, 13: 30 (10 pp), 2016 (5 tables, 34 references)

Abstract: A survey was conducted in 2015 of 159 female and 210 male approved, adult Canadian medical marijuana users (mean age 40.8 years) as to how they consumed cannabis. The most frequent form of delivery of medical marijuana was using a vaporizer (53 percent) and smoking a joint (47 percent). The majority of vaporizer users reported using a portable vaporizer (67 percent) followed by a stationary vaporizer (42 percent) and e-cigarette or vape pens (19 percent). The main reason for using medical marijuana was for pain relief (58 percent). The main reasons for vaporizer use was to reduce the negative health impacts of smoking. Oral ingestion and vaporizers were perceived as more expensive than smoking a joint.

Table: Prevalence of Modes of Delivery of Cannabis in 364 Medical Marijuana Users in Canada

Mode of Use of Cannabis	Ever Use (%)	Current Use (%)	Preferred (%)
Smoking a joint	74.2%	47.0%	23.1%
Smoking a pipe	61.3%	25.8%	4.9%
Smoking a bong/water pipe	53.6%	21.4%	8.5%
Smoking a blunt	38.7%	4.7%	1.1%
Using a vaporizer	65.9%	52.7%	28.3%
Eating in foods	64.1%	31.0%	7.1%
Drinking	29.9%	5.5%	1.6%
Taking a pill	28.6%	3.3%	0.8%
Using a spray	8.2%	1.1%	0.3%
Other	10.4%	8.0%	4.7%

Source: Adapted from Shiplo et al, 2016

This study presents a general picture of the current state of medical cannabis use among a sample of approved users in Canada. The findings indicate that approved users have tried multiple modes of delivery, but using a vaporizer was the most commonly used and most preferred mode. The findings suggest that increasing availability and lowering the cost of vaporizers is likely to reduce the prevalence of smoking medical cannabis even further, with the added benefits of reducing harm linked to smoking. Currently, it is unclear what, if any, guidance is being provided to medical cannabis users from physicians, health authorities, or licensed producers with respect to modes of delivery.

Reference Number: 10115

BIEHL, J.R., AND E.L. BURNHAM. "Cannabis Smoking in 2015. A Concern for Lung Health?" *Chest,* 148: 596–606, 2015 (3 tables, 2 figures, 39 references)

Abstract: A general review of the effects of cannabis smoking on lung health was conducted. Approximately 7 to 9 percent of the population in Colorado and Washington state report using cannabis at least monthly. Among regular users, 25 to 32 percent used marijuana daily and averaged approximately four joints per day. Users in general rarely consumed only tobacco or only cannabis. THC has a suppressive effect on the immune cell function. The main inhalation methods of cannabis are blunts (cannabis is rolled into a cigar with the tobacco removed); bong (smoke is bubbled through water); dabbing (cannabis concentrate is burned on a hot nail); g-pen (cannabis dissolved in wax and smoked through an e-cigarette); hookah (cannabis mixed with tobacco and burned with charcoal and the smoke is bubbled through water); joint (cannabis rolled in paper and smoked like a cigarette); pipe (cannabis smoked in a glass pipe); and vaporizer (cannabis is heated below burning temperature and vapor (not smoke) is inhaled).

Table: Advantages and Disadvantages of Various Methods of Inhaling Cannabis

Mode of Inhaling Cannabis	Advantages	Disadvantages
Blunt	Inexpensive, can smoke larger quantity of cannabis than joint	Made from cigar paper, smoke is harsh, and difficult to roll
Bong	Water can trap some of harmful products of combustion	Expensive, easily broken not as portable
Dabbing	Concentrated dabs are easy to conceal and potent psychoactive effects	Cumbersome to use, prone to burn injuries
G-pen	More discrete, no visible smoke or strong odour ("stealth toking"), no combustion products	Little regulation or uniformity of products inhaled, use rising among youth
Hookah	Can smoke with multiple people, higher volume of smoke	Mixed with tobacco, combustion products potentially more damaging to lungs
Joint	Small and convenient	Fragile, difficult to roll
Pipe	Can be inhaled directly, producing more rapid psychoactive effects	Glass pipes can break, possible to inhale harmful resin
Vaporizer	No smoke odour, no products of combustion	Expensive, not portable, no safety regulations

Source: Adapted from Biehle and Burnham, 2015

Increasing prevalence of cannabis consumption in the United States and continued predominant use through an inhaled route suggest an immediate and far-reaching impact on lung health.

1.02 DISTRIBUTION

THC and other fat-soluble cannabinoids are distributed throughout the body according to the fat content of the tissues (10201, 10203), whereas alcohol is distributed in the total body water. Hence, tissues that contain a high THC content will contain a low alcohol content. In addition, whereas alcohol simply dissolves into the blood, THC requires blood carrier proteins (10202).

The initial rapid decline in blood THC concentration after smoking is due to its rapid redistribution into the fat tissues and not to the elimination by the liver (10201, 10203).

Physical exercise, food deprivation, or dieting do not significantly increase the blood THC concentrations and will not cause a reoccurrence of the psychoactive effects of THC (10205, 10207).

Reference Number: 10201

NAHAS, G.G. "The Pharmacokinetics of THC in Fat and Brain: Resulting Functional Responses to Marijuana Smoking." *Human Psychopharmacology Clinical and Experimental*, 16: 247–55, 2001 (12 figures, 17 references)

Abstract: A general review of the pharmacokinetics of THC and its resulting effects, such as a pleasant sensory perception (PSP), was conducted. Following bolus IV administration, there is a dramatic drop in plasma THC concentration as it is absorbed by fat (half-life of about fifty seconds). There is a slow, terminal decrease in plasma THC of up to a half-life of seven days, a result of the slow return of unmetabolized THC from the fatty tissues to the blood. A 15 percent reabsorption of THC occurs from the bile back into the liver, which also accounts for the slow elimination end phase of THC.

> Rapid uptake of THC in fat and its slow release, associated with a rate limited uptake into the brain-blood barrier, could be a general phylogenetic mechanism to protect the brain from toxic exposure to fat-soluble xenobiotics or other psychoactive drugs with a similar pharmacokinetic profile.

Reference Number: 10202

FANALI, G., Y. CAO, P. ASCENZI, V. TREZZA, T. RUBINO, D. PAROLARO, AND M. FASANO. "Binding of delta-9-Tetrahydrocannabinol and Diazepam to Human Serum Albumin." *International Union of Biochemistry and Molecular Biology Life*, 63: 446–51, 2011 (5 figures, 34 references)

Abstract: Approximately 6 percent of cannabis users report past-month use of diazepam compared to 0.4 percent of non-cannabis users. Different drugs can bind to different sites of human serum albumin (HSA), which is an important plasma carrier protein. In vitro studies were conducted on the binding of THC and diazepam to HSA. The drugs bind to different sites of HSA and so do not interfere with each other.

> On this basis, both drugs bind to HSA without affecting their binding properties reciprocally, indicating the additive and synergistic anxiolytic effects observed during the co-administration of the two drugs are not modulated by concomitant binding to HSA.

Reference Number: 10203

REEVE, V.C., J.D. GRANT, W. ROBERTSON., H.K. GILLESPIE., AND L.E. HOLLISTER. "Plasma Concentrations of delta 9-Tetrahydrocannabinol and Impaired Motor Function." *Drug and Alcohol Dependence*, 11: 167–75, 1983 (3 tables, 2 figures, 10 references)

Abstract: Thirty-seven male and twenty-two female cannabis users (ages 20-52 years) smoked a marijuana cigarette (18 mg THC) until they were high. Forty-one subjects smoked only one cigarette, sixteen smoked two, and four smoked three to four cigarettes. Blood samples were collected at 0, 5, 30, 90, and 150 minutes after smoking and analyzed for THC by RIA. The subjects were tested on Roadside Sobriety Tests (Romberg, finger to nose, finger count, heel to toe, and hands pat) by police officers. If the THC measured at five minutes were ignored, failures with RSTs were associated with plasma concentrations of THC above 25 to 30 ng/mL. Overall, 94 percent of subjects failed to pass the test 90 minutes after smoking and 60 percent after 150 minutes.

> The kinetics of THC are peculiar in that, being a highly lipid-soluble drug, it enters the brain relatively rapidly, although with a perceptible delay in proportion to serum concentrations. Once there, it tends to

remain, even at a time when serum concentrations approach or reach zero. These properties of the drug have made it very difficult to relate either objective impairment or subjective estimates of intoxication to prevailing serum concentrations.

Reference Number: 10204

STROUGO, A., L. ZUURMAN, C. ROY, J.L. PINQUIER, J.M.A. VAN GERVEN, A.F. COHEN, AND R.C. SCHOEMAKER. "Modelling of the Concentration-Effect Relationship of THC on Central Nervous System Parameters and Heart Rate–Insight into its Mechanisms of Action and a Tool for Clinical Research and Development of Cannabinoids." *Journal of Psychopharmacology*, 22: 717–26, 2008 (2 tables, 5 figures, 36 references)

Abstract: Twelve male subjects received 2, 4, 6, or 8 mg THC or placebo at 1.5-hour intervals using a Volcano vaporizor. Frequent blood samples were collected and plasma THC, 11-OH-THC, and THCCOOH were measured. Various parameters such as alertness, HR, and body sway were measured. Plasma THC concentrations decreased bi-exponentially in accordance with a fast distribution and gradual elimination. The initial rapid disappearance is due to the high lipophilicity of THC and rapid disappearance from the plasma due to rapid penetration into the highly vascularized tissue such as brain and heart. A two compartmental model with an initial and terminal half-life of 3.81 minutes and 68.4 minutes was required for the model. An increase in the between dose variability in bioavailability was 24 percent, due to inadequate inhalation due to coughing.

This suggests that the effect of THC on the different responses could be due to different sites of action or different physiological mechanisms.

Reference Number: 10205

WESTIN A.A., G. MJONES, O. BUCHARDT, O.M. FUSKEVAG, AND L. SLORDAL. "Can Physical Exercise or Food Deprivation Cause Release of Fat-Stored Cannabinoids?" *Basic and Clinical Pharmacology and Toxicology*, 115: 467–71, 2014 (3 tables, 1 figure, 14 references)

Abstract: After smoking a single marijuana cigarette, serum THC concentrations are typically below detection after twelve hours, whereas the primary metabolite THCCOOH (11-nor-9-carboxy-delta 9 THC) can be detected in the serum for one week and in the urine for about two weeks. In chronic cannabis users, THC and THCCOOH can be detected in the blood for one month and THCCOOH for up to three months in the urine. Blood and urine samples were collected over seven days in one female and five male, heavy, chronic users (ages 25-35 years) undergoing rehab and analyzed for THC and THCCOOH respectively by LC-MS/MS. A CC ratio was determined in the urine by dividing urine THCCOOH by creatinine. At the beginning of the study, the THC concentration range from 0 to 3.6 ng/mL and THCCOOH from 35.4 to 175.5 ng/mL. On days three and five, the subjects were randomly assigned to forty-five minutes of treadmill exercise and twenty-four-hour food deprivation.

> To summarize, neither exercise at moderate intensity for forty-five minutes nor twenty-four-hour food deprivation caused significant elevations in blood or urine cannabinoid levels in our six human subjects. Our results are in accordance with data from a similar study where only slight and transient THC plasma elevations were noted during exercise and none during fasting. We conclude that exercise and fasting in regular cannabis users are unlikely to cause sufficient concentration changes to hamper interpretation in drug testing programs.

Reference Number: 10206

WESTIN, A.A., M.A. HUESTIS, K. AARSTAD, AND O. SPIGSET, "Urinary Excretion of 11-Nor-9-Carboxy-delta 9-Tetrahydrocannabinol in a Pregnant Woman Following Heavy Chronic Cannabis Use." *Journal of Analytical Toxicology*, 33: 610–14, 2009 (1 table, 1 figure, 23 references)

Abstract: Urine screens routinely detect THCCOOH and typically employ a cutoff of 50 ng/mL. Cannabis use can be detected in urine after a single dose for one to five days and in chronic users for up to thirty-six to ninety-five days. A twenty-year-old pregnant woman had consumed 5 g of cannabis resin hash for several months. Urine THCCOOH concentration (by LC-MS) and creatinine concentrations were determined. She was advised not to consume cannabis. Her first urine sample was 348.1 ng/mL (CC ratio of 110.3) and declined to 3.9 ng/mL (CC ratio of 5.0) at day eighty-four.

> We present data on the elimination time of THCCOOH in a pregnant woman following long-term heavy cannabis use. The final conclusion by

the laboratory medical staff was that there had not been new cannabis intake after the first specimen.

Reference Number: 10207

WONG, A., M.E. MONTEBELLO, M.M. NORBERG, K. ROONEY, N. LINTZERIS, R. BRUNO, J. BOOTH, J.C. ARNOLD, AND I.S. MCGREGOR. "Exercise Increases Plasma THC Concentrations in Regular Cannabis Users." *Drug and Alcohol Dependence,* 133: 763–67, 2013 (3 figures, 16 references)

Abstract: Fourteen regular cannabis users (ages 19 to 40 years) were divided into fasting and non-fasting groups (no breakfast) after abstaining from cannabis use overnight. Blood samples were collected before and after thirty-five minutes of moderate exercise on a stationary bicycle. Plasma THC and THCCOOH concentrations were determined by LC/MS and the limits of quantitation were 0.5 ng/mL for THC and 5 ng/mL for THCCOOH. The mean baseline plasma THC before exercise was 3.7 ng/mL and for THCCOOH was 74.2 ng/mL. Lack of food had no effect and exercise did not increase THCCOOH. However, THC was significantly elevated immediately post-exercise, but not two hours later. BMI was positively correlated with the increase in plasma THC.

Here we demonstrate that exercise enhances plasma THC levels in regular cannabis users. The lack of a fasting effect may reflect the modest duration of fasting used, which was associated with only a modest increase in fat utilization related to exercise. Overall, these results suggest that exercise may elevate blood THC levels by releasing dormant THC from fat stores. These data suggest the interpretation of blood THC levels in roadside and workplace might be complicated by recent exercise.

1.03 ELIMINATION

THC is eliminated in two phases after it is smoked. There is an initial rapid decrease in THC due mainly to its rapid distribution into the fat tissues, followed by a slow, steady release of the THC from the fatty tissues back into the blood and slow elimination by the liver and feces. Low blood concentrations of THC can be detected in heavy chronic users for almost a month (10307). The longer the person has consumed cannabis (e.g., twenty-two years versus two years), the longer THC will be detected in the blood (10301). The prolonged elimination of THC from the blood may complicate DUIC cases (10302, 10306, 10307).

The active metabolite (11-OH-THC) produced by the liver may be more potent than THC (10305).

Reference Number: 10301

KARSCHNER, E.L., E.W. SCHWILKE, R.H. LOWE, W.D. DARWIN, R.L. HERNING, J.L. CADET, AND M.A. HUESTIS. "Implications of Plasma Delta 9-Tetrahydrocannabinol, 11-Hydroxy-THC and 11-nor-9-Carboxy-THC Concentrations in Chronic Cannabis Smokers." *Journal of Analytical Toxicology*, 33: 469–77, 2009 (3 tables, 3 figures, 45 references)

Abstract: Plasma THC, 11-OH-THC, and THCCOOH concentrations were determined by GC/MS in six male and twelve female chronic cannabis users (ages 21 to 36 years) during seven days of abstinence, for a total of 126 plasma samples. All participants had consumed alcohol in the past month and sixteen smoked cigarettes. A plasma THC > 2 ng/mL occurred in 9, 6, 5, 6, 5, 4, and 4 patients on days 1 to 7 respectively. A plasma 11-OH-THC concentration > 2 ng/mL occurred in 4, 3, 1, 0, and 0 of the patients during days 1 to 7 respectively. Plasma cannabinoid concentrations were not correlated with BMI or fat of the chronic user. The patients who smoked for the longest period (twenty-two years) had THC detected longer and had the smallest decrease with time. The patient who smoked for the shortest time (two years) had the greatest decrease in THC.

> On the other hand, blood THC concentrations at the time of an accident are likely much higher than at the time blood is collected by clinical staff or police, which is generally two to four hours after an accident. Thus, although per se limits may be useful in cases where impairment cannot be documented by a sobriety test, drug recognition expert's examination or other measures of performance, limits as high as 2–5 ng/mL would prevent conviction of many drugged drivers who had documented poor performance with much lower THC concentrations at the time of the blood collection. Jones et al clearly showed that 77 to 90 percent of Swedish motor vehicle operators from 1995 to 2004, who recently smoked cannabis, would escape criminal charges if a 5 ng/mL whole blood limit were applied.

Reference Number: 10302

KARSCHNER, E.L., E.W. SCHWILKE, R.H. LOWE, W.D. DARWIN, H.G. POPE JR., R. HERNING, J.L. CADET, AND M.A. HUESTIS. "Do delta 9-Tetrahydrocannabinol Concentrations Indicate Recent Use in Chronic Cannabis Users?" *Addiction*, 104: 2041–48, 2009 (2 tables, 2 figures, 45 references)

Abstract: Whole blood cannabinoid concentrations were determined in thirteen female and twelve male frequent cannabis users (ages 21 to 38 years) in a secure research facility over seven days. Blood THC > 11-OH THC except in four participants on day one. On day one, blood THC > 1 ng/mL was detected in five participants (25 percent) and the highest blood THC was 7 ng/mL. A blood THC> 1 ng/mL was found in three participants.

> In summary, we found highly variable but often substantial whole blood THC concentrations in chronic cannabis users for many days after last drug exposure. These findings may be relevant for legislation employing THC concentrations to define intoxication and accident culpability.

Reference Number: 10303

REITER, A., J. HAKE, C. MEISSNER, J. ROHWER, H.J. FRIEDRICH, AND M. OEHMICHEN. "Time of Drug Elimination in Chronic Drug Abusers Case Study of 52 Patients in a Low Step Detoxification Ward." *Forensic Science International*, 119: 248–53, 2001 (6 tables, 29 references)

Abstract: Forty-two male (mean age 24.3 years) and ten female (mean age 20.7 years) heroin addicts had urine and blood samples collected daily for three weeks while undergoing treatment in a detoxification ward. Serum and urine THCCOOH and THC concentrations were determined by GC/MS at a detection limit of 10 ng/mL. The mean serum and urine THCCOOH concentrations initially were 23.8 and 260.4 ng/mL respectively. The mean THCCOOH detection time was 34.0 hours (3.4 to 74.3 hours in serum and 260.4 hours (0.1 to 433.3 hours) in urine).

> We could not detect THC in the serum of a single volunteer; according to the literature, the detection time should be five to twelve hours. THCCOOH by contrast could be detected in the serum for up to seventy-four hours.

Reference Number: 10304

LEE, D., M.M. BERGAMASCHI, G. MILMAN, A.J. BARNES, R.H.C. QUEIROZ, R. VANDREY, AND M.A. HUESTIS. "Plasma Cannabinoid Pharmacokinetics After Controlled Smoking and *Ad libitum* Cannabis Smoking in Chronic Frequent Users." *Journal of Analytical Toxicology*, 39: 580–87, 2015 (2 tables, 4 figures, 45 references)

Abstract: Ten male and one female chronic marijuana smokers had frequent blood samples collected after smoking a single 5.9 percent THC cannabis cigarette and after *ad libitum* smoking. Plasma THC, 11-OH-THC, and THCCOOH concentrations were determined by GC/MS. Median plasma maximum concentrations were 28.3 ng/mL (THC), 3.9 ng/mL (11-OH-THC), and 47.0 ng/mL (THCCOOH) after a single cigarette and 83.5, 14.2, and 155 ng/mL after *ad libitum* smoking respectively. Cannabinoid detection rates in seven smokers, four to five days after *ad libitum* smoking were 92.9 percent (THC > 0.5 ng/mL), 35.7 percent (11-OH-THC > 1 ng/mL), and 100 percent (THCCOOH > 0.5 ng/mL).

Smoking multiple cannabis cigarettes led to higher Cmax and AUC compared with smoking a single cigarette. The chronic frequent cannabis smokers exhibited extended detection windows for plasma cannabinoids, reflecting a large cannabinoid body burden.

Reference Number: 10305

LEMBERGER, L., R. MARTZ, B. RODDA, R. FORNEY, AND H. ROWE. "Comparative Pharmacology of delta-9-Tetrahydrocannabinol and its Metabolite 11-OH-delta-9-Tetrahydrocannabinol." *The Journal of Clinical Investigation*, 52: 2411–17, 1973 (3 tables, 5 figures, 18 references)

Abstract: Nine male occasional marijuana smokers (ages 22 to 24 years) were administered on various occasions either radioactively labelled 11-OH-THC or THC (1 mg dissolved in 1 mL of absolute alcohol) IV within one minute. The maximum psychological high occurred within two to three minutes after injection with 11-OH-THC, but approximately fifteen minutes after THC administration. The heart rate increased by 20 to 70 ppm after 11-OH-THC and 20 to 55 ppm after THC. Approximately 22 percent of 11-OH-THC was excreted in the urine after one week and 50 percent was excreted in the feces and is similar to the excretion of THC.

In general, the results of this present investigation indicate that in man, 11-OH-THC at the dose used is more potent than delta-9-THC, and further suggests that the psychological effects of delta-9-THC are dependent upon its conversion to an active metabolite.

Reference Number: 10306

SKOPP, G., AND L. POTSCH. "Cannabinoid Concentrations in Spot Serum Samples 24–48 Hours after Discontinuation of Cannabis Smoking." *Journal of Analytical Toxicology*, 32: 160–64, 2008 (3 tables, 24 references)

Abstract: Random serum samples were collected from sixteen heavy (> 1 joint/day), fifteen moderate (< 1 joint/day), and six light (< 1 joint/week) cannabis users who claimed twenty-four- to forty-eight-hour abstinence. Serum THC, 11-OH-THC, and free 11-THCCOOH were determined by GC/MS. A serum THC > 1 ng/mL was detected in eight heavy, three moderate, and one light user.

Although the authors are aware of the small study number, the present findings appear to indicate that low levels of THC along with OH-THC may not unequivocally prove a recent use of hashish or marijuana. Depending on the frequency and intensity of drug use, detection of psychoactive cannabinoids seems possible over a time period of more than twenty-four to forty-eight hours after abstaining from cannabis smoking.

Reference Number: 10307

BERGAMASCHI, M.M., E.L. KARSCHNER, R.S. GOODWIN, K.B. SCHEIDWEILER, J. HIRVONEN, R.H.C. QUEIROZ, AND M.A. HUESTIS. "Impact of Prolonged Cannabinoid Excretion in Chronic Daily Cannabis Smokers Blood on Per Se Drugged Driving Laws." *Clinical Chemistry*, 59: 519–26, 2013 (2 tables, 2 figures, 40 references)

Abstract: Thirty male chronic daily (median nine joints per day) cannabis smokers (median age 28 years) had blood samples collected every day for thirty-three days. Blood THC, 11-OH-THC, and THCCOOH concentrations determined by GC/MS. The limits of quantification were 0.5 ng/mL for THC and THCCOOH, and 0.5 ng/mL for 11-OH-THC. All subjects were also alcohol consumers. Upon admission, the blood THC concentration was 1.4 ng/mL (range 0.3 to 6.3 ng/mL). The maximal blood THC detected was > 2 ng/mL after nine days. The blood 11-OH-THC was < 1 ng/mL after one day and not detected for the rest of the time. The maximal blood THCCOOH concentrations did not drop below 1 ng/mL until thirty-one days. Sweden and Australia have a zero tolerance for illegal drugs. If a 5 ng/mL THC limit was employed in Sweden, 90 percent of the drivers would not have been prosecuted and 60 percent would not be prosecuted with a 1 ng/mL limit.

> In conclusion, our results demonstrate, for the first time as far as we are aware, that cannabinoids can be detected in blood of chronic daily cannabis smokers during a month of sustained abstinence. This is consistent with the time course of persisting neurocognitive impairment reported in recent studies. There is a strong public safety need to reduce morbidity and mortality from cannabis-impaired driving. Extended residual THC excretion in chronic daily cannabis smokers complicates prosecution. Establishment of per se THC legislation might achieve such a reduction in motor vehicle injuries and deaths. Per se alcohol legislation improved the prosecution of drunk drivers and dramatically reduced alcohol-related deaths. By analogy, one way to protect the public from drugged drivers is to establish legislation making it illegal to smoke cannabis and drive.

1.04 GENERAL PHARMACOKINETICS

Men generally obtain a higher blood THC concentration than women, which may be due in part to the differences in fat content between genders (10404). Women also tend to develop more dizziness, anxiety, and depression after cannabis use than men (10104). Low oral doses of THC are safely tolerated by older persons with dementia (10401). Heavy cannabis users typically obtain higher blood THC concentrations after smoking than occasional users (10408). After oral consumption of cannabis, the blood 11-OH-THC concentration may predict stronger dose effects (10406).

Reference Number: 10401

AHMED, A.I.A., G.A.H. VAN DEN ELSEN, A. COLBERS, C. KRAMERS, D.M. BURGER, M.A. VAN DER MARCK, AND M.G.M.O. RIKKERT. "Safety, Pharmacodynamics and Pharmacokinetics of Multiple Oral Doses of Delta-9

Tetrahydrocannabinol in Older Persons with Dementia." *Psychopharmacology,* 232: 2587–95, 2015 (4 tables, 3 figures, 35 references)

Abstract: Ten patients with dementia (mean age 77 years) received for twelve weeks oral THC (0.75 mg and 1.5 mg) or placebo twice daily for three days followed by a four-day washout period. Frequent blood samples were collected, and plasma THC and 11-OH-THC concentrations were measured by LC/MS. The mean maximum blood THC were 0.5 and 1.0 ng/mL and the mean maximum 11-OH-THC were 1.5 and 1.8 ng/mL for the low and high THC doses respectively.

> Our findings show that low THC doses are safe and well tolerated by frail, older persons with dementia. Oral THC was rapidly absorbed, showing dose-linear pharmacokinetics with maximum plasma concentrations being reached between one and two hours after dosing, although there was considerable inter-individual variability. Overall, THC showed smaller pharmacodynamics effects in frail, older individuals than expected on the basis of data for young healthy adults. These reassuring data warrant further pharmacodynamic and efficacy studies with higher THC doses in older patients with dementia.

Reference Number: 10402

AZORLOSA, J.L., S.J. HEISHMAN, M.L. STITZER, AND J.M. MAHAFFEY. "Marijuana Smoking: Effect of Varying delta 9 Tetrahydrocannabinol Content and Number of Puffs." *Journal of Pharmacology and Experimental Therapeutics*, 261: 114–22, 1992 (2 tables, 3 figures, 31 references)

Abstract: Seven male cannabis users (ages 19 to 28 years) smoked 4, 10, or 25 puffs from a marijuana cigarette containing 1.75 or 3.55 percent THC on six separate occasions. Plasma THC concentrations were determined by blood samples collected by an indwelling catheter and analyzed by RIA. The mean plasma THC concentrations were 56.9, 98.6, and 171.9 ng/mL for the 1.75 percent THC and 89.4, 172.6, and 268.4 ng/mL for the 3.55 percent THC after 4, 10, and 25 puffs respectively. The mean heart rate increased by up to 36 bpm for the high dose THC after 25 puffs. Various performance tests such as divided attention and DSST were conducted.

> The study showed that subjective measures were more sensitive to marijuana effects than were performance measures and that large individ-

ual differences in extent of performance impairment were apparent at higher plasma THC.

Reference Number: 10403

DESROSIER, N.A., S.K. HIMES, K.B. SCHEIDWEILER, M. CONCHEIRO-GUISAN, D.A. GORELICK, AND M.A. HUESTIS. "Phase I and II Cannabinoid Disposition in Blood and Plasma of Occasional and Frequent Smokers Following Controlled Smoked Cannabis." *Clinical Chemistry*, 60: 631–43, 2014 (4 tables, 2 figures, 25 references)

Abstract: Blood and plasma THC, 11-OH-THC, THCCOOH, cannabidiol (CBD), cannabinol (CBN), THC-glucuronide, and THCCOO-glucuronide were determined by LC-GC/MS in frequent blood samples collected via an indwelling catheter in fourteen frequent and eleven occasional marijuana smokers before and after smoking one 6.8 percent THC joint. The overall median blood to plasma ratios were 0.68, 0.63, 0.63, 0.59, 0.84, and 0.47 for THC, 11-OH-THC, THCCOOH, CBD, CBN, and THCCOO-glucuronide respectively. Overall blood and plasma cannabinoid concentrations were higher in frequent smokers compared to infrequent smokers. The median (range) of detecting a blood THC > 5 ng/mL was 3.5 hours (1.1 to > 30 hours) in frequent smokers and 1.0 hour (0-2.1 hours) in the occasional smokers. THC appears in plasma after the first puff and peaks before the last puff of the marijuana cigarette. THC is rapidly metabolized to 11-OH-THC, which peaks approximately thirteen minutes after smoking and reaching 10 percent of THC concentration. 11-OH-THC is metabolized to THCCOOH, which increases to a maximum over the first hour of smoking and plateaus after two to four hours. CBD/CBN ratio and THC-glucuronide could be used as inclusionary markers of recent use.

Cannabis-smoking history plays a major role in cannabinoid detection. These differences may impact clinical and impaired driving drug detection. The presence of cannabidiol, cannabinol, or THC-glucuronide indicates recent use, but their absence does not exclude it.

Reference Number: 10404

FATTORE, L., AND W. FRATTA. "How Important are Sex Differences in Cannabinoid Action?" *British Journal of Pharmacology*, 160: 544–48, 2010 (2 figures, 35 references)

Abstract: A general review of the differences between genders in cannabinoid action using human and animal studies. Boys are more likely to be heavy users than girls (6 percent versus 2 percent respectively). Women report significantly more dizziness than men. Men are more sensitive to the subjective effects of THC and have higher blood THC concentrations than women. Cannabinoids exert a greater effect on food intake and energy balance in men than in women and women develop more anxiety and depression from cannabis use.

> Yet, cannabinoid pharmacodynamics and pharmacokinetics may also be important, as sex differences in cannabinoid effects may be due, at least in part, to differences in muscle mass and the tissue distribution between males and females.

Reference Number: 10405

GROTENHERMEN, F. "Pharmacokinetics and Pharmacodynamics of Cannabinoids." *Clinical Pharmacokinetics*, 42: 327–60, 2003 (6 tables, 15 figures, 339 references)

Abstract: An excellent and well written review of the pharmacokinetics and dynamics of cannabinoids — mainly THC. The pharmacokinetics of THC vary according to its route of administration. With oral use, absorption is slow and erratic — maximal plasma THC concentration occurring after 60 to 120 minutes, but occasionally to four to six hours and even multiple peaks. About 90 percent of the THC in blood is distributed to the plasma bound to lipoproteins. Time course of plasma THC concentration fits an open 2, 3, 4, or even 5 compartmental models. THC passes to breast milk about 0.2 percent of the THC ingested by the mother. There are 100 different metabolites of THC. The major reason for the slow elimination of THC is the slow re-diffusion of THC from the body fat and other tissues into the blood. The terminal half-life is twenty-five to thirty-six hours for THC, twelve to thirty-six hours for 11-OH-THC, and twenty-five to fifty-five hours for THCCOOH. THC can induce tachycardia and increase oxygen demand and cause peripheral vasodilation and orthostatic hypotension.

> THC is thermolabile and photolabile. Storage leads to a cumulative decrease in THC content through oxidation of THC to CBN. Within forty-seven weeks, the THC content of marijuana (dried leaves and flowers of

Cannabis sativa) decreased by 7 percent with dare and dry storage at 5°C and by 13 percent at 20°C. Dronabinol rapidly degrades in acid solutions.

Reference Number: 10406

VANDREY, R., H.E.S. HERMANN, J.M. MITCHELL, G.E. BIGELOW, R. FLEGEL, C. LODICO, AND E.J. CONE. "Pharmacokinetic Profile of Oral Cannabis in Humans: Blood and Oral Fluid Disposition and Relation to Pharmacodynamic Outcomes." *Journal of Analytical Toxicology*, 41: 83–99, 2017 (6 tables, 6 figures, 29 references)

Abstract: Nine male and nine female healthy drug-free subjects (mean age 26 years) consumed brownies containing either 10, 25 or 50 mg THC. Whole blood and expectorated oral fluid samples were obtained for up to nine days later. Cannabis containing 11 percent total THC, 0.1 percent CBD, and 0.8 percent CBN was baked into the brownies at the laboratory. The powdered cannabis was baked at 121°C for thirty minutes to convert the inactive THCA into THC. THC concentrations were determined by an ELISA screen and LC/MS/MS. Blood 11-OH-THC and THCCOOH concentrations were determined by LC/MS/MS. OF THCCOOH were measured by ELISA and LC/MS/MS. Computerized cognitive/psychomotor tests such as the Digit Symbol Substitution Test (DSST) and the Divided Attention Task (DAT) were conducted, as well as cardiovascular and subjective measures. The subjective drug effect after oral ingestion occurred from thirty to sixty minutes after consumption and was sustained for ninety to 180 minutes and gradually decreased after eight hours. Impairment in DSST and other psychomotor tests occurred at the 25 and 50 mg dose but not the 10 mg dose. The maximum blood THC concentrations were 1.0, 3.5 and 3.3 ng/mL for the three doses respectively. High THC concentrations occurred in the OF samples immediately after the oral consumption of the cannabis-infused brownies (ten to thirty minutes) and rapidly declined over two hours. This was due to the THC being deposited in the oral cavity by chewing the brownies and would unlikely occur if encapsulated oral cannabis products such as dronabinol were ingested. Cannabis ingestion can cause dry mouth and 2.6 percent of OF samples could not be provided due to this effect.

Table: Mean Maximum Blood Concentrations of THC, 11-OH-THC, and THCCOOH, and Mean Time to Achieve the Maximum Blood Concentration After Oral Ingestion

Dose	Mean THC Maximum (ng/mL)	Mean Time to THC Maximum (hrs)	Mean 11-OH-THC Maximum (ng/mL)	Mean Time to 11-OH THC Maximum (hrs)	Mean THCCOOH Maximum (ng/mL)	Mean Time to THCCOOH Maximum (hrs)
10 mg	1.0 ng/mL	0.9	1.0 ng/mL	1.3	7.2 ng/mL	3.2
25 mg	3.5 ng/mL	2.6	3.3 ng/mL	3.0	21.3 ng/mL	3.3
50 mg	3.3 ng/mL	2.3	3.2 ng/mL	1.8	29.3 ng/mL	3.3

Source: Adapted from Vandrey et al, 2017

Interestingly, blood levels of THC, 11-OH-THC, and THCCOOH were moderate to highly correlated with subjective drug effect at all three doses. The strength of the correlation between THC and subjective drug effects decreased with increasing THC dose, but the strength of correlations between 11-OH-THC increased with increasing THC dose administered, suggesting that 11-OH-THC may be a more valid analyte for predicting stronger dose effects. Significant correlations were also observed between psychoactive blood cannabinoids and DSST percent correct, but these correlations were highest at the 10 mg dose when there was no impairment relative to baseline task performance. The use of blood cannabinoid levels as a predictive biomarker of intoxication or impairment following oral cannabis exposure is further complicated by the fact that the levels observed in this study are comparable to those likely to be measured in frequent cannabis users during periods of extended abstinence when no intoxication or impairment is evident.

Reference Number: 10407

WOODHOUSE, E.J. "Confirmation of the Presence of 11-Hydroxy delta-9-Tetrahydrocannabinol in the Urine of Marijuana Smokers." *American Journal of Public Health,* 62: 1394–96, 1972 (2 tables, 1 figure, 9 references)

Abstract: Four male experienced cannabis smokers (aged 21-28 years) smoked marijuana (0.6 to 5 percent THC) over a period of twelve hours. All urine samples voided by the subjects over that time period were collected and analyzed for 11-OH-THC and 11-OH-CBN after organic extraction, Thin Layer Chromatography, and MS. The marijuana samples smoked contained approximately equal amounts of THC and CBN and no detectable CBD. Control urine samples from three subjects not exposed to cannabis were also collected and analyzed.

> The conclusion drawn from this investigation is that 11-hydroxy-delta-9-tetrahydrocannabinol is present in the hydrolyzed urine of marijuana smokers. Other cannabinoids, especially 11-hydroxy-cannabinol, are indicated. The results are qualitative as yet but do indicate that similar metabolic processes are occurring when marijuana is smoked as occur when tetrahydrocannabinol is injected.

Reference Number: 10408

TOENNES, S.W., J.G. RAMAEKERS, E.L. THEUNISSEN, M.R. MOELLER, AND G.F. KAUERT. "Comparisons of Cannabinoid Pharmacokinetic Properties in Occasional and Heavy Users Smoking a Marijuana or Placebo Joint." *Journal of Analytical Toxicology*, 32: 470–77, 2008 (2 tables, 2 figures, 27 references)

Abstract: Four female and eight male occasional and three female and nine male heavy users (20 to 31 years of age) smoked a placebo or a 13 percent THC cannabis cigarette (median dose 33 mg) within ten minutes. Blood samples were collected frequently for up to eight hours and the serum THC, 11-OH-THC, and THCCOOH concentrations were measured by GC/MS. A positive serum THC concentration was observed in ten of the twelve heavy cannabis users at baseline (1.3 to 12.3 ng/mL). The peak serum THC concentrations were higher in heavy users than occasional users. The half-life of THC after smoking cannabis was 1.0 to 5.9 hours, compared to 17.5 to 42.5 hours after smoking placebo.

> The present study on cannabinoid pharmacokinetic properties in cannabis and placebo conditions indicates that occasional users (use < four times a month) exhibit no cannabinoids in the sober state, but comply with established pharmacokinetics. Heavy users reach higher THC concentrations in the cannabis condition despite equal doses and a standardized smoking procedure; however, the pharmacokinetic properties of THC, THC-OH, and THCA are not markedly different, especially when the values are corrected for the initial concentrations. The placebo condition revealed that heavy users might accumulate an amount

of THC that leads to cannabinoid concentrations in sober phases that resemble concentrations found in occasional users after acute cannabis use. Therefore, data obtained from heavy users have to be critically evaluated and further research in monitoring cannabinoids in heavy users after short- and long-term abstinence seems necessary.

Reference Number: 10409

FABRITIUS, M., B. FAVRAT, H. CHTIOUI, G. BATTISTELLA, J-M. ANNONI, M. APPENZELLER, K. DAO., E. FORNARI, E. LAUER, J-F. MALL, P. MAEDER, P. MANGIN, C. STAUB, AND C. GIROUD. "THCCOOH Concentrations in Whole Blood: Are They Useful in Discriminating Occasional from Heavy Smokers?" *Drug Testing and Analysis*, 6: 155–63, 2014 (3 tables, 4 figures, 25 references)

Abstract: The blood THC and THCCOOH were determined by MS/MS in twenty-five occasional and twenty-three heavy male cannabis smokers (ages 18 to 30 years) before and after smoking a 7.7 mg THC (700 mg, 11 percent), or a placebo (< 0.1 percent). The terminal half-life of THCCOOH is very long.

> Whole blood THCCOOH concentrations of heavy smokers determined in a controlled administration study greatly exceeded those measured in the occasional user's group. Therefore, we can take advantage of this difference to estimate in which category of smokers the drivers belong. A level of THCCOOH higher than 40 ug/L is strongly correlated with a heavy consumption of cannabis, whereas a concentration below 3 ug/L suggests occasional use.

1.05 EFFECTS OF ALCOHOL AND OTHER DRUGS

The mean blood THC concentration tends to increase if smoked with the co-consumption of alcohol or tobacco (as a blunt) (10502-6). Cannabis use appears to have no effect on the viral load of HIV-treated patients and increased their weight more than placebo (10501). The combination of Viagra with cannabis use has been associated with a myocardial infarction (10507). The oral consumption of cannabis tends to slow the rate of gastric emptying (10508).

Reference Number: 10501

ABRAMS, D.I., J.F. HILTON, R.J. LEISER, S.B. SHADE, T.A. ELBEIK, F.T. AWEEKA, N.L. BENOWITZ, B.M. BREDT, B. KOSEL, J.A. ABERG, S.G. DEEKS, T.F. MITCHELL, K. MULLIGAN, P. BACCHETT, J.M. MCCUNE, AND M. SCHAMBELAN. "Short-Term Effects of Cannabinoids in Patients with HIV-1 Infection." *Annals Internal Medicine*, 139: 258–66, 2003 (3 tables, 2 figures, 44 references)

Abstract: The short-term effect of cannabis use on viral load in HIV-infected patients was determined over a twenty-one-day period. Sixty-two HIV patients were randomly assigned to a 3.95 percent THC marijuana cigarette, 2.5 mg of dronabinol or a placebo capsule, three times daily before meals. HIV RNA levels, CH4+ and CD8+ cell subsets, and pharmacokinetic analysis of protease inhibition were determined at the start and throughout the study. Most patients were men (89 percent) and 62 percent were older than 40 years of age. Patients in the placebo condition gained a median of 1.1 kg, and patients using cannabis gained 3.0 kg (smoking) and 3.2 kg (oral).

This study provides evidence that short-term use of cannabinoids, either oral or smoked, does not substantially elevate viral load in individuals with HIV infection who are receiving stable antiretroviral regiments containing nelfinavir or indinavir.

Reference Number: 10502

COOPER, Z.D. AND M. HANEY. "Comparison of Subjective, Pharmacokinetic and Physiological Effects of Marijuana Smoked as Joints and Blunts." *Drug and Alcohol Dependence*, 103: 107–13, 2009 (5 figures, 26 references)

Abstract: Joints usually consist of marijuana rolled in standard cigarette paper. Blunts are made by removing tobacco from a cigar and replacing it with marijuana and were popularized by American hip-hop culture. The cigar leaf contains tobacco and nicotine, which may interact with the cardio-vascular and subjective effects of cannabis. Twelve female and twelve male blunt smokers (ages 21 to 45 years) inhaled either a marijuana blunt or cigarette (0, 1.8, and 3.6 percent THC). Plasma THC and nicotine concentrations and exhaled CO concentrations were determined. The mean THC concentrations were 12.4 ng/mL for men and 15.4 ng/mL for women. The cigar leaf produced no detectable blood nicotine concentrations. There was no difference in HR between joints or blunts.

Table: Mean Peak Plasma THC Concentration after Smoking a Low and High Dose Marijuana, Smoked as Joints or Blunts.

	Smoked as Joints	Smoke as Blunts
Low Dose Cannabis (1.8% THC)	50 ng/mL	77 ng/mL
High Dose Cannabis (3.6% THC)	60 ng/mL	85 ng/mL

Source: Adapted from Cooper and Haney, 2009

Using identical smoking procedures, marijuana smoked as joints affords greater THC plasma levels and subjective intoxicating effects compared to blunts yet blunts produce equal increases in heart rates and greater increases in carbon monoxide levels than joints. Thus, smoking marijuana in tobacco leaf increases the risks of marijuana by enhancing carbon monoxide exposure and heart rate compared to marijuana smoked in paper, risks that may be especially marked in women.

Reference Number: 10503

HUNAULT, C.C., J.C.H. VAN EIJKEREN, T.T. MENSINGA, I. DE VRIES, M.E.C., LEENDERS, AND J. MEULENBELT. "Disposition of Smoked Cannabis with High delta 9-Tetrahydrocannabinol Content: A Kinetic Model." *Toxicology and Applied Pharmacology,* 246: 148–53, 2010 (3 tables, 4 figures, 26 references)

Abstract: The standard NIDA joint contains 900 mg of pure cannabis, which has approximately 9 to 16 mg of THC for the lowest dose and 34 mg THC for the highest dose. In Europe, most of the cannabis smoked is mixed with tobacco (in this experiment, 300 mg of cannabis and 700 mg of tobacco). Twenty-four male cannabis users (ages 18 to 33 years) smoked marijuana cigarettes containing 0, 29.3, 49.1, and 69.4 mg THC. Blood samples were collected frequently for the next eight hours after smoking and the serum THC concentrations were determined by LC/MS. The median serum maximum THC concentrations were 114.5, 153.5, and 202.0 ng/mL for each dose respectively. A two compartmental open pharmacokinetic model was developed.

The model offers insight into the pharmacokinetics of THC in recreational cannabis users smoking cannabis containing high doses of THC mixed with tobacco. The model is an objective method for providing serum THC concentrations up to eight hours after smoking with a high THC content (up to 23 percent).

Reference Number: 10504

BALLARD, M.E. AND H. DE WIT. "Combined Effects of Acute, Very-Low-Dose Ethanol and Delta 9-Tetrahydrocannabinol in Healthy Human Volunteers." *Pharmacology and Biochemistry of Behavior,* 97: 627–31, 2011 (3 tables, 1 figure, 48 references)

Abstract: Five female and six male subjects (mean age 25 years) consumed placebo alcohol/THC; 0.1 and 0.2 g/kg alcohol and 2.5 mg oral THC (marinol). Subjective and physiological tests were conducted at forty and seventy minutes after the beverage was consumed. BrACs were measured with an Alco-Sensor III. DSSTs were also conducted. THC did not affect BrACs. THC decreased the desire for alcohol.

> Our data provided no evidence of synergistic effects of acute combinations of very-low-dose ethanol and THC on subjective or physiologic response or on cognitive performance.

Reference Number: 10505

LUKAS, S.E. AND S. OROZCO. "Ethanol Increases Plasma delta 9 Tetrahydrocannabinol (THC) Levels and Subjective Effects after Marihuana Smoking in Human Volunteers." *Drug and Alcohol Dependence,* 64: 143–49, 2001 (1 table, 2 figures, 35 references)

Abstract: About 70 percent of marijuana users reported combining it with alcohol to get a better high. Twenty-two male marijuana smokers consumed a placebo, 0.35, and 0.7 g/kg alcohol over eighteen minutes and then smoked either a placebo, 1.26 percent, or 2.53 percent THC cannabis cigarettes. Frequent blood samples were collected and plasma THC concentrations were determined, as well as subjective effects. In a previous study, marijuana smoke was found to slow the absorption of alcohol. Alcohol increased the initial plasma THC concentrations but not in the declining phase.

> These data suggest that ethanol may increase the absorption of THC, resulting in an increase in the positive subjective mood effects of smoked marijuana and contributing to the popularity of this drug combination.

Reference Number: 10506

HARTMAN, R.L., T.L. BROWN, G. MILAVETZ, A. SPURGIN, D.A. GORELICK, G. GAFFNEY, AND M.A. HUESTIS. "Controlled Cannabis Vaporizer Administration: Blood and Plasma Cannabinoids with and without Alcohol." *Clinical Chemistry*, 61: 850–59, 2015 (4 tables, 2 figures, 40 references)

Abstract: Ten female and twenty-two male cannabis smokers (ages 21–42 years) drank a placebo or alcohol (calculated to obtain a BAC of 0.065 g/100mL) within ten minutes. After drinking, the subjects inhaled placebo THC, low THC (2.9 percent), and high THC (6.7 percent) within ten minutes. Blood samples were collected before and frequently after inhalation for up to 8.3 hours. Blood and plasma cannabinoid concentrations were measured by LC-MS/MS. Nineteen subjects completed all six alcohol/cannabis doses. The mean peak THC blood concentration was 32.7 and 42.2 ng/mL for the low and high dose THC respectively with no alcohol consumption, and 35.3 and 67.5 ng/mL with alcohol. Higher THC and 11-OH-THC concentrations in the blood may be due to increased absorption of THC. Alcohol had little effect on cannabis metabolism. If a 1 ng/L THC cutoff was chosen, approximately 17 percent of the subjects were positive 8.3 hours after inhalation. If a 5 ng/mL cutoff was chosen, approximately 21 percent were positive after 2.3 hours.

Table: Mean Maximum Blood THC and 11-OH-THC Concentrations (ng/mL) with and without Prior Consumption of Alcohol.

	Blood THC (Low Dose)	Blood THC (High Dose)	Blood 11-OH-THC (Low Dose)	Blood 11-OH-THC (High Dose)
No Alcohol	32.7 ng/mL	42.2 ng/mL	2.8 ng/mL	5.0 ng/mL
Alcohol	35.3 ng/mL	67.5 ng/mL	3.7 ng/mL	6.0 ng/mL

Source: Adapted from Hartman et al, 2015

Vaporization is an effective THC delivery route. The significantly higher blood THC and 11-OH-THC Cmax values with alcohol possibly explain increased performance impairment observed from cannabis-alcohol combinations. Chosen driving-related THC cutoffs should be considered carefully to best reduce performance impairment windows. Our results will help facilitate forensic interpretation and inform the debate on drugged driving legislation.

Reference Number: 10507

MCLEOD, A.L., C.J. MCKENNA, AND D.B. NORTHBRIDGE. "Myocardial Infarction Following the Combined Recreational Use of Viagra and Cannabis." *Clinical Cardiology,* 25: 133–34, 2002 (6 references)

Abstract: Sildenafil citrate (Viagra) is metabolized mainly by the cytochrome P450 3A4 liver enzyme system that also metabolizes cannabis. A forty-one-year-old man was admitted to hospital for chest pains about twelve hours after smoking cannabis and taking one tablet of Viagra. He was treated with aspirin, beta blockers, and low molecular weight heparin. He had suffered a recent myocardial infarction (MI).

Previous literature has drawn attention to an association between Viagra use and MI. Postulated mechanisms include ischemia, increased shear stress, and coronary steal resulting from widespread vasodilation. This is the first reported case indicating the potential interaction between Viagra and cannabis. Through cytochrome P450 3A4, inhibition plasma levels of Viagra increase along with its physiological and adverse effects.

Reference Number: 10508

MCCALLUM, R.W., I. SOYKAN, K.R. SRIDHAR, D.A. RICCI, R.C. LANGE, AND M.W. PLANKEY. "Delta-9-Tetrahydrocannabinol Delays Gastric Emptying of Solid Food in Humans: A Double-Blind Randomized Study." *Aliment Pharmacology and Therapeutics,* 13: 77–80, 1999 (2 figures, 18 references)

Abstract: Nine male and four female subjects (ages 19 to 30 years), with some marijuana exposure, consumed a placebo or 10 mg/m^2 THC and a radioactively labelled test meal, which consisted of beef stew and a cracker. THC significantly slowed gastric emptying from 30 minutes to 94.2 minutes. The mean plasma THC concentrations were approximately 3 ng/mL, 10 ng/mL, and 8 ng/mL at one, two, and three hours respectively.

Delta-9-tetrahydrocannabinol delay in the emptying of solids may be helpful in understanding some THC-drug interactions. For example, THC slows the absorption of alcohol and pentobarbital. Although alcohol is absorbed to some extent from the stomach, it has to reach the small intestine to be fully absorbed, and a delay in gastric emptying slows the absorption of alcohol. Similar changes in the pharmacokinetics of other drugs, including orally administered anti-neoplastic agents, should also be considered. Because nausea is a psychological event that depends on sensory afferents such as pain, we can speculate that THC may reduce nausea by altering sensory input into the central nervous system.

CHAPTER 2

Blood Cannabinoids

The concentrations of THC and other cannabinoids in the blood are approximately 100,000 times less than that of alcohol. Hence, the methods used to analyze alcohol, such as headspace gas chromatography and the breathalyzer, do not apply to this drug. Instead, blood cannabinoid analysis requires more sensitive and sophisticated instruments, such as gas chromatography-mass spectrometry (GC-MS) or liquid chromatography-mass spectrometry (LC-MS) or even LC-MS-MS. Cannabinoid concentrations differ in blood compared to serum/plasma as they are bound to carrier proteins found in the serum/plasma portion of the blood and not the red blood cells.

2.01 METHODS OF ANALYSIS

The analyses of THC and other cannabinoids are conducted by immunoassays (as a screen) and then confirmed by laboratory-based mass spectrometers of one type or another. The first type of immunoassay was RIA or radio-immunoassay (20101). Other immunoassay techniques include ELISA (enzyme-linked immunosorbent assay), EMIT (enzyme-multiplied immunoassay technique) or FPIA (fluorescence polarization immunoassay).

Various types of mass spectrographic techniques are employed for the confirmation and quantification of the immunoassay screens (20102-5). An automated method has been described (20106).

Reference Number: 20101

ZIMMERMAN, E.G., E.P. YEAGER, J.R. SOARES, L.E. HOLLISTER, AND V.C. REEVE. "Measurement of delta-9-Tetrahydrocannabinol (THC) in Whole Blood Samples from Impaired Motorists." *Journal of Forensic Sciences*, 28: 957–62, 1983 (1 table, 3 figures, 12 references)

Abstract: Radio-immunoassay (RIA) was employed to analyze the THC concentration of 10 uL of serum or hemolyzed blood. There were no significant interferences of this method with other THC metabolites or other cannabinoids. Of the 1,792 blood samples collected from drivers in California who were driving erratically and analyzed, 14.4 percent were positive for THC (> 5.5 ng/mL).

> Sophisticated laboratory simulation and real-life driving studies support the view that marijuana in standard doses detrimentally affects driving performance. These findings are especially disturbing in view of the significant incidence and broad age of marijuana smoking adults. In conclusion, psychoactive THC was found in 14.4 percent of a large population of erratic motorists whose blood was analyzed by RIA. The range of blood THC levels was narrow, and use was spread over a broad age range. This preliminary effort represents the first large-scale field survey using quantitative analysis of delta-9-tetrahydrocannabinol in forensic specimens. This initial experience should facilitate and amplify a program designed to set forth the epidemiology of marijuana use in motorists and possible behavioural correlates.

Reference Number: 20102

SCURLOCK, R.D., G.B. OHLSON, AND D.K. WORTHEN. "The Detection of delta 9 Tetrahydrocannabinol (THC) and 11-nor-9-Carboxy-delta 9-Tetrahydrocannabinol (THCA) in Whole Blood Using Two-Dimensional Gas Chromatography and EI Mass Spectrometry." *Journal of Analytical Toxicology*, 30: 262–66, 2006 (6 figures, 9 references)

Abstract: A method to simultaneously measure THC and its metabolite THCCOOH using a two-dimensional gas chromatograph (i.e., 2 GC columns) and an electron ionization (EI) MS as whole blood samples is described. Sixty-three different drugs were tested on this system and none caused interference with the THC and THCCOOH results.

The 2D-GC-MS system described here is a relatively inexpensive addition to common GC ovens that enables an improvement in detection limits of cannabinoids by greatly reducing matrix interference.

Reference Number: 20103

HARTMAN, R.L., T.L. BROWN, G. MILAVETZ, A. SPURGIN, D.A. GORELICK, G.R. GAFFNEY, AND M.A. HUESTIS. "Effect of Blood Collection Time on Measured delta 9-Tetrahydrocannabinol Concentrations: Implications for Driving Interpretation and Drug Policy." *Clinical Chemistry,* 62: 367–77, 2016 (4 tables, 2 figures, 40 references)

Abstract: In the US, blood samples are usually not collected in DUIC cases until approximately 1.5 to 4 hours after the incident. Thirteen male and five female cannabis users (ages 21 to 37 years) drank a placebo or a low dose alcohol (target BAC 0.065 g/100mL) within ten minutes and ten minutes later inhaled a vaporized placebo, 2.9 percent or 6.9 percent THC over ten minutes. Frequent blood samples were collected and after protein precipitation the THC was measured by LC-MS/MS. BrACs were measured by an Alco-Sensor IV. The mean blood maximum THC concentration occurred at ten minutes after inhalation and were 38.2 ng/mL without and 47.9 ng/mL with alcohol consumption. The blood THC concentrations decreased 74 percent in the first thirty minutes and 91 percent by 1.4 hours. Only eleven subjects had a blood THC concentration > 5 ng/mL after 3.3 hours. In occasional smokers, THC is detected for a median of four hours (range one to six hours) after smoking a single 54 mg THC cigarette.

Forensic blood THC concentrations may be lower than common per se cutoffs, despite greatly exceeding them while driving. Concentrations during driving cannot be back-extrapolated because of unknown time after intake and interindividual variability in rates of decrease.

Reference Number: 20104

SCHWOPE, D.M., K.B. SCHEIDWEILER, AND M.A. HUESTIS. "Direct Quantification of Cannabinoids and Cannabinoid Glucuronides in Whole Blood by Liquid Chromatography Tandem Mass Spectrometry." *Analytical Bioanalytical Chemistry,* 401: 1273–83, 2011 (7 tables, 1 figure, 36 references)

Abstract: A method for the quantification of THC, THC-glu, 11-OH-THC, THCCOOH, THCCOOH-glu, CBD, and CBN was developed using LC/MS/MS in 0.5 mL of blood. The blood was initially protein precipitated by acetonitrile followed by solid-phase extraction (SPE) before analysis.

This method is the first robust, sensitive, and specific LC-MS/MS technique for direct detection and quantification of several cannabinoids and two cannabinoid glucuronides in human whole blood yielding a comprehensive cannabinoid whole blood profile following cannabis intake. The rapid and simple extraction and sixteen minute analysis are beneficial; however, care should be taken to prevent buildup of phospholipids and other matrix components leading to increased HPLC backpressure and loss of resolution. This method is utilized for several controlled cannabinoid administration studies and will provide whole blood pharmacokinetic and cannabinoid stability data useful to clinicians and forensic toxicologists interpreting whole blood cannabinoid concentrations often obtained during DUID cases and other investigations. This new analytical method for cannabinoids in whole blood offers advantages in sensitivity and spectrum of cannabinoid analytes included over existing LC-MS/MS and GC-MS assays and when applied to controlled cannabinoid administration studies may improve our ability to interpret cannabinoid whole blood results.

Reference Number: 20105

SIMOES, S.S., A.C. AIENJO, AND M.J. DIAS. "Qualitative and Quantitative Analysis of THC, 11-hydroxy-THC and 11-nor-9-carboxy THC in Whole Blood by Ultra-Performance Liquid Chromatography/Tandem Mass Spectrometry." *Rapid Communications in Mass Spectrometry,* 25: 2603–10, 2011 (4 tables, 1 figure, 30 references)

Abstract: A method is described to determine the concentration of THC, 11-OH-THC, and THCCOOH in whole blood using solid-phase extraction followed by Ultra-Performance liquid chromatography/tandem mass spectrometry (UPLC-MS/MS). The limit of quantitation (LOQ) was 0.5 ng/mL compared to 3 ng/mL of other methods of analysis.

A UPLC/MS/MS method was developed and fully validated for the confirmation and quantitation of THC, 11-OH-THC, and THC-COOH in whole blood samples. The method has all the advantages of UPLC/MS/MS with a reduced run time and improved sensitivity and selectivity compared with other methodologies, such as HPLC/MS/MS and GC/MS. The method provided very good precision and accuracy in the linear range 0.5-100 ug/L, using 500 uL of sample. The method was successfully used in proficiency tests and applied to authentic samples.

Reference Number: 20106

PURSCHKE, K., S. HEINL, O. LERCH, F. ERDMANN, AND F. VEIT. "Development and Validation of an Automated Liquid-Liquid Extraction GC/MS Method for the Determination of THC, 11-OH-THC and Free THC-Carboxylic Acid (THC-COOH) from Blood Serum." *Analytical Bioanalytical Chemistry*, 408: 4379–88, 2016 (5 tables, 4 figures, 30 references)

Abstract: An automated method was developed to determine the concentration of THC, 11-OH-THC, and THCCOOH using 0.5 mL of serum and a dual-stage liquid-liquid extraction method. The two-step liquid-liquid extraction was automated using a Multi-Purpose Sample equipped with different modules, such as a shaker, centrifuge, and evaporator. Cooling of the samples (4°C) is required for long-running analysis sequences for cannabinoid stability. The limits of detection and quantification were 0.3 and 0.6 ng/mL for THC; 0.1 ng/mL and 0.8 ng/mL for 11-OH-THC, and 0.3 ng/mL and 1.1 ng/mL for THCCOOH respectively.

These are the main achievements and benefits:

- The automated method saves manual work and reduces the risk of human errors. This makes analysis quality projectable and more independent of the human factor;
- By overlapping samples preparation and GC/MS run, the comprehensively automated method has a throughput of twenty-two samples per day compared to twenty samples per day with the manual workflow. Eighty-three minutes is needed for a single analysis (including samples preparation, GC/MS analysis, and the required blank analysis.), meaning that results are available eighty-three minutes after putting a single sample onto the autosampler;
- The automated method can be employed for all types of sera except postmortem samples;
- The automated system proved to be rugged and is employed in our daily routine in the institute;

- The analysis system can be used for other matrices (e.g., saliva or urine) and other liquid-liquid extraction workflows also outside the field of forensic toxicology and is therefore of general interest;
- Other liquid-liquid extraction workflows in our laboratory are actually under consideration for automation.

2.02 SERUM, PLASMA, AND RBCS

The distribution of THC and other cannabinoids between the serum, plasma, and red blood cells (RBC) is more variable than for alcohol as THC is not water soluble and does not distribute to the RBCs, and it is highly bound to plasma carrier proteins. Alcohol is just dissolved in the blood according to the water content of the serum, plasma, or blood and is not bound to plasma carrier protein.

A good rule of thumb to convert the blood THC concentration into the serum/plasma THC concentration is to multiple by approximately two times. Thus a *blood* THC concentration of 3 ng/mL is equivalent to a *serum/plasma* THC concentration of 6 ng/mL. If the impaired driving cannabis law is written in terms of blood THC limits, it may be complicated if the driver's serum/plasma samples were analyzed, rather than whole blood (20101-2).

Reference Number: 20201

SCHWILKE, E.W., E.L. KARSCHNER, R.H. LOWE, A.M. GORDON, J.L. CADET, R.I. HERNING, AND M.A. HUESTIS. "Intra- and Inter-Subject Whole Blood/Plasma Cannabinoid Ratios Determined by 2-Dimensional Electron Impact GC-MS with Cyrofocusing." *Clinical Chemistry,* 55: 1188–95, 2009 (3 tables, 3 figures, 25 references)

Abstract: The whole blood/plasma ratios of three cannabinoids were determined in 187 samples from thirty-two cannabis users by GC-MS. The whole blood concentrations of cannabinoids are approximately one-half that of plasma due to its high plasma protein binding and poor distribution into the erythrocytes (also known as red blood cells). Blood cannabinoids decreased by more than 20 percent when stored at -20°C and room temperature for two weeks but was less than 20 percent when stored at 4°C. The mean blood/plasma ratios were 0.39 for THC, 0.56 for 11-OH-THC, and 0.37 for THCCOOH.

Intra- and inter-subject whole blood/plasma THC and THCCOOH ratios will aid interpretation of whole blood cannabinoid data.

Reference Number: 20202

SCHWOPE, D.M., E.L. KARSCHNER, D.A. GORELICK, AND M.A. HUESTIS. "Identification of Recent Cannabis Use: Whole-Blood and Plasma Free and Glucuronidated Cannabinoid Pharmacokinetics Following Controlled Smoked Cannabis Administration." *Clinical Chemistry,* 57: 1406–14, 2011 (2 tables, 3 figures, 37 references)

Abstract: Nine male and one female cannabis smokers (ages 19 to 46 years) smoked one joint (6.8 percent THC; 0.25 percent CBD; 0.21 percent CBN) *ad libitum* over ten minutes. Blood and plasma concentration of THC, 11-OH-THC, THCCOOH, CBD, and CBN were measured by LC/MS/MS within twenty-four hours of the collection of the blood samples. Detection of THC-glucuronide (THC-glu) may be a marker of recent cannabis use as it is rapidly removed from the blood and plasma. High THCCOOH-glucuronide (-glu) concentrations may indicate chronic, daily cannabis users.

Table: The Time to Maximum Blood (Plasma) Concentration and Concentration at Maximum, 1 Hour, and 6 Hours after Smoking 1 Cannabis Cigarette (6.8% THC)*

Cannabinoid	Time to Maximum Concentration (hours)	Maximum Concentration (ng/mL)	Concentration at 1 hour (ng/mL)	Concentration at 6 hours (ng/mL)
THC	0.26 (0.26)	50 ng/mL (76)	10 ng/mL (18)	1.4 ng/mL (2.6)
11-OH-THC	0.26 (0.26)	6.4 ng/mL (10)	3.5 ng/mL (4.9)	ND (1.2)
THCCOOH	0.40 (0.50)	41 ng/mL (67)	27 ng/mL (43)	16 ng/mL (26)
CBD	0.25 (0.25)	1.3 ng/mL (2.0)	ND (ND)	ND (ND)
CBN	0.27 (0.25)	2.4 ng/mL (3.6)	ND (1.2)	ND (ND)
THC-gluc	0.50 (0.50)	0.7 ng/mL (3.6)	ND (0.6)	ND (ND)
THCCOOH-gluc	2.0 (2.0)	89 ng/mL (190)	74 ng/mL (150)	58 ng/mL (100)

* Note: ND = Not Detected

Source: Adapted from Schwope et al, (2011)

Human whole-blood cannabinoid data following cannabis smoking will assist whole blood and plasma cannabinoid Interpretation while furthering identification of recent cannabis intake.

2.03 STORAGE AND PRESERVATION

THC is highly lipophilic and will adhere to untreated types of glass or plastics causing low concentrations. Grey-top vacutainers (containing the preservative sodium fluoride) are better for the longer-term storage of blood cannabinoids than green-top vacutainers, (which contain heparin) and should be stored at -20°C (20302-3).

Reference Number: 20301

SKOPP, G., AND L. POTSCH. "Stability of 11-Nor delta 9 carboxy-tetrahydrocannabinol Glucuronide in Plasma and Urine Assessed by Liquid Chromatography-Tandem Mass Spectrometry." *Clinical Chemistry*, 48: 301–6, 2002 (3 tables, 3 figures, 30 references)

Abstract: Free THCCOOH has been proposed as a marker for heavy, chronic cannabis use. In urine free THCCOOH occurs in minute amounts for only a few days after cannabis use. The vast majority of THCCOOH in urine is glucuronidated. Plasma and urine samples were spiked with THCCOOH glucuronate and free THC and stored at -20°, 4°, 20°, and 40°C for up to ten days and analyzed by LC-MS-MS. THCCOOglu is stable in both urine and serum at -20°C, but at other temperatures THCCOOgluc from THCCOOH and the rate of formation increased with increasing temperature.

The in vitro degradation of THCCOOglu prevents clinical conclusion based on the metabolite pattern or the concentration of unconjugated THC-COOH in samples stored at >4°C for prolonged periods.

Reference Number: 20302

TOENNES, S.W. AND G.F. KAUERT. "Importance of Vacutainer Selection in Forensic Toxicological Analysis of Drugs of Abuse." *Journal of Analytical Toxicology*, 25: 339–43, 2001 (3 figures, 18 references)

Abstract: Two blood samples were collected from six drug-free subjects into grey-top (NaF) and red-top (no additive) vacutainers and spiked with THCCOOH. In addition, 147 actual cases in grey- and red-top vacutainers were analyzed as well. Cannabinoid, amphetamine, opiates, and cocaine were analyzed, initially by an Abbott FPIA immunoassay and then by GC-MS. In the fluoride-preserved blood samples, the THC-

COOH enzymatic results were 50 percent that of the other tube, due to hemolysis. On average, 90 percent of the fluoride samples and 32 percent of the other samples had lower results of THC, probably due in part to the fluoride stabilizing THCCOOH-glucuronide and preventing formation of THCCOOH.

A stability study with the THCCOOH acyl glucuronide showed that it is unstable in unpreserved serum, which could explain our observations.

Reference Number: 20303

SCHEIDWEILER, K.B., S.K. HIMES, N.A. DESROSIERS, AND M.A. HUESTIS. "In Vitro Stability of Free and Glucuronidated Cannabinoids in Blood and Plasma Collected in Plastic Gray-Top Sodium Fluoride Tubes Following Controlled Smoked Cannabis." *Forensic Toxicology*, 34: 179–85, 2016 (1 table, 2 figures, 29 references)

Abstract: Blood and plasma THC, 11-OH-THC, THCCOOH, CBD, CBN, THC-glucuronide, and THCCOOH glucuronide concentrations were determined by LC/MS/MS from subjects who smoked 6.8 percent THC cigarettes, which were pooled into low and high THC concentrations. The samples were stored in 6 mL Becton-Dickenson gray plastic tubes containing sodium fluoride and potassium oxalate. The samples were re-analyzed after one week at room temperature, one to twenty-six weeks at 4°C, and one to fifty-two weeks at -20°C. Differences of greater than +/- 20 percent were considered significant. THC concentrations were stable in blood and plasma for at least one week at room temperature. Blood THC concentrations were stable for twenty-six weeks at 4°C and -20°C.

Blood and plasma specimens collected via gray-top tubes should be stored at -20°C for < twelve weeks to assure accurate quantitative results of all major and minor cannabinoid markers.

CHAPTER 3

Oral Fluid Cannabinoids

The chapter on oral fluid (OF) cannabinoids is one of the largest in this book, as it reflects the importance of oral fluid in the detection of THC in suspected cannabis-impaired drivers. The methods of analyses are similar to that of blood or urine, in which there is an initial screen by immunoassay (IA) in the field, which result in a colour change or measured by a simple portable instrument. A blood sample can then be collected or another oral fluid sample for the THC concentration to be confirmed by a laboratory-based mass spectrometric method.

Oral fluid is excreted primarily by three glands, the parotid, submaxillary, and sublingual, with a flow rate varying up to several millilitres per minute. Oral fluid mainly consists of water and contains only 0.3 percent protein. Oral fluids should not be referred to as saliva and should only be collected using a scientific collection device, which collects OF in a pad. The sample is preserved using a buffer solution in the collection device to prevent THC loss. Samples such as expectorated spit or mechanically/chemically stimulated saliva should not be collected as the drug ratios are different than for passively collected OF samples.

Oral fluids provide the best sample (besides blood) to determine recent use of cannabis and its impairing effect on driving.

3.01 METHODS OF ANALYSIS

The screening oral fluid tests in the field are all based on immunoassay techniques that can be confirmed with another oral fluid or blood sample, which is sent to the forensic laboratory for MS analysis (30102, 30103,

30104). Early immunoassay screening tests were more unreliable and inaccurate than the tests currently employed (30101). The detection of the metabolite THCCOOH can rule out passive exposure to cannabis smoke (30102, 30103). The detection time for THC in OF ranged from four to twenty-two hours after smoking (30104).

Reference Number: 30101

LALOUP, M., M.D.M.R. FERNANDEZ, M. WOOD, G. DE BOECK, V. MAES, AND N. SAMYN. "Correlation of delta 9-tetrahydrocannabinol Concentrations Determined by LC-MS-MS in Oral Fluid and Plasma from Impaired Drivers and Evaluation of the On-Site Drager DrugTest." *Forensic Science International*, 161: 175–79, 2006 (3 tables, 18 references)

Abstract: Oral fluid (using the Intercept device) and blood samples were collected from 139 suspected drug-impaired drivers in Belgium between 2004 and 2005. The roadside OF test for cannabis (Drager DrugTest) was also conducted. OF and plasma were analyzed for THC by LC-MS-MS. If a plasma THC cutoff of 2 ng/mL was employed, a 5.2 ng/mL THC cutoff in OF showed a 91.6 percent sensitivity and a specificity of 88.6 percent. The Drager DrugTest only showed an accuracy of less than 66 percent and so is not recommended.

> The overall results of the study indicated a good accuracy of 84.9 - 95.7 percent (depending on the cutoff used for plasma analysis) when correlating THC detection in oral fluid and plasma, suggesting that oral fluid is a good predictor of actual cannabis influence.

Reference Number: 30102

MOORE, C., C. COULTER, S. RANA, M. VINCENT, AND J. SOARES. "Analytical Procedure for the Determination of the Marijuana Metabolite 11-nor-delta 9-Tetrahydrocannabinol-9-Carboxylic Acid in Oral Fluid Specimens." *Journal of Analytical Toxicology*, 30: 409–12, 2006 (2 tables, 3 figures, 9 references)

Abstract: THCCOOH was measured in oral fluid samples collected with the Quantisal collection device. The extraction efficiency was 80 percent. The method employed two-dimensional chromatography and MS. The method was tested on a forty-six-year-old male marijuana smoker. The cannabis metabolite THCCOOH was detected in all OF samples.

The presence of THCA [i.e., THCCOOH] minimizes the argument for passive exposure to marijuana in drug-testing cases.

Reference Number: 30103

BARNES, A.J., K.B. SCHEIDWEILER, AND M.A. HUESTIS. "Quantification of 11-Nor-9-Carboxy-delta 9 Tetrahydrocannabinol in Human Oral Fluid by Gas Chromatography-Tandem Mass Spectrometry." *Therapeutic Drug Monitoring*, 36: 225–33, 2014 (1 table, 2 figures, 26 references)

Abstract: A sensitive and specific method for the detection of THC-COOH in oral fluids using GC/MS/MS was described. THCCOOH is an inactive metabolite of THC and its detection can distinguish passive from active exposure to cannabis. The Quantisal and Oral-Eze collected systems, which collect 1 mL of OF which is added to 2–3 mL of buffer to stabilize and preserve the drug concentration, was employed in the evaluation. Potential interferences from eighty structurally similar drugs or metabolites were tested and did not cause a problem with this method of analysis. The total imprecision of the method (coefficient of variation) was 3.6 to 7.3 percent. The limit of detection was 7.5 ng/mL.

This method was applied to the analysis of oral fluid specimens collected from individuals participating in controlled cannabis studies and will be effective for distinguishing passive environmental contamination from active cannabis smoking.

Reference Number: 30104

DESROSIERS, N.A., D. LEE, D.M. SCHWOPE, G. MILMAN, A.J. BARNES, D.A. GORELICK, AND M.A. HUESTIS. "On-Site Test for Cannabinoids in Oral Fluid." *Clinical Chemistry*, 58: 1418–25, 2012 (2 tables, 2 figures, 18 references)

Abstract: One female and nine male, chronic, daily cannabis smokers who last smoked two days earlier on average, smoked a 6.8 percent THC cannabis cigarette. Oral fluid samples were collected by the Drager Drug Test 5000 and Quantisal collection devices at 0.5 hours prior to and up to twenty-two hours after smoking the cannabis cigarette. The Drug Test 5000 samples were analyzed within fifteen minutes of collection using a roadside instrument that employed lateral flow immunoassay. The THC results at a 5 ng/mL cutoff were obtained in 8.5 minutes. The

OF was collected nearly simultaneously by the Quantisal collection devices and were analyzed for THC, 11-OH-THC, THCCOOH, CBD, and CBN by 2D GC/MS. Four of the test subjects already had a positive THC OF result before smoking the cannabis cigarette. The diagnostic sensitivity of the Drug Test 5000 was 86 to 91 percent at a cutoff of 5 ng/mL. Insufficient OF volumes occurred in only 1.5 percent of the samples. THC OF-detected times ranged from four to twenty-two hours.

> In the new Drug Test 5000 on-site test with a 5 ug/L cutoff, a longer elution time and lateral flow time (8.5 minutes for THC vs 5 minutes for other drugs) enhances analyte recovery. The lower cutoff provided higher diagnostic sensitivity compared to previous versions and other currently available POC OF tests. The Drug Test 5000 offered the highest diagnostic sensitivity achieved to date compared to other point of care devices for THC OF detection. In addition, the Analyzer provided an objective digital readout, reducing subjectivity. The Drug Test 5000 appears highly promising as a diagnostically sensitive on-site device for workplace, pain management, drug treatment, and roadside drugged driving monitoring, although further research is required to ensure that field performance results are similar to those obtained in a controlled setting.

3.02 COMPARISON OF ORAL FLUID AND BLOOD/PLASMA AND URINE CONCENTRATIONS (LABORATORY)

Oral fluid THC concentrations follow a similar rapid decrease after smoking as plasma or blood THC concentrations (30302, 30203, 30206) and is a better indicator of active cannabis use than urine (30207). A high OF/plasma THC ratio of > 1000:1 indicates very recent marijuana smoking (30208). The mean OF/blood THC ratio in tested drivers in one study was 31:1 (30303).

Oral consumption of dronabinol (intact tablet and not chewed) do not routinely produce significant OF THC concentrations but oromucosal sprays and chewed cannabis-infused food products do (30205). Clearly observable blood in the OF sample can affect the THC results (30204). Rinsing the mouth or eating and drinking shortly before collection will lower the OF drug test results (30303). There is no difference in OF THC concentration collected from either the right or left side of the mouth (30207). OF roadside THC testers have been found to have a 92 percent accuracy (30201). The window of detection of cannabis use is longer for oral fluid THCCOOH than for THC (30208).

Reference Number: 30201

BEIRNESS, D.J., AND D.R. SMITH. "An Assessment of Oral Fluid Drug Screening Devices." *Canadian Society of Forensic Science Journal*, 9 pp, December 2016 (2 tables, 10 references)

Abstract: A total of 646 paired oral fluid samples were collected from volunteers during DECP (Drug Evaluation and Classification Program) courses, who all admitted to consuming drugs. One oral fluid sample was analyzed by one of three Point of Contact OF screening devices (Alere DDS2, Drager Drug Test 5000, or Securetec DrugWipe 6S) and compared to OF collected using a Quantisal device and analyzed by GC-MS or LC-MS/MS. The overall specificity for THC was 0.955, false alarm rate was 0.045, and accuracy was 0.923. The devices were not good at detecting benzodiazepines or amphetamine. OF could not be collected in two cases except for Securetec, which did not have an issue due to the small volume of OF required.

> POC oral fluid screening devices could prove to be valuable tools for the police in the detection of drug-impaired drivers. It will, however, be necessary to establish the legal and policy parameters for their use. One approach is to provide the use of drug screening devices in a manner similar to that for alcohol screening devices. Drivers suspected of drug use would be required to provide a sample of oral fluid to be analyzed using an approved POC oral fluid screening device. A positive result could lead to a demand for a more comprehensive drug influence evaluation by a DRE and/or demand for a blood sample. Provinces and territories may also consider using POC oral fluid screening devices as grounds to issue an immediate short-term administrative license suspension comparable to the administrative sanctions currently issued for having a blood alcohol concentration between 50 and 80 mg/dL [.05 and .08 g/100mL] in most jurisdictions in Canada.

Reference Number: 30202

HUESTIS, M.A. AND E.J. CONE. "Relationship of delta 9 Tetrahydrocannabinol Concentrations in Oral Fluid and Plasma after Controlled Administration of Smoked Cannabis." *Journal of Analytical Toxicology*, 28: 394–99, 2004 (2 tables, 4 figures, 23 references)

Abstract: Six male cannabis users smoked a placebo, 1.75 or 3.55 percent THC cigarettes. Frequent oral fluid and plasma samples were collected as well as urine samples. OF was collected under saliva-stimulated conditions (citric acid type of candy) and expectorated into a tube and analyzed by RIA. For one subject it was analyzed by GC-MS. Within twelve hours both oral fluid and plasma THC concentrations were less than 1 ng/mL. When very recent passive exposure to cannabis smoke can be ruled out, a positive oral fluid test provides credible evidence of active cannabis use.

The deposition of THC in oral fluid followed a similar time course as plasma THC following smoked cannabis administration under controlled dosing conditions. Transmucosal absorption of THC into blood is the likely explanation of the close relationship between oral fluid and plasma. After cannabis administration, an initial high concentration of THC was observed in the first oral fluid specimen that was attributed to initial contamination of oral fluid after smoking. The elevated THC concentrations in oral fluid dissipated within thirty minutes following smoked cannabis and were followed by a slower decline of sequestered THC in a similar manner as plasma THC. Although there was greater variability in oral fluid THC concentrations than in plasma, oral fluid concentrations at these times were found to closely mimic plasma THC concentrations.

Reference Number: 30203

KAUERT, G.J., J.G. RAMAEKERS, E. SCHNEIDER, M.R. MOELLER, AND S.W. TOENNES. "Pharmacokinetic Properties of delta 9-Tetrahydrocannabinol in Serum and Oral Fluid." *Journal of Analytical Toxicology*, 31: 288–93, 2007 (1 table, 1 figure, 24 references)

Abstract: Nine male and one female cannabis users smoked a low dose (18.2 mg THC) and a high dose (36.5 mg THC) marijuana cigarette containing 13 percent THC within ten minutes. Frequent blood samples were collected and the THC, 11-OH-THC, and THCCOOH concentrations were determined by GC/MS. Saliva samples were collected using an Intercept DOA Oral Specimens Collection Device without intentional stimulation of saliva flow. The mean peak serum THC concentrations were 47.8 ng/mL and 79.1 ng/mL respectively and decreased to less than 1 ng/mL after six hours. The mean elimination half-lives were 1.4 hours for THC, 2.0 hours for 11-OH-THC, and 3.4 hours for THCCOOH. Biphasic elimination showed a steep decline in the first one to two hours followed by a slower decrease. The mean OF: serum THC ratio was 46 and 36:1 for the low and high THC doses respectively.

> In conclusion, the similar elimination rates of THC in serum and oral fluid are considered accidental and the mechanism of elimination from oral fluid cannot be explained to date. The high differences in OF/S ratios, especially after using different collection procedures, are not a reliable base for correlating THC concentrations in oral fluid and serum, although it appears to contradict the conclusion of Huestis and Cone.

Reference Number: 30204

LEE, D., D.M. SCHWOPE, G. MILMAN, A.J. BARNES, D.A. GORELICK, AND M.A. HUESTIS. "Cannabinoid Disposition in Oral Fluid after Controlled Smoked Cannabis." *Clinical Chemistry*, 58: 748–56, 2012 (2 tables, 4 figures, 39 references)

Abstract: Nine male and one female cannabis smokers (ages 18 to 45 years) smoked a singe 6.8 percent THC cigarette after fifteen to twenty hours of cannabis abstinence. THC, THCCOOH, CBD, and CBN were determined in frequent oral fluid samples by a two-dimensional GC/MS. Oral fluids samples were collected using a Quantisal device consisting of a cellulose pad that turns blue to indicate that 1.0 mL of OF has been collected and a plastic tube that contains 3 mL of a stabilizing buffer. Maximum THC concentrations occurred at or before the first samples collected, fifteen minutes after the start of smoking (maximum 644 ng/mL). All samples were THC positive at six hours and four of the six samples were positive at twenty-two hours. THCCOOH is not present in cannabis smoke and so reflects hepatic or oral mucosal metabolism following systematic THC ingestion. Clearly observable blood occurred in OF samples in one subject and can affect OF results. OF volume was < 1 mL in twenty-two of the eighty-six samples collected within two hours of smoking.

The current proposed THC confirmation cutoffs > 1ug/L (DRUID) and >2 ug/L (SAMHSA) offer longer detection times but do not adequately protect against the possibility of passive cannabis smoke contamination. Cutoffs including THCCOOH with or without THC minimize the issue of possible exposure, although large inter-subject variability in THCCOOH detection windows was observed. We noted in this study and in previous work that THCCOOH generally provides a longer detection window than THC.

Reference Number: 30205

LEE, D., R. VANDREY, G. MILMAN, M. BERGAMASCHI, D.R. MENDU, J.A. MURRAY, A.J. BARNES, AND M.A. HUESTIS. "Oral Fluid/Plasma Cannabinoid Ratios Following Controlled Oral THC and Smoked Cannabis Administration." *Analytical and Bioanalytical Chemistry* 405: 7269–79, 2013 (1 table, 5 figures, 38 references)

Abstract: THC's high lipophilicity (fat solubility) results in extensive adsorption to oral mucosal membrane following smoking with mucosal adsorption into the blood. Oral fluid and plasma concentrations of THC, 11-OH THC, THCCOOH, CBD, and CBN were determined by GC/MS in one female and ten male chronic marijuana smokers (ages 25 to 51 years). There were four five-day sessions of 0, 30, 60, and 120 mg of oral THC followed by a five-puff smoked cannabis inhalation. Oral fluid was collected using a Quantisal device. 11-OH THC detected was rare, only 6 percent of specimens were positive and more were positive > 0.5 hours after smoking. The OF/P ratio for THC was high (median 6.1) within one hour of smoking and was a median of 2.1 by thirteen to seventeen hours after smoking. Median OF/P ratios for THCCOOH were median 0.3 to 2.5 and were more consistent.

OF/P THC but not THCCOOH ratios were significantly influenced by oral cavity contamination after smoking or oromucosal spray of cannabinoid products followed by time-dependent decreases. Establishing relationships between OF and plasma cannabinoid concentrations is essential for making inferences of impairment or other clinical outcomes from OF concentrations.

Reference Number: 30206

LEE, D., G. MILMAN, A.J. BARNES, R.S. GOODWIN, J. HIRVONEN, AND M.A. HUESTIS. "Oral Fluid Cannabinoids in Chronic Daily Cannabis Smokers during Sustained Monitored Abstinence." *Clinical Chemistry* 57: 1127–37, 2011 (2 tables, 3 figures, 36 references)

Abstract: Five hundred and seventy-seven oral fluid (OF) samples were collected from twenty-eight male chronic daily cannabis smokers, using the Quantisal device and THC, CBD, CDN, and THCCOOH concentrations were determined by GC/MS. Cutoffs of OF THC > 2 ng/mL and THCCOOH > 20 ng/mL restricted the cannabis detection window to under forty-eight hours. THCCOOH is not in cannabis smoke and is not due to oral mucosal contamination, unlike other cannabinoids.

Inclusion of multiple cannabinoid cut-offs accounted for residual cannabinoid excretion in OF from chronic daily cannabis smokers and could reduce the potential for positive test results from passive cannabis smoke exposure and lead to greatly improved test interpretations.

Reference Number: 30207

NIEDBALA, R.S., K.W. KARDOS, D.F. FRITCH, S. KARDOS, T. FRIES, AND J. WAGA. "Detection of Marijuana Use by Oral Fluid and Urine Analysis Following Single-Dose Administration of Smoked and Oral Marijuana." *Journal of Analytical Toxicology,* 25: 289–303, 2001 (4 tables, 6 figures, 28 references)

Abstract: The primary route of cannabinoids entry into the oral fluid appears to be direct deposition in the oral cavity during oral, intranasal, and smoked administration. Residues of THC are sequestered on oral tissues and appear in oral fluid. OF samples were collected using an Intercept device that collected on average 0.4 mL of OF and diluted with buffer and preservative solution (3:1). OF THC was determined using EIA (1 ng/mL cutoff) and confirmed by GC-MS/MS (0.5 ng/mL) cutoff. Urine THCCOOH was also analyzed by EIA and GC-MS/MS. There were no significant differences in OF THC concentration, whether collected from the right or left side of the mouth. Detection of OF THC was for thirty-four hours by GC-MS/MS and fifty-eight hours for urine THCCOOH by GC-MS/MS. Urine THCCOOH could not be detected until four to six hours after use.

In conclusion, drug testing is intended to identify individuals in numerous situations that have ingested or smoked THC. These situations may include police actions or pre-employment testing. The actual number of positives identified and confirmed as positive in most situations may actually be small as compared to the population at large. Therefore, drug testing will function mostly as a deterrent to drug use. Oral fluid, given its window of detection and convenience of use, offers an easy means of collection with reliable testing. Furthermore, the collection between plasma and oral fluid shown in this study suggests that oral fluid is a better indicator than urine for active drug use.

Reference Number: 30208

MILMAN, G., D.M. SCHWOPE, E.W. SCHWILKE, W.D. DARWIN, D.L. KELLY, R.S. GOODWIN, D.A. GORELICK, AND M.A. HUESTIS. "Oral Fluid and Plasma Cannabinoid Ratios after Round-the-Clock Controlled Oral delta-9-Tetrahydrocannabinol Administration." *Clinical Chemistry*, 57: 1597–606, 2011 (1 table, 5 figures, 40 references)

Abstract: Ten male cannabis smokers (ages 18 to 32 years) who had smoked cannabis within twenty-four hours of admission to a secure facility consumed 20 mg capsules of dronabinol (marinol) every four to eight hours with increasing frequency for eight days. Blood and OF samples (using a Quantisal device) were collected simultaneously and analyzed for THC, 11-OH-THC, and THCCOOH by 2-D GC/MS. Thirty-six plasma samples and forty-four OF samples were collected from each subject. All 360 plasma samples were positive for THC (up to 67.6 ng/mL). All ten plasma samples and nine OF samples were positive for THC at admission. Oral fluid THC was only detected in 7 percent of the samples collected in the last two to seven days. THCCOOH was found in all 360 plasma samples (up to 498 ng/mL at 6.7 days) and in 354 of the 360 OF samples (highest 1,088 ng/mL). A high OF/plasma THC ratio and high OF THC/THCCOOH ratios indicated recent cannabis smoking. Oral fluid THC primarily reflects smoked cannabis, not oral administration.

OF monitoring does not reliably detect oral dronabinol intake. The time course of THC and THCCOOH concentrations in plasma and OF were different after repeated oral THC doses and high interindividual variation was observed. For these reasons, OF cannabinoid concentrations cannot predict current plasma concentrations.

3.03 COMPARISON OF ORAL FLUID AND BLOOD/ PLASMA AND URINE CONCENTRATIONS (EPIDEMIOLOGICAL, FIELD)

One problem with field studies of the OF and blood/plasma THC ratio is the time difference between when the OF sample is collected and the time that the blood is collected. The longer the delay between OF and blood collection, the higher the apparent OF: blood/plasma ratio (30306). OF screening provides a more reliable indicator of cannabis use in drivers than self-reports by drivers (30307, 30308). OF samples are less personally intrusive and less prone to adulteration than urine samples (30301). Urine cannabinoid testing may miss very recent cannabis use compared to OF, as several hours are required for the metabolite THC-COOH to appear in the urine sample (30303). Rinsing of the mouth or eating food will reduce the oral fluid THC concentration (30303).

Reference Number: 30301

YACOUBIAN JR., G.S. AND E.J. CONE. "A Comparison between the Intercept Oral Fluid Collection Device and Urinalysis among Baltimore City Probationers." *Journal of Criminal Justice*, 34: 413–24, 2006 (9 Tables, 26 References)

Abstract: A comparison was conducted between on-site oral fluid testing to confirm laboratory urinalysis testing for cannabis, benzodiazepines, and opiates in 223 adult probationers in Baltimore during 2004. The Intercept Oral Fluid Collection device was employed. The overall agreement between the Intercept device and urinalysis ranged from 90 percent (marijuana) to 99 percent (benzodiazepines). There were twenty probationers who were cannabis negative by OF screen and positive by urinalysis. Seventy-two per cent of probationers and 88 percent of probation staff preferred OF over urine.

> The collection of urine specimens requires a bathroom, may necessitate gender specific collectors, and requires strict monitoring of the collection process to assure that the specimens have not been adulterated. With OF specimens, these issues are virtually eliminated. OF specimens can

be collected in any environment, by either gender and without concern for adulteration. After considering issues of personal invasiveness, ease of collection, cost, accuracy, and any consequences associated with false positive or false-negative results, policy-makers and practitioners in the criminal justice field should determine if these rates of agreement are high enough to consider replacing or augmenting UA with OF analysis.

Reference Number: 30302

LOGAN, B.K., A.L.A. MOHR, AND S.K. TALPINS. "Detection and Prevalence of Drug Use in Arrested Drivers Using the Drager Drug Test 5000 and Affiniton DrugWipe Oral Fluid Drug Screening Devices." *Journal of Analytical Toxicology,* 38: 444–50, 2014 (6 tables, 25 references)

Abstract: Roadside oral fluid drug screening using the Drager Drug Test 5000 (DDT 5000) and Affiniton DrugWipe were conducted on ninety-two drivers arrested for DUI in the Miami, Florida, area. The drivers also provided a urine sample and another OF sample for later analysis at a forensic laboratory. There were sixty-nine male and twenty-two female drivers (ages 18 to 79 years). Cannabinoids were the most common drug detected, followed by cocaine, amphetamine, and opiate. The confirmation rate for cannabinoids was 93 percent (OF) and 67 percent (urine) for the DDT 5000 and 67 percent (OF) and 60 percent(urine) for the DrugWipe. For drivers with a BrAC < 0.08 g/100mL, 22 percent were positive for marijuana and benzodiazepines. For drivers with a BrAC > 0.08 g/100mL, 39 percent were positive for another drug and 22 percent were positive for a cannabinoid.

The use of OF drug testing devices like the DDT 5000 and DrugWipe offers the ability to rapidly obtain a screening result in the field at the time of a traffic stop. In this evaluation, both devices were highly effective in generating confirmable positives in either urine or OF, although the confirmation rate was consistently higher when OF was used as the confirmatory specimen.

Reference Number: 30303

LANGEL, K., H. GJERDE, D. FAVRETTO, P. LILLSUNDE, K.L. OIESTAD, S.D. FERRARA, AND A.G. VERSTRAETE. "Comparison of Drug Concentrations between Whole Blood and Oral Fluid." *Drug Testing Analysis*; 6: 461–71, 2014 (3 tables, 6 figures, 56 references)

Abstract: Oral fluid and whole blood concentrations from volunteers and persons suspected of drug impaired driving in Finland, Norway, Italy, and Belgium for THC and various other drugs were analyzed by GC/MS. Oral fluid samples were collected with a Saliva Sampler. The mean OF/B ratio for THC was 31:1 and median was 14:1. Despite the variable results, OF would be a suitable matrix in DUID cases, especially if zero tolerance laws are adopted. Detecting high OF concentrations could be a sign of recent drug use, especially for THC. THC is a very lipid-soluble, highly plasma protein bound, and weakly acidic drug.

> Rinsing of the mouth or eating and drinking will also reduce the concentration in OF and cause additional variation. Huestis and Cone showed that THC concentration in OF was several times higher than in plasma during the first half hour after smoking a single cannabis cigarette (15.8 mg or 33.8 mg) and then decreased rapidly. This indicates that finding a high concentration of THC in OF is likely a sign of very recent cannabis consumption.

Reference Number: 30304

GJERDE, H., J. MORDAL., A.S. CHRISTOPHERSEN, J.G. BRAMNESS, AND J. MORLAND. "Comparison of Drug Concentrations in Blood and Oral Fluids Collected with Intercept Sampling Device." *Journal of Analytical Toxicology*, 34: 204–9, 2010 (2 tables, 43 references)

Abstract: Oral fluid and blood samples were collected from ninety psychiatric patients admitted to hospital and twenty-two drugged drivers in Norway between 2004 and 2007. Ten were positive for THC. The Intercept collection pad was placed between the cheek and gums or under the tongue for two to five minutes. The volume of oral fluid collected ranged from 0.2 to 1.8 mL (median 0.6 mL). The median OF: whole blood ratio for THC was 4.7.

> Our findings indicate that drug concentrations in oral fluid may not be used to accurately estimate drug concentrations in the blood.

Reference Number: 30305

CASOLIN, A. "Comparison of Urine and Oral Fluid for Workplace Drug Testing." *Journal of Analytical Toxicology*, 40: 479–85, 2016 (5 tables, 1 figure, 22 references)

Abstract: Urine and oral fluid samples were collected from 1,500 workers employed in Sydney Trains and New South Wales. Each year, a minimum of 25 percent of all rail safety workers must be selected to undertake random drug testing. Drugs were detected in 56 (3.7 percent) of the urine samples and 8 (0.5 percent) of the oral fluid samples. The detection time for drugs is generally longest in hair, followed by urine, sweat, oral fluid, and blood.

> Urine, therefore, is recommended as being the testing matrix of choice for routine random drug testing in safety-sensitive industries in Australia. This study has also confirmed that urine drug testing may miss very recent use of cannabis by a previously abstinent person and thus both urine and oral fluid would provide a greater level of assurance and could be indicated in a similar way to that considered and endorsed by Commissioner Cambridge.

Reference Number: 30306

WILLE, S.M.R., E. RAES, P. LILLSUNDE, T. GUNNAR, M. LALOUP, N. SAMYN., A.S. CHRISTOPHERSEN, M.R. MOELLER, K.P. HAMMER, AND A.G. VERSTRAETE. "Relationship Between Oral Fluid and Blood Concentrations of Drugs of Abuse in Drivers Suspected of Driving Under the Influence of Drugs." *Therapeutic Drug Monitor*, 31: 511–19, 2009 (4 tables, 7 figures, 66 references)

Abstract: Blood and oral fluid samples were collected from drivers suspected of DUID in Belgium, Germany, Finland, and Norway as part of the ROSITA 2 project. Oral fluid samples were collected using the Intercept collector, which involved inserting the device in the mouth for three minutes, after first wiping a few times between the lower teeth and cheeks. The interval between the collection of OF and blood samples was less than one hour for 90 percent of the samples. THC and other drug concentrations were determined by GC/MS or LC/MS. The time interval between OF and blood collection has an effect on the ratio. The ratio increases as the time between OF and blood sampling increases. The median OF: Blood THC ratio was 15.4:1 (range 0.01–568.9:1). The estimated median OF: Plasma (serum) ratio would be estimated to be about 8.5:1.

The wide range of the ratios for the different drugs of abuse in this study does not allow reliable calculations of the blood concentrations from oral fluid concentrations. Limitations of this study are the unknown time of last administration, dose, and route of administration, and the unknown exact oral fluid sample volume obtained from the Intercept devices. These limitations, together with the interlaboratory analytical variation, resulted in a wider range of OF: B ratios compared with published experimental studies. Nevertheless, these data reflect the realistic variability of the OF: B ratios in drivers after ingestion of drugs.

Reference Number: 30307

VAN DER LINDEN, T., P. SILVERANS, AND A.G. VERSTRAETE. "Comparison between Self-Report of Cannabis Use and Toxicological Detection of THC/THCCOOH in Blood and THC in Oral Fluid in Drivers in a Roadside Survey." *Drug Testing and Analysis*, 6: 137–42, 2014 (2 tables, 1 figure, 31 references)

Abstract: A roadside survey was conducted of 2,957 drivers in Belgium between 2008 and 2009 to determine the self-reported use of drugs and medicine in the last two weeks and the time of last intake. In addition, a blood sample and an oral fluid sample (using StatSure Saliva Sampler) were collected. THC was determined in OF by UPLC-MS/MS. THC and THCCOOH were determined by GC/MS after an initial enzymatic screen. Eighty-one subjects self-reported cannabis use and thirty-four had a positive THC in OF, whereas only eight were positive for THC in blood and twenty-seven were positive in blood for THCCOOH. There were forty-seven drivers who did not report cannabis use but were positive with OF and five were positive for THC in blood.

Although in other settings the use of self-report turned out to be a good indicator of cannabis use, the presented data suggests that self-report is not the ideal measurement to detect driving under the influence of cannabis. The idea of a possible retribution or penalty associated with a positive answer might have a great impact on how the questionnaire is completed. Analysis of biological samples is more accurate.

Reference Number: 30308

TOENNES, S.W., G.F. KAUERT, S. STEINMEYER, AND M.R. MOELLER. "Driving Under the Influence of Drugs – Evaluation of Analytical Data of

Drugs in Oral Fluid, Serum, and Urine and Correlation with Impairment Symptoms." *Forensic Science International,* 152: 149–55, 2005 (6 tables, 25 references)

Abstract: Blood and oral fluid samples were collected from 168 drivers suspected of driving under the influence of drugs (DUID) in Germany during 2001. Urine samples were not collected from all drivers as some refused to provide them and so a comparison was made of 131 cases in which urine, OF, and blood were collected. The OF was collected using a Draeger Drug test system and analyzed for THC, 11-OH-THC, THCCOOH, and other drugs by GC/MS. The serum from the blood was analyzed using an immunoassay screen and GC/MS. Urine drug determination was determined on-site without any confirmation. A SAC > 0.050 g/100mL was found in twenty-two of the 168 drivers and were excluded from the evaluation of impairment symptoms. OF agreed with serum THC detection in 90.8 percent of the samples, whereas urine agreed with serum in only 71 percent of the cases. The agreement of urine with serum increased to 94.7 percent if other serum cannabinoids were considered as well. The impairment classification of the driver by the police and medical officer agreed for 65.1 percent of the drivers. Of drivers with a positive serum THC concentration, however, agreement between the police and medical officer was 31.9 percent. An additional 27.7 percent were classified as impaired by the police officer alone.

From the study, it is concluded that drug detection in oral fluid is more closely related to drugs present in serum and is superior to urine testing. Drug screening in oral fluid is an effective method to detect drug-use and to suggest an influence of psychoactive substances in drivers.

3.04 COLLECTION, STORAGE, AND PRESERVATION

For the best stability of cannabinoids in OF, the sample should be diluted with a buffer solution, not exposed to direct bright lights, and be refrigerated (30404, 30406, 30407, 30409). OF samples with low volume should also be analyzed and not rejected (30402). Spitting is not a recommended procedure for collecting oral fluid samples (30403). THC adheres to the serum separator gel found in some blood tubes, causing a substantial loss of the drug (30407).

Reference Number: 30401

CROUCH, D.J. "Oral Fluid Collection: The Neglected Variable in Oral Fluid Testing." *Forensic Science International*, 150: 165–73, 2005 (5 tables, 2 figures, 31 references)

Abstract: A review was conducted on the effect of the type of collection and storage of oral fluid on the drug concentration. OF pH in healthy subjects is usually between 6.2 and 7.4. OF codeine concentrations obtained by spitting were 3.6 times higher than for acid stimulation OF and higher than other non-stimulated collection devices. Collection volume can also affect drug detection. The OF THC concentration stability at -20°C was 87 percent, at 4°C it was 55 percent and at 21°C was 61.2 percent after two weeks. After three weeks, it was 72 percent, 62 percent, and 15 percent respectively.

Compared to collecting a blood or urine specimen, collecting an OF specimen is relatively easy and much less invasive. However, collecting a valid representative OF specimen takes insight into the collection process and its related effects. Oral contamination has been demonstrated with cocaine, THC, heroin, and codeine.

Reference Number: 30402

GJERDE, H., P.T. NORMANN, AND A.S. CHRISTOPHERSEN. "The Prevalence of Alcohol and Drugs in Sampled Oral Fluid is Related to Sample Volume." *Journal of Analytical Toxicology*, 34: 416–18, 2010 (4 tables, 10 references)

Abstract: Saliva samples were collected from 10,816 Norwegian drivers during a roadside survey between 2005 and 2006 using Intercept Oral Specimen Sampling Device, and from 10,928 drivers between 2008 and 2010 using the StatSure Saliva Sampler. The prevalence of alcohol/drugs was found to be greater in saliva samples with a smaller volume of saliva collected. A positive oral fluid alcohol concentration was found in 4.5 percent of the samples < 0.6 mL in volume and decreased to 0.4 percent in samples > 1.25 mL in volume for the StatSure Saliva Sampler.

Our recommendation is that samples of oral fluid with smaller volume than required by the analytical methods should not be discarded but instead be analyzed using a smaller sample volume, if necessary, after dilution. If not analyzed positive drug cases will be missed and the total prevalence of alcohol and drugs in the population being studied will be underestimated.

Reference Number: 30403

HOUWING, S., B.E. SMINK, S-A. LEGRAND, R.P.M. MATHIJSSEN, A.G. VERSTRAETE, AND K.A. BROOKHUIS. "Repeatability of Oral Fluid Collection Methods for THC Measurement." *Forensic Science International*, 223: 266–72, 2012 (3 tables, 2 figures, 31 references)

Abstract: A total of 117 sets of oral fluid samples were collected from customers at a Netherland coffee shop using the StatSure Saliva Sampler (collection pad under the tongue) or spitting into a propylene tube in duplicate. Collection was done in an adjoining room ventilated with windows to prevent contamination. The mean THC concentration using StatSure was 50.4 and 69.3 ng/mL for the first and second sample, and 135.5 and 70.1 ng/mL for spitting for the first and second samples respectively. But both devices had less than 30 percent margin of error for the two consecutive samples. The Belgian OF THC limit is 10 ng/mL. Austria and Belgium use OF for enforcement of DUIC.

The repeatability of both the StatSure collection method and the ordinary spit tubes was low when applied to subjects who had consumed Cannabis very recently. Furthermore, THC concentrations were higher in samples obtained by spitting than samples collected with StatSure.

Reference Number: 30404

GENTILI, S., R. SOLIMINI, R. TITTARELLI, G. MANNOCCHI, AND P. BUSCARDO. "A Study on the Reliability of an On-Site Oral Fluid Drug Test in a Recreational Context." *Journal of Analytical Methods in Chemistry*, 1234581, 10 pp, 2016 (6 tables, 32 references)

Abstract: Eighty-three young people at a disco in Rome were tested with the DrugWipe AS oral screening device for methamphetamine, amphetamine, MDMA, cocaine, opiates, and cannabis. The tongue of the person is wiped five to ten times and tested on-site. Another OF sample was collected and analyzed for drugs by GC/MS. There was a 50 percent decrease in OF THC concentration after seven days storage at room temperature. No preservatives were used by DrugWipe SA.

From the results obtained in the present study, the DrugWipe SA device has been shown to be a practical, easy way of sampling and a non-time-consuming procedure for screening drug of abuse testing in oral fluid. The device has proven to be not sensitive and accurate enough for cannabis, but acceptable for other drugs of abuse.

Reference Number: 30405

MILMAN, G., D.M. SCHWOPE, D.A. GORELICK, AND M.A. HUESTIS. "Cannabinoids and Metabolites in Expectorated Oral Fluid Following Controlled Smoked Cannabis." *Clinica Chimica Acta,* 413: 765–70, 2012 (5 tables, 1 figure, 28 references)

Abstract: Nine male and one female cannabis users (mean age 31 years) smoked a marijuana cigarette (6.8 percent THC, 0.25 percent CBD, 0.21 percent CBN) within ten minutes. The subjects then spit into a polypropylene tube for up to twenty-two hours, and these were analyzed for THC, THCCOOH, 11-OH-THC, CBD, and CBN by GC/MS. Only two samples were positive for 11-OH-THC. Maximum OF THC concentration occurred before or at 0.25 hours (mean 2629 ng/mL) and decreased to 282 ng/mL at one hour and 13.5 ng/mL at three hours. CBD and CBN were present in two-thirds of the samples.

THCCOOH in OF suggests no passive contamination and CBD and CBN suggests recent cannabis smoking. Seventeen alternative cutoffs were evaluated to meet the needs of different drug testing programs.

Reference Number: 30406

LEE, D., G. MILMAN, D.M. SCHWOPE, A.J. BARNES, D.A. GORELICK, AND M. HUESTIS "Cannabinoid Stability in Authentic Oral Fluid after Controlled Cannabis Smoking." *Clinical Chemistry,* 58: 1101–9, 2012 (1 table, 4 figures, 40 references)

Abstract: THC, CBD, CBN, and THCCOOH concentrations were determined by GC/MS in ten OF samples collected by the Quantisal collection device and ten expectorations from cannabis smokers who smoked a 6.8 percent THC marijuana joint. The samples were analyzed after one and four weeks storage at 4°C and at -20°C for four and twenty-four weeks. THC degrades when exposed to air, acid, increased temperature, and light. It adsorbs readily to glass, plastic, and particulate matter. The

Quantisal collection pad collects 1 mL of OF and is then placed into 3 mL of elution/stabilizing buffer resulting in a 1:4 OF dilution. The expectorant was collected in a polypropylene tube. THC was stable in Quantisal OF under all storage conditions. THCCOOH was less stable. Cannabinoids were also less stable in expectorant sample.

Overall, cannabinoids in OF collected with Quantisal device were generally stable for four weeks at 4°C. Greater instability at -20°C could be in part due to poorer stabilizing ability of the Quantisal buffer at freezing temperatures. Even with reduced stability, after twenty-four weeks at -20°C, THC, THCCOOH, and CBD were stable in more than 44 percent of participants' Quantisal OF samples; in expectorated OF <13 percent were stable. Thus, for cannabinoid OF testing, the Quantisal collection device is preferred over expectoration for sampling. We also suggest performing analyses within four weeks of storage at 4°C, at least until further research documents stability beyond this time.

Reference Number: 30407

MOORE, C., M. VINCENT, S. RANA, C. COULTER, A. AGRAWAL, AND J. SOARES. "Stability of delta 9-tetrahydrocannabinol (THC) in Oral Fluid Using the Quantisal Collection Device." *Forensic Science International*, 164: 126–30, 2006 (1 table, 3 figures, 15 references)

Abstract: The Quantisal oral fluid collection device collects approximately 1 mL and turns the volume indicator a blue colour. It is diluted into 3 mL of buffer for a total volume of 4 mL. In vitro testing was conducted on the stability of spiked THC on its stability in OF. After fourteen days of refrigeration (2° to 8°C), the THC concentration decreased to 90.5 percent, whereas storage at room temperature (22-28°C) THC decreased to 71.1 percent of the original concentration. THC loss in serum separator tubes was greater and decreased to 70.3 percent after three days and 38.5 percent after fourteen days storage. THC adheres to the polystyrene serum separator causing substantial losses. Extended exposure under fluorescent lights should also be avoided.

In contrast, our results using Quantisal collection device show that if fluorescent light and plastic surfaces are avoided (e.g., serum separator is not allowed to remain in the sample), along with refrigeration of the specimen, or storage in the dark, THC extraction in excess of 80 percent for the collection buffer and loss due to degradation is less than 20 percent over two weeks, making it a good candidate to oral fluid collection.

Reference Number: 30408

TURFUS, S.C., M. CHU, D. GEROSTAMOULOS, AND O. DRUMMER. "An Assessment of the Stability of MDMA, Methamphetamine and THC in Oral Fluid." *Australian Journal of Forensic Sciences*, 46: 397–410, 2014 (5 figures, 23 references)

Abstract: The stability of the drugs THC, MDMA, and methamphetamine in OF samples collected by the police using a RapiScan collection device with a 2:1 buffer was determined. One OF sample is given to the driver for independent drug analysis. Approximately 2,500 OF samples are analyzed at the forensic laboratory in Victoria, Australia, using LC/MS/MS. When stored at -20°C for thirteen to thirty-nine months, the OF THC concentrations tended to be higher but still within +/- 30 percent of the initial concentration. Upon storage at a fluctuating temperature between room temperature to 60°C, there was a decrease in the THC concentration by 61 to 79 percent after one week and 70 to 87 percent after two weeks storage. There was no significant change in THC concentration when stored at room temperature for four weeks.

The results of this investigation indicate that samples should be analyzed promptly after collection to minimize the impact of variables associated with sample storage — such as temperature and length of time — on the concentrations of proscribed drugs in oral fluid. Regarding the sample that is given to the subject in the event of a contested case, THC concentrations should be interpreted in light of this investigation. Exposure to high temperature results in a substantial reduction of the concentration of THC. As the storage condition of this sample may not always be known, or the personal testimony may not always be adequately confirmed, this indicates that there should be thorough documentation of storage conditions and, if they cannot be ascertained, then there could be reconsideration of the recommendations.

Reference Number: 30409

SCHEIDWEILER, K.B., M. ANDERSSON, M.J. SWORTWOOD, C. SEMPIO, AND M.A. HUESTIS "Long-Term Stability of Cannabinoids in Oral Fluid after Controlled Cannabis Administration." *Drug Testing and Analysis*, 9: 143–47, 2017 (2 figures, 19 references)

Abstract: The stability of oral fluid THC, THCCOOH, THCV, CBD, and CBG was determined at 4°C for one, two, and three months. All OF samples were collected with the Quantisal device in which 1 mL of sample is collected and the collection pad is placed in a tube containing 3 mL of a stabilizer buffer. The OF samples were collected from fifteen cannabis users who smoked a joint containing 6.99 percent THC, 0.2 percent CBD, and 0.44 percent CBN, and were analyzed by LC/MS/MS after solid-phase extraction.

Quantisal-collected OF specimens should be stored at 4°C for no more than two months to assure accurate quantitative results for THC, THCCOOH, THCV, CBD, and CBG. However, if only THC is monitored, OF results were within 79 percent of baseline at three months for all participants. These data clarify OF cannabinoid stability and should be helpful for clinical and forensic drug testing laboratories in timing analyses and assisting interpretation of results for court/defense requested OF sample re-analysis after one to three months storage. Given the inconsistency of cannabinoids storage stability reported for other devices, we caution extrapolating our findings for Quantisal-collected OF to other collection devices.

3.05 PASSIVE INHALATION

Passive inhalation typically only occurs in OF samples for the first thirty minutes after exposure to cannabis smoke without ventilation (30503-4). It can be detected by the presence of THCCOOH, a metabolite of THC that is not found in marijuana smoke (30502). Some of the results showing passive inhalation have been due to the collection of OF in an environment with cannabis smoke contamination. Police should ensure the OF samples are not collected near where marijuana is smoked, such as the driver's car, to ensure no contamination (30503).

Reference Number: 30501

MOORE, C., C. COULTER, D. UGES, J. TUYAY, S. VAN DER LINDE., A. VAN LEEUWEN, M. GARNIER, AND J. ORBITA JR. "Cannabinoids in Oral Fluid Following

Passive Exposure to Marijuana Smoke." *Forensic Science International*, 212: 227–30, 2011 (4 tables, 1 figure, 11 references)

Abstract: Five male and five female subjects (ages 22 to 25 years) spent three hours passively inhaling marijuana smoke in two Dutch coffee shops. The subjects provided oral fluid samples before and during exposure using a Quantisal collection device, and THC, 11-OH-THC, THCCOOH, CBD, and CBN were measured by ELISA and GC-MS. The OF samples were collected outside the coffee shop. After one hour exposure the OF THC ranged from 0 to 3.8 ng/mL; after two hours, 0 to 6.8 ng/mL, and after three hours, 1.3 to 17 ng/mL. All samples were greater than 1 ng/mL twelve to twenty-two hours later. CBD was not detected and neither was the metabolite THCCOOH.

In accordance with other passive exposure studies, it has been demonstrated that THC was absorbed by volunteers under realistic conditions when exposed to marijuana smoke. The concentrations detected in some volunteers after only two hours of exposure were above proposed cut-offs for both screening and confirmatory assays.

Reference Number: 30502

NEWMEYER, M.N., N.A. DESROSIER, D. LEE, D.R. MENDU, A.J. BARNES, D.A. GORELICK, AND M.A. HUESTIS. "Cannabinoid Disposition in Oral Fluid after Controlled Cannabis Smoking in Frequent and Occasional Smokers." *Drug Test Analysis*, 6: 1002–10, 2014 (3 tables, 4 figures, 26 references)

Abstract: Oral fluid samples were collected for up to thirty hours from seventeen male and seven female frequent and occasional smokers (ages 18 to 45 years) using an Oral-Eze device (absorptive cotton pad turns blue after 1 mL of OF collected and has 2 mL of stablizing buffer). The subjects smoked a single marijuana cigarette (6.8 percent THC). THC, CBD, CNB, 11-OH-THC, and THCCOOH concentrations were determined using GC/MS. The active metabolite 11-OH-THC was only detected in five frequent and three occasional smokers and never exceeded 1.2 ng/mL. Low OF volume occurred mainly within the first two hours after smoking and had a higher positivity rate than samples collected with full volume. The addition of a cutoff of THCCOOH > 20 ng/L (0.02

mg/mL) prevented an acute passive inhalation false positive along with THC > 1 to 2 ng/mL.

Our data illustrate the effectiveness of the Oral-Eze device for OF collection and the impact of self-administered smoked cannabis history on OF cannabinoids results and the ability to improve interpretation and tailor OF cannabinoid cutoffs to fulfill the detection window needs of a given program.

Reference Number: 30503

NIEDBALA, R.S., K.W. KARDOS, D.F. FRITCH, K.P. KUNSMAN, K.A. BLUM, G.A. NEWLAND, J. WAGA, L. KURTZ, M. BRONSGEEST, AND E.J. CONE. "Passive Cannabis Smoke Exposure and Oral Fluid Testing II. Two Studies of Extreme Cannabis Smoke Exposure in a Motor Vehicle." *Journal of Analytical Toxicology*, 29: 607–15, 2005 (9 tables, 2 figures, 13 references)

Abstract: Four passive and four cannabis smokers were in an eight passenger van, while each cannabis user smoked one marijuana cigarette containing 5.4 percent THC (and 10.4 percent THC in two studies). Oral fluid was collected in the van or outside the van using the Intercept Oral Specimen Collection Device. OF THC and THCCOOH concentrations were determined by GC/MS. It was found that environmentally exposed collection contained 3–14 ng/mL THC contamination. The OF THC concentration was up to 1.2 ng/mL and all were zero after two hours. Mean peak serum THC was 596 ng/mL in smokers and ranged from 45 to 1080 ng/mL and occurred in the first oral fluid sample after smoking.

Overall, these studies indicate that collection of specimens outside of an area of possible smoke contamination is necessary for accurate determination of passive exposure effects on oral fluid testing. Even after extreme conditions employed in these studies, the results suggest that passive cannabis smoke exposure is not of concern in the use of oral fluid testing in the workplace.

Reference Number: 30504

NIEDBALA, R.S., K. KARDOS, S. SLAMONE, D. FRITCH, M. BRONSGEEST, AND E.J. CONE. "Passive Cannabis Smoke Exposure and Oral Fluid Testing." *Journal of Analytical Toxicology*, 28: 546–52, 2004 (3 tables, 2 figures, 10 references)

Abstract: During the smoking of a marijuana cigarette, 23 to 30 percent of THC is destroyed by pyrolysis, 20 to 30 percent is delivered by mainstream smoke to the user, and 40 to 50 percent is released into the ambient air as side-stream smoke. Four cannabis-free male subjects sat in a small (36 m^3) sealed room while five cannabis smokers inhaled one cigarette each (1.75 percent THC) for the first twenty minutes. All subjects remained in the room for four hours. Oral fluid and urine specimens were collected. THC and THCCOOH concentrations were determined by GC-MS/MS. Oral fluid was originally screened for cannabinoids by EIA (cutoff 3 ng/mL).

The risk of positive oral fluid tests for THC resulting from passive cannabis smoke was limited to approximately thirty minutes after exposure. THC concentration in oral fluid of passive subjects were highest at the conclusion of smoking and declined in a linear fashion within forty-five minutes below the cutoff concentration. In contrast, THC concentrations in cannabis smokers were considerably higher and generally remained positive through the four-hour session at the proposed DHHS cutoff concentration of 4 ng/mL for oral fluid. It is concluded that the risk of positive oral fluid tests from possible cannabis smoke inhalation is limited to a period of approximately thirty minutes following exposure.

3.06 MISCELLANEOUS

False oral fluid THC results are not produced by common food items such as orange juice, coffee, or mouthwash (30601). Detection of THCCOOH in the oral fluid can rule out passive inhalation of cannabis (30603). High oral fluid CBN and CBD concentrations may indicate the use of the oromucosal spray, sativex (30604). Previous alcohol consumption did not affect the oral fluid THC concentration at four hours (30602).

Reference Number: 30601

LEE, D., AND M.A. HUESTIS. "Current Knowledge on Cannabinoids in Oral Fluid." *Drug Testing and Analysis*, 6: 88–111, 2014 (6 tables, 4 figures, 248 references)

Abstract: Cannabis is the most widely abused illicit drug; globally, there are 119 to 224 million users (3–5 percent). Cannabis contains over 500 chemical compounds, including more than 100 cannabinoids. Oral fluid

(OF) testing offers simple, no-invasive, observed (making adulteration more difficult), safer, and less biohazard risk. OF consists of 97 percent water and contains electrolytes, enzymes, protein glycoproteins, mucous, bacteria, cells, and food debris. Healthy adults produce 0.5 to 1.5 L of OF per day. When cannabis is smoked, inhaled, or sprayed in the mouth, the oral mucosa is extensively contaminated. The OF/blood THC ratio is quite wide. A roadside study of 277 drivers showed a range of 0.01 to 568:1 with a mean of 15.4:1, and so blood THC cannot be predicted from OF THC. OF collection can include passive drool, expectoration, or OF collection devices (including a pad or sponge filter and buffer for stability). Common food items such as Listerine mouthwash, OJ, and coffee do not produce false screening results. Two commercial adulterants (Clear Chance, Fizzy Flush, and Test Spit in Klein) do not change THC concentration. Passive smoke inhalation produces up to 18 ng/mL immediately afterwards and decreases to zero in fifteen to thirty minutes. THCCOOH was not detected in passive inhalation.

> OF clearly offers many advantages as an alternative matrix for monitoring cannabis use. The reliability of the test results depends on the reliability of the overall testing process from collection, transportation/storage, and analysis to data interpretation. We present valuable information for establishing appropriate OF testing procedures.

Reference Number: 30602

TOENNES, S.W., K. SCHNEIDER, C. WUNDER, G.F. KAUERT, M.R. MOELLER, E.L. THEUNISSEN, AND J.G. RAMAEKERS. "Influence of Ethanol on the Pharmacological Properties on Delta-9 Tetrahydrocannabinol in Oral Fluid." *Journal of Analytical Toxicology,* 37: 152–58, 2013 (3 tables, 25 references)

Abstract: Seventeen heavy cannabis users (ages 19 to 37 years) consumed a placebo, 0.5, and 0.7 g/kg alcohol and smoked marijuana three hours later. Oral fluid samples were collected and analyzed for delta-9 THC by GC/MS and by onsite tests (Drager DrugTest 5000 and DrugWipe 5+). In addition, a roadside evaluation of the DrugTest 5000 was conducted between 2009 and 2010. The consumption of alcohol did not significantly affect THC pharmacokinetics. The mean oral THC concentration at four hours after smoking were 112, 109, and 105 ug/kg for the placebo, low, and high alcohol concentrations respectively.

The present study investigated the impact of drinking a social dose of an ethanol-containing beverage on THC concentrations in oral fluid and its pharmacokinetic properties in chronic users. No significant differences were observed between alcohol dosing conditions. Drinking 300 mL of a beverage had no relevant impact on oral fluid THC concentrations or on-site test results.

Reference Number: 30603

MILMAN, G., A.J. BARNES, D.M. SCHWOPE, E.W. SCHWILKE, W.D. DARWIN, R.S. GOODWIN, D.L. KELLY, D.A. GORELICK, AND M.A. HUESTIS. "Disposition of Cannabinoids in Oral Fluid after Controlled Around-the-Clock Oral THC Administration." *Clinical Chemistry*, 56: 1261–69, 2010 (4 tables, 1 figure, 33 references)

Abstract: Ten chronic marijuana smokers (ages 18 to 37 years) consumed thirty-seven doses each of 20 mg synthetic THC (dronabinol/Marinol) every four to eight hours over eight days. Oral fluid (OF) samples were collected using the Quantisal OF collection device and were analyzed for THC, 11-OH-THC, THCCOOH, CBD, and CBN by 2-D GC/MS. Overall, 440 OF samples were collected. THCCOOH was detected in 98.2 percent of the OF samples and ranged up to a concentration of 1,117.9 ng/mL. THC was detected in only 20.7 percent of the samples and generally decreased from the time of admission. The active metabolite 11-OH-THC was not detected. CBD and CBN were detected in only three and eight samples at a maximum concentration of 2.1 and 13 ng/mL respectively.

We show that THC in OF appears to primarily reflect previously self-administered smoked cannabis rather than diffusion from the bloodstream after controlled oral administration. THCCOOH concentrations gradually increased with continuous oral THC doses and were detected in relatively high concentrations twenty-three hours after the last dose. THCCOOH measurement not only identifies cannabis exposure, but also minimizes the possibility of passive inhalation of cannabis smoke and consequently may serve as a good biomarker for detection of cannabis use.

Reference Number: 30604

LEE, D., E.L. KARSCHNER, G. MILMAN, A.J. BARNES, R.S. GOODWIN, AND M.A. HUESTIS. "Can Oral Fluid Cannabinoid Testing Monitor Medication

Compliance and/or Cannabis Smoking During Oral THC and Oro-mucosal Sativex Administration?" *Drug and Alcohol Dependence*, 130: 68–76, 2013 (2 tables, 6 figures, 48 references)

Abstract: Eleven male and three female cannabis smokers (ages 19 to 43 years) provided six oral fluid (OF) samples over 10.5 hours after consuming synthetic oral THC (dronabinol at 5 mg and 15 mg), or the oromucosal spray Sativex (5.4 mg THC, 5.0 mg CBD; and 16.2 mg THC, 15.0 mg CBD) and placebo. The OF samples were collected using Quantisal collection devices and THC, CBD, CBN, 11-OH-THC, and THCCOOH were determined by 2-D GC/MS. After consuming the oral synthetic THC, the OF THC concentration decreased rapidly (due to previous residual cannabis smoking), and CBD and CBN were rarely detected. After the use of the Sativex spray, OF THC, CBD, and CBN were increased greatly, peaking at 0.25 to 1 hour. The mean CBD/THC and CBN/THC ratios were between 0.82 and 1.34, and 0.04 and 0.06 respectively, reflecting the cannabinoid composition of Sativex.

In summary, this study is the first to characterize OF cannabinoids after single oral THC or Sativex administration. After oral THC, OF cannabinoid concentrations primarily reflected residual excretion from cannabis smoking. Following Sativex, THC, CBD, and CBN were significantly elevated, with CBD concentrations as high and CBN concentration more than ten times lower than THC concentrations. THCCOOH concentration increases were less evident and observed only after high-doses Sativex. These data indicate that cannabinoid elimination patterns after oral THC and Sativex are markedly different from those after cannabis smoking. Lack of measurable THC, CBD, and CBN in OF following oral THC, and high OF CBD/THC ratios after Sativex, distinguish oral and sublingual drug delivery routes from cannabis smoking. Low THCCOOH/THC ratios suggest recent Sativex and smoked cannabis exposure. These data signify that relapse to smoked cannabis during oral THC pharmacotherapy for cannabis dependence, but not compliance with medication, should be evident with OF cannabinoid monitoring. In contrast, compliance with Sativex pharmacotherapy should be clearly observed by the high CBN/THC ratio as compared to that following cannabis smoking.

Reference Number: 30604

CHAPTER 4

Cannabinoids in Breath, Urine, Hair, Sweat, and Biomarkers of Cannabis Use

4.01 BREATH CANNABINOIDS

The breath alcohol section was the largest in my previous book, *Wigmore on Alcohol*, but is the smallest section in this book. Breath testing for THC is not yet practical as the THC blood concentration is about 1/100,000 times less than alcohol, and THC does not dissolve in water vapour, which is a major component of exhaled breath. The current methods are not practical for enforcement of DUIC as multiple exhalations (up to thirty times) are required to detect such low levels of THC (40101, 40102). THC is detected mainly in the aerosol particles in the breath and not in the vapor (40104).

Reference Number: 40101

STEPHANSON, N., S. SANDQVIST, M.S. LAMBERT, O. BECK. "Method Validation and Application of a Liquid Chromatography-Tandem Mass Spectrometry Method for Drugs of Abuse Testing in Exhaled Breath." *Journal of Chromatography B,* 985: 189–196, 2015 (5 tables, 3 figures, 33 references)

Abstract: Breath has become an emerging alternative matrix for drug testing. The underlying mechanism for making this possible is due to the formation of aerosol particles from the airway lining fluid by the breathing process. These aerosol particles may become contaminated with drugs present in the body. A collection device that selectively collects the micrometer aerosol particles on a filter was developed. The analysis of the drug is a challenge due to pg concentration. The method is fully validated for THC and other drugs. The breath samples were collected by exhaling 30L of breath into a bag, which took one to three minutes and an electrostatic filter collected the microparticle and separated it from the saliva. Breath samples were obtained from 1,096 random workplace testing subjects. A positive drug finding was found in thirty-nine cases (3.6 percent), Amphetamine was found in twenty-five cases, THC in eight cases, and cocaine in four cases. A matrix effect was observed with up to a 50 percent loss in THC concentration.

One advantage of breath sampling over oral fluid is that the sampling process more often is successful due to a problem with a dry mouth making oral fluid sampling sometimes to fail. Since adulteration often is a concern in drug testing, exhaled breath sampling may provide a procedure not only more convenient for the donor but also easier to control for the collector.

Reference Number 40102

TALPINS, S.K., E. HOLMES, T. KELLEY-BAKER, H.C. WALLS, AND T. KIMBAL. "Breath Testing for Cannabis. An Emerging Tool with Great Potential for Law Enforcement." *Between the Lines*, 25: 1–3, 2017 (11 references)

Abstract: The legal importance of developing a reliable breath testing for cannabis is discussed. One method captures a sample of the driver's breath for later analysis by LC/MS at a forensic laboratory. Another method uses field asymmetric ion mobility spectrometry (FAIMS) to determine breath cannabis concentration at the roadside.

In summary, researchers and entrepreneurs are developing methods and devices that could facilitate the identification of recent cannabis use and, when combined with DUID investigations, including field impairment testing result, improve DUID detection and prosecution. We encourage groups concerned with saving lives on our highways, including highway safety officers, enforcement leaders, prosecutors, traffic safety resource prosecutors (TSRP), toxicologists, safety advocates, and others to support the development and use of new technologies, address the policy issues revolving around them, and develop strategies to take advantage of them as appropriate.

Reference Number: 40103

HIMES, S.K., K.B. SCHEIDWEILER, O. BECK, D.A. GORELICK, N.A. DESROSIERS, AND M.A. HUESTIS. "Cannabinoids in Exhaled Breath following Controlled Administration of Smoked Cannabis." *Clinical Chemistry*, 59: 1780–789, 2013 (5 tables, 1 figure, 36 references)

Abstract: THC, THCCOOH, and CBN concentrations were measured in the breath of thirteen (nine male, four female) chronic and eleven (eight male, three female) occasional cannabis users (ages 19 to 41 years) by LC/MS/MS after smoking a 6.8 percent THC cigarette. Breath samples were collected frequently up to twenty-one hours after smoking ceased, using a SensAbuse device, which contains a polymeric filter pad enclosed in a plastic collection chamber. The subjects breathed normally through their nose and exhaled through a mouthpiece into the pad-containing chamber for three minutes. The mouthpiece was discarded, and the chamber was sealed at both ends and stored at -20°C. Methyl alcohol as an organic solvent was added to the pad for analysis. THC was the major cannabinoid detected in the breath. No sample contained THCCOOH and only one breath sample contained CBN. THC breath concentrations decreased significantly with time in both groups. Breath THC was detected in occasional smokers for 1.49 hours and 2.0 hours for chronic smokers.

> These first breath cannabinoid data following controlled cannabis administration suggest that the cannabinoid detection window in breath is short, ranging from 0.5 to 2 hours, and reflects parent THC only. Breath cannabinoids have a short detection window, coinciding with possible impairment one to two hours after smoking, making this alternative matrix applicable for DUID and for case workplace cannabinoid drug testing; however, the driving impairment window extends beyond the detectability of breath cannabinoids.

Reference Number: 40104

LJUNGKVIST, G., S. ULLAH, A. TINGLEY, K. STEIN, B. BAKE, P. LARSSON, A-C ALMSTRAND, E. VIKLUNG, O. HAMMAR, S. SANDQVIST, P. BECK, AND A-C. OLIN. "Two Techniques to Sample Non-Volatiles in Breath-Exemplified by Methadone." *Journal of Breath Research*, 12: 9 pp, 2017 (3 tables, 2 figures, 38 references)

Abstract: Exhaled breath contains particles or aerosols which contain non-volatile substances including drugs such as THC or methadone. The main components of these particles, which are derived from the respiratory tract lining fluid (RTLF), consisted mainly of lipids and proteins. Ten male and four female subjects (ages 26 to 60 years) undergoing methadone maintenance were tested on the SensAbuse and the PExA aerosol collection devices. The OF (by Quantisal) and collected breath samples were analyzed for methadone and codeine by LC/MS. The PExA method collects only small particles from the RTLF between 0.5 and 7.0 uM in diameter. The SensAbuse filters particles between 0.5 and 20 uM in diameter and had 100 times the methadone concentration than by the PExA method.

The results show that methadone was present in all samples using both methods, but when using the method based on impaction, the concentration of methadone in exhaled breath was less than 1 percent of the concentration collected by the method based on filtration. Optimizing the breathing pattern to retrieve particles from small airways did not increase the amount of exhaled methadone collected by the filtration method. The contamination-form codeine present in the oral cavity was only detected in samples collected by the impaction method. We conclude that methadone is distributed in the respiratory tract lining fluid of the small airways. The samples collected by the filtration method most likely contained a contribution from the upper airways/oral fluid in contrast to the impaction method.

4.02 URINE

Urine is the major testing sample for cannabis use for workplace and US federal testing and concentrates mainly on the THC metabolite THC-COOH. Unlike alcohol (which has a 1.3:1 urine blood ratio), the urine THCCOOH concentration cannot be converted into a blood THC concentration (40209, 40210). An additional complication is that some of the THCCOOH is free in the urine and some has been glucuronidated (i.e., attached to glucuronide) (40208). Creatinine should also be measured in the urine to detect tampering of the sample due to dilution effects. The temperature of the urine sample upon collection is typically measured as well to prevent substitution of the sample. On-site urine cannabinoid testing has been found to have a false positive rate of < 1 percent (40205).

THC and its active metabolite 11-OH-THC are rarely found in urine samples as they are not water soluble (40207). There was a loss of THC-COOH in urine samples stored at room temperature (40213, 40216) and in low pH urine (40208). Freezing urine provides the maximal storage stability for cannabinoids (40216). Efavirenz used in the treatment of HIV/AIDS did not cause a false positive urine cannabinoid test result (40215).

The higher the initial urine THCCOOH result, the longer the time the urine cannabinoid test will be positive (40217).

Reference Number: 40201

STEPHANSON, N., M. JOSEFSSON, R. KRONSTRAND, AND P. BECK. "Accurate Identification and Quantification of 11 nor-delta 9 tetrahydrocannabinol-9-carboxylic Acid in Urine Drug Testing: Evaluation of a Direct High Efficiency Liquid Chromatographic-Mass Spectrometric Method." *Journal of Chromatography B,* 871: 101–8, 2008 (6 tables, 5 figures, 43 references)

Abstract: A LC/MS/MS method to determine the concentration of THCCOOH (also known as THCA) in urine without an initial solid- or liquid-phase extraction is described. A comparison was conducted between 116 drug patient urine samples using the existing GC/MS method and there was an overall 98.3 percent agreement. The coefficient of variation was less than 5 percent and the method was linear from 2 to 1000 ng/mL for THCCOOH.

> The present study demonstrated for the first time that direct analysis of THCA in urine, being used as a marker for cannabis intake, can be performed by the validated LC/MS/MS method. The simplicity of this method, achieved by direct injection of urine, should have advantages over earlier GC/MS and LC/MS methods urine SPE procedures or LLE procedures.

Reference Number: 40202

WEI, B., L. WANG, AND B.C. BLOUNT. "Analysis of Cannabinoids and Their Metabolites in Human Urine." *Analytical Chemistry,* 87: 10183–87, 2015 (2 tables, 3 figures, 15 references)

Abstract: An ultrahigh performance liquid chromatography coupled with tandem mass spectrometry (UHPLC/MS/MS) method was developed to detect THC, 11-OH-THC, THCCOOH, CBD, and CBN in urine samples. This method is ten to one hundred times more sensitive than those reported in other methods. Positive electrospray ionization mode (ESI) was employed to obtain this sensitivity. This level of sensitivity was developed in order to assess and monitor secondhand marijuana smoke exposure. At room temperature (25°C), approximately 80 percent of the total CBD, CBN, and THC were lost after twenty-four hours but only 5 percent of the initial 11-OH-THC and 12 percent of the initial THCCOOH urine concentrations. At 4°C, approximately 10 to 30 percent of the total THC, CBD, and CBN decomposed after three days but no significant losses occurred at -20°C.

The validation results indicated that this method was accurate (average inter/intraday bias < 10 percent), precise (inter/intraday imprecision < 10 percent) and fast (6 min run time). In addition, sample preparation throughout was greatly improved using an automation liquid handling system, meeting the needs for potential large-scale population studies.

Reference Number: 40203

SCHEIDWEILER, K.B., N.A. DESROSIERS, AND M.A. HUESTIS. "Simultaneous Quantification of Free and Glucuronidated Cannabinoids in Human Urine by Liquid Chromatography-Tandem Mass Spectrometry." *Clinica Chimica Acta*, 413: 1839–847, 2012 (6 tables, 1 figure, 41 references)

Abstract: A LC/MS/MS method was developed to determine the concentration of THC, 11-OH-THC, THCCOOH, CBD, CBN, THC-glu, and THCCOOH-glu in 0.5 mL of urine. The cannabinoids in the urine samples were extracted prior to analysis using a Bond Elut Plexa or Styre Screen supported liquid extraction (SLE).

The method was a robust, sensitive, and specific LC/MS/MS method for simultaneous direct quantification of THC, 11-OH-THC, THCCOOH, cannabidiol, cannabinol, THC-glucuronide, and THCCOOH-glucuronide in human urine. SLE provided a fast and simple sample preparation approach while achieving efficient recoveries for the most extensive panel of cannabinoids and cannabinoid glucuronides in any urine method to date. Our current method achieved adequate sensitivity, specificity, analytical recovery, imprecision, and linear ranges that indicate applicability of this method for clinical, drug treatment, forensic, workplace, and driving under the influence of drugs (DUID) testing. Instability at room temperature 4°C and after freeze/thaw cycles indicated that THC, cannabidiol, and cannabinol likely will not be useful indicators for determining time of last cannabis intake. Prolonged urinary cannabinoids excretion in abstinent chronic cannabis smokers' urine complicates identifying recent cannabis intake in drug treatment, pain management, forensic, and workplace testing. Direct quantification of THC-glucuronide and THCCOOH-glucuronide in urine could assist in determining recent cannabis intake.

Reference Number: 40204

MCDONNELL, M.G., F. ANGELO, A. SUGAR, C. RAINEY, D. SREBNIK, J. ROLL., R. SHORT, AND R.K. RIES. "A Pilot Study of the Accuracy of Onsite Immunoassay Urinalysis of Illicit Drug Use in Seriously Mentally Ill Outpatients." *American Journal of Drug and Alcohol Abuse,* 37: 137–40, 2011 (1 table, 12 references)

Abstract: The accuracy of onsite immunoassay of urine from forty-two outpatients (ages 25 to 60 years) with drug abuse and serious mental illness (SMI) was determined. The urine was screened onsite using the Integrated EZ Split Key Cup that has an internal thermometer to determine the urine temperature (90 to 100° F) that detects tampering attempts. The cutoff for detection of THCCOOH in urine was 50 ng/mL. One immunoassay urine sample from each outpatient was randomly sent to an external laboratory to determine the drug concentration by GC/MS. The GC/MS tests identified cocaine use in 26 percent of the outpatients, cannabis in 10 percent of the outpatients, and opioids in 7 percent of the outpatients. The average creatinine levels in the urine (which can also detect dilution of the sample) were within an acceptable range (99 mg/dL). The accuracy of the immunoassay for cannabinoids was 98 percent. There was no association of inaccurate immunoassay results based on ethnicity, gender, age or creatinine levels.

Results of this pilot study support the accuracy of low-cost onsite immunoassay screening tests for drug use in adults with co-occurring drug dependence and SMI, most of whom were prescribed psychotropic medications. When errors did occur, they were more likely a result of under-identification of use rather than false positive results, as 71 percent (i.e., five of seven) of inaccurate immunoassay results were false negatives. When legal chain of custody and confirmatory testing is not required, onsite urinalysis provides an inexpensive and accurate clinical tool for assessing recent drug use in persons with CUD. A positive urinalysis at treatment intake is one of the most robust predictors of subsequent drug use during treatment. Therefore, onsite drug testing at treatment intake can provide valuable treatment planning information, identifying those at highest risk of relapse.

Reference Number: 40205

CROUCH, D.J., R.K. HERSCH, R.F. COOK, J.F. FRANK, AND J.M. WALSH. "A Field Evaluation of Five On-Site Drug Testing Devices." *Journal of Analytical Toxicology*, 26: 493–99, 2002 (7 tables, 23 references)

Abstract: Five on-site urine drug testing devices were evaluated on 800 specimens collected from DUI arrestees in Texas and New York between 1998 and 1999. The cut-off level for THCCOOH was 50 ng/mL. Thirty-six per cent (288/800) of the urine samples were positive for drugs and were confirmed by GC-MS. The false positive and negative rate for THCCOOH was less than 1 percent.

The most significant findings from this study were that the devices had few false negative and false positive results. Therefore, they effectively identified DUI arrestees with drugs in their urine.

Reference Number: 40206

KARSCHNER, E.L., A.J. BARNES, R.H. LOWE, K.B. SCHEIDWEILER, AND M.A. HUESTIS. "Validation of a Two-Dimensional Gas Chromatography Mass Spectrometry Method for the Simultaneous Quantification of Cannabindiol, delta-9-Tetrahydrocannabinol (THC), 11-Hydroxy-THC and 11-nor-9-carboxy-THC in Plasma." *Analytical Bioanalytical Chemistry* 397: 603–11, 2010 (4 tables, 1 figure, 26 references)

Abstract: A sensitive method to determine the concentration of CBD, THC, 11-OH-THC, and THCCOOH at concentrations as low as 0.125 to 0.25 ng/mL in 1 mL of plasma was described. The cannabinoids were extracted from the plasma by solid-phase extraction and derivatized. The analysis was conducted using a two-dimensional gas chromatography/

mass spectrometry (2D GC/MS) method. Two capillary, fused silica chromatographic columns were employed. This method was developed to detect the low cannabinoid concentrations that appear after the use of the Sativex oral spray.

> To our knowledge, this is the first analytical method to measure not only CBD, but also THC, 11-OH-THC, and THCCOOH concentrations at or below 0.25 ng/mL in plasma. This robust and sensitive method permits simultaneous quantification of multiple cannabinoid analytes in human plasma and will be applied to clinical specimens from controlled oral THC and Sativex administration. This complex instrumental method should be applicable to multiple biological matrices, following matrix validation, and should be highly useful for clinical research, forensic toxicology, workplace drug testing, and DUID programs.

Reference Number: 40207

DESROSIERS, N.A., D. LEE, M. CONCHEIRO-GUISAN, K.B. SCHEIDWEILER, D.A. GORELICK, AND M.A. HUESTIS. "Urinary Cannabinoid Disposition in Occasional and Frequent Smokers: Is THC-Glucuronide in Sequential Urine Samples a Marker of Recent Use in Frequent Smokers?" *Clinical Chemistry*, 60: 361–72, 2014 (4 tables, 2 figures, 33 references)

Abstract: The urine THC, 11-OH-THC, THCCOOH, cannabidiol, cannabinol, THC-glucuronide, and THCCOOH-glucuronide concentrations were determined by LC-MS/MS in fourteen frequent and ten occasional cannabis smokers (seventeen males, seven females, ages 19 to 41 years), for up to thirty hours after smoking one marijuana cigarette (6.8 percent THC). No urine sample had measureable THC, 11-OH-THC, cannabidiol, or cannabinol concentrations. Only THCCOOH, THC-glucuronide, and THCCOOH-glucuronide were detected. THC glucuronide concentrations peaked at 0.6 to 7.9 hours after smoking. At the newly adopted THCCOOH World Anti-Doping Agency, decision limit of 175 ng/mL were found in only 50 percent of the frequent smokers and none of the occasional smokers for zero to six hours after smoking.

> THCCOOH, THC-glucuronide, and THCCOOH-glucuronide concentrations were significantly higher in frequent than in occasional smokers. Furthermore, a creatinine-normalized THC-glucuronide absolute percent difference > 50 percent between two consecutive urine sam-

ples with the first of the consecutive samples > 2 ug/g may be used as a marker of recent smoking within six hours of the first sample collected in frequent smokers.

Reference Number: 40208

JAMERSON, M.H., J.J. MCCUE, AND K.L. KLETTE. "Urine pH, Container Composition, and Exposure Time Influence Adsorptive Loss of 11 nor delta 9 tetrahydrocanninol-9 Carboxylic Acid." *Journal of Analytical Toxicology*, 29: 627–31, 2005 (2 tables, 2 figures, 13 references)

Abstract: The stability of THCCOOH in urine under different pH, containers, and storage time studied in urine samples spiked at 7.5, 15, 60, and 500 ng/mL THCCOOH. THCCOOH is the primary unconjugated metabolite found in urine. There is a dramatic adsorptive loss of THCCOOH by up to 50 percent at low pH (4.6).

Furthermore, the data indicate that the adsorptive loss of 11-nor delta 9 THCCOOH is dependent on solution-container exposure time and is similar between containers of two distinct compositions. There, results suggest that for optimal analytical control performance, solution pH and control processing times are critical elements.

Reference Number: 40209

MARSOT, A., C. AUDEBERT, L. ATTOLINI, B. LACARELLE, J. MICALLEF, AND O. BLIN. "Comparison of Cannabinoid Concentrations in Plasma, Oral Fluid and Urine in Occasional Cannabis Smokers after Smoking Cannabis Cigarette." *Journal of Pharmacy and Pharmaceutical Sciences*, 19: 411–22, 2016 (5 tables, 3 figures, 45 references)

Abstract: About 95 to 99 percent of the THC is bound to proteins, mostly lipoproteins, and a small fraction to albumin in plasma. The chronic use of THC can induce cytochrome P450 and result in a higher rate of clearance. Frequent blood, urine, and oral fluid samples were collected from eighteen male cannabis users (ages 20 to 28 years) after smoking a 500 mg marijuana cigarette (4 percent THC). Plasma, urine, and OF were analyzed for THC, 11-OH-THC, and THCCOOH by GC/MS. The percentage of THC excreted was 1.9 percent (0.2 to 7.5 percent). The median OF/plasma THC ratio decreased from 82.6 at one minute to 10.3 at six hours.

Direct prediction of plasma THC concentrations from oral fluid concentration is not available regardless of large observed concentrations in this biological fluid. On the other hand, urine THCCOOH concentrations could estimate plasma THC concentrations. However, THCCOOH is a metabolite whose development also presented a wide variability of concentrations and, moreover, is an inactive metabolite, and will not reflect performance impairment. Results from this study support the interpretations that positive oral fluid THC results or positive urine fluid results are indicative of a recent cannabis exposure. There, data also provide valuable information on how to connect plasma, oral fluid, and urinary cannabinoid concentrations after smoking a cannabis cigarette.

Reference Number: 40210

ODELL, M.S., M.Y. FREI, D. GEROSTAMOULOS, M. CHU, AND D.I. LUBMAN. "Residual Cannabis Levels in Blood, Urine and Oral Fluid Following Heavy Cannabis Use." *Forensic Science International*, 249: 173–80, 2015 (3 tables, 27 references)

Abstract: Twelve female and nine male heavy cannabis users (ages 18 to 52 years) were admitted to two detoxification units and provided blood, urine, and oral fluid samples daily for up to seven days drug abstinent. Blood and OF were analyzed for THC by LC-MS/MS with a LOD of 1 ng/mL. Urine was analyzed for THCCOOH using LC-MS/MS. The mean THC concentrations for blood were 7.1, 4.0, 3.4, 3.1, 2.2, 2.0, and 1.9 ng/mL for days one to seven respectively. The mean OF THC concentrations were 28.1, 1.6, and 1.1 ng/mL for days one to three respectively. The mean urinary THCCOOH concentrations (not corrected for creatinine) were 1470, 974, 637, 373, 351, 335, and 303 ng/mL for days one to seven respectively.

The implications for forensic practitioners who have to interpret THC toxicology from the witness box are challenging. THC kinetics in heavy users appear to be highly variable and there is no easy interpretation that will allow a useful estimation of time and of use from a single measurement. The daily THC blood concentrations and urinary THC-COOH concentrations both showed expected patterns of monotonic decline over the whole seven days of the study. However, the high daily variation in each makes it challenging to interpret these levels in the usual forensic situation where there is usually only one measurement of these analytes available from a single set of specimens taken at a variable period after an incident under forensic investigation.

Reference Number: 40211

ROTH, K.D.W., N.A. SIEGEL, R.W. JOHNSON JR., L. LITAUSZKI, L. SALVATI JR., C.A. HARRINGTON, AND L.K. WRAY. "Investigation of the Effects of Solution Composition and Container Material Type on the Loss of 11 nor-delta 9 THC-9-Carboxylic Acid." *Journal of Analytical Toxicology*, 20: 291–300, 1996 (8 tables, 8 figures, 16 references)

Abstract: Water and urine samples (pH 5.9 and 0.1 percent sodium azide) were spiked with THCCOOH and its storage stability was measured in different containers. THCCOOH concentrations were measured by the immunoassay TDX-FLx. The THCCOOH loss during pipetting was also determined.

THCCOOH losses ranging from 0 to 9.7 ng/cm^2 and concentration reductions to 46 percent of starting values were measured. XPS indicated the presence of fluorine-labeled THCCOOH at materials surfaces. A half-life of ten minutes was calculated for THCCOOH losses from urine stored in high density polyethylene at room temperature. Sample handling losses during pipetting were determined and ranged from 1.1 to 7.9 ng per aliquot.

Reference Number: 40212

SCHWILKE, E.W., R.G. GULLBERG, W.D. DARWIN, C.N. CHIANG, J.L. CADET, D.A. GORELICK, H.G. POPE, AND M.A. HUESTIS. "Differentiating New Cannabis Use from Residual Urinary Cannabinoid Excretion in Chronic, Daily Cannabis Users." *Addiction*, 106: 499–506, 2010 (2 tables, 3 figures, 18 references)

Abstract: A model was developed from frequent urine samples collected from forty-eight daily cannabis users (ages 20 to 38 years) in which the THCCOOH and creatinine concentrations were determined by GC/MS. It was evaluated in sixty-eight other subjects.

These models provide clinicians, toxicologists, probation and parole officers, and medical review officers with the first validated method for differentiating new cannabis use from residual cannabinoid excretion in chronic daily cannabis users.

Reference Number: 40213

SKOPP, G., AND L. POTSCH. "An Investigation of the Stability of Free and Glucuronidated 11-Nor-delta 9-Tetrahydrocannabinol-9-caboxylic Acid in Authentic Urine Samples." *Journal of Analytical Toxicology*, 28: 35–40, 2004 (3 tables, 1 figure, 25 references)

Abstract: The stability of THCCOOH and THCCOOglu in thirty-eight urine samples from cannabis users were determined by LC/MS after storage at -20, 4, and 20°C for fifteen days and at 40°C for five days. Spiked urine samples were also tested at different pH. THCCOOH and THCCOOglu were stable at -20°C but at higher temperatures the THCCOOglu decreased with time and the THCCOOH increased. Free THCCOOH was not originally detected in twenty of the thirty-eight fresh urine samples. There was a loss of THCCOOH as well as THCCOOglu in urine samples stored at 20°C, probably due to bacterial and fungal action, as these samples became cloudy.

Also, the detection of unconjugated THCCOOH in urine has been suggested as an indication of heavy cannabis use. In light of the present findings, its reliability as a marker for frequent drug consumption seems questionable, for usually the transport of a urine specimen from the collection site to the forensic laboratory requires two days at least.

Reference Number: 40214

PAPA, P., L. ROCCHI, L.M. ROLANDI, M. DI TUCCIO, M. BIFFI, AND A. VALLI. "Illicit Drugs in Emergency Department Patients Injured in Road Traffic Accidents." *Annali dellIstituto Superiore di Sanita*, 53: 35–39, 2015 (4 tables, 2 figures, 13 references)

Abstract: Blood and urine samples were screened for drugs in 730 injured drivers involved in motor vehicle collisions in Italy. The blood THC limit for driving is 2 ng/mL. The proportion of drugs detected in the blood was cocaine (5.7 percent), THC (3.7 percent), opiates (1.4 percent), methadone (1.4 percent) and amphetamines (0.2 percent). Cannabinoids were detected in 14 percent of the samples but THC > 2 ng/mL in 3.7 percent.

The presented data confirm the low value of urine results for DUID aim, even if immunoassay urinary screening remains a simple and reliable tool to select cases for the more complex quantitative blood analysis.

Reference Number: 40215

KOH, H.C., W-Y. LEE, L.Z. EH, N.J. ISMAIL, P.S. TEE, A. OTHMAN, AND T. MURGAYA. "Efavirenz Does Not Cause False-Positive Urine Cannabis Test in HIV-Infected Patients on Highly Active Anti-Retroviral Therapy." *Medical Journal of Malaysia,* 68: 249–252, 2013 (2 tables, 11 references)

Abstract: Efavirenz is a commonly used drug as part of a three-drug cocktail for the treatment of HIV/AIDS and has been reported to give a false positive urine cannabis screen result. Urine samples were collected from thirty-seven male and fourteen female patients (ages 23 to 73 years) taking Efavirenz. The urine was screened for cannabinoids (THCCOOH) using an immunoassay screen (AxSYM Cannabinoid Assay from Abbott USA). All tested negative for cannabis except for one patient who admitted to using cannabis the day before.

Efavirenz does not cause false positive urine cannabis test with the AxSYM Cannabinoids Assay. Certification documents from doctors are therefore unnecessary.

Reference Number: 40216

DESROSIERS, N.A., D. LEE, K.B. SCHEIDWEILER, M. CONCHEIRO-GUSAN, D.A. GORELICK, AND M.A. HUESTIS. "In Vitro Stability of Free and Glucuronidated Cannabinoids in Urine Following Controlled Smoked Cannabis." *Analytical Bioanalytical Chemistry,* 406: 785–92, 2014 (1 table, 3 figures, 29 references)

Abstract: The stability of THC, 11-OH-THC, THCCOOH, cannabinol, THC-glucuronide, and THCCOOH-glucuronide was determined in pooled urine samples from twelve male and four female cannabis users (ages 19 to 37 years) by LC/MS/MS. The subjects smoked a 6.8 percent (54 mg) THC, 0.25 percent CBD, and 0.21 percent CBN for up to ten minutes. Urine samples were collected within six hours of smoking and pooled together to form a high cannabinoid concentration urine pool. The high concentration pool was diluted 5:1 with drug free urine to form a low cannabinoid concentration urine pool. The urine samples were stored at -20°C, 4°C, and room temperature for up to one year. The urine pH increased over time and after six months storage at 4°C the median increase was 0.44 pH units. Polypropylene tubes were used for storage, which absorb less cannabinoids than polyethylene tubes. THC, CBD, and CBN were never detected in urine. Initially, 11-OH-THC was not detected but appeared in the urine after one week storage at room temperature. At room temperature, the THCCOOH concentration increased and the THCCOOH-glucuronide concentration decreased.

> In summary, frozen storage provided optimal cannabinoid stability in urine, with THC-glucuronide and THCCOOH-glucuronide being stable for up to six months. Analysis should be conducted within three months if non-hydrolyzed THCCOOH or THCCOOH-glucuronide quantification is required. These data will aid those interpreting urinary cannabinoid results, as changes in concentration between repeat analyses can be explained with consideration of storage length.

Reference Number: 40217

GOODWIN, R.S., W.D. DARWIN, C.N. CHIANG, M. SHIH, S-H. LI, AND M.A. HUESTIS. "Urinary Elimination of 11 Nor-9-Carboxy-9-tetrahydrocannabinol in Cannabis Users during Continuously Monitored Abstinence." *Journal of Analytical Toxicology,* 32: 562–69, 2008 (2 tables, 3 figures, 19 references)

Abstract: The time course of the THCCOOH elimination in urine was studied in forty-six male and fourteen female cannabis users (ages 18 to 45 years) who had twenty-four-hour monitored abstinence in a closed research unit for up to thirty days. A total of 6,158 urine samples were screened by immunoassay and considered positive if the concentration was 50 ng/mL or more. The screening results by immunoassay were confirmed by GC/MS and the urine creatinine concentration was measured as well. In 60 percent of the subjects the maximum creatinine normalized urine THCCOOH concentration occurred in the first urine sample. In 40 percent of the subjects, the peak THCCOOH could take as long as 2.9 days after admission. The body mass index (BMI), an indication of body fat, was significantly correlated with the day of the last positive urine sample, i.e., the more fatty tissues in the body (higher BMI), the longer it took for the THCCOOH urine samples to become below 50 ng/mL. During abstinence, the release of THC from the fatty tissues to the blood is highly variable. The subjects were divided into three groups according to their initial urine THCCOOH concentrations of 0-50, 51-150, and > 150 ng/mL. The higher the initial urine THCCOOH concentration, the longer THCCOOH was excreted into the urine.

Table: Mean Day of Urine First Negative THCCOOH Test and Time of Last Positive THCCOOH Test in Three Groups with Initial Urine THCCOOH of 0-50 ng/mL, 51 to 150 ng/mL, and >150 ng/mL.

Initial Urine THCCOOH Concentration	Mean Time of First Negative Urine Sample (Days)	Mean Time of Last Positive Urine Sample (days)
0- 50 ng/mL	0.6 days	4.6 days
51 – 150 ng/mL	3.2 days	9.7 days
>150 ng/mL	4.7 days	15.4 days

Source: Adapted from Goodwin et al, 2008

This study monitored cannabis users on a closed research unit under continuous medical surveillance during cannabis abstinence for up to thirty days. The greater the creatinine-corrected initial THCCOOH concentration, the greater the interval until the first negative and first positive specimens. Cannabis users who present with an initial normalized THCCOOH concentration > 150 ng/mL can be expected to have detection rates between 60 and 100 percent for twenty-eight days after the first negative urine tests. These data increase our understanding of THCCOOH urinary elimination and provide guidelines for the interpretation of urine cannabinoid test results. They also suggest appropriate detection windows for differentiating new cannabis use from residual drug excretion based on creatinine-normalized THCCOOH urine data.

Reference Number: 40218

DZODZOMENYO, S., A. STOLFI, D. SPLAINGARD, E. EARLEY, O. ONADEKO, AND M. SPLAINGARD. "Urine Toxicology Screen in Multiple Sleep Latency Test: The Correlation of Positive Tetrahydrocannabinol, Drug Negative Patients and Narcolepsy." *Journal of Clinical Sleep Medicine*, 11: 93–99, 2015 (4 tables, 3 figures, 13 references)

Abstract: Drugs can influence the results of multiple sleep latency tests (MSLT). The effect of having a positive urine cannabinoid test on MLST was conducted on 383 patients (ages 5 to 20 years, mean age 13.3 years).

A positive urine cannabinoid test was found in fourteen patients (4 percent) ages 13 to 20 years, and thirty-eight (10 percent) had a positive drug urine test in total. Forty-three percent of the patients with positive urine cannabinoid tests had findings of narcolepsy with MSLT, compared with 24 percent of the negative urine drug screens.

> Because of the recent movement towards decriminalization and legalization of marijuana in the US, with recreational marijuana laws now approved in two states (Colorado and Washington) and medicinal/decriminalized marijuana laws approved in twenty states, awareness of the potential effects of marijuana use on MSLT findings seems important to address, with future studies needed. Our findings highlight and support the importance of obtaining a urine drug screen especially in any pediatric patients under thirteen years of age with MSLT findings consistent with narcolepsy prior to making this diagnosis. Urine drug screening would also be important in any population studies looking at the prevalence of narcolepsy in adolescents, especially with the recent trend in changing marijuana decriminalization and legalization.

Reference Number: 40219

YONKERS, K.A., H.B. HOWELL, N. GOTMAN, AND B.J. ROUNSAVILLE. "Self-Report of Illicit Substance Use Versus Urine Toxicology Results from at-risk Pregnant Women." *Journal of Substance Abuse*, 16: 372–89, 2011 (3 tables, 1 figure, 36 references)

Abstract: Urine toxicology screens for cannabis and cocaine were compared with self-reported drug use in 168 pregnant women. The urine THCCOOH cutoff was 50 ng/mL. Approximately 78 percent of the pregnant women who had a positive urine cannabinoid test reported using cannabis in the past twenty-eight days.

> In sum, our analysis of pregnant substance users found a good agreement with one-month self-report of either cocaine or marijuana use and urine toxicology reports. Many women who screened positive reported use later than suggested by the toxicology screening test, particularly for cocaine. Positive reports of drug use during the prior month may indicate to clinicians that a patient is also currently using drugs.

4.03 HAIR

Hair is a biological sample that can detect cannabis use for the greatest period of time, but it is difficult to determine exposure to cannabis compared to use (40304, 40305, 40307, 40310). THC may be detected in hair samples due to the handling of cannabis rather than its use (40307). It is recommended that the metabolite THCCOOH be analyzed to assist in determining use of this drug (40307). Washing the hair samples with methanol prior to analysis will assist in preventing environmental cannabis smoke from contaminating the hair (40310).

Reference Number: 40301

BEASLEY, E., S. FRANCESE, AND T. BASSINDALE. "Detection for Mapping of Cannabinoids in Single Hair Samples through Rapid Derivatization and Matrix-Assisted Laser Desorption Ionization Mass Spectrometry." *Analytical Chemistry,* 88: 10328–334, 2016 (1 table, 6 figures, 49 references)

Abstract: A matrix-assisted laser desorptive ionization mass spectrometry (MALDI-MS) was developed to detect cannabinoids in human hair samples. The method can detect the metabolites of THC; 11-OH-THC, THCCOOH, and THCCOOHglu and so can distinguish between use and unintentional exposure. In plant material THC degrades into CBN and CBD.

The use of MALDI imaging and profiling to detect cannabinoids in hair samples following in situ derivatization is presented. The method shows, for the first time, potential to detect cannabinoids from a single hair.

Reference Number: 40302

MUSSHOFF, F., D.W. LACHENMEIER, L. KROENER, AND B. MADEA. "Automated Headspace Solid-Phase Dynamic Extraction for the Determination of Cannabinoids in Hair Samples." *Forensic Science International,* 133: 32–38, 2003 (3 tables, 4 figures, 35 references)

Abstract: A fully automated procedure for detecting cannabinoids (THC, CBN, and CBD) in hair samples is described using headspace solid-phase dynamic extraction (HS-SPDE) followed by on-coating derivatization and GC/MS. All three cannabinoids were found in twenty hair samples of cannabis abusers. No cannabinoids were detected in hair samples from non-drug users. The main metabolite of THC (THCCOOH) was rarely found in hair samples except at very low concentrations and typically more sensitive methods using MS/MS are required.

> Compared with conventional methods of hair analysis, this automated HS-SPDE-GC-MS procedure is substantially faster. It is easy to perform without using solvents and with minimal sample quantities, and it yields the same sensitivity and reproducibility. Compared to SPME, we found a higher extraction rate, coupled with a faster automated operation and greater stability of the device.

Reference Number: 40303

AGIUS, R. AND P. KINTZ. "Guidelines for European Workplace Drug and Alcohol Testing in Hair." *Drug Testing and Analysis*, 2: 367–376, 2010 (11 references)

Abstract: The European Workplace Drug Testing Society (EWDTS) has developed guidelines for drug and alcohol testing in hair. The main concern with hair testing is environmental contamination that can confuse drug exposure with actual drug use. In general, an organic solvent wash is required for hair samples to remove such substances as hair wax, followed by aqueous washes. Immunoassay screening methods such as ELISA need to be confirmed by GC/MS or LC/MS.

> Cannabinoids, Immunochemical test: A THC concentration of 0.05 ng/mg must produce a positive result. Chromatographic Test: Recommended cut-off: THC < 0.05 ng/mg, THC-COOH < 2 pg/mg. Confirmation of THC-COOH is required to definitively prove the use of cannabinoids.

Reference Number: 40304

HUESTIS, M.A., R.A. GUSTAFSON, E.T. MOOLCHAN, A. BARNES, J.A. BOURLAND, S.A. SWEENEY, E.F. HAYES, P.M. CARPENTER., AND M.L. SMITH. "Cannabinoid Concentrations in Hair from Documented Cannabis Users." *Forensic Science International*, 169: 129–136, 2007 (2 tables, 1 figure, 24 references)

Abstract: Thirty-eight male chronic cannabis users (ages 21 to 42 years) provided 53 head hair samples (approximately 100 mg, cut as close to the scalp as possible) and analyzed by immunoassay (ELISA). The hair samples were also analyzed for THC and THCCOOH by GC/MS/MS. Thirty-eight hair samples were collected upon admission to a secure facility, 15 hair samples were collected after controlled administration of two 2.7 percent THC marijuana cigarettes and two hair samples after ingestion of oral THC in hemp oil. Nineteen samples (36 percent) had no detectable THC or THC (at LOQ of 1.0 and 0.1 pg/mg hair). Two hair samples (3.8 percent) had only THC detected, fourteen (26 percent) had only THCCOOH detected, and in eighteen (34 percent) both THC and THCCOOH were detected. The detection rate in daily users was 85 percent and was 52 percent in non-daily users of cannabis. There was a difference in the detection rate in hair samples collected from black or Caucasian subjects.

For many drugs the parent compound is in much higher concentration in hair than water-soluble metabolites and this is also true for cannabinoids. Concentrations ranged from 3.4 to > 100 pg THC/mg hair compared to 0.1 to 7.3 pg THCCOOH /mg hair.

Reference Number: 40305

MOOSMANN, B., N. ROTH, AND V. AUWATER. "Finding Cannabinoids in Hair Does Not Prove Cannabis Consumption." *Scientific Reports*, 5: 14906, 6 pp, 2015 (1 table, 3 figures, 24 references)

Abstract: THC-A, THC, and THCCOOH have been detected in forensic hair samples. THC-A (delta 9-tetrahydrocannaboinolic acid) is a non-psychoactive biosynthetic precursor of THC and is the main cannabinoid in fresh plant material. When heated by smoking or baking, THC-A is converted into THC. The chemical instability of THC-A can artefactually elevate THC concentration in hair. THCCOOH hair concentrations are very low in hair and require expensive instrumentation. One volunteer consumed 50 mg THC-A over a thirty-day period and achieved a maximum serum concentration of 2,120 ng/mL. No THC-A could be detected in hair, sweat, or sebum samples. The proportion of THC-A in smoke is 1 percent. Two subjects consumed 2.5 mg of dronabinol (THC three times a day for thirty days). No positive THC concentrations were detected in head, body, or beard hair, but THCCOOH could be detected. In beard hair samples, THCCOOH could be detected for up to eleven weeks after the last THC intake. THC findings in hair cannot be regarded as proof of cannabis consumption.

> Not over-interpreting THC or THCCOOH findings in hair is of upmost importance in child protection cases, but also in context of workplace testing and any forensic application. Practitioners who work with results of hair analysis should be aware of these limitations and the severe consequences false conclusions could entail.

Reference Number: 40306

TAYLOR, M., R. LEES, G. HENDERSON, A. LINGFORD-HUGHES, J. MACLEOD, J. SULLIVAN, AND M. HICKMAN. "Comparison of Cannabinoids in Hair with Self-Reported Cannabis Consumption in Heavy, Light and Non-Cannabis Users." *Drug and Alcohol Review,* 36: 220–26, 2017 (3 tables, 1 figure, 21 references)

Abstract: Hair THC, 11-OH-THC, and THCCOOH, and CBD and CBN concentrations were determined in 1-3 centimetre segments of hair from forty-one non-users, thirty-eight light users and twenty-six heavy users of cannabis. The hair samples received two methyl alcohol washes followed by an overnight soak in methyl alcohol. A solid-phase extraction was conducted before GC/MS/MS analysis. The 3 centimetre sections of hair (corresponding to exposure approximately two to three months ago) gave the highest percentage of cannabinoids detected. THC was detected in 0 percent of the non-users, 39 percent of the light users and 77 percent of the heavy cannabis users. The cutoff concentrations for a positive test were 0.05 ng/mg for THC, CBD, and CBN, and 0.4 pg/mg for 11-OH-THC and THCCOOH.

Table: Percent Positive Hair Cannabinoids Detected in Non-, Light, and Heavy Users of Marijuana

Cannabinoid	Non-User of Cannabis (% Positive)	Light User of Cannabis (% Positive)	Heavy User of Cannabis (% Positive)
THC	0%	39%	77%
11-OH-THC	0%	3%	19%
THCCOOH	0%	11%	54%
CBD	0%	11%	19%
CBN	0%	29%	73%

Source: Adapted from Taylor et al 2017

Our study has identified hair cannabinoids to be a useful test to detect heavy cannabis user; however, this testing method is unreliable when applied to low to moderate frequency cannabis users. Furthermore, we were unable to use hair testing to determine the quantity of cannabis used by an individual in a specified time frame. As a result, the real life application of hair testing for cannabis use is likely to be limited and might not be applicable to epidemiological surveys of the general population.

Reference Number: 40307

MOOSMANN, B., N. ROTH, AND V. AUWATER. "Hair Analysis for delta 9-Tetrahydrocannabinol Acid A (THCA-A) and delta 9 Tetrahydrocannabinol (THC) after Handling Cannabis Plant Material." *Drug Test Analysis*, 8: 128–32, 2016 (1 table, 3 figures, 26 references)

Abstract: Hair analysis is commonly performed for THC as THCCOOH is at a lower concentration and is a more expensive test to conduct. TH-CAA can be detected but it is not incorporated into hair via the blood stream. Thus, the presence of THCAA is probably due to handling plant material. Ten subjects rolled one joint on each of five consecutive mornings (500 mg, 8.9 percent THCAA, 1.39 percent THC, and 0.2 percent CBN) and were not allowed to wash their hands for three hours. Urine samples were collected before and after exposure and all were negative for THCCOOH. The analytical findings may be wrongly classified as proof of consumption or at least passive exposure to cannabis smoke and could have severe consequence in child welfare cases.

It can be concluded that at least parts of the THC as well as almost all of THCA-A found in routine hair analysis derive from external contamination caused by direct transfer through, for example, contaminated fingers. The two tested cannabinoids with their high lipophilicity can be transferred onto the hair surface and incorporated into the hair shaft.

Reference Number: 40308

SKOPP, G., P. STROHBECK-KUEHNER, K. MANN, AND D. HERMANN. "Deposition of Cannabinoids in Hair: After Long-Term Use of Cannabis." *Forensic Science International*, 170: 46–50, 2007 (1 table, 1 figure, 52 references)

Abstract: Hair THC, CBN, and CBD concentrations were determined in twelve male, heavy, chronic cannabis users and ten controls. Incorporation of cannabinoids into hair is weak compared to cocaine or codeine and cannabis smoke, weathering, and exposure to sunlight can alter the concentrations. THC is not expected to accumulate in sweat. The sum of THC, CBD, and CBN was correlated with cannabis use within the last three months. No THC, CBD, or CBN were detected in the control hair. During smoking CBN was formed from THC and small amounts of CBD were oxidized into THC, hence the sum of all three components is a better predictor of cannabis use.

In spite of numerous influences on a hair assay result, an increase in major cannabinoid concentration in hair with increasing dose was evident.

Reference Number: 40309

MOORE, C., F. GUZALDO, AND T. DONAHUE. "The Determination of 11-nor-delta 9-Tetrahydrocannabinol-9-Carboxylic Acid (THC-COOH) in Hair Using Negative Ion Gas Chromatography-Mass Spectrometry and High-Volume Injection." *Journal of Analytical Toxicology*, 25: 555–58, 2001 (2 tables, 2 figures, 10 references)

Abstract: The detection of THCCOOH is indicative of drug ingestion as opposed to environmental contamination (from smoke) as it is a metabolite of THC. A GC/MS method is described to determine hair THC-COOH concentrations as low as 0.5 pg/mg. The hair samples were first washed, incubated in sodium hydroxide, and then solid-phase extraction before analysis.

Table: Concentrations of THCCOOH Found in the Hair of Six Cannabis Users and Three Non-Users

Self-Reported Frequency of Smoking Cannabis	Hair THCCOOH Concentration (pg/mg)
Smoking Daily for 30 years (3 persons)	0.060 to 1.39
Smoking Daily for 17 Years (1 person)	0.81
Smoking Once a Month (1 person)	Negative
Smoking Once a Week for 20 years (1 person)	12.9
Non-User Who Lives with a User (1 person)	Negative
Non-Users (2 persons)	Negative

Source: Adapted from Moore, Guzaldo, and Donahue (2001)

This is the first report of the determination of THC-COOH in hair using a bench top GC-MS with high volume injection. The assay is used routinely for the analysis of workplace specimens that have previously been screened positively for cannabinoids using microplate enzyme immunoassay. Using ammonia as a reagent gas, the LOD was 0.3 pg/mg and the LOQ was 0.4 pg/mg. Monitoring one or two ions would probably increase the sensitivity of the assay.

Reference Number: 40310

THORSPECKEN, J., G. SKOPP, AND L. POTSCH. "In Vitro Contamination of Hair by Marijuana Smoke." *Clinical Chemistry*, 50: 596–602, 2004 (3 tables, 42 references)

Abstract: Samples of natural dark blonde, drug-free hair was divided into various strands. One set of strands was not treated, another was moistened with water, one was greased with artificial sebum, and another with artificial sweat and sebum. Another hair sample was bleached and another permed. Before exposure to marijuana smoke, the cut ends of all the hair fibres were sealed with nail polish to prevent drug uptake by the cross sections of the hair. The hair samples were exposed to marijuana smoke for sixty minutes. The cannabis used contained 86 mg/g THC and 0.4 mg/g CBN; CBD could not be detected. After cannabis smoke exposure, the hair was then treated with various washing procedures (e.g., methanol, dichloromethane) before analysis by GC/MS. Cannabinoid concentrations were lowest in the untreated hair, increased in damp hair, and were the highest in greased hair. There were no significant cannabinoid concentration differences between bleached or permed hair. External contaminants were completely removed by washing in methanol or dichloromethane in untreated hair samples only.

Table: THC Concentrations in Hair Samples without and with Washing (Three times with 5 mL of Methanol)*

Hair Treatment	THC Concentration before Washing (ng/g)	THC Concentration after Washing (ng/g)
Untreated	7.6	ND
Damp	19.5	ND
Sebum	8.6	0.4
Sebum/Sweat	5.9	0.1
Bleached	3.6	0.3
Permed	3.5	ND

* Note: ND = not detected

Source: Adapted from Thorspecken, Skopp, and Potsch, 2004

Exposure of hair to marijuana smoke yields detectable cannabinoids depending on concentrations in the air, hair care habits, and cosmetic treatment. Environmental marijuana smoke exposure may produce false-positive or falsely increased test results in hair.

4.04 SWEAT

It is difficult to detect THC in sweat patches as it binds to the patch and degrades at skin temperatures and when exposed to air (40401). It is even more difficult to detect THC in sweat patches if the person has consumed cannabis orally compared to smoking (40402).

Reference Number: 40401

SAITO, J., A. WTSADIK, K.B. SCHEIDWEILER., N. FORTNER, S. TAKEICHI, AND M.A. HUESTIS. "Validated Gas Chromatographic-Negative Ion Chemical Ionization Mass Spectrometric Method for delta 9-Tetrahydrocannabinol in Sweat Patches." *Clinical Chemistry*, 50: 2083–90, 2004 (4 tables, 1 figure, 26 references)

Abstract: A sensitive gas chromatography-negative ionization mass spectrometry (GC/MS) method was developed to measure THC in human sweat patches (PharmChek). Patches are typically worn for seven days. The THC from the patches were extracted with 3 mL of methanol-0.2 mmol/L sodium acetate buffer (pH 5.0) in a reciprocating shaker for thirty minutes. Solid-phase extraction columns (CleanScreen) were employed. The dried extracts were derivatized with trifluoracetic acid and analyzed by GC/MS. The limit of detection was 0.2 ng of THC/patch. It was difficult to detect THC as it binds to the patch material and degrades as it is exposed to air and room temperatures and the even-higher skin temperatures.

Preliminary data from patches worn for consecutive twenty-four-hour periods by a cannabis user during the first days of abstinence demonstrate the usefulness of this method for measuring THC from sweat patches worn for monitoring cannabis use. In addition, this is the first report identifying the potential adsorption of THC to the sweat patch or the degradation of THC on the patch that likely affects the minimum detectable dose of THC in sweat patches worn by cannabis users. These patch adsorption findings further document the need for controlled cannabis administration studies to evaluate the usefulness of sweat testing for THC.

Reference Number: 40402

HUESTIS, M.A., K.B. SCHEIDWEILER, T. SAITO, N. FORTNER, T. ABRAHAM, R.A. GUSTAFSON, AND M.L. SMITH. "Excretion of delta 9 Tetrahydrocannabinol in Sweat." *Forensic Science International*, 174: 173–77, 2008 (2 tables, 1 figure, 27 references)

Abstract: Sweat patches were analyzed for THC in seven male and four female daily cannabis users each week for four weeks of abstention. The sweat patches were applied to the chest or abdomen and THC was determined by GC/MS. The mean THC/sweat patch was 3.85, 1.47, 0.73, and 0.73 ng/patch after one to four weeks abstinence respectively. Sweat patches were also analyzed in one female and six male subjects who consumed multiple doses of oral THC, up to 14.8 mg daily. No patches had THC above the LOQ and shows that THC does not readily enter sweat after oral ingestion. The subjects had plasma THC concentrations of less than 6.1 ng/mL compared to the patients smoking 15.8 mg THC, who had maximum plasma THC concentrations of 84.3 ng/mL.

> Results of our clinical study indicate that daily cannabis users will excrete THC into sweat in concentrations above SAMHSA cutoff of 1 ng/patch. During abstinence, negative patches are expected after one week, but some may have a longer washout period of four weeks or more. The sensitivity of sweat patches to detect new drug use following cannabis smoking is not known and required an independent, controlled, smoked cannabis administration study. Our results indicate that patients who take THC orally up to 14.8 mg daily either intentionally or unknowingly will not produce a positive sweat patch using a cutoff concentration of 0.4 ng THC/patch.

Reference Number: 40403

VOSS, A., K. WITT, T. KASCHOWITZ, W. POITZ, A. EBERT, P. ROSER, AND K-J. BAR. "Detecting Cannabis Use on the Human Skin Surface via an Electronic Nose System." *Sensors*, 14: 13256–72, 2014 (3 tables, 6 figures, 41 references)

Abstract: An electronic nose (eNose) was developed to analyze human body odour to detect cannabis use in humans. An applicator carrying a specific sensor array containing semiconductor metal oxide sensors (SMOS) is applied to the skin surface. The sensors can be adjusted to detect different gases, mainly hydrocarbons, especially C1 to C8. Tobacco smokers (mean age 27 years) and twenty cannabis smokers (mean age 26 years) and who did not smoke cannabis or tobacco for at least twelve hours were tested. Sensors were samples ten times over thirty minutes. The accuracy of the device was 92 percent.

> This study shows that an electronic nose system has the ability to differentiate between human body odour of subjects using cannabis and normal tobacco-smoking subjects. We demonstrate that not only metabolite changes caused by disease are detectable from the skin surface, but that it is also possible to identify drug (here cannabis) consumption. This study provides evidence that after a necessary validation, a low-cost, portable, and fast working eNose system could be useful for health protection and for security agencies.

4.05 BREAST MILK/MECONIUM

As THC is fat soluble, it will appear in the breast milk of a mother who uses cannabis and thus expose the developing suckling child to potential adverse effects (40502, 40506, 40509). Meconium is the first bowel movement of the newborn and can be tested for drug exposure to the fetus for approximately the last three months before birth. The mean birth weight of neonates was lower in cannabis using mothers than non-cannabis using mothers (40508).

Reference Number: 40501

GRAY, T.R., A.J. BARNES, AND M.A. HUESTIS "Effect of Hydrolysis on Identifying Prenatal Cannabis Exposure." *Analytical Bioanalytical Chemistry*, 397: 2335–347, 2010 (5 tables, 2 figures, 17 references)

Abstract: Meconium is the first neonatal feces, which begins forming in the twelfth to sixteenthth week of gestation and reflects fetal exposure to drugs and other toxins in the last trimester. It is considered the gold standard for detecting prenatal exposure. Approximately 5 percent of American women (ages 18 to 44 years) reported using cannabis during pregnancy in 2008. A 2D GC/MS method for the identification of THC, 11-OH-THC, and THCCOOH in human meconium was developed. It was determined that an enzymatic-alkaline tandem hydrolysis before analysis increased the rate of detection of cannabinoids by a factor of two. Alkaline hydrolysis is best for THCCOOH-glu and enzymatic hydrolysis is best for THC-glu.

> In conclusion, hydrolysis is critical for efficient cannabinoid analysis in meconium. Maximal identification of cannabis-exposed neonates and the widest range of cannabis biomarkers can be achieved by employing enzyme-alkaline tandem hydrolysis.

Reference Number: 40502

WARNER, T.D., D. ROUSSOS-ROSS, AND M. BEHNKE. "It's Not Your Mother's Marijuana: Effects on Maternal-Fetal Health and the Developing Child." *Clinical Perinatology*, 41: 877–94, 2014 (3 tables, 99 references)

Abstract: A review was conducted on the effect of cannabis during pregnancy. There are 99 references. Approximately 5 percent of pregnant women use cannabis, which increases to 16.5 percent of pregnant women ages 15 to 17 years. Studies on the effects of marijuana on fetal-related complications and child development are inconclusive.

> Given that today's marijuana is six to seven times more potent and more likely to be consumed in greater average amounts by younger users, continued surveillance is warranted and may reveal more significant short- and long-term harms. The practice for physicians who care for marijuana-using pregnant women is being shared by shifting societa pressures. Increasingly, marijuana is being thought of as medicine by the general public, as evidenced by medical marijuana laws. Pro-marijuana advocacy efforts may lead to perceptions about marijuana being relatively safe and result in increased use by several groups, including pregnant women.

Reference Number: 40503

MARCHEI, E., D. ESCUDER, C.R. PALLAS, O. GARCIA-ALGAR, A. GOMEZ, B. FRIGULS, M. PELLEGRINI, AND S. PICHINI. "Simultaneous Analysis of Frequently Used Licit and Illicit Psychoactive Drugs in Breast Milk by Liquid Chromatography Tandem Mass Spectrometry." *Journal of*

Pharmaceutical and Biomedical Analysis 55: 309–16, 2011 (4 tables, 2 figures, 32 references)

Abstract: A GC/MS/MS method was developed to determine the concentration of cannabinoids (THC, 11-OH-THC, and THCCOOH) in 0.5 mL of breast milk.

Milk samples collected from a mother declaring cannabis smoking showed the presence of THC and OH-THC together with NIC [nicotine] and COT [cotinine], confirming that cannabis was consumed with tobacco and that THCCOOH, the acid metabolite, was not present in this sample.

Reference Number: 40504

WILLIAMSON, S., L. JACKSON, C. SKEOCH, G. AZZIM, AND R. ANDERSON. "Determination of the Prevalence of Drug Misuse by Meconium Analysis." *Archive of Diseases in Childhood. Fetal and Neonatal Edition.*, 91: F291–F292, 2006 (2 tables, 7 references)

Abstract: Meconium is the first stool sample of a newborn and is composed of materials ingested during the time the infant spends in the uterus, used as mucous, amniotic fluids, bile, and water. Drug metabolites accumulate in the meconium after sixteen-weeks' gestation. Meconium samples were collected from 400 newborns in the Glasgow Royal Maternity Hospital in 2001. Cannabis, cocaine, amphetamines, and other drugs were screened by immunoassay and confirmed by GC/MS.

The overall prevalence of misuse of benzodiazepines and opiates could not be concluded from this pilot study, but for drugs that can only be procured by the illicit route, prevalence of 2.75 percent for cocaine, 1.75 percent for amphetamine, and 13.25 percent for cannabinoids were found in this population.

Reference Number: 40505

ROBERSON, E.K., W.K. PATRICK, AND E.L. HURWITZ. "Marijuana Use and Maternal Experiences of Severe Nausea during Pregnancy in Hawai'i." *Hawai'i Journal of Medicine and Public Health,* 73: 283–87, 2014 (1 table, 35 references)

Abstract: The self-reported prevalence of marijuana use of 4,735 women before and after pregnancy on Hawai'i between 2009 and 2011 was determined. Six percent reported using cannabis in the month before pregnancy and 2.6 percent during pregnancy. Approximately 21 percent of pregnant women reported severe nausea. The women who reported severe nausea used cannabis more frequently (3.7 percent) than those who did not have nausea (2.3 percent).

> Hawai'i women who reported severe nausea during pregnancy were significantly more likely to report use of marijuana during pregnancy than those who did not report severe nausea during pregnancy. As medical marijuana use has been legal in the state of Hawai'i since the year 2000, this finding could indicate use of marijuana as an anti-emetic (either with or without a prescription from a licensed health provider) among those experiencing severe morning sickness. However, marijuana use before pregnancy was also associated with an increased likelihood of severe nausea, although the difference was not statistically significant. These preliminary findings warrant further research into the subject with special attention paid to the relatively rare but increasingly documented cannabinoid hyperemesis syndrome (CHS).

Reference Number: 40506

GARRY A., V. RIGOURD, A. AMIROUCHE, V. FAUROUX, S. AUBURY, AND R. SERREAU. "Cannabis and Breastfeeding." *Journal of Toxicology*, D 596149, 5 pp, 2009 (1 table, 28 references)

Abstract: THC is fat soluble and is excreted into human breast milk in moderate amounts. It is estimated that during one feeding, the infant would ingest 0.8 percent of the weight-adjusted maternal intake of one joint. The THC milk/plasma ratio in heavy cannabis users is 8:1. Maternal cannabis use may affect the quantity and quality of human breast milk. The newborn may also be exposed to THC by passive absorption from second hand smoke or dermal contact.

> In conclusion, clinical and pharmacokinetic data indicate that cannabis use is dangerous during breastfeeding for the child. Observed effects in breastfed infants like sedation or reduced muscular tonus could be due not only to cannabis but also other drugs or medications (psychotropic, antiepileptic, etc.) that mothers are likely to take. Mothers who

are drug addicts and want to breastfeed their infant must be sustained by a multidisciplinary team. A substitution treatment like methadone should be chosen in order to stop drug use and to protect their child from drug side effects.

Reference Number: 40507

COLES, R., T.T. CLEMENTS, G.J. NELSON, G.A. MCMILLIN, AND F.M. URY "Simultaneous Analysis of the delta 9-THC Metabolites 11-nor-9-Caroxy-delta 9-THC and 11-Hydroxy-delta 9-THC in Meconium by GC-MS." *Journal of Analytical Toxicology*, 29: 522–27, 2005 (2 tables, 7 figures, 10 references)

Abstract: A method was described to determine THCCOOH and 11-OH-THC in neonate's meconium by solid-phase extraction and GC-MS. Meconium samples are more complicated than urine due to the presence of lipids, tissues, salts, and other substances. The LOD for both metabolites was 5 ng/g.

This study describes a simple solid-phase extraction method and an optimized hydrolysis method that allow the preparation and analysis of both metabolites in a single extract.

Reference Number: 40508

GRAY, T.R., R.D. EIDEN, K.E. LEONARD, G.J. CONNORS, S. SHISLER, AND M. HUESTIS. "Identifying Prenatal Cannabis Exposure and Effects of Concurrent Tobacco Exposure and Neonatal Growth." *Clinical Chemistry*, 56: 1442–450, 2010 (3 tables, 33 references)

Abstract: Eighty-six pregnant women self-reported cannabis and tobacco consumption during pregnancy. Oral fluid samples were taken each trimester from the expecting mothers and meconium samples from the neonate and analyzed for cannabinoids and cotinine (a metabolite of nicotine) by immunoassay and LC/MS/MS. Thirty-eight women (44 percent) self-reported cannabis use during pregnancy, which decreased to twenty-two in the second trimester and fourteen in the third trimester. Twenty meconium samples (23 percent) were positive for one or more cannabinoids. Cannabis-smoking women were more likely to smoke tobacco as well, and smoked similar numbers of cigarettes as the non-cannabis-using smokers. Cannabis use caused a greater variability of measures of neonatal growth.

Table: Neonatal Growth Comparisons Independent of Tobacco Results, According to Meconium Cannabinoid Results

	Cannabinoid-negative Meconium (n=66)	Cannabinoid-positive Meconium (n=20)
Mean estimated gestational age at delivery (months)	39	39
Mean birth weight (grams)	3429	2853
Mean head circumference (cm)	34.4	33.0
Mean length (cm)	50.8	48.8

Source: Adapted from Gray et al, 2010

Cannabis exposure was associated with decreased birth weight, reduced length, and smaller head circumference, even after data were controlled for tobacco co-exposure. Prenatal cannabis exposure was associated with fetal growth reduction. Meconium testing primarily identifies prenatal cannabis exposure occurring in the third trimester.

Reference Number: 40509

GUNN, J.K.L, C.B. ROSALES, K.E. CENTER, A. NUNEZ, S.J. GIBSON, C. CHRIST, AND J.E. EHIRI. "Prenatal Exposure to Cannabis and Maternal and Child Health Outcomes: A Systematic Review and Meta-Analysis." *British Medical Journal Open*, 6: 8 pp, 2016 (1 figure, 53 references)

Abstract: A detailed review and meta-analysis was conducted of twenty-four studies regarding the effects of cannabis use during pregnancy. The OR of anemia in the mother was 1.36 times greater in cannabis users than non-users. Infants exposed to cannabis in utero had an increased OR of 1.77 times for a low birth weight and 2.02 times more likely to require placement in neonatal intensive care.

Use of cannabis during pregnancy may increase adverse outcomes for women and their neonates. As use of cannabis gains social acceptance, pregnant women and their medical providers could benefit from health education on potential adverse effects of cannabis use during pregnancy.

CHAPTER 5

Effects of Cannabinoids on Driving Ability

The effects of THC on driving ability has been studied almost as much as alcohol. The study of THC, however, is more difficult than for alcohol, as THC is such a low concentration in the blood (1/100,000th that of alcohol) and there was no simple reliable method for measurement in the breath. In addition, THC shows a biphasic elimination pattern (very rapid just after smoking and a prolonged end phase), unlike the uniform linear elimination of alcohol.

Some early studies did not measure blood THC concentrations and so could not determine how efficiently (if any) the test subject inhaled the cannabis smoke and so may have been measuring essentially THC-free subjects. In addition, the early studies used cannabis cigarettes legally supplied by US government growing operations and had low THC concentrations of less than 3–4 percent. More recent studies use a more realistic concentration of 8–15 percent THC or even higher.

The studies on the effects of THC on driving ability can be divided into five main types:

- Laboratory studies of various components of the driving task
- Laboratory studies using driving simulators
- Closed-course driving of motor vehicle
- Actual highway driving observations
- Field, epidemiological, or case-control studies of motor vehicle collisions

Physical signs or tests such as the standardized field sobriety tests (SFST) or drug recognition and evaluation (DRE) can assist in determining driving impairment due to cannabis or other drugs. Alcohol combined with THC causes more significant impairment of driving ability, which is of concern, as about 40 percent of drivers recently arrested for DUIC in Colorado also had a positive BAC.

Synthetic cannabinoids are not detected in the usual oral fluid or urine cannabinoid tests and cause a much greater impairment in driving ability than botanical cannabinoids. Some proposed countermeasures for DUIC include a zero tolerance for THC. Proposed per se blood THC limits in Canada are a lower penalty limit of 2 to 5 ng/mL and a higher penalty limit of 5 ng/mL or greater. Also, the BAC limit is lowered from .08 to .05 g/100mL if the blood contains 2.5 ng/mL of THC or more. This is to account for the additional impairment caused by the combination of both drugs.

5.01 LABORATORY STUDIES

The most controlled method of determining the effects of THC on driving ability is in the laboratory. The well-known time-distorting effects of THC can impair driving ability (50121). Some tolerance to the effects of some aspects of THC on driving impairment was found in heavy cannabis users (50117, 50122). Cannabis-impaired drivers tend to focus more on self than on the external task (50102). Cannabis also impaired divided attention tasks, which are an important safety aspect of driving (50207). Accuracy of a visual attention task decreased with increasing THC dose (50104). No differences in genders were found in cognitive testing after smoking a joint (50110). The use of higher potency skunk or sinsemilla cannabis causes more consistent impairment of executive functioning, tacking, and motor impulse control (50116). Impairment in a critical tracking task occurred at serum THC concentrations between 2 to 5 ng/mL (50115).

Reference Number: 50101

ADAMS, A.J., B. BROWN, G. HAEGERSTROM-PORTNOY, M.C. FLOM, AND R.T. JONES. "Marijuana, Alcohol and Combined Drug Effects on the Time Course of Glare Recovery." *Psychopharmacology*, 56: 81–86, 1978 (1 table, 6 figures, 11 references)

Abstract: Ten male subjects (ages 20 to 32 years) were administered a placebo, 075 mL/kg alcohol, 8 and 15 mg of THC, and 0.75 mL/kg alcohol and 15 mg THC, and were tested on a glare recovery task. Pupil size was not affected by alcohol. BrACs were determined with an Omicron Intoxilyzer, and the mean peak BrACs were 0.058 g/100mL (alcohol alone) and 0.052 g/100mL (alcohol and 15 mg THC). It is suggested that smoking THC may delay the gastric absorption of alcohol. Both alcohol and marijuana delayed glare recovery for at least two hours after ingestion.

> Although our experiments were performed under photopic light conditions, questions about night vision and the effect of alcohol and marijuana on glare recovery obviously arise. It is likely that similar alcohol- and marijuana-induced dysfunction occur during night-time activity.

Reference Number: 50102

BATTISTELLA, G., E. FORNARI, A. THOMAS, J-F. MALL, H. CHTIOUI, M. APPENZELLER, J-M. ANNONI, B. FAVRAT, P. MASEDER, AND C. GIROUD. "Weed or Wheel! fMRI, Behavioural, and Toxicological Investigations of How Cannabis Smoking Affects Skills Necessary for Driving." *PLOS ONE* 8: e52545, 2013 (4 tables, 7 figures, 86 references)

Abstract: Thirty-one male occasional cannabis users (ages 18 to 30 years) smoked an 11 percent THC joint (approximately 42 mg THC) or a placebo and were tested on various psychomotor skills (e.g., CTT), fMRI tracking tasks, and other measures. Various questionnaires were also completed (VAS). Blood samples were collected, and blood THC concentrations were determined. The highest blood median concentrations were 87.4 ng/mL (ranged 16.8 to 167.9 ng/mL). Time perception and attention were affected by cannabis.

> In conclusion, we have shown that in occasional smokers, cannabis globally altered the activity of the main brain networks involved in cognition despite the low THC concentrations. Subjects might be more attracted by intrapersonal stimuli (self) instead of orientating attention to task performance and this results in an insufficient allocation of task-orientated resources. Effects on BOLD response were associated with the subjective evaluation of the state of confusion. By contrast, we failed to find any quantitative correlation between the THC levels measured in whole blood and either the BOLD signal or the psycho-

motor performance. These results bolster the zero tolerance policy that prohibits the presence of any amount of THC in the blood while driving.

Reference Number: 50103

GREENBERG, H.S., S.A.S. WERNESS, J.E. PUGH, R.O. ANDRUS, D.J. ANDERSON, AND E.F. DOMINO. "Short-Term Effects of Smoking Marijuana on Balance in Patients with Multiple Sclerosis and Normal Volunteers." *Clinical Pharmacology and Therapeutics*, 55: 324–28, 1994 (2 tables, 1 figure, 12 references)

Abstract: Five male and five female patients with multiple sclerosis (MS) and ten gender- and age-matched control subjects were tested in a computer-controlled dynamic posturography before and after smoking one marijuana cigarette (1.5 percent THC) or placebo (extracted marijuana) over ten minutes.

Surprisingly, neither extracted marijuana nor active marijuana smoke inhalation had a discernible effect in patients or control subjects on standard clinical neurologic examination of motor, sensory, cerebellar, or reflex testing. Patients often had the subjective feeling that they were clinically improved, yet postural responses of both normal subjects and patients were adversely affected in terms of noise variance; the negative effect was greatest in the patients. This observation provides evidence that single exposures to marijuana smoke interfere sufficiently with sensory-motor signal processing to cause even the normal subjects with visual stabilization to revert to a safer postural strategy than the energy-minimizing one. Smoking marijuana increased the response delay in patients with eyes closed but not in the normal subjects. This may be caused by interference with sensory processing when visua cues are removed.

Reference Number: 50104

BOCKER K.B.E., J. GERRITSEN, C.C. HUNAULT, M. KRUIDENIER T.T. MENSINGA, AND J.L. KENEMANS. "Cannabis with High delta 9 THC Affects Perception and Visual Selective Attention Acutely: An Event-Related Potential Study." *Pharmacology, Biochemistry and Behavior*, 96: 67–74, 2010 (2 tables, 6 figures, 66 references)

Abstract: The average THC content of sinsemilla or skunk has increased to about 50 mg in western Europe and 63 mg in the US. Twenty-four male cannabis users (two to eighteen joints per month) between the ages of 18 and 33 years consumed placebo cannabis or joints containing 29.3, 49.2, and 69.4 mg of THC on four separate occasions. The joint also contained tobacco. The whole joint was smoked in about twenty-two minutes. Serum concentration of THC, 11 OH-THC, and THCCOOH were determined from blood samples collected fourteen times during the testing. The serum THC concentrations peaked within fifteen minutes and were 7.2, 12, and 14 ng/mL respectively. A visual attention task was performed two hours post-smoking and EEGs were determined. Response speed and standard deviation increased and accuracy decreased with increasing THC dose from 29.3 to 69.4 mg.

> Performance requiring attentional resources such as vehicle control may be compromised several hours after smoking cannabis cigarettes containing high doses of THC, as presently available in Europe and Northern America.

Reference Number: 50105

BROWN, B., A.J. ADAMS, G. HAEGERSTROM-PORTNOY, R.T. JONES, AND M.C. FLOM. "Effects of Alcohol and Marihuana on Dynamic Visual Acuity I. Threshold Measurements." *Perception and Psychophysics*, 18: 441–46, 1975 (2 tables, 4 figures, 12 references)

Abstract: Dynamic visual acuity (DVA) is the resolution of detail in moving targets and is a complex task involving precise sensory and motor coordination. Ten subjects consumed either a placebo, 0.5, or 1.0mL/kg of 95 percent v/v ethanol. BrACs were determined by an Omicron Intoxilyzer. The mean peak BrACs were 0, 0.025, and 0.080 g/100mL respectively. Eye movements were recorded in subjects following targets presented under low or high contrast. For the low contrast test, there was significant impairment at both alcohol doses; for high contrast, only the high alcohol dose produced significant impairment of DVA.

> To summarize, alcohol and marijuana produced significant dose-related reductions in dynamic visual acuity. The reduction of DVA produced by alcohol was greater than for equivalent doses of marijuana and we suggest that this difference was produced by differential oculomotor

effects of the two drugs. We have speculated that since DVA correlates well with accident records, reduction in DVA under alcohol may be an important contributing factor in alcohol-related traffic accidents.

Reference Number: 50106

BURNS, M. AND H. MOSKOWITZ. "Alcohol, Marihuana and Skills Performance." *Alcohol, Drugs and Traffic Safety*, Vol III, L. Goldberg (editor) Stockholm, T80, 954–68, 1980 (2 tables, 7 figures, 9 references)

Abstract: Twelve male subjects (ages 22 to 33 years) participated in one training and four treatment conditions. The treatment conditions were placebo/placebo, placebo/alcohol, marijuana/placebo, and marijuana/alcohol. Alcohol was consumed within thirty minutes at a dose of 0.58 g/kg. The marijuana dose was 200 ug THC/kg. BrACs were determined with a GC. The mean peak BrAC was 0.069 g/100mL. The subjects were tested on a Compensatory Tracking task, a Divided Attention task, an Information Processing task, a Critical Tracking task, and a Visual Short-Term Memory task.

Subjects reached a mean peak BAC of 0.06 percent when given alcohol alone and all tasks except short-term memory were statistically significantly degraded. The results of this study strongly indicate that drivers under the combined influence of alcohol and marijuana have an increased likelihood of initiating a crash. For the majority of tasks carried out by subjects in the study, the combined use of alcohol and marijuana produced additional decrements in performance. Since all of the tasks (with the possible exception of that involving short-term memory) involved skills that are components of driving performance, clearly the conclusion is compelled that the combined use of alcohol and marijuana produces increased risks for the user and for other members of the traffic population.

Reference Number: 50107

CHAIT, L.D., AND J.L. PERRY. "Acute and Residual Effect of Alcohol and Marijuana, Alone and in Combination on Mood and Performance." *Psychopharmacology,* 115: 340–49, 1994 (2 tables, 3 figures, 49 references)

Abstract: Ten male and four female subjects (ages 21 to 34 years) who were alcohol and marijuana users consumed either alcohol or placebo and marijuana or placebo. The subjects consumed the alcohol within twenty minutes at a dose of 0.6 g/kg for males and 0.5 g/kg for females. The subjects smoked the marijuana or placebo and then the alcohol administration was repeated two hours later. The BrACs were determined with an Alco-Sensor and the mean peak BrAC was 0.088 g/100mL. The subjects were tested on subjective effects and various psychomotor tasks after the drug administration and the next day to determine if there were hangover effects.

> In summary, acute administration of marijuana either alone or in combination with alcohol did not have effects on mood or psychomotor/cognitive performance the following day.

Reference Number: 50108

SPRONK, D., G.J.H. DUMONT, R.J. VERKES, AND E.R.A. DE BRUIJN. "Acute Effects of Delta-9-Tetrahydrocannabinol on Performance Monitoring in Healthy Volunteers." *Frontiers in Behavioral Neuroscience,* 5, Article 59, 1–11, 2011 (1 table, 3 figures, 80 references)

Abstract: Eight male and two female regular cannabis users (mean age 20.8 years) inhaled 4, 6, and 6 mg of THC or placebo using a vaporizer. The subjects inhaled the doses from the vaporizer bag within two to three minutes. Blood samples were collected and plasma THC concentrations were determined. An EEG was recorded during the performance of a speeded choice reaction task and error-related negativity (ERN) was measured. The mean peak plasma THCs ranged from 60 to 89 ng/mL and the lowest mean plasma THC concentrations ranged from 9.5 to 17.8 ng/mL.

> To conclude, our findings suggest that administration of THC has a diminishing effect on human performance monitoring as reflected by reduced ERN amplitudes. Given the small size of the study consisting of only 10 subjects, the results should be considered as preliminary and need to be confirmed with larger samples. Nevertheless, the results are relevant for several reasons. First, THC is the most important component of cannabis, which is a drug that is recreationally used by many people over the world. The study provides a better understanding of the risks of cannabis use during performance of complex functions like driving, which require a high level of performance monitoring. Second,

as THC is increasingly examined and applied for clinical applications, mapping the potential (cognitive) side effects are crucial aspects of patient's safety and drug compliance. We, for the first time, demonstrated that activation of the endocannabinoid system influences the ERN. We believe that the results of this study have extended our understanding of the cognitive effects associated with cannabinoids. The effects of cannabinoids on performance monitoring, and cognitive process in general, need further evaluation.

Reference Number: 50109

WEINSTEIN, A., O. BRICKNER, H. LERMAN, M. GREEMLAND, M. BLOCH, H. LESTER, R. CHISIN, Y. SARNE, R. MECHOULAM, R. BAR-HAMBURGER, N. FREEDMAN, AND E. EVEN-SAPIR. "A Study Investigating the Acute Dose-Response Effects of 13 mg and 17 mg delta 9-Tetrahydrocannabinol on Cognitive-Motor Skills, Subjective and Autonomic Measures in Regular Users of Marijuana." *Journal of Psychopharmacology*, 22: 441–51, 2008 (3 tables, 4 figures, 35 references)

Abstract: Four female and ten male regular cannabis users (mean age 27 years) who smoked at least one joint a day for at least five years were tested on computerized virtual maze tasks and gambling tasks. The subjects smoked a placebo cigarette or a cigarette containing 13 or 17 mg of pure THC and not the other cannabinoids. After smoking 17 mg THC, but not for the 13 mg dose, the regular cannabis users hit the walls more often in the maze test and decision making was affected.

Impaired accuracy of movement and increased collisions with maze walls in subjects on 17 mg THC is an important finding. Accurate movement is required for activities such as walking, driving, sportive activity, and flying. One of the important aspects of these activities is the ability to keep the body or the vehicle in the centre of the road.

Reference Number: 50110

ANDERSON, B.M., M. RIZZO, R.I. BLOCK, G.D. PEARLSON, AND D.S. O'LEARY. "Sex, Drugs and Cognition: Effects of Marijuana." *Journal of Psychoactive Drugs*, 42: 413–24, 2010 (3 tables, 4 figures, 52 references)

Abstract: Thirty-five female and thirty-five male occasional marijuana users (ages 18 to 31 years) consumed either a placebo cannabis cigarette or one containing 2.9 percent THC (22.9 mg). Thirty minutes later the subjects were administered a battery of neurophysiological tests, including attention, time estimation, cognitive flexibility, and visuospatial processing. Over 44 percent of the women requested to discontinue smoking the joint compared to 0 percent of the men.

> This study assessed sex differences in the effects of acute marijuana on cognition in thirty-five men and thirty-five women. As expected, marijuana did not have an impact on selective and divided attention, cognitive flexibility, and time estimation. No sex by drug interactions were found for cognitive testing, however, psychological response to the smoking session was striking, in that women requested to discontinue the marijuana cigarette more often than men. Despite receiving a smaller dose of marijuana, women under the influence of marijuana had a non-statistically significant slower reaction time to task switching, suggesting cognitive flexibility may be a key area to focus on in future research examining sex differences in marijuana's effects.

Reference Number: 50111

HEISHMAN, S.J., K. ARASTEH, AND M.L. STITZER. "Comparative Effects of Alcohol and Marijuana on Mood, Memory and Performance." *Pharmacology. Biochemistry and Behavior*, 58: 93–101. 1997 (4 figures, 62 references)

Abstract: Five male subjects (ages 18 to 26 years) consumed a placebo, 0.25, 0.5, and 1.0 g/kg ethanol or four, eight, or sixteen puffs of a marijuana cigarette. BrACs were determined with an Alcosensor III and the mean peak BrACs were 0.010, 0.030, and 0.090 g/100mL respectively. Plasma THC concentrations were also determined. Various psychomotor and subjective tests were conducted.

> In summary we have demonstrated that a range of alcohol and marijuana doses produced comparable subjective effects and performance impairment. The high dose of alcohol (1.0 g/kg, 30 minutes BAC = 90 mg/dL) and marijuana (16 puffs, 3.55 percent THC, immediate post-smoking THC level = 188 ng/mL) produced identical subjective ratings of perceived impairment at very similar degrees of actual impairment on the DSST and a test of word recall.

Reference Number: 50112

HOLLISTER, L.E., AND H.K. GILLESPIE. "Marihuana, Ethanol and Dextroamphetamine. Mood and Mental Function Alterations." *Archives of General Psychiatry,* 23: 199–203, 1970 (4 tables, 9 references)

Abstract: Eleven male and one female subjects were administered marijuana (median dose 32 mg THC), ethanol (57 g), dextroamphetamine (15 mg), or a marijuana placebo at random over weekly intervals. Subjects were given various psychomotor tests, including rod and frame, simple RT, Digit Symbol Substitution Tests, and measurements of subjective moods.

Dextroamphetamine produced the greatest changes in mood, decreasing drowsiness and increasing stimulation and activity. Dextroamphetamine tended to improve performance on psychomotor tests, the other two drugs tended to impair it. Time estimation was longer with marijuana than with other treatments. Ethanol and marijuana increased simple reaction time. Marijuana and ethanol were most alike in their effect with the particular exception of the alteration in time perception produced by the former drug.

Reference Number: 50113

LINDGREN, J.-E., A. OHLSSON., S. AGURELL, L. HOLLISTER, AND H. GILLESPIE. "Clinical Effects and Plasma Levels of delta 9-Tetrahydrocannabinol (THC) in Heavy and Light Users of Cannabis." *Psychopharmacology,* 74: 208–12, 1981 (2 tables, 3 figures, 9 references)

Abstract: Two female and sixteen male light or heavy cannabis users (ages 19 to 36 years) smoked a 1.64 percent THC, 0.23 CBN, 19 mg THC to obtain a desired high and were then administered 5 mg of THC dissolved in 95 percent ethanol solution IV or a placebo. Frequent blood samples were collected, and plasma THC concentrations were determined by MS. The mean peak plasma THC occurred at three minutes after smoking and were 98 ng/mL and 67 ng/mL for heavy and light users respectively. The mean peak plasma THC occurred at three minutes after IV administration and were 288 ng/mL for the heavy and 302 ng/mL for the light users respectively.

Not surprisingly, both heavy and light users showed more clinical effects following IV administration of THC as compared with smoking of cannabis. What was somewhat unexpected was the fact that heavy users did not appear to be particularly tolerant to either clinical effects of the drug. On the whole, their responses, adjusted for some minor differences in plasma concentrations of THC achieved, were entirely comparable to those of light users.

Reference Number: 50114

D'SOUZA, D.C., M. RANGANATHAN, G. BRALEY, R. GUEORGUIEVA, Z. ZIMOLO, T. COOPER, K. PERRY, AND J. KRYSTAL. "Blunted Psychotomimetic and Amnestic Effects of Delta-9-Tetrahydrocannabinol in Frequent Users of Cannabis." *Neuropsychopharmacology*, 33: 2505–516, 2008 (3 tables, 4 figures, 92 references)

Abstract: Fourteen male and eight female control subjects (mean age 29 years) and twenty-one male and nine female frequent cannabis users (mean age 24.8 years) were administered a placebo, 2.5 mg, or 5 ng THC by IV within two minutes. A cognitive/behavioural battery and field sobriety tests were conducted. Frequent blood samples were collected and plasma THC and THCCOOH were determined by radioimmunoassay (RIA). The mean peak plasma THC concentrations at ten minutes were 82 ng/mL and 119 ng/mL respectively. There were no significant differences in plasma THC between the two groups. Frequent users had poorer immediate, delayed, and cued recall with placebo than controls but performed better than controls at the 5 mg THC dose. Heart rate increased in a dose-dependent manner, without any group differences. THC increased commission and omission errors in both groups on vigilance testing.

Delta-9-tetrahydrocannabinol (1) produced transient psychotomimetic effects and perceptual alterations; (2) impaired memory and attention; (3) increased subjective effects of high; (4) produced tachycardia; and (5) increased serum cortisol in both groups. However, relative to controls, frequent users showed blunted responses to the psychotomimetic, perceptual altering, cognitive impairing, anxiogenic and cortisol increasing effects of delta-9-tetrahydrocannabinol but not to its euphoric effects. Frequent users also had lower prolactin levels. These data suggest that frequent users of cannabis are either inherently blunted in their response and/or develop tolerance to the psychotomimetic perceptual altering, amnestic, endocrine, and other effects of cannabinoids.

Reference Number: 50115

RAMAEKERS, J.G., M.R. MOELLER, P. VAN RUITENBEEK, E.L. THEUNISSEN, E. SCHNEIDER, AND G. KAUERT. "Cognition and Motor Control as a Function of Delta 9-THC Concentration in Serum and Oral Fluid. Limits of Impairment." *Drug and Alcohol Dependence*, 85: 114–22, 2006. (3 tables, 3 figures, 44 references)

Abstract: Six female and fourteen male recreational cannabis users (ages 19 to 29 years) smoked a placebo THC, 250 ug/kg THC, and 500 ug/kg THC cannabis cigarette (13 percent THC) on three separate occasions. Frequent blood and oral fluid samples were collected and analyzed for THC, 11-OH-THC, and 11-THCCOOH in serum and THC in OF by GC/MS. Various psychomotor tests were conducted including critical tracking tasks, stop signal task, and Tower of London. At sixty minutes, the mean serum THC was 10.4 and 6.1 ng/mL and the mean OF was 356 ng/g and 142 ng/g for the high and low doses respectively. The correlation between serum and OF THC concentrations was 0.84.

In summary, the present study showed a strong and linear relation between THC in serum and oral fluid. Linear relations between the magnitude of performance impairment and THC in oral fluid and serum, however, were low. Classification of performance into observations showing either impairment or no impairment provided a much better insight into the relation between serum THC and performance impairment. An initial shift toward impairment was evident in the critical tracking task for serum THC concentrations between 2 and 5 ng/mL. At concentrations between 5 and 10 ng/mL approximately 75 to 90 percent of the observations were indicative of impairment in all three performance tasks. At THC concentrations > 30 ng/mL the proportion of impaired observations increased to a full 100 percent in all three performance tasks. It is concluded that serum THC concentrations between 2 and 5 ng/mL established the lower and upper range of a legal THC limit.

Reference Number: 50116

RAMAEKERS, J.G., G. KAUERT, P. VAN RUITENBEEK, E.L. THEUNISSEN, E. SCHNEIDER, AND M. MOELLER. "High-Potency Marijuana Impairs Executive Function and Inhibitory Motor Control." *Neuropsychopharmacology*, 31: 2296–303, 2006 (1 table, 4 figures, 45 references)

Abstract: Most human performance studies have used low potency cannabis (4 percent THC), but the mean THC content in the US and Europe has increased to 10 percent, and sinsemilla has been found with up to 20 percent THC. Six female and fourteen male light users of marijuana (ages 19 to 29 years) received THC placebo, 250 ug/kg THC, and 500 ug/kg THC on three occasions at least seven days apart and were tested on critical tracking task, stop signal task, Iowa gambling task, and Tower of London. The tests were conducted at fixed intervals for up to 6 hours after dosing. Blood samples were collected at 5 minutes, 1, 3, and 6 hours, and serum THC concentrations were determined by GC-MS. The mean serum THC concentrations were 93.6, 10.6, 3.0, and 1.3 ng/mL at the high dose at 5 minutes, 1, 3, and 6 hours respectively. High potency marijuana consistently impaired executive functioning in the Tower of London task and impaired tracking performance and motor impulse control which lasted for up to 6 hours.

Use of higher dose of THC in controlled studies may offer a reliable indication of THC induced impairment as compared to lower doses of THC that have traditionally been used in performance studies.

Reference Number: 50117

RAMAEKERS, J.G., G. KAUERT, E.L. THEUNISSEN, S.W. TOENNES, AND M.R. MOELLER. "Neurocognitive Performance during Acute THC Intoxication in Heavy and Occasional Cannabis Users." *Journal of Psychopharmacology*, 23: 266–77, 2009 (3 tables, 4 figures, 48 references)

Abstract: Twelve occasional and twelve heavy cannabis users (seventeen males and seven females) smoked a placebo or marijuana (13 percent THC) within ten minutes and were tested on various psychomotor tasks such as CTT, divided attention, and Tower of London. Frequent blood samples were collected and serum THC, 11-OH THC, and THCCOOH concentrations were determined by GC/MS. The mean baseline serum THC concentration was 3.4 ng/mL and 1.6 ng/mL (11-OH THC), whereas for the infrequent smokers the results were zero. The mean peak serum THC was 120.9 ng/mL (heavy) and 49.7 ng/mL (light), which occurred six minutes after the end of smoking. THC increased subjective high and heart rate of occasional and heavy users to the same degree.

In conclusion, the present study demonstrated that an acute dose of 500 ug/kg THC produces impairment of critical tracking, divided attention, and motor impulse control in occasional cannabis users. In heavy cannabis users, performance impairment was limited to a loss of motor impulse control at high concentrations. Together, these data suggest that cannabis use history strongly determines the behavioural response to single doses of THC.

Reference Number: 50118

RAMAEKERS, J.G., J.H. VAN WEL, D.B. SPRONK., S.W. TOENNES, K.P.C. KUYPERS, E.L. THEUNISSEN, AND R.J. VERKES. "Cannabis and Tolerance: Acute Drug Impairment as a Function of Cannabis Use History." *Scientific Reports,* www.nature/scientific reports, srep26843, 8 pp, 2016 (2 tables, 4 figures, 36 references)

Abstract: Approximately 4 percent of the global population use cannabis and 10 percent of those develop a daily use pattern. Ninety-six male and twenty-six female cannabis users, who ranged from infrequent to daily use, were administered 300 ug/kg THC via a vaporizer using 11-12 percent THC plant material, a single dose of 300 mg cocaine, or a placebo. Various neurocognitive tests (CCT, SST, and DAT). Plasma THC, 11-OH-THC, THCCOOH, cocaine, and BZE concentrations were determined. The mean plasma baseline THC was 1.57 ng/mL, 11-OH-THC was 0.62 ng/mL, and THCCOOH was 20.9 ng/mL. The mean peak plasma THC concentration was 73.8 ng/mL. The acute effects of cannabis and cocaine on neurocognitive performances were similar in all types of cannabis users and showed no tolerance.

The present demonstration of absence of tolerance to cannabis impairment has important implications for risk perception in frequent users. It implies that neurocognitive function of daily or near daily cannabis users can be substantially impaired from repeated cannabis use during and beyond the initial phase of intoxication. As a consequence, frequent cannabis use and intoxication can be expected to interfere with neurocognitive performance in many daily environments such as school, work, or traffic.

Reference Number: 50119

SCHWOPE, D.M., W.M. BOSKER, J.G. RAMAEKERS, D.A. GORELICK, AND M.A. HUESTIS. "Psychomotor Performance, Subjective and Physiological Effects and Whole Blood Delta 9-Tetrahydrocannabinol Concentrations in Heavy, Chronic Cannabis Smokers Following Acute Smoked Cannabis." *Journal of Analytical Toxicology*, 36: 405–12, 2012 (1 table, 4 figures, 42 references)

Abstract: Nine male and one female chronic cannabis smokers (ages 19 to 46 years) inhaled one 6.8 percent THC cannabis cigarette. Frequent blood samples were collected and the THC, 11-OH-THC, and THCCOOH were determined in blood and plasma using a MS-MS. The subjective VAS, BP, HR, and psychomotor performance (critical tracking and divided attention task) were measured for up to six hours after smoking. Peak THC concentrations and VAS occurred at fifteen minutes after smoking. (Mean peak THC was 55 ng/mL.) There was a lack of correlation between blood THC concentration and observed effects until after the distribution phase.

> THC significantly increased VAS responses and heart rate with concentration-effect curves demonstrating counter-clockwise hysteresis. No significant difference was observed for critical tracking or divided attention task performance in this cohort of heavy, chronic cannabis smokers.

Reference Number: 50120

THEUNISSEN, E.L., G.F. KAUERT, S.W. TOENNES, M.R. MOELLER, A. SAMBETH, M.M. BLANCHARD, AND J.G. RAMAEKERS. "Neurophysiological Functioning of Occasional and Heavy Cannabis Users during THC Intoxication." *Psychopharmacology*, 220: 341–50, 2012 (4 tables, 3 figures, 44 references)

Abstract: Eight male and four female occasional cannabis users (mean age 23 years) and nine male and three female heavy cannabis users (mean age 23 years) smoked a placebo (800 mg tobacco) or cannabis cigarette (13 percent THC, 260 mg THC, and 540 mg tobacco) over ten to fifteen minutes. The subjects were tested on various psychomotor tasks such as divided attention task (DAT) and the stop signal task (SST). Event-related potentials (ERP) were measured by EEG during the testing. Blood samples were collected immediately after smoking and every fifteen minutes for the first hour. Serum THC, THCCOOH, and 11-OH-THC were measured by GC/MS. The mean peak plasma THC concentration was 120.9 ng/mL for heavy users and 49.1 ng/mL for occasional users. Performance on the SST was impaired for both groups but performance on the DAT was impaired only in the occasional users group.

> In the DAT, THC significantly decreased P100 amplitude in occasional but not in heavy cannabis users. P300 amplitude in the DAT was significantly decreased by THC in both groups. The N200 peak in the SST was not affected by treatment in either of the groups. Performance in the SST was impaired in both groups after THC treatment, whereas performance in the DAT was impaired by THC only in the occasional users groups.

Reference Number: 50121

SEWELL, R.A., A. SCHNAKENBERG, J. ELANDER, R. RADHAKRISHNAN, A. WILLIAMS, P.D. SKOSNIK, B. PITTMAN, M. RANGANATHAN, AND D.C. D'SOUZA. "Acute Effects of THC on Time Perception in Frequent and Infrequent Cannabis Users." *Psychopharmacology*, 226: 401–13, 2013 (3 tables, 1 figure, 131 references)

Abstract: THC activates CB1 receptors in the brain and is consistently reported to disrupt time estimation in the seconds to minutes range. Cannabis users frequently report a subjective slowing of time. The cannabis smoker's perception that external time is passing slowly is consistent with the subject's internal time passing more quickly. A time estimation task and time production tasks were determined in ten frequent (six male, four female) and thirty-four infrequent (twenty-seven male, seven female) cannabis smokers (ages 18 to 35 years). The subjects were administered a placebo, low (0.01 to 0.02 mg/kg), medium (0.03 to 0.04 mg/kg), and high (0.05 mg/kg) doses of THC IV. There were no baseline differences between frequent and infrequent smokers, which indicates that chronic exposure to cannabis does not alter time perception. THC effects on time perception were not dose related.

> THC transiently impaired time estimation and production in the seconds range. Even the lowest dose of THC, much less than that seen with recreational cannabis, produced changes in time perception. The effects

disappeared after a few hours. These temporal processing changes may or may not have functional consequences, which were not measured for this study. However, seconds range temporal processing is relevant to many everyday tasks; for example, driving, playing music, and using power tools. Processes underlying time perception from milliseconds to minutes may be particularly relevant to cognition as measures of temporal precision in humans correlated well with measures of general intelligence and working memory. Furthermore, time deficits are characteristic of disorders such as schizophrenia, autism, and attention-deficit hyperactivity disorder, suggesting that time alterations may be an endophenotype of psychiatric disease.

Reference Number: 50122

DESROSIERS, N.A., J.G. RAMAEKERS, E. CHAUCHARD, D.A. GORELICK, AND M.A. HUESTIS. "Smoked Cannabis, Psychomotor and Neurocognitive Effects in Occasional and Frequent Smokers." *Journal of Analytical Toxicology*, 39: 251–61, 2015 (1 table, 5 figures, 59 references)

Abstract: Smoked cannabis, effects on psychomotor function, risk taking, working memory, and subjective and physiological conditions were determined in fourteen frequent and eleven occasional cannabis users (eighteen men and seven women, ages 18 to 45 years) after smoking one 6.8 percent THC cigarette (54 mg THC). Frequent blood samples were collected and blood THC, 11-OH-THC, THCCOOH, CBD, and CBN were determined by LC-MS/MS. Baseline blood THC concentrations were not detected in the occasional user and a mean of 2.1 ng/mL in the frequent users. Blood THC concentrations were 32.3 ng/mL in frequent and 17.4 ng/mL in occasional smokers at 0.5 hours. HR increases and BP decreases were greater in occasional smokers, suggesting a tolerance effect.

We documented significant differences between occasional and frequent cannabis smokers in psychomotor, subjective, and physiological effects following cannabis smoking, with weaker effects in frequent smokers, suggesting tolerance development. Impairment domains included those that play a key role in a driver's ability to accurately control a car or to react to events on the road.

5.02 DRIVING SIMULATOR STUDIES

There is an increase in the veering or swaying of the car as measured by the standard deviation of lane position (SDLP) with increasing THC in driving simulator studies (50201, 50203). Oral ingestion of the prescription drug, dronabinol, can impair driving ability (50205). Driving simulator performance is more impaired when alcohol and THC are combined (50201).

Reference Number: 50201

DOWNEY, L.A., R. KING, K. PAPAFOTIOU, P. SWANN, E. OGDEN, M. BOORMAN, AND C. STOUGH. "The Effects of Cannabis and Alcohol on Simulated Driving: Influences of Dose and Experience." *Accident Analysis and Prevention*, 50: 879–86, 2013 (4 tables, 3 figures, 33 references)

Abstract: Forty-nine male and thirty-one female subjects (ages 21 to 35 years) were tested on a driving simulator (CyberCAR LITE) for six sessions involving the consumption of alcohol to obtain BACs of 0, 0.030, or 0.050 g/100mL and the smoking of a marijuana cigarette containing no THC, 1.8 percent, or 3 percent THC. Blood samples were collected before the experimental sessions and 20 and 60 minutes after the cessation of the smoking of the marijuana. The consumption of alcohol occurred over a 40-minute period and after a 20-minute wait, the marijuana cigarette was smoked over a 10-minute period. The driving simulation occurred under daytime or nighttime conditions and under freeway or city driving conditions. Each driving scenario took approximately 5 minutes to complete for a total simulated driving time of 20 minutes.

Driving simulator performance was more impaired in the THC and alcohol combined conditions. Consistent with past research, the level of THC detected in the blood is higher when THC is consumed with alcohol than when cannabis is consumed alone, and regular cannabis users returned higher levels of THC in plasma than non-regular users. Generally, regular cannabis users displayed more driving errors than non-regular cannabis users.

Reference Number: 50202

HARTMAN, R.L., T.L. BROWN, G. MILAVETZ, A. SPURGIN, R.S. PIERCE, D.A. GORELICK, G. GAFFNEY, AND M.A. HUESTIS. "Cannabis Effects on Driving

Lateral Control with and without Alcohol." *Drug and Alcohol Dependence*, 154: 25–37, 2015 (6 tables, 3 figures, 65 references)

Abstract: Thirteen male and five female occasional cannabis users (ages 21 to 37 years) drank placebo or low dose alcohol and inhaled 500 mg placebo, low (2.9 percent THC), or high (6.7 percent THC) vaporized cannabis over ten minutes. Breath blood and OF samples were collected on five occasions. The subjects drove the National Advance Driving Simulator in Iowa City for forty-five minutes. At a blood THC of 5 ng/mL there was a 4.1 percent increase in SDLP and at 10 ng/mL there was a 8.2 percent increase. These results were similar to a BAC of 0.050 g/100mL (6.7 percent) and 0.080 g/100mL (11 percent increase). THC and alcohol effects were additive in which a blood concentration of 5 ng/mL and 0.050 g/100mL alcohol had a similar SDLP as 0.080 g/100mL BAC.

SDLP was a sensitive cannabis-related lateral control impairment measure. During drive, blood THC > 8.2 ng/mL increased SDLP similar to notably impairing alcohol concentrations. Despite OF's screening value, OF variability poses challenges in concentration-based interpretation.

Reference Number: 50203

LENNE, M.G., P.M. DIETZE, T.J. TRIGGS, S. WALMSLEY, B. MURPHY, AND J.R. REDMAN. "The Effects of Cannabis and Alcohol on Simulated Arterial Driving: Influences of Driving Experience and Task Demand." *Accident Analysis and Prevention,* 42: 859–66, 2010 (5 tables, 2 figures, 35 references)

Abstract: Twenty-five experienced (seven years +) and twenty-two young novice drivers (< 2 years) consumed a placebo, 0.4 and 0.6 g/kg alcohol and placebo, one joint (19 mg THC), or two joints (38 mg THC). The subjects alternated consuming alcohol after each puff of marijuana. The mean BACs were 0, 0.020, and 0.050 g/100mL, and the mean blood THC concentrations were 0, 7.4, and 12.0 ng/mL respectively. The drivers were tested on a simulated computerized driving task.

In this study we examined the effects of cannabis, alone and in combination with alcohol, on the simulated driving performance of inexperienced and experienced drivers. Moderate workload was imposed by having the drivers undertake a car-following task while driving, or by measuring reactions to signs while driving. Task demand was manipulated through the completion of both tasks simultaneously. We expected that active cannabis and active alcohol would impair performance. However, the pattern of findings was mixed. Cannabis did impair simulated driving as evidence by increased variability in speed, headway, and lateral position, in accord with previous research. In most cases these effects were dose-dependent. The decrements in standard deviation of lateral position for high dose cannabis were greater than those observed in the high alcohol condition. RTs were also slower in the high dose cannabis condition. Performance in the cannabis conditions was associated with an increase in mean headway and a decrease in mean speed. These effects of cannabis were observed at levels similar to those believed to be indicative of performance impairment. Alcohol was found to have fewer effects on performance. In support of our earlier work, alcohol did increase variability in speed and lateral position, while also increasing steering variability, however there was no effect on RT.

Reference Number: 50204

LIGUORI, A., C.P. GATTO, D.B. JARRETT, W.V. MCCALL, AND T.W. BROWN. "Behavioral and Subjective Effects of Marijuana Following Partial Sleep Deprivation." *Drug and Alcohol Dependence*, 70: 233–40, 2003 (1 table, 4 figures, 51 references)

Abstract: Five male and two female cannabis users (ages 22 to 35 years) were tested on six occasions with placebo, 2 percent, or 3.5 percent THC marijuana after a regular sleep and after partial sleep deprivation (PSD). A 25-minute test battery was conducted, which included a computerized driving test and was conducted at 2, 62, and 122 minutes after smoking ended. No blood THC concentrations were determined.

Thus, while PSD increased the dose-dependence of THC effects on heart rate and subjective impairment, it did not enhance the effects of marijuana on standing balance and brake latency.

Reference Number: 50205

MENETREY, A., M. AUGSBURGER, B. FAVRAT, M.A. PIN, L.E. ROTHUIZEN, M. APPENZELLER, T. BUCLIN, P. MANGIN, AND C. GIROUD. "Assessment of Driving Capability Through the Use of Clinical and Psychomotor Tests in Relation to Blood Cannabinoids Levels Following Oral Administration of 20 mg Dronabinol or of a Cannabis Decoction Made with 20 or

60 mg delta 9 THC." *Journal of Analytical Toxicology*, 29: 327–38, 2005 (1 table, 5 figures, 53 references)

Abstract: Eight male occasional smokers of cannabis (ages 22 to 30 years) consumed a placebo, 20 mg dronabinol, and 16.5 or 45.7 mg THC (in a milk mixture). Blood was collected at 0, 1.0, 2.5, 4.0, 5.5, 7.0, 10, and 24 hours after ingestion and blood THC, 11-OH-THC, and THCCOOH concentrations were measured by GCMS. Various psychomotor and driving simulator tests were conducted. Two of the eight subjects were withdrawn from the study due to anxiety or altered perception. The high dose THC milk mixture induced vomiting. The mean peak blood THC concentrations were 2.8, 3.8, and 8.4 ng/mL for the dronabinol, low, and high THC milk mixtures respectively at one hour. The highest peak 11-OH-THC and THCCOOH were 12.8 ng/mL and 66.2 ng/mL respectively at 2.5 hours for the high dose THC milk mixture. The sum of THC and 11-OH-THC provides a better estimation impairment after oral ingestion than THC alone for oral ingestion only.

Table: Tracking Test (Percent of Time-Simulated Car in the Lane) at 2.5, 4, 5.5, and 10 Hours after Drug Administration.

Drug	2.5 Hours	4 Hours	5.5 Hours	10 Hours
Placebo	88%	84%	86%	88%
20 mg THC dronabinol	75%	70%	72%	85%
16.5 mg THC decoction	65%	68%	79%	86%
45.7 mg THC decoction	48%	68%	65%	78%

Source: Adapted from Menetrey et al, 2005

The willingness to drive was significantly hampered after all treatments. Important effects were also noticed with the road signs testing and the tracking test. Altogether, the results indicate that oral ingestion of cannabis or dronabinol in medium and high doses can severely impair several performance skills required for safe driving.

Reference Number: 50206

RONEN, A., P. GERSHON, H. DROBINER, A. RABINOVICH, R. BAR-HAMBURGER, R. MECHOULAM, Y. CASSUTO, AND D. SHINAR. "Effects of THC on Driving Performance, Physiological State and Subjective Feelings Relative to Alcohol." *Accident Analysis and Prevention*, 40: 926–34, 2008 (3 tables, 5 figures, 28 references)

Abstract: Ten male and four female cannabis users (mean age 26 years) were exposed to six experimental conditions and were tested on a computerized driving task of a thirty-four mile driving scenario at 55 mph. The subjects smoked two doses of marijuana cigarettes (13 and 17 mg THC), drinking to obtain a BAC of 0.05 g/100mL, and were tested twenty-four hours after smoking the high dose THC.

> In conclusion, based on our results, smoking the active ingredient in marijuana, THC, at dosages of 13 mg and 17 mg, may impair driving ability in recreational users of marijuana and can lead to unsafe driving. These effects are dose dependent, and are reflected in all three types of measurement techniques used: performance, subjective sensations, and physiological. The higher dose of THC (17 mg) was found to be more potent than the lower dose (13 mg), causing higher increase in heart rate and a greater feeling of discomfort and physical effort while driving after smoking. In terms of performance, the effects of 0.05 percent BAC seem to be similar to those of the low-level (13 mg) THC cigarettes, although subjects drove faster after alcohol compared to driving sessions after THC smoking. No THC-related effects were measurable twenty-four hours after smoking the high (17 mg) level of THC.

Reference Number: 50207

ANDERSON, B.M., M. RIZZO, R.I. BLOCK, G.D. PEARLSON, AND D.S. O'LEARY. "Sex Differences in the Effects of Marijuana on Simulated Driving Performance." *Journal of Psychoactive Drugs*, 42: 19–30, 2010 (2 tables, 2 figures, 63 references)

Abstract: Thirty-five female and fifty male occasional marijuana smokers (mean age 21 years) smoked a placebo or active (2.9 percent THC, 22.9 mg) cannabis cigarette. They were required to smoke the entire cigarette, but one male and eight female subjects discontinued smoking. The subjects then drove for fifteen minutes on a computerized, simulated, rural two-lane highway at 55 mph. During driving there were a series of unexpected traffic situations, such as an emergency vehicle or a dog crossing the road. No gender differences in driving performance after cannabis use were observed.

> The study assessed sex differences in the effects of acute marijuana use on driving performance in a double-blinded, placebo-controlled,

between-subjects design. Under the influence of active marijuana, participants exhibited increased drowsiness, although this did not appear to affect their driving. Participants under the influence of marijuana failed to benefit from prior experience on a distractor task as evidenced by a decrease in speed and a failure to show expected practice effects. This study supports existing literature that marijuana does affect simulated driving performance, particularly on complex tasks such as divided attention. It is anticipated that many teenagers and young adults driving under the influence of marijuana are doing so while conversing with friends in the car, listening to music, talking on the cell phone, and/or text messaging others. These behaviours divide the driver's attention and are particularly dangerous under the influence of marijuana.

5.03 CLOSED COURSE DRIVING STUDIES

Both alcohol and cannabis used at doses found in social situations were found to impair driving performance in cars driven in a closed course (50301, 50302).

Reference Number: 50301

CASSWELL, S. "Cannabis and Alcohol: Effects on Closed-Course Driving Behavior." 7th International Conference on Alcohol, Drugs and Traffic Safety, I.R. Johnston (editor), 238–46, 1977 (4 tables, 3 figures, 23 references)

Abstract: A study was conducted of thirteen cannabis users, (ages 20 to 30 years) who drove an instrumented car over a 3.68 km long track for eight laps for a total driving time of thirty-five minutes. The subjects drove under four conditions: placebo, alcohol only, marijuana only, and alcohol and marijuana. Subjects consumed alcohol adjusted for body weight to achieve a BAC of 0.100 g/100mL. The subjects smoked one joint containing either 3.12 or 6.24 mg of THC.

Table: Mean Distance (Metres) from the Traffic Sign at which the Correct Recognition Was Made after Placebo, Alcohol, and/or Cannabis Use

Drug Condition	Distance from 5-Letter Sign (metres)	Distance from 7-Letter Sign (metres)
Placebo	59 m	42 m
Alcohol Only	57 m	37 m

Drug Condition	Distance from 5-Letter Sign (metres)	Distance from 7-Letter Sign (metres)
Marijuana Only	54 m	38 m
Alcohol and Marijuana	55 m	39 m

Driving in many traffic conditions is a self-paced task. The individual's driving behaviour depends upon a match between perceived risk and the amount of risk or emotional tension he or she is prepared to tolerate. It appears from the present results that the drug treatments may have had different effects upon performance measures indicative of the drivers' perception or tolerance of risk. The pattern following MO (marijuana only) of control use similar to that following placebo treatment and of consistently slower speeds suggest that in a self-paced driving task such as this, drivers compensate for what they perceived as adverse effects on driving ability by maintenance of control effort and perhaps attempting to reduce the rate of required information processing by driving more slowly. By contrast, the alcohol-related speed increased and changes in steering control provides confirmation of the disinhibitory effect on driving performance already indicated by epidemiological studies of alcohol and road traffic. There were several indications that performance under the combined effects of the two drugs was affected detrimentally by both.

Reference Number: 50302

ATTWOOD, D.A., R.D. WILLIAMS, L.J. MCBURNEY, AND R.C. FRECKER. "Cannabis, Alcohol, and Driving: Effects on Selected Closed Course Tasks." *Alcohol, Drugs, and Traffic Safety*, Vol. III, L. Goldberg (editor), T80, Almqvist and Wiksell International, Sweden, 938–53, 1980 (1 table, 8 figures, 13 references)

Abstract: Eight male occasional drinkers and moderate cannabis users (ages 20 to 28 years) drove an instrumented car over a 1.7 km closed course. The subjects were divided into four conditions: placebo and placebo, placebo and alcohol, THC and placebo, and THC and alcohol. There were sixty-two variables measured during driving, including velocity maintenance, car following, and car following with variable velocity. The subjects consumed 1.25 g/kg ethanol or 0.63 g/kg ethanol within ten minutes. A maintenance dose was given throughout the experiment. Both BrACs and BACs were determined. The mean BACs were approximately 0.050 and 0.100 g/100mL. The subjects smoked three joints for a total dose of 150 ug/kg THC. Blood THC concentrations were not measured.

> The results of the driving task analyses suggest that alcohol and marijuana, when taken in quantities normally associated with social use, adversely affect performance on tasks that are typical of everyday driving situations. That is, no exaggerated courses on manoeuvres were employed to demonstrate the effects. Moreover, the data obtained from the driving tasks suggest that the effects of alcohol and marijuana are additive when the drugs are taken together.

5.04 HIGHWAY DRIVING STUDIES

After smoking cannabis, there is detectable impairment of driving ability in real life highway situations (50401-04). Dronabinol (oral THC) was found to impair driving in both occasional and heavy cannabis users, especially in regards to car weaving (SDLP) (50404).

Reference Number: 50401

KLONOFF, H. "Marijuana and Driving in Real-Life Situations." *Science*, 186: 317–24, 1974 (6 tables, 1 figure, 12 references)

Abstract: Forty-three men and twenty-one women (mean age 24 years) were assigned to one of three groups: smoking low (5 mg THC), high (8 mg THC), and placebo marijuana. The subjects drove a car around a closed course that included tasks such as slalom, tunnel, and emergency braking before and after drug/placebo administration. Some subjects also drove a car in Vancouver traffic between 12:00 noon and 8:00 p.m. The distance driven was approximately 26 km and driving time was approximately forty-six minutes. The smoking of marijuana potentiated the stress of driving under closed course and real conditions and caused a 22 percent increase in heart rate.

> It is evident that the smoking of marijuana by human subjects does have a detrimental effect on their driving skills and performance in a restricted driving area and that this effect is even greater under normal conditions of driving on city streets. The effect of marijuana however

is not uniform for all subjects, but is in fact bidirectional; whether or not a significant decline occurs in driving ability is dependent both on the subject's capacity to compensate and on the dose of marijuana. For those subjects who improved their performance, the explanation may lie in overcompensation and possibly the sedative effect of the drug.

Reference Number: 50402

LAMERS, C.T., AND J.G. RAMAEKERS. "Visual Search and Urban City Driving Under the Influence of Marijuana and Alcohol." *Human Psychopharmacology. Clinical and Experimental*, 16: 393–401, 2001 (2 tables, 3 figures, 42 references)

Abstract: Eight male and eight female subjects (ages 21 to 40 years) were tested in an instrumented car driving the City Driving Test (forty minutes duration) under four conditions: Alcohol (0.5 g/kg male, 0.43 g/kg female) and 100 ug/kg THC; placebo and THC; alcohol and placebo; and placebo and placebo. The subjects were recreational users of both drugs. The alcohol was consumed within fifteen minutes after a standard meal and BrACs were determined with a Lion SD-4 breath alcohol analyser. Additional doses of alcohol were consumed to maintain the BrAC at approximately 0.050 g/100mL. Eye movements were measured during the driving, and driving performance was noted by a licensed driving instructor. The mean BACs were between 0.035 and 0.042 g/100mL.

It is clear from the present results that the effects of low doses of marijuana and alcohol on urban driving proficiency and visual search were mild. Yet, it is well to remember that the dose of neither drug was particularly high. The marijuana dose was only a third of the dose preferred by cannabis smokers, whereas the alcohol dose produced BACs that were well below the legal limit in most countries. One can safely assume that drivers in the real world occasionally drive after consuming more or either or both in combination. If they do, our results suggest that their frequency of visual search for traffic would be considerably less than observed in the present study.

Reference Number: 50403

VELDSTRA, J.L., W.M. BOSKER, D. DE WAARD, J.G. RAMAEKERS, AND K.A. BROOKHUIS. "Comparing Treatment Effects of Oral THC on Simulated and On-the-Road Driving Performance: Testing the Validity of Driving

Simulator Research." *Psychopharmacology*, 232: 2911–919, 2015 (2 tables, 2 figures, 40 references)

Abstract: Ten female and fourteen male subjects (mean age 24 years) consumed 10 mg or 20 mg (synthetic THC) dronabinol (Marinol) or placebo. On-the road tests using an instrumented car and computer-simulated driving in the lab tasks were conducted two to four hours after drug administration. The on-the-road tests were conducted two to four hours after drug administration and the computer simulator tests four to five hours after ingestion. Blood samples were collected at 1.5, 4.25, and 6 hours after drug administration, and serum THC, 11-OH-THC, and THCCOOH concentrations were determined by GC/MS. The mean serum THC concentrations were 5.7, 2.8, and 2.5 ng/mL for the low dose and 7.5, 3.7, and 4.2 ng/mL for the high dose at their respective times.

The driving simulator was proven to be sensitive for demonstrating dronabinol-induced effects, particularly at higher doses. Treatment effects of dronabinol on weaving were comparable with driving on the road but inter-individual variability seemed higher in the simulator than on the road, which may have potential effects on the clinical inferences made from simulator driving. Car following on the road and in the simulator were, however, not comparable.

Reference Number: 50404

BOSKER, W.M., K.P.C. KUYPERS, E.L. THEUNISSEN, A. SURINX, R.J. BLANKESPOOR, G. SKOPP, W.K. JEFFREY, C. WALLS, C.J. VAN LEEUWEN, AND J.G. RAMAEKERS. "Medicinal Delta 9-Tetrahydrocannabinol (Dronabinol) Impairs On-the-Road Performance of Occasional and Heavy Cannabis Users but Is Not Detected in Standardized Field Sobriety Tests." *Addictions*, 107: 1837–844, 2012 (2 tables, 3 figures, 26 references)

Abstract: Twelve occasional and twelve heavy cannabis users (fourteen male and ten female), mean age 23.6 years, consumed a placebo, 10 mg, or 20 mg of dronabinol (THC). Blood samples were collected at baseline, 1.5, 4.25, and 6 hours after drug administration. Driving tests were conducted between 2 and 4 hours and SFST at 4.5 and 5 hours. The driving test involved driving an instrumented car on a primary road for one hour at a constant speed and standard deviation of lane position (SDLP) or weaving was measured, as well as the time to speed adaptation. The other driving test was car following for twenty-five minutes. The mean blood THC concentrations were 1.8 ng/mL for the occasional and 6.3 ng/mL for the heavy cannabis users at 4.25 hours for the 20 mg dose.

Table: Standard Deviation of Lane Position (SDLP) and Time to Speed Adaptation (TSA) in a Car-Following Task

Test	Cannabis Use	Placebo	10 mg Dronabinol	20 mg Dronabinol
SDLP (cm)	Occasional	17.9 cm	20.4 cm	22.1 cm
	Heavy	19.7 cm	21.0 cm	21.4 cm
TSA (seconds)	Occasional	2.5	4.1	2.9
	Heavy	3.1	3.6	3.8

Source: Adapted from Bosker et al, 2012

Dronabinol (medical tetrahydrocannabinol) impairs driving performance in occasional and heavy users in a dose-dependent way, but to a lesser degree in heavy users, possibly due to tolerance. The Standardized Field Sobriety Test is most sensitive to clinically relevant driving impairment caused by oral tetrahydrocannabinol.

5.05 FIELD (EPIDEMIOLOGICAL STUDIES)

Epidemiologic studies have confirmed that the impairment of various skills due to cannabis found in the laboratory lead to an increased risk of motor vehicle collisions and impairment in actual driving situations found on the highways (50501, 50504). As the blood THC concentration increases, the involvement of cannabis in fatal road traffic collisions increases (50503). Unlike alcohol-related motor vehicle collisions, cannabis-related collisions tend to be spaced throughout the week, rather than on weekends, and involve more multi-vehicle collisions as opposed to the preponderance of single motor vehicle collisions that occur with alcohol (50511, 50518, 50527). Acute cannabis consumption doubles the risk of fatal motor vehicle collisions (50505, 50522). The mean blood THC concentration in arrested drivers has increased in Norway in the past decade from 4.0 to 6.6 ng/mL, whereas the mean BAC has remained relatively constant (50531). Alcohol is commonly used together with cannabis, causing greater driver impairment (50502, 50515). It was estimated that currently DUIC costs are over $1 billion annually in Canada (50529).

The presence of CBD does not decrease the involvement of THC in driving impairment (50533).

Reference Number: 50501

NSC COMMITTEE ON ALCOHOL AND OTHER DRUGS. "Position of the Use of Cannabis (Marijuana) and Driving." *Journal of Analytical Toxicology*, 37: 47–49, 2013 (32 references)

Abstract: The position statement of the National Safety Council Committee on Alcohol and Other Drugs is presented.

> Laboratory-based impairment experiments identified divided attention tasks and executive functions as the most sensitive to cannabis' effects. Studies evaluating actual driving performance demonstrated dose-dependent THC impairment in road tracking, even following low to moderate THC doses that were required due to safety concerns. Driving under the influence of cannabis is an important public safety concern. Impaired driving endangers those both inside and outside the driver's vehicle. Smoking or eating cannabis with or without alcohol before driving is a common occurrence and increases the risks of motor vehicle accidents and fatalities. The position of the NSC COAD is that smoking or ingesting cannabis, THC, or synthetic cannabinoids before or during driving increases the risk of death or injury to the driver and the public.

Reference Number: 50502

ALVAREZ, F.J., AND I.F.M.C. DEL RIO. "Cannabis and Driving: Results from a General Population Survey." *Forensic Science International*, 170: 111–16, 2007 (3 tables, 1 figure, 27 references)

Abstract: The self-reported incidence of cannabis use and driving was determined in 1,266 male and 1,234 female subjects (ages 14 to 70 years) in Spain during 2004. Fifteen per cent reported cannabis use within the previous years (20 percent in male, and 11 percent in female). The mean initiation age for cannabis use was 17 years. Alcohol consumption was frequent among cannabis users. Of the cannabis users, 11 percent of the males and 8 percent of the females reported driving under the influence of cannabis.

> The present study shows that driving under the influence of cannabis and being a passenger in a vehicle driven by a person under the influence of cannabis are frequent behaviours; these were reported by 9.7

and 19.8 percent respectively of present year cannabis users. For the total population, these figures represent 1.5 and 31 percent respectively.

Reference Number: 50503

ANDREWS, R., K.G. MURPHY, L. NAHAR, AND S. PATERSON. "Cannabinoid Concentrations Detected in Fatal Road Traffic Collision Victims Compared with a Population of Other Postmortem Cases." *Clinical Chemistry*, 61: 1256–264, 2015 (3 tables, 3 figures, 37 references)

Abstract: Blood THC, 11-OH-THC, THCCOOH, CBD, CBN, and other drug and alcohol concentrations were determined in 100 fatal road traffic collisions (RTC) and 114 non-RTC cases from London and SE England between 2011 and 2013. Cannabinoid-positive RTC cases had a significantly lower median age (24 years) than non-RTC cases (39 years). The median THC, 11-OH-THC, and THCCOOH concentrations were 2.6, 1.8, and 7.3 ng/mL in non-RTC cases, and 4.2, 2.2, and 11.9 ng/mL in RTC cases. No drugs were detected in 68 percent of the RTC cases. Twenty-one RTC blood samples were positive for cannabinoids, none of which had other drugs detected and exceeded the number of RTC cases in which there was a BAC > 0.080 g/100mL. A positive blood THC concentration was detected in 90 percent of the RTC cases and 59 percent of the non-RTC cases. In March 2015, new drugged driving legislation was enacted in the UK. The limit for THC was set at 2 ng/mL.

Table: Percentage of Cases for Non-RTC (comparison) and RTC Cases at Each THC Concentration Group.

THC Concentration (ng/mL)	Non-RTC (% at Each THC Concentration Range)	RTC (% at Each THC Concentration Range)
Not Detected	79%	11%
0 – 3.5	60%	40%
3.5 – 5	40%	60%
> 5	20%	80%

Source: Adapted from Andrews et al, 2015

Our work supports the idea that cannabis use plays a role in fatal RTCs. However, given the mixed role of our participants in these RTCs (driver, passenger, pedestrian), further work is required to determine whether driving under the influence of cannabis should be a priority focus for legislation, and the utility of current and future laws regarding cannabis use and driving.

Reference Number: 50504

ASBRIDGE, M., J.A. HAYDEN, AND J.L. CARTWRIGHT. "Acute Cannabis Consumption and Motor Vehicle Collision Risk: Systematic Review of Observational Studies and Meta-Analysis." *British Medical Journal*, 344: e536, 2012 (1 table, 4 figures, 58 references)

Abstract: Self-reported driving under the influence of cannabis (i.e., > one hour after smoking) increased in Canada from 1.9 percent to 4 percent between 1996–7 and 2004. The percentage of cannabis positive drivers in Europe using roadside testing ranged between 0.3 and 7.4 percent. A meta-analysis and systematic review was conducted using 9 studies (out of 222) on the presence of THC (usually > 1 ng/mL) in the blood of drivers involved in serious or fatal MVCs. Rates of cannabis use in these drivers ranged from 1 to 7 percent in controls and 2 to 15 percent for drivers. Acute cannabis consumption approximately doubles the risk of fatal MVCs.

After a systematic review of the literature, this meta-analysis of studies examining acute cannabis consumption and motor vehicle collisions with adequate control groups found a near doubling of risks of a driver being involved in a motor vehicle collision resulting in serious injury or death. The increased risk was most evident for high quality studies, case-control studies, and studies of fatal collisions. To our knowledge, this meta-analysis is the first to examine the association between acute cannabis use and risk of motor vehicle collisions in real life settings. This review is important to enhancing our understanding of the effects of cannabis consumption on collision risk, and provides a more definitive statement on the direction that efforts in public policy and intervention should take in addressing road safety. These results converge with those from experimental studies (laboratory, simulator, and forensic), suggesting that cannabis impairs performance of cognitive and motor tasks necessary for safe driving, increasing the risk of collision.

Reference Number: 50505

ASBRIDGE, M., C. POULIN, AND A. DONATO. "Motor Vehicle Collision Risk and Driving Under the Influence of Cannabis: Evidence from Adolescents in Atlantic Canada." *Accident Analysis and Prevention*, 32: 1025–34, 2005 (3 tables, 89 references)

Abstract: A survey was conducted of 6,087 senior high school students in Atlantic Canada during 2002 and 2003. The prevalence of DUIC was higher (15.1 percent) than DUIA (11.7 percent) in these students. The risk of being involved in a MVC was increased two times in DUIC than in the cannabis-free adults. In Manitoba in 2001 (using cannabis within one hour of driving), 19 percent of students thought there was nothing wrong with DUIC, compared to 4 percent who thought there was nothing wrong with DUIA.

Because alcohol consumption is still considerably more prevalent than marijuana consumption, the fact that the use of these two substances in combination with driving has reached near parity suggests that teens are relatively less likely to drive after drinking than they are after using marijuana. This may reflect the concerted efforts in the past twenty years to deter drunk driving, compared to the much more limited efforts to deter the drug impaired driving.

Reference Number: 50506

AUGSBURGER, M., N. DONZE, A. MENETREY, C. BROSSARD, F. SPORKET, C. GIROUD, AND D. MANGIN. "Concentration of Drugs in Blood of Suspected Impaired Drivers." *Forensic Science International* 153: 11–15, 2005 (2 tables, 1 figure, 15 references)

Abstract: The blood and urine drug concentrations were determined in 440 drivers suspected of driving under the influence of drugs in Switzerland between 2002 and 2003. Ninety-one percent of the drivers were men and the mean age was 28 years (range 16 to 81 years). In 11 percent of the blood samples and 8 percent of the urine samples, no drug or alcohol could be detected. The most commonly detected drugs were cannabinoids (59 percent), alcohol (46 percent), benzodiazepines (12 percent), cocaine (13 percent), amphetamine (9 percent), and opiates (9 percent). The median blood THC concentration was 3 ng/mL (range 1 to 35 ng/mL). The median BAC was 0.125 g/100mL (range 0.014 to 0.310 g/100mL).

Because cannabis and alcohol are the most common recreational drugs used in Western countries among the young population, it is not surprising that cannabinoids and ethanol appear to be the most frequent substances measured in the blood of drivers suspected of DUID.

Reference Number: 50507

BEDARD, M., S. DUBOIS, AND B. WEAVER. "The Impact of Cannabis on Driving." *Canadian Journal of Public Health*, 98: 6–11, 2007 (5 tables, 1 figure, 37 references)

Abstract: The ORs of potentially unsafe driving reactions (Driver-Related Factors) before the FMVC were determined in fatally injured drivers in the US between 1993 and 2003, using the FARS data. The drivers were between 20 and 49 years of age and had a positive test for cannabis and a negative BAC. Of the 32,543 drivers tested, 1,647 (5 percent) were positive for cannabis. The OR for risky driving before the FMVC due to cannabis use was 1.29 (adjusted for age, gender, and driving record).

Cannabis had a negative effect on driving, as would be predicted from human performance studies. This finding supports the need for interventions to decrease the prevalence of driving under the influence of cannabis and indicates that further studies should be conducted to investigate the dose-response relationship between cannabis and safe driving.

Reference Number: 50508

BEIRNESS, D.J., AND E.E. BEASLEY. "A Roadside Survey of Alcohol and Drug Use among Drivers in British Columbia." *Traffic Injury Prevention*, 11: 215–21, 2010 (2 tables, 5 figures, 14 references)

Abstract: A roadside survey was conducted of 1,533 drivers between 9:00 p.m. and 3:00 a.m. on Wednesday to Saturday nights in BC during June 2008. BrACs were measured with an Intoxilyzer 400D. Oral fluid was also collected and tested for the presence of psychoactive drugs. A positive BrAC was found in 19 percent of the drivers in 1995, which declined to 8 percent in 2008. A BrAC > 0.080 g/100mL was found in 2 percent of the drivers in 1995 and 2.7 percent of the drivers in 2008. Drivers with a BrAC > 0.050 g/100mL increased from 2 percent between 9:00 p.m. and 10:30 p.m. to 12 percent between 1:30 a.m. and 3:00 a.m. Male drivers accounted for 78 percent of all drinking drivers. Cannabis was found in 5 percent of the drivers, cocaine in 5 percent, and opiates in 1 percent.

The pattern of drug use by drivers differed somewhat from the well-known patterns of drinking and driving. For example, whereas the incidence of alcohol use by drivers increases during the late-night hours, and is more common on weekend nights, drug use among drivers appears to be distributed more consistently across day and time.

Reference Number: 50509

BIECHELER, M.-B., J-F. PEYTAVIN, THE SAM GROUP, F. FACY, AND H. MARTINEAU. "SAM Survey on Drugs and Fatal Accidents: Search of Substances Consumed and Comparison Between Drivers Involved Under the Influence of Alcohol or Cannabis." *Traffic Injury Prevention*, 9: 11–21, 2008 (5 tables, 6 figures, 29 references)

Abstract: SAM is a French acronym for Stupeficiants et Accidents Mortels de la circulkation routiere (i.e., Drugs in Fatal Accidents). In France, the legal BAC of 0.05 g/100mL was introduced in 1995, and in 1999, all drivers involved in FMVCs had blood/urine drug tests conducted. The role of drugs/alcohol was determined in 16,391 drivers involved in FMVCs in France between 2001 and 2003. Alcohol/drugs were found in 26 percent of the drivers. A BAC > 0.050 g/100mL occurred in 21 percent of the drivers, cannabis in 7 percent, opiates in 1.3 percent, amphetamines in 0.6 percent, and cocaine in 0.3 percent of the drivers. Drivers with cannabis or cannabis/alcohol combination were found mainly in the younger age groups (20 to 24 years and 25 to 29 years). Drivers with a BAC > 0.050 g/100mL are overrepresented in the 20- to 44-year group.

Table: Index of Responsibility (Percent Responsible/Percent Not Responsible) According to the Presence of Alcohol and/or Cannabis)

Drug Combination	Responsibility Index
Cannabis Alone (THC > 1 ng/mL)	2.3 X
Alcohol Alone (BAC > 0.05 g/100mL)	9.4 X
Alcohol and Cannabis	14.1 X

Source: Adapted from Biecheler et al, 2008

Over and beyond the increasingly precise evidence of the role of cannabis as a factor of risk in road accidents at the level of a given population (quantified risk), substantial progress has been made in the observational system itself: biological environments, thresholds, and testing devices adapted to road use. Given the laboriousness of the current system, entailing urine tests in a medical environment, saliva tests that are usable by police are very eagerly awaited. While none of the commercial devices currently available have been able to show sufficient precision when compared with blood tests, substantial progress has been made in this area over the past few years and work is continuing. Correlations between saliva/blood concentrations of THC (analogous to air/blood concentrations for alcohol) create the hope that devices usable in road surveys will emerge, opening the way to other epidemiological studies on the model used by Borkenstein in the case of alcohol and to easier means of prevention on the road.

Reference Number: 50510

BLOWS, S., R.Q. IVERS, J. CONNOR, S. AMERATUNGA, M. WOODWARD, AND R. NORTON. "Marijuana Use and Car Crash Injury." *Addiction*, 100: 605–11, 2005 (2 tables, 28 references)

Abstract: Self-reported cannabis use in the three hours prior to driving and the marijuana use over the previous year were determined in 571 cases of serious MVCs and 588 control drivers in the Auckland area between 1998 and 1999. There was a 3.9 times OR in MVC for recent marijuana use and 9.5 times for chronic use.

This population-based control study suggests that habitual marijuana use is associated with a ten-fold increase in the risk of crash injury. The relationship between both habitual and acute marijuana use and car crashes is complex and likely to be related to other risk-taking behaviours, particularly risky driving.

Reference Number: 50511

BRUBACHER, J.R., H. CHAN, W. MARTZ, W. SCHREIBER, M. ASBRIDGE, J. EPPLER, A. LUND, S. MACDONALD, O. DRUMMER, R. PURSSELL, G. ANDOLFATTO, R. MANN, AND R. BRANT. "Prevalence of Alcohol and Drug Use in Injured British Columbia Drivers." *British Medical Journal Open*, 6: 9pp, March 10, 2016 (2 tables, 3 figures, 48 references)

Abstract: Blood samples were collected from 1,097 drivers attending seven trauma centres in British Columbia between 2010 and 2012 and were analyzed for alcohol (GC), cannabis, or other drugs (LC/MS or GC). The blood was collected a median of 87.2 minutes after the MVC. The majority of drivers were male (64 percent) and 61 percent were between 20 and 50 years of age. Alcohol was detected in 17.8 percent of the drivers and 15.4 percent of the BACs were 0.080 g/100mL or greater. A positive blood THC concentration (> 0.2 ng/mL) was detected in 7.3 percent of the drivers, of which 3 percent had a blood THC > 3 ng/mL. A total of 12.6 percent of the drivers were cannabis users (THCCOOH was positive). Overall, alcohol or at least one impairing drug was detected in 40.1 percent of drivers and alcohol and cannabis were detected in 1.6 percent of the drivers. Approximately 15 percent of THC positive drivers had consumed alcohol. Drivers with a blood THC > 3 ng/mL were less likely to be male, less than 30 years of age, less likely to be involved in SMVCs, or during the night and weekends than drivers with BAC > 0.080 g/100mL.

Table: Odds Ratio (OR) of an Injured Driver with a BAC > 0.08 g/100mL or Blood THC > 3 ng/mL

	BAC > 0.08 g/100mL	Blood THC > 3 ng/mL
Gender (male vs female)	3.4 X	2.1 X
Age (<30 vs >30 years)	3.8 X	2.7 X
Crash Type (single vs multi-vehicle)	6.9 X	0.7 X
Night vs Day	15.3 X	1.4 X
Weekend vs Weekday	3.9 X	0.8 X
Admitted vs Discharged	1.8 X	1.2 X

Source: Adapted from Brubacher et al, 2016

After alcohol, cannabis was the next most commonly detected recreational drug. Like alcohol, cannabis impairs driving ability and increases the risk of crashes, although to a lesser extent than alcohol.

Reference Number: 50512

CHIPMAN, M.I., S. MACDONALD, AND R.E. MANN. "Being at Fault in Traffic Crashes: Does Alcohol, Cannabis, Cocaine or Polydrug Abuse Make a Difference?" *Injury Prevention*, 9: 343–48, 2003 (5 tables, 33 references)

Abstract: The adjusted relative risk (ARR) of MVC and at fault MVCs were determined in 411 drivers beginning treatment for alcohol/drug abuse compared to 518 control drivers in Toronto during 1994. Significant ARRs of 1.59 to 1.79 (for all MVCs) were found for abusers of cannabis, cocaine, or a combination, but not for alcohol abusers.

There is no evidence of interaction between alcohol and either cannabis or cocaine, nor is it associated with a statistically significant increase in crash risk either pre-treatment or post-treatment. This may reflect the sanctions that exist in the general driving population for alcohol that are specific to driving. Most studies linking alcohol to crash risk have been case-control studies and have established high blood alcohol concentrations at the time of the crash. If many of the subjects who seek treatment for abuse of alcohol do not drink and drive, this might explain the weak association we have observed.

Reference Number: 50513

CIMBURA, G., D.M. LUCAS, R.C. BENNETT, AND A.C. DONELSON. "Incidence and Toxicological Aspects of Cannabis and Ethanol Detected in 1,394 Fatally Injured Drivers and Pedestrians in Ontario (1982–1984)." *Journal of Forensic Sciences,* 35: 1035–41, 1990 (6 tables, 12 references).

Abstract: A twenty-nine-month study was conducted of 1,169 fatally injured drivers and 225 fatally injured pedestrians. THC was detected in the blood of 127 drivers (10.9 percent), however, only twenty did not have any detectable BAC. Ethanol was detected in 57.1 percent of the drivers. THC was detected in 7.6 percent of the pedestrians, and ethanol was detected in 53.3 percent of the pedestrians. And 84 percent of the drivers had a BAC > 0.08 g/100mL. Drivers of motorcycles had a much higher incidence of THC detected (22.4 percent).

The 57.1 percent incidence of ethanol found in the fatally injured drivers of this study is essentially unchanged from the previous study carried out in 1978 and 1979 in Ontario. The incidence of THC, however, has increased approximately three times to 10.9 percent, although a part of the increase is probably due to inter-study difference in analytical method.

Reference Number: 50514

DE BONI, R., M.C. BOZZETTI, J. HILGERT, T. SOUSA, L. VON DIEMEN, D. BENZANO, G. MENEGON, B. HOLMER., P. DUARTE, AND F. PECHANSKY. "Factors Associated with Alcohol and Drug Use among Traffic Crash Victims in Southern Brazil." *Accident Analysis and Prevention,* 43: 1408–413, 2011 (3 tables, 42 references)

Abstract: BrACs and salivary drug screening were determined in 361 drivers, 138 passengers, and 107 pedestrians involved in nonfatal MVCs attending hospitals in Porto Alegre, Brazil during 2008. BrACs were measured with an Alcosensor IV. The drivers were 91 percent male with a mean age of 28 years. The passengers were 39 percent male with a mean age of 26 years, and the pedestrians were 57 percent male with a mean age of 37 years. A positive BrAC was found in 8, 9, and 9 percent of these groups respectively. A positive salivary cannabinoid result was found in 13, 4, and 4 percent of these groups respectively. Brazil has one of the highest rates of MVCs in the world and has a mortality rate of 77 deaths/100,000 vehicles (compared to 17/100,000 in the US).

> There was no significant difference in the alcohol and drug use among the groups, except for marijuana, which was higher among the drivers. Such prevalence may be associated with the higher proportion of young men because this is the population with the highest consumption rates.

Reference Number: 50515

DRUMMER, O.H., J. GEROSTAMOULOS, H. BATZIRIS, M. CHU, J. CAPLEHORN, M.D. ROBERTSON, AND P. SWANN. "The Involvement of Drugs in Drivers of Motor Vehicle Killed in Australian Road Traffic Crashes." *Accident Analysis and Prevention,* 36: 239–48, 2004 (5 tables, 45 references)

Abstract: The drug and alcohol involvement in 3,398 fatally injured drivers in Australia between 1990 and 1999 was analyzed. The 1,694 drug/alcohol positive drivers were compared to the 1,704 drug/alcohol negative drivers and a culpability index was determined. The OR for a positive THC was 2.7 times for all drivers and 2.4 times for motorcyclists. The median blood THC detected was 12 ng/mL and 84 percent had a blood THC of 5 ng/mL or more. Alcohol was detected in 43 percent of the THC positive cases. The OR of culpability of drivers with a BAC > 0.05 g/100mL was 3 times greater than for THC. If only THCCOOH was detected, the OR was 0.9 times.

Table: Culpability Ratio (Drivers Responsible/Drivers Not Responsible) for Alcohol, THC, Benzodiazepines, and Opioids

Drug	Culpability Ratio
BAC > 0.05 g/100mL	34.1 X
Blood THC > 5 ng/mL	10.2 X

Drug	Culpability Ratio
Benzodiazepines (e.g., valium)	4.5 X
Opioids (e.g., morphine)	4.4 X

Source: Adapted from Drummer et al, 2004

> The present study presents good evidence that drivers killed in motor vehicle crashes and taking psychoactive drugs, particularly cannabis and strong stimulants, or two or more drugs in combination, were more likely to be responsible for the crash than those taking neither drugs nor alcohol. Moreover, the combination of psychoactive drugs with alcohol further increased the likelihood that drivers caused the crash in which they died. We conclude that THC, amphetamines, and combinations of psychoactive drugs significantly increase driver's risk of serious road crash.

Reference Number: 50516

FERGUSSON, D.M., L.J. HORWOOD, AND J.M. BODEN. "Is Driving Under the Influence of Cannabis Becoming a Greater Risk to Driver Safety Than Drink Driving? Findings from a Longitudinal Study." *Accident Analysis and Prevention*, 40: 1345–50, 2008 (2 tables, 1 figure, 41 references)

Abstract: The self-reported rates of alcohol and cannabis driving and active motor vehicle collision involvement was determined in 936 participants in a longitudinal Christchurch, NZ, birth cohort study at ages 21 to 25 years. The percentage of self-reported drinking and driving was similar to cannabis (27 percent vs 21 percent), but the frequency for cannabis and driving was 8.92 times compared to 3.52 times for alcohol.

> Within the limitations imposed by these caveats, the results of the present study may suggest that the increasing use of cannabis, coupled with declining rates of drink driving behaviours, may be producing a situation in which the risks of driving under the influence of cannabis are becoming greater than the risks of driving under the influence of alcohol. In turn, this conclusion raises complex questions about the need to regulate driving under the influence of cannabis and the mechanisms by which this end may be achieved.

Reference Number: 50517

HUESTIS, M.A. "Cannabis (Marijuana) — Effects on Human Behavior and Performance." *Forensic Science Review,* 14: 16–60, 2002 (4 tables, 3 figures, 484 references)

Abstract: A detailed review was conducted on the effects of cannabis on human behaviour and performance. The greatest period of cannabis use in the US was in the 1960s–70s, followed by a decline in the 1990s, and then began to increase among the young. Currently, 35 percent of American males and 39.6 percent of females, ages 12 to 17 years, smoked at least once in the past thirty days. Cannabinol is 10 percent as psychoactive as THC. THC is a tricyclic 21 carbon structure and is a volatile, viscous oil with a high fat solubility. THC binds readily to glass and plastic, which can be minimized by the storage of the solution in amber silyated glassware or have the solution in a basic solution or organic solvent. Cannabis cannot be classified as sedative, tranquilizer, stimulant, or hallucinogen. Behaviour changes: feelings of euphoria, relaxation, altered time perception, lack of concentration, impaired learning, and memory. Mood changes, panic reaction, and paranoia also occur after use of cannabis. The concentration of the active metabolite (11-OH-THC) is 50 to 100 percent of THC concentration after oral ingestion and 10 percent after smoking.

> Despite these limitations, a number of conclusions can be drawn. More than 300,000 people are killed and 10 million injured throughout the world each year in traffic accidents. Cannabinoids are the number one illicit drug detected in motor vehicle injuries, fatalities, and DUID cases, and frequently are found in combination with ethanol or other drugs. Critical skills needed for the safe operation of motor vehicles and other forms of transport can be impaired following cannabis use. Impaired functioning of psychomotor activities, including measures of coordination, tracking, and vigilance and cognitive behaviour including memory, learning, attention, information processing, decisionmaking, and perception have been reported following cannabis use. Most effects have been reported following cannabis use. Most effects returned to baseline within three to four hours, although some complex, divided attention tasks have indicated decrements in performance up to twenty-four hours after cannabis use.

Reference Number: 50518

JONES, A.W., F.C. KUGELBERG, A. HOLMGREN, AND J. AHLNER. "Five-Year Update on the Occurrence of Alcohol and Other Drugs in Blood Samples from Drivers Killed in Road Traffic Crashes in Sweden." *Forensic Science International*, 186: 56–62, 2009 (7 tables, 4 figures, 47 references)

Abstract: The alcohol and other drug involvement in drivers killed in MVCs in Sweden between 2003 and 2007 were determined. The mean BAC was 0.170 g/100mL (range 0.020 to 0.490 g/100mL). Twenty-two percent of drivers had a BAC > 0.020 g/100mL. Drugs other than alcohol were found in 18 percent of the cases. The most common illicit drugs were amphetamine and cannabis. Alcohol positive cases were overrepresented in single FMVCs versus multiple FMVCs.

The present study verifies that 22 percent of drivers killed in traffic crashes in Sweden had a BAC above the legal limit for driving (> 0.2 g/L) and this figure has remained remarkably constant over the past eight years. Likewise, the average BAC in driver fatalities (1.7 g/L, 170 mg/100mL, or 0.17 percent) had also remained remarkably constant over the past eight-years and is in good agreement with information from other countries. Lowering the proportion of alcohol-related crashes will not be easy and will require radical measures such as mandatory introduction of ignition interlock devices in all vehicles used by hardcore offenders. Illicit drugs were identified in 7.2 percent of all driver fatalities, which reinforces the conclusion that alcohol abuse and alcohol-induced impairment are the major human factors responsible for road-traffic crashes in Sweden.

Reference Number: 50519

JONES, A.W., A. HOLMGREN, AND F.C. KUGELBERG, "Driving Under the Influence of Cannabis: A 10-Year Study of Age and Gender Differences in the Concentrations of Tetrahydrocannabinol in Blood." *Addiction,* 101: 452–61, 2008 (6 tables, 4 figures, 57 references)

Abstract: The age, gender, and blood THC concentrations (by GC/MS) were determined in blood samples of 8,794 apprehended drivers in Sweden between 1995 and 2004. Approximately 18 to 30 percent of all DUID suspects had measureable amounts of THC in the blood (> 0.3 ng/mL). The mean age of the cannabis users was 33 years (ages 15 to 66 years) and 94 percent were male. The mean, median, and highest blood THC concentrations were 2.1, 1.0, and 67 ng/mL respectively. The blood THC concentration was < 1.0 ng/mL in 43 percent of the cases and below 2.0 ng/mL in 61 percent of the cases. The blood THC concentration was higher when it was the only drug detected, 3.6 ng/mL vs 1.8 ng/mL in multi-drug users and 2.3 ng/mL for alcohol and THC users.

The concentration of THC in blood at the time of driving is probably a great deal higher than at the time of sampling (30 to 90 minutes later). The notion of enacting science-based concentration limits of THC in blood (e.g., 3-5 ng/mL) as discussed in some quarters would result in many individuals evading prosecution. Zero-tolerance or limit of quantitation laws are a much more pragmatic way to enforce DUID legislation.

Reference Number: 50520

JONES, C.G.A., W. SWIFT, N.J. DONNELLY, AND D.J. WEATHERBURN. "Correlates of Driving Under the Influence of Cannabis." *Drug and Alcohol Dependence*, 88: 83–86, 2007 (2 tables, 17 references)

Abstract: The characteristics of 320 Australian drivers who reported using cannabis in the previous year were determined. The potential prediction of driving under the influence of cannabis (DUIC), i.e., smoking cannabis within one hour of driving was determined. Late-onset cannabis use in female drivers (16 years +) were less likely to DUIC. Only 53 percent believed that cannabis increased accident risk and 80 percent felt that they would be unlikely to be caught DUIC.

Use of multiple drugs, believing that DUIC does not increase accident risk, and cannabis dependence all predicted likelihood of DUIC. There was an interaction between age of first cannabis use and gender, whereby earlier-onset cannabis use predicted DUIC among women.

Reference Number: 50521

KUMAR, S., Y.S. BANSAL, D. SINGH, AND B. MEDHI. "Alcohol and Drug Use in Injured Drivers: An Emergency Room Study in a Regional Tertiary Care Centre of North West India." *Journal of Clinical and Diagnostic Research*, 9: HC01–HC04, 2015 (3 tables, 1 figure, 17 references)

Abstract: Urine drug and alcohol screening was conducted on 200 injured drivers in Northwest India between 2013 and 2014. If the UAC was positive, the BAC was determined by GC. Alcohol/drugs were found in 55 percent of the drivers. Alcohol was found in 41 percent of the drivers, opiates in 13 percent, cannabis in 7 percent, and benzodiazepines in 7 percent. The BACs ranged from 0.020 to 0.391 g/100mL. The legal BAC for driving in India is 0.030 g/100mL.

> This study has shown that drivers are consuming not only alcohol but other psychoactive drugs. Indian traffic regulatory authorities are penalizing drunk drivers by doing roadside breath alcohol testing with no protocols for drug screening. Appropriate measures should be adopted to also screen traffic offenders for psychoactive drugs.

Reference Number: 50522

LAUMON, B., B. GADEGBEKU, J.L. MARTIN, M-B. BIECHLER, AND THE SAM GROUP. "Cannabis Intoxication and Fatal Road Crashes in France: Population Based Case-Control Study." *British Medical Journal*, 331: 1371, Dec. 10, 2005 (5 tables, 1 figure, 31 references)

Abstract: A study was conducted of 6,766 fatally injured drivers at fault and a control group of 3,006 fatally injured drivers not at fault in FMVCs in France between 2001 and 2003. Of all drivers, 681 (7 percent) had a positive blood THC concentration (> 1 ng/mL), 2,096 (21 percent) had a BAC > 0.05 g/100mL, and 285 (3 percent) were positive for both. The odds ratio of a driver with a positive blood THC concentration being at fault were 1.54 times (1-2 ng/mL), 2.13 times (3-4 ng/mL), and 2.12 times (> 5 ng/mL). The OR for alcohol are 2.70 times (BAC < 0.05 g/100mL), 6.29 times (0.05 to 0.08 g/100mL), 7.56 times (0.08 to 0.12 g/100mL), 13.2 times (0.12 to 0.200 g/100mL), and 39.6 times (BAC > 0.200 g/100mL). The OR for an at fault driver was 1.78 times for any detected blood THC concentration, and 9.51 times at any positive BAC.

> The risk of responsibility for fatal traffic crashes while driving under the influence of cannabis has a significant dose effect that shows a causal relation between cannabis and crashes.

Reference Number: 50523

LENGUERRAND, E., J-L. MARTIN, A. MOSKAL, R. GADEGBEKU, B. LAUMON, AND THE SAM GROUP. "Limits of the Quasi-Induced Exposure Method When Compared with the Standard Case-Control Design. Application to the Estimation of Risks Associated with Driving Under the Influence of Cannabis or Alcohol." *Accident Analysis and Prevention,* 40: 861–68, 2008 (3 tables, 41 references)

Abstract: The odds ratios for the involvement of alcohol or cannabis in 10,748 drivers involved in FMVCs in France between 2001 and 2003 using the standard case control or quasi-induced exposure (QIE) methods were determined.

Table: Comparison of the Odds Ratio for Alcohol and Cannabis Using the Standard Case Control and QIE Models

Drug	Standard Case-Control	QIE Clean Crash	QIE Single MVC
Positive Blood THC (> 1 ng/mL)	1.8 X	1.7 X	1.9 X
Positive BAC	8.6 X	7.5 X	19.2 X

Source: Adapted from Lenguerrand et al, 2008

On the contrary, the standard case-control approach with crash responsibility as disease of interest, also known as responsibility analysis, has provided information that is very useful for assessing the public health implications of alcohol and cannabis on French roads: 2.5 percent of the fatal crashes that occurred between 2001 and 2003 may therefore have been caused by cannabis and 29 percent by alcohol.

Reference Number: 50524

LIU, C., Y. HUANG, AND J.C. PRESSLEY. "Restraint Use and Risky Driving Behaviors Across Drug Types and Drug and Alcohol Combinations for Drivers Involved in a Fatal Motor Vehicle Collision on U.S. Roadways." *Injury Epidemiology*, 3: 9, 2016 (3 tables, 2 figures, 28 references)

Abstract: The mechanisms through which drug and/or alcohol contribute to FMVCs were determined using the FARS data in the US between 2008 and 2013 for 79,932 fatally injured drivers. More than half (54.6 percent) of the drivers tested positive for alcohol and/or drugs. Drug and alcohol use was higher in drivers aged 20 to 24 years (23.3 percent) and 24 to 44 years of age (47.4 percent). Males also accounted for the majority of drivers using drugs (67.5 percent), alcohol (81.9 percent), and both drugs and alcohol (79.5 percent). The OR of a driver being unbelted was 3.7 times for both cannabis and alcohol, 3.5 times for alcohol only, and

2 times for depressants and stimulants. Unbelted drivers were 4 times as likely to die in the crash compared to the unbelted driver.

Table: Odds Ratio of Driving Error/Violation with Cannabis, Alcohol, or Combination

Driving Error	Cannabis	Alcohol	Cannabis and Alcohol
Lane Violation	1.48 X	1.48 X	1.50 X
Speed Violation	1.42 X	1.68 X	2.36 X
Reckless Violation	1.55 X	2.29 X	2.37 X

Source: Adapted from Liu et al, 2016

In summary, the results of our study indicate that substance and alcohol use among drivers is associated with lower restraint use, increased driving violations, and driving errors, and that these violations vary by substance and substance combination. Our results also indicate that the presence of drug and drug and alcohol combinations exacerbate risky behaviours, such as driving unrestrained and making driving violations typically viewed as being associated with higher fatality.

Reference Number: 50525

MACDONALD, S., R. MANN, M. CHIPMAN, B. PAKULA, P. ERICKSON, A. HATHAWAY, AND P. MACINTYRE. "Driving Behavior under the Influence of Cannabis or Cocaine." *Traffic Injury and Prevention*, 9: 190–94, 2008 (2 tables, 2 figures, 23 references)

Abstract: A survey was conducted on 1,021 persons in treatment for the abuse of cannabis or cocaine regarding the effects of these drugs on driving ability. Driving under the influence of cannabis was reported by 75 percent of those undergoing treatment for cannabis.

When comparing the physical effects of cannabis and cocaine, paranoia or nervousness was reported more frequently for cocaine (56.7 percent) than for cannabis (43.5 percent). Poor concentration was more often reported as an effect of cannabis (21.1 percent) than cocaine (11.6 percent). Overall, the rank order of the physical effects for cocaine and cannabis were similar. However, then respondents described how these drugs affected their driving behaviour and a dramatically different pattern emerged. For driving under the influence of cocaine, 29.7 percent of the responses indicated that reckless driving was a common behaviour compared to 2.4 percent of the responses for driving under the influence of cannabis. Conversely, 39.9 percent of those who drove under the influence of cannabis reported the attempt to drive more carefully or cautiously compared with 19 percent for driving under the influence of cocaine. A higher proportion of responses by the cannabis subjects (27.9 percent) indicated that they drive normally when under the influence of cannabis, compared with 11.8 percent of cocaine subjects who drove under the influence of cocaine.

Reference Number: 50526

MURA, P., P. KINTZ, B. LUDES, J.M. GAULIER, P. MARQUET, S. MARTIN-DUPONT, F. VINCENT, A. KADDOUR, J.P. GOULLE, J. NOUVEAU, M. MOULSMA, S. TILHET-COARTET, AND O. POURRAT. "Comparison of the Prevalence of Alcohol, Cannabis and Other Drugs between 900 Injured Drivers and 900 Control Subjects: Results of a French Collaborative Study." *Forensic Science International* 133: 79–85, 2003 (5 tables, 4 figures, 24 references)

Abstract: Blood alcohol and other drug concentrations were determined in 900 drivers admitted to hospitals in France as a result of trauma, and compared to 900 age-matched controls who attended these hospitals for non-traumatic reasons. Urine or sweat samples were also collected to distinguish heroin administration from other opiates. A BAC > 0.050 g/100mL was found in 26 percent of the injured drivers compared to 9 percent in controls. A BAC > 0.200 g/100mL was found in 10 percent of the injured drivers and 2 percent of the controls. The odds ratio (OR) of alcohol, THC only, THC and alcohol, morphine, and benzodiazepines were 3.8, 2.5, 4.6, 8.2, and 1.7 respectively. Positive blood THC concentrations decreased from 21 percent to less than 0.1 percent of the drivers and their age increased from 18 to > 50 years of age.

Table: Percent of Injured Drivers with a Positive BAC or Positive Blood THC with Age

Age of Driver (Years)	% Positive BAC	% Positive THC
18 to 22 years	30.4%	21.0%
23 to 26 years	21.1%	18.9%
27 to 30 years	33.3%	10.3%
31 to 39 years	33.3%	4.2%
40 to 49 years	26.3%	3.4%
50 years +	15.4%	0.1%

Source: Adapted from Mura et al 2003

This study confirms the high prevalence of the use and/or abuse of psychoactive compounds in the French population. This is particularly true for cannabis in the young population. Furthermore, our results demonstrate a higher prevalence of alcohol, cannabinoids, and the combination of these two compounds in blood samples from drivers involved in road accidents than those from controls, and consequently suggest a causal role for these compounds in road crashes.

Reference Number: 50527

POULSEN, H., R. MOAR, AND C. TRONCOSO. "The Incidence of Alcohol and Drugs in Drivers Killed in New Zealand Road Crashes 2004–2009." *Forensic Science International*, 223: 364–70, 2012 (6 tables, 2 figures, 45 references)

Abstract: Blood alcohol and other drug concentrations were determined in 1,046 drivers killed in MVCs in New Zealand between 2004 and 2009. The BAC limit for drivers less than 20 years of age in New Zealand is 0.030 g/100mL and alcohol may be purchased at the age of 18 years. Twenty-four percent of the victims were women and 76 percent were men. Alcohol or other impairing drugs were detected in 500 deceased drivers (48 percent). One hundred and thirty-five drivers (27 percent) had consumed alcohol alone, 96 (19 percent) used cannabis alone, and 142 (28 percent) used alcohol and cannabis. The BACs of the 351 alcohol positive drivers ranged from 0.005 to 0.354 g/100mL (mean 0.152 g/100mL). The blood THC concentrations ranged from 0.1 to 44 ng/mL (mean 5.6 ng/mL). The prevalence of alcohol used by deceased drivers in New Zealand has decreased from 41 percent to 34 percent over a ten-year period.

Table: Alcohol and Cannabis Detected in Drivers of Single or Multi-Vehicle Fatal Motor Vehicle Collisions (FMVC)

Drug Detected in Driver	Single Vehicle FMVC (%)	Multi-Vehicle FMVC (%)
Alcohol Alone	23.0%	5.1%
Cannabis Alone	7.6%	10.0%
Alcohol and Cannabis	21.0%	7.5%

Source: Adapted from Poulsen, Moar, and Troncoso, 2012

Almost half of the drivers killed in New Zealand roads over a five-year period had used a potentially impairing drug. Use of cannabis by these drivers was almost as prevalent as the use of alcohol. When compared with studies of a similar nature from other countries, the use of cannabis in New Zealand, either alone or in combination with other drugs, is very high. The proportion of drivers who had used impairing drugs such as sedatives, stimulants, or opioids was similar to those seen in other studies.

Reference Number: 50528

WALSH, G.W., AND R.E. MANN. "On the High Road: Driving Under the Influence of Cannabis in Ontario." *Canadian Journal of Public Health*, 90: 260–63, 1999 (2 tables, 23 references)

Abstract: Cannabis was present in 3.7 percent of fatally injured Ontario drivers between 1978 and 1979 and increased to 10.9 percent between 1986 and 1989. A survey was conducted of Ontario drivers, ages 18 years or older, between 1996 and 1997, who drove within one hour of smoking cannabis. Only 1.9 percent of the drivers drove within one hour after smoking cannabis. The odds of DUIC decreases for drivers ages 25 years or older. The OR of DUIC is significantly lower for those who completed high school or university. Forty-seven percent of those who reported DUIC also reported driving after drinking.

Since 1.9 percent of all drivers reported DUIC, we might expect, if we assume that cannabis use had no impact on collision, that cannabinoids would be detected in about 1.9 percent of the drivers killed or injured in collisions. Instead, taking the most recent Ontario data available, Stoduto et al detected cannabinoids in 13.9 percent of their sample of injured drivers. That is, the proportion of injured drivers who tested positive for cannabinoids is about seven times higher than what would be expected based on the findings on DUIC in the Ontario general population of drivers.

Reference Number: 50529

WETTLAUFER, A., R.O. FLORICA, M. ASBRIDGE, D. BEIRNESS, J. BRUBACHER, R. CALLAGHAN, B. FISCHER, G. GMEL, S. IMTIAZ, R.E. MANN, A. MCKIERNAN, AND J. REHM. "Estimating the Harms and Costs of Cannabis-Attributable Collision in the Canadian Provinces." *Drug and Alcohol Dependence*, 173: 185–90, 2017 (2 tables, 3 figures, 48 references)

Abstract: This study quantifies the costs of cannabis-related traffic collision in the Canadian provinces. Between 3.4 to 5.5 percent (mean 4.1 percent) of licensed drivers in Canada have driven under the influence of cannabis (DUIC). The highest rates of DUI were 16 to 19 years of age and decreased with increasing age. The RR of fatal collisions was 2.17 times and 1.80 times for injuries for DUIC. Various other statistical traffic measures were employed to develop the costs. Cannabis-attributed traffic collisions were estimated to have caused 745 deaths, 4,407 injuries, and 7,794 persons in property damage only collision. It is estimated that the total costs attributed to cannabis-related traffic collisions are over $1 billion.

> Our results suggest that cannabis has a substantial impact on collision rates in Canada and represents a substantial economic burden. Youth and young adults were overrepresented in all three levels of traffic collisions, leading to higher cannabis-attributable harms and costs among this age group.

Reference Number: 50530

WHITEHILL, J.M., F.P. RIVARA, AND M.A. MORENO. "Marihuana-Using Drivers, Alcohol-Using Drivers and Their Passengers: Prevalence and Risk Factors among Underage College Students." *Journal of the American Medical Association Pediatrics,* 168: 618–24, 2014 (5 tables, 39 references)

Abstract: A telephone survey was conducted of 315 first year college students (ages 18 to 20 years) from two large universities on marijuana and alcohol use, and driving and riding as a passenger. In the prior month, 20.3 percent of the students used marijuana, and among them, 43.9 percent of the male and 8.7 percent of the female students drove after use. Most students (65.1 percent) drank alcohol, and among this group, 12.0 percent of the male and 2.7 percent of the female students drove after drinking.

> This study found that underage male college students who used marijuana in the past twenty-eight days had a high prevalence of driving after marijuana use and riding with a marijuana-using driver. This was more than double the prevalence of driving or riding after alcohol-use among current alcohol users. Our findings were consistent with other studies, demonstrating that for alcohol, the behaviours of driving after

substance use and riding with friends who have been using are strongly associated. Driving after drinking also increased the risk of driving after marijuana use. An older age of first marijuana use was associated with a 20 percent reduction in the risk of driving after marijuana use for each year increment in the age of first use. As expected, a higher percentage of the respondents' friends reported to be using marijuana indicated an increased risk of riding with a marijuana-using driver. Our finding that using only marijuana increased the risk of substance-impaired driving is logically consistent with other studies, indicating that driving after marijuana use is perceived as safer than driving after alcohol use and done more frequently.

Reference Number: 50531

VINDENES, V., D.H. STRAND, L. KRISTOFFERSEN, F. BOIX, AND J. MORLAND. "Has the Intake of THC by Cannabis Users Changed Over the Last Decade? Evidence of Increased Exposure by Analysis of Blood THC Concentrations in Impaired Drivers." *Forensic Science International*, 226: 197–201, 2013 (1 table, 2 figures, 25 references)

Abstract: Blood samples were collected from suspected DUID drivers in Norway between 2000 and 2010. As well, the drivers underwent a physician examination for drug impairment. THC only was detected in 1,747 drivers, alcohol only in 38,796, and amphetamines only in 2,493 drivers. The mean blood THC concentration increased gradually from 4.0 ng/mL in 2000 to 6.6 ng/mL in 2010 (a 58 percent increase). The mean BAC increase over the same time period was 3 percent and the mean blood amphetamine concentration was 16 percent over that time period. The mean age of the THC drivers was 25.7 years, of the alcohol drivers was 36.0 years, and of the amphetamine drivers was 32.2 years. The mean time from driving to the collection of the blood sample decreased 17 minutes from 2.01 hours in 2000 to 1.73 hours in 2010. When cannabis is smoked, the peak blood THC concentration occurs within minutes, followed by a rapid alpha phase elimination over the next hour, and a slow beta elimination phase (half-life of 24 hours). Thus a 17-minute reduction in the time of sampling would not significantly change the blood THC concentration, as most drivers would be in the beta phase at the time the blood samples were collected.

Table: Mean BAC and Mean Blood THC Concentrations in Blood Samples Collected from DUID Drivers in Norway between 2000 and 2010

Year	Mean BAC (g/100mL)	Mean Blood THC (ng/mL)
2000	0.152	4.0
2002	0.148	3.6
2004	0.151	5.5
2006	0.149	5.0
2008	0.151	5.3
2010	0.150	6.6

Source: Adapted from Vindenes et al 2013

Our study indicates that THC concentrations in blood samples from Norwegian drivers suspected of DUID have increased substantially over the last years, a phenomenon not seen for the amphetamines or ethanol.

Reference Number: 50532

WOODALL, K.L., B.L.C. CHOW, A. LAUWERS, AND D. CASS. "Toxicological Findings in Fatal Motor Vehicle Collisions in Ontario, Canada." *Journal of Forensic Sciences*, 60: 669–74, 2015 (2 tables, 4 figures, 28 references)

Abstract: Detailed forensic toxicological analyses were conducted on 229 fatally injured drivers in Ontario between 2011 and 2012. The ages of the drivers ranged from 15 to 92 years. Seventy-six percent were male and 24 percent were female drivers. No drugs or alcohol were detected in 44.1 percent of the drivers, alcohol only in 12.2 percent, drugs only in 28.4 percent, and in 15.3 percent alcohol and drugs were detected. The most common drugs detected were cannabis (22 percent of the drug positive cases), followed by benzodiazepines (17 percent), and antidepressants (17 percent). Single MVCs accounted for 43 percent of FMVCs. The incidence and BAC of drivers was greater in single FMVCs compared to multiple, but the incidence of drugs did not vary between single and multiple FMVCs.

This study indicates the importance of comprehensive toxicological testing in FMVC drivers. The findings reveal that, although alcohol and cannabis are the most common findings, a wide variety of drugs are observed in this type of death investigation.

Reference Number: 50533

HAVIG, S.M., G. HOISETH, M.C. STRAND, R.A. KARINEN, G-W. BROCHMANN, D.H. STRAND, L. BACHS, AND V. VINDENES. "THC and CBD in Blood Samples and Seizures in Norway: Does CBD Affect THC-Induced Impairment in Apprehended Subjects?" *Forensic Science International*, 276: 12–17, 2017 (6 tables, 36 references)

Abstract: Blood THC and CBD concentrations were measured in 6,134 suspected DUID drivers in Norway between 2013 and 2015. The blood samples were originally screened for THC, CBD, and other drugs by LC/MS/MS, and confirmation and quantitation for THC and CBD was by GC/MS. A comparison of the Clinical Test of Impairment (CTI) results as determined by a physician was conducted in 705 drivers, in which only THC and/or CBD were detected. The Norwegian limits for blood THC for driving are 1.3 ng/mL, 3.1 ng/mL, and 9.4 ng/mL. CBD was detected in 4,632 drivers (76 percent) of 6,134 drivers, and in 13 cases, only CBD was detected and not THC. The LOQ for CBD in this study was much lower than previous ones (0.16 ng/mL). As the blood THC concentration of the DUID drivers increased, the percentage of cases in which CBD was detected increased. The mean blood THC concentration for all samples was 4.3 ng/mL and the mean blood CBD concentration was 0.98 ng/mL, resulting in a mean THC/CBD ratio of 5.6. The mean blood THC and CBD concentrations were 8.7 ng/mL, 1.3 ng/mL, 6.3 ng/mL, and 1.0 ng/mL for those drivers considered impaired or not impaired by CTI respectively. In seized marijuana samples in Norway, the THC/CBD ratio was 200:1 for cannabis and 2:1 for hash.

Table: Percentage of Positive CBD Cases, Mean CBD Blood Concentrations, and THC/CBD Ratio in DUID Drivers with Increasing Blood THC Concentration

Blood THC Concentration Range (Norwegian Limits)	< 1.3 ng/mL	1.3 to 3.1 ng/mL	3.1 to 9.4 ng/mL	> 9.4 ng/mL
% CBD Positive Cases	49%	88%	93%	94%
Mean CBD Concentration	0.18 ng/mL	0.64 ng/mL	1.4 ng/mL	3.2 ng/mL
Mean THC/CBD Ratio	3.0	4.0	5.7	13.1

Source: Adapted from Havig et al, 2017

Among subjects apprehended in Norway, more than three-quarters of blood samples that tested positive for THC also tested positive for CBD, suggesting frequent consumption of high CBD cannabis products, which is consistent with the high hashish seizure rate in Norway. For subjects testing positive for THC and/or CBD only in blood, impairment as measured by a CTI could be related to THC concentrations but not to CBD concentrations. Our results indicate that CBD alone does not cause impairment, while THC does, and that CBD does not appear to protect against THC-induced impairment, in a naturalistic setting. Comparing traffic accidents with non-accident DUID cases, we found significantly higher THC concentration and the THC/CBD ratio in the non-accident group compared with the accident cases. The time elapsed between incident and blood sampling was conversely significantly higher in the accident cases, which could in part explain this finding. Although former studies have suggested CBD as a marker of cannabis smoking within the last hour, our findings also incidentally reveal that CBD may be detected in blood for more than two hours after intake.

Reference Number: 50534

MARTIN, J.-L., B. GADEGBEKU, D. WU, V. VIALLON, AND B. LAUMON. "Cannabis, Alcohol and Fatal Road Accidents." *PLOS ONE,* 12: e0187320, 16 pp, 2017 (6 tables, 1 figure, 40 references)

Abstract: Three-hundred characteristics were determined in 3,622 fatal motor vehicle accidents that occurred in metropolitan France during 2011. Alcohol, cannabis, and narcotic concentrations were determined in 4,059 drivers. Responsibility for the FMVC was assessed and divided into five groups with increasing responsibility. The mean crude OR for FMVC was 19.7 times for alcohol, 3.45 times for cannabis, and 2.2 times for opioids. The prevalence of cannabis use was lower in drivers greater than 35 years of age. Moped drivers had the highest prevalence of cannabis and alcohol use, followed by motorcyclists. The prevalence of drivers with a THC > 1 ng/mL and BAC > 0.05 g/100mL was 0.3 percent in not responsible drivers, and 6.0 percent for responsible drivers.

Table: Blood THC and Alcohol Concentrations and the Odds Ratio of Responsibility for a Fatal Motor Vehicle Collision

Driver Blood Drug Concentration	OR of Person Responsible for FMVC
THC < 1 ng/mL	1.0 X
THC 1-3 ng/mL	1.35 X
THC 3 – 5 ng/mL	3.59 X

Driver Blood Drug Concentration	OR of Person Responsible for FMVC
THC > 5 ng/mL	1.59 X
THC > 1 ng/mL	1.65 X
BAC < .05 g/100mL	1.0 X
BAC .05 to .08 g/100mL	6.40 X
BAC .08 to .120 g/100mL	8.30 X
BAC 0.12 to 0.20 g/100mL	24.4 X
BAC > .20 g/100mL	44.4 X
BAC > .05 g/100mL	17.8 X

Source: Adapted from Martin et al, 2017

Almost a decade separates the present study from a similar one conducted in France and there have been numerous developments in the intervening years. Even so, the prevalence of drivers responsible for causing fatal accidents under the influence of alcohol or narcotics has stayed remarkably stable, as have the proportion of fatal accidents, which could in theory be prevented if no drivers ever exceeded the legal limits. The overall number of deaths from traffic accidents has dropped sharply during this period, and the number of victims attributable to alcohol and/or cannabis declined proportionally. Alcohol remains the main problem in France. It is just as important to note that one in two drivers considered to be under the influence of cannabis was also under the influence of alcohol. With risks cumulating between the two, it is particularly important to point out the danger of consuming them together.

5.06 PHYSICAL SIGNS AND TESTS

Typically, the ability of the Drug Recognition Examiner (DRE) has been found to be much poorer in the detection and classification of drugs in the laboratory than in the field. In the field, DREs have an approximately 90 percent accuracy in determining drug intoxication (50603, 50617), whereas in the laboratory, accuracy drops to around 50 percent or less (50612). Some of the reasons for this difference are:

- In the field there are other physical symptoms, such as the odour of cannabis or injection marks on the arm or the finding of drug paraphernalia on the driver, that are cues not present in laboratory studies.

Reference Number: 50534

- In the field during the interview with the suspected driver, DREs often receive incriminating statements about drug use. Interviews are not usually conducted in laboratory studies.
- Typical drug concentrations and use are usually much higher in the field than in controlled laboratory studies.
- DREs may have speculated more freely about possible drug use in the laboratory studies, as there were no serious criminal consequences as occur in the field (50612).

Common signs of cannabis intoxication include red eyes, dilated and slow pupils, and increased pulse rate (50601, 50605), and overlap with some symptoms of alcohol intoxication (50608). Horizontal gaze nystagmus does not usually occur in drivers impaired by cannabis (50608, 50615), but does appear frequently in drivers under the influence of synthetic cannabinoids (50620). There was a positive correlation between the signs of intoxication and OF THC concentrations (50610), as well as blood THC concentrations (50614). SFST are considered a valuable screening tool for detection of cannabis impairment of driving ability (50618). One study found the one leg stand (OLS) to be a more useful test in the SFST to assess cannabis impairment than the walk and turn (WAT) (50618). The accuracy of drug evaluation classification reports by the police in Canada was nearly 90 percent for cannabis detection (50603).

Reference Number: 50601

OHLSSON, A., J-E. LINDGREN, A. WAHLEN, S. AGURELL, L.E. HOLLISTER, AND H.K. GILEPSIE. "Plasma delta-9-tetrahydrocannabinol Concentrations and Clinical Effects after Oral and Intravenous Administration and Smoking." *Clinical Pharmacology and Therapeutics,* 28: 409–16, 1980 (2 tables, 3 figures, 21 references)

Abstract: Eleven male cannabis users (ages 18 to 35 years) smoked a 19 mg THC cigarette or consumed a chocolate cookie containing 20 mg of THC or had 5 mg of THC injected over two minutes. Frequent blood samples were collected, and plasma THC concentrations were determined by GC/MS. The mean plasma THC curve for smoking and IV were essentially parallel. Peak plasma concentrations occurred within three minutes for both IV (219 ng/mL) and smoking (77 ng/mL). The peak plasma THC after oral injection occurred mainly at 60 to 90 minutes but was at 240 and 300 minutes in two individuals. Red eyes are the most reliable clinical sign, and for IV and smoking occurred at 3 to 10 minutes and 30 to 60 minutes for oral ingestion. In general, redden conjunctivae occurred as long as the plasma THC concentration was greater than 5 ng/mL. Increased pulse rate is the second highly reliable sign. After IV and smoking, the median pulse rate increased 34 to 40 bpm. After oral ingestion, the pulse rate increased by 26 bpm.

> Of the two major clinical signs of cannabis intoxication, increased pulse rate and conjunctival injection, the latter was clearly the most sensitive indicator of both intoxication and measureable THC in plasma. For many years it has been a practice in our laboratory, and no doubt in others, to dismiss subjects from marijuana experiments only after all conjunctivae injection had disappeared. This procedure is now proven to be both conservative and justified.

Reference Number: 50602

STARK, M.M., K. ENGLEHART, B.F. SEXTON, R. TUNBRIDGE, AND P. JACKSON. "Use of a Pupillometer to Assess Change in Pupillary Size Post-Cannabis." *Journal of Clinical Forensic Medicine*, 10: 9–11, 2003 (1 table, 1 figure, 7 references)

Abstract: The pupil size of fourteen volunteers was measured with a Procyon Pupillometer Model P2000SA before and thirty minutes after smoking a placebo, low dose cannabis (11.5 mg THC), high dose cannabis (18 mg THC), and resin (4.7 mg THC). There was an increase in pupil diameter after consuming cannabis, on average from 0.041 to 0.395 mm. The pupil size was also measured by medical doctors using a reference card fifteen minutes after smoking ceased.

Table: Number of Increases, Decreases, and No Change in Pupil Size as Measured by Medical Doctors Using a Reference Card

	Number in Increased Pupil Size (dilated)	Number Decreased Pupil Size (constricted)	No Change
High Dose (14 cases)	11	2	1
Low Dose (14 cases)	8	3	3
Resin (13 cases)	3	6	4

Source: Adapted from Stark et al, 2003

These findings with a Pupillometer and clinically of an increase in pupil size post-cannabis appear contradictory to previous research literature and require further evaluation.

Reference Number: 50603

BEIRNESS, D.J., E. BEASLEY, AND J. LECAVALIER. "The Accuracy of Evaluations by Drug Recognition Experts in Canada." *Canadian Society Forensic Science Journal*, 42: 75–79, 2009 (2 tables, 2 references)

Abstract: Drug Evaluation and Classification (DEC) reports and toxicological findings of 1,349 drivers arrested by the RCMP were assessed for accuracy. Stimulants were found in 47 percent of the toxicology reports, followed by cannabis (38 percent), and narcotic analgesics (34 percent). Ninety-two percent of the opinions of the DRE matched the drug class detected. No psychoactive drugs were found in forty-five cases (3.4 percent).

Table: Drug Type and Measures of Accuracy for DEC (DRE) Reports

	Cannabis	Stimulants	Narcotics	Depressants
Sensitivity	0.791	0.926	0,858	0.568
Specificity	0.982	0.928	0.955	0.975
False Alarm	0.018	0.072	0.045	0.025
Miss Rate	0.209	0.074	0.141	0.432
Accuracy	0.873	0.893	0.885	0.867

Source: Adapted from Beirness, Beasley, and Lecavalier, 2009

In conclusion, the results of this study demonstrate that DEC evaluations conducted by Canadian police officers trained as Drug Recognition Experts are accurate and provide support for the use of the DEC program in Canada as a procedure to collect the evidence required to enforce Canada's new drug-impaired driving laws.

Reference Number: 50604

BOORMAN, M., AND K. PAPAFOTIOU. "The Victorian Legislative Framework for Testing Drivers for Impairment Caused by Drugs Other than Alcohol: An Evaluation of the Characteristics of Drivers Detected From 2000 to 2005." *Traffic Injury Prevention*, 8: 217–23, 2007 (5 tables, 17 references)

Abstract: The characteristics of 460 drivers convicted for driving while impaired by drugs in Victoria, Australia, between 2000 and 2005 were determined. In Victoria, suspected drivers are administered a SFST and a blood sample is collected. The convicted drivers were 80 percent male with an average age of 30 years and 7 percent admitted alcohol consumption. Poly drug use was found in 82 percent of the drivers. Using SFST, the police officers identified drug impairment correctly in 89 percent of the cases.

Table: Common Drug Types Detected in Male and Female Drivers Arrested for Driving Under the Influence of Drugs.

Gender	THC	Depressants	Opioids	Amphetamines	Anti-depressants	MDMA	Analgesics
Males (n= 293)	32%	56%	35%	19%	6%	3%	2%
Females (n= 79)	29%	72%	34%	19%	11%	11%	3%

Source: Adapted from Boorman and Papafotiou, 2007

The results presented support the use of SFSTs to identify drivers who are impaired by drugs and have consumed a combination of drugs. The data indicate that males with an average age of 30 are most likely to consume depressants, opioids, cannabis, and amphetamines and drive while impaired by these drugs.

Reference Number: 50605

BOSKER, W.M., E.I. THEUNISSEN, S. CONEN, K.P.C. KUYPERS, W.K. JEFFREY, H.C. WALLS, G.F. KAUERT, S.W. TOENNES, M.R. MOELLER, AND J.G. RAMAEKERS. "A Placebo-Controlled Study to Assess Standardized Field Sobriety Tests Performance During Alcohol and Cannabis Intoxication in Heavy Cannabis Users and Accuracy of Point of Collection Testing Devices for Detecting THC in Oral Fluid." *Psychopharmacology*, 223: 439–46, 2012 (2 tables, 1 figure, 27 references)

Abstract: Fifteen male and five female heavy cannabis users (mean age 24 years) underwent three alcohol dosing conditions that were designed to achieve steady-state BACs of 0, 0.050, and 0.070 g/100mL over a five-hour period. In addition, the subjects smoked a THC cigarette (400 ug/kg) at three hours after alcohol dosing. SFSTs were conducted at five hours after alcohol dosing and blood and oral fluid samples were collected. Oral THC concentrations were determined with a Drager Drug Test 5000 and Securetec Drugwipe. The mean BACs were 0.037 and

0.051 g/100mL respectively at the time of the SFST. Cannabis/alcohol was related to performance in the one leg stand test.

> Taken together, the results indicated that the SFST were mildly sensitive to THC use in heavy users, probably because many of the participants have developed behavioural tolerance to THC-induced impairments. SFST were sensitive to low levels of alcohol in combination with THC as indicated by increments in the number of participants rated as impaired on HGN, OLS, and total SFST score.

Reference Number: 50606

BRAMNESS, J.G., H.Z. KHIABANI, AND J. MORLAND. "Impairment due to Cannabis and Ethanol: Clinical Signs and Additive Effects." *Addiction,* 105: 1080–87, 2010 (3 tables, 1 figure, 49 references)

Abstract: A Clinical Test for Impairment (twenty-seven clinical tests and observations) was conducted by physicians on drivers arrested by the police for impaired driving. A comparison was made of CTIs for 589 drivers who tested positive for THC alone and 894 for THC and alcohol, 3,180 drivers with alcohol alone, and 79 drivers who tested negative. A relationship between blood THC concentrations occurred with the eye tests including conjunctival injection (bloodshot eyes), dilated pupils, and slow or no reaction of the pupil to light. The percentage considered impaired by the physician was 45 percent if THC < 1.6 ng/mL and 53 percent at THC > 1.60 ng/mL. When a low BAC occurred in the drivers (< 0.050 g/100mL), it increased to 91 percent at THC < 1.60 ng/mL and 93 percent at THC > 1.6 ng/mL. At a BAC of more than 0.050 g/100mL, it was 97 percent at THC < 1.6 ng/mL and 100 percent at THC > 1.6 ng/mL.

Table: Percent of Arrested Drivers Considered Impaired by Examining Physicians at Various Blood Alcohol and THC Concentrations

	THC Not Detected	Low Blood THC Concentration (0.3 to 1.6 ng/mL)	High Blood THC Concentrations (> 1.6 ng/mL)
BAC Not Detected	14%	45%	53%
Low BAC (0.001 to 0.050 g/100mL)	77%	91%	93%
High BAC (> 0.050 g/100mL)	95%	97%	100%

Source: Adapted from Bramness, Khiabani, and Morland, 2010

This study demonstrates that cannabis impairs driving ability in a concentration-related manner. The effect is smaller than for ethanol. The effect of ethanol and cannabis taken simultaneously is additive. Conjunctival injection, dilated pupils, and slow pupil reactions are among the few signs to reveal THC influence.

Reference Number: 50607

BROOKOFF, D., C.S. COOK, C. WILLIAMS, AND C.S. MANN. "Testing Reckless Drivers for Cocaine and Marijuana." *The New England Journal of Medicine*, 331: 518–22, 1994 (2 tables, 39 references)

Abstract: A total of 175 drivers were stopped in Memphis, Tennessee, during 1993 for reckless driving, and 150 provided urine samples. The urine was tested at the roadside using an immunoassay test to detect cocaine or cannabis metabolites at a concentration of 330 ng/mL for benzoylecgonine and 100 ng/mL for THCCOOH respectively. Fifty-nine percent of the drivers were positive for these drugs, 13 percent for cocaine, 33 percent for cannabis, and 12 percent for both drugs. The drivers also performed a SFST. In a prescreening, 52 percent of the drivers admitted to using cannabis.

Simple behavioural tests have been a mainstay of the effort to detect impaired drivers, but these tests are not effective in detecting drug intoxication. The field sobriety tests currently used by police officers to evaluate impaired drivers were specifically designed to detect people under the influence of alcohol. We found, for example, that many police officers relied on the presence of nystagmus to make the assessment of intoxication, but drugs that dilate or constrict the pupils (with the exception of methaqualone) do not cause nystagmus.

Reference Number: 50608

DECLUES, K., S. PEREZ, AND A.A. FIGUEROA. "A 2-Year Study of delta 9-Tetrahydrocannabinol Concentrations in Drivers: Examining Driving and Field Sobriety Test Performance." *Journal of Forensic Sciences*, 61: 1664–70, 2016 (10 tables, 26 references)

Abstract: A study was conducted of 363 suspected DUID drivers who tested positive only for blood THC in Orange County between 2010 and 2012. One hundred and sixteen drivers (55.9 percent) received a DRE as well. The age range of the drivers was from 16 to 67 years (mean 24.5 years) and 92 percent were male. Blood THC concentrations ranged from 2 to 60 ng/mL (mean 9 ng/mL, median 6 ng/mL). The average time between first police contact and blood draw was 152 minutes for non-DRE cases and 193 minutes for DRE cases. SFSTs were conducted. Less than 10 percent of the drivers failed HGN and about one-third showed a lack of smooth pursuit (LOSP). Approximately 90 percent of drivers showed two-plus cues of impairment for WAT test. A total of 1,204 whole blood samples were confirmed to contain THC, but only 363 (30 percent) contained only THC.

Table: Number of HGN Cues Shown by THC Positive Drivers in Percent

Number of HGN Cues Observed	% of THC Drivers
0	78.6%
2	12.3%
4	2.9%
6	5.8%

Source: Adapted from Declues, Perez and Figueroa, 2016

Not every individual suspected of being under the influence of cannabis with THC in their blood performed poorly on every FST. This is further evidence that the FST symptomology, along with the presence of THC in the blood, should be used in totality to make the opinion of impairment for purposes of driving. Tolerance and the complexity of THC pharmacodynamics likely contributed to the lack of correlation to psychomotor task performance to THC concentrations. In conclusion, the driving behaviours seen in THC-impaired drivers are similar to those seen in alcohol-impaired drivers. This is likely due to an overlap in effects as well as a limited number of ways impairment can manifest in driving. In addition, the field sobriety tests proved to be sensitive to impairment by marijuana.

Reference Number: 50609

PORATH-WALLER, A.J., D.J. BEIRNESS, AND E.E. BEASLEY. "Toward a More Parsimonious Approach to Drug Recognition Expert Evaluations." *Traffic Injury Prevention*, 10: 513–18, 2009 (4 tables, 14 references)

Abstract: Seven hundred and forty-two completed Canadian Drug Evaluation and Classification (DEC) single drug evaluations were analyzed by a regression procedure. The drug classifications were CNS stimulant, narcotic analgesics, and cannabis. Currently, the DEC evaluation consists of over 100 separate pieces of information and lasts approximately thirty-five to forty minutes. Nine clinical indicators that significantly enhanced the prediction of drug category were:

- Pulse rate
- Systolic blood pressure
- Condition of eyes and eyelids
- Lack of convergence
- Hippus (rhythmic dilation and contraction of pupil)
- Reaction to light
- Rebound dilation
- Presence of injection sites

The overall correct drug classification rate was 81 percent.

> The findings from this study suggest that DREs can focus on a limited set of signs and symptoms when determining the category of drug ingested by the suspect without significantly compromising the accuracy of evaluations.

Reference Number: 50610

DOWNEY, L.A., R. KING, K. PAPAFOTIOU, P. SWANN, E. OGDEN, M. BOORMAN, AND C. STOUGH. "Detecting Impairment Associated With Cannabis With and Without Alcohol on the Standardized Field Sobriety Tests." *Psychopharmacology*, 224: 581–89, 2012 (3 tables, 2 figures, 21 references)

Abstract: Thirty-one female and forty-nine male cannabis and alcohol-using subjects (ages 21 to 35 years) smoked a placebo, 1.8 percent, and 3 percent THC cigarettes twenty minutes after the consumption of alcohol to obtain a low BAC (< 0.050 g/100mL) or high BAC (> 0.050 g/100mL). BrACs were determined and blood samples were collected twenty minutes and sixty minutes after smoking. The mean BrACs were 0.040 g/100mL for the low and 0.070 to 0.080 g/100mL for the high alcohol dose. The mean blood THC was approximately 40 to 50 ng/mL at sixty minutes for both cannabis-dosing conditions. SFSTs were conducted including HGN, WAT, and OLS. An additional vertical gaze nystagmus test was conducted, in which head movement jerks (HMJ) were determined. HMJ increased the number of subjects classified as impaired. At the low alcohol and low THC dose, 28 percent failed the SFST, which increased to 35 percent at the high alcohol and high THC dose.

> The current results highlight the limited ability of the SFST to identify drug consumption in the absence of any evidence of driving impairment or physiological indicators.

Reference Number: 50611

FIERRO, I., J.C. GONZALEZ-LUQUE, AND F.J. ALVAREZ. "The Relationship between Observed Signs of Impairment and THC Concentration of Oral Fluid." *Drug and Alcohol Dependence*, 144: 231–38, 2014 (3 tables, 1 figure, 39 references)

Abstract: A study was conducted of the comparison of thirty-one external signs of drug impairment as determined by especially trained police and oral fluid THC in 2,632 Spanish drivers between 2008 and 2009. BrACs were determined with an Alcotest 6810 and OF drugs by the Drager Drug Test 5000. OF samples were collected for confirmatory analysis by LC-MS/MS. An OF THC cutoff of 27 ng/mL and BrAC of 0.050 g/100mL were employed. There were 2,146 alcohol/drug negative drivers, 253 THC positive drivers, 201 alcohol only, and 32 THC and alcohol positive drivers. The OR for showing any sign of impairment increased with increasing OF THC concentration. For BACs > 0.050 g/100mL, the OR for showing any sign was twenty-nine times.

Table: Odds Ratio of Showing Any Sign of Impairment According to the Driver's OF THC Concentration

OF THC Concentration (ng/mL)	OR of Showing Sign of Impairment
0.00	1.00 X
< 3.00 ng/mL	1.70 X
3.01 to 25.00 ng/mL	3.78 X
25.01 to 100 ng/mL	7.22 X
> 100 ng/mL	16.55 X

Source: Adapted from Fierro et al, 2014

> This study shows the superiority of on-site OF devices versus the observation of signs of impairment for detecting drivers who have been exposed to THC. In addition, a positive concentration-effect relationship was found between OF THC concentration and impairment. The study

was carried out on a representative random sample of Spanish drivers from a real life roadside survey.

Reference Number: 50612

HEISHMAN, S.J., E.G. SINGLETON, AND D.J. COUCH. "Laboratory Validation Study of Drug Evaluation and Classification Program: Ethanol, Cocaine, and Marijuana." *Journal of Analytical Toxicology*, 20: 468–83, 1996 (8 tables, 1 figure, 43 references)

Abstract: Fourteen male and four female subjects (ages 23 to 40 years) who were drug users consumed a placebo, 0.28, and 0.52 g/kg ethanol over five minutes. Cocaine and marijuana were also administered. The subjects were evaluated by 28 DRE (Drug Recognition Examiners) who administered a battery of tests, i.e., Drug Evaluation and Classification (DEC). Blood samples were also collected, and the mean peak plasma ethanol concentrations were 0.024 and 0.054 g/100mL.

Using discriminant function analysis, it was found that seventeen to twenty-eight variables of DRE evaluation predicted the presence or absence of each of the three drugs, with a high degree of sensitivity and specificity and low rates of false positive and false negative errors. The five best predictive variables were nearly as accurate as the entire subset of seventeen to twenty-eight variables. When DRE is concluded, subjects were impaired by ethanol or drugs or both, their predictions were consistent with biological analysis in 51 percent of the cases.

Reference Number: 50613

KELLER, T., A. KELLER, E. TUTSCH-BAUER, AND F. MONTICELLI. "Driving Under the Influence of Drugs and Alcohol in Salzburg and Upper Austria during the Years 2003-2007." *Legal Medicine*, 11: S98–S99, 2009 (5 references)

Abstract: A study was conducted of alcohol and other drugs detected in 1,167 blood samples from drugged drivers in Austria arrested between 2003 and 2007. A newly developed road-site test system, Check 23, was also evaluated in urine samples. The drugs detected were cannabis (50 percent), opiates (20 percent), amphetamines (18 percent), cocaine (15 percent), and benzodiazepines (20 percent). Alcohol was found in only 7 percent of the samples analyzed.

> For the first time it could be shown that infrared pupillography can be used as a predictor of the presence of, at least on the central nervous system, a substance in the blood of a subject suspected to be under the influence of drugs or medication.

Reference Number: 50614

KHIABANI, H.Z., J.G. BRAMNESS, A. BIOURNEBOE, AND J. MORLAND. "Relationship between THC Concentration in Blood and Impairment in Apprehended Drivers." *Traffic Injury Prevention*, 7: 111–16, 2006 (2 tables, 1 figure, 37 references)

Abstract: The police physician Clinical Test of Impairment (CTI) and blood THC concentrations as determined by GC/MS were compared in 456 drivers in Norway between 1997 and 1999, in which THC was the only drug detected. The median blood THC concentration was 2.2 ng/mL (range 0.3 to 45.3 ng/mL). Male drivers had a higher blood THC concentration than female drivers (2.2 ng/mL vs 1.3 ng/mL). There was no difference in the blood THC concentration of regular users and non-regular users, but regular users were less likely to be judged impaired. Drivers who had signs of IV use were more likely to be judged impaired. The OR of being judged impaired increased from 1.7 times at THC of 0.8 to 1.6 ng/mL to 3.2 times at THC > 10.2 ng/mL.

> In conclusion, a positive relationship between the concentration of THC in blood and the risk of being assessed as impaired observed in this study is compatible with the assumption of concentration dependent negative effect of cannabis upon driving performance previously indicated by experimental and accident culpability studies.

Reference Number: 50615

KIBBY, T., AND S.E. HALCOMB. "Toxicology Observation: Nystagmus after Marijuana Use." *Journal of Forensic and Legal Medicine*, 20: 345–46, 2013 (9 references)

Abstract: The presence of lateral or vertical gaze nystagmus of less than 45° during SFSTs usually is indicative of intoxication by a sedative drug (including alcohol and barbiturates) but not marijuana. A 25-year-old male presented to an ED with a three-day history of persistent visual disturbances and dizziness. He admitted to smoking 4 grams (approximately eight joints) of marijuana and consumed several beers two days before attending hospital. The urine was positive for cannabinoids, but no alcohol was detected.

> This case is presented as a possible exception to the generalization that marijuana is not associated with nystagmus.

Reference Number: 50616

PAPAFORTIOU, K., J.D. CARTER, AND C. STOUGH. "The Relationship between Performance on the Standardized Field Sobriety Tests, Driving Performance, and the Level of Tetrahydrocannabinol (THC) in Blood." *Forensic Science International* 155: 172–78, 2005 (1 figure, 23 references)

Abstract: Fourteen female and twenty-six male subjects (ages 20 to 35 years) who had previously smoked marijuana were administered a placebo, low (1.74 percent THC), or high (2.93 percent THC) doses. The subjects were then administered the standardized field sobriety test and a driving simulator test. Seven blood samples were collected and the blood THC concentrations were determined by GC/MS. Immediately after smoking ceased the blood THC concentrations were 55 ng/mL (low) and 71 ng/mL (high). One hundred and twenty-five minutes later the blood THC concentrations were 2.5 ng/mL (low) and 2.4 ng/mL (high). An additional sign, head movements or jerks (HMJ), was found to occur when the subjects were tested on horizontal and vertical gaze nystagmus. There was no significant impairment in the simulator driving thirty minutes after smoking ceased, but significant impairment occurred at eighty minutes after smoking.

> In conclusion, the results of the present study indicate that the consumption of cannabis cigarettes containing either 1.74 or 2.93 percent THC significantly impairs performance on both the SFSTs and on driving behaviour. Furthermore, the results suggest that performance on the SFSTs provides a moderate predictor of driving impairment following the consumption of THC. Given that the level of THC in the blood does not provide an accurate and reliable indicator of whether driving performance is impaired, data obtained from the administration of SFSTs may provide important information concerning drug intoxication and driver fitness.

Reference Number: 50617

PAPAFORTIOU, K., J.D. CARTER, AND C. STOUGH. "An Evaluation of the Sensitivity of the Standardized Field Sobriety Tests (SFSTs) to Detect Impairment due to Marijuana Intoxication." *Psychopharmacology* 180: 107–14, 2005 (4 figures, 21 references)

Abstract: Fourteen female and twenty-six male subjects (ages 21 to 35 years) were assessed on SFSTs after smoking a placebo, 1.74 percent THC, and 2.93 percent THC marijuana cigarette at 5, 55, and 105 minutes after smoking. Seven blood samples were collected, and blood THC concentrations were determined using GC/MS. At the highest THC concentration, 46 percent were classified as impaired at 5 minutes, 41 percent at 55 minutes, and 28 percent at 105 minutes. When head movements or jerks (HMJ) were included, the detection rate increased by 10 percent.

> These findings suggest that impaired performance on the SFSTs is positively related to the dose of THC administered and that the inclusion of HMJ as a scored sign in the SFSTs improves their predictive validity when testing for THC intoxication.

Reference Number: 50618

PORATH-WALLER, A.J., AND D.J. BEIRNESS. "An Examination of the Validity of the Standardized Field Sobriety Test in Detecting Drug Impairment Using Data from the Drug Evaluation and Classification Program." *Traffic Injury Prevention*, 15: 125–31, 2014 (6 tables, 17 references)

Abstract: The use of the SFSTs are embedded in the DEC procedure. An analysis of 2,142 DEC tests (HGN, OLS, and WAT) was conducted in Canada between 1995 and 2009 and confirmed by toxicological tests. The study showed less impairment due to cannabis in the WAT test compared to the OLS test.

Table: Odds Ratio of Showing Signs in One Leg Stand (OLS) Test for Cannabis-Impaired Drivers

Sign in OLS	Odds Ratio (OR)
Swayed while balancing on one leg	1.33 X
Used arms to maintain balance	1.30 X
Hopped during test to maintain balance	0.69 X
Put raised foot down	1.04 X

Source: Adapted from Porath-Waller and Beirness, 2014

Reference Number: 50617

These findings provide support for the use of the SFST as a screening tool for law enforcement to identify impairment in persons who have used CNS stimulants, CNS depressants, cannabis, or other narcotic analgesics.

Reference Number: 50619

SHINAR, D., E. SCHECHTMAN, AND R.P. COMPTON. "Drug Identification Performance on the Basis of Observable Signs and Symptoms." *Accident Analysis and Prevention*, 37: 843–51, 2005 (4 tables, 23 references)

Abstract: The Drug Evaluation and Classification Program (DECP) was conducted by police officers on fifty-four subjects who had prior drug use. The police relied only on the physical tests alone and were not allowed to interview the subject. Placebo and two doses of drugs were tested (codeine, alprazolam, amphetamine, and marijuana). Police correctly identified impairing drugs in 31 percent of the cannabis subjects, 43 percent of alprazolam subjects, and 37 percent of the codeine subjects in this laboratory simulation with low drug doses.

In summary, it appears that the officers tended to base their diagnosis primarily on one or two signs or symptoms and then ignore the remaining signs and symptoms, even if they were inconsistent with the DECP recommended guidelines for the identification of that drug impairment. This reinforces the conclusion that the officers have difficulty in simultaneously evaluating all the information available in all the observed signs and symptoms.

Reference Number: 50620

PETERSON, B.L., AND F.J. COUPER. "Concentrations of AB-CHMINACA and AB-PINACA and Driving Behavior in Suspected Impaired Driving Cases." *Journal of Analytical Toxicology*, 39: 642–746, 2015 (5 tables, 1 figure, 19 references)

Abstract: A review was conducted of fifty-eight suspected impaired driving cases involving synthetic cannabinoids (SC), AB-CHMINACA, or AB-PINACA in Washington state during 2014. SCs were measured by LC-MS/MS or GC/MS in blood. The drivers were 95 percent male with a mean age of 28 years (ages 18 to 61 years). DREs were conducted on twenty drivers. The most common reason for stopping the driver was due to extreme lane veering, unconscious at the wheel, or a single motor vehicle collision with a parked car. HGN was observed in 50 to 60 percent of the drivers at lower concentrations of the drugs, not higher, as occurs with HGN with alcohol.

Table: Frequency of DRE Indicators, Drivers under the Influence of the Synthetic Cannabinoids (AB-PINCA and AB-CHMINACA) Compared to Plant Cannabis Indicators

Indicator	Cannabis Indicator	AB-PINACA Indicator	AB-CHMINACA Indicator
Horizontal gaze nystagmus	None	Present (60%)	Present (50%)
Vertical gaze nystagmus	None	Present (20%)	Present (40%)
Lack of convergence	Present	Present (70%)	Present (30%)
Pupil size	Normal to dilated	Normal to dilated (100%; 20% dilated)	Normal to dilated (100%; 30% dilated)
Reaction to light	Normal	Normal (60%)	Normal (60%)
Pulse (beats per minute)	Elevated	Elevated (10%)	Elevated (40%)
Blood pressure	Elevated	Lower (70%)	Lower (60%)
Body temperature	Normal	Normal (60%)	Normal (80%)

Source: Adapted from Petersen and Couper, 2015

Overall, several physiological indicators varied from those typically observed with marijuana use. The majority of these cases had very poor driving; subjects were involved in an accident, found passed out in a vehicle, or were called in as a suspected impaired driver. Slurred speech, confusion, lack of coordination/dexterity, and lethargy were commonly observed.

5.07 COUNTERMEASURES

One effective countermeasure for driving under the influence of cannabis is by more effective enforcement of the alcohol legal countermeasures and decreasing the BAC limit from 0.08 to 0.05 g/100mL (50705). It was estimated that 350,000 illegal drug-using drivers are arrested and taken off the road each year in the US by enforcing alcohol-impaired laws (50705). The typical blood THC limits range between 1 to 5 ng/mL (50702, 50709). Cannabis use increases in countries in which cannabis is

Reference Number: 50620

considered a harmless drug (50708), and proper health messages about its risk are important to reduce its harm (50710). To better protect public health, cannabis should be regulated like tobacco and not like alcohol (50710).

Reference Number: 50701

DUPONT, R.L., R.B. VOAS, J.M. WALSH, C. SHEA, S.K. TALPINS, AND M.M. NEIL. "The Need for Drugged Driving Per Se Laws: A Commentary." *Traffic Injury Prevention*, 13: 31–42, 2013 (81 references)

Abstract: A commentary on the need for per se drug limits in impaired driving is presented. Alcohol per se laws have increased the use of BACs to prosecute offenders, make it more efficient and transparent, and encouraged the development of sophisticated breath testing instruments. The International Association of Chiefs of Police have developed a drug evaluation and classification program (DEC). Twenty years after the DRE was introduced, the DRE completed on average only 5.5 enforcement evaluations a year. There should be an underage zero tolerance law.

Zero tolerance DUID laws can be integrated into current AID laws and law enforcement procedures in a way that not only does not adversely affect DUID enforcement, but also enhances drug driving efforts.

Reference Number: 50702

GROTENHERMEN, F., G. LESON, G. BERGHAUS., O.H. DRUMMER, H-P. KRUGER, M. LONGO, H. MOSKOWITZ, B. PERRINE, J.G. RAMAEKERS, A. SMILEY, AND R. TUNBRIDGE. "Developing Limits for Driving Under Cannabis." *Addiction*, 102: 1910–17, 2007 (2 figures, 32 references)

Abstract: An international team of DUID experts evaluate a per se limit for THC using experimental and epidemiological studies. During the first hour of the cannabis high, no unimodal relationship between impairment and THC concentration exists, however the blood THC concentrations during this time clearly exceed the legal limit. During the later phases of a cannabis high (more than two hours after smoking), the THC in the blood is a meaningful indicator of impairment. Acute impairment of driving ability typically caused driving impairment for three hours. A meta-analysis was conducted of sixty-six studies in which marijuana was smoked and twenty-one with oral intake of cannabis.

> Using current scientific evidence on cannabis-induced impairment of psychomotor skills and the related accident risk, this paper suggests a range of 7-10 ng/mL THC in the serum [3.5 to 5 ng/mL in blood] for an initial non-zero per se limit. It offers reasonably reliable separation of drivers whose driving is in fact impaired from cannabis from those who are not impaired. Inadequate evidence from epidemiological studies suggests the need for review and possible revision in future. Our findings also suggest using a zero limit for legal determination of impairment by cannabis, which in practice corresponds to the limit of detection for THC in blood, would classify inaccurately many drivers as driving under the influence of, and being impaired by, the use of cannabis.

Reference Number: 50703

HUESTIS, M.A. "Deterring Driving Under the Influence of Cannabis [Editorial]." *Addiction,* 110: 1697–98, 2015 (16 references)

Abstract: This short editorial is about determining drivers under the influence of marijuana.

> A two-tier system with reduced penalties for per se THC violations, and more severe penalties for documented impairment, appears to deter cannabis use and driving. Public education on drugged driving may also play a role in reducing serious injuries and fatalities. Cannabis is the number one illicit drug identified in motor vehicle crashes and fatalities. Public health and safety on the roads require that we develop policy and legislation to address and assess cannabis-impaired driving.

Reference Number: 50704

JOHNSON, M.B., T. KELLY-BAKER, R.B. VOAS, AND J.H. LACEY. "The Prevalence of Cannabis-Involved Driving in California." *Drug and Alcohol Dependence,* 123: 13 pp, 2012 (4 tables, 19 references)

Abstract: Oral fluid samples and breath tests were conducted for approximately 900 weekend nighttime drivers in six jurisdictions in California in the fall of 2010. OF was screened for drugs using ELISA and confirmed by GC/MS or LC/MS/MS. Eighty-two drivers tested positive for THC (8.5 percent) and thirteen were positive for both THC and alcohol (1.3 percent). Of the eighty-two drivers who tested positive for THC and asked if they had taken any drugs or medication that may affect driving, only two (2.5 percent) reported using cannabis.

Table: THC Prevalence Rates in Drivers by Jurisdiction

Jurisdiction	% THC Drivers
Anaheim (Orange County)	6.0%
Bakersfield (near Ventura County)	6.3%
Eureka (northern California)	18.3%
Fresno (Fresno County)	4.3%
San Rafael (Contra Costa County)	15.5%
Torrance (Los Angeles County)	6.3%

Source: Adapted from Johnson et al, 2012

There is a strong need to educate the public that combining cannabis and driving can be hazardous and to communicate that state laws provide officers with a mechanism for arresting drivers when there is evidence of driving impairment.

Reference Number: 50705

VOAS, R.B., J.H. LACEY, K. JONES, M. SCHERER, AND R. COMPTON. "Drinking Drivers and Drug Use on Weekend Nights in the United States." *Drug and Alcohol Dependence*, 130: 215–21, 2013 (2 tables, 35 references)

Abstract: A roadside survey was conducted in the US on weekend nights from July to November 2007. Of the 8,384 drivers surveyed, 85 percent provided a breath sample, 70 percent an oral fluid sample, and 39 percent a blood sample. A regression analysis was conducted on 5,912 drivers who provided a breath sample and an oral fluid or blood test. Approximately 11 percent of non-drinking drivers were using illegal drugs and 26 to 33 percent of the drivers with a BAC > 0.080 g/100mL also used illegal drugs. Medicinal drug use occurred in 4 percent of the non-drinking drivers and in 2 percent of the drivers with a BAC > 0.080 g/100mL. The association of BAC and drug use implies that programs such as sobriety checkpoints for alcohol and lowering the BAC limit to .05 g/100mL will also increase the rate of apprehensions of drugged drivers. In addition, it is less likely that alcohol-impaired drivers will be found with prescription drugs. It is estimated that about 350,000 illegal drug-using drivers are arrested and taken off the roads each year in the US by enforcing alcohol-impaired driving laws (DWI).

Table: Odds Ratio (OR) of Any Illegal Drug Use, Cannabis Use, Cocaine Use, or Prescription Drug Use and BAC of 8,384 Drivers Tested at a Roadside Survey

BAC of Driver	OR of Any Illegal Drug Use	OR of Cannabis Use	OR of Cocaine Use	OR of Prescription Drug Use
Less than 0.08 g/100mL	4.1 X	4.2 X	4.2 X	0.7 X
More than 0.08 g/100mL	4.0 X	3.5 X	3.5 X	0.9 X

Source: Adapted from Voas et al, 2013

The relationship between a high BrAC and drug use also suggests that programs of laws that increase the arrests of drinking drivers, such as conducting sobriety checkpoints or lowering the BAC limit from 0.08 to 0.05, will increase the apprehension of drugged drivers. In sum, it appears that under the current alcohol-orientated DWI enforcement system, a substantial number of drug-using drivers is arrested. This offers opportunities for increasing the apprehension of drug-using drivers by strengthening alcohol enforcement.

Reference Number: 50706

PACULA, R., L.B. KILMER, A.C. WAGENAAR, F.J. CHALOUPKA, AND J.P. CAULKINS. "Developing Public Health Regulations for Marijuana: Lessons from Alcohol and Tobacco." *American Journal of Public Health,* 104: 1021–28, 2014 (1 table, 93 references)

Abstract: Until November 2012, no modern jurisdiction had removed the prohibition for the commercial production, distribution, and sale of marijuana — including The Netherlands — but now Colorado and Washington have done so. The following public health recommendations for cannabis (based on tobacco and alcohol) are to keep prices high, have a state monopoly, restrict and carefully monitor licences, limit types of products sold, limit marketing, restrict public consumption, and measure and prevent impaired driving. Limiting public consumption reduces secondhand exposure to smoke and reduces the extent to which marijuana is seen by youth as socially acceptable or normative.

Restrictions on where marijuana can be consumed could also reduce the probability that marijuana and alcohol be used concurrently. Because of the evidence on how concurrent use increases the risk of a traffic crash, restricting place of consumption could have important implications for impaired driving. For example, use could be restricted to establishments that do not allow alcohol to be consumed or to private residences. However, if concurrent use leads to a decrease in alcohol consumption for some individuals, this could also produce some benefits (e.g., reduction in aggression). We cannot predict how concurrent use will influence social welfare under legalization. Researchers should pay close attention to this relationship.

Reference Number: 50707

WILSON F.A., J.P. STIMPSON, AND J.A. PAGAN. "Fatal Crashes from Drivers Testing Positive for Drugs in the US, 1993–2010." *Public Health Reports*, 129: 342–50, 2014 (1 table, 4 figures, 43 references)

Abstract: An analysis was conducted of 60,560 drivers who tested positive for at least one drug between 1993 and 2010 using the FARS data. In 2010, cannabis only was detected in 998 drivers, cocaine only in 145 drivers, methamphetamine in 95 drivers, and prescription drugs in 2,363 drivers. Ninety percent of persons 65 years or older have prescription expenses compared to 58 percent of those under 65 years of age.

Table: Characteristics of Cannabis Only Drivers Involved in an FMVC in the US, 2010

Characteristics	% of Cannabis Only Drivers
Gender	
Male	83.3%
Female	17.0%
Mean Age (years)	30.5 years
Age (in years)	
16 to 29	59.9%
30 to 49	29.4%
>50 years	10.7%
Injury Outcome	
Not Injured	8.4%
Nonfatal Injury	18.3%
Fatal Injury	73.3%
Positive BAC	
Yes	40.4%
No	59.6%

Characteristics	% of Cannabis Only Drivers
Census Region of Crash	
Northeast	13.0%
Midwest	32.4%
South	30.7%
West	20.3%

Source: Adapted from Wilson, Stimpson and Pagan, 2014

> [A] large fraction of drugged drivers involved in fatal crashes tested positive for cannabis. Unless policy-makers address this issue, perhaps by increasing penalties for drugged driving in localities with greater accessibility to cannabis, the high incidence in drugged driver's use of cannabis will likely continue. Currently, eighteen states plus Washington, DC, have legalized medical marijuana and more state legislatures are considering similar policies. At the same time, current state drug policies may not be effective in addressing the threat of drugged driving on traffic safety.

Reference Number: 50708

CUNNINGHAM. J.A., J. BLOMQVIST, A. KOSKI-JANNES, AND C. RAITASALO. "Societal Images of Cannabis Use: Comparing Three Countries." *Harm Reduction Journal*, 9: 21 (3 pp), 2012 (1 table, 6 references)

Abstract: A survey on cannabis use and beliefs was conducted on 740 people in Finland, 1,098 in Sweden, and 864 in Canada. The percent of cannabis use in the past twelve months was 4.4 percent in Finland, 1.7 percent in Sweden, and 11.9 percent in Canada. The percent who had never used cannabis was 83.4 percent in Finland, 84.5 percent in Sweden, and 58.9 percent in Canada.

Table: Cannabis Use and Public Opinion in Canada, Finland, and Sweden

	Canada	Finland	Sweden
Cannabis Use			
% past 12 months	11.9%	4.4%	1.7%
% prior to past 12 months	29.2%	12.2%	13.8%
% never	58.9%	83.4%	84.5%

	Canada	Finland	Sweden
Mean seriousness of cannabis as a societal problem (1= not at all serious, 10 = extremely serious)	5.6	6.6	8.2
% say very high risk of addiction if they try it	11.4%	31.8%	27.1%

Source: Adapted from Cunningham et al, 2012

Cannabis is perhaps the best example of a drug for which societal attitudes could be expected to vary. This is because it lies at the cusp between illegal and legal in some countries. In Canada, for example, attitudes toward cannabis have become more favourable over the past decades. Further, the use of cannabis for medical purposes is now legal in Canada and there have been ongoing initiatives to decriminalize this drug. In countries such as Sweden and Finland, use of cannabis is still a criminal offence with no special consideration given for the use of the drug for medical purposes. In addition, there has been a long history of demonizing cannabis as a serious drug of abuse. How do these variations regarding the legal nature of cannabis use correspond with societal attitudes regarding cannabis use? The three countries in this cross-national survey display quite different attitudes toward cannabis. Canada viewed cannabis as having minimal risk, both as a problem for society as well as for the person as a drug that is unlikely to result in addiction if it is tried. Participants in Sweden and Finland were considerably more concerned about cannabis as a problem in their society, with Sweden displaying the most concern and Finland scoring somewhere between Sweden and Canada. Interestingly, these differences appear to mirror actual levels of cannabis use in each country where more than 40 percent of Canadians report having tried cannabis at least once, while less than 20 percent of people in Sweden and Finland report ever trying cannabis.

Reference Number: 50709

WONG, K., J.E. BRADY, AND G. LI. "Establishing Legal Limits for Driving Under the Influence of Marijuana." *Injury Epidemiology*, 1: 26, 2014 (2 tables, 61 references)

Abstract: There are three legislative approaches to drugged driving: effect-based (tests/physical observations of impairment), per se laws, and zero tolerance laws. Two-tier systems in the EU penalize for any amount of drug detected with low penalty and high penalty for impairment. THC is extremely lipid soluble. THC and THCCOOH are detected in plasma bound to lipoproteins, and so the THC concentration in whole blood is approximately one-half that in blood. There is little THCCOOH metabolite in OF. OF is more reflective of recent use of cannabis than urine. Peak OF THC concentration of 5800 ng/mL has been reported immediately after smoking due to contamination of mucosa. The window for detected cannabinoids in breath is 0.5 to 2 hours.

Table: Legal THC Thresholds in Various European Countries

Country	Legal THC Limit
Belgium	1.0 ng/mL in blood serum
Denmark	1.0 ng/mL in blood
Finland	1.0 ng/mL in blood; 5 ng/mL THCCOOH in blood
France	1.0 ng/mL in blood
Germany	1.0 ng/mL in blood serum
Ireland	2.0 ng/mL in blood; 5 ng/mL THCCOOH in blood
Italy	0.5 ng/mL either THC or THCCOOH in blood
Netherlands	3.0 ng/mL in blood; 5.0 ng/mL in serum
UK	2.0 ng/mL in blood; 10 ng/mL THCCOOH in blood

Adapted from Wong, Brady and Li, 2014

There is compelling evidence that marijuana use impairs cognitive functions and driving skills and increases crash risk. Due to the limitations of impairment-based and zero tolerance laws, governments are increasingly adopting per se limits at which a driver is legally defined as being impaired to safely operate a motor vehicle.

Reference Number: 50710

BARRY, R.A., AND S. GLANTZ. "A Public Health Framework for Legalized Retail Marijuana Based on the US Experience: Avoiding a New Tobacco Industry." *PLOS Medicine* 13: e1002131, 2016 (1 table, 55 references)

Abstract: To protect public health, cannabis should be treated like tobacco and not alcohol. It should be subject to a robust, determined reduction program based on successful evidence from the tobacco control program. A voluntary alcohol advertising ban in media outlets in which 30 percent of the audience is less than 21 years of age still allows aggressive marketing in *Sports Illustrated* and *Rolling Stone*. American youths (ages 12 to 20 years) are exposed to 45 percent more beer and 27 percent more spirits advertisements than legal drinking age adults. Privatizing tobacco and alcohol sales has led to intensified marketing efforts, lower prices, more effective distribution, and an industry that will aggressively oppose any public health effort to control use. A state monopoly on cannabis would even better protect public health. Health messages for cannabis should include the risk of dependence, cardiovascular, respiratory, and neurological risks, and cancer, and warn against driving a vehicle or operating machinery and the risks of co-use of tobacco and alcohol.

> It is important that jurisdictions world-wide learn from the US experience and implement concurrently, with full legalization, a public health framework for marijuana that minimizes consumption to maximize public health. A key goal of the public health framework would be to make it harder for a new, wealthy, and powerful marijuana industry to manipulate the policy environment and thwart public health efforts to minimize use and associated health problems.

5.08 CANNABIS AND ALCOHOL/OTHER DRUGS

Approximately 40 percent of blood samples obtained by the police in Colorado, which contained a blood THC concentration of > 2 ng/mL, also contained alcohol (50801). When alcohol is consumed with cannabis, this increases the odds ratio of fatal crash involvement from approximately two times (THC alone), to twenty-five times (alcohol and THC) (50805). THC combined with alcohol use in a driver can result in serious impairment even at low concentrations (50807, 50809, 50810).

For example, car weaving (SDLP) was measured with low (2 percent THC) and moderate (4 percent THC) cannabis combined with a BAC of 0.040 g/100mL in an instrumented car on the highway under the supervision of a sober co-driver. It was found that the amount of weaving at the low THC dose and 0.04 g/100mL BAC was the same amount of car weaving as occurred at a BAC of 0.09 g/100mL. At the moderate THC dose and 0.04 g/100mL BAC, the amount of weaving was the same as occurs at a BAC of 0.140 g/100mL alone (50810). It can be expressed as:

Low Cannabis (2% THC) + 0.04 g/100mL BAC = 0.09 g/100mL BAC

Moderate Cannabis (4% THC) + 0.04 g/100mL BAC = 0.14 g/100mL BAC

The odds ratio of the driver being unbelted and speeding increases when THC is combined with alcohol or other drugs. Drivers who were cannabis users were about twice as likely to use alcohol and three times as likely to use cocaine as drivers who were not cannabis users (50812).

Reference Number: 50801

URFER, S., J. MORTON, V. BEALL, J. FELDMANN, AND J. GUNESCH. "Analysis of delta-9 Tetrahydrocannabinol Driving under the Influence of Drugs Cases in Colorado from January 2011 to February 2014." *Journal of Analytical Toxicology*, 38: 575–81, 2014 (4 tables, 3 figures, 19 references)

Abstract: Whole blood samples were submitted to ChemTox Laboratories in Boulder, Colorado, by law enforcement agencies in DUI and DUID cases between 2011 and 2014. All blood samples were analyzed for alcohol by headspace GC. A cannabinoid screen was conducted in 4,235 samples and a positive THCCOOH result was obtained by ELISA, of which 1,848 blood samples were confirmed for THC by GC/MS or LC-MS/MS. The overall mean blood THC concentration was 8.1 ng/mL and ranged from 2 to 192 ng/mL. The median blood THC was approximately 6 ng/mL of blood that was collected within one hour of the stop and decreased to approximately 5.5 ng/mL in blood samples collected one to two hours after the stop. In blood samples collected more than two hours after the stop, the median THC concentration was 4 ng/mL.

Table: Distribution by Percent of 1,598 THC Positive Blood Samples and Alcohol

Drug	%
THC only (> 2 ng/mL)	62%
THC (> 2ng/mL) and BAC > 0.05 g/100mL	32%
THC (> 2ng/mL) and BAC < 0.05 g/100mL	6%

Source: Adapted from Urfer et al, 2014

It is possible that public opinion regarding THC intoxication and driving may be similar to traditional views regarding DUI of alcohol; a commonly cited misconception about DUI is that everyone does it. This reinforces the attitude that occasionally driving while impaired, or only driving when it is perceived as absolutely necessary, is not a dangerous activity. This is reflected in attitudes toward THC impairment: many drivers not only believe that current DUI laws do not apply to marijuana use, but that they actually drive better high. It is important to promote awareness of the fact that although drivers under the influence of THC may be able to compensate for some of its impairing effects through exaggeratedly cautious driving, they are not equipped to respond appropriately to unforeseen driving circumstances and still present a major danger to public safety. All these factors indicate that public education concerning THC impairment should also be a priority.

Reference Number: 50802

HUNAULT, C.C., T.T. MENSINGA, K.B.E. BUCKER, C.M.A. SHIPPER, M. KRUDENIER, E.C. LEENDERS, I. DE VRIES, AND J. MEULENBELT. "Cognitive and Psychomotor Effects in Males after Smoking a Combination of Tobacco and Cannabis Containing Up to 69 mg delta-9-tetrahydrocannabinol (THC)." *Psychopharmacology*, 204: 85–94, 2009 (4 tables, 4 figures, 32 references)

Abstract: Twenty-four male cannabis users (mean age 24 years) smoked four joints over four days. Each joint contained 700 mg of tobacco and 300 mg of cannabis (placebo, 9.8 percent, 16.4 percent, and 23.1 percent THC respectively). Frequent blood samples were collected and serum THC, 11-OH-THC, and THCCOOH concentrations were determined using a Drug Control test. The subjects performed various cognitive and psychomotor tests, such as short-term memory, divided attention, and sustained attention. Vomiting occurred in 12 percent of the THC administrations overall and in 22 percent at the high dose THC. Smoking increased from 19.0 minutes for placebo, to 21.6, 23.1, and 24.4 minutes with increasing THC concentration. Slower RT occurred from 37 minutes to 5 hours after the onset of smoking. The number of errors and poorer motor control occurred with increasing THC. The mean peak THC concentrations were approximately 22, 45, and 65 ng/mL with increasing dose. Nicotine increased impairment in motor control and increased the heart rate.

Table: Mean Simple Reaction Time in Milliseconds (ms) with Increasing THC Dose and Time Since Smoking

Time Tested after Smoking Marijuana	Placebo	Low Dose THC (9.8%)	Medium Dose THC (16.4%)	High Dose THC (23.1%)
37 min	230 ms	247 ms	252 ms	271 ms
180 min	230 ms	259 ms	263 ms	280 ms
300 min	227 ms	249 ms	253 ms	256 ms

Source: Adapted from Hunault et al, 2009

In conclusion, the linear relationship between THC dose and cognitive, psychomotor and subjective effects continued at THC concentrations up to 69 mg. Effects were observed for participants already used to cannabis. If cannabis smokers are unable to titrate to a high feeling corresponding to a desired plasma THC level when smoking cannabis cigarettes, cannabis with high THC concentrations may be of greater concern for public health and safety than cannabis with lower THC concentrations.

Reference Number: 50803

DUBOIS, S., N. MULLEN, B. WEAVER, AND M. BEDARD. "The Combined Effects of Alcohol and Cannabis on Driving: Impact on Crash Risk." *Forensic Science International*, 248: 94–100, 2015 (3 tables, 2 figures, 58 references)

Abstract: The prevalence of driving under the influence of cannabis, alcohol, or both were determined in drivers ages 20 years or older who had a least one unsafe driving action (UDA) before the FMVC, compared to control drivers who did not have any UDA, using FARS data between 1999 and 2008. The prevalence of alcohol and THC increased from 2 percent in 1991 to 10 percent in 2008. Each 0.010 g/100mL increase in BAC increased the OR of a UDA by approximately 10 percent. Drivers who were positive for THC alone had a 16 percent increase in UDA. When alcohol and THC were combined, the OR of a UDA increased an additional 9 percent for each 0.010 g/100mL increase in BAC greater than either alcohol or THC alone. Of the 7,734 drivers positive for THC, approximately 56 percent were positive for alcohol and 31 percent for another drug.

Drivers positive for both agents had greater odds of making an error than drivers positive for either alcohol or cannabis only. Further research is needed to better examine the interaction between cannabis concentration levels, alcohol, and driving. This research would support enforcement agencies and public health educators by highlighting the combined effect of cannabis at low BAC levels.

Reference Number: 50804

CHIHURI, S., G. LI, AND Q. CHEN. "Interaction of Marijuana and Alcohol on Fatal Motor Vehicle Crash Risk: A Case Control Study." *Injury Epidemiology*, 4:8 2017 (7 tables, 69 references)

Abstract: A case control study was conducted of the incidence of alcohol alone, THC alone, and THC and alcohol in 1,944 fatally injured drivers in the US between 2006 and 2008, and 7,719 control drivers who participated in the 2007 US National Roadside Survey of Alcohol and Drug Use by Drivers. Overall 12.2 percent of the fatally injured drivers had a positive cannabis test compared to 5.9 percent of the controls. A positive BAC was detected in 57.8 percent of the fatally injured drivers compared to 7.7 percent of the controls. The adjusted ORs were 16.33 for alcohol alone, 1.54 for THC alone, and 25.09 for alcohol and THC.

Table: Adjusted Odds Ratio of Fatal Crash Involvement for Alcohol Only, Marijuana Only, and Alcohol and Marijuana Detected in Drivers

Drug Detected	Adjusted OR
Alcohol Alone	16.3 X
Marijuana Alone	1.5 X
Alcohol and Marijuana	25.1 X

Source: Adapted from Chihuri, Li and Chen, 2017

Alcohol use and marijuana use are each associated with significantly increased risks of fatal crash involvement. When alcohol and marijuana are used together, there exists a positive synergistic effect on fatal crash risk on the additive scale.

Reference Number: 50805

BOGSTRAND, S.T., M. LARSSON, A. HOLTAN, T. STAFF, V. VINDENES, AND H. GJERDE. "Associations Between Driving Under the Influence of Alcohol or Drugs, Speeding and Seatbelt Use Among Fatally Injured Car

Drivers in Norway." *Accident Analysis and Prevention*, 78: 14–19, 2015 (4 tables, 1 figure, 34 references)

Abstract: An in-depth analysis was conducted on 369 fatally injured drivers in Norway between 2005 and 2010. Blood samples were analyzed for alcohol and fifteen commonly used drugs. Forty percent of drivers had a BAC > 0.020 g/100mL and/or drug equivalent. For alcohol alone, the OR of no seatbelt use was 8.0 times and for speeding it was 5.2 times. For alcohol/drug impairment, the ORs were 4.6 times and 3.4 times respectively. About 30 percent of fatally injured drivers were repeat offenders previously convicted of DUI in Norway. It is estimated that only 0.2 percent of all drivers have a BAC > 0.020 g/100mL.

Table: Odds Ratio of Being Unbelted or Speeding in Fatal Motor Vehicle Collisions According to Alcohol and Drug Use

Alcohol/Drug Use by Driver	Odds Ratio for Being Unbelted	Odds Ratio for Speeding
Alcohol only	8.0 X	5.2 X
THC only	0.9 X	3.1 X
Alcohol and drugs	4.6 X	3.4 X
Illicit drugs only	2.3 X	2.7 X

Source: Adapted from Bogstrand et al, 2015

> We found that the majority of drivers with a fatal outcome in RTCs who were impaired by alcohol or drugs were unbelted or had speeded. Significantly smaller proportions of the sober drivers with a fatal outcome were unbelted or had speeded. The substances most clearly associated with being unbelted or speeding were alcohol and amphetamines.

Reference Number: 50806

PAPE, H., I. ROSSOW, AND E.E. STORVOLL. "Under Double Influence: Assessment of Simultaneous Alcohol and Cannabis Use in General Youth Populations." *Drug and Alcohol Dependence* 101: 69–73, 2009 (2 tables, 45 references)

Abstract: The combined intake of alcohol and cannabis is the most widespread form of polydrug substance use in the US and UK. A survey was conducted on 16,813 adolescents (ages 14 to 20 years) in Norway in 2003 and 2004. The prevalence of alcohol and cannabis use was 7 percent and the overall prevalence of cannabis use was 8 percent. Surveys were also conducted in thirty-five European countries. The prevalence of alcohol and cannabis users exceeded 50 percent in all countries.

Because adolescents most often combine cannabis with alcohol, their use of the drug may be more harmful than assumed. The results also indicate that cannabis is a complement rather than a substitute for alcohol, suggesting that policies that reduce adolescent drinking may reduce the use of cannabis as well.

Reference Number: 50807

PEREZ-REYES, M., R.E. HICKS, J. BUMBERRY, A.R. JEFFCOAT, AND C.E. COOK. "Interaction between Marihuana and Ethanol: Effects on Psychomotor Performance." *Alcoholism: Clinical and Experimental Research*, 12: 268–76, 1988 (1 table, 9 figures, 40 references)

Abstract: Six male subjects (ages 22 to 29 years) who were moderate users of marijuana and alcohol were tested under six conditions. Placebo alcohol, placebo marijuana, 0.42 g/kg alcohol, placebo marijuana/marijuana, and 0.85 g/kg alcohol and placebo marijuana/marijuana. The alcohol was consumed within thirty minutes after an overnight fast. Frequent blood samples were collected, and the BACs were determined by GC. Plasma THC concentrations were also determined. The heart rate, subjective ratings of intoxication, and accuracy and latency of response to a computerized task (Simulator Evaluation of Drug Impairment) were measured. The mean peak BACs for the low alcohol dose was 0.069 and 0.058 g/100mL for the placebo and marijuana conditions respectively. For the high alcohol dose, the mean peak BACs were 0.113 and 0.118 g/100mL for the placebo and marijuana conditions respectively. The mean peak plasma THC concentration was 133 ng/mL.

Under the experimental conditions of the study, the results clearly indicate that a) marijuana alone produced a significant overall reduction in accuracy and prolongation of reaction time, b) the low dose of ethanol alone did not produce significant changes in psychomotor performance or enhance the effects of marijuana, and c) the combination of the high ethanol dose with marijuana produced additional detrimental effects on performance and these effects may be synergistic.

Reference Number: 50808

RAMAEKERS, J.G., H.W.J. ROBBE., AND J.F. O'HALON. "Marijuana, Alcohol and Actual Driving Performance." *Human Psychopharmacology*, 15: 551–58, 2000 (4 figures, 31 references)

Abstract: Nine female and nine male marijuana and alcohol users (ages 20 to 28 years) consumed alcohol or placebo and then smoked either a placebo or marijuana cigarette (at a 100 or 200 ug/kg dose). The subjects consumed 0.6 g/kg alcohol over thirty minutes. The BrACs were determined by a Lion S-D4 Breath Alcohol Analyzer. Additional alcohol doses were consumed to maintain a BrAC of between 0.035 to 0.050 g/100mL during the driving tests. The subjects drove a specially instrumented car with dual controls in the presence of licensed driving instructors to ensure safety. Performance deficits were minor after alcohol alone and moderate for both THC doses, but dramatically greater when alcohol and THC were combined.

> It is clear from the present results that THC and alcohol combined produce serious impairment. Unfortunately, traffic police would not easily have recognized the level of impairment if the present subjects had been drugged driving under ordinary circumstances. None of the subjects would test positive on alcohol because their BAC values were below the legal limit in almost any country. Detection of marijuana use would also be highly unlikely.

Reference Number: 50809

RAMAEKERS, J.G., G. BERGHAUS, M. VAN LAR, AND O.H. DRUMMER. "Dose Related Risk of Motor Vehicle Crashes after Cannabis Use." *Drugs and Alcohol Dependence*, 73: 109–19, 2004 (2 tables, 2 figures, 56 references)

Abstract: A review was conducted as to the effect of THC on MVCs as measured in epidemiological studies and experimental studies of cannabis and performance. A comparison of the effect of oral versus smoked cannabis on psychomotor tasks was conducted. Maximal performance impaired appears to occur at THC concentrations > 14 ng/mL in plasma (7 ng/mL in blood).

> It is absolutely clear from epidemiological and experimental studies that the combination of alcohol and THC plays a major role in performance

impairment and motor vehicle crashes. The epidemiological evidence shows that the combination of alcohol and THC is overrepresented in injured and dead drivers and in particular in those responsible for the accident occurring. Experimental studies have shown that alcohol and THC combined can produce severe performance impairment even when given at low doses. The combined effect of alcohol and cannabis on performance and crash risk appears additive in nature, i.e., the effects of alcohol and cannabis combined were always comparable to the sum of the effects of alcohol and THC when given alone.

Reference Number: 50810

ROBBE, H. "Marijuana's Impairing Effects on Driving Are Moderate When Taken Alone but Severe When Combined with Alcohol." *Human Psychopharmacology*, 13: S70–S78, 1998 (1 table, 5 figures, 13 references)

Abstract: Road tracking and car following were assessed during two driving tests conducted on a restricted road and two on public highways after the use of marijuana alone or in combination with alcohol. In one test, nine male and nine female subjects were tested under six conditions (placebo/placebo; placebo/ 100 ug/kg THC; placebo/ 200 ug/kg THC; alcohol/ 100 ug/kg THC; and alcohol/ 200 ug/kg THC). The subjects then drove eighty kilometres on a public highway. The BACs during driving were approximately 0.040 g/100mL. There was no correlation between plasma THC, THCCOOH, and impairment of driving ability due to the delay between brain and plasma concentrations. There was impairment in all driving tasks with a positive BAC.

Although the effects of marijuana alone in driving performance are not dramatic in the present studies, they do imply a loss of driving ability that could be serious in other situations, for example, when combined with other drugs such as alcohol. The last study in this present series was designed to test this possibility and showed that the contribution of THC with alcohol, sufficient of attaining a BAC of 0.04 percent, has very severe effects on driving performance. Thus, subjects with BACs below the per se definition of intoxication drove in a manner one would expect for drivers operating about the limit when they had smoked marijuana after drinking alcohol. That the subjects were able to safely demonstrate their impairment while under the influence of both drugs was on occasion only possible because of the driving instructor's intervention. Had these individuals attempted to drive alone under similar circumstances, it is quite possible that one or more would have caused a serious traffic accident.

Reference Number: 50811

RONEN, A., H.S. CHASSIDIM, P. GERSHON, Y. PARMET, A. RABINOVICH, R. BAR-HAMBURGER, Y. CASSUTO, AND D. SHINAR. "The Effect of Alcohol, THC and Their Combination on Perceived Effects, Willingness to Drive and Performance of Driving and Non-Driving Tasks." *Accident Analysis and Prevention*, 42: 1855–65, 2010 (1 table, 9 figures, 36 references)

Abstract: Seven male and five female subjects (ages 24 to 29 years) were tested on a driving simulator after placebo alcohol, placebo THC; alcohol and placebo THC; alcohol placebo and THC; and alcohol and THC. The alcohol dose was calculated to obtain a BAC of 0.050 g/100mL and verified by breath alcohol tests. The active cigarette contained 13 mg of THC. The subjects were also tested twenty-four hours later after the alcohol and THC administration condition. Five of the twelve subjects had a collision with alcohol and THC, three out of twelve had a collision with THC alone, and two out of twelve with alcohol alone. No subjects had a collision under placebo treatment.

Table: Percent of Drivers Involved in a Collision and Drug Condition

Drug Condition	% of Drivers Involved In a Collision
Placebo	0%
Alcohol only	17%
THC only	25%
THC and Alcohol	42%

Source: Adapted from Ronen et al, 2010

In conclusion, the results indicated that the overall effect of the combination of THC and alcohol had greater effects and caused more impairments than the two drugs separately. Despite the fact that the subjects could clearly feel the effects of alcohol (0.05 percent BAC) or marijuana (THC in this study, 13 mg), and despite the blind design, they were still willing to drive under the influence.

Reference Number: 50812

SCHERER, M., R.B. VOAS, AND D. FURR-HOLDEN. "Marijuana as a Predictor of Concurrent Substance Use among Motor Vehicle Operators." *Journal of Psychoactive Drugs*, 45: 211–17, 2013 (4 tables, 35 references)

Abstract: The rates of marijuana use, abuse, and dependence were determined in 7,734 drivers from the 2007 US National Roadside Survey conducted on Friday and Saturday nights. Oral fluid and blood samples were collected, and drug concentrations were measured by LC/MS after being screened by immunoassay. BACs were determined in breath using a roadside Intoxilyzer 400. Six thousand, seven hundred and eighty-five drivers were non-users of cannabis, 672 were cannabis users, 165 were classified as having cannabis abuse, and 112 were dependent on cannabis.

Table: Percent of Cannabis Non-Users, Users, and Users with Abuse and Dependence and Other Drug Use in Drivers

Other Drug Use	Cannabis Non-Users	Cannabis Users
BAC < 0.08 g/100mL	6.5%	12.2%
BAC > 0.08 g/100mL	1.6%	3.7%
Cocaine Use	2.5%	7.1%
Opioid Use	3.1%	4.8%
Benzodiazepine Use	1.2%	2.1%

Source: Adapted from Scherer et al, 2013

As the popularity of marijuana increases among the general population, and as the legalization of marijuana appears increasingly possible, the need to understand the role of this substance in everyday life becomes an imperative. The findings from the current study underscore the need to update current interventions geared toward DUI offenders. The current study also begins to illustrate the concerns associated with marijuana use among drivers. Specifically, that marijuana is the most used substance among drivers, and that its use predicts the concurrent use of other substances that may impede driving to some extent. In an attempt to address concerns associated with marijuana use and driving, it may be necessary to further develop educational components discussing the use of substances other than alcohol in basic driver's education classes. Enhancing protocols to tailor DUI interventions and driver's education classes to include marijuana use may be valuable in addressing these concerns.

CHAPTER 6

Effects of Cannabis on Health and Other Behaviours

Currently, alcohol is by far the most common drug detected in medico-legal or coroner's cases. THC, though, is a close second. It is like a "me-too" drug, any problems that alcohol causes, can also be caused by THC, although perhaps not to as great an extent. Unlike alcohol, THC can cause psychosis, paranoia, and a detachment from reality that can lead to risky situations, especially in regard to falls from a height.

Prolonged, daily cannabis use is also associated with various health problems, such as cannabinoid hyperemesis syndrome, heart attacks, thrombosis, stroke, and various lung diseases. Edible cannabis poses even more risks than smoking, especially for children who have seen a large increase in ER admissions due to accidental exposure to THC by this route in gummy bears and other cannabis-infused candies and cookies. Edible cannabis may soon pose a risk similar to alcohol as a "date rape drug."

The combination of both drugs causes greater impairment, especially in driving, and can also increase the risk of dependence on both drugs. Withdrawal symptoms tend to be greater with the use of both drugs than with each drug singly.

6.01 ADOLESCENTS

THC affects the developing adolescent brain to a much greater extent than the adult brain (60105, 60106, 60118). The well-known effects of cannabis on memory and learning cause adolescent users to have a greater risk of not completing high school or obtaining a university degree, and consequently being unemployed (60104, 60108, 60109, 60121). Liberalization of cannabis policy has been found to increase adolescent use of this drug (60107, 60117). High school cigarette smokers were ten times as likely to use cannabis, too (60111). There is an association between early cannabis use and other drug use (60113, 60116). Current, occasional cannabis-using secondary school students in France were 2.1 times more likely to have a suicide attempt, 3.2 times as likely to have a depressive mood, and 5.5 times as likely to have violent behaviour (60101).

Reference Number: 60101

HUAS, C., C. HASSLER, AND M. CHOQUET. "Has Occasional Cannabis Use among Adolescents Also to be considered as a Risk Marker?" *European Journal of Public Health,* 18: 626–29, 2008 (2 tables, 26 references)

Abstract: A survey was conducted of 16,532 French secondary school students (ages 12 to 19 years) on cannabis use and violent behaviour, suicide attempts, and depressive mood. Sixty-eight percent of students never tried cannabis, 16 percent at least once, 8 percent were current occasional users, and 8 percent were heavy current users. Compared to never users, current occasional users had an OR of 2.1 times for suicide attempts, 3.2 times for depressive mood, and 5.5 times for violent behaviour.

> But our data highlighted that the distance between heavy consumers and occasional consumers is quite less important than that between occasional consumers and non-consumers. So, contrary to the general opinion, the risk is also related to occasional use, not only to regular use.

Reference Number: 60102

MONSHOUWER, K., S. VAN DORSSELAER, J. VERDURMEN, T. TER BOGT, R. DE GRAFF, AND W. VOLLENBERGH. "Cannabis Use and Mental Health in Secondary School Children. Findings from a Dutch Survey." *British Journal of Psychiatry* 188: 148–53, 2006 (3 tables, 24 references)

Abstract: A survey was conducted on cannabis use and mental health of 5,551 adolescents (ages 12 to 16 years) in The Netherlands. Past year prevalence of cannabis use was 1.8 percent in those aged 12 years, 17.2 percent in those aged 14 years, and 31.0 percent in those aged 16 years. After adjusting for confounding factors, cannabis use was linked to delinquent and aggressive behaviour but not to withdrawn behaviour and depression.

In a country with a liberal drug policy like The Netherlands, cannabis use is associated with aggression and delinquency, just as in other countries. Cannabis use was not associated with an internalizing problem. Alcohol use and regular smoking were strong confounding factors.

Reference Number: 60103

LEE, C.M., C. NEIGHBORS, AND B.A. WOODS. "Marijuana Motives: Young Adults' Reasons for Using Marijuana." *Addictive Behaviors*, 32: 1384–94, 2007 (6 tables, 23 references)

Abstract: A survey was conducted on 634 high school graduates in Washington state (mean age 18 years, 58 percent male, and 42 percent female) of cannabis users as to their motives to start using this drug. Of the 490 participants who reported using cannabis in the last year, 67.3 percent reported experiencing at least one negative consequence related to its use. The most common negative consequences were change in personality (32 percent), neglecting responsibilities (31 percent), or going to school or work while high (24 percent).

Table: Motives for Marijuana Use and Percent Endorsing the Motive

Motive Category	% Endorsing Motive
Enjoyment/fun (e.g., be happy, get high, enjoy feeling)	52.1%
Conformity (e.g., peer pressure, friends do it)	42.8%
Experimentation (e.g., new experience, curiosity)	41.3%
Social enhancement (e.g., bonding with friends, hang out)	25.7%
Boredom (e.g., something to do, nothing better to do)	25.1%
Relaxation (e.g., to relax, helps me sleep)	24.6%
Coping (e.g., depressed, relieve stress)	18.1%
Availability (e.g., easy to get, it was offered)	13.7%
Relative low risk (e.g., no health risk, no hangover)	10.9%
Alter perception or perspectives (e.g., to enhance experiences, makes things more fun)	10.6%

Source: Adapted from Lee et al, 2007

This research is the first study we are aware of to qualitatively assess marijuana use motives by asking students for their own reasons for using marijuana. Further, this study found that those emerging adult, incoming freshmen who use marijuana for habit, altered perceptions, activity enhancement, enjoyment/fun, rebellion, or coping reasons are at greater risk for frequent marijuana use and/or negative consequences.

The present research also suggests that some type of marijuana use is seen as normative and experimental. In fact, students who say they use marijuana for experimental reasons appear to report relatively lower levels of marijuana use and marijuana-related problems.

Reference Number: 60104

MAGGS, J.L., J. STAFF, D.D. KLOSKA, M.E. PATRICK, P.M. O'MALLEY, J. SCHULENBERG. "Predicting Young Adult Degree Attainment by Late Adolescent Marijuana Use." *Journal of Adolescent Health*, 57: 205–11, 2015 (3 tables, 39 references)

Abstract: A longitudinal study was conducted of thirteen cohorts of high school students in the US between 1990 and 2002 and subsequent attainment of a four-year university degree at ages 23/24 and 25/27, involving 4,925 students (54 percent female). Marijuana use at age 19/20 was divided into non-users, infrequent users (1–5 occasions per month), and frequent users (6+ occasions per month). The percentages of these groups were 84 percent, 9 percent and 7 percent respectively. The study was controlled for eighteen other risk factors for not obtaining a university degree.

In a national sample, late adolescent frequent marijuana users were less likely to attain bachelor's degrees by their mid-twenties compared to infrequent users and non-users, independent of adolescent risk factors but not of adolescent substance use. Infrequent users and non-users did not differ in degree attainment.

Reference Number: 60105

GRUBER, S.A., M.K. DAHLGREN, K.A. SAGAR, A. GONENC, AND S.E. LUKAS. "Worth the Wait: Effects of Age of Onset of Marijuana Use on White Matter and Impulsivity." *Psychopharmacology,* 231: 1455–65, 2014 (4 tables, 68 references)

Abstract: Twenty-five (eighteen male, seven female) chronic, heavy cannabis smokers and eighteen healthy controls had an MRI of white matter microstructures determined, as well as self-reported impulsivity. The chronic marijuana smokers were divided into eleven early onset smokers (mean age 14.5 years) and fourteen later onset smokers (mean age 17.9 years). The mean urinary THCCOOH concentrations before MRI was 406 ng/mL for the early onset and 744 ng/mL for the later onset cannabis users. Fractional anisotropy (FA) is a measure of directionality and coherence in the white matter fibres of the brain, and was reduced in marijuana smokers. It was even more reduced in the early onset marijuana smokers. Self-reported impulsivity was greater in cannabis users as well and was correlated with FA scores, especially in early onset smokers.

> Findings from this study suggest that chronic, heavy MJ smokers have lower white matter fibre tract integrity relative to non-MJ-smoking participants, and that earlier age of MJ onset is associated with lower FA levels. Further, MJ smokers demonstrated higher levels of reported impulsivity relative to control participants, which is related to FA levels, specifically within the early onset MJ groups. Notably, lower FA levels are associated with higher reported impulsivity within this sample, suggesting a specific relationship between white matter organization and impulsivity in those individuals who begin smoking MJ prior to age 16. Taken together, these findings reinforce the idea that early onset of MJ use negatively impacts white matter development and is associated with behavioural impulsivity, a combination that may have enduring negative effects, particularly on the developing brain. Data from this study highlight the importance of early identification of MJ use among emerging adults and the need for efforts aimed at delaying or preventing the onset of MJ use.

Reference Number: 60106

MOKRYZ, C., T.P. FREEMAN, S. KORKKI, K. GRIFFITHS, AND H.V. CURRAN. "Are Adolescents More Vulnerable to the Harmful Effects of Cannabis than Adults? A Placebo-Controlled Study in Human Males." *Translational Psychiatry*, 6: e961, 2016 (1 table, 4 figures, 91 references)

Abstract: An estimated 13 percent of 15- to 16-year-olds in Europe and 23 percent of 15- to 17-year-olds in the US have taken cannabis in the previous year. Twenty adolescent (ages 16 to 17 years) and twenty adult (ages 24 to 28 years) cannabis users inhaled placebo cannabis (< 0.3 percent THC) and cannabis (12 percent THC) using a Volcano Medic vaporizer operating at 210°C. The subjects inhaled a balloon full of the vapor. The subjects were then tested in memory and response inhibition; HR, BP, and subjective drug effects were also measured. Adolescents reported feeling less stoned, less dry mouth, and less cognitive disorganization than adults. The adults were markedly more anxious and less alert than the adolescents. Adolescents wanted more of the drug than adults, who wanted less cannabis after drug use. Adolescents did not show more memory impairment but had inhibitory process impairment and were less accurate at the stop-signal test.

> These findings have important implications for public health, especially given the current changes in legislation that are making cannabis more available and may influence adolescent use in several parts of the globe. If adolescents do not feel satiated after an acute dose of the drugs while also experiencing fewer negative effects, they may well use more cannabis in a smoking session than adults, potentially contributing to the increased risk of long-term harms associated with younger age of use, including addiction. In turn, adult's experience of more negative effects of cannabis may limit their use and reduce their risk of harms, which would concur with the declining prevalence of cannabis use seen from early adulthood.

Reference Number: 60107

SHI, Y., M. LENZI, AND R. AN. "Cannabis Liberalization and Adolescent Cannabis Use: A Cross-National Study in 38 Countries." *PLOS ONE*, November 25, 2015, 15 pp (5 tables, 1 figure, 47 references)

Abstract: A study on self-reported cannabis use (ever, use in past year, regular) and types of cannabis control policies was conducted on 172,894 adolescents (age 15 years) in the 2001/2002, 2005/2006, and 2009/2010 cross-sectional Health Behaviour in School-Aged Children (HBSC) survey of thirty-eight European and North American countries. Overall, 4.6 percent of the boys and 2.1 percent of the girls surveyed used cannabis regularly. The highest percentage of boys who used cannabis regularly was in the US and Canada at 10.9 percent. The highest percentage of girls using cannabis regularly was 7.2 percent in Canada and 6.5 percent in the US. Boys were more likely to use cannabis than girls and were less affected by cannabis liberalization. Depenalization was associated with higher odds of past-year use (1.4 times) and regular use (1.23 times). Partial prohibition was associated with higher odds of regular use (2.39 times). The correlation between cannabis liberalization and regular use was only significant after the policy had been introduced for more than five years.

Our study showed that the liberalization policy in general was associated with higher levels of cannabis use and depenalization, and partial prohibition policies were particularly correlated with regular use. The correlation was heterogeneous between genders and between short- and long-term effects. Efforts to prevent cannabis use among adolescents are recommended in countries that have embraced liberalization policies, with particular attention to gender differences.

Reference Number: 60108

SILINS E., L.J. HOWARD, G.C. PATTON, D.M. FERGUSSON, C.A. OLSSON., D.M. HUTCHINSON, E. SPRY, J.W. TROUMBOUROU, L.D. DEGENHARDT, W. SWIFT, C. COFFEEY, R.J. TAIT, P. LETCHER, J. COPELAND, AND R.P. MATTICK. "Young Adult Sequelae of Adolescent Cannabis Use: An Integrative Analysis." *Lancet Psychiatry*, 1: 286–93, 2014. (2 tables, 2 figures, 38 references)

Abstract: A study was conducted on the association of the frequency of cannabis use before the age of 17 years (i.e., never, less than monthly, monthly or more, weekly, and daily) and seven developmental outcomes up to age 30 years. Three long-running longitudinal studies from Australia and New Zealand involving 2,537 to 3,765 participants was assessed. The adjusted OR of attaining a high school diploma was 0.78 times for less than monthly to 0.37 times for daily use. For degree attainment, it was 0.78 times for less than monthly and 0.38 times for daily use. The risk of cannabis dependence was 2.06 and 17.95 times respectively, other illicit drug use was 1.67 and 7.80 times respectively, and suicide attempt 1.62 and 6.82 times respectively. There was no significant increase in social assistance or depression.

Table: Frequency of Marijuana Use before the Age of 17 Years and Adjusted Odds Ratio (OR) of Young Adult Outcome Compared to Non-users (OR=1.0)

Young Adult Outcome	Monthly Cannabis Use	Weekly Cannabis Use	Daily Cannabis Use
High School Completion	0.62 X	0.47 X	0.37 X
Degree Attainment	0.62 X	0.49 X	0.38 X
Cannabis Dependence	4.2 X	8.7 X	18.0 X
Other Illicit Drug use	2.8 X	4.7 X	7.8 X
Suicide Attempt	2.6 X	4.2 X	6.8 X

Source: Adapted from Silins et al, 2014

Adverse sequelae of adolescent cannabis use are wide ranging and extend into young adulthood. Prevention or delay of cannabis use in adolescence is likely to have broad health and social benefits. Efforts to reform cannabis legislation should be carefully assessed to ensure they reduce adolescent cannabis use and prevent potentially adverse developmental effects.

Reference Number: 60109

FERGUSSON, D.M., L.J. HORWOOD, AND N. SWAIN-CAMPBELL. "Cannabis Use and Psychosocial Adjustment in Adolescence and Young Adulthood." *Addiction*, 97: 1123–35, 2002 (4 tables, 49 references)

Abstract: A twenty-one-year longitudinal study in New Zealand assessed the frequency of cannabis use in 1,265 children between the ages of 14 and 21 years with measures of psychosocial outcome, such as crime, depression, and suicide attempts. Other studies have reported linkages between cannabis use and adverse outcomes, such as delinquency, antisocial behaviour, dropping out of school, reduced educational achievement, unemployment, mental illness, risky sexual behaviour, affiliation with delinquent peers, and divorce, even when adjusted for confounding factors.

This is the third study in which we have examined the linkages between cannabis use and psychosocial adjustment in this cohort. As the data has accumulated, a number of consistent conclusions have emerged about the linkages between cannabis use and adjustment in adolescence and young adulthood. The conclusions are: a) cannabis and particularly regular cannabis use is associated with a dramatic increase in risks of other forms of illicit drug use, even when confounding is taken into account; b) cannabis use and particularly regular cannabis use is associated with smaller but detectable increases in crime, depression, and suicidal behaviours, even when confounders are taken into account; and c) the adverse effects of cannabis on adjustment seem to be most pronounced for younger users and decline with increasing age.

Reference Number: 60110

MILLER, S.M., J.T. SIEGEL, Z. HOHMAN, AND W.D. CRANO. "Factors Mediating the Association of the Recency of Parent's Marijuana Use and their Adolescent Children's Subsequent Initiation." *Psychology of Addictive Behaviors*, 27: 848–53, 2012 (2 tables, 1 figure, 59 references)

Abstract: The interaction of parent's recent use of marijuana (RMU) and the child's subsequent marijuana initiation was determined in 1,399 parent-child (ages 12 to 17 years) pairs from a National Survey of Parents and Youth conducted in the US between 1999 and 2004. Children of parents who used marijuana were 2.3 times more likely to use cannabis than children of parents who never used cannabis.

> There is no doubt that teenage drug use is related to many personal and environmental features, but a significant factor in adolescent's marijuana initiation and use may be the expectations arising from their close and long-term interaction with parents. The implications of this possibility should not be minimized. There may be little we can do to alter behaviour that occurred many years in the past, but the effects of that behaviour may be attenuated. Making salient to parents the importance of the drug-relevant messages they convey to their children and the subtle, implicit cues of which they must be aware may help reduce the odds of their abstinent children initiating marijuana use. Most parents, for example, are unaware that marijuana's potency has risen steadily over the past thirty years, as have the drug's attendant dangers. This suggests that youth drug prevention efforts may be profitably directed toward parents who would prove more open and nonreactive than the primary prevention target, their children.

Reference Number: 60111

KONG, G., N. SINGH, D. CAMENGA, D. CAVALLO, AND S. KRISHNAN-SARIN. "Menthol Cigarette and Marijuana Use among Adolescents." *Nicotine and Tobacco Research*, 15: 2094–99, 2013 (2 tables, 34 references)

Abstract: A survey of drug and tobacco use was conducted on 837 high school students in Connecticut in 2010. Lifetime marijuana use for all students was 33 percent and past 30-days marijuana use was 21 percent. Thirteen percent reported smoking cigarettes in the last 30 days and 55 percent of smokers smoked menthol cigarettes. Compared to non-smokers, smokers were over ten times more likely to be lifetime cannabis users and to have used cannabis in the last 30 days. Menthol cigarette smokers were over five times more likely to have lifetime cannabis use than other smokers.

In conclusion, cigarette smoking is associated with marijuana use, and smokers smoking menthol cigarettes further increased the odds of marijuana use. These findings suggest that more research on the dual use of marijuana and menthol cigarettes is needed to inform the development of prevention and treatment of substance use, as well as public health policy in targeting these substances.

Reference Number: 60112

MEIER, M.H., M.L. HILL, P.J. SMALL, AND S.S. LUTHAR. "Associations of Adolescent Cannabis Use with Academic Performance and Mental Health: A Longitudinal Study of Upper Middle-Class Youth." *Drug and Alcohol Dependence*, 156: 207–12, 2015 (5 tables, 47 references)

Abstract: The marijuana, alcohol, and tobacco use and academic performance (SAT score and GPA) were determined in 254 students from an upper-middle-class US community through four years of high school, from the age of 14/15+ years to age 17/18 years. The socio-economic status (SES) of the students would not be low. Ninety-seven students (38 percent) had used cannabis in high school and forty-eight students (19 percent) used cannabis on a monthly basis for two or more years of high school. Persistent cannabis use, as well as tobacco and alcohol use, were all associated with lower Grade Point Average (GPA) and greater externalizing symptoms in the twelfth grade.

Adolescents from an upper-middle-class community who used cannabis persistently had lower GPA and more externalizing symptoms in the twelfth grade, even after accounting for ninth grade GPA and externalizing symptoms. These findings suggest that socio-economic disadvantage and related risks that tend to be uncommon in upper-middle-class communities cannot fully account for associations of cannabis use with poorer academic performance and mental health. Findings are consistent with studies from adolescents from diverse socio-economic backgrounds, which demonstrate that associations between cannabis use and poorer educational achievement and greater externalizing behaviour are robust to controls for SES.

Reference Number: 60113

DEGENHARDT, L., C. COFFEY, J.B. CARLIN, W. SWIFT, E. MOORE, AND G.C. PATTON. "Outcomes of Occasional Cannabis Use in Adolescence: 10-Year

Follow-up Study in Victoria, Australia." *The British Journal of Psychiatry*, 196: 290–95, 2010 (2 tables, 2 figures, 31 references)

Abstract: A ten-year study (1992–2003) was conducted of 1,943 high school students, from ages 14.9 to 24 years, on the association between cannabis use and psychosocial and drug use outcomes at age 24 years in Victoria, Australia, compared to non-users. One-third of the students used cannabis within the last six months throughout the study and of these, approximately two-thirds reported only occasional use and one-third at least weekly. There was an association between early onset cannabis use and subsequent drug involvement (i.e., the gateway effect). The association may be due to cannabis causing the maturing adolescent brain to become more sensitive to drug effects.

Table: Odds Ratio or Risk of Psychosocial Outcomes and Substance Use at 24 Years of Age in Occasional and at Least Weekly Cannabis Users

Adolescent Cannabis Use	Welfare	Depression/ Anxiety	Alcohol Dependence	Nicotine Dependence	Cannabis Dependence	Other Illicit Drug Use
Occasional	1.2 X	1.2 X	1.6 X	3.1 X	7.1 X	3.1 X
At Least Weekly	2.4 X	1.3 X	2.6 X	5.0 X	9.3 X	12 X

Source: Adapted from Degenhardt et al, 2010

Occasional adolescent cannabis use was associated with higher levels of drug use in young adulthood compared with non-users. The confounding effect of tobacco use for a number of outcomes suggests possible mediating effects of underlying risk taking behaviours in increasing risk for some adverse psychosocial outcomes. Exaggerated messages about severe harms of occasional cannabis use would be unfounded and at odds with the experience of this group. Yet, interventions to reduce escalation of both cannabis and other drug use among occasional users do seem warranted. Given that occasional users are unlikely to present to specialized services, this message might be best delivered through screening in primary care or community-level health education.

Reference Number: 60113

Reference Number: 60114

CHUN, T.H., A. SPIRITO, L. HERNANDEZ, A.M. FAIRLIE, H. SINDELAR-MANNING, C.A. EATON, AND W. LEWANDER. "The Significance of Marijuana Use among Alcohol Using Adolescent ED Patients." *Academic Emergency Medicine*, 17: 63–71, 2010 (4 tables, 1 figure, 47 references)

Abstract: An assessment was conducted of 113 adolescent patients (ages 13 to 17 years) presenting to ED with evidence of recent alcohol use and concurrent cannabis use, between 2003 and 2007 in southern New England. Fifty-seven percent of the adolescent patients reported using alcohol only (AO) and 43 percent reported alcohol and marijuana use (AM). Other illicit drug use was reported by 22 percent of AM subjects, compared to only 2 percent of the AO patients. AM adolescents had a greater likelihood of increased alcohol and tobacco use compared to AO.

Table: Alcohol, Tobacco, and Illicit Drug Use in Alcohol Use Only (AO) and Alcohol and Marijuana Use (AM) Adolescent Trauma Patients

Substance Use	Alcohol Use Only	Alcohol and Marijuana Use
Cigarettes per Day (mean)	0.37	5.63
Days Drinking per Month (mean)	1.90	3.67
Days Binge Drinking per Month (mean)	0.73	2.48
Percent Using Other Illicit Drugs	2%	22%

Source: Adapted from Chun et al, 2010

Adolescents who use both AM report greater substance use and more risk factors for substance abuse than AO using adolescents. Screening for a history of marijuana use may be important when treating adolescents presenting with an alcohol-related event. Alcohol and marijuana co-use may identify a high risk population, which may have important implications for ED clinicians in the ED care of these patients, providing parental guidance and follow-up care.

Reference Number: 60115

JACOBUS, J., S. BAVA, M. COHEN-ZION, O. MAHMOOD, AND S.F. TAPERT. "Functional Consequences of Marijuana Use in Adolescents." *Pharmacology and Biochemistry of Behavior*, 92: 559–65, 2009 (86 references)

Abstract: A review was conducted of studies on the neuropsychological functioning brain structure, brain function, and subjective and objective measures of sleep in relation to adolescent cannabis use. Almost half of all American Grade 12 students have used marijuana and 6 percent use it daily.

> Adolescent marijuana use has been associated with risky behaviours, reduced educational performance, and increased probability of later psychiatric problems. Adolescents who use marijuana heavily tend to show some disadvantages in attention, verbal learning, and memory and processing speed that persists beyond one-month abstinence, but largely remits after three months of sustained abstinence. Adolescent onset marijuana use has been linked to abnormalities in brain structure, including reduced gray matter and increased white matter volume, reduced fronto-parietal white matter integrity, hippocampal volumes that are not appropriately linked to memory level, prefrontal cortex volumes that are larger than expected in female users but smaller in male users, and increased cerebral blood flow in male users. The effects of marijuana use on brain function are detectable after a month of abstinence, so are not solely due to recent marijuana use, and are characterized by increased activation in parietal, superior temporal, hippocampal, and posterior cingulate regions during working memory demands and increased parietal and frontal activation during response inhibition.

Reference Number: 60116

GREEN, K.M., R.J. MUSCI, R.M. JOHNSON, P.A. MATSON, B.A. REBOUSSIN, AND N.S. IALONGON. "Outcomes Associated with Adolescent Marijuana and Alcohol Use among Urban Young Adults: A Prospective Study." *Addictive Behaviors,* 53: 155–60, 2016 (3 tables, 1 figure, 56 references)

Abstract: Alcohol and cannabis use were studied in 608 urban children from ages 6 to 25 years in Baltimore. Alcohol and cannabis use from Grades 8 to 12 were assessed and revealed four types of use: (1) Non-user (47 percent), (2) Moderate alcohol use (28 percent), (3) moderate alcohol/increasing cannabis use (12 percent), and (4) high dual use (13 percent). Negative outcomes in adulthood were associated with all three types of alcohol and/or cannabis use. All user groups had higher rates of substance dependence than non-users. The high dual use group had the lowest rate of high school graduation and the moderate alcohol users/increasing cannabis group had an increased risk of having a criminal justice record. Cannabis use increased the risk of addiction to other substances.

> Among urban youth, heterogeneous patterns of alcohol and marijuana use across adolescence are evident, and these patterns are associated with distinct outcomes in adulthood. These findings suggest a need for targeted education and intervention efforts to address the needs of youth using both marijuana and alcohol, as well as the importance of universal early preventative intervention efforts.

Reference Number: 60117

MILLER, A.M., R. ROSENMAN, AND B.W. COWAN. "Recreational Marijuana Legalization and College Student Use: Early Evidence." *SSM Population Health,* 3: 649–57, 2017 (8 tables, 3 figures, 22 references)

Abstract: Recreational marijuana legalization (RML) induces more students to use marijuana by lowering one or more costs of using it, such as the threat of punishment, price/availability, lack of social acceptability, and the inherent desire to be law abiding. Washington state legalized the recreational use of cannabis in 2012 and the first retail stores opened in July 2014. A survey was conducted on cannabis/alcohol/tobacco and illicit drug use in the past thirty days of 13,335 undergraduate students (average age 23 years) at Washington State University between 2006 and 2015. The results were compared to survey data from the National College Health Assessment. The increase in marijuana use at WSU was greater than the national trend and the increase in cannabis use was greatest among female, black, and Hispanic students. There was a similar increase in underage students as well.

> It is likely that RML affects factors other than legality, which drive the increase in use. We find evidence that some students may have waited to use until they could legally obtain marijuana from authorized distributors, but the most significant increase in use occurred after RML and before marijuana was available in a legal market. We also find that underage students (for whom marijuana use continues to remain illegal) had as big of a response as legal-age students. Changes in price, availability, social acceptability, and perhaps reduced law enforcement are likely to affect students of all ages, whereas only legal-age students

experience a direct change in the law. Finally, we find evidence that students did not significantly change their use of tobacco, alcohol, or illegal drugs simultaneously with changes in marijuana.

Reference Number: 60118

POPE JR., H.G., A.J. GRUBER, J.I. HUDSON, G. COHANE, M.A. HUESTIS, D. YURGELUN-TODD. "Early Onset Cannabis Use and Cognitive Deficits: What Is the Nature of the Association?" *Drug and Alcohol Dependence* 69: 303–10, 2003 (3 tables, 49 references)

Abstract: A series of ten neuropsychological tests were conducted on 122 long-term, heavy cannabis users (ages 30 to 55 years) and eighty-seven comparison subjects who had minimal exposure to cannabis. All subjects abstained from cannabis use for twenty-eight days. The cannabis users were divided into sixty-nine early onset cannabis users (before age 17 years) and fifty-three later onset users. Early onset cannabis users showed poorer cognitive performance than later onset users or control subjects, especially in verbal IQ.

Table: Neuropsychological Tests Showing Significant Cognitive Impairment in Early and Late Onset Cannabis Users and Controls.

Test	Early Onset Cannabis User	Late Onset Cannabis User	Control
Verbal IQ	103.5	115.6	117.8
Word Memory–total recall (BSRT)	115.4	119.4	121.0
Word Memory 30 Minute Delay (BSRT)	9.2	9.3	10.3
Wisconsin Card Sorting Test	7.8	7.5	8.5

Source: Adapted from Pope Jr et al, 2003

The difference may reflect (1) innate differences between groups in cognitive ability antedating first cannabis use; (2) an actual neurotoxic effect of cannabis on the developing brain; or (3) poorer learning of conventional cognitive skills by young cannabis users who have eschewed academics and diverged from the mainstream culture.

Reference Number: 60119

MALHOTRA, C., N. SHARMA, R. SAXENA, AND G.K. INGLE. "Drug Use among Juveniles in Conflict with the Law." *Indian Journal of Pediatrics* 74: 353–56, 2007 (1 table, 18 references)

Abstract: The pattern of drug use in thirty-four children (ages 13 to 17 years) at an observation home for boys in Delhi in September 2005 was determined. Substances commonly used included smokeless tobacco products, smoked cigarettes, marijuana, alcohol, and volatile substances.

> The results of the present study showing progression of drug use in youth from non-use to tobacco and alcohol use to marijuana and ultimately to other drugs is suggested by a number of other cross-sectional and longitudinal studies.

Reference Number: 60120

ZHANG, C., J.S. BROOK, C.G. LEUKEFELD, AND D.W. BROOK. "Trajectories of Marijuana Use from Adolescence to Adulthood as Predictors of Unemployment Status in the Early Forties." *American Journal of Addictions*, 25: 203–9, 2016 (3 tables, 1 figure, 44 references)

Abstract: Longitudinal data of 548 (approximately 50 percent female) participants between the ages of 14 to 43 years were analyzed as to cannabis use and unemployment at age 43 years. Five types of cannabis users were identified: chronic users/decreasers (8.3 percent), quitters (18.6 percent), increasing users (7.3 percent), chronic occasional users (25.6 percent), and non-users/experimenters (40.2 percent). Chronic users/decreasers had 3.5 times higher risk of unemployment than non-users.

> The relation between chronic marijuana use since early adolescence and later unemployment may be due to the chronic marijuana users' reduced working productivity, which may manifest as a lack of motivation to work, diminished cognitive function, and mental and physical health problems.

Reference Number: 60121

PALAMAR, J.J., M. FENSTERMAKER, D. KAMBOUKOS, D.C. OMPAD, C.M. CLELAND, AND M. WEITZMAN. "Adverse Psychosocial Outcomes Associated with Drug Use Among US High School Seniors: A Comparison of Alcohol and Marijuana." *American Journal of Drug and Alcohol Abuse*, 40: 438–46, 2014 (7 tables, 45 references)

Abstract: A detailed survey was conducted of 4,249 high school seniors who used both alcohol and marijuana; 2,949 who used alcohol alone, and 240 who used marijuana alone, between 2007 and 2011. The percentage of adverse events increased with increased drug use. Marijuana use was more likely to hurt relationships with teachers, parents, and supervisors. Cannabis use was associated with less energy and less interest in activities and lower performance at work or school. Alcohol use was more likely to be associated with unsafe driving practices (20 percent vs 9 percent respectively).

There were also numerous significant differences by sex for both drugs, with females more likely to report most adverse outcomes related to alcohol and marijuana use compared to males. Females were particularly more likely to report engaging in behaviours they regretted, feeling less stable emotionally, and thinking less clearly due to alcohol use. Sex differences were generally not as large for marijuana, but females were more likely to report less energy and less emotional stability and more psychological effects compared to males.

Reference Number: 60122

BRIERE, F.N., J.S. FALLU, A. DESCHENEAUX, AND M. JANOSZ. "Predictors and Consequences of Simultaneous Alcohol and Cannabis." *Addictive Behaviors*, 36: 785–88, 2011 (2 tables, 17 references)

Abstract: The simultaneous use of alcohol and cannabis is common among adolescents. This study was conducted of 6,589 Grade 7 students in Quebec and followed them to Grade 10. Approximately one-third of the Grade 10 students reported at least one episode of simultaneous alcohol and cannabis use. Simultaneous users consumed more alcohol and cannabis than students who consumed alcohol only, cannabis only, or both drugs non-simultaneously. Simultaneous use was associated with four times greater odds of reporting three or more problems the following year.

Simultaneous use was associated with an increased risk of subsequent problems in this final model, indicating a unique effect of mixing alcohol and cannabis in the same episode, as opposed to using the two substances in separate occurrences.

Reference Number: 60122

6.02 AGGRESSION/IMPULSIVITY/VIOLENCE

Cannabis, to a lesser extent than alcohol, triggers some aggressive, violent, impulsive, or criminal behaviour (60205, 60209, 60210). The aggression may occur in part during cannabis withdrawal and not due to the psychoactive effect of THC (60202, 60207). The risk of non-partner violence was doubled after cannabis use (60210).

Reference Number: 60201

CUNRADI, C.B., M. TODD, AND C. MAIR. "Discrepant Patterns of Heavy Drinking, Marijuana Use, and Smoking and Intimate Partner Violence: Results of the California Community Health Safety Study of Couples." *Journal of Drug Education* 45: 73–95, 2015 (2 tables, 43 references)

Abstract: The risk of interpersonal violence was determined in 2,000 couples in California with discrepant (either husband or wife) or concordant (both husband and wife) pattern of heavy drinking, marijuana use, and smoking cigarettes. Among the couples in the study, 6.7 percent reported male to female partner violence (MFPV) and 9.7 percent reported female to male partner violence (FMPV). The mean age was 41.9 years. Approximately 80 percent of the couples were classified as non-heavy drinkers. Approximately 90 percent of the couples did not use marijuana in the last year and 90 percent did not smoke tobacco.

> For both heavy drinking and marijuana use, the results of the fully adjusted model (model 8) showed that couples with discrepant use patterns were twice as likely to experience aggression compared to couples who do not engage in these substance use behaviours. Specifically, discrepant heavy drinking wives were at an increased risk for MFPV; discrepant marijuana use husbands were at increased risk for FMPV. A potential explanation for these findings is that the wife's heavy drinking or the husband's marijuana use may be deemed unacceptable by their spouse, which could lead to conflict and thereafter aggression.

Reference Number: 60202

DE SOUZA FERNANDES PERNA, E.B., E.L. THEUNISSEN, K.P.C. KUYPERS, S.W. TOENNES, AND J.G. RAMAEKERS. "Subjective Aggression During Alcohol and Cannabis Intoxication Before and After Aggression Exposure." *Psychopharmacology*, 233: 331–40, 2016 (2 tables, 3 figures, 53 references)

Abstract: Twenty heavy alcohol users, twenty-one regular cannabis users, and twenty controls (mean age 23 years) were administered two aggression tests, and subjective aggression was assessed before and after drug/placebo administration. The alcohol consumed was enough to obtain a BAC of 0.080 g/100mL and 300 ug/kg THC using a Volcano vaporizer (12 percent THC marijuana) was administered to the cannabis users. Blood testosterone and cortisol concentrations were determined as well. The mean serum THC, 11-OH-THC, and THCCOOH before aggression tests were 46.5, 3.9, and 27.7 ng/mL respectively. The mean BrAC was 0.079 g/100mL.

> It is concluded that alcohol facilitated feelings of aggression, whereas cannabis diminished aggressive feelings in heavy alcohol and regular cannabis users respectively.

Reference Number: 60203

HAGGARD-GRANN, U., J. HALLQVIST, N. LANGSTROM, AND J. MOLLER. "The Role of Alcohol and Drugs in Triggering Criminal Violence: A Case-Crossover Study." *Addiction*, 101: 100–8, 2006 (2 tables, 60 references)

Abstract: A study was conducted of the alcohol/drug use of 133 violent criminal offenders in Sweden between 2002 and 2003. There were 118 male (88 percent) and 15 female offenders with a mean age of 35 years (range 17 to 76 years). Fifty-nine percent of the offenders were exposed to alcohol in the past twenty-four hours prior to the violent act and 6 percent to cannabis. The mean relative risk of violent offence was 13.2 times greater with alcohol.

> Alcohol, with or without simultaneous use of benzodiazepines, strongly triggered criminal violence. Hence, our results support the importance of interventions aimed at decreasing alcohol consumption in individuals at risk for violence. In contrast, regular doses of benzodiazepines and antidepressants seem to inhibit criminal violence.

Reference Number: 60204

MCDONALD, J., L. SCHLEIFER, J.B. RICHARDS, H. DE WIT. "Effects of THC on Behavioral Measures of Impulsivity in Humans." *Neuropsychopharmacology,* 28: 1356–65, 2003 (1 table, 5 figures, 44 references)

Abstract: Eighteen male and nineteen female cannabis users (mean age 23 years) were administered a capsule containing a placebo, 7.5, or 15 mg THC (marinol). Various psychomotor tasks were conducted, such as DSST, Digit Span, Strop Test, and Go/no go task. Heart rate increased in a dose-response manner and maximal ratings occurred eighty minutes after consumption. There were no gender differences in the effects of THC.

These results suggest that THC may increase certain forms of impulsive behaviour while not affecting other impulsive behaviours. The dissociations between the four measures of impulsivity suggest that impulsivity is an assemblage of distinct components, rather than a unitary process.

Reference Number: 60205

ANSELL, E.B., H.B. LAW, M.J. ROCHE, AND R. SINHA. "Effects of Marijuana Use on Impulsivity and Hostility in Daily Life." *Drug and Alcohol Dependence,* 136–42, March 2015 (2 tables, 2 figures, 71 references)

Abstract: Twenty-six female and seventeen male participants (mean age 23.7 years), of whom 21 percent were positive in a urine screen for cannabinoids, reported their daily alcohol consumption, tobacco use, recreational cannabis use, impulsivity, and interpersonal hostility over fourteen days. Marijuana use was associated with increased impulsivity on the same day and next day after use. Increased hostile behaviour and perception of hostility occurred on the same day as cannabis use.

Marijuana use is associated with changes in impulse control and hostility in daily life. This may be one route by which deleterious effects of marijuana are observed for mental health and psychosocial functioning. Given the increasing prevalence of recreational marijuana use and the potential for legalization in some states, further research on the potential consequences of marijuana use in young adult's day-to-day life is warranted.

Reference Number: 60206

RICHER, I., AND J. BERGERON. "Driving Under the Influence of Cannabis: Links with Dangerous Driving, Psychological Predictors and Accident Involvement." *Accident Analysis and Prevention*, 41: 299–307, 2009 (7 tables, 72 references)

Abstract: Seventy-five male drivers (ages 17 to 49 years) who self-reported driving under the influence of cannabis were measured for dangerous driving behaviour. Seventy-two were tested for unsafe driving behaviour in a driving simulator.

> The results show an association between DUIC and self-reported, negative emotional driving but not one with aggressive driving. Therefore, the hypothesis asserting that DUIC is positively related to aggressive driving could not be corroborated. DUIC drivers reported higher levels of anger while driving; nevertheless, they do not admit to being more aggressive toward other drivers. These results support previous studies showing that anger on the road does not always lead to aggressive driving.

Reference Number: 60207

SMITH, P.H., G.G. HOMISH, K.E. LEONARD, AND R.L. COLLINS. "Marijuana Withdrawal and Aggression among a Representative Sample of U.S. Marijuana Users." *Drug and Alcohol Dependence*, 132: 63–68, 2013 (3 tables, 1 figure, 35 references)

Abstract: The incidence of general and relationship aggression was determined in a general population of US cannabis users based on data from the 2001–2002 and 2004–2005 National Epidemiologic Survey on Alcohol and Related Conditions. Marijuana may be tied to aggression through withdrawal symptoms in which some heavy cannabis users have exhibited changes in mood and behaviour and experienced aggression and irritation during abstinence. There was no increase in general aggression during withdrawal but 60 percent higher odds of relationship aggression during withdrawal by marijuana users with a history of aggression.

> One explanation for the differential findings between relationship aggression and general aggression stems from the transitive nature of marijuana withdrawal. Previous research suggests that marijuana withdrawal symptoms peak after two to six days of abstinence and may last up to two weeks. Individuals tend to interact more frequently with their partners than others, and hence may be more likely to interact with their partner during periods of withdrawal.

Reference Number: 60208

BUTTERS, J.E., R.G. SMART, R.E. MANN, AND M. ASBRIDGE. "Illicit Drug Use, Alcohol Use and Problem Drinking Among Infrequent and Frequent Road Ragers." *Drug and Alcohol Dependence*, 80: 169–75, 2005 (3 tables, 32 references)

Abstract: A survey was conducted of 2,421 adults (18 years of age and older) in Ontario during 2002 on the association of past year drug/alcohol use and road rage. Eighty percent of drivers reported drinking in the last twelve months (12 percent problem drinking), 11 percent indicated cannabis use, and 1 percent cocaine/amphetamine use. The OR of frequent road ragers was 1.7 times for alcohol problems, 1.4 times for cannabis use in the last twelve months, and 29 times for ecstasy users.

Serious road ragers may be individuals immersed in a more deviant lifestyle, incorporating relatively frequent rule breaking behaviour and a general disregard for legal sanctions. The extent to which these findings represent pharmacological effects, psychosocial processes, or both, is an important topic for future research.

Reference Number: 60209

REINGLE, J.M., S.A.S. STARAS, W.G. JENNINGS, J. BRANCHINI, AND M.M. MALDONADO-MOLINA. "The Relationship between Marijuana Use and Intimate Partner Violence in a Nationally Representative, Longitudinal Sample." *Journal of Interpersonal Violence,* 27: 1562–78, 2012 (2 tables, 46 references)

Abstract: A longitudinal study was conducted on 9,421 adolescents and young adults (ages 15 to 26 years) regarding the association between marijuana use and intimate partner violence in four waves of interviews (i.e., 1994–1995, 1995–1996, 2001–2002, and 2007–2008). The data was obtained from the National Longitudinal Study of Adolescent Health (Add Health) in the US. More than 50 percent of those surveyed reported cannabis use and 30 percent reported some form of intimate partner violence at Wave 4. Twelve percent were victims only, 4.7 percent were perpetrators only, and 11.9 percent reported being both.

Among young adults, all analyzed patterns of marijuana use during adolescence and early adulthood were associated with a 1.2 to 2.4 times increased risk of intimate partner violence perpetration and victimization. This study expands on prior research linking marijuana use with intimate partner violence by using a longitudinal design and recognizing the overlap between perpetration and victimization in intimate partner violence. Specifically, we found that any use of marijuana during adolescence and young adulthood increases the risk of intimate partner violence. Consistent users were at greatest risk of perpetration and victimization.

Reference Number: 60210

CUNNINGHAM, R.M., R. MURRAY, M.A. WALTON, S.T. CHERMACK, M. WOJNAR, P. WOZNIAK, B.M. BOOTH, AND F.C. BLOW. "Prevalence of Past Year Assault among Inner-City ED Patients." *Annals of Emergency Medicine*, 53: 814–23, 2009 (1 table, 3 figures, 91 references)

Abstract: Risk factors for non-partner violent assault (NPV) were determined in 10,744 patients (mean age 36.4 years) attending an Emergency Department in Flint, Michigan, between 2006 and 2008. Overall 14 percent of the patients surveyed reported violence with a non-partner in the previous year. Some risk factors were being male, single, and unemployed. Drug and alcohol use in the previous thirty days were also risk factors.

Table: Substance Use in the Past 30 days and Odds Ratio (OR) of Any Non-Partner Violence

Substance Use in Past 30 Days	OR of Any Non-Partner Violence
Alcohol only	1.73 X
Marijuana	2.36 X
Cocaine	3.10 X
Prescription drug	1.43 X
Substance Use Treatment in Last 3 Months	1.70 X

Source: Adapted from Cunningham et al, 2009

Each year more than 37 million patients visit emergency departments (EDs) with injuries. Of these visits, approximately 17 percent are related to violence or assault. Research from multiple disciplines suggests that violent injury is non-random and is best predicted by past experience and behaviour. Among fatal injuries, 20 percent are related to interpersonal violence. Assault-related injuries have reached epidemic numbers, exceeding two-million persons annually, with homicide as a leading cause of death among young adults. Often, in non-intimate partner violence, the victim and assailant know each other, with friends or relatives involved in the majority of gun-related violence. Nationally, more individuals report victimization by friends or acquaintances than by spouses or dating partners. Among women in the ED, prior research finds that half of assault-related injuries were perpetrated by a non-partner, underscoring the importance of understanding violence outside of intimate partner relationships.

Reference Number: 60211

BROOK, J.S., J.Y. LEE., S.J. FINCH, AND D.W. BROOK. "Developmental Trajectories of Marijuana Use from Adolescence to Adulthood: Relationship with Using Weapons Including Guns." *Aggressive Behaviors*, 40: 229–37, 2014 (3 tables, 1 figure, 35 references)

Abstract: The trajectories of cannabis use and violent behaviour were determined in 838 inner city Grade 7 to 10 students in New York City in 1990 (T1), 1994–1996 (T2), 2000–2001 (T3), and 2004–2006 (T4). Cannabis use in this group was divided into non-users (45 percent), quitter (17 percent), moderate (18 percent), and increasing chronic user (7 percent).

Table: Odds Ratio (OR) of Violent Behaviour Compared to the Cannabis Non-user for Various Marijuana Use Trajectories

	OR of Shooting or Hitting Someone with a Weapon (gun or club)	OR of Holding a Weapon (gun or club) to Someone	OR of Stealing without Using a Weapon
Increasing Chronic User	3.37 X	3.49 X	2.13 X
Moderate User	1.98 X	1.91 X	0.97 X
Quitter	1.70 X	2.88 X	0.39 X

Source: Adapted from Brook et al, 2014

The findings of this study have implications for public policy, prevention, and treatment. As noted earlier, our results indicate that young ethnic minority men who are on a trajectory of increasing chronic marijuana use over adolescence and young adulthood are more likely to engage in physical violence involving use of weapons. Therefore, it is important for public policy, including education, to focus on this very vulnerable and problematic group. The findings also provide information for prevention and treatment. Interventions in emerging adulthood and adulthood should focus on decreasing the increasing chronic marijuana group, and the moderate marijuana trajectory group. This may lower the rates of violent behaviour with the use of guns. As regards public policy, eased regulation regarding marijuana use could conceivably result in an increase in violent behaviour.

Reference Number: 60212

PETERS, E.N., R.F. LEEMAN, L.M. FUCITO, B.A. TOLL, W.R. CORBIN, AND S.S. O'MALLEY. "Co-Occurring Marijuana Use Is Associated with Medication Nonadherence and Non-Planning Impulsivity in Young Adult Heavy Drinkers." *Addictive Behaviors,* 37: 420–26, 2012 (3 tables, 58 references)

Abstract: One hundred and twenty-two heavy drinkers (ages 18 to 25 years) participated in an eight-week, randomized clinical trial of placebo-controlled naltrexone use. They were divided into seventy-one subjects who did not use cannabis in the previous three months and twenty-four who used cannabis two times or more a week. Various self-assessment measures, such as impulsivity and medication compliance, were determined. Co-occurring heavy alcohol and marijuana use was significantly associated with non-planning impulsivity and a history of both unintentional (OR = 3.30) and purposeful (OR = 3.98) nonadherence to medication.

> In conclusion, young adult heavy drinkers with co-occurring marijuana use presenting for an alcohol reduction clinical trial reported several high risk clinical characteristics that may portend worse treatment outcomes.

Reference Number: 60213

AMARO, H., L.E. FRIED, H. CABRAL, AND B. ZUCKERMAN. "Violence During Pregnancy and Substance Use." *American Journal of Public Health,* 80: 575–79, 1990 (4 tables, 29 references)

Abstract: Physical and/or sexual violent incidents were determined in 1,243 pregnant women in Boston between 1984 and 1987. Violent incidences were reported by ninety-two women (7 percent) during pregnancy and an additional 3 percent reported violent incidences in the three months prior to pregnancy, but not during pregnancy. The women who were victims of violence during pregnancy were 2.27 times more likely to have a cannabis user as a partner and 2.35 times as likely to have a cocaine user as a partner but there was no increase in risk of violence if the partner consumed alcohol. As the pregnant women increased their consumption of alcohol, cannabis, or cocaine, there was an increasing risk of violence.

> The findings of this study support previous reports on the prevalence of violence during pregnancy. Of greater importance are the results that provide evidence of a strong relation between violence during pregnancy and the use of alcohol by the pregnant woman and the use of illicit drugs by her male partner. A number of previous studies have shown that abused women are at greater risk of using heavier quantities of alcohol and prescription and non-prescription drugs than women who are not abused. While the cause and effect relationship between use of alcohol and experience of violence is unclear; there are indications that women who are abused may self-medicate with alcohol, illicit drugs, and prescription medication in order to cope with the violence.

6.03 CANNABINOID HYPEREMESIS SYNDROME (CHS)

Cannabinoid Hyperemesis Syndrome (CHS) appears to be a paradoxical reaction to cannabis use, first reported in 2004 in Australia (60301). Cannabis is usually associated with the relief of nausea and vomiting and an increase in appetite and weight, especially in male users. But after chronic use, usually over several years, severe cyclical vomiting and abdominal pain can develop, which are typical symptoms of CHS. Sufferers of this syndrome mistakenly continue using cannabis or increase its use, as cannabis is known as an anti-emetic (60301, 60303, 60304, 60310).

The three main phases of CHS are:

Proximal phase: This phase is variable in duration and consists of nausea, fear of vomiting, and abdominal discomfort. The symptoms are more common in early middle-age adults who have been chronically using marijuana since adolescence.

Vomiting phase: The vomiting phase is manifested by intense, persistent nausea and vomiting and retching that can occur up to five times per hour and has been described by patients as overwhelming. The CHS sufferers find relief in hot bathing and showering in hot water. Indeed, one patient attended hospital as he ran out of hot water at home. Patients typically visit EDs on numerous occasions, as ER physicians are generally unaware of CHS. Numerous unnecessary clinical tests are

Reference Number: 60213

typically conducted, such as radiologic abdominal imaging, colonoscopy, and blood tests, which yield normal results.

Recovery phase: The recovery phase begins with cessation of cannabis use. Within one week, the patients were experiencing a substantial decrease and eventual cessation of cyclic vomiting and abdominal pain. The tendency to take hot showers declines as well. CHS will reoccur as soon as cannabis use is resumed (60319).

CHS is not well recognized by physicians, especially in EDs, and so numerous ED attendances occur, and unnecessary clinical tests conducted before the proper diagnosis is made (60302, 60309, 60312, 60316). On average, a person suffering from CHS attended hospital on 7.1 occasions (60317). Legalization of marijuana in Colorado caused a twofold increase in persons attending hospital as a result of cyclical vomiting (60305). The excessive hot water showering or bathing can result in a red-brown rash over the body, known as thermal ketosis, which also appears in persons exposed to fires or close, long contact with laptop computers (60310).

Reference Number: 60301

ALLEN, J.H., G.M. DE MOORE, R. HEDDLE, AND J.C. TWARTZ. "Cannabinoid Hyperemesis: Cyclical Hyperemesis in Association with Chronic Cannabis Abuse." *Gut*, 53: 1566–70, 2004 (4 tables, 25 references)

Abstract: Ten cases of cannabinoid hyperemesis in South Australia are described. In all cases, chronic cannabis abuse predated the onset of cyclical vomiting. Nine of the ten patients developed obsessive hot bathing/showering, which relieved the symptoms of nausea and vomiting. Seven patients ceased marijuana use and remained symptom free. Three patients continued to smoke cannabis and suffered relapses. Two of the three again ceased cannabis use and no longer had cyclical vomiting. The third refused to quit and remains ill.

> The compulsion to have multiple hot showers or baths exhibited by these chronic cases is not trivial. It is clinically important to both nurse and doctor as it flags these patients on the ward. Their ready identification should lead to a reduction in morbidity for the patients and cost to the health service. The consequences of this discovery bear further consideration. The paradoxical effect of its action must raise concerns about the long-term tolerability of marijuana. Furthermore, it would

also appear clinically prudent to exclude cannabis as an underlying cause in other cyclical illnesses, such as atypical abdominal and pelvic pain. Cannabis abstention, with urine drug screen monitoring, can be titrated against a clinical course. Finally, we feel that this disorder is an important differential diagnosis for unexplained vomiting, particularly in communities tolerant of cannabis. The diagnosis can be considered or discounted with the aid of an inexpensive consented drug screen.

Reference Number: 60302

HERMES-LAUFER, J., L.D. PUPPO, I. INAN, F-X. TROILLET, AND O. KHERAD. "Cannabinoid Hyperemesis Syndrome: A Case Report of Cyclic Severe Hyperemesis and Abdominal Pain with Long-Term Cannabis Use." *Case Reports in Gastrointestinal Medicine*, 2016, 4 pp (19 references)

Abstract: A 26-year-old man attended hospital on three occasions as a result of recurrent vomiting and abdominal pains. He had used cannabis twice a day for ten years. Symptoms were resistant to all treatments except for hot showers. He was diagnosed with CHS and the symptoms stopped when he stopped using cannabis.

The Cannabis Hyperemesis Syndrome is a challenging differential diagnosis in patients who present with cyclic vomiting and abdominal pain with a history of cannabis use. Recognition of this syndrome is important in order to avoid costly and unnecessary clinical testing and to help the patient understand and break the cycle of drug use.

Reference Number: 60303

JONES, J.L. AND K.E. ABERNATHY. "Successful Treatment of Suspected Cannabinoid Hyperemesis Syndrome Using Haloperidol in the Outpatient Setting." *Case Reports in Psychiatry,* Article ID 3614053, 3 pp, 2016 (15 references)

Abstract: An 18-year-old female cannabis user presented to hospital with persistent vomiting and nausea. She increased her cannabis use to relieve the symptoms by up to two to three joints per day and was diagnosed with Cannabinoid Hyperemesis Syndrome (CHS). She refused to give up cannabis, was prescribed haloperidol (5 mg/day), and the nausea and vomiting ceased.

From a public health perspective, 22.2-million persons, aged 12 or older, in the United States were current users of cannabis in 2014 and this number has continued to rise each year, since 2002, according to the National Survey on Drug Use and Health. At present, there are no reliably effective treatment regimens for patients with CHS who refuse to discontinue cannabis use, including conventional antiemetics. Pharmacologic studies indicate that haloperidol may act indirectly on CB1 receptors to relieve nausea, vomiting, and abdominal pain. Our findings in this case study are consistent with case reports from the emergency department setting and suggest the need for further studies to evaluate the efficacy of haloperidol in the treatment of refractory CHS.

Reference Number: 60304

IACOPETTI, C.L., AND C.D. PARKER. "Cannabinoid Hyperemesis Syndrome: A Case Report and Review of Pathophysiology." *Clinical Medicine and Research,* 12: 65–67, 2014 (12 references)

Abstract: A 33-year-old man with a history of post-traumatic stress, hypertension, and GERD presented at hospital after two days of severe nausea and intractable vomiting. He has intermittent recreational marijuana use for many years, which gradually increased to daily use in the past two years. His cyclical vomiting required five hospital admissions. He had frequent hot showers to control his vomiting. The half-life of THC is initially 2 hours in the first 8 hours after administration and then up to 12.6 weeks extended to 4 weeks. High levels of CBD may play a role in the development of CHS.

Clinicians should be aware that cannabis can have paradoxically emetogenic effects in some habitual users and that the pathognomonic features of cannabinoid hyperemesis syndrome are recurrent bouts of vomiting and symptom relief with hot water bathing. Increased awareness of CHS could reduce the expense and potential morbidity of extensive diagnostic work-ups for these patients.

Reference Number: 60305

KIM, H.S., J.D. ANDERSON, O. SAGHAFI, K.J. HEARD, AND A.A. MONTE "Cyclic Vomiting Presentations Following Marijuana Liberalization in Colorado." *Academic Emergency Medicine.* 22: 694–99, 2015 (1 table, 1 figure, 16 references)

Abstract: The rate of cyclic vomiting (cannabis-induced hyperemesis) ER presentations was determined at two Denver hospitals before and after legalization of cannabis in Colorado. A total of 2,574 ER visits were reviewed and cyclic vomiting was identified in thirty-six patients over 128 visits. The patients were mainly female (71 percent) with a mean age of 31 years. The prevalence of cannabis hyperemesis increased from 41 per 113,262 ER visits to 87 per 125,095 ER visits after liberalization (i.e., 3.6/10,000 vs 7.0/10,000).

> In this retrospective study, we observed that the prevalence of cyclic vomiting presentations nearly doubled after the liberalization of medical marijuana in Colorado. This increase was accompanied by an increase in self-reported marijuana usage and serves as a crucial first step in establishing a formal diagnosis of cannabinoid hyperemesis syndrome.

Reference Number: 60306

SIMONETTO, D.A., A.S. OXENTENKO, M.L. HERMAN, AND J.H. SZOSTEK. "Cannabinoid Hyperemesis: A Case Series of 98 Patients." *Mayo Clinic Proceedings*, 87: 114–19, 2012 (4 tables, 1 figure, 25 references)

Abstract: A review was conducted of ninety-eight case reports of patients with cannabinoid hyperemesis syndrome between 2005 and 2010. All ninety-eight patients were younger than 50 years of age (mean age 32.3 years). Ninety-one percent reported relief of symptoms with a hot shower.

> Cannabinoid hyperemesis should be considered in younger patients with long-term cannabis use and recurrent nausea, vomiting, and abdominal pain.

Reference Number: 60307

SONTINENI, S., S. CHAUDHARY, V. SONTINENI, AND S.J. LANSPA. "Cannabinoid Hyperemesis Syndrome: Clinical Diagnosis of an Under Recognized Manifestation of Chronic Cannabis Abuse." *World Journal of Gastroenterology*, 15: 1264–66, 2009 (4 tables, 1 figure, 25 references)

Abstract: A 22-year-old man presented at hospital with recurrent episodes of nausea, refractory vomiting, and colicky epigastric pain at least twice a day for one week. He has been treated on two occasions in ER for severe vomiting in the last two months. Taking a hot bath relieved his symptoms.

Table: Clinical Criteria for Cannabinoid Hyperemesis Syndrome

Essential for Diagnosis
Long-term cannabis use
Major Features
Severe cyclic nausea and vomiting
Resolution with cannabis cessation
Relief of symptoms with hot showers or baths
Abdominal pain
Weekly use of marijuana
Supportive Features
Age less than 50 years
Weight loss > 5 kg
Morning predominance of symptoms
Normal bowel habits
Negative laboratory, radiographic, and endoscopic test results.

Source: Adapted from Simonetto et al, 2012

> Given the high prevalence of chronic cannabis abuse worldwide and the paucity of reports in the literature, clinicians need to be more attentive to the clinical features of this under-recognized condition.

Reference Number: 60308

SULLIVAN, S. "Cannabinoid Hyperemesis." *Canadian Journal of Gastroenterology*, 24: 284–85, 2010 (17 references)

Abstract: The classic features of CHS are (1) chronic heavy use of cannabis, (2) recurrent episodes of severe nausea and intractable vomiting, (3) abdominal pains, (4) temporary relief of the symptoms by taking a hot shower or bath, and (5) resolution of the problem when cannabis use is stopped. The shortest length of heavy use of cannabis before CHS was eighteen months.

> Chronically, the only therapy reported to be of benefit is cessation of cannabis use. How quickly it helps is uncertain, but my impression is that once the patient leaves the emergency department, they will not return if they stop using cannabis. However, symptoms return within weeks if cannabis use is restarted.

Reference Number: 60309

SUN, S., AND A.E. ZIMMERMANN. "Cannabinoid Hyperemesis Syndrome." *Hospital Pharmacy* 48: 650–55, 2013 (1 table, 21 references)

Abstract: CHS is a recently described condition of cyclical vomiting related to long-term cannabis use. There are three phases of CHS: (1) Prodromal phase, which can last for months or years. The patient develops early morning nausea, fear of vomiting, and abdominal discomfort. The symptoms are most common in 20 to 50 year olds who have been consistently using cannabis since adolescence. The patient may increase the use of cannabis in the belief that cannabis will assist in preventing nausea. (2) Hyperemetic phase: intensely, persistent vomiting and retching described as an overwhelming incapacitation resulting in decreased food intake and food aversion. There is a weight loss of typical > 5 kg. A learned behaviour of frequent hot baths or showers becomes compulsive. (3) Recovery phase: begins with cannabis cessation and relative wellness and normal eating habits. Weight loss is regained and a return to regular bathing frequency. A return to cannabis use will lead to a reoccurrence of CHS.

CHS is potentially under-recognized and under-diagnosed in the ED and it should be considered in the differential diagnostic in long-term cannabis use patients with CHS symptoms to avoid unnecessary extensive diagnostic work-up, including invasive radiologic imaging.

Reference Number: 60310

CHEUNG, E., C. NG, AND J. FOOTE. "A Hot Mess: A Case of Hyperemesis." *Canadian Family Physician*, 60: 633–37, 2014 (1 table, 18 references)

Abstract: A 29-year-old man presented to hospital after having more than ten episodes of vomiting in the past eight hours. He was a regular cannabis smoker (1 to 3 joints per day) and had used cocaine more than two weeks ago and alcohol more than three days ago. He was diagnosed with Cannabinoid Hyperemesis Syndrome (CHS). CHS may be due to THC causing sensitivity of CB1 receptors in the brain leading to pro-emetic CB1 activity in the gut overriding the antiemetic CB1 properties in the brain. The typical bathing or showering in hot water to alleviate the symptoms of CHS may divert blood from the periphery, reducing the stimulation of CB1 receptors in the gut and offering temporary relief. The patient refused to believe that he had CHS.

It is worthwhile to note that most chronic marijuana users will reject the association between their cannabis use and hyperemesis because of having been asymptomatic despite years of cultural belief that cannabis has antiemetic properties.

Reference Number: 60311

KRAEMER, R.R., R.M. LA HOZ, AND J.H. WILLIG. "Some Like It Hot: Erythema Ab Igne due to Cannabinoid Hyperemesis." *Journal of General Internal Medicine*, 28: 1522, 2013 (2 figures, 5 references)

Abstract: A 42-year-old man with cyclical vomiting due to chronic cannabis use was admitted to hospital for severe nausea and vomiting. He took five to six hot showers a day to relieve these symptoms. A red to brown pigmented rash was seen on his trunk and arms. This rash was consistent with erythema ab igne (EAI) or thermal ketosis, which also appear in people working by open fires, excessive use of heating pads, and on the thighs of frequent portable computer or laptop users.

Cannabinoid hyperemesis, a syndrome of cyclical vomiting from chronic marijuana use, has been associated with compulsive bathing, which ameliorates the nausea. The linkage of cannabinoid hyperemesis and EAI due to compulsive bathing is a new association of this classic heat-associated skin lesion. The patient was discharged without complication.

Reference Number: 60312

PATTERSON, D.A., E.L. SMITH, M. MONAHAN, A. MEDVECZ., B. HAGERTY, L. KRIJGER, A. CHAUHAN, AND M. WALSH. "Cannabinoid Hyperemesis and Compulsive Bathing: A Case Series and Paradoxical Pathophysiological Explanation." *Journal of the American Board of Family Medicine*, 23: 790–93, 2010 (17 references)

Abstract: Cannabis hyperemesis syndrome (CHS) was first described in 2004 in a series of nine patients. In the current study, CHS was observed in four male chronic cannabis users (ages 20 to 43 years of age). All had cyclical vomiting and compulsive hot bathing. It is thought that hot bathing caused a redistribution of blood flow from the gut to the skin, which brings relief to the patient.

> We report four cases of chronic cannabinoid use in patients, leading to a cyclic vomiting syndrome with compulsive hot-water bathing. With the recent legalization of medical marijuana in numerous states, we suspect that cannabinoid hyperemesis will become a more frequently encountered diagnosis. As these cases demonstrate, expensive and invasive diagnostic, medical, and surgical treatments could be avoided with an accurate history and knowledge of this phenomenon. Family physicians should be aware of this increasing clinical syndrome.

Reference Number: 60313

CHANG, Y.H., AND D.M. WINDISH. "Cannabinoid Hyperemesis Relieved by Compulsive Bathing." *Mayo Clinic Proceedings*. 84: 76–78, 2009 (17 references)

Abstract: A 25-year-old female long-term cannabis user (six to seven years) presented to the ED with nausea, vomiting, and abdominal pain, which lasted for several days. She showered for as much as four hours at a time and left her hospital room to use a neighbour's shower. After forty-eight hours, her symptoms disappeared. A 23-year-old male chronic cannabis user (two to three times a day for nine years) came to the ED after a day of nausea, vomiting, and abdominal pain, and after using all the hot water in his house. He was treated with anti-emetic drugs.

> Cannabinoid hyperemesis is a clinical syndrome characterized by repeated vomiting and associated learned compulsive hot-water bathing behaviour due to long-term marijuana use. Research has identified type 1 cannabinoid receptors in the intestinal nerve plexus that have an inhibitory effect on gastrointestinal motility. This inhibitory effect may lead to hyperemesis in marijuana users. The thermoregulatory role of endocannabinoids may be responsible for the patient's need to take hot showers. We report two cases of cannabinoids hyperemesis that demonstrate this unusual adverse effect of marijuana use.

Reference Number: 60314

PRICE, S.L., C. FISHER, R. KUMAR, AND A. HILGERSON. "Cannabinoid Hyperemesis Syndrome as the Underlying Cause of Intractable Nausea and

Vomiting." *Journal of the American Osteopathic Association*, 111: 166–69, 2011 (14 references)

Abstract: A 30-year-old man was admitted to hospital after three days of nausea, diffuse abdominal pain, and continued vomiting. He initially denied drug use but when confronted by his positive urine cannabinoid result, he admitted to chronic use of cannabis for years. He was treated for pain, nausea, and vomiting and eventually his symptoms disappeared. By the fourth day of his hospitalization, he had taken nineteen hot showers.

Cannabinoid hyperemesis syndrome is a newly recognized diagnosis related to cannabis toxicity. The adverse effects of chronic cannabis use are still under investigation, and the mechanism of cannabis leading to intractable nausea and vomiting is still unclear. With the widespread use of this substance, both recreationally and therapeutically, the paradoxical effect of cannabinoid hyperemesis syndrome deserves further attention. The goal of this present case report is to raise awareness of the potential adverse effects of cannabis and the importance of obtaining a thorough history, including questions regarding illicit substance abuse. When questioning a patient's social history, it may be worthwhile to inquire about hot showering patterns, especially in those who deny or minimize their use of illicit drugs. Clinicians should have heightened awareness when intractable nausea and vomiting is unresponsive to anti-emetics but relieved with hot showering. When encountering this unusual presentation, clinicians should consider illicit cannabis abuse in addition to organic disease as a possible cause. This consideration may prevent further unnecessary work-up and health-care costs for patients with cannabinoid hyperemesis syndrome.

Reference Number: 60315

WILD, K., AND H. WILSON. "Cannabinoid Hyperemesis." *British Medical Journal Case Reports*, 3 pp, 2010 (14 references)

Abstract: A 21-year-old female chronic cannabis user (heavy smoking for seven years) presented at the ED with a four-week history of sudden onset vomiting, nausea, and anorexia. After examination and further tests (her urine drug screen was positive for cannabinoids), she was diagnosed with cannabinoid hyperemesis and treated with IV fluids and anti-emetics. Since her discharge, she has had several additional episodes of cyclical vomiting, all related to continuing cannabis use. The patient is now seeking cognitive behavioural therapy to become completely abstinent.

Cannabis use and its potency has increased over recent years, hence it is likely consumers are being exposed to higher doses of the drug. A new clinical syndrome titled cannabinoid hyperemesis emerged in 2004, which has since been described by several authors. It is characterized by episodic vomiting often relieved by hot-water bathing or showering. These symptoms arise after heavy chronic cannabis use and abstinence leads to symptom resolution. Cannabinoids have been found to have an antiemetic effect at CB1 receptors in the central nervous system (CNS), but, paradoxically, chronic cannabis use results in hyperemesis. It has been proposed that accumulation of the drug leads to delayed gastric emptying and at toxic levels results in gastric stasis, hence counteracting the antiemetic effect. It is probable that the condition is underreported in the literature and under-diagnosed in clinical and emergency settings.

Reference Number: 60316

MOHAMMED, F., K. PANCHOO, M. BARTHOLEMEW, AND D. MAHARAJ. "Compulsive Showering and Marijuana Use: The Cannabis Hyperemesis Syndrome." *American Journal of Case Reports,* 14: 326–28, 2013 (19 references)

Abstract: A 26-year-old male heavy cannabis user (four joints a day for two years) attended hospital after suffering from abdominal pain and frequent vomiting for three weeks. The nausea was relieved by taking up to fifteen hot showers a day. He was counselled on abstinence from marijuana, and although he did not enter a substance abuse program, he was cannabis-free and symptom-free at the six-month follow-up.

Cannabis (or more affectionately referred to on the street as marijuana or ganja) is one of the frequently used illicit drugs both internationally and in the Caribbean islands. Cannabis has several well-known effects on the gastrointestinal system. More recently and less well recognized is the cannabinoid hyperemesis syndrome (CHS), which is typified by the tetrad of cyclical vomiting, abdominal pain, compulsive hot showering, and chronic marijuana use. The rarity of the condition can lead to a diagnostic dilemma resulting in extensive and expensive investigation with a delay in treatment. We report the first cases of CHS in the Caribbean and highlight the need for being aware of this differential in chronic marijuana smokers, particularly for those who have access to high potency, genetically engineered marijuana.

Reference Number: 60317

GALLI, J.A., R.A. SAWAYA, AND F.K. FRIENDENBERG. "Cannabinoid Hyperemesis Syndrome." *Current Drug Abuse Review*, 4: 241–249, 2011 (1 figure, 76 references)

Abstract: THC causes a significant delay in gastric emptying. Patients with CHS usually remain misdiagnosed for a considerable time; the average number of ER visits is 7.1. Daily marijuana use is characteristic of CHS and is often reported as three to five times per day. Hot bathing may reduce cannabis-induced disequilibrium of the thermoregulatory system. Cannabis increases core temperature while decreasing skin temperature, which increases blood flow to skin and dissipates excess core heat. CHS is a recurrent disorder interspersed with symptom-free intervals.

In clinical practice CHS is most often confused with cyclic vomiting syndrome (CVS). In fact, patients with CHS are often mislabeled as having CVS and vice versa. Confusion exists in the medical literature secondary to a failure to recognize chronic marijuana use as a source of vomiting.

6.04 CARDIOVASCULAR EFFECTS

Cannabis use is associated with the risk of heart attacks (myocardial infarction) and, to a lesser extent, strokes. The relative risk of a MI is 4.8 times greater within an hour of smoking cannabis (60405). The reasons for the risk of MI increasing with smoking cannabis includes the increasing stress on the heart by an increase in heart rate, changes in blood pressure, an increase in oxygen demand by the heart with a corresponding decrease in oxygen available, due to the carbon monoxide in cannabis smoke (60401, 60402, 60405, 60409). Atrial and ventricular fibrillation induced by smoking cannabis may cause blood clots resulting in strokes (60403, 60404, 60411, 60412, 60420). Cannabis use was found to increase vascular age (60414). Some of the adverse cardiovascular effects of cannabis may be due to co-existing tobacco use as well.

Contrary to popular beliefs that cannabis is a harmless, natural plant and flower and has never caused fatalities, its use has been associated with sudden cardiac deaths, which, although rare, is still a risk that cannabis users should be aware of (60407, 60409).

Reference Number: 60401

JOHNSON, S., AND E.F. DOMINO. "Some Cardiovascular Effects of Marihuana Smoking in Normal Volunteers." *Clinical Pharmacology and Therapeutics,* 12: 762–68, 1971 (5 figures, 10 references)

Abstract: Twenty male subjects (ages 21 to 33 years) smoke one to five marijuana cigarettes containing 0.5 percent or 2.9 percent THC. ECGs, BP, and HR were measured. The increase in HR was dose-related and the maximum HR was within 30 minutes after smoking and persisted for at least 90 minutes. BP was elevated and correlated with HR. Premature ventricular contractions (PVCs) were observed in some subjects.

Although no deaths have been reported from marijuana intoxication alone, the tachycardia, hypertension, and PVCs it can produce indicate that marijuana should be used with caution by people with heart disease. Like nicotine and caffeine, marijuana may be a cause of PVCs in susceptible individuals. This was a relatively rare finding and may be due to smoking rather than pure THC.

Reference Number: 60402

ZACHARIAH, S.B. "Stroke after Heavy Marijuana Smoking." *Stroke,* 22: 406–9, 1991 (2 figures, 28 references)

Abstract: A 34-year-old chronic tobacco (less than one pack/day) and cannabis user (seven joints/day) for fifteen years increased his cannabis use to fourteen joints/day. After smoking a joint, he suffered left arm and leg weakness, dizziness, and slurred speech and was admitted to hospital. He had suffered a stroke. A 32-year-old male, who smoked half a pack of tobacco a day for nine years and heavy cannabis use for fourteen years, also suffered a stroke after increasing his cannabis use. His urine and plasma were positive for cannabinoids.

I postulate that marked swings in blood pressure caused the strokes. Intravenous administration of THC produces systemic and ocular hypotension. Fluctuations in blood pressure have been well documented in healthy volunteers and marijuana users, and marijuana in particular can produce inconstant changes in pulse rate and blood pressure. Both of my patients were hypertensive without other risk factors for stroke at the time of hospital admission, although their blood pressure readings returned to normal in the weeks following the stroke with no medical treatment and abstinence from marijuana. I propose that the elevation of systemic blood pressure in my patients, who had both recently increased their amount of marijuana smoking, could be a reaction to cerebral vasospasm preceded by hypotension, which leads to cerebral infarction. It is also possible that tobacco smoking could have added to this problem.

Reference Number: 60403

MACINNES, D.C., AND K.M. MILLER. "Fatal Coronary Artery Thrombosis Associated with Cannabis Smoking." *Journal of the Royal College of General Practitioners*, 34: 575–76, 1984 (4 references)

Abstract: A 32-year-old man who had smoked marijuana that evening was admitted to hospital with chest pains. He later died and postmortem examination revealed a coronary thrombosis.

The smoking of cannabis causes changes in the cardiovascular system characteristic of stress. If cannabis were to increase the heart rate in a predisposed individual, it seems reasonable to suppose that angina could be precipitated, resulting perhaps in ischaemic damage. Furthermore, should psychoactive effects of the drug cause the patient to react in an atypical manner, he might not take suitable measures to relieve the angina, thus increasing the risk of damaging the myocardium or of precipitating an arrhythmia. The problem of cardiovascular disease associated with cannabis smoking will surely become more common as younger cannabis smokers begin to enter the risk years of ischaemic heart disease.

Reference Number: 60404

CANGA, Y., D. OSMONOV, M.B. KARATAS, G. DURMUS, E. ILHAN, AND V. KURBAS. "Cannabis: A Rare Trigger of Premature Myocardial Infarction." *Anadolu Kardiyol Derg*, 11: 271–75, 2011 (2 figures, 9 references)

Abstract: A 28-year-old man attended a clinic after chest pains lasting for twelve hours. He had been smoking cannabis three times a week for six years and twenty cigarettes a day for eight years. His last consumption of cannabis was two hours before the onset of pain. The patient had thrombosis and total occlusion of the proximal portion of the left anterior descending coronary artery. The clot was removed and the patient was discharged after six days in hospital.

We reported this case to attract attention that cannabis may be a much more common cause of myocardial infarction than is generally recognized. Clinicians should be more cautious about use of cannabis and similar illicit substances when taking medical histories.

Reference Number: 60405

MITTLEMAN, M.A., R.A. LEWIS, M. MACLURE, J.B. SHERWOOD, AND J.E. MULLER. "Triggering Myocardial Infarction by Marijuana." *Circulation*, 103: 2805–9, 2001 (2 tables, 1 figure, 35 references)

Abstract: A total of 2,624 male and 1,258 female patients (ages 20 to 92 years) were interviewed at sixty-four medical centres just after their myocardial infarction (MI) between 1989 and 1996. One hundred and twenty-four (116 male and 8 female) patients (3.2 percent) reported smoking marijuana within a year of their MI. Thirty-seven patients reported smoking cannabis within 24 hours and nine patients within one hour prior to their MI. The Relative Risk of MI was 4.8 times in the hour after smoking marijuana and declined rapidly thereafter. Marijuana is considered a rare trigger of acute MI but may pose an additional health risk in those patients with pre-existing artery disease.

Marijuana has several well-described effects on the cardiovascular system. For example, smoking marijuana is associated with a dose-dependent increase in resting heart rate of 20 percent to 100 percent. Blood pressure is typically increased in the supine position and postural hypotension, which is often symptomatic is common. Overall, there is a net increase in myocardial oxygen demand with a decrease in oxygen supply, which is due in part to an increase in carboxyhemoglobin; this results in a lower anginal threshold in patients with chronic stable angina. Furthermore, there are several reports of myocardial infarction occurring in close proximity to marijuana use in otherwise low-risk individuals.

Reference Number: 60406

FISHER, B.A.C., A. GHURAN, V. VADAMALAI, AND T.F. ANTONIOS. "Cardiovascular Complications Induced by Cannabis Smoking: A Case Report and Review of the Literature." *Emergency Medicine Journal*, 22: 679–80, 2005 (12 references)

Abstract: A 35-year-old woman attended hospital as a result of a one-month history of headaches. Her BP was 179/119 Hg. She smoked twenty cigarettes a day and marijuana. While at hospital, she smoked cannabis and approximately twenty to thirty minutes later, developed palpitations, chest pains, and shortness of breath. Her BP was 233/120 with a heartrate of 150 beats per minute. She was treated with flecainide IV. Her urine was positive for cannabinoids. She was prescribed amlodipine and atenolol, and two weeks post-discharge, her BP was 117/85.

> These recent reports confirm that cannabis use alone can result in cardiovascular complications. Furthermore, cannabis may often be used in combination with other recreational drugs, such as cocaine and amphetamines, which may have synergistic effects. A careful recreational drug history should always be elicited particularly when associated with unusual cardiovascular presentations and altered mental states.

Reference Number: 60407

BACHS, L., AND H. MORLAND. "Acute Cardiovascular Fatalities Following Cannabis Use." *Forensic Science International*, 124: 200–3, 2001 (1 table, 1 figure, 26 references)

Abstract: THC was detected in 180 blood samples out of 10,000 post-mortem cases analyzed at the National Institute for Forensic Toxicology in Norway between 1995 and 1999 by GC/MS. In 145 cases, there were other toxicological findings. In thirty-five cases, THC was the major toxicological finding and consisted of nine suicides, nine accidental deaths, and three homicides. Six cases were sudden deaths of unknown causes. The six victims were all male, ranging in age from 17 to 43 years, and had blood THC concentrations ranging from 2 to 22 ng/mL. An acute cardiovascular event was the probable cause of the deaths. CV effects are consistent with physiological findings after acute cannabis use. Significant tachycardia, conjunctival injection, increased limb flow and postural hypotension have been reported. After smoking a regular dose of cannabis (20 mg THC), the blood THC concentration will typically be 5 to 10 ng/mL one hour after smoking. There has been an age shift since the 1960s and 1970s, in that the cannabis user is now older and would presumably have a greater frequency of CV effects than the young cannabis user.

Table: Causes of Death Having Cannabis as the Major Toxicological Finding

Cause of Death	Number of Cases
Suicide	9
Accident	9
Somatic Illness	7
Sudden (probably cardiac)	6
Homicide	1

An acute cardiovascular event was the probable cause of death. In all cases, cannabis intake was documented by blood analyses. To our information, there were no heavy drug addicts in our material and the deceased individuals seemed to be occasional cannabis users.

Reference Number: 60408

BARBER, P.A., H.M. PRIDMORE, V. KRISHNAMURTHY, S. ROBERTS, D.A. SPRIGGS, K.N. CARTER, AND N.E. ANDERSON. "Cannabis, Ischemic Stroke and Transient Ischemic Attack. A Case Control Study." *Stroke,* 44: 2327–29, 2013 (2 tables, 12 references)

Abstract: Urine drug screens were conducted of 100 male and 60 female ischemic stroke/transient ischemic attack patients (ages 18 to 55 years) between 2009 and 2012 admitted to a New Zealand hospital. Twenty-five (15.6 percent) had positive urine cannabinoid tests. Patients with a positive screen were more likely to be men, Maori, and tobacco smokers and have worse outcomes at discharge. Thirteen of the 160 control patients (8.1 percent) test positive for cannabinoids. An increased OR for stroke/TIA was 2.3 times even after adjusting for age, gender, and ethnicity but not after adjusting for cigarette smoking.

Cannabis is generally perceived as having few serious adverse effects. This study suggests that this may not be the case.

Reference Number: 60409

HARTUNG, B., S. KAUFERSTEIN, S. RITZ-TIMME, AND T. DALRUP. "Sudden Unexpected Death under Acute Influence of Cannabis." *Forensic Science International*, 237: e11–e13, 2014 (31 references, 3 figures)

Abstract: In 2009 it was estimated that between 125- and 203-million people in the world population ages 15 to 64 years (2.8 to 4.5 percent), had consumed cannabis in the last year. There is little public awareness of potentially hazardous cardiovascular effects of cannabis. Smoking cannabis induces high heart rate, cardiac output, BP, and venous CoHB (compared to high nicotine cigarettes). Two males (ages 23 and 28 years) died unexpectedly under the acute influence of cannabis. The post-mortem blood THC concentrations were 5.2 and 1.9 ng/mL and blood 11-OH-THC concentrations were 1.8 and 0.8 ng/mL respectively.

The presented cases highlight the potentially hazardous cardiovascular effects of cannabis in putative healthy young persons.

Reference Number: 60410

LI, A.M., AND R. RASSEKH. "Hypotension Associated with Ingestion of Cannabinoids in Two Children with Cancer." *Canadian Medical Association Journal*, 188: 596–97, 2016 (10 references)

Abstract: A 2-year-old boy treated for cancer using chemotherapy was given (independent of medical advice) THC-CBD oil drops orally, increasing the dose from one drop to three drops three times a day. The child developed hypotension as his BP dropped to 50/30 mm Hg. The patient was administered a rapid 20 mL/kg bolus of normal saline and maintenance fluid support that corrected the hypotension. The parents insisted on continuing THC-CBD drops but at the lower doses, and the child's BP remained normal. A 4-year-old girl with a bone marrow transplant developed hypotension (80/33 mm Hg) after a few drops of THC-CBD oil. She was administered 20 mL/kg bolus and maintenance fluid therapy and her BP remained normal. The parents discontinued the THC-CBD drops.

The effects of cannabinoids in the pediatric population are not well described. In young children, the overarching symptom of cannabis toxicity appears to be somnolence or neurologic depression. Six cases of accidental marijuana ingestion by children seen in a children's hospital result in coma, all reversible with supportive care. Of the six children, one seventeen-month-old had documented hypotension. Other case reports have also described coma associated with cannabis toxicity in young children in the absence of reported blood pressure changes. A systematic review of the effects of cannabinoids for the control of chemotherapy-induced nausea showed a relative risk for hypotension of 2.23 (95 percent confidence interval 1.75 to 2.83) in thirty randomized trials involving adults and children given cannabinoids (nabilone, dronabinol or levonantgradol).

Reference Number: 60411

KOSIOR, D.A., K.J. FILLIPIAK, P. STOLARZ., AND G. OPOLSKI. "Paroxysmal Atrial Fibrillation in a Young Female Patient Following Marijuana Intoxication: A Case Report of Possible Association." *Medical Science Monitoring*. 6: 386–89, 2000 (2 figures, 18 references)

Abstract: A 24-year-old woman was admitted to hospital due to paroxysmal atrial fibrillation (140 bpm), nausea, vomiting, and unconsciousness within minutes after smoking a cannabis cigarette. The patient was administered IV fluids and metoprolol and recovered.

The occurrence of paroxysmal atrial fibrillation in a young patient without organic heart disease and its possible association with marijuana abuse might suggest the appearance of arrhythmias is quite often, especially in predisposed subjects.

Reference Number: 60412

LAZARO, I.J.S., L.A. BONET, M.J. SANCHO-TELLO, AND L. MARTINEZ-DOLZ. "Ventricular Tachycardia Due to Marijuana Use in a Heart Transplant Patient." *Revista Espanola Cardiologia*, 62: 459–61, 2009 (2 figures, 3 references)

Abstract: A 29-year-old man with a heart transplant for five years due to idiopathic dilated myocardiopathy. He developed sinus tachycardia and a vasospasm while smoking cannabis while he had a cardiac monitor.

We found it interesting in this case that, even though heart and coronary vessels were found denervated, they responded to the stimulus of marijuana, first with sinus tachycardia and later with a vasospasm.

Reference Number: 60413

ORSINI, J., C. BLAAK, S. RAJAYER, V. GURUNG, E. TAM, J. MORANTE, B. SHAMIAN, AND R. MALIK. "Prolonged Cardiac Arrest Complicating a Massive ST-Segment Elevation Myocardial Infarction Associated with Marijuana Consumption." *Journal of Community Hospital Internal Medicine Perspectives*, 6 pp, Sept. 7, 2016 (1 table, 3 figures, 40 references)

Abstract: Cannabis overdoses account for the third highest rate of illicit drug-related hospitalization after heroin and amphetamines. Approximately 18 to 37 percent of all acute recreational drug-related toxicity visits to ED are related to cannabis. A 40-year-old man developed clonic-tonic seizures followed by cardiac arrest while out at a party. The EMS arrived at the scene and a ventricular fibrillation rhythm was observed. Electrical cardioversion was delivered seven times. Urine toxicology screen was positive for THC but negative for other drugs. A LC-MS/MS urine assay was negative for synthetic cannabinoids. The serum ethyl alcohol concentration was 0.119 g/100mL. He was admitted to ICU but was brain dead. Autopsy revealed acute anterior-lateral septal posterior wall myocardial infarction with a mural thrombus in the left ventricle, as well as hypertensive and atherosclerotic heart disease as the main cause of death. A Table is provided listing thirty cases of cardiac arrests associated with marijuana consumption.

Despite the widespread use of marijuana, public awareness of the risk for potential cardiovascular complications remains low. Although uncommon, severe cardiovascular toxicity and death may develop from its consumption.

Reference Number: 60414

REECE, A.S., A. NORMAN, AND G.K. HULSE "Cannabis Exposure as an Interactive Cardiovascular Risk Factor and Accelerant of Organismal Ageing: A Longitudinal Study." *British Medical Journal Open*, 2016, 6 pp (2 tables, 3 figures, 61 references)

Abstract: Radial Arterial Pulse Wave Tonometry (RAPWT) was conducted on eleven cannabis only smokers, 504 tobacco only smokers, 114 tobacco and cannabis smokers, and 534 non-smokers in Brisbane, Australia. Arterial differences or vascular age was measured. The effect of cannabis use on vascular age was significant and was on average 11.84 percent in males. A dose-response relationship was demonstrated.

> Cannabis is an interactive cardiovascular risk factor (additional to tobacco and opioids), shows a prominent dose-response effect, and is robust to adjustment. Cannabis use is associated with an acceleration of the cardiovascular age, which is a powerful surrogate for the organismal-biological age. This likely underlies and bi-directionally interacts with its diverse toxicological profile and is of considerable public health and regulatory importance.

Reference Number: 60415

MATEO, I., A. PINEDO, M. GOMEZ-BELDARRAIN, J.M. BASTERRETEXA, AND J.C. GARCIA-MANCO. "Recurrent Stroke Associated with Cannabis Use." *Journal Neural Neurosurgery Psychiatry*, 76: 435–37, 2005 (1 figure, 27 references)

Abstract: A 36-year-old man suffered three ischaemic strokes over approximately 2.5 years after heavy hashish consumption.

> Establishing a causal relationship between drug consumption and stroke is not easy, and this relationship is usually based on a temporal link between drug use and the occurrence of stroke in young patients without any other vascular risk factors. Because cannabis use is so widespread, this could represent a causal relationship; in fact, due to their high liposolubility and persistence in fatty tissues, cannabis metabolites persist in urine for weeks and therefore their presence in a patient's stroke could merely represent prior use. This patient's case, however, is exceptional in that there was a close and clear-cut temporal relationship between drug intake and stroke, which occurred on three separate occasions. The repetition of events after exposure to cannabis previously undescribed, suggests a role for cannabis in this patient's stroke. A -cohol ingestion could also have contributed. The relationship between alcohol and ischaemic stroke is complex and whether binge drinking is associated with stroke is controversial. Nevertheless, the role of a coho in this patient's strokes was probably secondary, as he did not consume large amounts of the drug nor much higher levels than he was usec to consuming occasionally on weekends. However, hashish is an illega

drug in Spain, not subject to any regulation or control, and therefore other toxic substances could have been added during its manufacture.

Reference Number: 60416

TROJAK, B., S. LECLERQ, V. MEILLE, C. KHOUMRI, J-C. CHAUVET-GELINIER, M. GIROUD, B. BONIN, AND A. GISSELMANN. "Stroke with Neuropsychiatric Sequelae after Cannabis Use in Man: A Case Report." *Journal of Medical Case Reports,* 5: 264, 4 pp, 2011 (2 figures, 6 references)

Abstract: A 24-year-old male chronic cannabis user (up to five joints a day for four years) was found deeply unconscious twelve hours after he had fallen from a first-floor balcony. Before the fall, he had smoked ten joints that evening. He was unconscious for four days and an MRI showed bilateral multiple ischemic infarcts, which were not consistent with traumatic contusions. Upon regaining consciousness, he had behavioural disorders and a generalized clonic-tonic seizure.

Over the past few years, ischemic stroke associated with cannabis use has been reported in the literature. Typically, this accident concerns young, frequent cannabis smokers and usually occurs following cannabis consumption with simultaneous intake of alcohol, which is also thought to play a role in the cerebrovascular event. In most case reports, the outcome of the neurovascular event was favourable and the patients rapidly recovered from stroke within hours or a few days. Here we report the case of a young man who presented to our hospital with stroke that led to four days of deep coma followed by neuropsychiatric sequelae. Moreover, this stroke occurred in the absence of alcohol intoxication.

Reference Number: 60417

SATTOUT, A.H., AND M.F. NICOL. "Cardiac Arrest Following Cannabis Use: A Case Report." *Cases Journal,* 2: 208 3 pp, 2009 (11 references)

Abstract: A 15-year-old male suffered a cardiac arrest following use of alcohol and cannabis with friends. Paramedics arrived and CPR was in progress. After a single DC shock, a sinus rhythm was restored. At the hospital, the patient was intubated and ventilated. Urine drug screen was positive for THC but negative for other drugs. The patient suffered from ADHD and a history of cocaine and ecstasy abuse.

Recreational use of cannabis will remain on the rise with a number of potentially serious if not fatal consequences.

Reference Number: 60418

WOLFF, V., V. LAUER., O. ROUYER, F. SELLAL., N. MEYER, J.S. RAUL, C. SABOURDY, F. BOUJAN., C. JAHN, R. BEAUJEUX, AND C. MARESCAUX. "Cannabis Use, Ischemic Stroke, and Multifocal Intracranial Vasoconstriction. A Prospective Study in 48 Consecutive Young Patients." *Stroke*, 42: 1778–80, 2011 (1 table, 1 figure, 8 references)

Abstract: This study was conducted of forty-eight consecutive young patients (< 45 years of age) with acute ischemic stroke between 2005 and 2007. Urine drug screening was conducted and thirteen were positive for cannabinoids, all of whom admitted to smoking marijuana. Ten of the eleven patients with multifocal intracranial stenosis were cannabis users. During the days before the stroke, all binged on cannabis. Six patients who stopped cannabis use after the stroke had favourable outcomes.

In regard to this study, we have to conclude that cannabis is not as harmless as was thought and cerebrovascular risk when consumed is probably underestimated.

Reference Number: 60419

JOUANJUS, E., M. LAPEYRE-MESTRE, J. MICALLEF, J., ET AL. "Cannabis Use: Signal of Increasing Risk of Serious Cardiovascular Disorders." *Journal of the American Heart Association*, 3: 7 pp, 2014 (2 tables, 48 references)

Abstract: There were 1,979 reports of adverse cannabis-related events in French hospitals between 2006 and 2010, of which thirty-five were cardiovascular complications. The percentage of cannabis-related cardiovascular events increased from 1.1 percent in 2006 to 3.6 percent in 2010 of all cannabis-related complications. The cannabis-related cardiovascular event patients were mostly men (86 percent) with an average age of 34 years. In nine cases, the CV event lead to death.

Table: **Total Number of Adverse Cannabis-Related Events Reported by French Hospitals between 2006 and 2010 and Percent Related to Cardiovascular Complications**

Year	Number of Adverse Cannabis-Related Events	% of Adverse Cannabis Event Related to Cardiovascular Complications
2006	468	1.1%
2007	452	1.1%
2008	415	1.4%
2009	335	2.4%
2010	309	3.6%
Total	1979	1.8%

Source: Adapted from Jouanjus et al, 2014

Increased reporting of cardiovascular complications related to cannabis and their extreme seriousness (with a death rate of 25.6 percent) indicate cannabis as a possible risk factor for cardiovascular disease in young adults in line with previous findings. Given that cannabis is perceived to be harmless by the general public and that legalization of its use is debated, data concerning its danger must be widely disseminated. Practitioners should be aware that cannabis may be a potential triggering factor for cardiovascular complications in young people.

Reference Number: 60420

HACKAM, D.G. "Cannabis and Stroke. Systematic Appraisal of Case Reports." *Stroke*, 46: 852–56, 2015 (1 figure, 39 references)

Abstract: A review was conducted of thirty-four case reports involving sixty-four patients on the effect of cannabis use on the risk of strokes. Most cases (81 percent) showed a temporal relationship between cannabis use and stroke. In 70 percent of the cases, other sources except for cannabis use were excluded. In about 22 percent of the patients, another stroke occurred after re-exposure to cannabis. Other risk factors included tobacco and alcohol consumption (34 percent and 11 percent respectively).

This review suggests that the case reports linking cannabis with acute stroke are relatively robust, with high rates of temporality, exclusion of other causes of stroke, and substantial stroke recurrence in patients who resumed cannabis consumption during follow-up. In half, there were concomitant risk factors, such as tobacco and alcohol consumption.

Reference Number: 60421

GUNAWARDENA, M.D.V.M., S. RAJAPKSE, J. HERATH, AND N. AMARASENA. "Myocardial Infarction Following Cannabis Induced Coronary Vasospasm." *British Medical Journal Case Report* Nov 12: 3 pp, 2014 (17 references)

Abstract: A 29-year-old male heavy smoker presented to hospital with chest pains after smoking a potent form of marijuana known as Kerala Ganja or KG. He also had a tablet of LSD forty-eight hours prior. He was diagnosed with acute myocardial infarction and treated.

> Kerala Ganja, produced in Kerala, India, is a more potent preparation than conventional marijuana. Marijuana is a potential trigger for acute coronary syndrome in young patients without cardiac risk factors. Marijuana can cause coronary vasospasms. Kerala Ganja may have more potent vasospastic effects than marijuana. A history of substance abuse should be actively sought in patients presenting with acute coronary syndrome and normal coronary arteries.

Reference Number: 60422

YURTDAS, M., AND M.K. AYDIN. "Acute Myocardial Infarction in a Young Man; Fatal Blow of the Marijuana: A Case Report." *Korean Circulation Journal*, 5 pp, 2012 (1 table, 19 references)

Abstract: A 26-year-old man was admitted to hospital due to chest pain radiating to both arms for two hours. He smoked cannabis twice a week for eight years and his last consumption was three hours before the onset of symptoms. He also smoked ten to fifteen tobacco cigarettes a day. A large blood clot was detected in his right coronary artery. After treatment and a stent operation, he was released after four days. A table lists thirteen acute myocardial infarctions (AMI) associated with cannabis use, mainly in men in their thirties. One mechanism of cannabis-associated AMI is that its use may cause atrial fibrillation, which may result in clot formation.

> In conclusion, our report deals with the importance of awareness of the marijuana that may give rise to AMI, through the mechanisms discussed above, in apparently healthy young persons who occasionally or habitually use this drug.

Reference Number: 60423

BARANCHUK, A., A.M. JOHRI, C.S. SIMPSON, M. METHOT, AND D.P. REDFEARN. "Ventricular Fibrillation Triggered by Marijuana Use in a Patient with Ischemic Cardiomyopathy: A Case Report." *Cases Journal*, 1: 373 (4 pp), 2008 (1 table, 1 figure, 8 references)

Abstract: A 60-year-old male chronic cannabis user presented to hospital with a left eye orbital rupture sustained during a fall due to syncope shortly after smoking four bongs (rather than the usual two to three) of marijuana. He had a larger anterior myocardial infarction, severe three-vessel coronary artery disease and had an implantable cardioverter defibrillator (ICD). The ICD detected a ventricular fibrillation just before the fall and gave a 35 joules shock to stop it. He had received a similar shock several months earlier when he smoked four bongs.

Although marijuana is the most frequently used illicit drug worldwide, its effects on the cardiovascular system remains controversial. In our case, the patient described experiencing two syncopal events, each occurring after more than his usual marijuana exposure. Although this observation does not prove a cause-and-effect relationship, the timing of the events suggests that dose-dependent marijuana exposure may have led to ventricular fibrillation in this patient with coronary artery disease and structural heart disease. We hypothesize that the arrhythmic event was triggered by excessive catecholamine release.

Reference Number: 60424

JEHANGIR, W., M. STANTON, R. KHAN, P. SAHGAL, AND A. YOUSIF. "Did Cannabis Precipitate an STEMI in a Young Woman?" *Cardiology Research*, 6: 283–85, 2015 (2 figures, 5 references)

Abstract: A 27-year-old presented at hospital with a sudden onset of severe retrosternal pain. She had a history of cigarette smoking at age 9 years and frequent cannabis use. Her urine toxicology was positive for cannabinoids. She had an ST-segment myocardial infarction (STEMI)

Due to increasing support of the use of cannabis for medical and recreational purposes, it has become increasingly important to understand not only the medical benefits, but also the adverse consequences of its administration. This case report is another piece of evidence among others that is highlighting the potential cardiovascular effects of cannabis. Several case reports have emerged in recent years that demonstrate cannabis-induced cardiovascular events, such as myocardial infarction, arrhythmias, and sudden cardiovascular death. In vitro studies investigating the role of THC in platelet activation have demonstrated a potential pathophysiological insight into the role of cannabis in cardiovascular events. Further investigations into the association between cannabis use and cardiovascular events are warranted in order to fully appreciate the consequences of cannabis usage, both medical and recreational.

6.05 DEPENDENCE/CANNABIS USE DISORDER (CUD)

Cannabis is not a harmless drug as it does cause dependence, although it doesn't appear to be as severe for most people as tobacco or alcohol. Cannabis dependence occurs in about 11 percent of lifetime users with an increased risk for adolescents and daily users (60513). Approximately 4.3-million Americans are classified as having Cannabis Use Disorder (CUD), more than two times the number of cocaine and heroin abusers combined (60502). Some of the predictors for CUD is male gender, nicotine dependence, and high alcohol use (60503, 60505), and living alone (60509). Recreational cannabis users prefer high potency skunk over other types of cannabis, even though they admit it causes more memory impairment and paranoia than other types (60504).

The *Diagnostic and Statistical Manual of Mental Disorders* of the American Psychiatric Association (DSM-V) defines Cannabis Use Disorder (CUD) as a "problematic pattern of cannabis use leading to clinically significant impairment or distress" and lists eleven criteria, of which at least two are required to be defined as CUD, as follows:

- Tolerance
- Withdrawal
- Taken in larger amounts or over a longer period than intended
- Persistent desire or unsuccessful efforts to cut down or control cannabis use
- A great deal of time is spent in activities necessary to obtain cannabis, use cannabis, or recover from its effects
- Important social, occupational, or recreational activities are given up or reduced because of cannabis use

- Continued cannabis use, despite having persistent or recurrent social or interpersonal problems caused or exacerbated by the effects of cannabis
- Continued cannabis use, despite knowledge of having a persistent or recurrent physical or psychological problem that is likely to have been caused or exacerbated by cannabis
- Recurrent cannabis use in physically hazardous situations
- Recurrent cannabis use resulting in a failure to fulfill major role obligations at work, school, or home
- Craving or a strong desire or urge to use cannabis (60507)

The APA defines the severity of CUD as mild (2-3 criteria), moderate (4-5 criteria) or severe (6+ criteria). The storage of THC in the fatty tissues and its slow release results in a delayed or slower onset of withdrawal symptoms, unlike that which occurs for nicotine or alcohol, which are water soluble (60502). The use of tobacco and cannabis together causes more severe symptoms of CUD (60503, 60515). Ninety-five percent of all risky cannabis users were also risky users of alcohol and/or tobacco (60501).

The most common self-reported reason for attempting to quit or reduce cannabis use was "to save money," followed closely by "I didn't want to set a bad example for children," and "there is drug testing where I work" (60512).

In some cases, cannabis overdose can be confused with an opioid overdose, and the administration of naloxone has been found to assist in cannabis overdose cases as well (60621).

Reference Number: 60501

GMEL, G., J. GAUME, C. WILLI, P-A. MICHAUD, J. CORNUZ, AND J-B. DAEPPEN. "Challenging the "Inoffensiveness" of Regular Cannabis Use by Its Associations with Other Current Risky Substance Use: A Census of 20-Year-Old Swiss Men." *International Journal of Environmental Research and Public Health*, 7: 46–59, 2010 (4 tables, 1 figure, 54 references)

Abstract: A survey of 3,537 male Swiss army recruits (mean age 20 years) was conducted in 2007 regarding the occurrence of risky alcohol and tobacco use among risky cannabis users. Risky cannabis use was defined as at least twice weekly, risky tobacco use as daily smoking, and risky alcohol use as six or more drinks more than once a month or more than twenty drinks per week. Seventeen percent of all recruits were risky cannabis users but only 0.4 percent exclusively used cannabis. Ninety-five percent of all risky cannabis users also were risky users of alcohol and/or tobacco. Among non-risky alcohol users, the odds ratio (OR) for risky tobacco use (daily smoking) increases from one to more than thirteen times with risky cannabis use. Risky cannabis use was more strongly associated with risky alcohol use as the OR for risky alcohol use rose from 1 to 4.1 times when there was risky cannabis use.

Cannabis use is sometimes seen as a relatively inoffensive or harmless substance compared to legal substances such as tobacco and alcohol, but risky users appear to be more prone to engaging in other risky behaviours. The present study reveals that in the past six months, 95 percent of the subjects used either tobacco or alcohol in a risky way, and nearly two-thirds of them did both. Tobacco and alcohol use have been shown to be two of the three main risk factors for mortality and morbidity in developed societies. This is a major public health concern, since 17.2 percent of all young Swiss francophone men use cannabis in a risky way (i.e., at least twice per week).

Reference Number: 60502

RAMESH, D., J.E. SCHLOSBURG, J.M. WIEBELHAUS, AND A.H. LICHTMAN. "Marijuana Dependence: Not Just Smoke and Mirrors." *Institute for Laboratory Animal Research Journal*, 52: 295–308, 2011 (2 tables, 132 references)

Abstract: A detailed review of marijuana dependence as a result of prolonged and repeated administrations of THC in humans and laboratory animals is presented. The long half-life and other pharmacokinetic properties of THC results in a delayed expression of withdrawal symptoms. The number of Americans classified as having cannabis use disorder is 4.3 million, more than two times the number of cocaine and heroin abusers combined, even though 3 to 4 percent of cannabis users develop dependence, compared to 15 to 25 percent for cocaine.

Research has firmly established the existence of a clinically significant and distinct cannabis withdrawal syndrome characterized by anger, aggression, irritability, anxiety, or nervousness, decreased appetite or weight loss, restlessness, and sleep difficulties with strange dreams. Dependent individuals may continue to use marijuana to avoid these and other withdrawal symptoms. Laboratory animal models of cannabinoid withdrawal have been useful not only for characterizing and investigating the neurobiology of cannabinoid dependence, but also for assessing potential pharmacological agents for therapeutic use. However, not all positive results in preclinical testing translate to clinical success, probably because of the wide variety of symptoms, both physical and psychological, observed in humans.

Reference Number: 60503

BROOK, J.S., J.Y. LEE, S.J. FINCH, J. KOPPEL, AND D.W. BROOK. "Psychosocial Factors Related to Cannabis Use Disorders." *Substance Abuse*, 32: 242–51, 2011 (3 tables, 1 figure, 59 references)

Abstract: The association between various psychosocial factors and the risk of developing cannabis use disorder (CUD) was determined in 838 participants from New York City at the mean ages of 14.1, 19.2, 24.5, and 29.2 years. The risk for CUD was cumulative with the increasing number of psychosocial factors. Older adults were less likely to have CUD than younger adults.

Table: Predictors and Bivariate Odds Ratio (OR) of Cannabis Use Disorder at Mean Age of 29.2 Years.

Predictors of CUDs	Odds Ratio of CUD
Gender (male)	3.9 X
Impulsivity	1.5 X
Arguments with partner	1.4 X
Frequent skipping work	1.6 X
Nicotine dependence	1.6 X
High alcohol use	2.7 X
Problems with cannabis use	5.1 X

Source: Adapted from Brook et al, 2011

Cannabis abuse and dependence are related to indices of poor psychological well-being, such as symptoms of anxiety, depression, and psychosis. Frequent and/or long-term cannabis use, as is typical of cannabis use disorders (CUDs), is associated with measures of impaired physical well-being, such as upper respiratory symptoms. Given the harmful effects of CUDs, there is a clear public health imperative to identify the factors leading and contributing to their development and persistence. CUDs do not arise from a limited set of underlying causes, but out of a constellation of factors, across multiple domains. In particular, variables in the domains of personality attributes, family, peer, work, neighbourhood, and substance use all contribute to cannabis use and dependence. The prevalence of CUDs varies across demographic groups. In particular, males and younger adults (e.g., between the ages of 18 and 29 years) demonstrate higher rates of CUDs than females and older adults. As regards personality attributes, several recent longitudinal studies have found that personality traits associated with a syndrome of under-control, including impulsivity, disinhibition, and aggression, are related to the subsequent development of CUDs.

Reference Number: 60504

FREEMAN, T.P., AND A.R. WINSTOCK. "Examining the Profile of High-Potency Cannabis and Its Association with the Severity of Cannabis Dependence." *Psychological Medicine*, 45: 3181–89, 2015 (2 tables, 2 figures, 36 references)

Abstract: An on-line drug survey was conducted in Britain on cannabis use in 2,514 persons (mean age 24.24 years). Approximately 73 percent reported using skunk cannabis last year, 69 percent cannabis, and 59 percent resin. Skunk was classified by its users as giving the best high, the most paranoia, and memory impairment, and was the most preferred type and most available.

Table: Characteristics of Three Types of Marijuana as Rated by Cannabis Users (Percent)

Characteristic	Skunk	Other Marijuana Types	Resin
Best High	70%	12%	18%
Most Paranoid	78%	8%	14%
Most Memory Impairment	81%	4%	15%
Preferred Type	59%	20%	21%
Most Value for Money	35%	18%	47%

Source: Adapted from Freeman and Winstock, 2015

Use of high potency cannabis (skunk) is associated with an increased severity of dependence, especially in young people. Skunk is also rated as having stronger effects on memory impairment and paranoia than other types of cannabis but, at the same time, it produces the best high and is user's preferred type.

Reference Number: 60505

HASIN, D.S., T.D. SAHA, B.T. KERRIDGE, R.B. GOLDSTEIN, S.P. CHOU, H. ZHANG, J. JUNG, R.P. PICKERING, W.J. RUAN, S.M. SMITH, B. HUANG, AND B.F. GRANT. "Prevalence of Marijuana Use Disorder in the United States between 2001 and 2002 and 2012 and 2013." *Journal of the American Medical Association Psychiatry*, 72: 19 pp, December 2015 (3 tables, 89 references)

Abstract: The past year rate of cannabis use and cannabis use disorder (CUD) was determined in two US epidemiological studies in 2001 to 2002 (43,093 participants) and 2012 to 2013 (36,309 participants). The past year's prevalence of cannabis use was 4.1 percent in 2001 to 2002 and 9.5 percent in 2012 to 2013. The prevalence of DSM-IV CUD was 1.5 percent in 2001 to 2002 and increased to 2.9 percent in 2012 to 2013. The prevalence of CUD in cannabis users decreased from 35.6 percent to 30.6 percent.

In summary, while many in the United States think prohibition of recreational marijuana should be ended, this study and others suggest caution and the need for public education about the potential harms in marijuana use, including the risk for addiction. As is the case with alcohol, many individuals can use marijuana without becoming addicted. However, the clear risk for marijuana use disorders among users (approximately 30 percent) suggests that as the number of US users grows, so will the number of those experiencing problems related to such use. This information is important to convey in a balanced manner to health care professionals, policy-makers, and the public.

Reference Number: 60506

COHEN, N.L., A.J. HEINZ, M. ILGEN, AND M.O. BONN-MILLER. "Pain, Cannabis Species and Cannabis Use Disorders." *Journal of Studies on Alcohol and Drugs*, 77: 515–20, 2016 (1 table, 19 references)

Abstract: A study was conducted of 163 medical cannabis users (77 percent male) at a cannabis dispensary in California. The participants were heavy users, with 67 percent reporting use of cannabis at least thirty times in the last month. The preferred method of use was vaporizers (31 percent), joints or blunts (22 percent), pipes (22 percent), water pipes (16 percent), and oral ingestion (8 percent). The mean THC concentration in indica, sativa, and hybrid marijuana was 15.8 percent, 15.9 percent, and 20.8 percent respectively. The majority of individuals used cannabis for chronic pain relief. Individuals who used cannabis for chronic pain relief used the indica cannabis strain more often and had fewer cannabis use problems than those who did not use it for pain.

Findings also indicated that individuals who used cannabis for chronic pain were more likely to choose indica over sativa and the use of indica was associated with fewer cannabis problems. The observed pattern is in line with anecdotal evidence and previous research illustrating a preference for indica among individuals living with various chronic pain conditions.

Reference Number: 60507

FARMER, R.F., D.B. KOSTY, J.R. SEELEY, S.C. DUNCAN, M.T. LYNSKEY, P. ROHDE, D.N. KLEIN, AND P.M. LEWINSOHN. "Natural Course of Cannabis Use Disorders." *Psychological Medicine*, 45: 63–72, 2015 (1 table, 3 figures, 58 references)

Abstract: Cannabis Use Disorder (CUD) was assessed in 816 participants (59 percent female) between the ages of 16 and 30 years in the Oregon Adolescent Depression Project (OADP). The weighted lifetime prevalence of CUDs was 19.1 percent at an average onset age of 18.6 years. Of those diagnosed with a CUD episode, 81.8 percent eventually achieved recovery. The recurrence rate was 27.7 percent before the age of 30 years, and the mean time to recurrence was 46.1 months. Women achieved recovery significantly faster than men.

CUDs are relatively common, affecting about one in five persons in the OADP sample prior to age 30. Eventual recovery from index CUD episodes is the norm, although about 30 percent of those with a CUD exhibit a generally persistent pattern of problematic use extending sever years or longer.

Reference Number: 60508

BUCHOWSKI, M.S., N.N. MEADE, E. CHARBONEAU, S. PARK, M.S. DIETRICH, R.L. COWAN, AND P.R. MARTIN. "Aerobic Exercise Training Reduces Cannabis Craving and Use in Non-Treatment Seeking Cannabis-Dependent Adults." *PLOS ONE*, 6: e17465 (6 pp), 2011 (1 table, 3 figures, 39 references)

Abstract: Daily cannabis use and measures of craving for the drug were determined for one week prior to and during a daily thirty-minute treadmill training and during a two week follow-up in twelve non-treatment-seeking cannabis dependent adults. The average number of daily joints decreased from 5.9 before the aerobic exercise to 2.8 joints during the exercise and increased to 4.1 joints daily in the follow-up period.

> In summary, we found that participation in a supervised moderate exercise program could decrease cannabis use in association with reduced cannabis cue-induced craving in cannabis-dependent young adults who were not seeking treatment. Taken together, adequately powered controlled trial is warranted to test the efficacy of moderate exercise as a component of treatment for cannabis dependence under real-world conditions.

Reference Number: 60509

VAN DER POL, P., N. LIEBREGTS, R. DE GRAAF., D.J. KORF, W. VAN DEN BRINK, AND M. VAN LAAR. "Predicting the Transition from Frequent Cannabis Use to Cannabis Dependence: A Three-Year Prospective Study." *Drug and Alcohol Dependence*, 133: 352–59, 2013 (4 tables, 73 references)

Abstract: Frequent cannabis users are at a greater risk of becoming dependent on it. About 20 to 50 percent of daily cannabis users are dependent. This study followed 600 frequent cannabis users (ages 18 to 30 years) at 18 months and 36 months to determine the risk factors in developing cannabis dependence. Initially only 269 frequent cannabis users without prior cannabis were assessed and 199 completed the three-year evaluation. Over the three years, 73 frequent cannabis users developed dependence (37.2 percent). The risk factors of developing cannabis dependence for frequent cannabis users were different from the general population.

Table: Risk Factors of Developing Cannabis Dependence in Frequent Cannabis Users

Risk Factor	Odds Ratio of Developing Cannabis Dependence
Living alone	3.38 X
Using cannabis (also) during daytime	1.79 X
No pauses, smoking whole joint	1.84 X
Major financial crisis	2.44 X
Separation from someone important	2.14 X

Source: Adapted from van der Pol et al, 2013

In summary, our findings imply that young adult non-dependent frequent cannabis users are at considerable risk (37 percent) to develop cannabis dependence in the near future, especially when they show the following risk factors: CUD symptoms, coping motives for their (frequent) use of cannabis, acute stressful negative life events, and living alone. Unexpectedly, the actual level of cannabis exposure and the presence of stable vulnerability factors seem to be less significant.

Reference Number: 60510

STRASHNY, A. "Marijuana Admissions to Substance Abuse Treatment Aged 18 to 30: Early vs. Adult Initiation." *Substance Abuse and Mental Health Services Administration, The CBHSQ Report*, August 13, 2013, 7 pp (2 tables, 4 figures, 6 references)

Abstract: In 2010, there were 687,531 substance abuse admissions ages 18 to 30 years of age in the US. Of those, 340,412 were due to marijuana.

Research increasingly confirms that marijuana use is harmful. Acute symptoms of marijuana intoxication include impaired short-term memory, attention, judgment, and cognitive function, as well as increased heart rate. Symptoms that can persist for weeks after the immediate effects of marijuana have worn off include insomnia and, possibly, impaired memory and learning. When continued over years, a pattern of heavy, daily, or almost daily use can increase some health risks, including marijuana dependence, chronic cough, or respiratory impairment, cardiovascular disease, and adverse effects on psychosocial development and mental health.

Reference Number: 60511

FISCHER, B., S. IMTIAZ, K. RUDZINSKI, AND J. REHM "Crude Estimates of Cannabis-Attributable Mortality and Morbidity in Canada: Implications for Public Health Focused Intervention Priorities." *Journal of Public Health*, 38: 183–88, 2015 (66 references)

Abstract: A comparative risk assessment was conducted for cannabis-related morbidity and mortality for motor vehicle collisions, use disorders, mental health (psychosis), and lung cancer in Canada. It is estimated that 4 to 12 percent of MVA fatalities and/or injuries involve cannabis. Based on recent Canadian data, 1.3 percent of the general adult population have cannabis use disorder (CUD), which corresponds to 380,000 Canadians, of whom 33,000 were treated in Ontario in 2012–2013. It is estimated that 106 to 186 cannabis-attributable schizophrenia cases occur in Canada annually. It is also estimated that 130 to 280 lung cancer deaths occurred in Canada due to cannabis.

> Main findings are that the largest number of cases with cannabis-related harm consequences appears to occur through motor vehicle accidents and use disorders, whereas the number of cases of lung cancer and psychosis occur at a markedly smaller scale. In addition, only two of the domains — motor vehicle accidents and lung cancer — result in mortality outcomes. Based on these considerations, we conclude, based on our estimate, that motor vehicle accidents and use disorders form the majority of instances of cannabis-attributable disease burden in Canada, whereas lung cancer — despite a limited amount of mortality in this category — and psychosis lead to substantially less extensive burdens.

Reference Number: 60512

PACEK, L.R., AND VANDREY, R. "Cannabis Use History and Characteristics of Quit Attempts: A Comparison Study of Treatment-Seeking and Non-Treatment-Seeking Cannabis Users." *Experimental and Clinical Psychopharmacology*, 22: 517–23, 2014 (5 tables, 30 references)

Abstract: A detailed survey was conducted on 74 cannabis users who wanted to quit/reduce their cannabis use and were seeking formal treatment and 131 who did not, between 2008 and 2013. Treatment seekers were more likely to be female (43 percent vs 29 percent), older (33.4 years vs 29.7 years), and have longer cannabis histories. Treatment seekers had on average 7.4 quit attempts compared to 4.3 for non-treatment seekers. The longest quit time was 6.7 days for non-treatment seeking and 292.2 days for treatment seekers.

Table: Percentage of Self-Reported Reasons for Making a Quit Attempt for Non-Treatment-Seeking and Treatment-Seeking Subjects

Reason to Quit	Non-Treatment Seeking (%)	Treatment Seeking (%)
To save money	72.6%	87.7%
To prove to myself that I wasn't addicted	56.4%	67.1%

Reason to Quit	Non-Treatment Seeking (%)	Treatment Seeking (%)
To feel in control of my life	47.6%	71.2%
I don't want to be a bad example for children	47.6%	68.5%
To have more energy	42.7%	74.0%
To get more things done during the day	43.5%	64.4%
There is drug testing where I work	41.9%	52.0%
So that my hair and clothes won't smell like marijuana	26.6%	46.6%
To avoid burning holes in clothes/furniture	19.5%	27.4%

Source: Adapted from Pacek and Vandrey, 2014

Treatment seekers reported significantly more withdrawal symptoms during abstinence, more reasons for attempting to quit, and utilized a greater number of coping strategies during their most difficult quit attempt, but substance use characteristics between groups were similar. These findings, taken together, potentially characterized treatment-seeking cannabis users as being more motivated to attempt to quit using cannabis than non-treatment-seeking participants, but having more difficulty doing so.

Reference Number: 60513

MONTANARI, L., B. GUARITA, J. MOUNTENEY, AND N. ZIPFEL. "Cannabis Use among People Entering Drug Treatment in Europe: A Growing Phenomenon?" *European Addiction Research*, 23: 113–21, 2017 (1 table, 2 figures, 34 references)

Abstract: The trends in first time drug treatment entry for cannabis-related problems were determined in twenty-two European countries between 2003 and 2014. In 2014 an estimated 83-million Europeans (25 percent), ages 15 to 64 years, had used cannabis at least once in their lifetime. Around 1 percent of Europeans were daily or nearly daily cannabis users. Cannabis dependence occurs in about 11 percent of lifetime users with an increased risk for adolescents and daily users. Twenty-nine percent of all drug treatment admissions are for cannabis. The greatest number of first-time cannabis treatment admissions occurred in the UK, Germany, Spain, France, and Italy.

Table: **Number of First-Time Cannabis Treatment Admissions in Europe between 2003 and 2014**

Country	2003	2007	2011	2014
France	–	5,703	7,193	6,897
Germany	5,516	9,708	10,236	14,458
Ireland	982	696	1,367	1,696
Italy	–	5,538	5,781	5,267
Portugal	–	447	457	690
Spain	–	4,619	9,736	–
The Netherlands	1,635	2,732	4,034	3,429
The United Kingdom	5,289	12,251	15,107	15,895

Source: Adapted from Montanari et al, 2017

This paper has provided evidence of an increase in the overall treatment demand for cannabis-related problems in Europe with differentiated trends evident at the national level. It is apparent that many important questions central to the current policy debate remain unanswered. Nevertheless, people with cannabis-related problems represent an increasing proportion of treatment demands in specialized facilities and their needs are significantly different when compared to the needs of opioid clients, which have historically been the focus of public health interventions. National differences and contextual factors remain to be investigated, and improving the understanding of the profiles and needs of different sub-populations of cannabis clients is an important future research priority.

Reference Number: 60514

VAN DER POL, P., N. LIEBREGTS, T. BRUNT, J. VAN AMSTERDAM., R. DE GRAFF, D.J. KORF, W. VAN DEN BRINK, AND M. VAN LAAR. "Cross-Sectional and Prospective Relation of Cannabis Potency, Dosing and Smoking Behavior with Cannabis Dependence: An Ecological Study." *Addiction*, 9 pp, 2014 (4 tables, 2 figures, 30 references)

Abstract: The smoking behaviours and cannabis potency of the joint smoked were determined in a naturalistic setting in seventy-three male and twenty-three female Dutch heavy cannabis users. The users rolled their own joint and mixed in tobacco and then smoked it. The percent THC in the cannabis samples ranged between 1.1 to 24.7 percent (mean 12.4 percent) and when mixed with tobacco in a joint, it ranged between

0.24 to 15.7 percent (mean 3.6 percent). The total number of puffs ranged from three to forty and the total puff volume ranged from 0.15 to 2.54 litres. There was a repeat of these tests and measures 1.5 years later. Between the assessments, the number of dependence symptoms increased in one-third, decreased in one-third, and remained stable in one-third of the subjects. The severity (progression) of cannabis dependence was predicted by total puff volume, decrease in puff volume, and decrease in puff duration during the course of smoking joints, but not by the total number of puffs.

> Although experienced young adult cannabis users with a preference for stronger joints titrated their THC exposure to some extent by inhaling less smoke, in general, more potent cannabis was used in higher dosages, leading to a higher THC exposure compared to users preferring lower potency cannabis.

Reference Number: 60515

REAM, G.L., E. BENOIT, B.D. JOHNSON, AND E. DUNLAP. "Smoking Tobacco Along with Marijuana Increases Symptoms of Cannabis Dependence." *Drug and Alcohol Dependence*, 95: 199–208, 2008 (4 tables, 1 figure, 43 references)

Abstract: Smoking blunts and "chasing" marijuana with tobacco are popular among urban youth. Blunts are made from inexpensive cigars in which the tobacco is removed and replaced with about 1.5 grams of cannabis (about three joints), resulting in the concurrent consumption of nicotine and cannabinoids. A survey was conducted of 481 cannabis users in New York City who were younger than 35 years of age, on tobacco and cannabis use and cannabis dependence symptoms.

Table: Odds Ratio of Cannabis Dependence Symptoms Based on Concurrent Tobacco/Cannabis Use

	Spent more time using than intended	Neglected usual responsibilities	Wanted to cut down but could not	Preoccupied with use	Need more for desired effect
Used blunts in last 30 days	1.04 X	1.03 X	1.01 X	1.04 X	1.05 X

	Spent more time using than intended	Neglected usual responsibilities	Wanted to cut down but could not	Preoccupied with use	Need more for desired effect
Often chase marijuana/ tobacco	1.31 X	1.36 X	1.24 X	1.36 X	1.36 X

Source: Adapted from Ram et al, 2008

These data confirm that marijuana use practices of smoking blunts and chasing marijuana with tobacco uniquely contribute to cannabis dependence symptoms. There findings hold even after controlling for solitary marijuana use, frequency of marijuana joint/pipe use, tobacco use, and several demographic factors, including gender, race, age, recruitment location, and indicators of socio-economic status. Previous research using animal models, humans under laboratory conditions, ethnography to elicit users' own perspectives, and survey research focused on tobacco rather than marijuana dependence had already established conclusively that marijuana and tobacco interact in ways that have implications for abuse/dependence. The present analyses, however, may be the first to connect this interaction to actual user rituals/ practices involving concurrent use of marijuana and tobacco.

6.06 ED ATTENDANCE

One of the major causes of Emergency Department attendance due to cannabis intoxication is due to edible marijuana. Edible cannabis tends to be more toxic than smoked marijuana for four major reasons:

1) Difficulties in Titrating the Dose: The effects are not felt for approximately 60 to 90 minutes or longer, compared to only several minutes after smoking. This makes it difficult to adjust to the strength of the THC and encourages persons to eat more of the edible cannabis if they feel no effect and overdose (60601).
2) Highly Variable Absorption: The same amount of edible cannabis can produce highly variable blood THC concentrations, depending on its absorption rate through the stomach. Smoking and vaping provides more predictable blood THC concentrations.
3) Higher Concentrations of the Psychoactive Metabolite: Eating cannabis produces higher concentration of its psychoactive

Reference Number: 60515

metabolite 11-OH-THC due to first pass metabolism of THC by the liver, which is avoided when cannabis is smoked. Some researchers have found that 11-OH-THC is twice as psychoactive as THC and lasts twice as long (60601).

4) More Attractive and Easier to Consume: Eating cannabis-infused candies, baked goods, cookies, and other edibles is much more attractive and easier to do than trying to smoke "dried plant material." This has led to a substantial increase in ED visits by children, due to accidental cannabis intoxication (60603, 60606).

Most of the calls to the US Poison Centers regarding cannabis overdose involved cannabis-infused foods or beverages and 91 percent of the calls were from US states with decriminalized recreational/medical marijuana (60606). The increase in THC concentration in seized hashish samples in France was associated with more pediatric admissions and more children being admitted to hospital in a coma (60604). Psychosis, paranoia, tachycardia, and vomiting are common features seen in EDs as a result of a cannabis overdose (60608, 60610, 60620). Naloxone was used to treat a cannabis intoxication (60621).

There was one reported fatality involving an 18-year-old man who had an asystolic cardiac arrest while smoking cannabis and suffered a fatal hypoxic brain injury (60610).

Reference Number: 60601

BENJAMIN, D.M., AND M.J. FOSSLER. "Edible Cannabis Products: It Is Time for FDA Oversight." *The Journal of Clinical Pharmacology,* 56: 1045–47, 2016 (1 table, 2 figures, 10 references)

Abstract: A short report on the adverse effects and regulation of edible marijuana was presented. In September 2014, five high school students, ages 14 to 16 years, became sick after eating brownies laced with cannabis, which was sold by a classmate. Three vomited and two students became unconscious and were hospitalized. In February 2016, Colorado Regulators enacted new rules that each unit should have no more than 10 mg of THC and each package no more than 100 mg of THC. The FDA does not regulate edible cannabis and it does not meet even the basic standards of a drug like acetaminophen.

Smoked cannabis is absorbed into the pulmonary circulation and returned to the heart through the pulmonary vein. From the heart, it is distributed systemically, without passing through the liver. However, orally ingested THC is subject to both transmural absorption and metabolism in the gastrointestinal tract and first-pass hepatic metabolism, as it passes through the liver. As a result, THC is metabolized more extensively by the oral route leading to the synthesis of a much larger amount of 11-OH-THC metabolite than is generally formed following smoking. The 11-OH-THC metabolite is psychopharmacologically active and can combine its psychotropic effects with those of THC to produce a more robust psychotropic effect in the CNS. The magnitude of the effect of the combined 11-OH-THC and THC most likely was the cause of the psychotic reactions and loss of consciousness described in the cases reported above.

Reference Number: 60602

AL-SHIDHANI, T.A., AND V. ARORA. "Cannabis Exposure in an Omani Child. First Case Report from Oman." *Sultan Qaboos University Medical Journal*, 1: 511–14, 2011 (18 references)

Abstract: An Omani female child (age 2 years and 10 months) was brought to hospital by her parents due to drowsiness, lethargy, abnormal eye movements, and vomiting. She had ingested a blackish substance mixed with sand. Cannabinoids were detected in the child's vomit.

It is important for clinicians to consider substance abuse as a differential diagnosis for presentations similar to this case in other pediatric patients. Emergency medicine physicians should be able to detect suspicious behaviour as described above, supported by inconsistent information/history given by family members in order to provide appropriate immediate treatment and also initiate a follow-up case for the patient and possible also for the family.

Reference Number: 60603

MACCOUN, R.J., AND M.M. MELLO. "Half-Baked: The Retail Promotion of Marijuana Edibles (Perspective)." *The New England Journal of Medicine,* 372: 989–91, 2015 (1 figure, 5 references)

Abstract: A short review was conducted of the risk of the increasing popularity of edible marijuana. The attractive packaging of edible marijuana may be a tort law concept of attractive nuisance — being foreseeably likely to attract children who are unable to appreciate the risk involved. The US federal government does not regulate edible marijuana. Child-resistant packaging may be easily defeated by older children. The courts may assist in regulating cannabis-infused edibles by personal injury lawsuits brought against manufacturers by consumers who are injured from this product.

> Clear labelling regarding THC doses and recommended serving sizes, along with warning labels about the risks of overconsumption, are also commonsense measures but won't protect young children. We believe that regulations should also impose substantive restrictions on product formulation and packaging aimed at reducing the likelihood that minors and other consumers will confuse marijuana and non-marijuana products. Restricting the extent to which marijuana edibles can look and taste like familiar sweets could also keep the psychological barriers to marijuana initiation among children and adolescents from being lowered. Finally, regulations could seek to reduce the risk of overconsumption by controlling and standardizing THC content.

Reference Number: 60604

CLAUDET, I., S. MOUVIER, M. LABADIE, C. MANIN., A-P. MICHARD-LENOIR, D. EYER, AND D. DUFOUR, "Unintentional Cannabis Intoxication in Toddlers." *Pediatrics,* 140: e2017017, 10 pp, 2017 (4 tables, 3 figures, 44 references)

Abstract: A study was conducted of 235 hospital admissions of children less than 6 years of age in France, between 2004 and 2014, due to cannabis intoxication. Annual admission rates increased by a factor of thirteen and the number of severe admissions by a factor of twenty between 2004 and 2014. Seventy-one percent of admissions were 18 months or older. Seventy-two percent of the cannabis intoxication was due to hashish. The THC concentration of hashish in France has increased from 9.3 percent in 2004 to 20.7 percent in 2014. The resin is now in smaller olive-shaped pellets rather than 250 g bars.

Table: Number of Pediatric Admissions (with and without Coma) and the THC Concentration of Seized Hashish Samples in France between 2009 and 2014

Year	THC Concentration of Seized Hashish (%)	Number of Pediatric Admissions	Number of Admissions with Coma
2005	8.8%	5	1
2011	11.9%	15	2
2012	15.8%	25	5
2014	20.7%	62	18

Source: Adapted from Claudet et al 2017

Children are collateral victims of changing trends in cannabis use and prevailing THC concentration. Intoxicated children are more frequent, younger, and have intoxications that are more severe. This raises a real issue of public health.

Reference Number: 60605

BUI, Q.M., S. SIMPSON, AND K. NORDSTROM. "Psychiatric and Medical Management of Marijuana Intoxication in the Emergency Department." *Western Journal of Emergency Medicine*, 16: 414–17, 2015 (35 references)

Abstract: A 34-year-old woman with no previous psychiatric history presented to ED with erratic and disruptive behaviour. She was paranoid, grandiose, hyper-religious, and had auditory hallucinations. The patient admitted to consuming edible cannabis chocolates daily for the past week. Her THCCOOH level was over 500 ng/mL. After 48 hours her paranoia and hallucinations improved dramatically.

The medical risk of acute cannabis use is primarily cardiovascular in nature. THC enhances sympathetic tone, thereby increasing heart rate and blood pressure. Marijuana increases the risk of myocardial infarction within one hour of use and cardiovascular events have been reported in otherwise healthy patients.

Reference Number: 60606

CAO, D., S. SRISUMA, A.C. BRONSTEIN, AND C.O. HOYLE. "Characterization of Edible Marijuana Product Exposures Reported to United States

Poison Centers." *Clinical Toxicology*, 7 pp, 2016 (5 tables, 3 figures, 16 references)

Abstract: A total of 430 calls regarding edible marijuana overdoses were made to the US Poison Center between 2013 and 2015. Forty-nine percent were male and the median age was 18 years. The most common age groups were < 5 years (109), 13 to 19 years (78) and 20 to 29 years (59). The most common symptoms were drowsiness, lethargy (43 percent), tachycardia (31 percent), agitation (14 percent), and confusion (14 percent). Cardiovascular symptoms included hypertension (4 percent), chest pains (3 percent), and hypotension (1 percent). Twelve patients were admitted to CCU and three were intubated. Ninety-one percent of the calls occurred in states with decriminalized medical/recreational marijuana.

Table: Type of Cannabis Product and Percentage of Poison Centre Calls Involving that Product

Cannabis-Infused Product	Percent of Poison Centre Calls
Marijuana-containing food	49%
Marijuana-containing beverage	2%
Marijuana brownies	15%
Marijuana cookies	15%
Marijuana candies	19%

Source: Adapted from Cao et al, 2016

Edible marijuana exposures are increasing and may lead to severe respiratory depression.

Reference Number: 60607

CIPRIANI, F., A. MANCINO, S.M. PULITANO, M. PIASTRA, AND G.A. CONTI. "A Cannabinoid Intoxicated Child Treated with Dexmedetomidine: A Case Report." *Journal of Medical Case Reports*, 9: 152 (4 pp), 2015 (1 table, 1 figure, 15 references)

Abstract: A 19-month-old boy was admitted to hospital after eating something he had found on the ground in a park. He was lethargic with paroxysms of agitation. The baby could not be calmed down and so was administered dexmedetomidine and the agitation disappeared. Urine cannabinoids was positive.

Dexmedetomidine is a fairly safe and effective antidote for pediatric marijuana or natural cannabinoid exposures. Its properties and potential to allow for cooperative sedation make it a more attractive choice with fewer side effects than benzodiazepines or opioids.

Reference Number: 60608

FOGELMAN, S., C. RANGAN, J. KENNEDY, M. SANTOS, M. KIM, R. REPORTER, S.M. TEUTSCH, J.E. FIELDING, AND D. DIAMOND. "Inadvertent Ingestion of Marijuana–Los Angeles, California, 2009." *Morbidity and Mortality Weekly Report*, 58: 947–50, 2009 (2 tables, 9 references)

Abstract: A preschool teacher put brownies, which she had bought from a sidewalk vendor, on a table in the break room to share with staff. She also gave two brownies to her adult son. The brownies were later found to contain cannabinoids. Six persons ate the brownies and two attended hospital due to the adverse effects of edible marijuana. None of the persons affected had ever consumed cannabis. The one teacher who was tested was positive for the metabolite THCCOOH (27 ng/mL in serum and 66 ng/mL in urine). The sidewalk vendor who sold the brownies was never located and no charges were laid.

Table: Gender, Age, Symptoms, Time of Onset, and Duration for Six Persons Who Ate a Cannabis-Infused Brownie.

Gender/Age	Symptoms	Onset after Eating Brownie (min)	Duration of Symptoms (hrs)
Female, 25 years	Drowsiness, fatigue, weakness, dizziness, ataxia, numbness, tingling, dry mouth/throat, mouth irritation [attended hospital]	90 minutes	3.0 hours
Female, 32 years	Drowsiness, fatigue, weakness, dizziness, ataxia, altered mood, altered taste, numbness, palpitations	90 minutes	8.0 hours
Female, 21 years	Drowsiness, fatigue, weakness, dizziness, ataxia, headache, giddiness, numbness, altered taste, increase appetite, itching	80 minutes	10.0 hours

Gender/Age	Symptoms	Onset after Eating Brownie (min)	Duration of Symptoms (hrs)
Female, 22 years	Drowsiness, fatigue, weakness, dizziness, ataxia, headache, agitation, anxiety, numbness, tingling, muscle twitching, chills, dry mouth/throat, nausea, vomiting, shortness of breath, palpitations [attended hospital]	90 minutes	4.0 hours
Female, 33 years	Drowsiness, fatigue, dizziness, ataxia, anxiety, giddiness, numbness, tingling, muscle twitching, altered taste, shortness of breath	30 minutes	6.5 hours
Male, 24 years	Drowsiness, fatigue, ataxia, agitation, dry mouth/throat, loss of appetite, excessive sweating, burning eyes, itching eyes	180 minutes	6.0 hours

Source: Adapted from Fogelman et al (2009)

Similar episodes of inadvertent ingestion of marijuana occurred in Colorado in 1978 and in California in 1981, where persons unknowingly ingested marijuana in baked goods. The constellation of symptoms described in this report is similar to other instances in which persons reported drowsiness, fatigue, ataxia, and dizziness. Accidental marijuana ingestion has led to coma in children. Therefore, pediatricians should be alert to signs of accidental ingestion.

Reference Number: 60609

DAVIS, J.M., B. MENDELSON, J.J. BERKES, K. SULETA, K.F. CORSI, AND R.E. BOOTH. "Public Health Effects of Medical Marijuana Legalization in Colorado." *American Journal of Preventative Medicine*, 50: 373–79, 2016 (1 table, 3 figures, 24 references)

Abstract: An analysis was conducted of calls to poison centres mentioning marijuana- and cannabis-related outcomes in hospitals before and after 2009. Poison centre calls increased 0.8 percent per month and marijuana-related hospital discharges increased 1 percent per month.

This paper presented changes in marijuana related policy and public health outcomes over the time period of the study. The increases in MMR applicants and decreases in trends of marijuana-related arrests may be a direct result of policy changes. When taken with changes suggesting a decrease in the perceived risk of marijuana, these factors may mark increased use and increased acceptance of marijuana over this time period and be important components of deleterious public health outcomes. In addition to an increase in prevalence of marijuana use over this timeframe and increases in marijuana-related fatal motor vehicle crashes previously reported, this study identified increases in hospital discharges and poison centre calls and decreases in treatment entries and arrests in this time period.

Reference Number: 60610

DINES, A.M., D.M. WOOD, M. GALICIA, C.M. YATES, F. HEYERDAHL, K.E. HOVDA, I. GIRAUDON, R. SEDEFOVE, EURO-DEN RESEARCH GROUP, AND P.I. DARGAN. "Presentations to the Emergency Department Following Cannabis Use: A Multi-Centre Case Series from Ten European Countries" *Journal Medical Toxicology*, 11: 415–21, 2015 (3 tables, 24 references)

Abstract: A study was conducted of 2,189 recreational drug-related presentations to EDs over six months between 2013 and 2014, using the Euro-DEN (Drug Emergencies Network) data. Of these, 356 (16.2 percent) involved cannabis and 36 (1.6 percent) involved lone-use of cannabis. Of the 320 cases involving cannabis and another drug, alcohol was the most common other drug in 190 cases (59 percent), followed by benzodiazepines in 73 (23 percent). Of the thirty-five nonfatal lone cannabis cases, the most common reported clinical features were agitation/aggression in eight (23 percent), psychosis in seven (20 percent), unruly in seven (20 percent), and vomiting in eight (23 percent). Most patients (71 percent) received no treatment and thirty (86 percent) were discharged from the ED. There was one fatality involving an 18-year-old male who collapsed with an asystolic cardiac arrest while smoking cannabis and suffered hypoxic brain injury.

Table: Clinical Features of Thirty-five Non-fatal, Cannabis Only Cases

Clinical Feature	As the Only Clinical Feature	With Other Clinical Features
Agitation/Aggression	4	4
Psychosis	4	3
Anxiety	0	7

Clinical Feature	As the Only Clinical Feature	With Other Clinical Features
Vomiting	4	3
Chest Pains	1	3
Palpitations	0	3
Hallucinations	0	3
Seizures	1	1
Hypertension	0	2
Dyspnea (shortness of breath)	0	2
Headache	1	1

Source: Adapted from Dines et al, 2015

Although uncommon, severe toxicity, including cardiovascular toxicity and death, may be under-recognized and it is important the emergency physicians are aware of this.

Reference Number: 60611

GIROUD, C., M. DE CESARE, A. BERTHET, V. VARLET, N. CONCHA-LOZANO, AND B. FAVRAT. "E-Cigarettes: A Review of New Trends in Cannabis Use." *International Journal of Environmental Research and Public Health*, 12: 9988–0008, 2015 (4 figures, 54 references)

Abstract: The emergence of electronic cigarettes (e-cigs) has given cannabis smokers a new method of inhaling cannabis. The lower temperatures required to vaporize cannabis are safer and recreational users can vape undetected using deodorized extracts (stealth vaping). Most e-cigs use liquids, but some can use loose leaf with interchangeable coil heads. Between 2010 and 2014, US poison centres recorded some 2,405 e-cig exposure calls, most as inhalational, and eye and skin exposure in toddlers. Less than 1 percent THC, it is not considered to be a narcotic.

The most significant health concerns involve the vaping of cannabinoids by children and teenagers. E-cigs could provide an alternative gateway to cannabis use for young people. Furthermore, vaping cannabinoids could lead to environmental and passive contamination.

Reference Number: 60612

KIM, H.S., AND A.A. MONTE. "Colorado Cannabis Legalization and Its Effect on Emergency Care." *Annals of Emergency Medicine*, 68: 71–75, 2016 (2 figures, 27 references)

Abstract: Colorado legalized the use of medical marijuana in 2000, but it was not truly commercialized until the US Attorney General ceased prosecution of cannabis use and products in 2009. The number of registered medical marijuana licences in Colorado increased from 5,051 to 118,895. Recreational cannabis was legalized in 2014 in Colorado. The prevalence of hospitalizations for cannabis exposure doubled from 15 per 100,000 from 2001 to 2009 to 28 per 100,000 from 2010 to 2013. Unintentional cannabis exposure in children under 12 years of age increased from 0 out of 790 poison cases to 14 out of 588 poison cases after legalization.

> Edible marijuana products pose unique risks for pediatric exposure because of their brightly coloured packaging and formulation into candies and other sweets. In contrast to adult patients, pediatric patients typically present with central nervous system depression, potentially causing airway compromise or risk of aspiration. We recommend that pediatric patients younger than 6 years and presenting with central nervous system depression be observed until symptoms resolve either in the ED or in an inpatient setting. In pediatric patients aged 6 years or older, disposition should be determined according to a provider assessment of symptoms severity, patient comorbidities, and reliability of caregivers. Pediatric patients presenting without altered mental status may be discharged if they remain asymptomatic four hours after ingestion.

Reference Number: 60613

KIM, H.S., K.E. HALL, E.K. GENCO, M. VAN DYKE, E. BARKER, AND A.A. MONTE. "Marijuana Tourism and Emergency Department Visits in Colorado." *New England Medical Journal*, 374: 797–98, 2016 (1 figure, 3 references)

Abstract: The legalization of medical marijuana was approved in Colorado in 2000 and medical use and availability was increased in 2009. Retail sales of cannabis were approved in 2012 and retail sales began in 2014, although only in a few areas of the state that allow local dispensaries. ED visits due to cannabis intoxication were determined at an urban hospital in Aurora and statewide for both residents and non-residents. The rate of ED visits for tourists increased from 78 per 100,000 in 2012, to 112 per 100,000 in 2013, and to 163 per 100,000 in 2014. For residents, the rate increased from 70 to 86 to 101 per 100,000.

ED visits related to cannabis use appear to be increasing more rapidly among out-of-state residents than among Colorado residents. The initial educational efforts through mass media have focused primarily on Colorado residents. These data underscore the importance of point-of-sale education for visitors regarding the safe and appropriate use of marijuana products.

Reference Number: 60614

LIAKONI, D., P.C. DOLDER, K. RENTSCH, AND M.E. LIECHTI. "Presentations Due to Acute Toxicity of Psychoactive Substances in an Urban Emergency Department in Switzerland: A Case Series." *BMC Pharmacology and Toxicology*, 17: 25, 2016 (3 tables, 2 figures, 8 references)

Abstract: A study of 210 attendances at an ED at the University Hospital of Basel in Switzerland between 2014 and 2015 due to self-reported recreational drug use was conducted. The mean age of the patients was 33 years and 73 percent were male. Most patients were admitted on the weekends or at night. Approximately 50 percent of the patients reported the consumption of alcohol as well. The most commonly detected drugs were cannabis (70), cocaine (57), opioids (40) and benzodiazepines (38). There were two fatalities. The most common clinical observations were impaired consciousness, GCS < 15 (49 percent), tachycardia BPM > 100 (28 percent), anxiety, nervousness, or fear (23 percent), or unconsciousness (20 percent).

In conclusion, most medical problems related to recreational drug toxicity concerned cocaine and cannabis and mainly included sympathomimetic toxicity and/or psychiatric disorders. Similar to the previous year, cases with acute toxicity linked to NPS appear to be uncommon.

Reference Number: 60615

RODRIGUEZ-CASTRO, C.E., H. ALKHATEEB, A. ELFAR, F. SAIFUDDIN, A. ABBAS, AND T. SIDDIQUI. "Recurrent Myopericarditis as a Complication of Marijuana Use." *American Journal of Case Reports*, 15: 60–62, 2014 (2 figures, 6 references)

Abstract: A 29-year-old man attended hospital on two occasions, due to chest pain aggravated by coughing after deep inhalation and lying flat, and relieved while sitting or leaning forward. Prior to both occasions, he had smoked adulterated marijuana from Mexico. The symptoms resolved after ibuprofen therapy.

> In this case, we believe that the cause of myopericarditis may likely be related to the consumption of contaminated or adulterated cannabis, given the clinical history of using cannabis and subsequent hospitalization on two occasions with similar symptoms, similar laboratory findings, and hospital course.

Reference Number: 60616

LIAKONI, D., P.C. DOLDER, K. RENTSCH, AND M.E. LIECHTI. "Acute Health Problems due to Recreational Drug Use in Patients Presenting to an Urban Emergency Department in Switzerland." *Swiss Medical Weekly,* 145: 7 pp, 2015 (4 tables, 28 references)

Abstract: A study was conducted of 77,767 attendances at the ER of the University Hospital of Basel in Switzerland between 2013 and 2014. Of these attendances, 216 were related to the recreational use of drugs and 476 were due to alcohol. The most commonly reported drugs were cocaine (36 percent), cannabis (31 percent), and opioids (13 percent). The mean patient age was 31 years and 69 percent were male. In 44 percent of the cases, another drug was detected. The most frequent symptoms were tachycardia (31 percent), anxiety (27 percent), nausea or vomiting (23 percent), and arrhythmia (22 percent).

> In conclusion, most acute medical problems related to recreational drug toxicity were due to cocaine and cannabis use, and mainly included sympathomimetic toxicity and/or psychiatric disorders. Cases with acute toxicity linkage to novel psychoactive substances appear to be uncommon, with only two novel substances (pentylone and 2C-B) found. It could be that novel designer drugs are not frequently used or infrequently lead to ED attendance.

Reference Number: 60617

WANG, G.S., G. ROOSEVELT, M-C. LE LAIT, E.M. MARTINEZ, B. BUCHER-BARTELSOM, A.C. BRONSTEIN, AND K. HEARD. "Association of Unintentional Pediatric Exposures with Decriminalization of Marijuana in the United States." *Annals of Emergency Medicine,* 63: 1450–55, 2014 (3 tables, 2 figures, 22 references)

Abstract: In the US, according to the American Association of Poison Control Centers, there were 985 unintentional marijuana exposures in children age 9 and younger between 2005 and 2011. Four hundred and ninety-six exposures occurred in non-legal states, 93 in transitional states and 396 in decriminalized states. The median age of the victims was 1.5 to 2 years and 78 percent of the exposures were due to ingestion. The main clinical symptoms were drowsiness, lethargy, and ataxia. The OR of admission to critical care units was 3.4 times greater in transitional and decriminalized states compared to non-legal states. The call rate in non-legal states did not change between 2005 and 2011 but increased 30 percent in decriminalized states and 11.5 percent in transitional states. In approximately 95 percent of the patients, the symptoms disappeared within 24 hours.

As more states pass marijuana legislation and access to the drug is eased, the availability of high-concentration edible products may lead to an increase in symptomatic pediatric exposures. Ongoing surveillance is crucial in assessing the marijuana industry's effect on children and evaluating preventative efforts as it continues to spread. Decreasing the likelihood of ingestion offers the best strategy to minimize these childhood exposures because the increasing use and availability after decriminalization will be less amenable to public health interventions. We believe state lawmakers should consider requirements, such as child-resistant packaging, warning labels, and public education, when drafting marijuana legislation to minimize the effect on children.

Reference Number: 60618

WOODRUFF, S.I., C.T. MCCABE, M. HOHMAN, J.D. CLAPP, A.M. SHILLINGTON, K. EISENBERG, C.B. SISE, E.M. CASTILLO, T.C. CHAN, AND M.J. SISE. "Characteristics of Cannabis-Only and Other Drug Users Who Visit the Emergency Department." *Cannabis and Cannabinoid Research,* 1.1: 149–53, 2016 (1 table, 26 references)

Abstract: A study was conducted of the characteristics of 686 adult patients attending the EDs and trauma units of two Southern California hospitals, who reported drug use within the previous 30 days. There were 141 non-daily cannabis users, 253 daily cannabis users, and 292 other drug users. Approximately 19 to 22 percent of cannabis only users had problematic drug use. The mean age of the daily cannabis users was the youngest of the three groups (34.9 years).

> Although cannabis may be less harmful to individual health relative to other forms of drug use, heavier cannabis use is a concern because it may be associated with mental and physical health problems. Cannabis dependence does occur, and individuals often perceive themselves as unable to stop.

Reference Number: 60619

GRANT, P., AND P.A. GANDHI. "A Case of Cannabis-Induced Pancreatitis." *Journal of the Pancreas*, 5: 41–43, 2004 (9 references)

Abstract: A 29-year-old man attended an ED due to severe abdominal pain, nausea, and vomiting. Throughout his stay at hospital, he surreptitiously smoked cannabis, as he thought it would stop his abdominal pain, and each time he had a reoccurrence of pain due to pancreatitis. He had smoked cannabis heavily for three months prior to admission. He was advised to cease cannabis use and his pain resolved. Approximately 2 percent of pancreatitis cases are due to drug use.

> In conclusion, we have described a case of cannabis-induced pancreatitis. This is the first such case in the literature and it reinforces the fact that drug-induced or aggravated pancreatitis is a serious problem. Considering the frequent use of cannabis in the general population, this case should be kept in mind. The association needs to be explored but is problematic because of the difficulty in monitoring cannabis and getting patients to admit to drug use.

Reference Number: 60620

JOUANJUS, E., F. LEYMARIE, M. TUBERY, AND M. LAPEYRE-MESTRE. "Cannabis-Related Hospitalizations: Unexpected Serious Events Identified Through Hospital Databases." *British Journal of Clinical Pharmacology*, 71: 758–65, 2011 (4 tables, 30 references)

Abstract: Two hundred admissions that were due to cannabis use in six hospitals in Toulouse, France, between 2004 and 2007, were assessed. The patients were mainly men (77 percent) with a mean age of 28 years. It is estimated that the rate of hospital admissions increased from 1.15

per 1,000 regular cannabis users in 2004 to 3.20 per 1,000 in 2007. There were 619 adverse events reported in these patients. A total of seven myocardial infarctions were related to cannabis use, as well as seventeen extra-cardial vascular events (one man in his twenties died).

Table: Adverse Event Classification and the Percent of Patients Using Cannabis in that Classification*

Adverse Event Classification	% of Patients
Psychiatric Disorder	57.5%
Respiratory System Disorder	31.0%
Cardiovascular Disorder	29.0%
Gastro-intestinal Disorder	26.5%
Vision Disorder	5.5%
Obstetrics	1.5%
* Note: Some patients suffered more than one adverse event	

Source: Adapted from Jouanjus et al, 2011

In conclusion, our results suggest that the risk to develop serious adverse events is high in cannabis using populations. Although somatic complications are less frequent than psychiatric complications, they are serious disorders. Neurological, cardiovascular, and respiratory disorders are particularly involved. We probably under-evaluated the incidence of cannabis-related serious outcomes, but we have provided the first available estimates. We have looked beyond the well-known psychiatric reactions and provided estimates of serious cardiovascular and respiratory events. These results should encourage similar and perhaps better control research studies in other settings. Furthering the knowledge in the field of cannabis-related complications is necessary. The awareness thus generated should contribute to improved case detection and lead to care adjustments. The education of people at large is another point to consider.

Reference Number: 60621

RICHARDS, J.R., V. SCHANDERA, AND W. ELDER. "Treatment of Acute Cannabinoid Overdose with Naloxone Infusion." *Toxicology Communications*, 1: 29–33, 2017 (1 figure, 36 references)

Abstract: A 40-year-old heavy cannabis user was admitted to ED due to hypoventilation, hypothermia (34.2°C), and somnolence. The patient was administered naloxone IV, as it was thought to be an opioid overdose, and recovered. The initial blood THCCOOH concentration was 226 ng/mL. No drugs were detected in the urine screen except for a cocaine metabolite.

> In summary, our case represents evidence that naloxone may play a role in the treatment of cannabinoid toxicity, which may be explained by overlap between the endocannabinoid and endogenous opioid systems. Clinicians should not expect the dramatic reversal in hypoventilation and somnolence customarily observed with naloxone treatment of opioid overdose. Multiple and escalating doses of naloxone may be required to achieve effect, and a continuous infusion represents a logical method of delivery to counter the long half-life of cannabinoids. Further research into the use of naloxone for acute cannabinoid intoxication may offer insight into the varied human responses observed in prior controlled studies and case reports.

6.07 FIRES

Fires can result not only from tobacco but also from lighted cannabis cigarettes, although joints pose a lesser risk as they burn faster and extinguish easier than tobacco cigarettes. Illegal growing of marijuana in residential locations (grow-ops) have caused fires due to substandard wiring, and heat and high electricity demands from high-intensity lamps and blowers (60701). Fires and explosions have resulted from the production of butane hash oil (BHO) or dabs, which use highly volatile solvents such as butane to extract THC from marijuana (60702). Even the use of dabs can pose a risk as the method often involves using a blow torch to heat the "nail" to over 400°C. The risk of fires would also be increased as the user would be "high" while using the blow torch.

Reference Number: 60701

DIPLOCK, J., D. PLECAS, AND L. GARIS. "Targeting Marijuana Growing Operations in British Columbia." *University of the Fraser Valley, Centre for Public Safety and Criminal Justice Research, Report*, 22 pp, August 2013 (85 references)

Abstract: Illegal indoor residential marijuana-growing operations (grow-ops) have been a public safety concern in British Columbia. The grow-ops typically use large amounts of stolen electricity with substandard electrical wiring unable to take the increased electrical burden, and as consequence have resulted in numerous fires. A typical grower's rule of thumb is that for every 1,000-watt high intensity light, about one pound of marijuana can be harvested. The number of lights in residential grow-ops have increased over the years from an average of nine to nearly thirty.

> All growing operations pose some serious risks to British Columbia's communities, but indoor marijuana growing operations in residential buildings are perhaps the most problematic. According to research, indoor illegal marijuana production, particularly when done on a commercial scale, results in some sort of structural hazard or contamination in nearly all cases. These hazards are also shared by licensed medical operations. As residential houses are not originally designed to be ideal for indoor plant growing, buildings require substantial modifications to achieve a suitable environment. A number of extensive modifications are required, including increased electrical power, altered ventilation, structural changes, added watering apparatuses, increased air flow, dehumidification, increased levels of carbon dioxide, added cooling units, and anti-detection measures. There is a particularly dangerous trend of growers disconnecting the furnace and re-venting the exhaust to rooms used for growing marijuana. The clandestine nature of this criminal enterprise results in growers circumventing the legal systems in place for making these types of modifications to buildings, which often require specific training, certification and inspection to ensure safety standards are met. The substantially altered residence can present a number of hazards, including fires, electrical hazards, molds, and chemical residues.

Reference Number: 60702

BELL, C., J. SLIM, H.K. FLATEN, G. LINDBERG, AND W. AREK. "Butane Hash Oil Burns Associated with Marijuana Liberalization in Colorado." *Journal of Medical Toxicology*, 11: 422–25, 2015 (6 references)

Abstract: A study was conducted of twenty-nine cases of butane hash oil (BHO) burns associated with the manufacture of dabs that occurred in Colorado between 2008 and 2014. No cases occurred before medical cannabis liberalization, nineteen occurred during medical liberalization (2009–2013) and twelve since the 2014 legalization. The median age of the victims was 26 years (range 15 to 58 years), 72 percent were Caucasians and 90 percent were male.

> In summary, marijuana policy liberalization in Colorado has been associated with an unanticipated problem of increasing hydrocarbon flash burns due to BHO production. A combination of public health messaging, standardization of manufacturing processes, and worker safety regulations are needed to decrease the risks associated with BHO production.

Reference Number: 60703

STOGNER, J.M., AND B.L. MILLER. "Assessing the Dangers of Dabbing: Mere Marijuana or Harmful New Trend?" *Pediatrics,* 136: 3 pp, 2015 (1 table, 7 references)

Abstract: Dabbing is the inhalation of a concentrated THC product created through butane extraction and is known as butane hash oil (BHO). The process of creating these products is extremely dangerous (it is known as blasting), as butane is highly flammable and volatile. A number of fires, explosions, and severe burns have resulted from its production. In addition, the use of dabs may also be a fire hazard as a blow torch is often used to vaporize the dab for inhalation. The safety risks of BHO are similar to methamphetamine.

> Compared with flower cannabis use, dabbing is more complex and carries the risk of accidental injury. Young people may use the term "oil rig" to refer to their dabbing paraphernalia, which typically consists of a glass water pipe and a 4-to-6-inch hollow titanium rod called the nail. Nails have a concave surface area to dabs that extends beyond the pipe; nails are sometimes covered with a dome. The oil rig is prepared by heating the nail with a blowtorch. Once the nail is sufficiently heated, users place a dab onto the nail's exposed surface. The user inhales as the dab is vaporized by the heat in the nail, pulling its vapors through the nail and water. An under-appreciated risk associated with this technique is the open flame. Unlike the lighters used when smoking flower cannabis, which typically pose no more of a threat than a first-degree burn, a blow torch is often used to heat the nail to temperatures > 400°C. In addition to the risks inherent in using these types of heating devices while cognitively impaired, there are long-term health risks associated with inhaling off-gassing solder, rust from oxidized metal parts, and benzene, some

of which are increasingly related at higher temperatures. Extracts can also be consumed in other ways, such as the use of a modified electronic cigarette. These techniques avoid some of the indirect risks (e.g., fire) but are likely to be associated with similar health problems.

6.08 FLYING

Cannabis use impairs the ability to pilot a plane safely and may show a carry-over effect (60801, 60802). The incidence of drug violations in aviation employees was the lowest for flight crewmembers and highest for aviation screeners (60803). The most common drug detected was cannabis (60803).

Reference Number: 60801

YESAVAGE, J.A., V.O. LEIRER, M. DENARI, AND L.E. HOLLISTER. "Carry-Over Effects of Marijuana Intoxication on Aircraft Pilot Performance: A Preliminary Report." *American Journal of Psychiatry*, 142: 1325–29, 1985 (1 table, 1 figure, 12 references)

Abstract: Ten experienced male pilots (mean age 29 years) were tested on a computerized flight simulator before and one, four, and twenty-four hours after smoking a marijuana cigarette (19 mg THC). The mean performance on the flight task showed trends toward impairment twenty-four hours later.

The difficulty the subjects experienced in aligning and landing precisely at the centre of the runway is a particular cause for concern. It may be related to the trend toward more and larger aileron changes on approach. Elevator control seems less affected by the drug. It is important to note that the near doubling of the lateral deviation on a landing at twenty-four hours may be an extremely serious error.

Reference Number: 60802

MATHEW, R.J., W.H. WILSON, T.G. TURKINGTON, AND R.E. COLEMAN. "Cerebellar Activity and Disturbed Time Sense after THC." *Brain Research*, 797: 183–89, 1998 (5 tables, 2 figures, 51 references)

Abstract: Twenty-four female and twenty-two male cannabis users (mean age 30 years) received either a 0.15 mg/min or 0.25 mg/min infusion of THC for twenty minutes or a placebo. Brain blood flow was determined by a MRI and PET scans and behavioural correlations were measured. There was a correlation between decreased cerebellar blood flow and impaired time sense (time seemed to be slower). Most subjects, however, showed an increase in CBF. The cerebellum is associated with an internal timing system.

> Altered time sense after marijuana intoxication may have considerable clinical significance. As was pointed out earlier, a number of studies have indicated significant impairment of motor function when time sense is impaired. This is particularly important in situations where individuals under the influence of marijuana operate motor vehicles, heavy machinery, or aircraft.

Reference Number: 60803

LI, G., S.P. BAKER, Q. ZHAO, J.E. BRADY, B.H. LANG, G.W. REBOK, AND C. DIMAGGIO. "Drug Violations and Aviation Accidents: Findings from the U.S. Mandatory Drug Testing Programs." *Addiction,* 106: 1287–92, 2011 (2 tables, 1 figure, 26 references)

Abstract: Between 1995 and 2005, the Federal Aviation Agency recorded 4,977 post-accident drug tests and 1,129,922 random drug tests of aviation employees. Of these, there were 91 and 7,211 drug violations respectively. It was estimated that 1.2 percent of aviation accidents were attributable to drug violations. Of the drugs detected, 67.3 percent were cannabis, 23.9 percent were cocaine, 6.1 percent were amphetamines, and 2.1 percent were opiates. Overall, less than 1 percent of aviation employees tested positive for drugs by random testing.

Table: Percent of Drug Violations in Aviation Employees by Occupation in the United States, 2003 to 2005

Occupation	% with Drug Violations
Flight Crewmembers	0.05%
Air Traffic Controllers	0.26%
Flight Attendants	0.39%
Ground Security Coordinators	0.61%
Aircraft Dispatchers	0.68%
Aircraft Maintenance	1.00%
Aviation Screeners	1.16%

Source: Adapted from Li et al, 2011

Reference Number: 60803

> Contrasting the random testing data with the post-accident testing data enabled us to quantitatively assess the association between drug violation and the risk of accident involvement in aviation employees. The finding that aviation employees who test positive for illicit drugs are at a significantly increased risk of being involved in accidents is consistent with studies conducted in other industries and the estimated odds ratio is comparable to that associated with alcohol violations.

6.09 HOMICIDES

The most common drug detected in homicide victims besides alcohol is cannabis and involved mainly males (60901, 60902, 60905). Cannabis was detected over twice as frequently in homicide victims as suicide victims (60903, 60905).

Reference Number: 60901

ADEAGBO, B.A., C. CLARK, AND K.A. COLLINS. "Homicides Committed by Youth Assailants. A Retrospective Study." *American Journal of Forensic Medicine and Pathology*, 29: 219–23, 2008 (2 tables, 5 figures, 22 references)

Abstract: A study was conducted in South Carolina of seventy homicides committed by youth, ages 19 years or younger, between 1991 and 2006. Of the seventy victims, sixty-one (87 percent) were male and ranged in age from 0 (fetus) to 73 years. Cocaine/benzoylecgonine was detected in seventeen victims (20 percent), THC in twelve (14 percent), and alcohol in nine (11 percent).

> In conclusion, the current study shows that the youth assailants of homicides were predominately black men, 15 to 19 years of age with an age range of 4 to 19 years. The most common victim was a black man, 10 to 19 years of age. Fifty-six percent of the victims knew the youth assailant. The most common homicide location was the home, closely followed by the street. The most common weapon used to commit the homicide was a handgun, and most homicides had a motive of argument. Associations were identified between weapon and motives, victim age, victim gender, and location. Toxicology was often positive in the victims especially marijuana, cocaine, and ethanol.

Reference Number: 60902

DARKE, S., AND J. DUFLOU, "Toxicology and Circumstances of Death of Homicide Victims in New South Wales, Australia, 1996–2005." *Journal of Forensic Sciences*, 53: 447–51, 2008 (2 tables, 1 figure, 31 references)

Abstract: A drug and alcohol screen was conducted on 485 homicide victims in New South Wales, Australia, between 1996 and 2005. Seventy-one percent of the victims were male and the mean age of the victims was 35 years (range 15 to 60 years). A positive BAC was detected in nearly one-half of the victims and the median BAC was 0.140 g/100mL (range 0.010 to 0.480 g/100mL). The most commonly detected drugs were cannabis, opioids (morphine), and amphetamines. The most common drug combinations were alcohol and cannabis (11 percent), opioids and benzodiazepines (4 percent), and cannabis and psychostimulants (4 percent). A weekly cycle was noted for alcohol homicides consistent with weekend binge drinking. Alcohol was also the only drug to show diurnal differences.

Table: Percent of Homicide Victims in which Alcohol or Cannabis Were Detected According to the Day of Death

Day of Week	% Alcohol Positive	% Cannabis Positive
Monday	25%	19%
Tuesday	27%	24%
Wednesday	33%	14%
Thursday	41%	23%
Friday	42%	25%
Saturday	49%	26%
Sunday	49%	19%

Source: Adapted from Darke and Duflou, 2008

If we were to characterize a particularly high-risk circumstance for males, it would be in a public place, in the late evening/early morning, or on a weekend. For a female, the same scenario would apply, except that the risk would relate to a domestic dispute in a home environment.

Reference Number: 60903

DARKE, S., J. DUFLOU, AND M. TOROK. "Drugs and Violent Death: Comparative Toxicology of Homicide and Non-Substance Toxicity Suicide Victims." *Addiction*, 104: 1000–1005, 2009 (2 tables, 24 references)

Abstract: Toxicological analyses were conducted on 478 homicide and 1,245 non-substance toxicity suicide victims in Sydney, Australia, between 1997 and 2003. A positive BAC was detected in approximately 40 percent of the victims, with no group differences (median BAC was 0.120 g/100mL). Alcohol was more common among male victims (43 percent) than female victims (27 percent). Illicit drugs were detected in one-quarter of the victims, and cannabis, opiate, and psychostimulants were more prevalent in homicide than suicide victims.

Table: Percent of Drugs Detected in Homicide and Suicide Victims

Drug	Homicide (% detected)	Suicide (% detected)	Odds Ratio of Homicide Compared to Suicide
Alcohol	42.0%	38.7%	Not significant
Cannabis	22.1%	10.6%	2.39 X
Opioids	12.2%	8.3%	1.53 X
Prescription drugs	11.6%	26.5%	0.36 X

Source: Adapted from Darke, Duflou, and Torok, 2009

The current study illustrates graphically the extent of alcohol involvement in violent death. Alcohol was ubiquitous and, importantly, there was no group difference in prevalence. The levels of intoxication were clinically significant, with the median concentration being the equivalent of approximately six to eight standard drinks in men. While levels were comparable across groups, the intoxication of HOM cases was significantly higher than that of SUI cases. The implications of this finding are unclear. It may reflect, however, the effects of heavy intoxication on increased situational risk to involvement in violence, e.g., intoxicated involvement in street fights.

Reference Number: 60904

GALEA, S., J. AHERN, K. TARDIFF, A.C. LEON, AND D. VLAHOV. "Drugs and Firearm Deaths in New York City, 1990–1998." *Journal of Urban Health: Bulletin New York Academy of Science,* 79: 70–86, 2002 (3 tables, 3 figures, 31 references)

Abstract: Drug and alcohol toxicology tests were conducted on post-mortem blood and urine in victims of fatal firearm deaths, including homicides, suicides, and accidents. There were 11,133 firearm deaths in NYC between 1990 and 1998. The majority of the victims were male (91 percent) and most (88 percent) were homicides. The total number of firearm deaths decreased from 1,720 in 1990 to 526 in 1998. Over half of all firearm deaths had a postmortem toxicology result. Cannabis overtook cocaine or morphine as the illicit drug most associated with firearm deaths. Firearm deaths with positive alcohol results were consistently high throughout the nine years of this study.

> In summary, analysis of trends of firearm deaths and associated toxicology in New York City between 1990 and 1998 demonstrated the decreasing role of cocaine and heroin, with the former declining at a faster rate. Decline in firearm deaths that were both cocaine and opiate positive toxicologically started in 1990, before targeted police efforts to limit illegal firearms and enforce quality of life crimes that started in New York City in the mid-1990s. Firearm deaths toxicologically positive for cannabis, on the other hand, increased in the early 1990s and started to decline in the mid-1990s.

Reference Number: 60905

SHEEHAN, C.M., R.G. ROGERS, G.W. WILLIAMS IV, AND J.D. BOARDMAN. "Gender Differences in the Presence of Drugs in Violent Deaths." *Addiction,* 108: 547–55, 2013 (3 tables, 1 figure, 48 references)

Abstract: The association between the presence of alcohol, amphetamines, antidepressant, cocaine, marijuana, and opiates was determined in 1,003 homicide and 4,788 suicide victims that occurred in Colorado between 2004 and 2009. Alcohol was detected in 48.9 percent of the homicide and 30.1 percent of the suicide victims. Cannabis was present in 22.4 percent of the homicide and only 5 percent of the suicide victims. Homicide victims were 1.79 times (amphetamine), 2.03 times (marijuana), and 2.6 times (cocaine) respectively as likely to be detected in suicide victims as homicide victims.

> Suicide and homicide decedents are characterized by varying patterns of licit and illicit drug use that differ by gender. Drugs associated with homicide (marijuana, cocaine, and amphetamines) are stronger among males, while drugs associated with suicide are stronger among females (antidepressants and opiates). Taking these differences into consideration may allow for targeted interventions to reduce violent deaths.

6.10 MEMORY

Cannabis intoxication from smoking or oral ingestion, impairs short-term or working memory and learning (61002, 61005, 61006, 61009). Due to the memory impairment, many cannabis users had difficulty maintaining a coherent train of thought (61010). Cannabis users who reported no memory problem had a lower verbal and visual memory score (61007). Heavy cannabis users (daily for at least two years) had a greater susceptibility to false memories (61004) and still have memory problems even when not intoxicated (61006). Concurrent tobacco use may prevent in part the memory impairment due to cannabis intoxication and may account for the popularity of using both drugs (61008).

Reference Number: 61001

BARTHOLOMEW, J., S. HOLROYD, AND T.M. HEFFERNAN. "Does Cannabis Use Affect Prospective Memory in Young Adults?" *Journal of Psychopharmacology,* 24: 241–46, 2010 (2 tables, 39 references)

Abstract: The prospective memory (video-based memory task) was determined in forty-five cannabis users and forty-five non-users (median age 19 years).

> In conclusion, the results obtained from the objective prospective memory task in the present study suggest that prospective memory impairments are associated with cannabis use in young adults and these impairments should be added to the list of neuropsychological deficits associated with regular cannabis use.

Reference Number: 61002

CURRAN, H.V., C. BRIGNELL, S. FLETCHER, P. MIDDLETON, AND J. HENRY "Cognitive and Subjective Dose-Response Effects of Acute Oral Delta 9 Tetrahydrocannabinol (THC) in Infrequent Cannabis Users." *Psychopharmacology,* 164: 61–70, 2002 (1 table, 8 figures, 3 references)

Abstract: Fifteen male infrequent cannabis users (ages 18 to 30 years) consumed a placebo, 7.5, and 15 mg of oral THC on three occasions at one-week intervals. A battery of tests was conducted, including memory, choice, and simple RT and verbal fluency before and 1, 2, 4, 6, 8, 24, and 48 hours after dosing. Plasma THC and 11-OH THC were determined by GC/MS from blood samples collected via an indwelling catheter. The mean peak plasma THC concentration occurred at 2 hours and were approximately 4.5 ng/mL for the high and 1 ng/mL for the low doses respectively.

> These data demonstrate that oral delta 9 THC impaired episodic memory and learning in a dose-dependent manner, while sparing perceptual primary and working memory.

Reference Number: 61003

RANGANATHAN, M., AND D.C. D'SOUZA. "The Acute Effects of Cannabinoids on Memory in Humans." *Psychopharmacology*, 188: 425–44, 2006 (1 table, 5 figures, 136 references)

Abstract: A review was conducted on the acute effects of cannabinoids on memory.

> Acute administration of delta-9-THC transiently impairs immediate and delayed free recall of information presented after, but not before, drug administration in a dose- and delay-dependent manner. In particular, cannabinoids increase intrusion errors. These effects are more robust with the inhaled and intravenous route and correspond to peak drug levels. This profile suggests that cannabinoids impair all stages of memory, including encoding, consolidation, and retrieval.

Reference Number: 61004

RIBA, J., M. VALLE, F. SAMPEDRO, A. RODRIGUEZ-PUJADAS, S. MARTINEZ-HORAT, J. KULISEVSKY, AND A. RODRIGUEZ-FORNELLS. "Telling True from False: Cannabis Users Show Increased Susceptibility to False Memories." *Molecular Psychiatry*, 20: 772–77, 2015 (1 table, 4 figures, 47 references)

Abstract: Sixteen heavy cannabis users (daily for at least two years) and matched cannabis-naive subjects were tested as to their susceptibility to false memories using a memory test of words.

> Taken together, the present results indicate that long-term heavy cannabis users are at an increased risk of experiencing memory errors even when abstinent and drug-free. These deficits show a neural basis and suggest a subtle compromise of brain mechanisms involved in reality monitoring. Though subtle, the deficits bear similarities with alterations

observed in psychiatric and neurologic conditions and also with age-related cognitive decline. This lingering diminished ability to tell true from false may have medical and legal implications.

Reference Number: 61005

LANE, S.D., D.R. CHEREK, L.M. LIEVING, AND O.V. TCHEREMISSINE. "Marijuana Effects on Human Forgetting Functions." *Journal of the Experimental Analysis of Behavior,* 83: 67–83, 2005 (2 tables, 2 figures, 39 references)

Abstract: Acute cannabis use impairs working memory in humans. Three male and two female cannabis users (ages 21 to 34 years) with a negative urine drug screen (EMIT) were tested on a computerized memory test employing a delayed match to sample (DMTS) procedure, after smoking a placebo, 2.2 percent THC (M1), and 2.9 percent THC (M2) cigarettes. There were significant increases in heart rate after smoking M1 and M2. HR increases are among the most reliable indicators of cannabis use. The range of retention intervals for DMTS were 0.5, 4, 12, and 24 seconds. The marijuana-induced disruption in DMTS performance increased as the retention interval increased, with very little impairment with the short (0.5 seconds) retention interval but increasing impairment as the interval was increased. Cannabis impairs memory function by increasing the rate of forgetting.

The acute administration of smoke marijuana to adult humans produced changes in rates of forgetting but not in initial discriminability. Relative to performance after placebo administration, these impairments were a function of delay interval length. Specifically, delta-9-THC increased the slope parameter of negative exponential forgetting functions in all five subjects.

Reference Number: 61006

SOLOWIJ, N., AND R. BATTISTI. "The Chronic Effects of Cannabis on Memory in Humans: A Review." *Current Drug Abuse Reviews,* 1: 81–98, 2008 (1 table, 105 references)

Abstract: A review was conducted on the effects of chronic cannabis use on memory problems. Short-term memory problems are one of the most common problems associated with cannabis use.

Sufficient evidence has accumulated from relevant studies of cannabis users in the unintoxicated state to conclude that long-term heavy cannabis use is associated with impaired memory function, associated being the key operative, given the wide variety of studies reviewed in this paper. Our central tenet is that impaired memory function persists beyond the period of acute intoxication and is related to a variety of cannabis use parameters.

Reference Number: 61007

MCCLURE, E.A., J.B. LYDIARD, S.D. GODDARD, AND K.M. GRAY. "Objective and Subjective Memory Ratings in Cannabis-Dependent Adolescents." *American Journal of Addictions*, 24: 47–52, 2015 (3 tables, 37 references)

Abstract: A study was conducted on memory impairment of eighty-two male and thirty female cannabis-dependent adolescents (mean age 18.9 years) enrolled in a clinical cannabis-cessation program. Ten percent reported serious memory problems, 48 percent reported minor memory loss, and 42 percent reported there was no memory problem. Verbal and visual memory tests were conducted on the subjects. The subjects reporting minor memory problems on average performed better than those who reported no problem. The subjects who reported serious memory problems performed the worst on the memory tests. Female cannabis users on average obtained lower verbal and visual memory scores than males. Heavy cannabis users also performed worse on the memory tests than light users of cannabis.

Table: Self-Reported Cannabis-Related Memory Problems and Verbal and Visual Memory Test Scores [Note: A score of 100 is average for adolescents)

Self-Reported Memory problems	Verbal Memory Score (mean)	Visual Memory Score (mean)
"No problem"	92.7	93.1
"Minor problem"	103.7	102.2
"Serious problem"	80.2	91.3

Adopted from McClure et al (2015)

Participants reporting minor problems demonstrated the strongest performance on the memory tasks. This finding may suggest that these participants may be more likely to recognize or remember difficulties leading to some endorsement of problems with cannabis, but objectively are not experiencing cognitive deficits. Most notably and of greater concern is that participants reporting no problem were not classifying themselves correctly and appeared to have memory deficits when compared to other participants in this trial and normative scores for their age group.

Reference Number: 61008

SCHUSTER, R.M., N.A. CRANE, R. MERMELSTEIN, AND R. GONZALEZ. "Tobacco May Mask Poorer Episodic Memory Among Young Adult Cannabis Users." *Neuropsychology*, 29: 759–66, 2015 (1 figure, 2 tables, 38 references)

Abstract: Cannabis users have been shown to have memory impairments related to the severity of cannabis use and typically resolve after twenty-eight days of abstinence. In contrast, acute tobacco use has been shown to result in improvements in concentration and memory. Twenty-three female and forty-one male young cannabis users (mean age 20.8 years) were tested on the Hopkins Verbal Learning Test - Revisited (HVLT-R). More cannabis use was associated with poorer initial acquisition, total learning, and delayed recalls in HVLT-R, but only in sporadic tobacco use. Cannabis users who smoked tobacco consistently did not have significant impairment.

> In sum, these data provide important insight into a potential mechanism (i.e., attenuation of cognitive decrements) that might reinforce use of both substances and hamper cessation attempts among cannabis users who also smoke cigarettes. However, it is critical to underscore that these findings do not encourage tobacco use among cannabis users. Especially given that the effect sizes found in the current study were small to moderate, it is highly unlikely that any possible cognitive-enhancing effects would outweigh the numerous documented health risks from tobacco (e.g., cardiovascular disease, respiratory disease, reproductive effects, and cancer). Instead, these results are valuable due to their relevance in informing the development of more tailored and targeted intervention efforts for the growing number of individuals who use both cannabis and tobacco.

Reference Number: 61009

THEUNISSEN, E.L., P. HECKMAN, E.B. DE SOUSA, FERNANDES PERNA, K.P.C. KUYPERS, A. SAMBETH, A. BLOKLAND, J. PRICKAERTS, S.W. TOENNES, AND J.G. RAMAEKERS. "Rivastigmine but not Vardenafil Reverses Cannabis-Induced Impairment of Verbal Memory in Healthy Humans." *Psychopharmacology*, 232: 343–53, 2015 (6 tables, 1 figure, 52 references)

Abstract: Nine male and six female occasional cannabis users (mean age 21 years) received placebo, or 20 mg vardenafil or rivastigimine; and placebo, or 11 percent THC using a Volcano vaporizer on six occasions. Blood samples were collected at four different times and serum THC, 11-OH-THC, and THCCOOH concentrations were determined. The subjects were tested on a visual verbal learning task, prospective memory task, Sternberg memory test, stop signal task, and critical tracking and delayed attention tasks. All subjects under the influence of cannabis were impaired in all memory tasks, critical tracking, divided attention, and stop signal tasks for up to two hours after use. The mean peak serum THC concentrations were between 4.2 and 6.3 ng/mL and were unaffected by the two drugs. Pretreatment with rivastigimine improved delay and immediate recall memory but vardenafil had no such effects.

> Impaired learning and recall are among the most often reported cognitive deficits observed during cannabis intoxication. In particular, immediate recall, delayed recall, and recognition of items learned while under the influence of THC are impaired, whereas recall of items learned before cannabis administration is generally not affected while recalled in an intoxicated state. This suggests that THC specifically impairs acquisition and consolidation of information into memory but not its retrieval from memory.

Reference Number: 61010

ILAN, A.B., M.E. SMITH, AND A. GEVINS. "Effects of Marijuana on Neurophysiological Signals of Working and Episodic Memory." *Psychopharmacology*, 176: 214–22, 2004 (1 table, 3 figures, 75 references)

Abstract: Five female and five male casual marijuana smokers (ages 23-31 years) smoked a placebo or a marijuana cigarette (3.45 percent THC) in six puffs spaced fifty seconds apart, and were tested on working memory (WM) and episodic memory (EM). An electroencephalogram (EEG) was conducted during the testing. Responses in the working memory task were slower and less accurate after smoking marijuana and there was an increased tendency to erroneously identify distractor words in the episodic memory tests.

In conclusion, difficulty maintaining a coherent train of thought because of the intrusion of irrelevant information is part of the high that accompanies acute marijuana smoking. These intrusions may result from activated CB1 receptors disrupting the selective filtering of information into what is relevant and what should be forgotten. Such disruption may interfere with the temporal organization of information required in WM and EM. The results presented here suggest that subjects who became more intoxicated after marijuana smoking had difficulty manipulating information in WM and discriminating previously studied words from those that merely seem familiar.

Reference Number: 61011

SCHWEINSBURG, A.D., B.C. SCHWEINSBURG, K.L. MEDINA, T. MCQUEENY, S.A. BROWN, AND S.F. TAPERT. "The Influence of Recency of Use on fMRI Response during Spatial Working Memory in Adolescent Marijuana Users." *Journal of Psychoactive Drugs*, 42: 401–12, 2010 (3 tables, 3 figures, 7 references)

Abstract: Thirteen recent cannabis users (2 to 7 days abstinent), thirteen abstinent users (27 to 60 days abstinent), and eighteen non-using controls (all ages 15 to 18 years) had a functional magnetic resonance imaging (fMRI) conducted during a spatial working memory task (SWM).

In summary, heavy marijuana-using teenagers who had used within a week of scanning demonstrated greater frontal and insular brain response during SWM than marijuana users who had been abstinent for at least twenty-seven days. Interestingly, such frontal and insular activation was not observed in non-using control youths, suggesting that recent users recruit additional brain regions not normally utilized for this SWM task. There fMRI differences suggest increased working memory updating and inhibitory control among recent users despite similar task performance. Although cross-sectional, these results could indicate a change in neural strategy during the first month of abstinence, with less reliance on compensatory recruitment of frontal and insular regions. Finally, increased cognitive control and spatial working memory effort following recent use may have important implications for teens attempting abstinence, but longitudinal investigations are needed to verify these initial impressions.

6.11 MISCELLANEOUS

Over the last decade the percentage of Americans who perceive regular use of cannabis as a great risk declined from 51 percent to 40 percent. Only 24 percent of persons, ages 18 to 25 years, perceived regular cannabis use as a great risk (61110). One psychiatrist who warned of cannabis use in adolescents in a public lecture was harassed by middle-age male cannabis users who insisted that marijuana was a safe drug (61103). Digital clubbing has been reported to occur in heavy cannabis users (61101, 61102). Smoking cannabis is not recommended for the treatment of glaucoma (61111). One hour after smoking cannabis, handwriting appear larger and less legible with increased spacing and changes in the slant (61113). Cannabis (or alcohol) use does not increase creativity (61114). Although marijuana use has been associated with the munchies, cannabis users, in general have a lower body mass index (61115).

Reference Number: 61101

BARIS, Y.I., E. TAN, F. KALYONCU, M. ARTVINLI, AND A.A. SAHIN. "Digital Clubbing in Hashish Addicts." *Chest*, 98: 1545b–46, 1990 (5 references)

Abstract: Four cases of digital clubbing or hypertrophic osteoarthropathy are described in hashish addicts. It has also been reported in heroin addicts.

The pathogenesis of clubbing is still controversial. However, increased blood flow to the distal parts of the extremities has been noted in most studies. Besides many other systemic manifestations, hashish may produce signs of autonomic dysfunction. The administration of tetrahydrocannabinol (psychoactive compound of cannabis plants) in vivo results in a decline of neural synthesis and release of acetylcholine with a concomitant increase of catecholamines, which have vasodilatative properties on skeletal muscles. Adrenergic blockade to reverse the hypervascularity has been successful. We suggest that chronic use of hashish may elevate catecholamine levels and may cause vasodilatation of the peripheral arteries followed by digital clubbing.

Reference Number: 61102

SCHULLER, A., V. COTTIN, A. HOT, AND J-F. CORDIER. "Finger Clubbing and Altered Carbon Monoxide Transfer Capacity in Cannabis Smokers." *European Respiratory Journal*, 31: 473–81, 2008 (1 table, 5 references)

Abstract: A 26-year-old chronic tobacco and cannabis smoker (fifteen joints a day for ten years) had marked digital clubbing on his hands and feet. Pulmonary function tests were normal except for a decreased CO lung transfer capacity. The patient quit smoking tobacco and reduced his cannabis use to once a month and the clubbing disappeared. Another male chronic tobacco and cannabis (ten joints a day for eight years) smoker (age 27 years) also had marked finger clubbing and decreased CO lung transfer.

> The pathophysiology of cannabis-induced finger clubbing remains speculative. We hypothesize that the drug may increase the expression of vascular endothelial growth factor, alpha, or of its receptor. Cannabis-induced alteration of carbon monoxide transfer may be related to vascular changes and/or infiltration by pigmented macrophages of the alveolar interstitium and capillaries of the lung, as shown by autopsy analysis of cannabis smokers (also showing bronchiolar inflammation).

Reference Number: 61103

OSUCH, E. "Marijuana Use in Youth from Bench to Bedside to Longitudinal Outlook." *The Canadian Journal of Psychiatry*, 61: 316–17, 2016 (10 references)

Abstract: In September 2010, this psychiatrist gave a public lecture at a downtown library in London, Ontario, entitled "Marijuana Use in Youth: Is it as harmless as we'd like to think?" The talk was announced in the local newspaper, which received numerous hateful, rude, and accusatory comments online. She also received threatening emails and was heckled by several middle-age men during her talk.

> Thus, there are strong opinions about this matter, and they are highly polarized. There may be a dearth of reliable information to ground this conversation, but that depends on your perspective. Some, including

myself, would say that there is ample evidence that marijuana use by youth is problematic and believe that use of this substance among youth should not be prevented from increasing but should actually be decreased. There is a widespread perception, meanwhile, that marijuana use is harmless. This is particularly notable in the types of media used by youth, such as Twitter. In addition, I have heard from a youth and young adults in London and elsewhere that instructors at high schools and post-secondary schools have told them to use marijuana, "if they're going to use anything this weekend because it's safest." Combining the actual risks associated with marijuana use in youth and the belief that there is little to fear in its use, along with the lack of evidence for good and accessible treatments for youth with marijuana use disorders, paints a dismal picture. Vulnerability to harmful effects of marijuana appears to be even more pronounced for youth poised to interact with psychiatric and other mental health case treatment providers because of the existence of neuropsychiatric risk factors. This combination of facts suggests that there is a momentous storm coming toward us of upcoming need for psychiatric and addictions services that we have no clear way to adequately meet or prevent. As providers of care, this should be of concern.

Reference Number: 61104

FABER, M., A. VAN GASSE, V. SABATO, M.M. HAGENDORENS, C.H. BRIDTS, L.S. DE CLERCK, AND D.G. EBO. "Marijuana Allergy: Beyond the Joint." *Journal of Investigative Allergology and Clinical Immunology*, 25: 70–72, 2015 (1 figure, 9 references)

Abstract: A 24-year-old woman attended a clinic in 2012 with generalized urticarial, angioedema, and dyspnea after eating various nuts and fruits, but prior to eating, she smoked cannabis. The allergies worsened as she continued smoking cannabis.

> In conclusion, we report the case of a patient with genuine marijuana allergy and extensive cross-allergies. These cross-allergies are rapidly evolving and have extended beyond fruit and vegetables to involve wheat, tobacco, and Hevea latex. As this cross-reactivity appears to be associated with sensitization to an ns-LTP from cannabis, the term marijuana connection is proposed.

Reference Number: 61105

FISCHER, B., Y. MURPHY, P. KURDYAK, E. GOLDNER, AND J. REHM. "Medical Marijuana Programs: Why Might They Matter for Public Health and Why We Should Better Understand Their Impacts?" *Preventive Medicine Reports*, 2: 53–56, 2015 (68 references)

Abstract: A short review of Medical Marijuana Programs (MMPs) in the US and Canada and their problems was presented. There are sixty-eight references. Most of the Canadian MMP participants had a prior cannabis history and most increased their cannabis consumption (33 percent large and 32 percent small) post-MMP. Forty percent reported > 2 g/day of use and 42 percent reported > 2 episodes per day.

> The scope and quality of existing evidence characterizing potential health effects of MMPs are limited. This is partly an effect of the emerging nature of this area of knowledge, and also related to the fact that MMPs, at least in North America, were not primarily implemented as health interventions but rather came about as a consequence of developments in the ongoing political and legal struggles over cannabis control: in Canada, they were a consequence of constitutional court decisions; in US states, they were introduced in most instances following public ballot initiatives.

Reference Number: 61106

CARLINI, B.H., S.B. GARRETT, AND R.M. HARWICK. "Beyond Joints and Brownies: Marijuana Concentrates in the Legal Landscape of WA State." *International Journal of Drug Policy*, 42: 26–29, 2017 (2 figures, 30 references)

Abstract: The problem of Vaporizable Cannabis Concentrates (VCCs), a form of marijuana with a high THC concentration in Washington state, is discussed. Since the VCC method of consumption is vaporization, it is often seen as healthier than smoking low THC joints. In one print advertisement, one dab product with 80 percent THC is described as benign as a tropical vacation. It has been proposed that increasing illicit drug potency is due to drug prohibition, since highly potent drugs are easier to transport and conceal. But the opposite seems to be occurring in Washington state; after decriminalization and for-profit legalization.

Vaporizable Cannabis Concentration sales have increased 770 percent in Washington state from 2014 to 2016.

> The legalization model adopted in Washington is dissonant with the political rhetoric that made legalization possible. The political arguments of Initiative I-502 were centred on racial disparity in the criminal justice system and a public health approach to mitigate the impact of MJ legalization, which included a commitment to using a generous proportion of MJ excise tax revenues to fund MJ-related prevention, treatment, and research. Unfortunately, very modest gains have been made in terms of racial justice: while marijuana possession court filings plummeted since legalization, African-American adults continue to be 2.8 times more likely to have a misdemeanor cannabis charge than white, non-Hispanic adults. Similarly, the promise to protect public health had yet to materialize in a meaningful way: the original planned allocation of MJ excise taxes to fund prevention, treatment, and research have been roughly cut in half and — per initiative of state legislators — reallocated to the WA State General Fund. As for the topic of this article, the WA movement for MJ legalization was centred on the MJ plant and based on the relatively benign societal experiences of adults consuming MJ joints and brownies. The market-driven MJ industry is, however, transforming MJ into something different: a very potent and well-marketed product that most people were not aware existed when the Initiative passed.

Reference Number: 61107

VIDOT, D.C., G. PRADO, N. DE LA CRUZ-MONOZ, C. SPADOLA, M. CUESTA, AND S.E. MESSIAH. "Post-Operative Marijuana Use and Disordered Eating Among Bariatric Surgery Patients." *Surgery for Obesity and Related Diseases*, 12: 171–78, 2016 (4 tables, 35 references)

Abstract: The effect of cannabis use on eating disorders was determined on twelve male and thirty-eight female patients (mean age 28 years) who underwent bariatric weight loss surgery (WLS), mainly the Roux-en-Y Gastric Bypass procedure. Eighteen percent of the patients reported current cannabis use, 38 percent reported recent use, and 21.4 percent reported increased cannabis use post-WLS. A loss of controlled food intake was associated with current cannabis use and increased cannabis use post-WLS. Current or increased cannabis use post-WLS was also associated with higher scores on the eating disorder subscales.

Table: Percent of Patients with Yale Food Dependence Criteria According to Cannabis Use

Yale Food Dependence Criteria	Never Used Cannabis	Current Cannabis Use	Increasing Cannabis Use Since WLS
Loss of Control	5.3%	22.2%	33.3%
Too Much Time Spent to Obtain Food	9.1%	22.2%	50.0%
Skip Important Activities	4.5%	11.1%	16.7%
Diagnosis of Food Addiction/Dependence	9.1%	22.2%	33.3%

Source: Adapted from Vidot et al, 2016

Findings show marijuana use in post-WLS patients despite recommendations against use. A subgroup of WLS patients may be at risk for disordered eating post-WLS, particularly those who used marijuana before surgery and should be closely monitored for several years post-WLS.

Reference Number: 61108

FREISTHLER, B., AND P.J. GRUENEWALD. "Examining the Relationship between the Physical Availability of Medical Marijuana and Marijuana Use across Fifty California Cities." *Drug and Alcohol Dependence,* 143: 244–50, 2014 (3 tables, 31 references)

Abstract: A telephone survey was conducted on marijuana use of 8,853 persons living in fifty mid-size California cities and compared to the number of medical marijuana dispensaries and delivery services available in each city. On average, approximately 5.4 percent of those surveyed used cannabis and that ranged from city to city from 1.1 percent to 19.3 percent. Those surveyed on average used cannabis 3.02 times a week. White males who had higher incomes and higher levels of impulsivity and tolerance of deviance were more likely to use cannabis.

The current study finds that the total physical availability of medical marijuana through dispensaries and delivery services per roadway mile at the city-level is positively related to current marijuana use and greater frequency of use, controlling for a variety of demographic and personality characteristics. As expected, current physical availability of medical marijuana was unrelated to lifetime use.

Reference Number: 61109

LACHENMEIER, D.W., AND J. REHM. "Comparative Risk Assessment of Alcohol, Tobacco, Cannabis and Other Illicit Drugs Using the Margin of Exposure Approach." *Scientific Reports,* 5: 8126, 7 pp, 2015 (2 tables, 3 figures, 67 references)

Abstract: A comparative risk assessment of THC, alcohol, nicotine, diazepam, and other drugs was conducted using the margin of exposure (MOE) approach. The MOE is the ratio between the toxicological threshold and estimated human intake. The toxicological threshold is the median lethal drug dose from animal experiments. The toxicological threshold ranged from 2 mg/kg for heroin to 531 mg/kg for ethanol. The population exposure was based on sewage analysis and prevalence in Europe. On a population scale, only alcohol falls into the high risk category while the other drugs, cocaine, amphetamine, ecstasy, and benzodiazepines, had a MOE > 100 and cannabis had a MOE > 10,000.

> Nevertheless, as previously stressed, our finding should not be interpreted that moderate alcohol consumption poses a higher risk to the individual and their close contacts with regular heroin use. Much of the harm from drug use is not inherently related to consumption but is heavily influenced by the environmental conditions of drug use and this additional hazard is not included in a drug ranking based on animal toxicology.

Reference Number: 61110

OKANEKU J., D. VEARRIER, R.G. MCKEEVER, G.S. LASALA, AND M.I. GREENBERG. "Change in Perceived Risk Associated with Marijuana Use in the United States from 2002 to 2012." *Clinical Toxicology,* 53: 151–55, 2015 (2 tables, 2 figures, 24 references)

Abstract: Cannabis use and the perception of its risk was determined in 614,579 respondents between 2002 and 2012, using the US National Survey on Drug Use and Health. The percentage of those who perceived great risk in regular cannabis use decreased from 51.3 percent to 40.3 percent, whereas the percentage who perceived no risk increased from

5.7 percent to 11.7 percent. Increasing age resulted in increasing perceived risk. Males have lower rates of perceived risks than females.

Table: Percent of Respondents Who Characterize Regular Use of Marijuana as Associated with Great Risk according to Age in 2002 and 2012

Age Group (Years)	2002	2012
12 to 17 years	51.4%	43.5%
18 to 25 years	34.7%	24.1%
26 to 34 years	45.0%	29.5%
35 to 49 years	47.2%	40.7%
50 years and older	62.8%	47.7%

Source: Adapted from Okaneku et al, 2015

During the 2002– 2012 study period, there was a significant decrease in the perceived risk associated with occasional and regular marijuana use among residents of the United States. Younger age, male gender, and past month use were also associated with decreased perceived risk.

Reference Number: 61111

SUN, X., C.S. XU, N. CHADA, A. CHEN, AND J. LIU. "Marijuana for Glaucoma: A Recipe for Treatment or Disaster?" *Yale Journal of Biology and Medicine*, 88: 265–69, 2015 (1 table, 43 references)

Abstract: Glaucoma is associated with elevated intraocular pressure (IOP > 25 mm Hg) and causes irreversible vision loss. Medical marijuana and THC by smoking, oral, or IV administration can lower IOP by 25 percent in 60 to 65 percent of the patients. The effects last for four hours and require at least six to eight doses a day. Tolerance develops to the therapeutic effects and after several months the IOP is no longer lowered in most people. No THC eye-drops are possible because of its high fat solubility. THC works on CB ciliary cells, causing decrease in aqueous humor production and lowering IOP. Medical laser or surgical treatment can help cure glaucoma and eye drops are also available, which cause IOP reduction.

Medical marijuana has been shown to lower the IOP for brief periods of time but carries a greater side effect profile than standard therapeutic options. The daily dose amounts to maintain the IOP lowering effect is likely to lead to CUD [Cannabis Use Disorder] and result in physical and psychological harm to the patient.

Reference Number: 61112

VOGEL, I., P.M. VAN DE LOOIJ-JANSEN, C.L. MIELOO, A. BURDORF, AND F. DE WAART. "Risky Music Listening Behaviors and Associated Health Risk Behaviors." *Pediatrics*, 129: 1097–103, 2012 (4 tables, 35 references)

Abstract: A survey was conducted of 944 Dutch students (ages 15 to 25 years) on risky music listening behaviour that may induce hearing loss. Thirty percent of MP-3 player users exceeded safe hearing thresholds and 48 percent of disco goers exceeded safe levels of sound.

Table: Association of Cannabis or Hard Drug Use and Odds Ratio of Unhealthy Lifestyles

Drug Use	Risky MP3 Listening	Risky Music Venues Listening	Smoking	Binge Drinking
Cannabis use	2.28 X	1.66 X	9.71 X	5.29 X
Hard Drug use	1.22 X	1.76 X	2.96 X	3.47 X

Source: Adapted from Vogel et al, 2012

Risky MP3-player listeners used cannabis more often during the past four weeks. Students exposed to risky sound levels during discotheque and pop concert attendance were more often binge drinkers, and reported inconsistent condom use during sexual intercourse.

Reference Number: 61113

ZAKI, N.N., AND M.A. IBRAHEIM "Effect of Alcohol and Cannabis Sativa Consumption on Handwriting." *Neurobehavioral Toxicology and Teratology*, 5: 225–27, 1983 (1 figure, 7 references)

Abstract: Handwriting samples of five male subjects (ages 32 to 45 years) were obtained before, during, and one hour after smoking of cannabis sativa or consumption of 75 mL of wine. No blood drug concentrations were determined. There were no changes in handwriting immediately after the consumption of wine. One hour later there was expanded spacing and some changes in the slant of the writing and decreases in legibility. Immediately after smoking four cannabis cigarettes in the two subjects tested, the handwriting was larger, with some alterations in letter forms and base-line deviations. One hour after smoking, the letters remained larger and altered but there was no base line deviation.

It is concluded that the CNS depressant activity of both CS and alcohol are responsible for their effect on handwriting. It is suggested that while alcohol does affect the CNS, it does not greatly depress the CNS activity used to direct manipulative functions such as handwriting under the experimental conditions used. The changes in handwriting observed may be of some forensic value, i.e., especially during comparison of signatures for certain legalities. A suggested forged signature may reflect a true one obtained under the influence of cannabis or alcohol.

Reference Number: 61114

KOWAL, M.A., A. HAZEKAMP, L.S. COLZATO, H. VAN STEENBERGEN, N.J.A. VAN DER WEE, J. DURIEUX, M. MANAI, AND B. HOMMEL. "Cannabis and Creativity: Highly Potent Cannabis Impairs Divergent Thinking in Regular Cannabis Users." *Psychopharmacology*, 232: 1123–34, 2015 (2 tables, 4 figures, 59 references)

Abstract: Seven female and fifty-two male regular cannabis users were randomly divided into a placebo group, low THC (5.5 mg), and high THC (22 mg). The placebo and cannabis (19 percent THC) were delivered via a vaporizer. The subjects were tested on creativity tasks of convergent thinking (remote Association Task) and divergent thinking (Alternate Uses Tasks). Administration of the high dose marijuana was detrimental to divergent thinking and the low dose cannabis had no effect. Divergent thinking is an important component of creativity.

In any case, it can be claimed that the phenomological experience of a person intoxicated with cannabis might not necessarily reflect his or her actual performance. In particular, the frequently reported feeling of heightened creativity could be an illusion. In other words, smoking a joint may not be the best choice when in need of breaking the writer's block or overcoming other artistic inhibitions, and smoking several of them might actually be counter-productive.

Reference Number: 61115

SANSONE, R.A., AND L.A. SANSONE. "Marijuana and Body Weight." *Innovations in Clinical Neuroscience*, 11: 50–54, 2014 (30 references)

Abstract: The use of cannabis is often associated with snacking behaviour, known as the munchies. Stimulation of CB1 receptor sites (of which THC is a partial agonist) have been shown to stimulate feeding behaviour. In normal subjects, a low dose of cannabis (i.e., one cigarette) was found to have no effect on food intake, but two to three cigarettes increased snacking behaviour but not meal size.

Marijuana is a clinically controversial substance, but one potential medical benefit may be weight gain. According to available studies, appetite stimulation as well as weight gain may occur in patients with physical debilitation due to HIV/AIDS and/or cancer. However, while weight gain may occur, it is not greater than currently available agents for inducing weight gain (e.g., megestrol). As for the effects of marijuana on the body in the general population, use appears to be associated with a lower body mass index. This observation may be partially explained by differences in short-term versus long-term use, comorbid polydrug use, and/or the intriguing theory that food and drugs may compete for the same reward sites in the brain. Alternatively, marijuana may genuinely be a regulatory compound, increasing weight in those with low weight, but not in those who are normal or overweight.

Reference Number: 61116

BUSSE, F., L. OMIDI, K. TIMPER, A. LECHTLE, M. WINDGASSEN, E. KLUGE, AND M. STUMVOLL. "Lead Poisoning Due to Adulterated Marijuana [Letter]." *New England Journal of Medicine*, 385: 1641–42, 2008 (1 table, 1 figure, 3 references)

Abstract: Over a three-to-four-month period, twenty-nine patients (ages 16 to 33 years) were admitted to four different hospitals in the Leipzig area of Germany, with classic signs and symptoms of lead poisoning, including fatigue, abdominal cramps, and nausea. An additional ninety-five persons had elevated blood lead levels. They all smoked marijuana as a joint or in a water pipe. Left-over packages of cannabis were found to contain small lead particles.

The current working hypothesis of the police is that because of its high specific gravity and inconspicuous grayish colour, lead was used to increase the weight of street marijuana sold by the gram and thereby to maximize profits among dealers. In the material that was obtained, the lead content on average was 10 percent by weight, which translates into a profit increase of approximately 1,000 euros ($1,500.00) per kilogram of marijuana. Lead particles smoked in a joint, which can have a core temperature of 1,200°C, are very effectively absorbed in the respiratory tract. The medical community, including pediatricians, should consider adulterated marijuana as a potential source of lead intoxication.

Reference Number: 61117

NUSSBAUM, A.M., J.A. BOYER, AND E.C. KONDRAD. "'But My Doctor Recommended Pot': Medical Marijuana and the Patient-Physician Relationship." *Journal of General and Internal Medicine*, 26: 1364–67, 2011 (1 table, 1 figure, 20 references)

Abstract: In Colorado, a small group of fifteen physicians registered 49 percent of all medical marijuana patients and one physician alone registered 10 percent of all patients. Physicians were not required to have follow-up visits from patients prescribed medical marijuana to determine the benefits of this drug or if complications or side effects occurred. As of June 2011, there were 128,698 registered medical marijuana users in Colorado.

Table: Percentage of Reported Conditions of Colorado Medical Marijuana Registrants*

Qualifying Medical Conditions	% of Registrants Reporting Condition
Severe pain	94%
Muscle spasm	20%
Severe nausea	12%
Cancer	2%
Seizures	1%
Cachexia	1%
Glaucoma	1%
HIV/AIDS	1%

* Note: Some patients registered for multiple conditions

Source: Adapted from Nussbaum, Boyer, and Kondrad, 2011

In sum, Colorado's medical marijuana legislation and industry unburden physicians of their responsibilities to the welfare of their patients by allowing them to act out of insufficient scientific knowledge regarding the effectiveness and safety of marijuana. In this model, physicians are gatekeepers to an otherwise illegal substance, a very thin account of the relationship between a patient and physician. We believe physicians have further responsibilities to their patients than the medical marijuana legislation and industry require. If marijuana is to be available for medical use, we believe it ought to be regulated, approved, and prescribed like any other medical treatment. Until this occurs, we call on physicians to stop recommending marijuana. If physicians choose to recommend marijuana, we believe this should be done, at minimum, in the context of a longitudinal patient-physician relationship, in the absence of improper financial incentives for the physician with an honest acknowledgement to patients of the limited scientific knowledge regarding the safety and efficacy of medical marijuana and only when other, more rigorously studied, treatments have failed.

6.12 MOTORCYCLISTS

As expected, cannabis causes impairment of operating a motorcycle as well as cars, and was more often found in motorcyclists (61202).

Reference Number: 61201

DRUMMER, O.H., AND S. YAP. "The Involvement of Prescribed Drugs in Road Trauma." *Forensic Science International*, 265: 17–21, 2016 (2 tables, 34 references)

Abstract: The prescription drug, cannabis, and alcohol concentrations were determined in 2,638 fatally injured drivers in Australia between 2000 and 2013. Approximately 79 percent of the drivers were male and 53 percent were single motor vehicle collisions (SMVCs). The percentage of drivers positive for alcohol/drug was 50.5 percent. A BAC > 0.010 g/100mL was detected in 27.5 percent of the drivers, and a BAC > 0.079 g/100mL was found in 22.7 percent. A blood THC > 2 ng/mL was detected in 14.5 percent of the drivers. Cannabis use was highest in motorcyclists (18.7 percent) and lowest in truckers (5.8 percent). Culpability analysis of drivers with only THC detected had an OR of 3.0 times of a fatal MVC.

Drugs prescribed for medicinal reasons or obtained over the counter (anti-depressants, anti-psychotic, benzodiazepine, opioids, sedating anti-histamines) were present in 21.2 percent of fatally injured drivers on Victorian roads between 2000 and 2013; however, responsibility analyses did not show a significantly increased crash risk. There was a tendency for benzodiazepine positive drivers to have an increased OR over drug-free drivers, as has been shown in previous studies, but the relatively low numbers of cases where this drug group was found by itself may have precluded the ability to achieve statistical significance.

Reference Number: 61202

SODERSTROM, C.A., P.C. DISCHINGER, T.J. KERNS, AND A.L. TRIFILLIS. "Marijuana and Other Drug Use Among Automobile and Motorcycle Drivers Treated at a Trauma Center." *Accident Analysis and Prevention* 27: 131–135, 1995 (3 tables, 25 references)

Abstract: Serum THC, alcohol, cocaine, and PCP concentrations were determined in 225 automobile drivers and 106 motorcycle drivers attending a trauma centre during 1990 and 1991. A positive BAC was found in 35 percent of automobile drivers (mean SAC = 0.160 g/100mL) and 47 percent of motorcycle drivers (mean SAC = 0.141 g/100mL). A positive serum THC was found in 3 percent of the automobile drivers and 32 percent of the motorcycle drivers. The use rates for all drugs was higher in motorcycle drivers than in automobile drivers.

This study indicates that pre-injury marijuana use among automobile drivers admitted to a mid-Atlantic regional trauma centre has decreased markedly. The same has not occurred among cyclists. In addition, alcohol, cocaine, and PCP use was higher for the cyclists.

6.13 PEDESTRIANS

The most common drug detected in pedestrian fatalities besides alcohol was cannabis, which declined with increasing age of the victim (61301).

Reference Number: 61301

WALSH J.M., R. FLEGEL, R. ATKINS, L.A. CANGIANELLI, C. COOPER, C. WELSH, AND T.J. KERNS. "Drug and Alcohol Use Among Drivers Admitted to a Level-1 Trauma Center." *Accident Analysis and Prevention*, 37: 894–901, 2005 (2 tables, 3 figures, 23 references)

Abstract: Blood and urine samples were collected from 168 MVC victims (108 were drivers) who attended an ER in Maryland. Seventy-two percent of the injured drivers were male and one-third were 25 years of age or younger. Fifteen percent were positive for alcohol alone and another 16 percent for alcohol and another drug. Sixty-six percent of the drivers had a positive toxicology result. The mean BAC of drivers with alcohol alone was 0.172 g/100mL and with another drug was 0.175 g/100mL. The most commonly detected illegal drugs were marijuana, cocaine, and amphetamines. Marijuana use declined with increasing age.

> It appears that within our total MVC patient pool, passenger drug and alcohol use is roughly equivalent with that of the driver population, however, injured pedestrians tend to have higher rates of alcohol only and lower rates of drug plus alcohol than other MVCs. Drug and alcohol use in MVC victims was generally equivalent to that observed in trauma victims of other cases (i.e., violence, nonviolent/non MVC, industrial, sports injuries).

6.14 PSYCHOSIS/SCHIZOPHRENIA

Psychosis is a complicated mental disorder in which there is a loss of contact with reality and is associated with:

- Delusions
- Hallucinations
- Paranoia
- Disorganized thinking
- Disorganized talking

Cannabis use is associated with a three times greater risk of attending an ER with psychosis than with alcohol use (61411). The risk of psychosis increases with increasing use and potency of cannabis (i.e., skunk) (61402, 61403, 61407, 61414, 61417, 61423). Significant risks of psychosis also occur for inexperienced users of edible marijuana (61417). The use of synthetic cannabinoids pose the greatest risk of severe psychosis (61423). High CBD concentrations in marijuana help protect the user against developing psychosis (61410, 61421).

Schizophrenia is a more serious long-lasting mental disorder that is usually chronic and progressively deteriorating with the similar loss of contact with reality as psychosis and is also associated with long-term cannabis use (61405, 61419).

Reference Number: 61401

BARROWCLOUGH, C., L. GREGG., F. LOBBAN, S. BUCCI, AND R. EMSLEY. "The Impact of Cannabis Use on Clinical Outcomes in Recent Onset Psychosis." *Schizophrenia Bulletin*, 41: 382–90, 2015 (3 tables, 1 figure, 41 references)

Abstract: One hundred and ten patients (mean age 24 years) with a non-affective psychotic disorder with cannabis use or dependence in the UK were examined at baseline, 4.5, 9, and 18 months later. Cannabis use throughout this time period was determined.

> In conclusion, the findings from this methodologically robust study indicated that cannabis has no direct impact on the positive symptoms of psychosis in the early phase of psychosis. However, during this recent onset period, greater exposure to cannabis is associated with higher levels of depression possibly mediated by social factors; and reducing cannabis may lead to direct improvements in anxiety symptoms and better functioning.

Reference Number: 61402

DI FORTI, M., H. SALLIS, F. ALLEGRI, A. TROTTA, L. FERRARO, S.A. STILO, A. MARCONI, C. LA CASCIA, T.R. MARQUES, C. PARIANTE, P. DAZZAN, V. MONDELLI, A. PAPARELLI, A. KOLLIAKOU, D. PRATA, F. GAUGHRAN., A.S. DAVID, C. MORGAN, S.D. STAHL, M. KHONDOKER, J.H. MACCABE, AND R.M. MURRAY. "Daily Use, Especially of High-Potency Cannabis, Drives the Earlier Onset of Psychosis in Cannabis Users." *Schizophrenia Bulletin*, 40: 1509–17, 2014 (2 tables, 3 figures, 38 references)

Abstract: Psychotic patients with a history of cannabis use have an earlier age of onset of psychosis (AOP) by almost three years. Four hundred and ten first episode psychosis patients were studied between 2005 and 2010. Patients with cannabis exposure had an AOP of 28.2 years, versus 31.4 years for those who never used cannabis. Those who started cannabis use at age 15 years or younger had AOP of 27.0 years compared to 29.1 years for those who started > 15 years of age. Persons who used high potency cannabis (skunk) had the earliest AOP (25.2 years). The daily users of high potency marijuana had AOP six years earlier than non-cannabis users.

Table: Mean Age of Onset of Psychosis by Degree of Exposure to Cannabis.

Cannabis Use	Mean Age of Onset of Psychosis (Years)
Never used	31.4 years
Hash at weekends or less	31.1 years
Hash everyday	29.5 years
Skunk at weekends or less	26.5 years
Skunk everyday	25.2 years

Source: Adapted from Di Forti et al, 2013

> We confirm an association between cannabis use and earlier AOP and further show this to be independent of gender. Moreover, daily cannabis use and use of high potency cannabis are independently associated with a significantly higher hazard to make contact with services for psychosis at any given time. Finally, a younger age at first cannabis use (< 15 years) is associated with a younger AOP only in those who had used cannabis daily. All these findings support a true effect of cannabis use on AOP that is dose-dependent, similar to its effect on risk of developing a psychotic disorder.

Reference Number: 61403

DI FORTI, M., A. MARCONI, E. CARRA, S. FRAIETTA, A. TROTTA, M. BONOMO, F. BIANCONI, P. GARDNER-SOOD, J. O'CONNOR, M. RUSSO, S.A. STILO, T.R. MARQUES, V. MONDELLI, P. DAZZAN, C. PARIANTE, A.S. DAVID, F. GAUGHAN, Z. ATAKAN, C. IYEGBE, J. POWELL, C. MORGAN, M. LYNSKEY, AND R.M. MURRAY. "Proportion of Patients in South London with First-Episode Psychosis Attributable to Use of High Potency Cannabis: A Case-Control Study." *Lancet Psychiatry*, 2: 233–38, 2015 (4 tables, 2 figures, 29 references)

Abstract: A comparison was made between 410 patients with first episode psychosis and 370 population controls between 2005 and 2011 in South London. Thirty-three percent of the patients and 37 percent of the controls never used cannabis. Thirty percent of the patients and 11 percent of the controls used cannabis every day. Skunk cannabis has high potency THC and low cannabidiol. The risk of individuals having a psychotic disorder is three times greater for those who used skunk cannabis compared to those who never used cannabis and 5.4 times for daily skunk cannabis users. Samples of skunk cannabis seized in the London area had more THC than hash and virtually no cannabidiol (CBD).

Table: Odds Ratio of Psychosis with Increasing Use of Skunk.

Cannabis Use	Odds Ratio of Psychosis
Never used	1.0 X
Skunk less than once per week	1.90 X
Skunk on weekends	2.70 X
Skunk everyday	5.40 X

Source: Adapted from Di Forti et al, 2015

Our findings show the importance of raising public awareness of the risk associated with use of high potency cannabis, especially when such varieties of cannabis are becoming more available. The worldwide trend of liberalization of the legal constraints on the use of cannabis further emphasizes the urgent need to develop public education to inform young people about the risks of high potency cannabis.

Reference Number: 61404

DREWE, M., J. DREWE, AND A. RIECHLER-ROSSLER. "Cannabis and Risk of Psychosis." *Swiss Medical Weekly*, 134: 659–62, 2004 (43 references)

Abstract: A short general review was conducted on cannabis use and psychosis. Genetic variation of CB1 receptors are associated with an increased risk of developing cannabis abuse in schizophrenic patients.

Cannabis consumption modulates dopamine concentrations in certain brain areas and can thus induce or modulate the development of psychotic symptoms and psychosis. Cannabis in high doses may induce acute reversible (toxic) psychoses. Cannabis may also induce the manifestations of schizophrenia psychosis in vulnerable patients (dopamine stress) or at least trigger an earlier onset in this population. Young age is an additional risk factor for the development of psychosis. Concomitant cannabis consumption may affect the progression of schizophrenia psychoses and worsen the prognosis. Cannabis consumption is associated with a schizotypal personality; the causal relationship is not clear. Cannabis consumption can also lead to other psychiatric disorders including depression and may result in a severe loss of energy and cognitive disturbances.

Reference Number: 61405

HICKMAN, M., P. VICKERMAN, J. MACLEOD, G. LEWIS, S. ZAMMIT, J. KIRKBRIDE, AND P. JONES. "If Cannabis Use Causes Schizophrenia, How Many Cannabis Users May Need to be Prevented in Order to Prevent One Case of Schizophrenia? England and Wales Calculations." *Addiction*, 104:1856–61, 2009 (3 figures, 24 references)

Abstract: The adjusted risk ratio for psychosis was 2.1 times for heavy cannabis users.

Following the calculations above, if cannabis is related causally then the risk of schizophrenia in 1997–99 for men ages 20 to 24 was approximately 1 in 1,500 for heavy cannabis users, and 1 in 2,400 for light/heavy users. For women aged 20 to 24 the risk of schizophrenia was 1 in 4,000 for heavy cannabis users and 1 in 6,600 for light users.

Reference Number: 61406

PATEL, R., R. WILSON, R. JACKSON, M. BALL, H. SHETTY, M. BROADBENT, R. STEWART, P. MCGUIRE, AND S. BHATTACHARYYA. "Association of Cannabis Use with Hospital Admission and Antipsychotic Treatment Failure in First Episode Psychosis: An Observational Study." *British Medical Journal, Open*, 6, 2016: (3 tables, 2 figures, 38 references)

Abstract: A study was conducted of 2,026 persons attending South London and Mauddsley hospital with a first episode of psychosis (FEP) between 2006 and 2013. Outcomes of these patients were also determined up to five years later. Approximately 46 percent of FEPs had documented history of cannabis use and this was particularly common in patients who were male, single, and 16 to 25 years of age. Cannabis use was associated with 1.5 times the risk of frequency of hospital admission, 1.55 times the risk of compulsory admission and a greater number of days spent in hospital.

Cannabis use in patients with FEP was associated with an increased likelihood of hospital admission. This was linked to the prescription of several different antipsychotic drugs, indicating clinical judgment of antipsychotic treatment failed. Together, this suggests that cannabis use might be associated with worse clinical outcomes in psychosis by contributing toward failure of antipsychotic treatment.

Reference Number: 61407

SCHOELER, T., N. PETROS, M. DI FORTI, E. KLAMERUS, E. FOGLIA, O. AIJNAKINA, C. GAYER-ANDERSON, M. COLIZZI, D. QUATTRONE, I. BEHLKE, S. SHETTY, P. MCGUIRE, A.S. DAVID, R. MURRAY, AND S. BHATTACHARYYA. "Effects of Continuation, Frequency, and Type of Cannabis Use on Relapse in the First 2 Years after Onset of Psychosis: An Observational Study." *Lancet Psychiatry*, 3: 947–53, 2016 (3 tables, 1 figure, 25 references)

Abstract: Cannabis is the most commonly used illicit drug in patients with established psychosis. Two hundred and fifty-six patients with a first episode of psychosis between 2002 and 2013 were initially assessed. A follow-up assessment was conducted in 2015. Forty percent of the patients never used cannabis and 21 percent were regular cannabis users. Daily users of high potency cannabis (skunk) had worse outcomes or relapsed. Regular users of cannabis who stopped cannabis use at the start of the treatment had the best outcomes.

Table: Odds Ratio of Relapse of Psychosis with Cannabis Use

Cannabis Use	Odds Ratio of Risk of Relapse
Never user	1.24 X
Intermittent user	1.76 X
Continued user (hash)	1.82 X
Continued user (skunk, low frequency)	2.42 X
Continued user (skunk, high frequency)	3.28 X

Source: Adapted from Schoeler et al, 2016

Adverse effects associated with continual use of cannabis after the onset of a first episode of psychosis depend on the specific pattern of use. Possible interventions could focus on persuading cannabis-using patients with psychosis to reduce use or shift to less potent forms of cannabis.

Reference Number: 61408

SOLOMONS, K., V.M. NEPPE, AND J.M. KUYL. "Toxic Cannabis Psychosis Is a Valid Entity." *South African Medical Journal*, 78: 476–81, 1990 (4 tables, 35 references)

Abstract: A study was conducted of 100 black men admitted to a South African hospital with acute psychiatric symptoms. The patients had a history of recent dagga use and/or a positive urine cannabinoid test. The urine test was positive in twenty-nine cases (29 percent) and twenty-six were diagnosed with having toxic dagga psychosis. A history of dagga use was obtained from 45 percent of the patients. Dagga is a potent South African cannabis.

> The study demonstrated the heterogenic nature of toxic psychosis syndrome by documenting a variety of different clinical presentations, which included schizophrenia (42 percent), paranoia (26 percent), maniform psychosis (18 percent), and organic psychosis (16 percent).

Reference Number: 61409

SCHUBART, C.D., I.E.C. SOMMER, W.A. VAN GASTEL, R.L. GOETGEBUER, R.S. KHAN, AND M.P.M. BOKS. "Cannabis with High Cannabidiol Content Is Associated with Fewer Psychotic Experiences." *Schizophrenia Research*, 130: 216–21, 2011 (1 table, 2 figures, 36 references)

Abstract: A web-based survey was conducted on 1,877 cannabis users (mean age 23 years) in The Netherlands between 2008 and 2010 who used the same type of marijuana greater than 60 percent of the time. The THC, CBD, and CBN concentrations were measured in five cannabis products sold in The Netherlands: Dutch marijuana, imported marijuana, Dutch hashish, imported hashish, and the strongest marijuana sold in the coffee shops. The THC/CBD ratio ranged from 2.0 to 81.5:1. It was determined that 1,214 participants used high CBD cannabis and 663 used low CBD cannabis. In addition, self-reported scores of positive, negative, and depressive symptoms were determined.

> To our knowledge, this is the first large study to investigate the influence of cannabidiol content on the presence of psychiatric symptoms in cannabis users from the general population. The key finding of the current study is that cannabidiol mitigates the psychotic symptoms associated with cannabis use with a small, albeit significant, effect. Given the low dose of cannabidiol in joints as compared to oral administration in treatment studies, a larger effect could not be expected. The current data add to our knowledge of cannabidiol as a potential anti-psychotic agent, suggesting that cannabis types with high cannabidiol content are significantly less strongly associated with psychotic symptoms.

Reference Number: 61410

VALLERSNES, O.M., A.M. DINES, D.M. WOOD, C. YATES, F. HEYERDAHL, K.E. HOVDA, I. GIRAUDON, AND EURO-DEN RESEARCH GROUP. "Psychosis Associated with Acute Recreational Drug Toxicity: A European Case Series." *BMC Psychiatry*, 16: 293 (8 pp), 2016 (3 tables, 51 references)

Abstract: Psychosis was present in 348 (6.3 percent) of 5,529 cases of recreational drugs and novel psychoactive substances presenting at sixteen EDs in ten European countries between 2013 and 2014. The patients were mainly male (80 percent) with a median age of 29 years (24 to 38 years). The most common drugs detected were cannabis in ninety cases (26 percent), amphetamines in 87 (25 percent), and cocaine in 56 (16 percent).

In addition to the risk of inducing acute psychosis, regular use of several recreational drugs, especially amphetamine, methamphetamine, and cannabis, has been shown to be associated with later development of chronic psychosis or schizophrenia.

Table: Adjusted Odds Ratio of Psychosis According to Drug

Drug	Odds Ratio for Presenting to ER with Psychosis
LSD	3.1 X
Amphetamines	3.0 X
Cannabis	1.5 X
Alcohol	0.54 X

Source: Adapted from Vallersnes et al, 2016

Reference Number: 61411

ZVOLENSKY, M.J., J.R. COUGLE, K.A. JOHNSON, M.O. BONN-MILLER, AND A. BERNSTEIN. "Marijuana Use and Panic Psychopathology among a Representative Sample of Adults." *Experimental and Clinical Psychopharmacology*, 18: 129–34, 2010 (1 table, 17 references)

Abstract: The association between cannabis use and panic attacks and disorder were determined in 5,672 Americans (mean age 45 years, 53 percent women) between 2001 and 2003.

Table: Adjusted Odds Ratio for Panic Attack and Disorder after Lifetime or 12-Month Cannabis Use

	Adjusted Odds Ratio for Lifetime Marijuana Use	Adjusted Odds Ratio for 12-Month Marijuana Use
Lifetime Panic Attacks	1.62 X	1.27 X
12-Month Panic Attacks	1.27 X	1.65 X
Lifetime Panic Disorder	1.70 X	0.97 X
12-month Panic Disorder	1.44 X	1.10 X

Source: Adapted from Zvolensky et al, 2010

After adjusting for socio-demographic variables (age, marital status, income, education, race, and sex) and the presence of a lifetime substance disorder, lifetime marijuana use was significantly associated with increased odds of a lifetime panic attack history. Lifetime marijuana use was also significantly associated with an increased risk of current (past year) panic attacks; however, this relation was not significant when controlling for nicotine dependence. Lifetime marijuana use was significantly associated with increased odds of a lifetime diagnosis of panic disorder, as well as a current (past year) diagnosis of panic disorder. Current (past year) marijuana use was significantly associated with both lifetime and current panic attacks but not current or lifetime panic disorder.

Reference Number: 61412

WILKINSON, S.T., R. RADHAKRISHNAN, AND D.C. D'SOUZA, "Impact of Cannabis Use on the Development of Psychotic Disorders." *Current Addiction Reports*, 1: 115–28, 2015 (2 tables, 176 references)

Abstract: A review was conducted on the link between cannabis use and psychosis. Schizophrenia is the prototypical psychotic disorder and is characterized by hallucinations, delusions, amotivation, social withdrawal, and deficits in memory and attention. About 20 to 50 percent of individuals who use cannabis suffer transient hallucinations, paranoia, and dissociative symptoms.

In summary, exposure to cannabis is associated with a number of distinct syndromes, including (1) acute psychosis associated with cannabis intoxication, (2) acute psychosis that lasts beyond the period of acute intoxication, and (3) persistent psychotic disorders. Given the changing legal status of cannabis in the United States and elsewhere, research on the association of cannabis and psychosis (especially persistent psychotic disorders) has profound implications for public health and policy. As evidenced above, the cannabis psychosis relationship fulfills many but not all of the traditional criteria for causality. The strength of the association is modest but consistent; the relationship is biologically plausible, exhibits a dose-response effect, and in most studies, persistent psychosis is preceded by cannabis use (although few studies have taken into account the time of onset of negative symptoms). Similar to tobacco use and lung cancer, not everyone who has been exposed to cannabis develops a persistent psychotic disorder such as schizophrenia and not everyone diagnosed with schizophrenia has been exposed to cannabis. Therefore, cannabis exposure is neither necessary nor sufficient to cause a persistent psychotic disorder such as schizophrenia. More likely, cannabis may be a component cause that, in concert with known (specific genetic polymorphisms or history of childhood abuse) and unknown factors, contributes to the risk of schizophrenia.

Reference Number: 61413

STEFANIS, N.C., M. DRAGOVIC, B.D. POWER, A. JABLENSKY, D. CASTLE, AND V.A. MORGAN. "Age at Initiation of Cannabis Use Predicts Age at Onset of Psychosis: The 7- to 8-Year Trend." *Schizophrenia Bulletin*, 39: 251–54, 2013 (1 figure, 20 references)

Abstract: The time between the age of initiation of cannabis use and the age of onset of psychotic illness was determined in 997 cannabis users during 2010 in Australia. There was a linear association between the age of initiation and age of onset of psychosis, and this was on average between seven to eight years.

Cannabis may exert a cumulative toxic effect on individuals on the pathway to developing psychosis, the manifestations of which are delayed for approximately seven to eight years, regardless of the age at which cannabis use was initiated.

Reference Number: 61414

NIESINK, R.J.M., AND M.W. VAN LAAR. "Does Cannabidiol Protect against Adverse Psychological effects of THC?" *Frontiers in Psychiatry*, 4: article 150, 8 pp, 2013 (2 tables, 90 references)

Abstract: A review was conducted of the possible protective effect of CBD. Cannabis sativa contains more than eighty different cannabinoids. THC binds to CB1 receptors (CNS) and CB2 receptors (immune system). THC mimics endocannabinoids but is not rapidly broken down at the activation site and it activates all CB receptors throughout the brain. Cannabidiol is an antagonist to THC. Daily use of cannabis with high THC and low CBD increases the risk of psychosis.

Cannabis is not a safe drug. Depending on how often someone uses, the age of onset, the potency of cannabis that is used, and someone's individual sensitivity, the recreational use of cannabis may cause permanent psychological disorders. Many recreational users will never be faced with serious or permanent health deficits. However, for some users, the use of cannabis may cause undesirable psychological side effects, such as cognitive impairment, anxiety, and paranoia, and an increased risk of developing chronic psychosis and addiction.

Reference Number: 61415

KELLEY, M.E., C.R. WAN, B. BROUSSARD, A. CRISAFIO, S. CRISTOFARO, S. JOHNSON, T.A. REED, P. AMAR., N.J. KASLOW, E.F. WALKER, AND M.T. COMPTON. "Marijuana Use in the Immediate 5-Year Premorbid Period is Associated with Increased Risk of Onset of Schizophrenia and Related Psychotic Disorders." *Schizophrenia Research*, 171: 62–67, 2016 (3 tables, 1 figure, 41 references)

Abstract: The lifetime marijuana/alcohol/tobacco use was determined in 210 (159 male) first-episode psychosis patients (mean age 23.9 years) in the US between 2008 and 2013 in the five years prior to the onset of psychosis. Daily use of cannabis was associated with a 2.1 times increase in psychosis onset, even after controlling for alcohol/tobacco use. Cumulative marijuana exposure was associated with an increased rate of psychosis independent of gender and family history.

These data provide evidence of a clear temporal relationship between escalations in use in the five years pre-onset and an increased rate of onset; demonstrate that the strength of the association is similar pre- and post-onset of prodromal symptoms; and determine that early adult use may be just as important as adolescent use in these associations.

Reference Number: 61416

DI FORTI, M., C. MORGAN, P. DAZZAN, C. PARIANTE, V. MONDELLI, T.R. MARQUES, R. HANDLEY, S. LUZI, M. RUSSO, A. PAPARELLI, A. BUTT, S.A. STILO, B. WIFFEN, J. POWELL, AND R.M. MURRAY. "High-Potency Cannabis and the Risk of Psychosis." *The British Journal of Psychiatry*, 195: 488–91, 2009 (3 tables, 20 references)

Abstract: A study was conducted comparing the cannabis use of 202 male and 78 female patients (mean age 25 years) with a first episode of psychosis and of the cannabis use of 174 controls (no psychosis). Sixty-three percent of controls had never used cannabis compared to 57 percent of patients. But among those who used cannabis, 59 percent of the patients had used it for more than five years compared to 38 percent of the control group. In addition, 78 percent of patients used sinsemilla (skunk) cannabis, compared to only 31 percent of the control group. Cannabis was used every day by 77 percent of the patients compared to 33 percent of the controls.

It is generally accepted that drinking a glass of light wine every day is less likely to be associated with serious health consequences than drinking a daily bottle of whisky or vodka. Unfortunately, previous studies of the association between cannabis use and psychosis have not collected detailed information on the patterns of use or potency of the cannabis smoked. Our findings are the first to suggest that the risk of psychosis is much greater among those using sinsemilla (skunk) rather than occasional users of traditional hash. It is not surprising that those who use skunk daily seem to be the group with the highest risk of all. Unfortunately, sinsemilla (skunk) is displacing traditional cannabis preparations in many countries. Public education about the risks of heavy use of high potency cannabis is vital.

Reference Number: 61417

FAVRAT, B., A. MENETREY, M. AUGSBURGER, L.E. ROTHUIZEN, M. APPENZELLER., T. BUCLIN, M. PIN, P. MANGIN, AND C. GIROUD. "Two Cases of Cannabis Acute Psychosis Following the Administration of Oral Cannabis." *BMC Psychiatry*, 5: 17, 6 pp, 2005 (2 figures, 26 references)

Abstract: Two healthy male occasional cannabis users (both age 22 years) developed severe anxiety, psychosis, and paranoia approximately one hour after consuming 20 mg of dronabinol or 16.5 mg of a hemp milk THC decoction respectively in an experimental study. The effects persisted for up to four hours after consumption. The maximum whole blood concentrations of THC, 11-OH-THC, and THCCOOH were approximately 15 ng/mL, 20 ng/mL, and 50 ng/mL respectively. Typically, after oral ingestion 11-OH-THC blood concentrations are higher than THC, as occurred in these cases. Cannabis psychosis has been described before, as in 1958 when ten subjects developed severe anxiety, panic attacks, paranoid delusions, and depersonalization, and in 1969 when twelve soldiers in Vietnam had disorientation and hallucinations after their first use of cannabis.

> In conclusion, doctors and users should be aware of the increasing availability of oral cannabis in special drinks or food, as well as in medications under development. While the oral route of administration achieves only limited blood concentrations, significant psychotic reactions may occur. An increased incidence of psychotic episodes might be induced by this new trend and requires attention regarding this phenomenon in a public perspective.

Reference Number: 61418

LASEBIKAN, V., AND O.O. AREMU. "Cannabis Use and Associated Harms among Schizophrenia Patients in a Nigerian Clinical Setting: A Case-Control Study." *Frontiers in Psychiatry*, 7, Article 136, 9 pp, 2016 (4 tables, 1 figure, 43 references)

Abstract: Cannabis use and associated health problems were determined in 150 patients with schizophrenia and 150 matched control patients without schizophrenia in Nigeria. The alcohol, smoking, and substance involvement screening test (ASSIST) was administered. A significantly higher proportion of patients with schizophrenia were unmarried and unemployed compared to the control patients. The prevalence of cannabis use was 10.0 percent in patients with schizophrenia and 2.7 percent in controls.

> In conclusion, cannabis use is fourfold more prevalent in patients with schizophrenia. About one in every forty persons in a de facto primary case, in this instance, the general outpatient's department, a walk-in clinic, use cannabis. Cannabis use in patients with schizophrenia is associated

with moderate health risk. Although the present study has not established a causal relationship between cannabis use and schizophrenia, it should serve as a template for large-sample size prospective studies in Nigeria. Such study design may shed more light on the relationship between cannabis use and symptoms of schizophrenia.

Reference Number: 61419

GONZALEZ-PINTO, A., S. ALBERICH, S. BARBEITO, M. GUTIERREZ, P. VAGA, B. IBANEZ, M.K. HAIDAR, E. VIETA, AND C. ARANGO. "Cannabis and First-Episode Psychosis: Different Long-Term Outcomes Depending on Continued or Discontinued Use." *Schizophrenia Bulletin,* 37: 631–39, 2011 (3 tables, 3 figures, 35 references)

Abstract: Recent onset first-episode psychosis patients admitted to a Spanish general hospital psychiatric ward between 1997 and 1999 were divided into three groups according to cannabis use. Twenty-five patients had used cannabis continually (CU) before and after the psychotic episode; twenty-seven had used cannabis before the first psychotic episode and stopped using it (CUS); and forty had never used cannabis (NU). Approximately 50 percent of all three groups were women. The patients were assessed at years 1, 3, 5, and an additional follow-up was conducted at 8 years.

Table: Mean Global Assessment of Functioning (GAF) Score by Cannabis Use Group*

Years of follow-up	Never used cannabis	Used cannabis and stopped	Continued use of cannabis
Baseline	57	54	55
1 year	62	62	58
3 years	55	62	56
5 years	58	65	53
8 years	57	70	54

* Note: The higher the GAF score, the better the recovery

Source: Adapted from Gonzalez-Pinto et al, 2011

In conclusion, half of the patients with a first psychotic episode who used cannabis were able to stop using it during follow-up. Those patients who stopped using cannabis experienced a slow but steady improvement over time, both in functional outcome and negative symptoms. On the other hand, patients who continued using cannabis had a trend toward increasing negative symptoms over time and no improvement in functional outcome. All patients had improvement in functional outcome and positive symptoms over the long term.

Reference Number: 61420

MORGAN, C.J.A., AND H.V. CURRAN. "Effects of Cannabidiol on Schizophrenia-Like Symptoms in People Who Use Cannabis." *The British Journal of Psychiatry*, 192: 306–7, 2008 (1 figure, 11 references)

Abstract: Hair analyses were conducted on 140 drug and non-drug users for THCA/THC (indicates cannabis use) and cannabidiol (CBD). Fifty-four screened positive for cannabinoids. The subjects were divided into three groups: THC only (seven women, thirteen men, mean age 26.1 years); THC + CBD (six women, twenty-one men, mean age 27.8 years); and those with no cannabinoids detected in hair (twenty-seven women and fifty-eight men, mean age 26.7 years). Psychosis was assessed using the Oxford-Liverpool Inventory of Life Experiences and Peter's Delusion Inventory. A higher level of hallucinations-delusions occurred in the THC only group compared to the THC + CBD group and the negative cannabis group.

These preliminary findings may support previous work showing the antipsychotic properties of CBD in the laboratory. Moreover, this suggests smoking strains of cannabis containing CBD in addition to delta 9-THC may be protective against the psychotic symptoms induced by delta 9-THC alone.

Reference Number: 61421

KHAN, M.A., AND S. AKELLA. "Cannabis-Induced Bipolar Disorder with Psychotic Features: A Case Report." *Psychiatry*, 6: 44–48, 2009 (24 references)

Abstract: A 21-year-old man was hospitalized twice, one week apart, and diagnosed with cannabis-induced psychotic disorder. His urine drug tests were only positive for cannabinoids. He began using cannabis occasionally at the age of 14 years, but started using it on a daily basis, in increasing amounts four months prior to the admissions. On the second occasion, he was delusional and displayed extreme grandiosity and mood lability. He would talk to himself for hours. His diagnosis was updated to a bipolar disorder with psychotic features. He was treated and released after four months of hospitalization.

Several case studies and longitudinal studies have illustrated the link between acute psychosis and mania associated with cannabis. The most prominent features elicited are auditory hallucinations, paranoid feelings of being persecuted, depersonalization, de-realization, anxiety, grandiosity, and irritability. The debate remains as to whether or not cannabis can cause schizophrenia and bipolar disorder in an otherwise healthy individual. We presented a case of a young individual who was previously healthy and was high functioning, pursuing a bachelor's degree in chemistry with a 3.3 grade point average. His case is unique because we had the opportunity to observe him firsthand longitudinally over a four-month period, saw how cannabis use can cause psychotic symptoms, and followed him through his course as he developed a more severe affective and psychotic disorder.

Reference Number: 61422

MORRISON, P.D., V. ZOIS, D.A. MCKEOWN, T.D. LEE, D.W. HOLT, J.F. POWELL, S. KAPUR, AND R.M. MURRAY. "The Acute Effects of Synthetic Intravenous delta 9-tetrahydrocannabinol on Psychosis, Mood and Cognitive Functioning." *Psychological Medicine*, 39: 1607–16, 2009 (4 figures, 54 references)

Abstract: Twenty-two healthy male cannabis users (mean age 28 years) were administered a placebo or 2.5 mg dronabinol (THC) IV within 5 minutes. Blood samples were collected at 0, 1, 5, 15, 30, 60, and 120 minutes post-injection, and plasma THC and 11-OH-THC concentrations were determined by GC/MS. Various measures of mood and psychosis, as well as neuropsychological tests (verbal learning, digit spam), were determined. The mean peak plasma THC concentration varied from 96.1 to 206.6 ng/mL (mean 176.7 ng/mL) at 1 minute post-injection and peak plasma 11-OH-THC varied from 1.5 to 7.8 ng/mL (mean 4.4 ng/mL) at 5 minutes.

In conclusion, in a sample of healthy male subjects, pure synthetic IV preparation of THC elicited acute positive psychotic symptoms, anxiety, dysphoria, working memory/executive deficits, and, subsequently, feelings of tiredness. Our findings suggest that THC-induced positive psychotic symptoms are neither secondary to high levels of anxiety nor a cause of anxiety.

Reference Number: 61423

MURRAY, R.M., H. QUIGLEY, D. QUATTRONE, A. ENGLUND, AND M. DI FORTI. "Traditional Marijuana, High Potency Cannabis and Synthetic Cannabinoids: Increasing Risk for Psychosis." *World Psychiatry*, 15: 195–204, 2016 (1 table, 166 references)

Abstract: Currently there are 180 million cannabis users worldwide. A general review of the effects of cannabis is presented. THC impairs learning attention and memory in a dose-dependent manner. The problems with high potency cannabis and synthetic cannabinoids are described. Psychotic patients who continued cannabis use had higher relapse rates, longer hospital admissions, and more severe positive symptoms than other former users who discontinued cannabis or never users.

Epidemiological evidence demonstrates that cannabis use is associated with an increased risk of psychotic outcomes and confirms a dose-response relationship between the level of use and the risk of later psychosis. High potency cannabis and synthetic cannabis carry the greatest risk. Experimental administration of tetrahydrocannabinol, the active ingredient of cannabis, induces transient psychosis in normal subjects, but this effect can be ameliorated by co-administration of cannabidiol. This latter is a constituent of traditional hashish, but is largely absent from modern high potency forms of cannabis. Argument continues over the extent to which genetic disposition is correlated to, or interacts with, cannabis use, and what proportion of psychosis could be prevented by minimizing heavy use. As yet, there is no convincing evidence that cannabis use increased risk of other psychiatric disorders, but there are not such doubts concerning its detrimental effect on cognitive function. All of the negative aspects are magnified if use starts in early adolescence. Irrespective of whether use of cannabis is decriminalized or legalized, the evidence that it is a component cause of psychosis is now sufficient for public health messages outlining the risk, especially of regular use of high potency cannabis and synthetic cannabinoids.

6.15 RAILROAD/TRUCKS

Random drug, including cannabis, and alcohol testing has helped reduce its incidence in transportation accidents including railroads and trucking (61501, 61503).

Reference Number: 61501

COTHEN, G.C., AND R. SHAMBERGER. "Substance Abuse Countermeasures for the Railroad Industry." *Alcohol, Drugs and Driving*, 8: 241–63, 1992 (3 tables, 3 figures)

Abstract: The problem of alcohol and drugs in railroad accidents is reviewed. Between 1975 and 1984, a minimum of 48 train accidents had alcohol or drugs as a contributing causative factor, which resulted in thirty-seven fatalities, eighty injuries, and $34 million in property damage. Random drug and alcohol testing was introduced, and the employee is prohibited from remaining on duty if the BAC > 0.040 g/100mL. The percentage of positive alcohol/drug tests declined from 5.5 percent in 1987 to 1.5 percent in 1991. The most common drugs detected were alcohol, marijuana, and cocaine.

Post-accident toxicology programs are perhaps best to bridge the gaps between unexplained mass urinalysis findings (and lack of findings) and the drug abuse culture. In 1991, FRA reported only three marijuana positives in post-accident testing (out of 552 tests).

Reference Number: 61502

GIROTTO, E., A.E. MESAS, S.M. DE ANDRADE, AND M.M. BIROLIM. "Psychoactive Substance Use by Truck Drivers: A Systematic Review." *Occupational and Environmental Medicine*, 71: 71–76, 2014 (3 tables, 1 figure, 54 references)

Abstract: A systematic review was conducted of thirty-six studies on the psychoactive substances used by truck drivers in various countries. The use of these substances varied greatly between studies; alcohol (0.1 to 91 percent), marijuana (0.2 to 29.9 percent), and cocaine (0.1 to 8.3 percent).

In summary, the intake of psychoactive substances by truck drivers is a relatively frequent occurrence, although the prevalence varies according to the place and methodology employed. Furthermore, intake seems to be higher when working conditions are poor, and this can have a direct impact on the health of the individual truck drivers and society as a whole, due to the increase in traffic accidents.

Reference Number: 61503

LUND, A.K., D.F. PREUSSER, R.D. BLOMBERG, AND A.F. WILLIAMS. "Drug Use by Tractor-Trailer Drivers." *Journal of Forensic Sciences*, 33: 648–61, 1988 (9 tables, 9 references)

Abstract: A study was conducted of the incidence of alcohol and drugs in the blood and/or urine of 317 trailer truck drivers stopped during the week of December 15, 1986, in Tennessee. Of these, forty-two drivers refused to provide a sample. A positive BAC was determined in the blood of three drivers (0.010, 0.020, and 0.030 g/100mL) and a positive UAC but not BAC was detected in another driver. Fifty drivers (16 percent) had indications of marijuana (15 percent) or cocaine use (2 percent).

The effect of the detected drugs on the risk of crashes among truck drivers is difficult to estimate even with information about the concentration of the drugs in blood. Alcohol, the drug whose effects are best known, was found in less than 1 percent of drivers and in every case, the concentration was well below state per se or presumptive limits and even below the 0.04 g/dL limit for commercial vehicle drivers.

6.16 RESPIRATORY EFFECTS

Smokers of cannabis develop similar symptoms of bronchitis as cigarette smokers, such as morning cough, increased sputum production, and wheeze (61404). Smoking tainted or contaminated black market joints increased respiratory problems. Some of the contaminants detected in black market weed have included talc, aluminum, silicon, molds, fungi, PCP, and embalming fluids (61606, 61607, 61613). The practice of sharing joints has led to an increased risk of tuberculosis (61601) and HPV (Human Papilloma Virus) (61614). The typically prolonged breath holding in cannabis smokers can lead to the development of large bullae (air filled spaces), also known as vanishing lung disease (61608, 61609, 61612). There is an 8 percent increase in the risk of lung cancer for each joint year of smoking (i.e., one joint per day for a year or equivalent) (61611).

Reference Number: 61601

OELTMANN, J.E., E. OREN, M.B. HADDAD, L.K. LAKE, T.A. HARRINGTON, K. IJAZ, AND M. NARITA. "Tuberculosis Outbreak in Marijuana Users, Seattle, Washington, 2004." *Emerging Infectious Diseases*, 12: 1156–59, 2006 (2 tables, 1 figure, 15 references)

Abstract: A tuberculosis outbreak (TB) occurred in eleven men in Seattle as a result of frequent "hotboxing," which is the practice of smoking marijuana with others in a car with the windows closed, so that the exhaled smoke is repeatedly inhaled. Frequent cannabis use has been reported in TB patients before. The sharing of a water pipe (bong) has caused TB transmission, along with the practice of "shotgunning" (inhaling the smoked and exhaling it directly into another's mouth).

> This investigation noted that a similar activity, hotboxing, might have contributed to transmission. As with shotgunning, it promotes the sharing of exhaled smoke and air. One patient with smear-positive cavitary disease reported daily hotboxing with friends, often for most of the day. In addition, marijuana smoking might induce cough, creating an ideal environment for transmission. Many friends stayed and used marijuana at the single-bedroom apartment during the height of the outbreak. Furthermore, by nailing boards over the windows, ventilation was limited, creating an environment similar to that of hotboxing.

Reference Number: 61602

POLEN, M.R., S. SIDNEY, I.S. TEKAWA, M. SADLER, AND G.D. FRIEDMAN, "Health Care Use by Frequent Marijuana Smokers Who Do Not Smoke Tobacco." *Western Journal of Medicine*, 158: 596–601, 1993 (4 tables, 29 references)

Abstract: The medical records of 452 daily marijuana smokers were compared to 450 non-smokers of cannabis and tobacco between 1979 and 1985. Marijuana smokers consume fewer cigarettes per day than tobacco users, but they inhale longer and more deeply and retain smoke longer in the lungs.

> In summary, daily marijuana smoking appears to be associated with respiratory conditions, even among persons who never smoke tobacco. The association is consistent with a possible independent deleterious

> effect of marijuana smoking on respiratory health. Frequent marijuana use also appears to be intimately linked to alcohol consumption as a risk factor for injury-related and other medical cases.

Reference Number: 61603

TAYLOR D.R., D.M. FERGUSSON, B.J. MILNE, L.J. HORWOOD, T.E. MOFFITT, M.R. SEARS, AND R. POULTON. "A Longitudinal Study of the Effects of Tobacco and Cannabis Exposure on Lung Function in Young Adults." *Addiction*, 97: 1055–61, 2002 (4 tables, 29 references)

Abstract: The effect of tobacco and cigarette smoking on FEV1/FVC ratio was determined in a group of 900 subjects (ages 18 to 26 years) in the Dunedin study. The ratio was 77.4 in heavy cannabis smokers, mean age 26 years compared to 82.4 for non-users.

> The results of the present analysis suggest that cannabis use and daily tobacco smoking combine additively to influence their effects on lung function. Although the magnitude of the changes in lung function associated with cannabis exposure may not be clinically significant, the findings suggest that if cannabis smoking were continued over a prolonged period along with tobacco use, this may potentially lead to important lung pathology in later years.

Reference Number: 61604

HANCOX R.J., H.H. SHIN, A.R. GRAY, R. POULTON, AND M.R. SEARS. "Effects of Quitting Cannabis on Respiratory Symptoms." *European Respiratory Journal*, 46: 80–87, 2015 (4 tables, 1 figure, 33 references)

Abstract: The symptoms of bronchitis associated with smoking cannabis were determined in 1,037 young adults in the Dunedin study in New Zealand at ages 18, 21, 26, 32, and 38 years. Frequent cannabis use was defined as smoking at least fifty-two times a year. Cannabis use was also associated with tobacco use at each age. Between 68 to 83 percent of frequent cannabis users were also tobacco users. Reducing or quitting cannabis was associated with a reduction in cough, sputum, and wheeze to levels similar to non-users.

Table: Odds Ratio of Various Respiratory Symptoms in Current Cannabis Use Compared to Non-Users

Symptom	Odds Ratio Compared to Non-Users
Morning Cough	1.97 X
Sputum Production	2.31 X
Wheeze	1.55 X

Source: Adapted from Hancox et al, 2015

Frequent cannabis use is associated with symptoms of bronchitis in young adults. Reducing cannabis use often leads to a resolution of these symptoms.

Reference Number: 61605

PLETCHER, M.J., E. VITTINGHOFF, R. KALHAN, J. RICHMAN, M. SAFFORD, S. SIDNEY, F. LIN, AND S. KERTSZ. "Association between Marijuana Exposure and Pulmonary Function Over 20 Years. The Coronary Artery Risk Development in Young Adults (CARDIA) Study." *Journal of the American Medical Association*, 307: 173–81, 2011 (3 tables, 2 figures, 37 references)

Abstract: Pulmonary function tests, forced expiratory volume in one second (FEV1), and forced vital capacity (FVC), as well as tobacco and cannabis use were determined in 5,115 men and women (initially aged 18 to 30 years) from four US cities between 1985 and 2006. Fifty-four percent of the participants reported current marijuana or tobacco smoking. The median intensity of tobacco smoking was eight to nine cigarettes per day, compared to a median of two to three episodes of cannabis use in the last thirty days. With increasing cigarette smoking there was a decrease in FEV1 and FVC, on average of 332 mL and 229 mL respectively. With low cannabis use there was an increase in FEV1 and FVC. If the consumption of cannabis was more than twenty-five episodes a month, the FEV1 decreased.

Marijuana may have beneficial effects on pain control, appetite, mood, and management of other chronic symptoms. Our findings suggest that occasional use of marijuana for these or other purposes would not have significant adverse consequences on pulmonary function. It is more difficult to estimate the potential effects of regular heavy use, as this pattern of use is relatively rare in our study sample; however, our findings

> do suggest an accelerated decline in pulmonary function with heavy use, and a resulting need for caution and moderation when marijuana use is considered.

Reference Number: 61606

GILBERT, C.R., M. BARAM, AND N.C. CAVAROCCHI. "Smoking Wet. Respiratory Failure Related to Smoking Tainted Marijuana Cigarettes." *Texas Heart Institute Journal*, 40: 64–67, 2013 (2 figures, 18 references)

Abstract: Wet cannabis cigarettes are conventional joints that have been dipped into various liquids. In the 1970s, cannabis cigarettes were laced with PCP, also known to drug dealers and users as embalming fluids. Soon, mistakenly, the joints were dipped in real embalming fluids. A 20-year-old man and a 27-year-old woman were both admitted to hospital due to acute respiratory distress (ARDS) after smoking wet marijuana cigarettes.

> Our patients had similar presentations after similar temporal exposure to tainted marijuana cigarettes. We believe that smoke from tainted marijuana cigarettes could be an unrecognized cause of respiratory failure in young adults who present with an otherwise unclear origin of respiratory failure and ARDS. According to the available literature, the varying quantity and quality of ingredients in marijuana cigarettes can lead to presentations that range from cough to bronchospasms to severe respiratory failure. We recommend that the inhalation of smoke from tainted marijuana cigarettes be considered as the cause of SRDS in young adults, when the clinical context suggests it.

Reference Number: 61607

SCHEEL, A.H., D. KRAUSE, H. HAARS, I. SCHMITZ, AND K. JUNKER. "Talcum Induced Pneumoconiosis Following Inhalation of Adulterated Marijuana, A Case Report." *Diagnostic Pathology*, 7: 26–30, 2012 (3 figures, 9 references)

Abstract: A 29-year-old man was admitted to hospital with persistent fever, dyspnea, and cervical emphysema. He admitted to use of cut marijuana for several years, usually by water pipe smoking. Locally available cannabis was commonly adulterated by substances like sand (silicon) or talc (hydrated magnesium silicate). Histopathology and energy dispersive x-ray spectroscopy of the lungs revealed crystal deposits of silicon and magnesium of one to two micron size and small deposits of aluminum. The aluminum particles are probably due to a layer of aluminum foil commonly used in water pipes to cover the incinerated charcoal.

The exacerbated chronic interstitial lung disease in a 29-year-old patient could be attributed to his prolonged abuse of adulterated marijuana by histopathology and x-ray spectroscopy. Both size and elemental composition of mineralic deposits found in biopsies were compatible with inhaled talcum as the leading contaminant.

Reference Number: 61608

JOHNSON, M.K., R.P. SMITH, D. MORRISON, G. LASZLO, AND R.J. WHITE. "Large Lung Bullae in Marijuana Smokers." *Thorax,* 55: 340–42, 2000 (1 table, 4 figures, 11 references)

Abstract: Four male tobacco and cannabis users (ages 27 to 46 years) presented to hospital with multiple large upper zone lung bullae (also known as vanishing lung syndrome). Three of the men had relatively low exposure to tobacco.

Other than the psychoactive compound delta-9-tetrahydrocannabinol and other cannabinoid compounds in marijuana, and nicotine in the tobacco, smoke from the two substances is virtually identical. However, there are some fundamental differences when comparing the physical dynamics of smoking marijuana with smoking conventional tobacco. A draw on a marijuana joint involves on average a volume two-thirds larger, a depth of inspiration one-third greater, and a breath holding time four times longer than a draw on a cigarette. Indeed, barotrauma in the form of pneumonediastinum has been reported to occur while smoking marijuana. When this smoking practice is combined with the lack of filter tips on marijuana cigarettes, it leads to a fourfold greater delivery of tar and a five times greater increase in carboxyhemoglobin per cigarette smoked. Regular marijuana smokers experience more cough, sputum, and wheeze than non-smokers and similar levels of symptoms to tobacco smokers. Three to four joints of marijuana per day have been reported to give as many symptoms as an average of twenty-two tobacco cigarettes. The physiological effects of marijuana in terms of pulmonary function abnormalities are predominately in the large airway, producing measurable airways obstruction that returns to normal if the smoking habit is short lived.

Reference Number: 61609

MISHRA, R., R. PATEL, AND M. KHAJA. "Cannabis-Induced Bullous Lung Disease Leading to Pneumothorax." *Medicine,* 96: 19, 4 pp, 2017 (5 figures, 25 references)

Abstract: A 30-year-old man presented to ED with a sudden onset of a severe right-sided chest pain. He smoked cannabis daily for five years but did not smoke tobacco. A chest x-ray showed a right-sided pneumothorax. A CT scan showed a few apical bullae in the right lung. The urine was positive for cannabinoids and clubbing of his fingers was noted. The patient underwent chest tube drainage of the lung. Typical smoking of cannabis is associated with a 66 percent larger puff volume and a 33 percent increase in breathing depth and inhalation time compared with tobacco smokers. Marijuana smokers also tend to hold their breath four times longer than tobacco smokers. The patient denied he used breath holding maneuvers while smoking cannabis.

The prevalence of bullous lung disease among marijuana smokers, both in relation to the general population and to cigarette smokers, warrants further research. It is imperative that physicians educate patients and colleagues about the potential dangers of marijuana that is often used recreationally. This case report highlights the risk of bullous lung disease leading to pneumothorax following marijuana smoking.

Reference Number: 61610

GOODYEAR K., D. LAWS, AND J. TURNER. "Bilateral Spontaneous Pneumothorax in a Cannabis Smoker." *Journal of the Royal Society of Medicine,* 97: 435–36, 2004 (1 figure, 5 references)

Abstract: A 23-year-old man attended the Emergency Department in severe respiratory distress after two weeks of cough. Mobile radiography showed a bilateral pneumothorax with a complete collapse of the left lung. After needle decompression, chest drains were inserted bilaterally, which relieved the symptoms. He had smoked cannabis since the age of 13 years and now smoked it daily.

Though cannabis (marijuana) is an illegal drug in the UK, it is widely used in the 18 to 25 years age group. In those who smoke it, there are increasing reports of detrimental effects on the respiratory tract. An association between spontaneous pneumothorax and pneumomediastinum with marijuana has previously been described. A suggested mechanism is coughing while breath-holding in inspiration, for example, after taking a draw on a joint. Perhaps this was the explanation in the present case. Cannabis apart, the risk of pneumothorax seems to be increased by tobacco smoke and the two may be synergistic. Our patient was unusual in not regularly mixing them. The separate influence of cannabis is hard to investigate; moreover, patients may be reluctant to disclose information about use of other illicit drugs. For example, bilateral pneumothorax has been reported after cocaine smoking.

Reference Number: 61611

ALDINGTON, S., M. HARWOOD, B. COX, M. WEATHERALL, L. BECKERT, A. HANSELL, A. PRITCHARD, G. ROBINSON., AND R. BEASLEY. "Cannabis Use and Risk of Lung Cancer: A Case-Control Study." *European Respiratory Journal*, 31: 280–86, 2008 (3 tables, 41 references)

Abstract: New Zealand has a high rate of cannabis use (15 percent of adults) and rarely is cannabis mixed with tobacco. The frequency of cannabis use was determined in 79 cancer patients and 324 matched controls, all under the age of 56 years of age. There were 21 cannabis smokers in the cancer patients (27 percent) and 39 cannabis smokers in the control group (12 percent). The risk of lung cancer increased 8 percent for each joint year (i.e., one joint/day for one year or equivalent), compared to an increased risk of 7 percent for each pack year of cigarette smoking. The patients who had greater than 10.5 joint-years of exposure had 5.7 times the risk of lung cancer.

Table: Cannabis and Tobacco Use as Continuous Variables and Risk of Lung Cancer

Characteristic	Relative Risk of Lung Cancer
Pack-year of cigarette smoking	1.07 X
Joint-year of cannabis smoking	1.08 X

Source: Adapted from Aldington et al, 2008

Cannabis smoking may have a greater potential than tobacco smoking to cause lung cancer. Cannabis smoke is qualitatively similar to tobacco smoke, although it contains up to twice the concentration of the carcinogenic polyaromatic hydrocarbons. Cannabis cigarettes are less densely packed than tobacco cigarettes and tend to be smoked without filters to a smaller butt size, leading to higher concentrations of smoke inhaled. Furthermore, smokers of cannabis inhale more deeply and hold their breath longer, facilitating the deposition of the carcinogenic products in the lower respiratory tract. These factors are likely to be responsible for the fivefold greater absorption of carbon monoxide from a cannabis joint, compared with a tobacco cigarette of similar size, despite similar carbon monoxide concentrations in the smoke inhaled. Several studies have demonstrated pre-cancerous histological and molecular abnormalities in the respiratory tracts of cannabis smokers, and the carcinogenic effects of cannabis smoke have been demonstrated in vitro and in different in vivo animal models. Conversely, there is also evidence that delta-9-tetrahydrocannabinol may have anti-carcinogenic effects.

Reference Number: 61612

AUJAVEB, A., C. DONALD, AND S. DOE. "Breath Holding in a Marijuana Smoker." *Respiratory Medicine Case Reports*, 5: 69–72, 2012 (9 figures, 14 references)

Abstract: A 28-year-old man attended hospital due to chest pain after holding his breath for 2.5 minutes in a competition at a pub. He smoked cigarettes and cannabis regularly. He had a left pneumothorax (PTX), which was treated successfully. PTX has occurred in chronic marijuana smokers during Valsalva and breath holding maneuvers.

Marijuana is the most common illegal drug used in the UK. A history of marijuana smoking should be elicited in the respiratory history. Marijuana smoking can be associated with significant lung pathology and all physicians should be aware of the health implications.

Reference Number: 61613

GARGANI, Y., P. BISHOP, AND D.W. DENNING. "Too Many Moldy Joints: Marijuana and Chronic Pulmonary Aspergillosis." *Mediterranean Journal of Hematology and Infectious Diseases*, 3: 6 pp, 2011 (7 figures, 20 references)

Abstract: Two cases are presented of chronic pulmonary aspergillosis (CPA) involving extensive medical use of marijuana. Both patients were male (ages 35 and 47 years). The first patient smoked cigarettes but also five joints a day for four years to alleviate joint pain, which worsened his respiratory problems considerably. He had a right-side pneumothorax with pulmonary bullae. He was determined to have aspergillosis due to smoking fungal-contaminated cannabis and recovered after the appropriate treatment. The second patient smoked about twenty joints per day for thirty-four years. His respiratory function was so compromised that he could only walk ten yards. He also developed CPA from moldy cannabis, but later died.

Both tobacco and marijuana are commonly contaminated with fungi, and serology from marijuana smokers exhibits evidence of Aspergillus exposure. It remains to be seen whether fungal spores survive the burning process, indicating perhaps that exposure to Aspergillus comes from handling the marijuana rather than smoking it. It has been observed that IA presents earlier after immunocompromised among smokers than non-smokers. The way marijuana is smoked is different to that of tobacco in that the cigarettes or joints are usually smoked without a filter and are smoked down to a smaller butt. Users hold their breath for longer and use the Valsalva maneuver. These measures maximize the diffusion of the psychoactive compound. In doing so, however, they expose their lungs to a greater tar and carbon monoxide burden, as well as subjecting their lungs to greater pressure changes. This barotrauma from marijuana smoking has long been associated with the formation of bullae and subsequent pneumothoraxes. The association is so strong that some now recommend that patients presenting with spontaneous pneumothoraxes should be directly questioned about marijuana smoking.

Reference Number: 61614

ZWENGER S.R. "Bogarting that Joint Might Decrease Oral HPV among Cannabis Users." *Current Oncology,* 16: 5–7, 2009 (26 references)

Abstract: Human Papilloma Virus (HPV) can cause cancers of the throat and tongue. It is thought that the development of oral cancers in heavy cannabis users may be due to the transmission of HPV by various forms of sharing joints or smoking apparatus rather than cannabis per se. Thus, bogarting (i.e., not sharing) joints may decrease oral HPV and cancer in heavy marijuana users.

It certainly may not be the cannabis smoke that causes oral cancers in heavy cannabis users. Most people who have ever smoked cannabis have most likely done so by sharing a rolled cigarette or pipe in a group setting. The sharing and passing of these smoking devices from an oral HPV-infected individual to an uninfected individual could easily provide a route of transmission for the virus between users. Frequency and setting should therefore be considered two major factors that might contribute to the likelihood of acquiring oral HPV. Thus, the relationship between cannabis and various cancer types might not be from cannabis use itself, but from contracting high risk types of oral HPV that lead to cancer in later life.

Reference Number: 61615

REECE, A.S. "Severe Multisystem Dysfunction in a Case of High Level Exposure to Smoked Cannabis." *British Medical Journal Case Reports*, 10 pp, 2009 (3 figures, 23 references)

Abstract: A 56-year-old male heavy cannabis user (two to fourteen joints daily for twenty-five years) attended hospital with disabling shortness of breath. A CT scan of the chest revealed over forty bullae, the largest was 11 cm in diameter. He also had osteoporosis with multiple vertebrate crush fractures, hypertension, and increased vascular age (69.8 years), and had suffered a stroke. His dental health was poor, which he attributed to his strong sweets preference while he was stoned.

Cannabis lung disease can become very severe. Indeed, giant lung cysts can form in predisposed individuals. Cannabis can affect other body systems, such as the cardiovascular system, the bones, the brain, and the kidneys. There is a need to consider multisystem impacts in patients presenting with significant cannabis exposure. The impacts of cannabis-related mental disorders, such as depression, can be far reaching and severe for lifestyle and life path. The presence of multisystem disorders suggests that common underlying pathophysiological pathways may be implicated in several body systems. In view of the widespread use of cannabis, further investigation and elucidation in this area would appear to be a research priority.

Reference Number: 61615

Reference Number: 61616

GAO, Z., R. WOOD-BAKER, R. HARLE, K. MULLER, J. HAUSER, AND D.W. REID. "Bong Lung in Cystic Fibrosis: A Case Report." *Journal of Medical Case Reports*, 4: 371, 2010 (2 figures, 9 references)

Abstract: A 23-year-old man with cystic fibrosis was admitted to hospital with a one-week history of pleuritic chest pain, increased cough and sputum production, and deterioration in lung function. He admitted to several years of smoking marijuana using a bong and had typical symptoms of large apical lung bullae on high resolution computerized tomography scanning, and spontaneous pneumothoraces. The patient made a slow recovery over the next three weeks and was consulted about his cannabis use. The prevalence of smoking marijuana in cystic fibrosis patients has been reported to be as high as 20 percent.

> Our case highlights the importance of questioning young adult cystic fibrosis patients about illicit drug use and the utility of sputum cyto - ogy and computed tomography scanning when patients present with pneumothoraces and deterioration in clinical status.

6.17 SEXUAL ASSAULTS/BEHAVIOUR

After alcohol, cannabis is the most common drug detected in sexual assault victims (61702, 61703, 61711). Cannabis use has been found to increase risky sexual behaviour (61706, 61708, 61712). Cannabis is the most frequently detected drug in cases with multiple illicit drugs (61709). Cannabis-infused edibles may become a similar date-rape drug as alcohol (61710).

Reference Number: 61701

DU MONT, J., AND M.J. MCGREGOR. "Sexual Assault in the Lives of Urban Sex Workers: A Descriptive and Comparative Analysis." *Women and Health*, 39: 79–95, 2004 (4 tables, 45 references)

Abstract: A detailed study was conducted of 462 sexual assault victims seen at the Sexual Assault Service in a Vancouver hospital between 1993 and 1997. Ninety-six victims (21 percent) were identified as sex workers in police files. The sex worker victims were younger (range 14 to 42 years, mean 26 years), compared with the other sexual assault victims (mean age 28 years). Alcohol/marijuana use occurred in 23 percent of the sex workers and 59 percent of the other sexual assault victims. Positive sperm/semen samples occurred in 62 percent of the sex worker victims and 44 percent of other victims.

> Sexual assault examiners should be extra vigilant in assessing and providing care to sex workers, as our results show that, while less emotive in their presentation, they tend to suffer greater physical injury.

Reference Number: 61702

JONES, A.W., F.C. KUGELBERG, A.H. HOLMGREN, AND J. AHLNER. "Occurrence of Ethanol and Other Drugs in Blood and Urine Specimens from Female Victims of Alleged Sexual Assault." *Forensic Science International*, 181: 40–46, 2008 (5 figures, 57 references)

Abstract: Toxicological analyses were conducted on 1,806 female sexual assault victims (mean age 24 years) in Sweden between 2003 and 2007. There was an increase in the number of sexual assault cases during the summer months. Thirty-one percent of the cases were negative for both drugs and alcohol. Alcohol alone was detected in 43 percent of the cases and with other drugs in an additional 12 percent of the cases. The BACs ranged from 0.010 to 0.370 g/100mL (mean 0.124 g/100mL). The BAC was positively correlated with the age of the victim. The most common drugs detected were cannabis (THC) in 100 cases, diazepam in 88 cases, amphetamines in 86, and paracetamol in 68. The mean blood THC concentration detected was 1.2 ng/mL.

Table: Drugs Found in the Blood and Urine of Female Sexual Assault Victims

Drugs Detected	Number of Times Detected	Mean Age of Victim	Mean Blood Drug Concentration
Alcohol	882	25 years	0.124 g/100mL
Cannabis	100	25 years	1.2 ng/mL
Diazepam (valium)	88	32 years	0.35 mg/L
Amphetamine	86	29 years	0.22 mg/L
Codeine	29	36 years	0.06 mg/L

Source: Adapted from Jones et al, 2008

> Cannabis was the most prevalent illicit drug (N=100) as verified by analysis of THC in blood or carboxy-THC in urine. The mean and median

concentration of THC in blood of 0.0012 and 0.0006 mg/L respectively suggests fairly recent use of this illicit drug. Because cannabis is normally smoked, this surely reflects voluntary use of cannabis or marijuana.

Reference Number: 61703

JUHASCIK, M.P., A. NEGRUS, D. FAUGNO, L. LEDRAY, P. GREENE, A. LINDER, B. HANER, AND R.E. GAENSSLEN. "An Estimate of the Proportion of Drug-Facilitation of Sexual Assault in Four US Localities." *Journal of Forensic Sciences*, 52: 1396–1400, 2007 (5 tables, 25 references)

Abstract: Urine and hair drug analyses were conducted on 144 victims of sexual assault at four US medical centres between 2002 and 2004. Alcohol consumption was admitted by 46 percent of the victims, marijuana by 9 percent, cocaine by 6 percent, and amphetamine by 3 percent. Opiate and benzodiazepine use were not admitted but were detected in 10 percent of the victims.

However, taking sexual advantage of another person who is impaired because of voluntary drugs (and/or alcohol) use is also drug-facilitated sexual assault.

Reference Number: 61704

LANE, S.D., D.R. CHEREK, O.V. TCHEREMISSINE, L.M. LIEVING, AND C.J. PIETRAS. "Acute Marijuana Effects on Human Risk Taking." *Neuropsychopharmacology*, 30: 800–9, 2005 (1 table, 2 figures, 84 references)

Abstract: Marijuana use has been associated with risky sexual behaviour, and chronic use may serve as a predictor of HIV risk. After alcohol, marijuana is the second most common drug found in MVCs and FMVCs. Marijuana is associated with criminal behaviour, robbery, attempted homicide, drug trafficking, and delinquency in adolescents and young adults. Five male and five female occasional cannabis users (ages 19 to 38 years), who had a urine EMIT cannabinoid < 50 ng/mL, smoked a placebo, half a joint of 1.77 percent THC, a full joint of 1.77 percent THC, and a full joint of 3.58 percent THC. It normally required three to four days to meet the clean urine requirement. At the high dose, the HR increased by 31.9 beats per minute, and systolic BP decreased by 2.4, and diastolic by 0.9 mm Hg. The risk-taking task presented subjects with a choice of a risky or non-risky, and the subjects were rewarded with money.

Table: Some Responses after Smoking Placebo, One-half of 1.77%, 1.77%, and 3.58% THC Joints

Response	Placebo	One-half of 1.77% THC	1.77% THC	3.58% THC
Mean change in heart rate	1.83	8.70	21.40	31.90
"Feel effects of cannabis"	1.33	2.60	3.10	3.30
Mean change in number of risky choices	-1.07	4.60	4.80	28.40

Source: Adapted from Lane et al, 2005

The increase in risk taking observed at the 3.58 percent THC does supports epidemiological evidence indicating that risky behaviour may be related to the level or chronicity of marijuana use. Previous laboratory studies of acute marijuana effects on aggression, response inhibition, risky driving maneuvers, and complex decision making collectively suggest that marijuana may engender disinhibition at doses sufficient to produce a state of intoxication. In the present study, it is possible that the effect on risk taking was observed only with the 3.58 percent THC cigarettes because only this dose created a requisite level of impairment to disrupt inhibitory processes. Impairment in inhibitory processes provides a possible mechanism through which marijuana may influence risky decision making.

Reference Number: 61705

MADEA, B., AND F. MUSSHOFF. "Knock-Out Drugs: Their Prevalence, Modes of Action, Means of Detection." *Deutsches Arzteblatt International,* 106: 341–47, 2009 (2 tables, 25 references)

Abstract: An overview of the use of knock-out drugs in crimes such as robbery and sexual assaults was conducted. Criminals use drugs to facilitate sexual assault by inducing sedation and sleep, affecting the memory and altering behaviour, with the intention of lowering inhibitions and increasing alleged sexual desire.

The most frequently used drug in cases of sexual assault is still alcohol (40 percent to 60 percent), followed by illegal drugs (cannabis, cocaine). The presence of involuntarily consumed medications and drugs of abuse is demonstrated by routine toxicological analysis in only a relatively few cases (2 percent). The substances most commonly found are benzodiazepines, followed by other hypnotics. In Europe, the illegal substance gamma-hydroxybutyric acid (GHB), Liquid Ecstasy, often mentioned as a date-rape drug, is only rarely detected with sufficient medicolegal certainty.

Reference Number: 61706

MORGAN, E., B. SKAATHUN, S. MICHAELS, L. YOUNG, A. KHANNA, S.R. FRIEDMAN, B. DAVIS, D. PITRAK, AND J. SCHNEIDER. "Marijuana Use as a Sex-Drug is Associated with HIV Risk among Black MSM and Their Network." *AIDS Behavior,* 20: 600–7, 2016 (4 tables, 34 references)

Abstract: A study was conducted on the cannabis use of 202 Black Men having Sex with Men (BMSM). Sixty percent used cannabis in general and 21 percent used it as a sex drug. Marijuana use as a sex drug was associated with participation in group sex and sex without a condom.

Of the reasons marijuana use is either not disaggregated or is excluded from analyses that examine HIV risk is because of common perceptions that it is not associated with HIV acquisition, as compared to other drugs typically described in the literature. In fact, analyses of marijuana and HIV risk are few and have mixed conclusions.

Reference Number: 61707

MULLINS, M.E. "Laboratory Confirmation of Flunitrazepam in Alleged Cases of Date Rape." *Academic Emergency Medicine* 6: 966–68, 1999 (9 references)

Abstract: Drug analyses were conducted on 1,077 urine samples from alleged sexual assault victims. Flunitrazepam was detected in only six cases (0.6 percent), GHB in forty-six (4 percent), marijuana in 200 (18 percent), and alcohol in 400 (36 percent).

Although flunitrazepam has become synonymous with date-rape drug in American culture, its documented occurrence remains rare. Ethanol remains the most common intoxicant detected among sexual assaults.

Reference Number: 61708

SCHUSTER, R.M., N.A. CRANE, R. MERMELSTEIN, AND R. GONZALEZ. "The Influence of Inhibitory Control and Episodic Memory on the Risky Sexual Behavior of Young Adult Cannabis Users." *Journal of International Neuropsychology*, 18: 827–33, 2012 (1 table, 1 figure, 31 references)

Abstract: Cannabis is associated with risky sexual behaviour (RSB), including more partners, earlier age of initiation, and less frequent use of protection. Forty-one male and twenty-four female cannabis users (mean age 21 years) were assessed for RSB and neurocognitive functioning using the Hopkins Visual Learning Test-Revised, the Iowa Gambling Task, the Go Stop Go task, and the Balloon Analogue Risk task.

> Despite these limitations, our findings indicate that poorer neurocognitive performance on measures of episodic memory and risk taking are associated with more RSB among young adult cannabis users. Importantly, the relationship of cannabis use with RSB is influenced by decision-making and risk-taking performance, with only those who perform more poorly showing significant relationships. Thus, poorer neurocognitive performance among cannabis users may present a significant public health concern, given the role of RSB as a vector for HIV. Our results suggest that strategies at reducing cannabis use or remediating specific neurocognitive deficits may help to reduce RSB and sex-related negative consequences in this population.

Reference Number: 61709

SCOTT-HAM, M., AND F.C. BURTON. "Toxicological Findings in Cases of Alleged Drug-Facilitated Sexual Assault in the United Kingdom over a 3-Year Period." *Journal of Clinical and Forensic Medicine*, 12: 175–86, 2005 (12 tables, 5 figures, 37 references)

Abstract: Drug screening was conducted on 1,014 cases of claimed drug-facilitated sexual assaults at the Forensic Science Service London Laboratory between 2000 and 2002. Alcohol was detected in 470 cases (46 percent), and illicit drugs in 344 cases (34 percent). Cannabis was the most common drug detected (26 percent), followed by cocaine (11 percent). In twenty-one cases (2 percent), a sedative or disinhibiting drug was detected, including MDMA, GHB, diazepam, and temazepam. No Rohypnol (flunitrazepam) was detected in any case. Cannabis was a frequent drug detected in cases with multi-illicit drugs.

Table: Twenty-Three Sexual Assault Cases in which Three or More Illicit Drugs Were Detected

Drug Combination	Number of Cases with alcohol	Number of Cases without alcohol
Cannabis + cocaine + ecstasy	2	7
Cannabis + cocaine + heroin	2	3
Cannabis + ecstasy + amphetamine	2	3
Cannabis + amphetamine + cocaine	2	1
Cannabis + amphetamine + cocaine + ketamine	0	1
Ecstasy + amphetamine + cocaine	1	0

Source: Adapted from Scott-Ham and Burton, 2005

The importance of recreational illicit drug use, with or without concurrent alcohol consumption, is also noteworthy in these cases. Over half of the cases (65 percent) contained either alcohol and/or an illicit drug or drugs. Clearly, alcohol consumption and use of illicit drugs should be considered a significant risk factor in such cases.

Reference Number: 61710

FRIESE, B., M.D. SLATER, R. ANNECHINO, AND R.S. BATTLES. "Teen Use of Marijuana Edibles: A Focus Group Study of an Emerging Issue." *Journal of Primary Prevention*, 37: 303–9, 2016 (2 tables, 10 references)

Abstract: Focus groups among thirty-nine high school teens (ages 15 to 17 years) in the San Francisco area were conducted on how cannabis was consumed. Teen perceptions of the pros of edible cannabis use is no smell and no smoke and a lower risk of getting caught at school. Some of the cons are they don't know the dosage of THC in edibles, homemade edibles taste bad, and you could pass out and get raped. Youth have access to edibles from dispensaries.

Table: Teens' Perceptions of Pros and Cons of Edible Cannabis

Pros of Edible Use	Cons of Edible Use
No smell, no smoke Smoking is unattractive for girls Lower risk of getting caught at school Lower risk of lip cancer	Do not know what is in homemade edibles Could be spiked with something else *Could pass out and get raped (emphasis added)* Homemade edibles taste bad Do not know the dosage of edibles (especially homemade) Can kill you High can be very intense and long-lasting

Source: Adapted from Friese et al, 2016

Desspite these limitations, this research provides important preliminary insights. Edibles are seen as having distinctive advantages (especially by females) and distinctive risks. These findings may be used to inform future quantitative and qualitative research and the development of interventions. For example, interventions could restrict the sale of edibles with strong youth appeal, e.g., lollipops, candy, brownies, or cookies, or make them visually distinctive so that it would be more difficult for youth to consume at school. Furthermore, youth should be educated about the risks of edible use, in particular, the dangers of consuming excessive amounts of THC.

Reference Number: 61711

SLAUGHTER, L. "Involvement of Drugs in Sexual Assault." *Journal of Reproductive Medicine*, 45: 425–30, 2000 (7 tables, 26 references)

Abstract: Urine samples collected within seventy-two hours of a sexual assault were analyzed for drugs and alcohol from 2,003 victims in forty-eight US states between 1996 and 1999. Alcohol was detected in 24 percent, cannabinoids in 19 percent, cocaine in 11 percent, oxazepam in 10 percent, amphetamine in 6 percent, GHB in 4 percent, and flunitrazepam in 0.4 percent of the samples.

This and other studies support the notion that public attention should be redirected to the substances that are detected most frequently in victims of sex crimes: alcohol and marijuana. Additionally, it should be better understood that with moderate to heavy consumption, these drugs have properties similar to those of both GHB and FN: intoxication, disinhibition, and amnesia.

Reference Number: 61712

PARKS, K.A., R.L. COLLINS, AND J.L. DERRICK. "The Influence of Marijuana and Alcohol Use on Condom Use Behavior: Findings from a Sample of Young Adult Female Bar Drinkers." *Psychology and Addictive Behavior*, 26: 888–94, 2012 (3 tables, 1 figure, 36 references)

Abstract: The effects of alcohol and cannabis on risky sexual behaviour (failure to use a condom) was determined in 251 American women (average age 21 years) who attended bars at least once a week. Daily information was collected over a twelve-week period using a computer-based interactive voice response system and monthly in-person interviews. Overall, 60 percent of sexual activity occurred without the use of a condom. The OR of not using a condom was 1.2 times for alcohol only, 1.1 times for cannabis only, and 2.4 times for alcohol and cannabis use before sexual activity. The degree of sexual assertiveness of the woman moderated the drug effects.

> Our findings do not provide support for a simple additive or interactive effect of alcohol and marijuana on risky sexual behaviour, but rather suggest that the use of these two substances interacts with existing individual vulnerabilities to further increase the chance of engaging in risky sexual behaviour.

Reference Number: 61713

BELLIS, M.A., K. HUGHES, A. CALAFAT, M. JUAN, A. RAMON, J.A. RODRIGUEZ, F. MENDES, S. SCHNITZER, AND P. PHILLIPS-HOWARD. "Sexual Uses of Alcohol and Drugs and the Associated Health Risks: A Cross Sectional Study of Young People in Nine European Cities." *BMC Public Health*, 8: 155 (11 pp), 2008 (5 tables, 32 references)

Abstract: A survey was conducted of the sexual practices and alcohol/drug use in 1,341 participants (ages 16 to 35 years) in nine European cities, who routinely attended pubs, bars, and nightclubs. Participants were significantly more likely to have had sex under the age of 16 years if they had used alcohol (OR 3.47), cannabis (OR 4.19), cocaine (OR 5.73), or ecstasy (OR 9.35) before the age of 16. Any cannabis use was associated with risky sex, without a condom or birth control, and use of both cannabis and ecstasy was associated with having regretted sex.

Table: Percent of Male Alcohol/Drug Users Who Intentionally Employ Them for Sexual Purposes

Reason Drug Used for Sex	% Male Alcohol Users	% Male Cannabis Users	% Male Cocaine Users	% Male Ecstasy Users
Prolong Sex	16.9%	13.0%	28.2%	15.7%
Enhance Sensation and Arousal	11.9%	23.2%	33.0%	28.1%
Facilitate Sexual Encounter	34.1%	13.7%	14.6%	13.5%
Unusual/Exciting Sexual Activity	15.7%	13.0%	22.3%	28.1%

Source: Adapted from Bellis et al, 2008

An epidemic of recreational drug use and binge drinking has resulted in millions of individuals routinely consuming substances that alter the sexual decisions they make and increases the chance of unsafe and regretted sex. However, for many, substance use is now an integral part of their strategic approach to sex and, as such, an additional factor that locks them into continued use. Tackling substances with both physiological and psychological links to sex requires approaching substance use and sexual behaviour in the same way that young people experience them: as part of the same social process.

6.18 SPORTS

Cannabis is the third most common drug detected in athletics (61802). Cannabis use is more common in contact sports than non-contact sports (61808). Professional tennis is a sport under strict anti-doping control, and cannabis and cocaine are the main drugs detected. Alcohol consumption is not banned (61809).

Reference Number: 61801

CAMPOS, D.R., M. YONSMINE, AND R. DE MORALES MOREAU "Marijuana as Doping in Sports." *Sports and Medicine,* 33: 395–99, 2003 (3 tables, 1 figure, 130 references)

Abstract: The role of cannabis in sports was reviewed. Tests for cannabinoids usage are typically conducted in urine for 11 nor (delta 9 tetrahydrocannabinol) 9-carboxylic acid (THCCOOH). The main metabolite of THC at a cutoff of > 15 ng/mL. The number of positive urine for cannabis between 1998 and 2002 was 3 percent in soccer, 5 percent in volleyball, 1 percent in cycling, and 3 percent in horse racing. Cannabinoids can reduce anxiety but have no ergogenic potential in sport.

> The ethical aim to protect athletes from the psychoactive effects of delta-9-THC and reaffirm principles for a better quality of life has led the IOC to propose sanctions against the use of all products of cannabis.

Reference Number: 61802

HUESTIS, M.A., I. MAZZONI, AND O. RABIN. "Cannabis in Sport: Anti-Doping Perspective." *Sports Medicine*, 41: 949–966, 2011 (2 tables, 1 figure, 135 references)

Abstract: Since 2004, the World Anti-Doping Agency has prohibited the use of cannabis in all sports during competition. The potential of cannabis to enhance sports performance, the risk cannabis poses to athletes, and its violation of the spirit of sport are discussed in relation to this ban. Passive inhalation of THC is discussed. Cannabis contains over 400 different chemicals and at least 61 cannabinoids. Smoking and pyrolysis may produce an additional 2,000 compounds. CBD possess anxiolytic, antipsychotic, and alerting properties and modulate the effect of THC. CBN is 10 percent as psychoactive as THC. Physiological effects include tachycardia, conjunctival injection (red eyes), dry mouth, increased appetite, vasodilation, and bronchodilation. Smoking produces rapid changes in HR, pronounced hypotension, and dizziness in about 25 percent of individuals, ten minutes after smoking. CB1 receptors are located in the CNS and associated with short-term memory impairment, impairment of motor inhibition, decision making and inhibitory control. Smoked cannabis can decrease anxiety, fear, depression, and tension. THC appears immediately at high concentrations in OF due to the exposure of the oral mucosa to THC in smoke and decreases in approximately thirty-five to forty minutes. Urine THCCOOH does not exceed the 15 ng/mL threshold unless passive inhalation occurs under extreme conditions. Approximately 7.7 percent of drug infractions of WADA since 2004 involve cannabis and it is the third most commonly detected drug in athletics. Sanctions for the first positive test range from a warning to a two-year bar, with recurring infractions resulting in a lifetime ban.

Recent advances in understanding the endogenous cannabinoid system demonstrates its important role in many critical functions that could positively affect sports performance. This fact, together with the detrimental health effects of cannabis and its violation of the spirit of sport, supports the prohibition of cannabis.

Reference Number: 61803

BUCKMAN, J.F., D.A. YUSKO, S.G. FARRIS, H.R. WHITE, AND R.J. PANDINA. "Risk of Marijuana Use in Male and Female College Student Athletes and Nonathletes." *Journal of Studies on Alcohol and Drugs* 72: 586–91, 2011 (1 table, 36 references)

Abstract: Self-reported cannabis use was determined in 392 undergraduate student athletes (mean age 19.9 years) from seventeen different teams and 504 non-athlete students (mean age 20.0 years). The prevalence of past-year marijuana use was 50 percent in male non-athletes, 37 percent in male athletes, 48 percent in female non-athletes, and 25 percent in female athletes. In addition, non-athletes used cannabis more frequently than athletes. The risk factors for cannabis use were being white, smoking cigarettes in the past year, having high sensation-seeking scores, and misperceiving normative student marijuana use. Smoking cannabis can undermine athletic performance as it decreases alertness, increases reaction time, and accelerates muscle fatigue.

Table: Frequency of Past-Year Marijuana Use in Male and Female Athletes and Non-Athletes Who Smoked Cannabis

Frequency of Use	Male Athletes	Male Non-Athletes	Female Athletes	Female Non-Athletes
Infrequent	66%	30%	85%	48%
Monthly	14%	25%	13%	33%
Weekly	17%	19%	0%	11%
Daily	3%	26%	3%	7%

Source: Adapted from Buckman et al, 2011

For all individuals, marijuana use carries a high potential for negative consequences, particularly related to legal ramifications and health. Beyond this, athletes contend with the possibility of impairing their athletic performance and losing their eligibility to compete if they use marijuana.

Reference Number: 61803

Reference Number: 61804

LAURE, P., AND C. BINSINGER. "Doping Prevalence among Preadolescent Athletes: A 4 Year Follow-Up." *British Journal of Sports Medicine*, 41: 660–63, 2007 (3 tables, 22 references)

Abstract: All of the students (initially 3,594) who started sixth grade in eastern France were studied over the next four years as to drug use and doping in athletics. Initially 1.2 percent of the group reported using doping agents to improve performance at least once in the last six months, which increased to 3.0 percent four years later. The most common doping agents used were salbutamol (45.4 percent), corticosteroids (10.2 percent), cannabis (6.3 percent), and other stimulants or anabolic agents (38.0 percent).

Table: Global Odds Ratio of Using Doping Agents and Recreational Drug Use in Pre-Adolescent Athletes

Recreational Drug Use	Global OR of Doping
Tobacco	5.9 X
Alcohol	7.3 X
Alcohol Intoxication	4.2 X
Cannabis	7.8 X

Source: Adapted from Laure and Binsinger, 2007

> The present findings support our previous ones: young athletes who use doping agents are more likely to be boys, invest much time in training, are ready users of psychoactive substances, and, importantly, they appear to be in some distress (do not feel happy, low self-esteem, high trait anxiety). Furthermore, at least six months previously, they have said that they had been tempted to try a prohibited drug. Adults responsible for young children should be alerted by these signs, even though the results are from an epidemiological study and therefore must be applied to individual people with care.

Reference Number: 61805

BERGAMASCHI, M.M., AND J.A.S. CRIPPA. "Why Should Cannabis be Considered Doping in Sports?" *Frontiers in Psychiatry*, 4, Article 32, 2 pp, May 2013 (14 references)

Abstract: The current World Anti-Doping Agency (WADA) standard for doping is a urine THCCOOH concentration > 15 ng/mL. Cannabis smoking can be helpful for extreme sports, as it improves muscular relaxation, reduces anxiety, and can extinct fear memories. Cannabis use can also have detrimental effects on sports performance (such as decreasing alertness). Spice or synthetic cannabinoids will not be detected on standard drug screening tests and neither will other cannabinoids, such as CBD.

The non-psychoactive cannabidiol (CBD) is anxiolytic in humans following a single dose; decreased anxiety and fear memories extinction after oral CBD intake may enhance sports performance with no violation in the Code, as no THCCOOH is detected in the urine. One way to protect athletes' health and to promote health, fairness, and equality is to include any illicit drugs, their constituents, and analogs in the anti-doping program. The sports may assist in creating educational programs for youth and athletes as a way to keep them away from drugs and to preserve the intrinsic value about the spirit of sport.

Reference Number: 61806

HARCOURT, P.R., H. UNGLIK, AND J.L. COOK. "A Strategy to Reduce Illicit Drug Use Effective in Elite Australian Football." *British Journal of Sports Medicine*, 46: 943–45, 2012 (2 tables, 11 references)

Abstract: Urine drug testing was conducted on players of the Australian Football League (AFL) over seven years. The number of drug tests were increased each year and focused on high risk times, during non-game periods. There were no positive tests on match days and a reduction from nineteen illicit drug positives to six positive tests on non-match days. The number of positive urine cannabinoid tests decreased from six in 2005 to zero in 2011.

There is a suggestion that more testing may reduce illicit drug use and this study supports this supposition, given the decrease in positive tests with greater test numbers. Professional football players in England report widespread use of recreational drugs in an environment of low testing; only 66 percent had been tested in the previous two years and 60 percent felt they were unlikely to get tested that year. It would appear that more testing is likely to impact athlete behaviour.

Reference Number: 61807

VELIZ, P.T., C.J. BOYD, AND S.E. MCCABE. "Competitive Sport Involvement and Substance Use among Adolescents: A Nationwide Study." *Substance Use and Misuse*, 50: 156–65, 2015 (5 tables, 29 references)

Abstract: The association between different types of competitive sports and substance use was determined in 21,049 participants in grade 8 to 10 during 2010 and 2011. The sports were divided into high contact (football, wrestling, hockey), semi-contact (baseball, basketball, soccer), and non-contact (cross country, swimming).

Table: The Odds Ratio (OR) of Participants in Contact, Semi-Contact, and Non-Contact Sports of Substance Use, Compared to Non-Participants of Sports

Type of Sports	OR of Alcohol in Past 30 Days	OR of Cigarettes in Past 30 Days	OR of Cannabis Use in Past 30 Days	OR of Other Illicit Drugs in Past 30 days
Contact Sports	1.63 X	1.30 X	1.24 X	1.13 X
Semi-Contact Sports	1.16 X	1.04 X	1.18 X	1.31 X
Non-Contact Sports	0.88 X	0.795 X	0.795 X	1.10 X

Source: Adapted from Veliz, Boyd, and McCabe, 2015

In conclusion, the results of this study provide support for the hypothesis that participation in competitive sports is associated with substance use among secondary school students, especially among participants in high-contact sports. The findings regarding physical contact demonstrate the importance of considering different levels of physical contact. Adolescents who participate in high-contact sports had higher odds of engaging in substance use when compared to other adolescents who did not participate in these types of sports. Parents, educators, and policy-makers need to be aware that the promise of sport is not a monolithic force that stretches across all youth participants, and may fall short in providing a necessary forum to establish healthy practices across the life course.

Reference Number: 61808

MAQUIRRIAN, J. "Epidemiological Analysis of Doping Offences in the Professional Tennis Circuit." *Journal of Occupational Medicine and Toxicology*, 5: 30 (6pp), 2010 (5 tables, 14 references)

Abstract: Tennis is a professional sport under strict anti-doping control. Between 2003 and 2009, an average of 1,906 urine samples were collected annually and tested for drugs and doping agents. Fifty-two doping violations were reported between 2003 and 2009 for a positive rate of 0.38 percent. During Grand Slam tournaments, the doping rate was 0.18 percent. Alcohol consumption is not prohibited. Stimulants were detected in 32.6 percent of the positive samples, cannabis in 23.0 percent, anabolics in 11.5 percent, and diuretics and masking agents in 11.5 percent.

> In summary, this study showed that the incidence of positive doping samples among professional tennis players is quite low, supporting the assumption that there is no evidence of systematic doping in tennis. This study confirmed that social drugs misuses (marijuana and cocaine) constitute the main problem of doping in tennis. All out of competition EPO and GH analyses were negative. Male and wheelchair tennis players showed higher risk of infringing the doping code than their female and non-handicapped counterparts.

6.19 SUICIDE/DEPRESSION

Acute cannabis intoxication can cause confusion, psychosis, and loss of balance, which causes an increased risk of jumping or falling from a height (61901, 61906, 61909). The OR for suicidal ideation was 2.9 times greater for young people who used cannabis eleven or more times a year (61908, 61912, 61915, 61916). The risk for suicide was 2.90 times for alcohol dependence and 3.96 times for cannabis dependence (61902). A suicide attempt in a patient prescribed marijuana by a doctor is described (61913).

Reference Number: 61901

LUNDHOLM, L., I. THIBLIN, B. RUNESON, A. LEIFMAN, AND A. FUGELSTAD. "Acute Influence of Alcohol, THC, or Central Stimulants on Violent Suicide:

A Swedish Population Study." *Journal of Forensic Sciences*, 59: 436–40, 2014 (2 tables, 41 references)

Abstract: A study was conducted of the characteristics of 13,352 male and 5,542 female suicide victims comparing drug use in violent and non-violent methods, in Sweden between 1994 and 2009. Twenty-three percent were positive for alcohol, 1.3 percent for central stimulants, and 0.7 percent for THC. The most common methods for suicide were hanging (37 percent) and poisoning (27 percent). THC positive victims were less likely to commit suicide by drowning or firearms but were 1.6 times as likely to jump from a height. Twelve percent of the THC positive group jumped compared to 6 percent of the alcohol and drug negative groups.

Table: Adjusted Odds Ratio According to Suicide Method and Use of Alcohol, Cannabis, or Central Stimulants

Suicide Method	Alcohol	THC	Central Stimulants
Hanging	0.67 X	0.81 X	1.17 X
Drowning	0.56 X	0.51 X	0.34 X
Firearm	0.78 X	0.36 X	0.63 X
Sharp Force	0.24 X	0.70 X	1.53 X
Jumping from Height	0.44 X	1.62 X	1.12 X

Source: Adapted from Lundholm et al, 2014

Cannabis is mostly used for its relaxing effect, but the drug has several psychiatric side effects. Jumping from a height is a method related to psychopathology and cannabis is associated with confusion and drug-related psychosis.

Reference Number: 61902

CHACHAMOVICH, E., L.J. KIRMAYER., M. HAGGARTY, M. CARGO, R. MCCORMICK, AND G. TURECKI. "Suicide among Inuit: Results from a Large Epidemiologically Representative Follow-Back Study in Nunavut." *Canadian Journal of Psychiatry*, 60: 268–75, 2015 (4 tables, 39 references)

Abstract: An analysis was conducted of 120 suicides by Inuit that occurred between 2003 and 2006 in Nunavut and control subjects. The OR for suicide was 2.90 times for alcohol dependence, 3.96 times for cannabis dependence in the last six months, and 2.38 times to have experienced childhood abuse.

At the individual level, clinical risk factors for suicide among Inuit are similar to those observed in studies with the general population and indicate a need for improved access to mental health services. The high rate of mental health problems among control subjects suggests the need for population-level mental health promotion.

Reference Number: 61903

DARKE, A.C., J. DUFLOU, AND M. TOROK. "Toxicology and Circumstances of Completed Suicide by Means Other than Overdose." *Journal of Forensic Sciences*, 54: 490–94, 2009 (2 tables, 23 references)

Abstract: The postmortem drug/alcohol concentrations were determined in 1,415 suicide victims in New South Wales between 1997 and 2003. A positive BAC (0.010–0.400 g/100mL) was found in 4 percent of the male and 27 percent of the female victims. Male victims were more likely to be positive for alcohol, cannabis, and psychostimulants and female victims for pharmaceuticals. Alcohol was more common where a suicide note was left and there were relationship problems.

Table: Percentage of Cases in which a Drug Was Detected in Male and Female Suicide Victims and the Odds Ratio According to Gender of Using that Drug

Drug Detected	Male (%)	Female (%)	Gender OR
Alcohol	43.8%	26.9%	2.12 X
Cannabis	11.4%	6.4%	1.87 X
Opioids	9.2%	9.5%	NS
Psychostimulant	7.3%	3.0%	2.52 X

Source: Adapted from Darke, et al, 2009

In summary, psychoactive substances played a significant role among both genders and across all circumstances.

Reference Number: 61904

DHOSSCHE, D.M., C.L. RICH, AND G. ISACSSON. "Psychoactive Substances in Suicides. Comparison of Toxicologic Findings in Two Samples." *American Journal of Forensic Medicine and Pathology*, 22: 239–43, 2001 (2 tables, 31 references)

Abstract: Toxicological analyses were conducted on 179 suicide victims in San Diego, California, between 1981 and 1982 and in 333 suicide victims in Mobile County, Alabama, between 1990 and 1998. The analyses were conducted on postmortem blood or tissue samples and the results were confirmed by GC/MS. A positive BAC was found in 33 percent and 30 percent of the victims respectively. Suicide victims were positive for alcohol, cocaine, or cannabis in 40 percent of both groups. Antidepressant drugs were found in 20 percent and 8 percent of the samples respectively.

> Detection of alcohol, cocaine, or cannabis in about 40 percent of suicides supports the clinical practice of discouraging consumption of these substances in depressed patients. Another challenge is the low rate of detection of antidepressants in suicide, which suggests undertreatment of depression in suicides. Continued reporting of routine comprehensive toxicologic findings in suicides is useful to monitor patterns of use of psychoactive substances in this group and to guide suicide prevention in clinical practice and public health policy.

Reference Number: 61905

HANCOCK-ALLEN, J.B., L. BARKER, M. VANDYKE, AND D.B. HOLMES. "Death Following Ingestion of an Edible Marijuana Product, Colorado, March 2014." *Morbidity and Mortality Weekly Report,* 64: 771–72, 2015 (8 references)

Abstract: A 19-year-old male naive cannabis user consumed part of a marijuana cookie containing 65 mg of THC. Approximately thirty to sixty minutes later, after having not felt any effects, he consumed the rest of the cookie. During the next two hours he exhibited erratic speech and hostile behaviour and jumped off the fourth floor balcony to his death. His postmortem blood contained 7.2 ng/mL THC and 49 ng/mL of delta 9-carboxy-THC. No other drugs were determined. Approximately 45 percent of Colorado's marijuana sales involve edible marijuana. Absorption is much slower orally as peak plasma THC concentrations occur at one to two hours, compared to five to ten minutes after smoking cannabis.

> Regulation of recreational marijuana edibles in Colorado continues to evolve. On the basis of initial surveillance data in Colorado and numerous cases of accidental overconsumption, on February 1, 2015, Colorado instituted new packaging and labeling rules requiring that edible

marijuana products contain no more than 10 mg of THC or have clear demarcation of each 10 mg serving.

Reference Number: 61906

PATTON, G.C., C. COFFEY, J.B. CARLIN, L. DEGENHARDT, M. LYNSKEY, AND W. HALL. "Cannabis Use and Mental Health in Young People: Cohort Study." *British Medical Journal*, 325: 195–98, 2002 (4 tables, 23 references)

Abstract: A survey was conducted between 1992 and 1998 of 1,601 students, ages 14 to 15 years, in forty-four schools in Victoria, Australia, regarding cannabis use and later depression and anxiety were followed for seven years. Approximately 60 percent of the participants had used cannabis by the age of 20 years and 7 percent were daily users. Seventy-one male participants (9.7 percent) and 188 female participants (22 percent) reported depression and anxiety. The OR for experiencing depression or anxiety in women increased from 0.87 to 1.9 to 8.6 times for increasing cannabis use from seldom to one to four times a week to daily use.

Table: Odds Ratio of Depression and Anxiety with Cannabis Use by Gender in 1,590 Young Adult Users

Cannabis Use	OR for Men	OR for Women
None to < 5 times ever	1.0 X	1.0 X
5 times ever to less than weekly	1.1 X	0.87 X
1-4 times per week	1.5 X	1.9 X
Daily	1.9 X	8.6 X

Source: Adapted from Patton et al, 2002

Frequent cannabis use in teenage girls predicts later depression and anxiety, with daily users carrying the highest risk. Given recent increasing levels of cannabis use, measures to reduce frequent and heavy recreational use seem warranted.

Reference Number: 61907

PEDERSEN, W. "Does Cannabis Use Lead to Depression and Suicidal Behaviors? A Population-Based Longitudinal Study." *Acta Psychiatrica Scandinavica*, 18: 395–403, 2008 (3 tables, 46 references)

Abstract: Cannabis use and depression and suicidal thoughts and attempts were determined in 2,033 Norwegians over a thirteen-year period (ages 14 to 27 years). The OR for suicide ideation and attempts was

2.9 times for those who used cannabis eleven or more times over the last year, but not significant for lesser use.

The conclusion is that cannabis use in the late adolescence and early twenties was associated with an increased risk of later suicide ideation and suicide attempts. However, no association with later depression was found.

Reference Number: 61908

PERRET, G., M. FLOMENBAUM, AND R. LA HARPE. "Suicides by Fall from Height in Geneva, Switzerland, from 1991 to 2000." *Journal of Forensic Sciences*, 48: 821–26, 2003 (3 tables, 20 references)

Abstract: A study was conducted of 197 suicides as a result of falls from heights in Geneva between 1991 and 2000. The victims ranged in age from 13 to 95 years (mean 52 years). Fifty-six percent of the victims were women and 44 percent were men. The age distribution of the suicide victims peaked at 20 to 29 years in men and 60 to 69 years in women. Most of the victims jumped from their home (62 percent), 14 percent from other buildings, and 13 percent from bridges. Half of the suicides from bridges were from the same bridge (the highest one in the Geneva area). Toxicological and alcohol testing was conducted in only 24 percent of the victims. A positive postmortem BAC was found in 35 percent of these cases, and alcohol and other drugs in 25 percent. Benzodiazepines, cannabis, and antidepressants were the most common drugs found. Alcohol testing alone was conducted in another 11 percent of the victims. Of all victims tested for alcohol, 22 percent had a BAC > 0.050 g/100mL.

Toxicology results showed that alcohol, cannabis, and benzodiazepines were found with the highest frequency. These substances may contribute to suicidal behaviour by suppressing fear and inhibition.

Reference Number: 61909

PERRET, G., A. ABUDUREHEMAN, M. PERRET-CATIPOVIC, M. FLOMENBAUM, AND R. LA HARPE. "Suicides in the Young People of Geneva, Switzerland from 1993 to 2002." *Journal of Forensic Sciences*, 51: 1169–73, 2006 (1 table, 6 figures, 28 references)

Abstract: A study was conducted of sixty-five suicides in Geneva between 1993 and 2002 in persons less than 25 years of age. Approximately three-quarters were male and one-quarter were female and the youngest victim was 12 years of age. The most common methods of suicide for male victims were firearms (38 percent), fall from height (30 percent), hanging (13 percent), and drowning (10 percent). The most common methods of suicide for female victims were fall from height (40 percent), firearms (20 percent), drug overdose (20 percent), hanging (13 percent), and drowning (7 percent). Toxicological testing was conducted in 41 percent of all deaths. Alcohol only was detected in 26 percent and alcohol/drug in another 15 percent of the victims. The most common drugs were benzodiazepines, cannabis, and cocaine.

> Toxicology results show a high percentage of drug or alcohol use in suicide victims. This was an incidental finding in the traumatic suicides. This has been described as a significant risk factor to commit suicide, especially among older adolescent male victims, probably due to the disinhibiting effects of these substances. The most frequent finding was cannabis (18 percent), cannabis and benzodiazepines (7 percent), and cocaine and morphine (7 percent).

Reference Number: 61910

PIPER, T.M., M. TRACY, A. BUCCIARELLI, K. TARDIFF, AND S. GALEA. "Firearm Suicide in New York City in the 1990s." *Injury Prevention,* 12: 41–45, 2006 (2 tables, 2 figures, 35 references)

Abstract: An analysis was conducted of 1,200 suicides by firearms that occurred in New York City between 1990 and 2000. The OR of cannabis being detected was 2.61, and was 1.3 times for alcohol and 1.44 times for cocaine.

> In multi-variable modelling, characteristics of suicide decedents associated with a greater likelihood of firearm suicide were male, of black race, residing in the outer boroughs, and use of cannabis.

Reference Number: 61911

DELFORTERIE, M.J., M. LYNSKEY, A.C. HUIZINK, H.E. CREEMERS, J.D. GRANT, L.R. FEW, A.L. GLOWINSKI, D.J. STATHAM, T.J. TRULL, K.K. BUCHOLZ, P.A.F. MADDEN, N.G. MARTIN, A.C. HEATH, AND A. AGRAWAL. "The Relationship between Cannabis Involvement and Suicidal Thoughts and Behaviors." *Drug and Alcohol Dependence*, 150: 98–104, 2015 (5 tables, 49 references)

Abstract: A twin-based study of cannabis use and suicidal ideation (SI), plan, and attempt was conducted in 9,583 individuals in a community-based twin sample from the Australian Twin Registry. The sample was 59 percent female and between 27 and 48 years of age. The OR of suicidal ideation was 1.28 to 2.00 and between 1.95 and 2.51 for unplanned suicide attempts, regardless of the duration of cannabis user compared to non-cannabis users.

Cannabis involvement is associated, albeit modestly, with SI and unplanned suicide attempts. Such attempts are difficult to prevent and their association with cannabis use and cannabis use disorder symptoms requires further study, including in different samples and with additional attention to confounders.

Reference Number: 61912

NUSSBAUM, A., C. THURSTONE, AND I. BINSWANGER. "Medical Marijuana Use and Suicide Attempt in a Patient with Major Depressive Disorder." *American Journal of Psychiatry*, 168: 778–81, 2011 (2 figures, 17 references)

Abstract: The medicalization of marijuana encourages regular use. Regular use of cannabis has a significant association with depression. A 29-year-old woman was admitted to hospital in Denver, Colorado, two hours after ingesting ethylene glycol in a suicide attempt. She has used marijuana since she was 18 years of age, when she obtained her medical marijuana licence and smoked at least a joint daily. In the months prior to her current suicide attempt, she doubled her daily use of cannabis. Her self-admitted periods of heaviest cannabis use were temporally associated with depressive episodes and suicide attempts. She was referred to an outpatient substance abuse program but declined to attend as she thought her marijuana use was not a problem, as it was prescribed by a doctor.

Finally, Ms. H's case shows our need for rigorous investigations into the effects of marijuana on medical and psychiatric conditions, especially in association with impulsivity and suicidality. The medical marijuana industry, a system that encourages chronic and frequent use of marijuana, has expanded dramatically, and the ways in which this development will alter patterns of marijuana use and abuse remain unclear.

Reference Number: 61913

WRIGHT, N.E., D. SCERPELLA, AND K.M. LISDAHL. "Marijuana Use is Associated with Behavioral Approach and Depressive Symptoms in Adolescents and Emerging Adults." *PLOS ONE*, 11: 17 pp, 2016 (2 tables, 2 figures, 101 references)

Abstract: The endocannabinoid system plays a major neurodevelopmental role as the primary brain endocannabinoid receptor CB1 has significantly greater binding in adolescents than in adulthood. The effect of marijuana use on anxiety, depression, impulsivity, and executive dysfunction was determined in forty-two marijuana users (smoked more than ten times in the last year) and forty-two healthy controls (smoked less than five times in the last year). The groups were balanced for gender. A drug urine toxicology screen was conducted on the subjects as they were to refrain from drug/alcohol use for seven days prior to testing. The urine was tested for cotinine, a biomarker of exposure to tobacco smoke. In the marijuana group, there was an increase in depressive symptoms and a decrease in fun-seeking and reward response. Female marijuana use has increased anxiety symptoms and increased disinhibition.

Table: Percentage of Marijuana Users and Controls with Elevated Clinical Symptoms Scores

Clinical Symptom	% with Elevated Scores in Marijuana Group	% with Elevated Scores in Control Group
Depression	7%	2%
Anxiety	2%	5%
Apathy	17%	14%
Disinhibition	21%	4%
Executive Dysfunction	36%	14%

Source: Adapted from Wright, Scerpella, and Lisdahl, 2016

This study is consistent with prior findings regarding increased depressive symptoms in marijuana users. The eCB system is downregulated in response to repeated THC binding to CB1, particularly in limbic regions, and the eCB system has been linked to increased mood symptoms, perhaps suggesting an underlying mechanism. In an independent study, our group previously reported that increased marijuana use was predictive of increased depressive symptoms in young adults without independent Axis I mood disorders. Further, we found that frontolimbic poorer white matter integrity and volume were related to increased depressive symptoms and apathy in adolescent and young MJ users. Marijuana use may therefore lead to white matter abnormalities, which in turn may lead to greater depressive symptoms. A recent meta-analysis has also reported that marijuana use increased the odds ratio of developing depression. Importantly, the present study excluded for independent mood disorders, so these findings may not generalize to youth who develop depression prior to their onset of marijuana use. In addition, the effect size demonstrated was small, indicating that the relationship between marijuana use and depressive symptoms may be subtle.

Reference Number: 61914

ILGEN, M.A., M.A. WALTON, R.M. CUNNINGHAM, K.L. BARRY, S.T. CHERMACK, P. DE CHAVEZ, AND F.C. BLOW. "Recent Suicidal Ideation among Patients in an Inner-City Emergency Department." *Suicide and Life-Threatening Behavior,* 39: 508–17, 2009 (2 tables, 31 references)

Abstract: A study was conducted of 2,388 male and 3,253 female patients (mean age 36.5 years) at an inner city Emergency Department in Flint, Michigan, between 2006 and 2007, as to suicidal thoughts and alcohol/drug use. Approximately 8 percent of the patients had suicidal thoughts within two weeks of their ED attendance and approximately 0.4 percent of all ED admissions were for treatment of attempted suicide and self-inflicted injury.

These findings suggest that many patients who do not initially report a suicide attempt have had significant suicidal thoughts within the past two weeks. Suicidal thoughts are most common in single parents with poorer mental health, more depressive symptoms, who have had some drug and alcohol treatment in the past three months, or those who have used cocaine or marijuana in the past thirty days. In order to identify patients at high risk for suicide seen in ED, expanding screening efforts beyond those explicitly for treatment for suicide should be considered.

Reference Number: 61915

RAJA, M., AND A. AZZONI. "Suicidal Ideation Induced by Episodic Cannabis Use." *Case Reports in Medicine*, 2 pp, 2009 (11 references)

Abstract: A 32-year-old man attended an ER for psychiatric help. He had smoked cannabis a few hours before and now felt hopelessness, anxiety, fear, and agitation, and had the impulse to commit suicide by falling from a height. He had a similar episode to commit suicide three years earlier after smoking cannabis, which was resolved in a few hours. He reported no stressful life events. His urine toxicology screen was only positive for cannabinoids. He was treated with 4 mg of risperidone and 1000 mg of valproate and was released the next day.

> On this background of definite association between cannabis use and suicidal ideation or behaviour, the reported case presents two original clinical aspects that deserve consideration. First, episodic assumption of cannabis, induced suicidal ideation abruptly. Second, suicidal ideation appeared independent of mood depression, stressors, or life events, suggesting that suicidality may be not a direct consequence of depression and appears to be a relatively independent psychopathological dimension. There seems to be no linear relation between the severity of depression and the risk of suicide. In some patients, high suicidal risk may be concomitant with relatively minor depressive states, while in others, extremely severe depression may be immune to suicidal risk.

6.20 TRAUMA/ACCIDENTS

Alcohol, cannabis, and cocaine are common drugs detected in trauma patients (62002, 62003, 62006). Cannabis use when combined with high levels of risk increased the risk for minor injuries at the workplace and outside the workplace (62005).

Reference Number: 62001

ANDERSEN, S.R., F. BIERING-SORENSEN, E.M. HAGEN, J.F. NIELSEN, F.W. BACH, AND N.B. FINNERUP. "Cannabis Use in Persons with Traumatic Spinal Cord Injury in Denmark." *Journal of Rehabilitative Medicine* 49: 152–60, 2017 (2 tables, 4 figures, 41 references)

Abstract: The use of cannabis in 537 spinal cord injury (SCI) patients in Denmark was determined. Twenty-six percent of SCI patients tried cannabis at least once. Of these, 75 percent were former cannabis users and 25 percent were current users. The most common negative effects of cannabis use were inertia, feeling quiet, absentmindedness, and risky behaviour.

Table: Negative Consequences of Cannabis Use in Forty-Eight Current Cannabis Users

Negative Consequences	Number Reporting this Negative Consequence (%)
Inertia	21 (44%)
Feeling quiet/subdued	18 (38%)
Seems distant/absentmindedness	9 (19%)
Risky behaviour	10 (21%)
Feeling depressed	4 (8%)

Source: Adapted from Andersen et al, 2017

The current study found the prevalence of current cannabis users among persons with traumatic SCI in Denmark to be slightly higher than previously reported in the Danish general population. This may be due to an increased risk of accidents among cannabis users. Most participants started using cannabis before their SCI and used it for recreational purposes, but some also reported some effects on pain and spasticity. Approximately 20 percent of those who had never tried cannabis stated that if cannabis were legal, they would try it in order to alleviate symptoms due to SCI. Cannabis use was associated with lower age, living in rural areas and larger cities, tobacco-smoking, high alcohol intake, and higher muscle stiffness. There is currently limited evidence for the use of medical cannabis for SCI-related pain and spasticity and there are concerns about side effects and long-term risks.

Reference Number: 62002

LEVY, R.S., C.K. HERBERT, B.G. MUNN, AND R.L. BARACK. "Drug and Alcohol Use in Orthopedic Trauma Patients: A Prospective Study." *Journal of Orthopedic Trauma*, 10: 21–27, 1996 (9 tables, 19 references)

Abstract: A toxicology screen including alcohol was conducted on 628 patients admitted to an inner-city hospital between 1993 and 1994. The most common reasons for attendance were falls (31 percent), fights (14 percent), gunshot wounds (12 percent), and MVCs (13 percent). The incidence of alcohol/drug positives was 56 percent. Alcohol was the most commonly detected drug (25 percent), followed by cocaine (22 percent) and marijuana (21 percent). The highest incidence of drug use was found in males ages 31 to 40 years of age.

Table: Incidence of Alcohol and Other Drugs Detected in Orthopedic Trauma Patients

Drug Detected	% Positive
Alcohol	25%
Cocaine	22%
Cannabis	21%
Opiates	11%
Benzodiazepines	8%
Barbiturates	4%

Source: Adapted from Levey et al, 1996

> We conclude that drug and alcohol use is widespread in patients presenting to inner-city trauma centres with orthopedic injuries. This information should be considered during all aspects of a patient's treatment, especially when considering surgical intervention.

Reference Number: 62003

MCDONALD, A., N.D. DUNCAN, AND D.I.G. MITCHELL. "Alcohol, Cannabis and Cocaine Usage in Patients with Trauma Injuries." *Western Indian Medical Journal*, 48: 200–2, 1999 (2 tables, 1 figure, 15 references)

Abstract: The serum alcohol concentration (SAC) and the presence of cannabinoid and cocaine metabolites in the urine were determined in 100 male and eleven female trauma patients (age 16-79 years) admitted to a Jamaican hospital during a three-month period. Thirty-five patients (32 percent) had a positive SAC and 71 percent of these had a SAC > 0.080 g/100mL. The urine was positive for cannabinoids in 36 percent of the patients and cocaine in 6 percent. Sixty-six percent of the road traffic accident victims, 70 percent of the victims of violence, and 39 percent of the victims of other accidents were positive for one or more of the drugs tested.

Despite these limitations, this study raises a number of important questions and suggests some differences between the pattern of substance abuse in Jamaica and developed countries.

Reference Number: 62004

WOOLARD, R., J. BAIRD, M.J. MELLO, C. LEE, M. HARRINGTON, T. NIRENBERG, B. BECKER, L. STEIN, AND R. LONGABAUGH. "Injuries, Negative Consequences and Risk Behaviors among Both Injured and Uninjured Emergency Patients Who Report Using Alcohol and Marijuana." *Journal of Emergencies, Trauma and Shock*, 2: 23–28, 2009 (1 table, 12 references)

Abstract: This study compared 266 uninjured to 249 injured ED patients who admitted to alcohol use in the last mouth and smoked marijuana in the last year, and determined their need and readiness for a Brief Intervention (BI). In both groups there are similar rates of binge drinking, marijuana use, driving under the influence of alcohol/marijuana, injury, and other negative consequences.

ED patients who admit to alcohol and marijuana use also use other hazardous substances and participate in high risk behaviours. In both injured and uninjured patients who admit using alcohol and marijuana, the ED visit is an opportunity to deliver BI to reduce alcohol and marijuana use and associated risk behaviours and the subsequent injury and negative consequences. Given their risk behaviours and experience of negative consequences, members of both injured and uninjured groups have an equal need for BI. Fortunately, in both groups, a high number of members express motivation to change.

Reference Number: 62005

WADSWORTH, E.J.K., S.C. MOSS, S.A. SIMPSON, AND A.P. SMITH. "A Community Based Investigation of the Association between Cannabis Use, Injuries and Accidents." *Journal of Psychopharmacology*, 20: 5–13, 2006 (6 tables, 54 references)

Abstract: A survey was conducted of 7,979 persons in Wales in 2001 regarding drug use and accidents, traffic accidents, injuries, and problems of memory or attention. The respondents were 58 percent female with a mean age of 45.6 years. Twelve percent reported using drugs in the last year, and of these, 59 percent reported using only cannabis. Overall,

11 percent of the respondents reported an accident, 2 percent a traffic accident, and 4 percent frequent minor accidents. There was no association between cannabis use and cognitive problems. Cannabis use, when combined with high levels of risk, increased the risk for minor injuries, both outside and at the workplace.

> Cannabis use was associated with a significant detrimental impact on safety. It is possible that this is linked to an amplification of other risk factors associated with accidents and injuries. This has potentially wide-reaching implications, particularly in the context of other work and lifestyle characteristics.

Reference Number: 62006

LI, G., A. CHANMUGAM, R. ROTHMAN, C. DISCALA, C.N. PAIDAS, AND G.D. KELEN. "Alcohol and Other Psychoactive Drugs in Trauma Patients Aged 10–14 Years." *Injury Prevention*, 5: 94–97, 1999 (2 tables, 1 figure, 28 references)

Abstract: A toxicological screen was conducted on 1,356 trauma patients (ages 10 to 14 years) and recorded in the US National Pediatric Trauma Registry between 1990 and 1995 and evaluated. One hundred and sixteen patients (9 percent) were positive for alcohol or other drugs (AOD). Twenty-four (1.8 percent) tested positive for alcohol and the BAC ranged between 0.007 to 0. 230 g/100mL. Cannabis was the most frequent drug detected, even more than alcohol, in 32 patients (2.4 percent).

Table: Percentage of Trauma Patients (Ages 10–14 Years) Who Were Alcohol or Other Drug (AOD) Positive by Mechanism of Injury

Mechanism of Injury	% Positive of Alcohol or Other Drug (AOD)
Shooting (173 cases)	15%
Beating (57 cases)	11%
Stabbing (51 cases)	10%
Pedestrian (261 cases)	8%
Motor Vehicle (264 cases)	7%
Falls (122 cases)	6%
Bicycle (203 cases)	5%

Source: Adapted from Li et al, 1999

It is recognized that injury presents a unique opportunity to initiate intervention for substance abuse. Comprehensive instruments for assessing alcohol and other drug abuse are readily available and clinical guidelines for referral and treatment have been developed. Clinical trials conducted in adults demonstrated that brief counseling can reduce alcohol consumption by over 40 percent in primary care settings as well as inpatient care settings. It is unclear, however, whether similar intervention programs can be successfully implemented in children and adolescents.

Reference Number: 62007

OYEFESO A., F. SCHIFANO, H. GHODSE, K. COBAIN, R. DRYDEN, AND J. CORKERY. "Fatal Injuries under the Influence of Psychoactive Drugs: A Cross-Sectional Exploratory Study in England." *BMC Public Health*, 6: 148, 2006 (3 tables, 5 figures, 19 references)

Abstract: A study was conducted of 3,803 drug-related deaths of persons ages 16 to 64 years. There were 119 male and 28 female victims of fatal injuries under the influence (FIUI) of drugs between 1999 and 2001 in England, which is about 4 percent of the total number of drug-related deaths. There were ninety intentional deaths (hanging, drowning) and fifty-one unintentional deaths (road traffic accidents, falls). The most frequent drugs detected were alcohol in combination with drugs (36 percent), cannabis (18 percent), sedative/hypnotics (18 percent), heroin (16 percent), and cocaine (16 percent). Cannabis was detected in 15.9 percent of the intentional and 23.5 percent of the unintentional FIUI deaths.

Table: Odds Ratio of Different Drugs in Unintentional FIUI Compared to Non-FIUI Cases

Drug	OR of Unintentional FIUI
Cannabis	18.6 X
Cocaine	4.3 X
Sedatives/Hypnotics	2.0 X
Alcohol in Combination	1.6 X
Opioids	0.9 X

The implication of cannabis in 23 percent of unintentional FIUI cases challenges the general assumption that cannabis does not contribute to premature mortality like other illicit drugs.

6.21 WITHDRAWAL/CANNABIS WITHDRAWAL SYNDROME (CWS)

The Cannabis Withdrawal Syndrome (CWS) occurs after cessation or decreasing of heavy or prolonged cannabis use and is followed by typical symptoms as defined by *The Diagnostic and Statistical Manual of Mental Disorders* of the American Psychiatric Association (DSM-V) including:

- Irritability, anger or aggression
- Nervousness/anxiety
- Sleep difficulty
- Decreased appetite or weight loss
- Depressed mood
- One or more of the following physical symptoms: abdominal pain, shakiness/tremors, sweating, fever, chills, or headache

CWS is defined as occurring if three or more of the symptoms develop within one week of quitting or decreasing cannabis use abruptly (62103, 62107). Some individuals find quitting cannabis is more difficult than quitting smoking cigarettes (62104). Adolescents who smoke tobacco are nineteen times more likely to relapse cannabis abstinence than non-smokers (62110). The oral synthetic analogue THC medication, Nabilone, has been found to decrease the cannabis withdrawal symptoms (62106).

Reference Number: 62101

BONNETT, U., AND U.W. PREUSS. "The Cannabis Withdrawal Syndrome: Current Insights." *Substance Abuse and Rehabilitation*, 8: 9–37, 2017 (2 tables, 3 figures, 130 references)

Abstract: A detailed review was conducted on the cannabis withdrawal syndrome (CWS). CWS occurs in about 90 percent of patients diagnosed with cannabis dependence. Adult cannabis dependents develop a more severe CWS than adolescent dependents. A more prolonged and heavier cannabis use predicts a stronger CWS. Regular cannabis use is related to a desensitization and downregulation of the CB1 receptors, which starts to reverse after two days of abstinence and generally returns to near normal functioning after about four weeks. Continuous exposure to alcohol leads to an increase in endocannabinoid levels that also results in a downregulation of CB1 receptors. Alcohol is co-used by 33 to

46 percent of regular cannabis users. Heavy tobacco use was associated with greater irritability during CWS of adolescents. Women seeking treatment for CWS have more frequent and more severe symptoms than men after quitting cannabis use.

Although there was early evidence from animal experiments and despite observations in humans in every decade, CWS entity was doubted before the 1990s, when a new cannabis wave started to roll in worldwide, particularly in affluent regions. This was related to a mounting number of patients seeking treatment due to various cannabis-related disorders, including cognitive deficits, psychosis, and dependence. Considering these populations and also non-treatment-seeking cannabis-dependent individuals, larger retrospective clinical trials demonstrated that discontinuation of regular cannabis use is frequently followed by waxing and waning behavioural mood and physical symptoms, such as weakness, sweating, restlessness, dysphoria, sleeping problems, anxiety, and cravings, which are subsequently positively associated with relapse to cannabis use.

Reference Number: 62102

ALLSOP, C., J. COPELAND, M.M. NORBERG, S. FU, A. MOLNAR, J. LEWIS, AND A.J. BUDNEY. "Quantifying the Clinical Significance of Cannabis Withdrawal." *PLOS ONE, 7*: e44864, 12 pp, 2012 (6 tables, 2 figures, 48 references)

Abstract: Thirty-two male and seventeen female dependent, non-treatment-seeking cannabis users (ages 18 to 57 years) were assessed for one week before, during a two-week monitored abstinence, and one month later. Cannabis abstinence was determined if the THCCOOH: creatinine was below 50 ng/mL. The common symptoms during the one-week abstinence were trouble getting to sleep, loss of appetite, feeling physically tense, mood swings, feeling irritated, imagining being stoned, and feeling restless. Higher levels of dependence on cannabis were associated with higher levels of functional impairment during cannabis withdrawal.

Table: Odds Ratio of Predicting Relapse during Cannabis Withdrawal According to Symptom

Withdrawal Symptom	Odds Ratio of Relapse
I had no appetite	1.44 X
I felt physically tense	3.74 X
I felt anxious	1.1 X
Life felt like an uphill struggle	1.6 X
I had trouble getting to sleep	0.58 X
I had mood swings	0.47 X

Source: Adapted from Allsop et al, 2012

Cannabis withdrawal is clinically significant because it is associated with functional impairment of normal daily activities, as well as relapse to cannabis use.

Reference Number: 62103

LEVIN, K.H., M.L. COPERSINO, S.J. HEISHMAN, F. LIU, D.L. KELLY, D.L. BOGGS, AND D.A. GORELICK. "Cannabis Withdrawal Symptoms in Non-Treatment Seeking Adult Cannabis Smokers." *Drug and Alcohol Dependence*, 111: 120–27, 2010 (2 tables, 55 references)

Abstract: A study was conducted of the withdrawal symptoms experienced by cannabis users in the Baltimore area. Of the 857 subjects who scheduled for the study session, 357 did not appear. A total of 469 cannabis users (58 percent male, 42 percent female) were studied. The mean age was 31 years (range 18 to 65 years) and 80 percent were African-American. The sample was mainly of low socio-economic status, the mean years of education was twelve. One-third did not complete high school, half were unemployed, and 73 percent had never married. Marijuana was smoked by 88.7 percent, blunts by 62.9 percent, hashish by 39 percent, and hashish oil by 14.5 percent. Most used legal psychoactive substances to help quit (70 percent caffeine, 75 percent alcohol, 79 percent tobacco). The frequency of cannabis use (joints per day) was associated with the severity of withdrawal but withdrawal symptoms occurred in individuals who used cannabis less than weekly.

Table: Some Characteristics of Cannabis Withdrawal Symptoms Reported by 469 Non-Treatment-Seeking Cannabis Smokers

Withdrawal Symptoms	Percent Reporting Symptom	Mean Days after Quitting
Craving for Cannabis	76%	3 days
Trouble Falling Asleep	47%	3 days
Feeling Anxious or Nervous	50%	3 days
Insulted, Yelled or Swore at a Person	29%	3 days
Upset Stomach	13%	3 days
Feeling Bored	50%	4 days
Feeling Sad, Depressed	45%	4 days
Feeling Angry	34%	4 days
Headaches	23%	4 days
Physical Discomfort	10%	4 days
Strange Dreams	20%	6 days
Threw or Broke Something	15%	6 days
Pushed, Grabbed or Slapped a Person	4%	6 days
Weight Loss	15%	12 days
Improved Memory	28%	13 days

Source: Adapted from Levin et al, 2010

In summary, we found that cannabis withdrawal is a common, clinically significant syndrome among adult users not seeking treatment and without other substance abuse or psychiatric comorbidity. Withdrawal was experienced by those using cannabis less than daily. Cannabis withdrawal may trigger relapse to cannabis use and thus is a legitimate focus of treatment efforts.

Reference Number: 62104

VANDREY, B., A.J. BUDNEY, J.R. HUGHES, AND A. LIGUORI. "A within Subject Comparison of Withdrawal Symptoms during Abstinence from Cannabis, Tobacco and Both Substances." *Drug and Alcohol Dependence*, 92: 48–54, 2008 (2 tables, 2 figures, 41 references)

Abstract: Six male and six female tobacco, cannabis, and alcohol users (mean age 28 years) had withdrawal symptoms assessed after nine days of smoking either cannabis, tobacco, or both. The Withdrawal Symptoms Checklist (WSC) was similar for cannabis and tobacco, but was more severe after cessation of both substances.

Table: Cannabis and Tobacco Daily Use and Rank Order of Withdrawal Difficulty with Cannabis (C), Tobacco (T), or Dual Use (D) in the Twelve Subjects

Subject #	Cannabis Use (times daily)	Tobacco (cigarettes daily)	Rank-Order
1	4	15	D > T > C
2	6	35	T > D > C
3	2	20	D > T > C
4	2	40	D > T > C
5	8	20	T > C > D
6	6	15	C > T > D
7	10	17	D > C > T
8	2	20	D > C > T
9	3	16	T > C > D
10	4	15	C > T > D
11	4	20	C > D > T
12	1	10	C > T > D

Source: Adapted from Vandrey et al, 2008

These limitations acknowledged, the results do suggest that the severity of the cannabis withdrawal syndrome is of comparable magnitude to that of the tobacco withdrawal syndrome. Tobacco withdrawal has been extensively researched, and by its inclusion in DSM-IV is judged to be clinically significant (substance withdrawal disorders must produce clinically significant distress to be included in DSM-IV). This observed similarity with tobacco withdrawal combined with several lines of evidence suggest that cannabis withdrawal is clinically significant as described in the introduction, suggest that cannabis withdrawal is clinically significant in a subset of heavy cannabis users and should be characterized in detail in the next iterations of the DSM and ICD manuals.

Reference Number: 62105

VANDREY, R., A. UMBRICHT, AND E.C. STRAIN. "Increased Blood Pressure Following Abrupt Cessation of Daily Cannabis Use." *Journal of Addiction Medicine*. 5: 16–20, 2011 (2 figures, 26 references)

Abstract: Eleven male and two female daily cannabis users smoked cannabis *ad libitum* for two days and were abstinent for three days. Blood pressure and heart rate were monitored. Systolic BP increased from a mean of 129.6 mm Hg to 139.8 mm Hg and diastolic BP increased from

74.8 mm Hg to 81.8 mm Hg after abstinence. HR also increased but was not statistically significant.

> Abrupt cessation of heavy cannabis use may cause clinically significant increases in blood pressure in a subset of users. Blood pressure should be monitored among those attempting to reduce or quit frequent cannabis use, particularly those with pre-existing hypertension.

Reference Number: 62106

HANEY, M., Z.D. COOPER, G. BEDI, S.K. VOSBURG, S.D. COMER, AND R.W. FOLTIN. "Nabilone Decreases Marijuana Withdrawal and a Laboratory Measure of Marijuana Relapse." *Neuropsychopharmacology*, 38: 1557–65, 2013 (2 tables, 3 figures, 46 references)

Abstract: Three female and eight male chronic marijuana smokers seeking treatment for cannabis dependence were administered a placebo, and 6 or 8 mg of nabilone orally daily. Both doses of nabilone decreased marijuana relapse and decreased withdrawal symptoms, but the 8 mg dose caused some decrease in psychomotor task performance. All participants who also smoked cigarettes and took nabilone did not decrease tobacco consumption.

> Nabilone significantly reversed characteristic symptoms of marijuana withdrawal, including worsened mood, disrupted sleep, and decreased food intake. Most critical for its potential clinical utility, both nabilone dose conditions also decreased a laboratory measure of marijuana relapse: participants chose to smoke fewer individual doses of marijuana while maintained on nabilone as compared with placebo. Nabilone significantly decreased relapse to active marijuana the first day it was available and persisted in decreasing marijuana self-administration on subsequent days of active marijuana use, even among those who have relapsed. This may have important clinical implications, as many patients in drug treatment eventually sample their abused drug after a period of abstinence, but a medication that prevents a return to pre-treatment levels of drug use can have a significant impact on long-term outcome.

Reference Number: 62107

CORNELIUS, J.R., T. CHUNG, C. MARTIN, D.S. WOOD, AND D.B. CLARK. "Cannabis Withdrawal is Common Among Treatment-Seeking Adolescents with Cannabis Dependence and Major Depression and is Associated with Rapid Relapse to Dependence." *Addictive Behavior*, 33: 1500–05, 2008 (2 tables, 25 references)

Abstract: Ninety-two male and seventy-eight female cannabis users (mean age 20.3 years) with a major depressive disorder were divided into 104 showing cannabis dependence, thirty-two with cannabis abuse, and thirty-four cannabis users without abuse or dependence. The subjects presented for treatment and the withdrawal symptoms were assessed.

Table: Withdrawal Symptoms and Percent of Cannabis Dependent and Cannabis Use Groups Experiencing Them*

Symptom	% in Cannabis Dependent Group	% in Cannabis Use Group
Craving Cannabis	81.6%	8.8%
Irritability	75.7%	8.8%
Restlessness	58.3%	5.9%
Anxiety	55.3%	2.9%
Depression	52.4%	5.9%
Change in Appetite	45.6%	2.9%
Trouble Sleeping	43.7%	2.9%
Trouble Concentrating	39.8%	5.9%
Tiredness, Drowsiness, Weakness	27.2%	2.9%
Anger, Violent Outbursts	27.2%	2.9%

* Note: These symptoms must increase during abstinence in order to be counted as positive

Source: Adapted from Cornelius et al, 2008

The most commonly reported specific withdrawal symptoms were cannabis craving, irritability, restlessness, anxiety, and depression. These findings are consistent with reports that common symptoms of cannabis withdrawal are primarily emotional and behavioural, not the medical physical symptoms sometimes observed with opioid, sedative, or alcohol withdrawal. The number of cannabis withdrawal symptoms was found to be significantly higher in the cannabis dependent group than among the two comparison groups of either cannabis abuse or those of cannabis user but without cannabis abuse or dependence. We found that the presence of cannabis withdrawal symptoms was associated with rapid reinstatement of cannabis dependence symptoms (rapid relapse), as had been hypothesized. This additional finding provides evidence to support the clinical significance of cannabis withdrawal symptoms in the clinical course of adolescents and young adults with cannabis dependence.

Reference Number: 62108

LERNER, A.G., C. GOODMAN, D. RUDINSKI, AND A. BLEICH "Benign and Time-Limited Visual Disturbances (Flashbacks) in Recent Abstinent High-Potency Heavy Cannabis Smokers: A Case Series Study." *Israeli Journal of Psychiatry Related Science*, 48: 25–29, 2011 (41 references)

Abstract: Eight male patients (mean age 29 years) diagnosed with Cannabis Use Disorder, who smoked high potency cannabis at least three times a day for at least five years, underwent detoxification. Two of the eight patients relapsed after two months. Six abstinent patients reported visual flashbacks for up to six months after ceasing cannabis use. The flashbacks are reported to be benign and short term (lasting up to a few months).

High potency cannabis may have some influence in the development of the presented visual side effects. The THC content varies between different sources and preparations of cannabis. Sophisticated cultivation such as hydroponic farming and plant-breeding techniques have greatly increased the potency of cannabis products. In the 1960s and 1970s, an average joint contained about 10 mg of THC. Now a joint made out of potent subspecies may contain around 150 mg of THC or 300 mg if laced with hashish oil. Given the fact that the effects of THC are dose-related and most of the research on cannabis was carried out in the 1970s using doses of 5–26 mg of THC, modern predisposed and vulnerable cannabis smokers may be exposed to doses of THC greater than in the past and risk and consequences might be greater.

Reference Number: 62109

HUGHES, J.R., S. NAUD, A.J. BUDNEY, J.R. FINGAR, AND P.W. CALLAS. "Attempts to Stop or Reduce Daily Cannabis Use: An Intensive Natural History Study." *Psychology Addictive Behavior* 30: 389–97, 2016 (1 table, 2 figures, 70 references)

Abstract: In the US, there are approximately five million daily users of cannabis. Daily cannabis use accounts for most of the harm, dependence, and treatment-seeking associated with cannabis use. One hundred and ninety-three daily users of cannabis who intended to stop or reduce their consumption in the next three months called an interactive voice response system every morning to report on cannabis use and withdrawal symptoms. The participants were surveyed six months after the study as to current cannabis use. The mean age of the participants was 32 years, half were men and half were unemployed. Most (72 percent) have a high school education and about half made a quit attempt at some point during the study. But only 8 percent of those trying to quit were abstinent at the six-month follow-up.

> This study replicates our prior findings that a) cannabis users trying to change make many and often rapid transitions among use as usual, reduction, and abstinence; b) reduction attempts are more common than abstinence attempts; c) quit and reduction attempts are short-lived and few participants achieve long-term abstinence; d) alcohol and drug use are not greater on abstinence days; and e) few users seek treatment. Novel findings include f) a greater number of days of abstinence or intentional reduction predicted a greater decline in cannabis dependence; g) most users do not prepare before their quit attempt; h) coping outcomes during abstinence predict increased duration of abstinence; i) tobacco use is less common on days of abstinence; and j) withdrawal symptoms occur even with short quit attempts.

Reference Number: 62110

HANEY, M., G. BEDI, Z.D. COOPER, A. GLASS, S.K. VOSBURG, S.D. COMER, AND R.W. FOLTIN. "Predictors of Marijuana Relapse in the Human Laboratory: Robust Impact of Tobacco Cigarette Smoking Status." *Biological Psychiatry*, 73: 242–48, 2013 (2 tables, 2 figures, 63 references)

Abstract: Adolescents who smoke tobacco are nine times more likely to smoke marijuana than non-smokers. The rates of tobacco cigarette use among marijuana smokers are greater than two times the US national average. Among adults in marijuana treatment, the marijuana and cigarette smokers had one-half as many cannabis negative urines and fewer weeks of abstinence than former cigarette smokers despite the same treatment. In this study, fifty-one chronic cannabis users, of which thirty-eight were also cigarette smokers, were assessed as to cannabis intoxication, withdrawal, and relapse in an inpatient setting. Forty-nine percent of the patients relapsed the first day active cannabis became available. Tobacco smokers were nineteen times more likely to relapse than non-smokers.

In sum, these data indicate that daily marijuana smokers have considerable difficulty maintaining abstinence from marijuana and the factor best predicting this failure to maintain abstinence is tobacco smoking status. Whether individuals are currently smoking tobacco cigarettes or have been recently abstinent does not alter these high relapse rates, suggesting that cigarette smoking does not directly or indirectly influence marijuana relapse. Rather, cigarette smoking in concert with daily marijuana use may reflect intrinsic factors, such as greater impulsivity or distress intolerance, which render these individuals susceptible to relapse. Overall, the data suggest that current cigarette smoking is a clinical marker for a greater risk of drug relapse including marijuana relapse.

Reference Number: 62111

ROOKE, S.E., M.M. NORBERG, AND J. COPELAND. "Successful and Unsuccessful Cannabis Quitters: Comparing Group Characteristics and Quitting Strategies." *Substance Abuse Treatment, Prevention and Policy*, 6: 30, 9 pp, 2011 (5 tables, 40 references)

Abstract: A study was conducted of the characteristics of successful and unsuccessful cannabis quitters consisting of ninety-nine male and sixty-six female (ages 18 to 70 years) marijuana users. Coping, environmental modification, and co-morbid mental health problems are important factors in the treatment of cannabis use disorder. Unsuccessful quitters focused on the desire to quit but did not sufficiently plan strategies for quitting. Some of the successful coping strategies were to find other ways to cope with stress and negative emotions (rather than using cannabis), find other ways to relax and to plan for coping with situations in which the person may be tempted to use cannabis. Unsuccessful quitters also had more symptoms of depression and stress.

The study found that lower education, higher cannabis dependence, higher exposure to other cannabis users, lower use of coping-related strategies, and psychological distress were associated with unsuccessful attempts to quit cannabis among a community sample. Future interventions for cannabis use may show increased success by tailoring treatments to target these demographics and placing an emphasis on the development of coping skills.

Reference Number: 62111

CHAPTER 7

Postmortem Cannabinoids

As THC is fat soluble, it is found mainly in the postmortem tissues that contain fat, and if cannabis is smoked prior to death, it will be found in high concentrations in the lungs (70101, 70102, 70107). Cannabinoids undergo less postmortem redistribution than would be expected in a fat-soluble drug (70102). Although vitreous humor is a good sample for alcohol analysis, it is a poor sample for THC analysis (70103). Cerumen (ear wax) may be an alternative specimen to show cannabis use (70109). Next of kin interviews found reported cannabis use in only 59 percent of the deceased who tested positive for cannabinoids (70111).

Reference Number: 70101

GRONEWOLD, A., AND G.A. SKOPP. "A Preliminary Investigation on the Distribution of Cannabinoids in Man." *Forensic Science International,* 210: e7–e11, 2011 (2 tables, 21 references)

Abstract: The postmortem femoral blood, heart blood, VH, brain, liver, lung, muscle, and kidney concentrations of THC, CBD, CBN, 11-OH-THC, THCCOOH, and THCCOOgluc were determined in five cases of sudden death by LC/MS/MS. Cannabinoids were hardly detected in VH. Muscle was a better matrix for postmortem cannabinoids than CSF.

Table: Postmortem THC Concentration in Various Tissues in the Case with the Highest Postmortem Femoral Blood THC Concentration

Postmortem Sample	THC Concentration (ng/mL)
Femoral Blood	5.8
Heart Blood	1.9
Bile	6.3
Vitreous Humor	Not detected
Gastric Contents	130
Brain	Not detected
Liver	Not detected
Lungs	1.4
Muscle	8.9
Kidneys	Not detected

Source: Adapted from Gronewold and Skopp, 2011

This is not unexpected for drugs like THC that are highly protein bound and lipophilic in nature are not at all or less extensively transferred into aqueous matrices, such as vitreous humor or cerebrospinal fluid. Accordingly, only THCCOOH or its glucuronide were detectable in low concentrations in the available liquor specimens. THC concentrations in the brain were low and metabolites could hardly be detected.

Reference Number: 70102

HOLLAND, M.G., D.M. SCHWOPE, R. STOPPACHER, S.B. GILLEN, AND M.A. HUESTIS. "Postmortem Redistribution of Delta 9-Tetrahydrocannabinol (THC), 11-Hydroxy-THC (11-OH-THC), and 11 nor-9-Carboxy THC (THCCOOH)." *Forensic Science International*, 212: 247–251, 2011 (2 tables, 2 figures, 29 references)

Abstract: Postmortem heart and iliac (leg vein) blood samples were collected from sixteen male and three female deceased with a positive cannabinoid urine screen. THC, 11-OH-THC, and THCCOOH were analyzed by GC/MS to determine if postmortem redistribution (PMR) occurs. Ten cases were positive for THC and 11-OH-THC. THCCOOH was present in all nineteen cases. The median heart/iliac blood ratio was 1.5, 1.6, and 1.8 for THC, 11-OH-THC, and THCCOOH respectively.

THC and its metabolites 11-OH-THC and THCCOOH undergo only modest PMR, much less than expected based on the lipophilic nature and the high Vd of cannabinoids. Average C:P ratios for all analytes were less than 2.0. There was a positive trend (albeit not statistically significant) of increasing PMR and postmortem interval between death and blood draw observed for all analytes.

Reference Number: 70103

HOLMGREN, P., H. DRUID, A. HOLMGREN, AND J. AHNER. "Stability of Drugs in Stored Postmortem Femoral Blood and Vitreous Humor." *Journal of Forensic Sciences*, 49: 820–25, 2004 (2 tables, 2 figures, 30 references)

Abstract: Femoral blood and vitreous humor alcohol/drug concentrations were determined before and after one year's storage at -20°C. The femoral blood sample and one vitreous humor sample had sodium fluoride (NaF) added and one vitreous humor sample had no NaF added. The stability of forty-seven drugs were determined. The mean initial femoral BAC was 0.175 g/100mL (range 0.039 to 0.360 g/100mL), which decreased to 0.161 g/100mL (range 0.030 to 0.340 g/100mL) after one year's storage at -20°C. The mean VHAC was 0.200 g/100mL (range 0.042 to 0.440 g/100 mL) sodium fluoride added and 0.121 g/100mL (range 0 to 0.310 g/100mL) without NaF added, after one year's storage. The mean THC concentration in femoral blood decreased from 3 ng/mL to 1 ng/mL. No THC was detected in the vitreous humor. VH represents the free unbound fraction and so a significant correlation was found between the degree of protein binding of the drug and its concentration in VH.

In summary, with the addition of a preservative and storage of postmortem femoral blood samples at -20°C, most substances in this study were stable for one year but a few exceptions were noted. Such changes during storage are important to be aware of when interpreting analytical results carried out a long time after the collection of the sample. Our results also support the opinion that VH is a useful alternative specimen to blood for drug analysis, particularly regarding the substances where we were able to establish a significant correlation between femoral blood and VH concentrations. Combined analysis of VH and femoral blood may also assist in the differentiation between acute and chronic intake. However, interpretation of concentrations in VH must be done with caution and should only be made regarding substances with known femoral blood-VH correlations.

Reference Number: 70104

LEMOS, N.P., AND E.A. INGLE. "Cannabinoids in Postmortem Toxicology." *Journal of Analytical Toxicology*, 35: 394–401, 2011 (1 table, 1 figure, 24 references)

Abstract: A study was conducted of thirty postmortem cases in which the screen was positive for cannabinoids and THC, 11-OH-THC, or THCCOOH was detected by GC/MS in peripheral, heart blood or urine. The deceased were twenty-eight men and two women (ages 19 to 65 years). THC was identified in twenty-eight central blood samples (mean 8.0 ng/mL) and all thirty peripheral blood samples (mean 16.1 ng/mL). THCCOOH was identified in all blood and urine samples. The mean THCCOOH concentration was 57 ng/mL in cardiac blood and 61 ng/mL in peripheral blood. 11-OH-THC was not found in all urine samples and in only four cardiac and six peripheral blood samples (mean 14.8 ng/mL and 11.3 ng/mL respectively).

Similarly, postmortem redistribution (PMR), although a well-publicized phenomenon, is not well characterized or understood. For example, THC appears on first glance to be a good candidate for PMR based on its relatively large volume of distribution of 10 L/kg and high plasma protein bound fraction. However, the distribution pattern observed in our thirty cases is clearly not consistent with that expectation.

Reference Number: 70105

LIN, D.-L., AND R.-L. LIN. "Distribution of 11-Nor-9-Carboxy-delata 9 Tetrahydrocannabinol in Traffic Fatality Cases." *Journal of Analytical Toxicology*, 29: 58–61, 2005 (4 tables, 1 figure, 5 references)

Abstract: THCCOOH concentrations were determined by GC/MS in postmortem urine, heart blood, vitreous humor, and bile from fifty traffic fatality cases in New Jersey. An alkaline hydrolysis was conducted on all samples to determine the free and glucuronidated THCCOOH concentrations. The highest concentration of THCCOOH was found in the bile and the lowest in VH, which was mainly undetectable. The mean bile to blood and urine to blood ratios were 242:1 and 196:1 respectively.

Because marijuana is not a high risk agent in overdose cases, most medical examiner/coroner offices do not include this drug in their routine analytical protocol. However, as the effects of drugs on human performance become a major concern in modern society, monitoring the presence of parent compounds and metabolites derived from the use of marijuana (the most abused substance) is likely to gain popularity.

Reference Number: 70106

MURA, P., P. KINTZ, V. DUMESTRE, S. RAUL, AND T. HAUET. "THC Can Be Detected in Brain While Absent in Blood." *Journal of Analytical Toxicology*, 29: 2005 (2 tables, 8 references)

Abstract: A study was conducted of twelve postmortem cases in which cannabinoids (THC, 11-OH-THC, and THCCOOH) were detected in the blood by GC-MS. Brain tissues were also analyzed for cannabinoids. In three cases, the blood THC concentration was < 0.2 ng/mL, while the brain THC concentrations were 1.6, 2.2, and 29.9 ng/mL respectively.

Table: Cannabinoid Concentrations in Blood and Different Areas of the Brain in One Case with a Positive Blood THC Concentration

Area of the Brain	THC Concentration	11-OH THC Concentrations	THCCOOH Concentration
Blood	5.4 ng/mL	2.8 ng/mL	38.3 ng/mL
Locus niger	35.6 ng/g	16.6 ng/g	28.8 ng/g
Hippocampus	17.9 ng/g	11.1 ng/g	28.8 ng/g
Occipital lobe	16.6 ng/g	11.7 ng/g	27.8 ng/g
Striatum-putamen pallidum	20.0 ng/g	14.7 ng/g	26.1 ng/g
Frontal lobe	12.6 ng/g	12.5 ng/g	12.5 ng/g
Spinal code	27.0 ng/g	12.0 ng/g	28.7 ng/g
Corpus callosum	38.6 ng/g	15.8 ng/g	16.8 ng/g

Source: Adapted from Mura et al, 2005

As a conclusion, our observations demonstrate that active constituents of cannabis may be present in the brain when they are no longer detectable in blood.

Reference Number: 70107

KEMP, P.M., P.S. CARDONA, A.K. CHATURVEDI, AND J.W. SOPER. "Distribution of delta 9-Tetrahydrocannabinol and 11-Nor-9-Carboxy-delta 9 Tetrahydrocannabinol Acid in Postmortem Biological Fluids and Tissues from Pilots Fatally Injured in Aviation Accidents." *Journal of Forensic Sciences*, 60: 942–49, 2015 (1 table, 39 references)

Abstract: Cannabinoids were detected in fifty-four male and one female, fatally injured pilots (mean age 45 years) in postmortem samples from 2,121 fatal aviation accidents that occurred in the US between 2005 and 2012. Cannabinoids were thus detected in only 2.7 percent of the fatally injured pilots. Blood and urine samples were screened for THCCOOH by immunoassays. Free THC and total THCCOOH were determined by GC/MS in blood and other postmortem tissues. Postmortem THC concentrations were highest in the lung tissues. The mean blood THC concentration in fatally injured pilots increased between 1997 and 2006, indicating an increase in marijuana potency.

Given that marijuana is usually consumed by smoking, the inhaled cannabinoids are introduced into the body through the pulmonary tract via the mouth, through the trachea, and into the lungs. Users generally inhale deeply and hold the smoke in their lungs for as long as possible to maximize absorption of the pharmacologically active compound, THC. Consequently, it seems reasonable to hypothesize that THC would be present in significant concentrations in postmortem lung tissue.

Reference Number: 70108

SCHROEDER, J.L., L.J. MARINETTI., R.K. SMITH, W.E. BREWER, B.L. CLELLAND, AND S.L. MORGAN. "The Analysis of Delta 9-Tetrahydrocannabinol and Metabolite in Whole Blood and 11-Nor-delta 9-Tetrahydrocannabinol-9 Carboxylic Acid in Urine using Disposable Pipette Extraction with Confirmation and Quantification by Gas Chromatography-Mass Spectrometry." *Journal of Analytical Toxicology*, 32: 659–66, 2008 (5 tables, 6 figures, 23 references)

Abstract: An improved and more rapid extraction technique for THC and THCCOOH was employed using disposable pipette extraction (DPX). The DPX is a unique solid-phase extraction method in which the loose sorbent, styrene divinylbenzene, is in the pipette tip and thus thoroughly mixes with the sample. The protein in the blood is precipitated and the urine samples were hydrolyzed using potassium hydroxide before analysis by GC/MS using single ion monitoring. Two postmortem cases are described using this method. In the first case, a 20-year-old man committed suicide by hanging and had a postmortem blood THC of 7 ng/mL and THCCOOH of 53 ng/mL. In the other case, a 48-year-old man was found dead beside his bicycle. The cause of death was due to cardiac dysrhythmia. His postmortem femoral blood contained 28 ng/mL THC and 176 ng/mL THCCOOH.

The DPX method has been validated for use in forensic case specimens for the analysis of THC and its metabolite(s) in blood and THC in urine. It is very reliable, fast, and easy to perform. This method is ideal for laboratories performing high throughput analyses because of the assembly line type of extraction technique. Sensitivity, accuracy, precision, and reproducibility for both blood and urine analysis have proven to be exceptional and would be an asset to any forensic laboratory. Other methods are just as sensitive using GC-MS but are generally more sensitive using LC-MS or LC-MS-MS. GC-MS was chosen to analyze these specimens because most laboratories have one or more of these instruments and are under extensive budget restrictions if operated by government entities. LC-MS and LC-MS-MS systems are often not an option for such laboratories.

Reference Number: 70109

MEIER, S.I., S.C. KOELZER, M. SCHUBERT-ZSILAVECZ, AND S.W. TOENNES. "Analysis of Drugs of Abuse in Cerumen: Correlation of Postmortem Analysis Results with Those for Blood, Urine and Hair." *Drug Testing and Analysis*, 9: 1572–85, 2017 (3 tables, 33 references)

Abstract: Cerumen (earwax) may be an alternative specimen for drug or cannabis analysis. Cerumen (using cotton swabs of both ears), urine, hair, and blood samples were collected from thirty-eight deceased drug abusers and analyzed for cannabinoids and other drugs by LC-TOF-MS and GC/MS. Cannabinoids were not routinely detected in blood samples but THCCOOH was detected in urine/bile in eighteen cases. In only one (of the eighteen cases) was THC detected in the cerumen, although CBN was detected in five cases and CBD in two cases. The metabolites 11-OH-THC or THCCOOH were never detected in cerumen.

Cerumen is a new alternative specimen to prove drug abuse. The time span for the detection of drugs covers not only recent ingestion but also past drug use. The present results suggest a detection time window in excess of that of urine but not as long as is possible with hair. Current problems with the detection of opiates and cannabinoids have to be resolved in order to use cerumen as an alternative to urine analysis for the assessment of drug abstinence.

Reference Number: 70110

LAUNIAINEN, T., AND I. OJANPERA. "Drug Concentrations in Post-Mortem Femoral Blood Compared with Therapeutic Concentrations in Plasma." *Drug Testing and Analysis*, 6: 308–16, 2014 (2 tables, 2 figures, 33 references)

Abstract: Drug concentration distributions were determined in the femoral postmortem blood in 57,903 Finnish autopsy cases between 2000 and 2011 and compared to therapeutic or typical drug concentrations in plasma. Seventy-five percent of the cases were male with a median age of 55 years compared to a median age of 59 years for female cases. In 43 percent of the cases, a postmortem femoral BAC > 0.02 g/100mL was detected and the median BAC was 0.190 g/100mL. A positive blood THC concentration was found in 347 cases with a mean (median) THC concentration of 5 ng/mL (2 ng/mL). The typical plasma THC concentration range in living subjects was estimated to be between 5 to 10 ng/mL. The postmortem blood/plasma concentration ratio for THC was determined to be 0.4:1. The PM/plasma ratio was 1 in 61 of the 129 drugs detected and < 1 in 22 drugs and > 1 in 36 drugs. A table lists the PM blood/plasma ratios for 129 different drugs.

> A PM blood/plasma relationship was introduced to illustrate how the median PM blood drug concentrations related to the established therapeutic ranges in plasma. In our study, most neutral and acidic drugs, such as benzodiazepines, anti-epileptics, non-steroidal, anti-inflammatory drugs, and paracetamol, had a median concentration within or below the therapeutic range exhibiting a PM blood/plasma relationship < 1. In particular, drugs that are extensively plasma bound, such as benzodiazepines and warfarin [and THC] had a lower PM blood concentration.

Reference Number: 70111

LEHRMANN, E., Z.R. AFANADOR, A. DEEP-SOBOSLAY, G. GALLEGOS, W.D. DARWIN, R.H. LOWE, A.J. BARNES, M.A. HUESTIS, J.L. CADET, M.M. HERMAN, T.M. HYDE, J.E. KLEINMAN, AND W.J. FREED. "Postmortem Diagnosis and

Toxicological Validation of Illicit Substance Use." *Addiction Biology*, 13: 105–17, 2008 (5 tables, 32 references)

Abstract: Antemortem illicit drug abuse was determined by case history, next of kin interviews, blood, urine, and/or brain and scalp hair drug analysis in forty-two postmortem cases. Overall case history and/or toxicology identified 33 cocaine, 29 cannabis, 10 PCP and 9 opioid cases. A positive cannabinoid result was found in twelve blood/urine cases and nineteen scalp cases. Next of kin interviews found cannabis use reported in seventeen cases.

Detection of the cannabis metabolite 11-nor-9-carboxytetrahydrocannabinol in hair testing circumvented the problem of test specificity for cannabis and increased the sensitivity of cannabinoid detection in cases with a cannabis use history from 32 percent by general toxicology to 64 percent by hair testing. It has been suggested that the low incorporation of cannabinoids into hair may significantly underestimate the number of true positive cases. This was not evident in the present study, as hair testing corroborated cannabis use in fourteen of seventeen cases with a lifetime cannabis use history and in all cases with a recent cannabis use, as evidenced by a cannabinoid-positive general toxicology. That 53 percent of cases with a cannabinoid-positive hair test had a cannabinoid positive general toxicology appears to be due to the different temporal perspectives afforded by the testing matrices, as fifteen of seventeen cases with a cannabinoid positive hair testing either had a cannabis-positive history and/or general toxicology. Cannabis use does, however, appear to be significantly underreported, in that many ME laboratories do not include cannabis testing in routine death investigations. Presently, only one-third of cannabinoid-positive cases detected in subsequent testing of blood and/or brain were identified by ME toxicology. These data suggest that currently active cannabis users can be reliably detected by hair testing and that hair testing offers a suitable matrix for determining recent and regular antemortem use.

Reference Number: 70111

CHAPTER 8

Various Cannabinoids and Related Compounds

8.01 BOTANICAL CANNABIS

There has been a worldwide increase in the potency of botanical cannabis, such as marijuana and hashish (80105, 80111, 80112, 80114), which has caused increases in public health risks such as driving under the influence of cannabis (DUIC) and psychological health problems. Since live marijuana plants are 80 percent water, seized samples by the police may decrease in weight by up to 80 percent as it dries out at ambient temperatures (80109) , and does not necessarily mean that the police were sampling the seized plants. Stored cannabis will also decrease in THC concentration if exposed to sunlight or oxygen (80104). Marijuana is a highly variable plant and the total cannabinoid content of seven identical plants grown beside each other under controlled indoor growing conditions ranged from 12 to 25 percent (80102).

Botanical cannabis contains many other volatile compounds, but the main distinction between cannabis and other related plants such as hops is the presence of THC and CBN (80101, 80102, 8012). Mature, budding cannabis plants have a stronger odour than non-mature plants and are the easiest drug to detect by drug-sniffing dogs, such as German Shepherds (80101, 80108).

Reference Number: 80101

WIEBELHAUS, N., D. HAMBLIN, N.M. KREITALS, AND J.R. ALMIRALL. "Differentiation of Marijuana Headspace Volatiles from Other Plants and Hemp Products Using Capillary Micro-Extraction of Volatiles (CMV)

Coupled to Gas-Chromatography-Mass Spectrometry (GC-MS)." *Forensic Chemistry*, 2: 1–8, 2016 (4 tables, 3 figures, 34 references)

Abstract: Currently the main method of illicit drug detection is by trained drug-sniffing canines. A new method to detect illicit drugs such as marijuana was developed to identify small quantities of drugs in a large space. A capillary micro-extraction of volatiles (CMV) pre-concentrates the volatiles in the air within minutes, which can then be analyzed by a GC-MS. Whole hop leaf, hemp paper, hemp fibres, ropes, seeds, a cigar, and marijuana samples were analyzed by this system. Of all the samples analyzed, hops showed the most similar volatile emissions to cannabis, although THC was not detected in hops. Of the sixteen volatiles found in the headspace of cannabis samples, only alpha-santalene, valencene, beta-bisabolene, and in some cases THC and cannabinol were detected and specific to the marijuana sample.

Table: Comparison of Major Volatile Organic Compounds Detected in Marijuana and Other Related Plants.*

Sample	Alpha Pinene	Beta Pinene	Beta Myrcene	Limonene	Beta Linalool	Beta Caryophyllene	Alpha Terpineol	tetrahydro-cannabinol	cannabinol
Marijuana	X	X	X	X	X	X	X	X	X
US Northern Brewer Hops	X	X	X	X	X	X			
Whole sterilized hemp seeds	X					X	X		
Handmade hemp paper									
Hemp rope									
Cigar (tobacco)				X					
Texas Sage	X					X			
Oakleaf Fig						X			
St. Augustine Grass	X	X							

* X = Detected.

Source: Adapted from Wiebelhaus et al, 2016

The capillary micro-extractor of volatiles (CMV) was found to be a viable complement to canine detection of illicit drugs, specifically marijuana. Its ability to collect trace amounts of volatile compounds within a short (approximately one minute) extraction time facilitates the development of a technique for field testing for the presence of marijuana plants. The CMV was shown as a suitable investigative tool and it was also found that such a device could detect a collection of volatile compounds that are characteristic to marijuana plants. These identified compounds provide marijuana a distinct chemical signature that can be compared to other samples. In order to determine that the volatile compounds identified are unique to marijuana headspace, a more diverse set of samples must be collected and analyzed. This will help establish a collective chemical profile of marijuana that may be used for comparisons. A database can then be created and utilized for detecting marijuana in multiple environments through use of the CMV sampling.

Reference Number: 80102

GIESE, M.W., M.A. LEWIS, L. GIESE, AND K.M. SMITH. "Development and Validation of a Reliable and Robust Method for the Analysis of Cannabinoids and Terpenes in Cannabis." *Journal of the Association of Official Agricultural Chemists International*, 98: 1503–22, 2015 (11 tables, 6 figures, 43 references)

Abstract: As of 2014, there have been over 545 different chemical compounds found in the cannabis plant, of which 140 are terpenoids. To analyze the cannabinoids and terpenes in dried plant material, approximately 5 to 7 grams of the marijuana flower or bud is homogenized in a stainless-steel coffee grinder and 1000 mg of the grounds are placed in a centrifuge tube with 2.0 mm of zirconia beads. Reagent grade ethanol, 4-biphenyl carboxylic acid (BPCA), and nonane (internal standard) are added and the sample is centrifuged twice. The extract is analyzed for cannabinoids using High Pressure Liquid Chromatography (HPLC) with a diode array detector. HPLC is preferred for cannabinoids to prevent degradation during analysis. The terpenes are measured using a Gas Chromatograph (GC) with a flame ionization detector. Cannabis is a highly variable plant and the cannabinoid content of the flowers is very inhomogeneous. In one study of seven identical cannabis plants that were grown indoors beside each other, the range of total cannabinoids was from 12 to 25 percent w/w, and the total terpenes from 1.4 to 2.2 percent. This variability is the reason why some medical marijuana manufacturers make extracts to ensure a more uniform product. The variation in THC within the plant is greater than the variability between plants.

The variability in raw materials is the principal reason why medical producers, such as GW Pharmaceuticals, produce standardized extracts to guarantee product uniformity. However, finished flowers remain popular products in the United States, and variation in this product is an important concept for dispensaries, patients, and legislators to understand when interpreting test results and enacting regulations.

Reference Number: 80103

DOS SANTOS, N.A., L.M. SOUZA, E. DOMINGOS, H.S. FRANCA, V. LACERDA JR., A. BEATRIZ, B.G. VAZ, R.T. RODRIGUES. V.V. CARVALHO, B.B. MERLC, R.M. KUSTER, AND W. ROMAO. "Evaluating the Selectivity of Colorimetric Test (Fast Blue BB salt) for the Cannabinoids Identification in Marijuana Street Samples by UV-Vis, TLC, ESI (+) FT-ICR MS and ESI (+) MS/MS." *Forensic Chemistry*, 1: 13–21, 2016 (1 table, 10 figures, 21 references)

Abstract: The principal screening test for cannabinoids used by the Brazilian Forensic Police is a colorimetric test called Fast Blue B or BB salt, which reacts with THC, CBN, or CBD in a basic media to form a reddish colour. Various analyses and tests were conducted to determine the chemical reaction with THC and Fast Blue B salt (FBBS) and Fast Blue BB salt (FBBBS).

The products of the colorimetric test, reaction between Fast Blue BB salt (FBBBS) and delta-9-THC present in marijuana samples, were identified using ESI (+)-FT-ICR MS. The colorimetric test using reagent FBBBS shows a reddish colour when in the presence of cannabinoids in samples of C. sativa L, and the selectivity of the reagent is higher than for the Fast Blue B salt (FBBS) in the presence of interferences such as J. decurrens Cham and P. cupana Kunth. The positive result for the colorimetric test using the reagent FBBBS was proved with UV-Vis analyses due to the appearance of a band in the visible region at approximately 471 nm.

Reference Number: 80104

LINDHOLST, C. "Long Term Stability of Cannabis Resin and Cannabis Extracts." *Australian Journal of Forensic Sciences*, 42: 181–90, 2010 (3 figures, 16 references)

Abstract: THC, THCA, CBN, and CBD concentrations were determined in cannabis, resin slabs (hash), and cannabis extracts after storage for up to four years at room temperature, 4°C, and -20°C, with and without exposure to sunlight. At room temperature there was an exponential decrease in THCA and a corresponding increase in THC. Due to the dense structure of cannabis resin slab, it is unlikely sunlight had a significant effect. But sunlight increases cannabinoid degradation.

Cannabinoid stability in cannabis material is influenced by light, temperature, and possibly also oxygen availability. The stability of acidic and neutral cannabinoids differs, with the acidic species being more susceptible to degradation. Knowledge about cannabinoid stability may ensure correct sample storage, handling, and interpretation of analytical results, thereby improving forensic intelligence information.

Reference Number: 80105

MEHMEDIC, Z., S. CHANDRA, D. SLADE, H. DENHAM, S. FOSTER, A.S. PATEL, S.A. ROSS, I.A. KHAN, AND M.A. ELSOHLY. "Potency Trends of delta 9-THC and Other Cannabinoids in Confiscated Cannabis Preparations from 1993 to 2008." *Journal of Forensic Sciences*, 55: 1209–17, 2010 (5 tables, 5 figures, 43 references)

Abstract: The cannabinoid concentrations were determined by GC in 46,211 samples seized in the US between 1993 and 2008. The types of samples analyzed were marijuana, sensemilla, Thai sticks, and ditchweed. Hashish and hash oil samples were also analyzed. The THC concentrations were ditchweed (0.3 to 0.5 percent), marijuana (3.4 to 6.1 percent), sinsemilla (3.8 to 6.2 percent), Thai sticks (0 percent), hashish (6.6 to 23.1 percent), and hash oil (16.5 to 24.9 percent) between 1993 and 2008 respectively. The CBD concentrations were lowest in sinsemilla (0.2 percent) and marijuana (0.4 percent).

The increase in cannabis potency is mainly due to the increase in the potency of non-domestic versus domestic samples.

Reference Number: 80106

MORGAN, C.J.A., T.P. FREEMAN, G.L. SCHAFER, AND H.V. CURRAN. "Cannabidiol Attenuates the Appetitive Effects of delta 9-Tetrahydrocannabinol in

Humans Smoking Their Chosen Cannabis." *Neuropsychopharmacology*, 35: 1879–85, 2010 (3 tables, 2 figures, 37 references)

Abstract: Seventy-two male and twenty-two female cannabis users (mean age 21.3 years) had the CBD: THC ratio determined of the marijuana they normally smoked. They were tested on two days, the intoxicated day, when they smoke a joint they brought with them before testing, and a drug-free day, when no cannabis or other drug was used for twenty-four hours. Thirty of the subjects with the lowest CBD: THC ratios and thirty-one subjects with the highest CBD: THC ratios were evaluated. The mean CBD: THC ratios were 0.02 for skunk, 0.24 for herbal cannabis, and 0.53 for resin. There was a reduced attentional bias to drug and food in intoxicated subjects smoking cannabis with a high CBD: THC ratio, and an overall reduction in the ratings of liking the drug stimuli.

When people are given a choice between marijuana cigarettes with different THC concentrations, those with higher THC content are preferred over those containing lower THC concentrations. The constituents of street cannabis have changed over the past decade or so with high THC/low CBD strains such as skunk and sinsemilla now dominating the market. This change was thought to be driven by user preference for lower CBD strains because of CBD's potential to modulate the psychotomimetic effects of the drug and reduce the stoned feeling. However, the findings of this study suggest instead that one reason may be CBD's capacity to modulate both the wanting and liking of THC without affecting the stoned feeling. Our results suggest that lower CBD in cannabis may result in greater salience of drug cues when intoxicated, potentially invoking more associative learning around drug cues in users of high THC/low CBD cannabis, which could speculatively result in a higher chance of later addiction. The research reported here also contributed to the growing body that suggests a range of potential therapeutic uses of CBD, including the ability to accurately modulate the reinforcing properties of drugs.

Reference Number: 80107

POLLIO, A. "The Name of Cannabis: A Short Guide for Non-Botanists." *Cannabis and Cannabinoid Research* 1: 234–38, 2016 (5 tables, 35 references)

Abstract: A short discussion on the classification of cannabis for the non-botanist is presented. The genus Cannabis (family Canabaceae) is indigenous to the wetlands of Asia. Only 5 percent of all angiosperms (i.e., flowering plants) have separate male and female flowers. They are called monoecious if male and female flowers occur on the same plant, and dioecious if there are separate male and female plants, as occurs with cannabis. Male cannabis plants have a shorter life cycle than female and are taller with slimmer shoots. Cannabis is wind-pollinated and so the male plant produces vast quantities of pollen that is spread over a wide geographical area (up to three miles or more). Four main groups or types of cannabis have been characterized as below.

1) Group of the non-narcotic plants, domesticated for stem fibre and/or oil seed in Western Asia and Europe, less low THC and high cannabidiol (CBD)
2) Group of the non-narcotic plants domesticated in East Asia, mainly China, low to moderate THC, high CBD
3) Group of the narcotic plants domesticated in South Central Asia, high cannabinoids, mostly THC
4) Group of the narcotic plants domesticated in South Asia (Afghanistan and neighbouring countries) contains both THC and CBD

Reference Number: 80108

RICE, S., AND J.A. KOZIEL. "Characterizing the Smell of Marijuana by Odor Impact of Volatile Compounds: An Application of Simultaneous Chemical and Sensory Analysis." *PLOS ONE* 10: 17 pp, December 10th, 2015 (1 table, 4 figures, 35 references)

Abstract: Mature budding plants have a more intense odour than non-mature plants, suggesting that the buds contain odorous compounds. German Shepherds are the best breed of dog to detect drugs. Marijuana is easiest to detect, followed by hashish, amphetamines, cocaine, and heroin. Odour Activity Analysis (OAA) was conducted on seized marijuana samples and analyzed using phase micro-extraction and GC/MS. Some of the VOCs detected were pinene, mycrene, limonene, linalool, and others, for a total of thirty-one compounds. Overall, odour of marijuana is time dependent and not affected, whether it is stored in a ziplock sandwich bag or a duffel bag. This study added an additional 200 VOCs to those already detected in cannabis.

This suggests that more attention should be focused on highly odorous compounds typically present in low concentrations, such as nonanal, deconal, o-cymene, and benzaldehyde, which have more potent odour impact than previously reported marijuana headspace volatiles.

Reference Number: 80109

WARNER, M.L., I. ALFORD, D.M. LAWRENCE, A.C. KOHL, S.J. WILLIAMS, AND D.T. YEATMAN. "Comparative Analysis of Freshly Harvested Cannabis Plant Weight and Dried Cannabis Plant Weight." *Forensic Chemistry,* 3: 52–57, 2017 (6 tables, 3 figures, 14 references)

Abstract: Live cannabis plants consist of nearly 80 percent water. After drying at room temperature, only 10 to 12 percent of this moisture will be retained. A 70 percent weight loss can occur over the course of three days at ambient temperature. Thirty-six freshly harvested cannabis plants from cannabis grow houses (grow-ops) were weighed. The minimum number of days for the sample to reach dryness was three days from the point of seizure to a maximum of nine days. The most significant weight loss occurred in one to three days and plateaued after a week.

Table: Average Cumulative Weight Loss, Initially Measured as 100 Percent on the First Day of Seizure

Days since Marijuana Seized	Cumulative Weight Loss (%)
0	100%
1	69%
2	41%
3	29%
4	26%
5	25%

Source: Adapted from Warner et al, 2017

Water is present is all living plants; therefore, fresh cannabis plants once harvested will dry, thereby decreasing in weight over time. This study evaluated the weight loss that occurs in freshly harvested cannabis plants that are stored in ambient temperature and humidity-controlled conditions.

Reference Number: 80110

SULLIVAN, N., S. ELZINGA, AND J.C. RABER. "Determination of Pesticide Residues in Cannabis Smoke." *Journal of Toxicology,* 6 pp, 2013 (3 tables, 1 figure, 13 references)

Abstract: The amount of pesticide residue was determined in the smoke of cannabis spiked with four common pesticides. Approximately 450 mg of spiked cannabis was ignited and 1.2 L minute vacuum sampling of the smoke was collected and analyzed by GC/MS. The percent recovery (i.e., concentration of the pesticide in the smoke) was determined after using a glass pipe, a water pipe without a filter, and a water pipe with a cotton filter.

Table: Percent Recovery of Four Pesticides after Three Different Modes of Smoking

Mode of Smoking	Pesticide	% Recovery
Glass pipe	Diazinon	61.5
	Paclobutrazol	67.4
	Bifenthrin	60.3
	Permethrin	69.5
Water pipe, no filter	Diazinon	42.2
	Paclobutrazol	49.5
	Bifenthrin	45.4
	Permethrin	59.9
Water pipe, cotton filter	Diazinon	0.08
	Paclobutrazol	10.2
	Bifenthrin	9.0
	Permethrin	10.9

Source: Adapted from Sullivan, Elzinga and Raber, 2013

Although pesticides are designed to degrade fairly quickly in the environment, it is evident from this study that some are highly resistant to pyrolysis and volatilize easily into the smoke stream, in agreement with previous studies noting the distillation behaviour of pesticides in mainstream smoke. Considering these results, high pesticide exposure through cannabis smoking is a significant possibility, which may lead to further health complications in cannabis consumers. This revelation certainly confounds previous meta-studies seeking to determine the possible negative consequences associated with long-term cannabis use, as our experience with a breadth of samples indicates a significant possibility that the negative consequences reported in these studies could have been the result of various chemical residue exposures resulting from the use of unregulated product supply chains. As more states legislate and regulate cannabis products, a strong regulatory approach will help to reduce the potential public health and safety consequences from pesticide exposure.

Reference Number: 80111

BURGDORF, J.R., B. KILMER, AND R.L. PACULA. "Heterogeneity in the Composition of Marijuana Seized in California." *Drug and Alcohol Dependence*, 117: 59–61, 2011 (2 figures, 22 references)

Abstract: THC and CBD concentrations were determined in 5,083 seized marijuana samples in California between 1996 and 2008. In border areas (with Mexico), the increase in median THC was from 4.52 to 6.84 percent. In the non-border areas of California, the increase was from 4.18 percent to 13.95 percent. The median concentration of CBD dropped from 0.24 percent in 1996 to 0.08 percent in 2008. The THC: CBD ratio for all seizures increased from 26.21:1 to 187.99:1.

> While the reasons behind the observed changes in THC and CBD levels fall outside of the scope of this study, one reason may be that growers are making greater use of plant strains that favour THC production over CBD production. Recent research suggests that sinsemilla marijuana tends to have higher levels of THC and lower levels of CBD. Sinsemilla is typically grown indoors and accounts for an important share of domestic production in California. Since Mexico is thought to be a major source of lower quality commercial grade marijuana, it is not surprising that the ratio is highest for seizures made away from the border.

Reference Number: 80112

SWIFT, W., A. WONG, K.M. LI, J.C. ARNOLD, AND I.S. MCGREGOR. "Analysis of Cannabis Seizures in NSW, Australia: Cannabis Potency and Cannabinoid Profile." *PLOS ONE,* 8: 9 pp, July 2013 (2 tables, 5 figures, 51 references)

Abstract: The THC concentration in cannabis over the last few decades has increased. In the US, herbal cannabis has increased in THC concentration from 3.4 percent THC to 8.8 percent THC and CBD has remained around 0.3 to 0.4 percent. A high THC/low CBD profile has been linked to poorer outcomes including an increased risk of psychosis. A commission in The Netherlands has recommended that cannabis with a THC concentration of 15 percent be classified as a hard drug. Australia has one of the highest rates of cannabis use in the world. THC, CBD cannabigerol (CNG), as well as their plant-based carboxylic acids, THC-A, CBD-A, CNG-A, and CBN, cannabichromere (CBC), and tetrahydrocannabivarin (CBV) were determined in samples seized by the police in New South Wales (NSW) between 2010 and 2011 from adults in possession of not more than 15 grams of dried cannabis (Cannabis Cautioning) and from green plant material (GPM) from thirteen different growers eradication programs in 2012. In smoking cannabis, approximately 30 percent of the THC-A is thought to convert to free THC. The mean THC concentration was 14.9 percent in samples (range 0.9 to 39.8 percent). The mean CBD was 0.14 percent (range 0–6.5 percent). There were few significant differences in the cannabinoid profile in marijuana grown indoors or outdoors, although the mean total THC was higher in indoor grown plants.

Table: Median Cannabinoid Concentrations in Cannabis Plants Grown Indoors or Outdoors

Cannabinoid	Indoor Grown	Outdoor Grown
Median Total THC Concentration	20.13%	14.07%
Median Total CBD Concentration	0.04%	0.04%
Median CBN Concentration	0.01%	0%
Median CBG	0.33%	1.09%

Source: Adapted from Swift et al, 2013

The pattern of high THC/low CBD cannabis has become a focus of concerns over the potential mental health impacts of current cannabis use patterns. Given existing data on the potential modulating effects of CBD on the adverse effects of THC, these data lend support to the proposition that cannabis currently available in Australia exhibits a profile that may render some cannabis users vulnerable to adverse mental health impact of their use.

Reference Number: 80113

ARNOLDI, S., G. RODA, E. CASAGNI, L. DELL'ACQUA, M.D. CAS, F. FARE, C. RUSCONI, G.L. VISCONTI, AND V. GAMBARO. "Characterization of the Volatile Components of Cannabis Preparations by Solid-Phase Micro-

Extraction Coupled to Headspace-Gas-Chromatography with Mass Detector (SPME-HSGC/MS)." *Journal of Chromatography, Separation Techniques*, 8: 6 pp, 2017 (5 tables, 5 figures, 13 references)

Abstract: The volatile components of seven seized hashish samples were determined by SPME-HSGC/MS. Solid-phase extraction is based on the adsorption of volatiles onto a coating of a suitable fibre followed by direct injection into the GC/MS. This method is more rapid and does not involve the use of solvents as occurs with liquid-liquid extraction. The internal standard chosen for this method was nonane.

Table: Characteristics and THC, CBD, and CBN Concentrations of Seized Hashish Samples

Sample Number	Description	% THC	% CBD	% CBN
2	Colour: dark brown; very hard texture	13.4	6.0	0.6
3	Colour: black; soft texture; malleable	9.8	5.8	0.6
4	Colour: light brown; hard texture	11.7	7.9	0.3
5	Colour: dark brown; compact texture	18.3	7.0	0.4
6	Colour: brown; soft texture	16.0	6.7	0.9
7	Colour: greenish-brown, very hard and compact texture	21.7	9.2	0.6

Source: Adapted from Arnoldi et al, 2017

The HS-SPME-GC/MS method studied herein allows the rapid and reproducible determination of the volatile components of Cannabis. This analysis could be particularly useful for the characterization of cannabis preparations (hashish) and to establish the region of origin and eventual links between different seizures. To this end, the parameters of the SPME and the analytical method were optimized using azulene and caryophyllene, two representative terpenes of hashish. Ten different hashish preparations were analyzed and the quantitative determination of Caryophyllene, the most abundant component, was carried out, using nonane as internal standard.

Reference Number: 80114

SOULEMAN, A.M.A., A.E-D.A. GAAFAR, O.M. ABDEL-SALAM, S.A. ELSHEBINEY. "Determination of delta-9-tetrahydrocannabinol Content of Cannabis Seizures in Egypt." *Asian Pacific Journal of Tropical Medicine*, 10: 311–14, 2017 (1 figure, 31 references)

Abstract: Extracts of cannabis were prepared from dried flowering tops and leaves (marijuana) and resin (i.e., hashish) from cannabis seizures in Egypt and analyzed for THC by HPLC. The THC content of marijuana was 9.55 percent without heating and 11.19 percent with heating. The resin had 18.34 percent THC without heating and 31.34 percent with heating. The increase in THC with heating due to the well-known effect of heating causing the decarboxylation of the inactive THCA to psychoactive THC.

> Cannabis abuse is a worldwide problem that seems on the rise. Studies indicate increased cannabis use and increased emergency department visits for the users of cannabis only and cannabis polydrug. THC is known for its negative impact on the motor and cognitive functions, e.g., verbal learning, memory, attention, risk-taking behaviour, and psychological disorders, such as schizophrenia. Increased THC content in available illicit cannabis could thus expose a risk for driving problems and psychological health.

8.02 SATIVEX/DRONABINOL/NABILONE

Sativex, dronabinol, and nabilone, which are THC-based, controlled pharmaceuticals, are legal in many countries. Sativex is one of the most promising pharmaceuticals, as it is an oromucosal spray that contains a 1:1 mixture of THC and CBD (80201). Using an oromucosal spray allows for faster absorption of the cannabinoids and avoids the first-pass effect of the liver, as with an oral ingestion. Avoiding the first-pass effect means that the formation of the psychoactive metabolite 11-OH-THC is minimized.

Dronabinol (brand name marinol) is a synthetically produced THC, which is identical to the plant-based THC and is consumed orally (80208). Dronabinol is dissolved in sesame oil to promote absorption of the drug. It will be detected in the typical urine cannabinoid drug screens.

Nabilone (brand name cesamet) is a synthetically produced cannabinoid similar but not identical to plant-based THC (80204, 80210). It will not produce a positive urine cannabinoid drug screen result.

Reference Number: 80114

Reference Number: 80201

RUSSO, E.B., G.W. GUY, AND P.J. ROBSON. "Cannabis, Pain and Sleep: Lessons from Therapeutic Clinical Trials of Sativex, a Cannabis Based Medicine." *Chemistry and Biodiversity,* 4: 1729–43, 2007 (1 table, 5 figures, 89 references)

Abstract: Sativex is an oromucosal spray that is a 1:1 mixture of THC and CBD in a base of 50 percent ethyl alcohol, 50 percent propylene glycol, and 0.05 percent peppermint flavouring. The drugs are extracted from plants selected to produce a high concentration of THC and one to produce a high concentration of CBD. The plants are harvested when about six-feet high before flowering and producing seeds. The entire plant is harvested, and CO2 extracted (a better solvent than other volatile organic compounds such as butane) to produce a concentrate of THC, CBD and other cannabinoids, and terpenes. The pump spray had an onset of activity in fifteen to forty minutes, which allows the patient to titrate the dose. Common adverse events with Sativex include headache, nausea, bad taste, oral stinging, dry mouth, dizziness, nausea, or fatigue, but not enough to require cessation of drug use.

Experience to date with Sativex in numerous Phase I to III studies in 2,000 subjects with 1,000 patient years of exposure demonstrate marked improvement in subjective sleep parameters in patients with a wide variety of pain conditions, including multiple sclerosis, peripheral neuropathic pain, intractable cancer pain, and rheumatoid arthritis with an acceptable adverse event profile. No tolerance to the benefit of Sativex on pain or sleep nor need for dosage increases have been noted on safety extension studies of up to four years, wherein 40 to 50 percent of the subjects attained good or very good sleep quality, a key source of disability in chronic pain syndromes that may contribute to patient's quality of life.

Reference Number: 80202

ROBSON, P. "Abuse Potential and Psychoactive Effects of delta 9-tetrahydrocannabinol and Cannabidiol Oromucosal Spray (Sativex), A New Cannabinoid Medicine." *Expert Opinion Drug Safety,* 10: 675–85, 2011 (4 tables, 5 figures, 48 references)

Abstract: A general review was conducted of the abuse potential of cannabis and Sativex. A short chronology of cannabis is included. Cannabis produces psychological dependence equivalent to alcohol but one-half that of physical dependence of alcohol. Physical dependence is a consistent pattern of bodily symptoms and signs that occur as a result of drug withdrawal or reduction. Psychological dependence is an intense longing to take the drug, triggered by environmental cues. The mean peak plasma THC concentration of equivalent amounts of THC was 156.7 ng/mL after smoking and 8.8 ng/mL as Sativex spray. The lower peak plasma THC concentration obtained by Sativex and its high CBD concentration reduces the side effects of this drug.

Table: Percent of Adverse Events after Using Sativex and after Placebo

Adverse Event	Sativex	Placebo
Disorientation	4%	0.5%
Disturbances in attention	3.7%	0.1%
Feeling drunk	2.9%	0.4%
Euphoric mood	2.2%	0.9%
Depression	1.9%	0.8%
Memory impairment	1.4%	0.1%
Dissociation	1.7%	0.1%

Source: Adapted from Robson, 2011

In clinical trials, intoxication scores have been low, and euphoria reported by only 2.2 percent of patients. Tolerance has not occurred, abrupt withdrawal has not resulted in a formal withdrawal syndrome, and no case of abuse or diversion has been reported to date.

Reference Number: 80203

RUSSO, M., R. DE LUCA, M. TORRISI, C. RIFICI, E. SESSA, P. BRAMANTI, A. NARO, AND R.S. CALABRO. "Should We Care About Sativex-Induced Neurobehavioral Effects? A 6-Month Follow-Up Study." *European Review for Medical and Pharmacological Sciences*, 20: 3127–33, 2016 (4 tables, 40 references)

Abstract: Sativex is a 1:1 mixture of THC and CBD approved for the treatment of Multiple Sclerosis (MS) and associated spasticity, spasm, and pain. Each spray delivers 2.7 mg of THC and 2.5 mg of CBD in an ethanol/propylene glycol solution. Forty MS patients were tested on clinical and neuropsychological measures before, 1 month, and 6 months after using Sativex. The initial number of sprays were increased gradually from 1 spray to 9 sprays per day. The main reported side effects were dizziness, dry mouth, nausea, and mild generalized weakness. There were no changes observed in the blood tests, blood pressure, or weight. One patient was removed from the study after one month of Sativex use (12 sprays per day) after developing psychotic symptoms, including suicidal ideation.

> Our findings show that Sativex treatment does not significantly affect the cognitive and neurobehavioural domains at a moderate dosage. However, the study supports the relevance of an extensive neuropsychological evaluation in patients who are selected for the drug administration, in an attempt to early detect the uncommon but important neurobehavioural side effects.

Reference Number: 80204

BEDI, G., Z.D. COOPER, AND M. HANEY. "Subjective, Cognitive, and Cardiovascular Dose-Effect Profile of Nabilone and Dronabinol in Marijuana Smokers." *Addictive Biology*, 18: 872–81, 2013 (1 table, 4 figures, 43 references)

Abstract: Four female and ten male heavy marijuana smokers received a placebo, and 2, 4, 6, 8 mg of nabilone and 10, 20 mg of dronabinol. Various tests and measures were conducted but no blood THC concentrations were determined. Nabilone (4, 6, 8 mg) and dronabinol increased the rating of good effect. Nabilone (2 mg) and dronabinol (10 mg) decreased systolic BP and there was a dose-dependent increase in heart rate.

> Thus, nabilone produced sustained dose-related increases in positive mood, few cognitive decrements, and lawful cardiovascular alterations. It had a longer time to peak effects than dronabinol and effects were more dose-related, suggesting improved bioavailability. Nabilone was well-tolerated by marijuana smokers, supporting further testing as a potential medication for marijuana dependence.

Reference Number: 80205

GORELICK, D.A., R.S. GOODWIN, E. SCHWILKE, D.M. SCHWOPE, W.D. DARWIN, D.I. KELLY, R.P. MCMAHON, F. LUI, C. ORTEMANN-RENON, D. BONNET, AND

M.A. HUESTIS. "Tolerance to Effects of High-Dose Oral delta 9-Tetrahydrocannabinol and Plasma Cannabinoid Concentrations in Male Daily Cannabis Smokers." *Journal of Analytical Toxicology*, 37: 11–16, 2013 (2 tables, 1 figure, 27 references)

Abstract: Thirteen male daily cannabis smokers (mean age 25 years) consumed 40 mg on Day 1, 100 mg on Days 2-4, and 120 mg on Days 5-6 of dronabinol (Marinol) and had BP, HR, and symptoms of subjective intoxication (VAS) assessed every thirty minutes for three hours after the morning THC dose. Plasma THC and 11-OH-THC concentrations were determined. The mean peak THC concentrations were approximately 30 ng/mL and 15 ng/mL for 11-OH-THC. The mean BP decreased from 129/75 to 120/62 and HR increased from 60 bpm to 68 bpm.

Table: Mean Morning Subjective and Cardiovascular Responses to Increasing Cumulative Doses of Oral THC

Variable	Day 1	Day 2	Day 4	Day 6
"Good drug affect"	1.5	17.7	13.0	8.2
"High"	3.4	17.7	11.3	8.3
"Stoned"	1.3	7.8	5.0	4.3
Systolic blood pressure (mm Hg)	129.1	121.4	120.4	119.6
Heart rate (beats per minute)	59.6	74.3	68.8	68.4

Source: Adapted from Gorelick et al, 2013

Six days of around-the-clock oral THC produced tolerance to subjective intoxication but not to cardiovascular effects.

Reference Number: 80206

LILE, J.A., T.H. KELLY, R.J. CHARNIGO, A.L. STINCHCOMBE, AND L.R. HAYS "Pharmacokinetic and Pharmacodynamic Profile of Supratherapeutic Oral Doses of delta 9-THC in Cannabis Users." *Journal Clinical Pharmacology*, 53: 680–90, 2013 (1 table, 4 figures, 40 references)

Abstract: The usual dose of dronabinol for appetite stimulation and anti-emetic therapy is 2.5 to 10 mg. Due to tolerance, 20 to 40 mg of dronabinol is recommended three to four times a day for cannabis use disorders. Four male and three female cannabis users (ages 18 to 25 years) were administered a placebo and six doses of oral THC in 15 mg increments for a maximum dose of 90 mg. Blood samples were collected hourly from an indwelling catheter and plasma concentrations of THC and 11-OH-THC were determined by LC/MS. Various other parameters such as HR, BP, and DSST were measured. HR increased with increasing dose, systolic but not diastolic BP was lower at low dose and higher at high doses. Fingertip temperature decreased but not oral temperature at higher doses.

> In conclusion, the present study contributes to the literature by demonstrating that, with dose escalation and cautious side effect monitoring, large doses of delta 9-THC can be administered to humans with a history of cannabis use, which might be useful for managing cannabis-use disorders.

Reference Number: 80207

MAY, M.B., AND A.E. GLODE. "Dronabinol for Chemotherapy-Induced Nausea and Vomiting Unresponsive to Antiemetics." *Cancer Management and Research*, 8: 49–55, 2016 (20 references)

Abstract: Chemotherapy induced nausea and vomiting (CINV) is one of the most common symptoms feared by patients. Dronabinol is a synthetic delta 9 THC pill. A meta-analysis was conducted of 1,366 patients in thirty randomized clinical trials between 1975 and 1996. For patients who smoked marijuana during chemotherapy, 70 to 100 percent experienced relief, compared to 76 to 88 percent of those who ingested oral THC.

> Current guidelines, as well as the FDA-approved indications, consider dronabinol's role to be in the management of breakthrough CINV. Dronabinol has a unique mechanism of action and adverse effect profile that should be considered when treating a patient with this medication.

Reference Number: 80208

MILMAN G., M.M. BERGAMASCHI, D. LEE, D.R. MENDU, A.J. BARNES, R. VANDREY, AND M.A. HUESTIS. "Plasma Cannabinoid Concentrations during Dronabinol Pharmacotherapy for Cannabis Dependence." *Therapeutic Drug Monitoring*, 36: 218–34, 2014 (1 table, 4 figures, 25 references)

Abstract: Dronabinol is a pure synthetic form of THC and since 1999 has been approved for the treatment of anorexia in AIDs and other wasting diseases and an anti-emetic agent in cancer patients undergoing chemotherapy. Pharmacokinetic profile of dronabinol differs markedly for smoke marijuana. Peak THC after smoking occurs before smoking ends and rapidly declines to about 10 percent of maximum serum THC after one to two hours. After dronabinol peak THC occurs two to four hours later. Dronabinol in sesame oil is 90 to 95 percent absorbed after oral consumption, but due to first pass metabolism, only 6 to 20 percent reaches the blood stream. Eleven daily cannabis smokers (ages 18 to 55 years) received 0, 30, 60, or 120 mg/day THC in dronabinol for five-day periods, each period separated by nine days of *ad libitum* smoking. At the end of each five-day period, the subjects smoked one 5.9 percent THC cigarette. Blood was collected on the first and fifth day and plasma THC 11-OH THC and THCOOH were determined by GC/MS. During placebo dosing all cannabinoids concentrations decreased while all cannabinoids increased after dronabinol administration.

During active dronabinol dosing, significant dose-dependent increases in THC and 11-OH-THC concentrations support withdrawal symptom suppression. THC concentrations after cannabis smoking were only distinguishable from oral THC doses for one hour, too short a period to feasibly identify cannabis relapse. THCCOOH/THC ratios were higher fourteen hours after overnight oral dronabinol abstinence but cannot distinguish oral THC dosing from smoked cannabis intake.

Reference Number: 80209

PLASSE, T.F., R.W. GORTER, S.H. KRASNOW, M. LANE, K.V. SHEPARD, AND R.G. WADLEIGH. "Recent Clinical Experience with Dronabinol." *Pharmacology, Biochemistry and Behavior,* 40: 695–700, 1991 (4 tables, 4 figures, 28 references)

Abstract: The synthetic THC, dronabinol (Marinol), comes in sesame oil capsules at 2.5, 5, and 10 mg doses. The drug is used as an anti-nausea and anti-emetic agent for patients undergoing chemotherapy. It also promotes weight gain and appetite in seven out of ten HIV patients.

Dronabinol has now been marketed in the US for four years. It has an extremely good safety profile. While side effects occur fairly often, they are usually mild and resolve quickly and without sequealae on discontinuation of treatment. Drug diversion and inappropriate prescribing of dronabinol have not been reported. In fact, physicians and patients often seem reluctant to use the medication because it is a cannabinoid.

Reference Number: 80210

WARE, M.A., AND E. ST ARNAUD-TREMPE. "The Abuse Potential of the Synthetic Cannabinoid Nabilone." *Addiction*, 105: 494–503, 2010 (2 tables, 4 figures, 57 references)

Abstract: Nabilone (Cesamet) is a synthetic THC prescription drug in Canada used for the treatment of nausea, vomiting, and pain. A detailed review of newspapers, the scientific literature, Statistics Canada, the RCMP Drug Reports, and interviews with police was conducted to determine if nabilone is used as a drug of abuse. Nabilone is consumed orally at a typical dose of 2 mg.

Although cannabis is illegal, it remains more widely accessible and available at a lower cost than nabilone. These characteristics make nabilone unattractive for drug users, although it is possible that interest will increase when generic and therefore less expensive nabilone options become available. The current study revealed, however, that nabilone has no known street value.

8.03 CANNABIDIOL (CBD)/HEMP

Cannabidiol (CBD), can be thought of as the Best cannabinoid. It is the major cannabinoid found in hemp (80304, 80305). It causes no psychoactive impairment and has been shown to decrease the harmful effects of THC (80311, 80314) and decrease anxiety (80310). Hemp seeds will not give a positive oral or urine cannabinoid test (80304, 80305). CBD has helped children with refractory epilepsy, but the CBD oil should be free of THC or adverse side effects may occur (80312). Ancient Chinese medicine contained high CBD and low THC concentrations (80313), unlike today's high potency medical marijuana.

Reference Number: 80301

HILL, K.P. "Medical Marijuana for Treatment of Chronic Pain and Other Medical and Psychiatric Problems. A Clinical Review." *Journal of the American Medical Association*, 313: 2474–83, 2015 (3 tables, 69 references)

Abstract: As of March 2015, twenty-three states and the District of Columbia had medical marijuana laws in place. A review was conducted of medical marijuana studies between 1948 and 2015, and twenty-eight randomized clinical studies of cannabinoids were found. Marijuana is potentially addictive, causing significant problems for work, school, and relationships in about 9 percent of adult and 17 percent of adolescent users. Regular marijuana use is associated with an increased risk of anxiety, depression, and psychotic illness, and use of marijuana can worsen these conditions as well. Regular marijuana use is associated with increased rates of respiratory tract infections, chronic bronchitis, and pneumonia.

> The primary cannabinoids contained in marijuana are delta 9 tetrahydrocannabinol (THC) and cannabidiol. THC produces the euphoria that comes from using marijuana, but it also can produce psychosis. Cannabidiol is not psychoactive and is thought to have anti-anxiety and possibly antipsychotic effects as well. Marijuana's therapeutic effects depend on the concentration of THC as a given formulation as well as the ratio of THC to cannabidiol because of cannabidiol's ability to mitigate the psychoactive effects of THC. As a result, the THC-cannabidiol ratio for many strains of marijuana has been engineered to achieve desired effects.

Reference Number: 80302

HINDOCHA, C., T.P. FREEMAN, G. SCHAFER C. GARDNER, R.K. DAS, C.J.A. MORGAN, AND H.V. CURRAN. "Acute Effects of Delta-9-Tetrahydrocannabinol, Cannabidiol, and Their Combination on Facial Emotion Recognition: A Randomized Double-Blind, Placebo-Controlled Study in Cannabis Users." *European Neuropsychopharmacology*, 25: 325–34, 2015 (1 table, 3 figures, 53 references)

Abstract: Cannabis contains hundreds of cannabinoids. The two most important are THC (partial agonist of CB1 receptor) and cannabidiol (CBD). THC and CBD have opposing psychological and emotional properties. Twenty-four light and twenty-four heavy (thirty-four male, fourteen female) cannabis users were tested on the effects of inhaled THC (8 mg), CBD (16 mg), and their combination (8 mg THC and 16 mg CBD and placebo) using a Volcano Medic Vaporizer on emotional facial recognition. The six basic emotions were happiness, sadness, anger, disgust, fearful, surprise, and neutral. The subjects also completed several questionnaires and VAS of subjective effect of being stoned. One-half of each group was rated low on schizotypy (proneness to psychosis). Both the

THC and CBD and THC alone produced feelings of being stoned, but not CBD alone.

> In summary, the findings of this study add to previous evidence that acute THC administration reduces cannabis users' ability to accurately identify facial emotions. Importantly, this study provides the first behavioural evidence that CBD subtly enhances emotional facial affect recognition and protects against the impairment produced by THC.

Reference Number: 80303

HOCH, E., U. BONNET, R. THOMASIUS, F. GANZER, U. HAVEMANN-REINECKE, AND U.W. PREUSS. "Risks Associated with the Non-Medicinal Use of Cannabis." *Deutsches Arzteblatt International*, 112: 271–78, 2015 (2 tables, 40 references)

Abstract: The THC content of cannabis has increased sharply in the past decade, whereas another active ingredient, cannabidiol (CBD), is no longer present in many strains. The anxiolytic, antipsychotic, antiemetic, and neuroprotective action of CBD may compensate for the adverse effects of THC. A review was conducted of the potential adverse physical and mental effects of intensive recreational use of cannabis. In Europe, cannabis consumption is the most common reason for a first drug treatment due to the use of an illegal drug and has increased from 45,000 in 2006 to 61,600 in 2011.

> The use of cannabis is widespread, extending from experimental consumption to dependence. Empirical data have now clearly shown that starting early in life and regularly using high amounts of cannabis for a long period of time increased the risk of various mental and physica disorders and endangers age-appropriate development.

Reference Number: 80304

HOLLER, J.M., T.Z. BOSY, C.S. DUNKLEY, B. LEVINE, M.R. PAST, AND A. JACOBS. "Delta 9 Tetrahydrocannabinol Content of Commercially Available Hemp Products." *Journal of Analytical Toxicology*, 32: 428–32, 2008 (3 tables, 1 figure, 22 references)

Abstract: Hemp seeds are the manufacturing starting point for the vast majority of hemp products. Hemp seeds are a good source of essential fatty acids. The THC content of seventy-nine different products ranging from oil to nutritional bars, snacks and candies and beverages were determined by GC/MS. No THC was detected in 86 percent of the products and none had a concentration greater than 7.8 ug/g.

> Results of the hemp products tested indicate the amount of THC present in commercially available products is significantly less in products available today than those reported in the past. As a result, the probability that these products will produce the urine THC metabolite levels greater than the DoD and HHS confirmation cutoff of 15 ng/mL is significantly reduced and should not be considered as a realistic cause for a positive urine analysis result.

Reference Number: 80305

LESON, G., P. PLESS, F. GROTENHERMEN, H. KALANT, AND M.A. ELSOHLY. "Evaluating the Impact of Hemp Food Consumption on Workplace Drug Tests." *Journal of Analytical Toxicology*, 25: 691–98, 2001 (2 tables, 3 figures, 39 references)

Abstract: Current Federal US law prohibits commercial farming of hemp. In the EU and Canada, industrial hemp grown for seeds and fibre must be less than 0.3 percent THC. In the US, seeds and oil have been imported from Canada and EU. Most drug testing programs in the US employ 50 ng/mL limit and 15 ng/mL for GC/MS confirmation of THC-COOH. Some programs employ 20 ng/mL screening and 10 ng/mL confirmation and some only use a screening test. Ten female and five males ingested four different doses of THC in oil at concentrations between 0.09 to 0.6 mg THC per day for ten days each. Urine samples were collected four to eight hours after oil ingestion and screened by RIA (radioimmunoassay). The urine THCCOOH concentration was confirmed by GC/MS. None of the subjects had positive screening between 0.09 and 0.45 mg/day. One subject screened positive at 50 ng/mL cutoff but was only 3 ng/mL by GC/MS. Eighty-two percent of the THC in hemp oil was free and THCA is typically less than 10 percent.

> In the present study daily ingestion of up to 0.6 mg of THC by fifteen subjects did not produce confirmed positive urine THC results at the 10 or 15 ng/mL GC-MS cutoffs. Currently practiced seed-cleaning methods appear to be successful in limiting THC concentrations in hemp oil

and hulled seeds to 5 ug/g and 2 ug/g respectively. At these THC residue levels, ingestion of 0.6 mg/day via hemp foods requires ingestion of unrealistically high amounts of such products.

Reference Number: 80306

MERRICK, J., B. LANE, T. SEBREE, T. YAKSH, C. O'NEILL, AND S.L. BANKS. "Identification of Psychoactive Degradants of Cannabidiol in Simulated Gastric and Physiological Fluid." *Cannabis and Cannabinoid Research*, 1: 102–12, 2016 (5 tables, 7 figures, 36 references)

Abstract: In recent epilepsy research, pediatric subjects receiving orally administered CBD showed a high incidence of adverse effects including somnolence (21 percent) and fatigue (17 percent), although CBD is non-psychoactive. An in vitro study was conducted to determine how CBD degrades in simulated gastric fluid. Due to CBDs limited aqueous solubility, a surfactant (1 percent dodecyl sulfate (SDS)) was added. The stability of CBD was tested in a physiologically buffered solution as well. The CBD in simulated gastric fluid was 85 percent degraded after sixty minutes and 98 percent after two hours, to delta 9 and delta 8 THC. In a patient treated with 700 mg of CBD, formulated in a lipid environment (oil-based solute), the total delta 9 and 8 THC degradation products would be 6.5 mg after thirty minutes, and 13 mg after sixty minutes, even if only 1 percent of the CBD was available.

SGF converts CBD into the psychoactive components delta 9 and delta 8 THC. The first order kinetics observed in this study allowed estimated levels to be calculated and indicated that the acidic environment during normal gastrointestinal transit can expose orally CBD treated patients to levels of THC and other psychoactive cannabinoids that may exceed the threshold for a physiological response. Delivery methods that decrease the potential for formation of psychoactive cannabinoids should be explored.

Reference Number: 80307

CRIPPA, J.A.S., A.C.S. CRIPPA, J.E.C. HALLAK, R. MARTIN-SANTOS, AND A.W. ZUARDI. "Delta-9-THC Intoxication by Cannabis-Enriched Cannabis Extract in Two Children with Refractory Epilepsy: Full Remission after Switching to Purified Cannabidiol." *Frontiers in Pharmacology*, 7: Article 359, 6 pp, 2016 (3 figures, 28 references)

Abstract: Although there are more than twenty different drugs approved for the treatment of epilepsy, approximately 30 percent of patients continue to have seizures. Two children (a 10-year-old girl and a 7-year-old boy) with treatment-resistant epilepsy showed THC intoxication after consuming edible CBD-enriched extractions. Symptoms included inappropriate laughter, ataxia, reduced attention, irritability, aggressiveness, and eye redness. The extract was found to contain 3-4 percent THC and 90 percent CBD. The extracts were replaced by purified CBD (99.6 percent) dissolved in corn oil (BSPG Pharm, Sandwich UK). The children attained full remission after switching to the purified CBD and the THC intoxication symptoms disappeared.

The two cases reported here highlight the need for cannabis-derived compounds produced according to good laboratory and manufacturing practices (GLP/GMP) that could lead to the development of medicines consistently produced and controlled by international regulatory standards. The use of handcrafted uncontrolled cannabis-based medicine by children and adolescents raises special concerns because of the well-known harmful long-term effects of delta 9-THC on the developing brain. The potentially toxic effects of delta 9-THC and other cannabis constituents, including cognitive impairment and chronic psychiatric disturbances, have not yet been studied in younger patients who might be more vulnerable than adults to potential long-term adverse effects. Therefore, randomized clinical trials using high-quality and reliable cannabis-derived substances without other impurities (e.g., solvents) are required to ascertain the safety and efficacy of cannabinoids as medicines.

Reference Number: 80308

PEACE, M.R., K.E. BUTLER, C.E. WOLF, J.L. POKLIS, AND A. POLKIS. "Evaluation of Two Commercially Available Cannabidiol Formulations for Use in Electronic Cigarettes." *Frontiers in Pharmacology*, 7: Article 279, 6 pp, 2016 (1 table, 1 figure, 34 references)

Abstract: E-cigarettes were developed as an alternative method for nicotine delivery but now are used for other drugs delivery. A battery heats a coil containing a wick saturated with an e-liquid (propylene glycol) or vehicular glycerin (VG). Two cannabidiol PG formulations were analyzed, Cloud 9 Hemp Easy Rider, and Yellow Brick Road by HPLC-MS/MS.

Ethanol was detected in the e-liquids. Both were labelled as containing 3.3 mg/mL CBD but contained 6.5 and 7.6 mg/mL respectively.

Vaping CBD would eliminate harmful combustion products of smoking, while still employing the advantages of inhalation over ingestion. As research continues to understand the effects of CBD and its potential properties, the e-cigarettes may prove a useful CBD delivery system.

Reference Number: 80309

ROSER, P., J. GALLINAT, G. WEINBERG, G. JUCKEL, I. GORYNIA, AND A.M. STADELMANN. "Psychomotor Performance in Relation to Acute Oral Administration of delta 9-Tetrahydrocannabinol and Standardized Cannabis Extract in Healthy Human Subjects." *European Archives for Psychiatry and Clinical Neuroscience*, 259: 284–92, 2009 (3 tables, 5 figures, 64 references)

Abstract: Twelve male and twelve female subjects (mean age 28 years) consumed either a placebo, cannabis extract (10 mg THC, 5.4 mg CBD), or THC (10 mg) on each of three consecutive weeks. Three female subjects did not finish the series due to panic attacks due to cannabis use during testing, and so the number of subjects was reduced from twenty-seven to twenty-four. Subjects did right- and left-hand tapping alone and while humming and reading before and two hours after the drug administration. A blood sample was collected two hours after the drug administration and plasma 11-OH-THC, THCCOOH, THC, and CBD concentrations were determined. The mean peak plasma THC was 1.2 to 1.9 ng/mL, 11-OH-THC was 2.5 to 5.0 ng/mL, and 23.8 to 36.4 ng/mL THCCOOH.

Psychomotor performance was assessed by using a finger tapping test series. Cannabis extract but not delta 9 THC revealed a significant reduction of right-hand tapping frequencies that was also found in schizophrenia. As to the pure delta 9-THC condition, left-hand tapping frequencies were correlated with the plasma concentration of the delta 9 metabolite 11-OH-THC. These effects are thought to be related to cannabinoid actions on CB1 receptors in the basal ganglia, the cerebral cortex, and cerebellum.

Reference Number: 80310

BERGAMASCHI, M.M., R.H.C. QUEIROZ, M.H.N. CHAGAS, D.C.G. DE OLIVEIRA, B.S. DE MARTINIS, F. KAPCZINSKI, J. QUEVEDO, R. ROESLER, N. SCHRODER, A.E. NARDI, R. MARTIN-SANTOS, J.E.C. HALLAK, A.W. ZUARDI, AND J.A.S. CRIPPA. "Cannabidiol Reduces the Anxiety Induced by Simulated Public Speaking in Treatment-Naive Social Phobia Patients." *Neuropsychopharmacology*, 36: 1219–26, 2011 (2 tables, 2 figures, 45 references)

Abstract: Generalized Social Anxiety Disorder (SAD) is one of the most common anxiety conditions and is associated with impairment in daily social life. Twelve male and twelve female subjects with SAD were divided into a CBD group and a placebo group and were compared with twelve subjects without SAD (healthy controls or HCs) in a simulated public speaking test (SPST). The subjects were required to present a four-minute speech about local public transit, which was videotaped. The CBD group consumed 600 mg CBD powder mixed in corn oil in a gelatin capsule eighty minutes before the simulated public speaking test. The placebo was only corn oil in an identical gelatin capsule.

> Pretreatment of SAD patients with CBD significantly reduced anxiety, cognitive impairment, and discomfort in their speech performance (S) and significantly decreased alert in their anticipatory speech (A). The cognitive impairment, discomfort, and alert of SAD patients who received CBD had similar results as the HC during the SPST. These preliminary results indicate that a single dose of CBD can reduce the anxiety-enhancing effect provoked by SPST in SAD patients, indicating that this cannabinoid inhibits the fear of speaking in public, one of the main symptoms of the disorder.

Reference Number: 80311

BHATTACHARYYA, S., P.D. MORRISON, P. FUSAR-POLI, R. MARTIN-SANTO, S. BORGWARDT, T. WINTON-BROWN, C. NOSARTI, C.M. O'CARROLL, M. SEAL, P. ALLEN, M.A. MEHTA, J.M. STONE, N. TUNSTALL, V. GIAMPIETRO, S. KAPUR, R.M. MURRAY, A. ZUARDI, J.A. CRIPPA, Z. ATAKAN, AND P.K. MCGUIRE. "Opposite Effects of delta 9-Tetrahydrocannabinol and Cannabidiol on Human Brain Function and Psychopathology." *Neuropsychopharmacology*, 35: 764–74, 2010 (2 tables, 5 figures, 50 references)

Abstract: Fifteen male infrequent cannabis users (mean age 27 years) were scanned with functional magnetic resonance imaging (fMRI) while performing a verbal memory task, a response inhibition task, a sensory processing task, and when viewing fearful faces following the administration of placebo, 600 mg CBD, or 10 mg THC orally. In the second experiment, three male and three female cannabis users (mean age 26 years) were administered 5 mg CBD or placebo IV, before 1.25 mg THC IV. The subjects were assessed as to psychotic symptoms by a psychiatrist.

Table: Mean Psychotic Symptoms as Assessed by a Psychiatrist after THC IV, and Pre-Administration of a Placebo or CBD

Time After THC IV (minutes)	Mean Psychotic Symptoms (Placebo Pre-treatment)	Mean Psychotic Symptoms (CBD Pre-Treatment)
0	7.0	7.0
30	12.0	9.0
90	8.5	7.5

Source: Adapted from Bhattacharyya et al, 2010

Overall, these data indicate that some of the effects of CBD on brain function and psychiatric symptoms are in opposite direction to those of delta 9-THC. How this might be achieved at a molecular level is uncertain. Although the effects of delta 9-THC are clearly mediated by central CB1 receptors, CBD may act through a range of other mechanisms, including inhibition of the uptake and hydrolysis of Anancamide. However, recent data suggest that CBD can also modulate the effect of delta 9-THC by binding to CB1 receptors. Our data are consistent with a potential therapeutic role of CBD in ameliorating the psychiatric consequences of cannabis use in the general population, and in patients with existing psychiatric disorders, particularly as conventional antipsychotic medication is relatively ineffective for such conditions. It also may have a role in the treatment of psychotic and anxiety disorders independent of cannabis use. From a public health point of view, one worrying implication of our results is that cannabis users may be at an increased risk of acute adverse psychological reactions following cannabis use, in light of the increasingly potent forms of cannabis with decreasing CBD content available on the street.

Reference Number: 80312

AGUIRRE-VELAZQUEZ, C.G. "Report for a Survey of Parents Regarding the Use of Cannabidiol (Medicinal Cannabis) in Mexican Children with Refractory Epilepsy." *Neurology Research International,* 2017, Article ID 2985729, 5 pp (3 tables, 2 figures, 15 references)

Abstract: Refractory epilepsy (RE) is a failure to respond to two or more antiepileptic drugs and occurs in 30 to 35 percent of the patients with epilepsy. Serious childhood epilepsies are characterized by frequent convulsions, delayed neurological development, and deterioration in the quality of life. A detailed survey was conducted of the parents of twenty-seven male and sixteen female children (mean age 7.6 years) with refractory epilepsy in Mexico. The children were treated mainly with RSHO-X (76.6 percent cannabidiol and 0.1 percent THC) and Charlotte's Web, marijuana with high CBD to THC ratio. In thirty-five cases (81.3 percent), there was a reduction in the number of seizures. In five cases (11.6 percent), there was no change and in two cases (4.6 percent), there was in increase in seizures. In controlled studies, the placebo effect can account for 20 percent of the results. There were only mild adverse effects in sixteen cases (37.2 percent), mainly increased appetite and disrupted sleep.

Table: Changes in Monthly Seizures Rates after Use of CBD

Categories of Improvement	% Reduction	% of Cases
Free from seizure	100%	16.0%
Significant	80 – 100%	25.5%
Moderate	50 – 80%	25.5%
Slight	25 – 50%	16.0%
Unchanged	±25%	11.6%
Worsening	> 25%	4.6%

Source: Adapted from Aguirre-Velazquez, 2017

The results of this study indicate that, from the viewpoint of the parents of children with RE, medicinal cannabis is useful as an add-on treatment for their children since it induces a significant reduction in the frequency, duration, and intensity of the seizures. It also improved aspects of the patients' quality of life in terms of their emotional and cognitive states, their sleep patterns, and their diet. There was an absence of serious adverse effects, with only some tolerable mild adverse effects experiences with this CBD-based treatment.

Reference Number: 80312

Reference Number: 80313

BRAND E.J., AND Z. ZHAO. "Cannabis in Chinese Medicine: Are Some Traditional Indications References in Ancient Literature Related to Cannabinoids?" *Frontiers in Pharmacology*, 8: Article 108, 11 pp, 2017 (3 figures, 49 references)

Abstract: Cannabis has long been used in China for fibre or as a seed crop. There are few references referring to cannabis as medicine or as a recreational drug. Pre-modern Chinese medical textbooks are known as "Benaco."

> Today cannabis landraces throughout most regions of China reflect fibre biotypes, and some provincial standards have followed international trends by defining fibre biotypes for cultivation as varieties containing < 0.3 percent THC by weight. In modern China, intermediate and drug biotypes have primarily been reported in isolated regions in the northwest province of Xinjiang and the southwest province of Yunnan. Drug use of cannabis in Xinxiang province was recorded along the Silk Road from the Qing Dynasty (1644–1911 CE) to the twentieth century, and was described in a report by the Russian explorer Shoqan Walikhanov in 1858; however, there is little evidence outside of Benaco literature that suggests that drug cannabis was known or used in other parts of ancient China. Furthermore, according to texts that focus on the history of drug prohibition in China, there is little evidence that cannabis was either abused or prohibited in China prior to the first documented seizures of imported cannabis products in Xinxiang in 1936. This stands in notable contrast to other drugs that have a well-documented history of regulation, medical use, abuse, and prohibition in China, such as opium and deleriant drugs derived from tropane alkaloid-containing plants, such as henbane and datura. On the whole, the abundance of references to hemp and the paucity of references to drug cannabis in early Chinese history suggests that fibre and drug varieties had diverged in ancient times. As cannabis is wind-pollinated and its biotype distinctions are genetically determined, the long-term and abundant cultivation of fibre-rich biotypes in China likely supplanted or diluted any drug biotypes that were once present.

Reference Number: 80314

WINTON-BROWN, T.T., P. ALLEN, S. BHATTACHARRYA, S.J. BORGWARDT, P. FUSAR-POLI, J.A. CRIPPA, M.L. SEAL, R. MARTIN-SANTOS, D. FLYTCHE, A.W. ZUARDI, Z. ATAKAN, AND P.K. MCGUIRE. "Modulation of Auditory and Visual Processing by Delta-9-Tetrahydrocannabinol and Cannabidiol: An fMRI Study." *Neuropsychopharmacology*, 36: 1340–48, 2011 (2 tables, 4 figures, 42 references)

Abstract: Fourteen male cannabis users (ages 20 to 42 years) consumed a placebo, 10 mg THC, or 600 mg CBD orally and performed various cognitive tasks while undergoing functional magnetic resonance imaging (fMRI). A urine drug screen was conducted before testing. The capsules were consumed one hour before the fMRI. Blood samples were collected at one and two hours after ingestion and THC and CBD concentrations were measured by GC/MS. The mean blood THC concentrations were 3.9 and 5.1 ng/mL and the mean CBD concentrations were 4.7 ng/mL and 17.0 ng/mL at one and two hours respectively. HR increased only with THC dose. Eight of the original eighteen subjects (44 percent) experienced frank psychotic symptoms and three withdrew from the study. THC and CBD had opposing effects on temporal activation during auditory processing but mixed effects on visual processing. The decrease of temporal activation by THC was associated with an increase in psychotic symptoms.

> Single acute doses of THC and CBD significantly modulated brain function in areas that process auditory and visual stimuli. These results are the first to demonstrate how the two major constituents of cannabis (THC and CBD) function on the sensory cortices, and how their effects are related to the induction of psychotic symptoms by cannabis. The data also provide further evidence that THC and CBD have distinct effects on regional brain activation, sometimes in opposite directions.

8.04 SYNTHETIC CANNABINOIDS

Synthetic cannabinoids have numerous street names, such as "Spice," "K2," "Black Mamba," or "Angry Birds" (80409).

The term "synthetic marijuana" is misleading and suggests that these drugs are well tolerated and not harmful, but they are actually much more dangerous and unpredictable than botanical cannabis/marijuana and so should be referred to as "synthetic cannabinoids" or SCs. Some of the main facts about SCs are:

- Synthetic cannabinoids are not botanical marijuana or cannabis
- Synthetic cannabinoids are more potent than cannabis
- Synthetic cannabinoids are ever-changing
- Synthetic cannabinoid research was "hi-jacked"
- Synthetic cannabinoids are dangerous drug with unpredictable human toxicity
- Synthetic cannabinoids have many street names
- Synthetic cannabinoids use is not limited to young people only
- Synthetic cannabinoids are easily obtained
- Synthetic cannabinoids are more addicting and have more unknown health consequences than botanical cannabis
- Over 90 percent of SC users have smoked cannabis previously, showing cannabis is a gateway drug to the use of SCs
- Synthetic cannabinoids cannot be detected by routine urine cannabinoid drug screens
- Synthetic cannabinoids are continually changing and being modified in clandestine labs or widely sold over the net, which makes law enforcement more complicated and difficult

Dr. John W. Hoffman and his colleagues synthesized and published research on synthetic cannabinoids over twenty years and has many SCs with his initials "JWH" to identify them (80401). SCs have caused severe poisoning, convulsions, seizures, hospitalization, and death (80432, 80433, 80439). Drivers impaired by SC were more likely to have a motor vehicle crash and have confusion, disorientation, and incoherent, slurred speech compared to marijuana users (80402). Another reason for the more severe consequences of SCs use is that they contain no CBD which would moderate these effects.

Reference Number: 80401

WILEY, J.L., J.A. MARUSICH, J.W. HUFFMAN, R.L. BAISTER, AND B.F. THOMAS. "Hijacking of Basic Research: The Case of Synthetic Cannabinoids." *Methods Rep RTI Press*, November 2011, 11 pp (2 figures, 35 references)

Abstract: John W. Hoffman graduated in chemistry from Harvard University and became a professor at Clemson, where his main research was on the synthesis of novel cannabinoids. He and his colleagues designed and synthesized JWH-018 and published their results over twenty years ago. Since his retirement, he has received increasing phone calls from law enforcement agencies, the military, and panicked parents about a "new" street drug or herbal called K2, or Spice, based on his research.

> Gathering and communicating knowledge are important aspects of the scientific endeavour. Yet presentation of data in public forums, such as scientific meetings and publications, makes it available not only to scientists, but also to others who may have different ideas about how to use research findings. A recent example of this type of hijacking is the introduction of synthetic cannabinoids that are sprayed on herbal products and consequently smoked for their marijuana-like intoxicating properties. Originally developed for the legitimate research purpose of furthering understanding of the cannabinoid system, these synthetic cannabinoids are being abused worldwide, creating issues for regulatory and law enforcement agencies that are struggling to keep up with the growing number of compounds of various structural motifs. Basic and clinical scientists need to provide advice now to facilitate decision-making about the health threats posed by this emerging problem.

Reference Number: 80402

CHASE, P.B., J. HAWKINS, J. MOSIER, F. JIMENEZ, K. BOESEN, B.K. LOGAN, AND F.G. WALTER. "Differential Physiological and Behavioral Cues Observed in Individuals Smoking Botanical Marijuana versus Synthetic Cannabinoid Drugs." *Clinical Toxicology*, 54: 14–19, 2016 (2 tables, 2 figures, 31 references)

Abstract: There are well over 400 synthetic cannabinoids developed for research purposes. DRE was conducted on sixteen drivers (mean age 20 years) using synthetic cannabinoids and compared with twenty-five drivers (median age 20 years) using marijuana. Normal ranges on the DRE protocol are HR (60–90 bpm), BR (120–140/70–90 mm Hg), and temperature 97.6 to 99.6°F. The average time from stop to DRE was one hour and the average time from stop to blood collection was 1 hour, 50 minutes, for synthetic cannabis and 1 hour and 34 minutes for botanical cannabis. CB1 receptors are located in CNS and enteric plexus and CB2 in the tissues of the immune system, leukocytes, spleen, tonsils, and lymph nodes (anti-inflammatory). Mean THC was 11 ng/mL and THC-COOH was 50 ng/mL in the arrested drivers using botanical cannabis.

Table: Percent of Drivers Using Botanical or Synthetic Cannabinoids Showing Various Clinical Symptoms

Clinical Symptom/Observation	% of Drivers Using Botanical Cannabis	% of Drivers Using Synthetic Cannabinoids
Motor vehicle crash	4%	31%
Confusion	0%	44%
Disorientation	0%	31%
Incoherent, slurred speech	12%	65%
Horizontal gaze nystagmus	12%	50%
Lack of convergence	96%	80%
Reddened conjunctivae	92%	69%
Higher pulse rate (> 90bpm)	60%	69%

Source: Adapted from Chase et al, 2015

Drivers under the influence of synthetic cannabinoids showed greater impairment (confusion, disorientation, and incoherent slurred speech) than drivers under the influence of marijuana in this population evaluated by DREs. These physical findings of synthetic cannabinoid intoxication and driver impairment are incompatible with safe driving and have the potential to lead to morbidity and mortality.

Reference Number: 80403

AKUTSU, M., K-I. SUGIE, AND K. SAITO. "Analysis of 62 Synthetic Cannabinoids by Gas Chromatography-Mass Spectrometry with Photoionization." *Forensic Toxicology*, 35: 94–103, 2017 (1 table, 4 figures, 12 references)

Abstract: A GC/MS method to detect sixty-two different synthetic cannabinoids was described. The method uses the GC/MS in the photoionization mode (PI) rather than the more common electron ionization (EI) mode or the more cumbersome chemical ionization (CI) mode. Photoionization uses ultraviolet light to deprive one electron from the target molecule with a low ionization threshold.

In this study, the mass spectra of sixty-two synthetic cannabinoids were recorded by the GC-PI-MS and the mass spectra for twenty compounds were measured by GC-EI-MS for comparison. Most of the mass spectra obtained from the sixty-two synthetic cannabinoids by GC-PI-MS showed very simple patterns of either molecular ion only or a molecular ion plus only one fragment peak, providing useful information on the molecular weight of the target compound. Therefore GC-EI/PI will be a useful tool for identifying synthetic cannabinoids contained in a dubious product.

Reference Number: 80404

CLAYTON, H.B., R. LOWRY, C. ASHLEY, A. WOLKIN, AND A.M. GRANT. "Health Risk Behaviors with Synthetic Cannabinoids versus Marijuana." *Pediatrics*, 138: 10 pp, 2017 (4 tables, 44 references)

Abstract: An analysis of the 2015 Youth Risk Behavior Study involving 15,624 high school students (grades 9 to 12) in the US was conducted. Approximately 61 percent of the students never used marijuana or synthetic cannabinoids (SC), 30 percent only used cannabis, and 9 percent have ever used synthetic cannabinoids. But 98 percent of the students who had ever used SC used marijuana as well.

Table: Prevalence (or Odds Ratio) of Various Health Behaviours According to Use of Marijuana or Synthetic Cannabinoids in US High School Students Compared to Non-Users

Health Behaviour	Ever Used Marijuana (prevalence)	Ever Used SCs (prevalence)
Drove when drinking alcohol	3.64 X	4.54 X
Physically forced sexual intercourse	2.20 X	2.87 X
In a physical fight	1.79 X	2.37 X
Attempted suicide	1.61 X	1.93 X
Used alcohol/drugs before last sexual intercourse	4.33 X	5.62 X
Did not use any method to prevent pregnancy	1.20 X	1.92 X

Source: Adapted from Clayton et al, 2017

Students who ever used synthetic cannabinoids were more likely than students who ever used marijuana only to have used marijuana before age 13 years, to have used marijuana more than once in the past thirty days, and to have used marijuana more than twenty times during the past thirty days. Several injury/violence behaviours were more prevalent among students who ever used synthetic cannabinoids compared with students who ever used marijuana only.

Reference Number: 80405

DAVIES, B.B., C. BAYARD, S.J. LARSON, L.W. ZARWELL, AND R.A. MITCHELL. "Retrospective Analysis of Synthetic Cannabinoid Metabolites in Urine of Individuals Suspected of Driving Impaired." *Journal of Analytical Toxicology*, 40: 89–95, 2016 (2 tables, 2 figures, 37 references)

Abstract: Synthetic cannabinoids are sprayed on herbal material (hence the names herbal incense, spice, K2) and smoked. A total of 526 urine samples from suspected impaired drivers in Washington, DC, between 2012 and 2013 were screened for twelve different synthetic cannabinoids (SCMs) by LC-MS. Nineteen cases (3.6 percent) were confirmed positive for SCs. Drugs other than SCs (mainly alcohol) were detected in 90 percent of the cases.

Table: Gender, Age, and Other Drugs Found in the Urine of Drivers with Synthetic Cannabinoid Metabolites Detected in the Urine

Case Number	Gender	Age (years)	Parent SC Detected	Other Drugs (concentration)
1	Male	28	UR-144	PCP (245.4 ng/mL)
2	Male	N/A	UR-144	THCCOOH (3,652.6 ng/mL)
3	Female	33	UR-144	Alcohol (0.26 g/100mL)
4	Female	30	UR-144	PCP (345.2 ng/mL) Acetone (0.016 g/1000mL)
5	Male	37	UR-144	Alcohol (0.23 g/100mL) THCCOOH (582.7 ng/mL)
6	Male	32	UR-144	None
7	Male	36	UR-144	PCP (1,133.2 ng/mL)
8	Female	35	UR-144	Alcohol (0.09 g/100mL) PCP (85.4 ng/mL)
9	Male	53	PB-22	Alcohol (0.07 g/100mL)
10	Male	45	UR-144	Alcohol (0.27 g/100mL)
11	Male	28	UR-144	Alcohol (0.19 g/100mL) THCCOOH (31.3 ng/mL)
12	Male	22	UR-144	Alcohol (0.14 g/100mL) THCCOOH (31.3 ng/mL)
13	Male	35	UR-144	Alcohol (0.11 g/100mL) THCCOOH (detected)
14	Female	33	UR-144	None
15	Male	N/A	JWH-073 JWH-018 AM2201	Alcohol (0.02 g/100mL)

Case Number	Gender	Age (years)	Parent SC Detected	Other Drugs (concentration)
16	Male	22	UR-144	Alcohol (0.20 g/100mL) THCCOOH (138.6 ng/mL)
17	Male	35	UR-144 JWH-073 JWH-018	Alcohol (0.03 g/100mL)
18	Male	29	UR-144	Alcohol (0.22 g/100mL)
19	Male	33	JWH-073 JWH-018 AM2201	Alcohol (0.33 g/100mL) THCCOOH (74.8 ng/mL)

Source: Adapted from Davies et al, 2015

SC identification, detection, and quantitation in forensic toxicology laboratories is challenging due to the evaluation and expansion of the designer drug market. When using a targeted LC-MS/MS method, continuous analytical modifications were required.

Reference Number: 80406

DOGAN, S., C. AKMAN, A. YILMAZ, U.M. KALAFAT, AND T. OCAK. "A Hypothermic Case with Giant Osborn Waves and Atrial Fibrillation after Using Synthetic Cannabinoid." *Anatolian Journal of Cardiology*, 16: 150–52, 2016 (3 figures)

Abstract: A 22-year-old man was found unconscious in a park after using SC. He was hypothermic (temperature below 35°C) and had atrial fibrillation and giant Osborn waves detected in the ECG.

Unconsciously, staying outside for an extended time in extreme cold is the most important cause of hypothermia. In recent years, a significant social problem is the increase in the number of people using synthetic cannabinoids (SC) in public places. A frequent result of SC use is severe deterioration in consciousness and perception.

Reference Number: 80407

GINSBURG, B.C., L.R. MCMAHON, J.J. SANCHEZ, AND M.A. JAVORS. "Purity of Synthetic Cannabinoids Sold Online for Recreational Use." *Journal of Analytical Toxicology*, 56: 666–68, 2012 (1 table, 1 figure, 11 references)

Abstract: The purity of synthetic cannabinoids JWH-018 and JWH-073 obtained from three online suppliers was determined by HPLC. The purity of the samples ranged from 75.6 percent to 98.0 percent, although the samples varied considerably in colour, texture, and odour.

It is concluded that adverse events following consumption of synthetic cannabinoid preparations is unlikely to be due to impurities or residue from the manufacturing process, but rather to effects of the active drug or interactions with other psychoactive chemicals from herbs blended into products marketed as cannabis alternatives.

Reference Number: 80408

TYNDALL, J.A., R. GERONA, G. DE PORTU, J. TRECKI, M-C. ELIE, J. LUCAS, J. SLISH, K. RAND, L. BAZYDLO, M. HOLDER, M.F. RYAN, P. MYERS, N. IOVINE, M. PLOURDE, E. WEEKS, J.R. HANLEY, G. ENDRES, D. ST. GERMAINE, P.J. DOBROWOLSKI, AND M. SCHWARTZ. "An Outbreak of Acute Delirium from Exposure to the Synthetic Cannabinoid AB-CHMINACA." *Clinical Toxicology*, 53: 950–56, 2015 (2 tables, 2 figures, 23 references)

Abstract: Between May 28, 2014 and June 8, 2014, thirty-five patients were treated at the University of Florida Medical Center in Gainesville after using the synthetic cannabinoid AB-CHMINACA obtained from a local smoke shop. Five patients had seizures and bradypnea and were intubated and treated in ICU. None died. Serum or plasma AB-CHMINACA concentrations were measured in thirteen patients and ranged from 0.4 to 14.3 ng/mL (median 8.3 ng/mL) by liquid chromatography/quadrupole time of flight mass spectrometry (LC/QTOF/MS).

Table: Percent of Patients with Differing Clinical Presentation

Clinical Presentation	% of Patients
Patients requiring intubation	14.3%
Patients with seizures	40.0%
Patients with ICU admissions	20.0%
Patients with tachycardia (> 100 bpm)	45.7%
Patients with hypertension (> 150/90)	17.1%
Patients with altered mental status (Glasgow Coma Scale < 14)	54.3%

Source: Adapted from Tyndall et al, 2015

The outbreak resulted in acute delirium and seizures and necessitated the hospitalization of ten individuals as well as medical evaluation for another twenty-five individuals. The prompt and coordinated response by EMS, the local public health department, treating clinicians, and law enforcement agencies, as well as the dissemination of public service announcements and control of the source of the implicated product, substantially curtailed the availability of the illicit compound and promoted a rapid and substantial community awareness of the event.

Reference Number: 80409

KEMP, A.M., M.S. CLARK, T. DOBBS, R. GALLI, J. SHERMAN, AND R. COX. "Top 10 Facts You Need to Know About Synthetic Cannabinoids: Not So Nice Spice." *American Journal of Medicine*, 129: 240–44, 2016 (1 table, 6 figures, 22 references)

Abstract: The drug commonly referred to as "Spice" is actually a group of several hundred types of synthetic cannabinoids. Between April 1 and May 31, 2015, Mississippi reported 1,243 ED visits due to adverse effects from synthetic cannabinoids, of which 10 percent required intensive care (ICU) admissions and resulted in an estimated seventeen deaths.

Table: Common Street Names for Synthetic Cannabinoids

Spice	Fake weed	Scooby Snax
K2	Gangsta	Sexy Monkey
Angry Birds	Mojo	Skunk
Bhang	Killa Gorilla	Smacked
Bliss	Moon Rocks	Smoking Santa
Black Mamba	Ninja	Tomcat
Bombay Blue	Mr Nice Guy	WANTED
Dr Feel Good	Outer Space	Yucatan

Source: Adapted from Kemp et al, 2016

Synthetic cannabinoids have emerged as a significant problem resulting in many emergency department visits and even fatalities. To counter this growing problem, it is imperative that providers be aware of these dangerous substances and their effects on patients.

Reference Number: 80410

LABAY, L.M., J.L. CARUSO, T.P. GILSON, R.J. PHIPPS, L.D. KNIGHT, N.P. LEMOS, I.M. MCINTYRE, R. STOPPACHER, L.M. TORMOS, A.L. WIENS, AND B.K. LOGAN. "Synthetic Cannabinoids Drug Use as a Cause or Contributory

Cause of Death." *Forensic Science International*, 260: 31–39, 2016 (6 tables, 12 references)

Abstract: Synthetic cannabinoid CB1 and CB2 receptor agonists were developed to provide therapeutic benefits claimed for botanical cannabis without its psychoactive effects. Twenty-five medical examiner cases in which synthetic cannabinoids were detected are presented.

The results show that some deaths are being attributed to synthetic cannabinoids with the highest risk being behavioural toxicity resulting in excited delirium, trauma, or accidents, and as contributing factors in subjects with pre-existing cardiopulmonary disease.

Reference Number: 80411

LAURITSEN, K.J., AND H. ROSENBERG. "Comparison of Outcome Expectancies for Synthetic Cannabinoids and Botanical Marijuana." *American Journal of Drug and Alcohol Abuse*, 42: 377–84, 2016 (2 tables, 1 figure, 31 references)

Abstract: A web-based study was conducted of 186 adults who used both synthetic and botanical cannabis and 181 adults who used only botanical cannabis. The most common reasons for using cannabis were relief of psychological or psychiatric symptoms (25 percent), relaxation (16 percent), relief of bodily pain (12 percent), enhancing one's mental state (7 percent), treating a medical condition (6 percent), and fun (5 percent). Synthetic cannabis is basically a second choice of botanical cannabis.

Given growing public acceptance of recreational and medical marijuana, coupled with negative perceptions and increasing regulation of synthetic cannabinoid compounds, botanical marijuana is likely to remain more available and more popular than synthetic cannabinoids.

Reference Number: 80412

LOGAN, B.K., L.E. REINHOLD, A. XU, AND F.X. DIAMOND. "Identification of Synthetic Cannabinoids in Herbal Incense Blends in the United States." *Journal of Forensic Sciences*, 57: 1168–80, 2012 (4 tables, 5 figures, 11 references)

Abstract: Synthetic cannabinoids sold over the internet as incense or a legal high were analyzed by TLC, GC/MS, HPLC, and LCTOF. Usually

1–3 g of a mixture of dried and crushed plant material (flowers, stems, or leaves) often with a perfumed aromatic odour. The mixture is sold as incense for burning and can be smoked in either cigarettes, joints, or pipes of the type labelled for marijuana smoking. The most common is K2 and is typically sold in a 2.5 X 2.5 inch metallic Mylar bag with a ziplock closure. The contents of the bag are 1–3 grams of dried and crushed plant material and have a perfumed aromatic odour like pot-pourri. Several samples analyzed contained drug-free material.

This drug market is extremely dynamic with more compounds being substituted for existing ones as legislation attempts to restrict their distribution and use. As there is no governance of this ad hoc drug discovery process, the naming conventions for newly synthesized compounds is likely to be confusing and inconsistent.

Reference Number: 80413

MCILROY, G., L. FORD, AND J.M. KHAN. "Acute Myocardial Infarction, Associated with the Use of a Synthetic Adamantyl-Cannabinoid: A Case Report." *BMC Pharmacology and Toxicology*, 17:2, 2016 (1 figure, 21 references)

Abstract: A 39-year-old man suffered a collapse and cardiac arrest. He smoked "Black Mamba" three hours before admission and urine toxicology was positive for synthetic cannabinoids.

Novel psychoactive compounds are constantly being developed and later prohibited in a cat and mouse game between the legal high manufacturers and governments. Synthetic cannabinoids represent an evolving drug class that are sold openly (although frequently labelled "not for alcohol consumption"), produce stimulant effects in those that smoke them, and are often undetectable on routine toxicology testing. However, because of their unregulated development, synthetic cannabinoids can have potentially serious side effects, putting those that use them at an unknown risk of harm.

Reference Number: 80414

MCKEEVER, R.G., D. VEARRIER, D. JACOBS, G. LASALA, J. OKANEKU, AND M.I. GREENBERG. "K2–Not the Spice of Life; Synthetic Cannabinoids and

ST Elevation Myocardial Infarction: A Case Report." *Journal of Medical Toxicology* 11: 129–31, 2015 (1 figure, 15 references)

Abstract: Synthetic cannabinoids have become widely used due to commercial availability, a perceived more intense high and not detected by routine immunoassay urine drug screens. They have a variety of names such as K2, Spice, Genie, Sense, Moon Rock, and Black Mamba. Synthetic cannabinoid use has been associated with tachycardia, agitation, vomiting, seizures, myocardial infarction, and transient ischemic attacks. A 16-year-old man attended hospital after using K2 rather than cannabis, to avoid the weekly urine drug tests while on parole. He suffered chest pains for twenty-four hours and his ECG showed ST elevation.

> To our knowledge, this is the first report of ST-elevation myocardial infarction in the setting of synthetic cannabinoid use without concomitant marijuana use.

Reference Number: 80415

ALADAG-CIFTDEMIR, N., I. YUCEL, R. DURAN, U. VATANSEVER-OZBEK, AND B. ACUANS. "A New Emerging Problem in Pediatric Emergency Units: Synthetic Cannabinoids." *The Turkish Journal of Pediatrics*, 58: 492–97, 2016 (1 table, 22 references)

Abstract: Six male and three female pediatric patients (ages 7 months to 17 years) attended the ED as a result of synthetic cannabinoids ingestion between 2013 and 2015 in Turkey. The 7-month-old girl was chewing an herbal substance containing SC that was used by her mother. The most common SC was Bonzai. Two patients required hospitalization. Use of SC by adolescents is increasing as it is inexpensive, easy to obtain, and difficult to detect.

Table: Clinical Findings of Pediatric Patients with Synthetic Cannabinoid Overdose

Case No.	Age/Gender	Admission Complaint	Additional Clinical Findings	Heart Rate (bpm)	Blood Pressure (mmHg)
1	16/male	Palpitation	Tachycardia Hypertension	150	146/88
2	14/female	Faintness	Vertigo Confusion	98	110/70

Case No.	Age/Gender	Admission Complaint	Additional Clinical Findings	Heart Rate (bpm)	Blood Pressure (mmHg)
3	12/male	Dizziness Drowsiness	Vertigo Tendency to sleep Skin rash Perioral cyanosis	82	90/50
4	17/male	Unconsciousness Generalized muscle Contractions	Somnolence Tremor Muscle spasm Mydriasis	100	115/63
5	17/female	Faintness Inability to speak	Tremor Incessant laughing Hypertension Tendency to sleep	76	190/120
6	15/male	Confusion	Tendency to sleep	76	108/70
7	12/male	Faintness	Confusion Tachycardia Mydriasis	120	120/70
8	15/male	Contractions Thirst	Muscle spasm Confusion	88	110/70
9	7 months/ female	Somnolence	Somnolence Increased oxygen saturation	90	80/50

Source: Adapted from Aladag-Ciftdemir et al, 2016

All the patients in our study have either expressed using Bonzai themselves or the witnesses have told that they use Bonzai, but the validation test has not been carried out. There may be clinical discrepancies between patients worldwide because ingredients of SC-containing substances may differ from each other in different locations and time periods. Probably more patients hiding their substance use admit to our pediatric emergency department with various symptoms. With the increase of awareness and information on this issue, we think that clinicians will more quickly recognize such patients.

Reference Number: 80416

MIR, A., A. OBAFEMI, A. YOUNG, AND C. KANE. "Myocardial Infarction Associated with Use of the Synthetic Cannabinoid K2." *Pediatrics,* 128: e6, 2011 (3 figures, 21 references)

Abstract: Three 16-year-old boys presented to ER with chest pains. All had ECGs that showed ST-segment elevation and all had used K2 within several days prior to presentation.

Although chest pain is a common presenting complaint of teenagers seen in emergency departments, chest pain from cardiac causes remains exceedingly rare. Use of illicit drugs causing chest pain and myocardial ischemia, however, must remain part of the differential diagnosis. Because synthetic cannabinoids do not currently show on routine toxicology screening tests, careful questioning is necessary to elicit a history of exposure to K2 or similar products.

Reference Number: 80417

MUSHOFF, F., B. MADEA, G. KERNBACH-WIGHTON, W. BUCKER, S. KNEISEL, M. HUTTER, AND V. AUWATER. "Driving Under the Influence of Synthetic Cannabinoids (Spice): A Case Series." *International Journal of Legal Medicine,* 128: 59–64, 2014 (2 tables, 48 references)

Abstract: Seven case reports are presented of impaired driving while under the influence of synthetic cannabinoids like Spice or K2. Synthetic cannabinoids have a much greater affinity to the CB1 receptors than THC, indicating a high potency. CB1 receptors are found in the brain and peripheral nervous system and affect perception, motor function, and sense of time. Low doses of synthetic cannabis in less than 1 ng/mL can cause impairment of driving ability.

Table: Some Adverse Clinical Effects of Spice

Central Effect	Cardiovascular Effects	Gastrointestinal Effects	Other Effects
Agitation	Cardiotoxicity	Nausea	Appetite changes
Anxiety	Chest pains	Vomiting	Brisk reflexes
Confusion	Tachyarrhythmia		Dilated pupils
Irritability	Tachycardia		Emesis
Memory changes			Somnolence
Psychosis			Tolerance
Sedation			Withdrawal/Drug dependence
Seizures			

Source: Adapted from Mushoff et al, 2014

In internet forums, it is advised to consume these products because neither quick test used by the police nor immunoassay-based routine drug testing procedures are able to detect these drugs. Therefore, in drug rehabilitation or abstinence programs, e.g., in the context of driving license issues, former cannabis users change to synthetic cannabinoids as a substitute. The bottom line is that police as well as forensic toxicologists and other groups need to become familiar with the effects of synthetic cannabinoid use and develop some awareness of the problem.

Reference Number: 80418

OBAFEMI, A.I., K. KLEINSCHMIDT, C. GOTO, AND D. FOUT. "Cluster of Acute Toxicity for Ingestion of Synthetic Cannabinoid-Laced Brownies." *Journal of Medical Toxicology*, 11: 426–29, 2015 (1 table, 26 references)

Abstract: Five male and six female staff (ages 20 to 57 years) of an inpatient unit of a large hospital consumed one brownie each that contained a synthetic cannabinoid receptor agonist (SCRA), AM-201, which was added by another staff member's son. The onset of symptoms occurred within one hour (most between 25 to 45 minutes) after ingestion, and lasted usually between two to four hours. Symptoms included memory impairment (91 percent), inappropriate giggling (36 percent), dry mouth (100 percent), blurring of vision (100 percent), and numbness and tingling sensation (100 percent). The urine screens for other drugs were negative.

Clinicians need to consider oral exposure to SCRAs as potential etiology in patients presenting with unexplained symptoms.

Reference Number: 80419

ORSINI, J., C. BLAAK, E. TAM, S. RAJAYER, J. MORANTE, A. YEH, AND A. BUTALA. "The Wide and Unpredictable Scope of Synthetic Cannabinoids Toxicity." *Case Reports in Critical Care*, 2015, 5 pp (3 figures, 38 references)

Abstract: A 41-year-old man was brought to ED after having a tonic-clonic seizure in the street. He had a history of polydrug abuse. A bag of K2 (spice), a synthetic cannabinoid, was found on his person. He suffered acute hypoxemic/hypercapnia respiratory failure resulting from acute congestive heart failure.

This case illustrates for health care workers the possible life-threatening adverse effects of synthetic cannabinoids abuse. Although there is no specific toxidrome associated with synthetic cannabinoids intoxication, clinicians should suspect their involvement in patients presenting with signs and symptoms of drug overdose.

Reference Number: 80420

PATTON, A.L., K.C. CHIMALAKONDA, C.L. MORAN, K.R. MCCAIN, A. RADOMINSKA-PANDYA, L.P. JAMES, C. KOKES, AND J.H. MORAN. "K2 Toxicity: Fatal Case of Psychiatric Complications Following AM2201 Exposure." *Journal of Forensic Sciences*, 58: 1676–80, 2013 (4 figures, 31 references)

Abstract: Synthetic cannabinoids (SC) first appeared in Europe in 2005 and in the US in 2009. A 23-year-old man with no known history of mental illness or drug addiction was found dead from self-inflicted knife wounds to the neck. Various smoking devices were found and packages labelled as "Mad Hatter Incense" and "ZAN-X Extra Relaxation," containing a green plant material, were found as well. Postmortem blood was found to contain 12 ng/mL AM2201 and its metabolite (2.5 ng/mL).

The case described here indicates the potential mortality associated with the psychiatric complications of SC exposure. As exhibited in this case, SC exposure is not typical of THC and can induce adverse responses commonly observed with PCP, cocaine, and methamphetamine overdose.

Reference Number: 80421

RIEDERER, A.M., S.L. CAMPLEMAN, R.G. CARLSON, E.W. BOYER, A.F. MANANI, P.M. WAX, AND J.A. BRENT. "Acute Poisonings from Synthetic Cannabinoids: 50 US Toxicology Investigators Consortium Registry Sites, 2010–2015." *Morbidity and Mortality Weekly Report*, 65: 692–95, 2015 (1 table, 2 figures, 10 references)

Abstract: Synthetic cannabis were initially research compounds produced in the 1980s, which are two to one hundred times more potent than THC and are now produced in illicit drug labs. The most common name for the synthetic cannabinoids are K2 and Spice. Between 2010 and 2015, there were 456 cases of synthetic cannabinoid intoxication at fifty hospitals throughout the US. Of these, 277 were sole and 179 combined with other drugs. During the same time period, only three cannabis cases were logged in and the majority were children and teenagers. Among the 456 synthetic cannabinoid cases, 83 percent were male and

27 percent between 13 and 18 years of age. The most common symptoms were agitation, CNS depression, coma, delirium, and toxic psychosis. Three deaths were recorded. There was a 330 percent increase in synthetic cannabis calls to US Poison Centers in the first four months of 2015.

> The increase in acute synthetic cannabinoid poisonings observed in toxic underscores the need for targeted prevention interventions. Educating the public on the potentially life-threatening consequences of synthetic cannabinoid use is important for countering the observed upward trend in synthetic cannabinoid poisonings.

Reference Number: 80422

VANDREY, R., K.E. DUNN, J.A. FRY, AND E.R. GIRLING. "A Survey Study to Characterize Use of Spice Products (Synthetic Cannabinoids)." *Drug and Alcohol Dependence*, 120: 238–41, 2012 (1 table, 21 references)

Abstract: An internet survey was conducted of 168 synthetic cannabis users in the US in 2011. The respondents were mainly male (83 percent), 92 percent consumed alcohol, 84 percent cannabis, 66 percent tobacco, 37 percent hallucinogens, and 34 percent prescription opioids. The mean age of first time use was 26 years and the mean number of daily uses was four times. Eighty-seven percent reported obtaining Spice products from retail vendors (head shops, gas stations), 38 percent obtained them from the internet, and 29 percent from friends. The primary reasons for use were curiosity (78 percent), liked the effect (58 percent), and relaxation (48 percent). Thirty percent reported using SCs to avoid a positive cannabinoid urine test. Most reported they believed Spice products were generally safe for human use.

Table: Percentage of Synthetic Cannabinoid Users and Subjective Positive and Negative Effects

		Never	Sometimes	Most of the Time	Every Time
Positive Effects	Felt a pleasant high	4%	17%	42%	37%
	Had increased appetite	27%	36%	23%	14%
	Felt stimulated/ energetic	32%	50%	15%	3%
	Unable to control laughter	51%	33%	11%	5%

		Never	Sometimes	Most of the Time	Every Time
Negative Effects	Had a dry mouth	22%	34%	30%	14%
	Had trouble remembering	36%	43%	16%	5%
	Felt heart racing	41%	43%	10%	6%
	Felt paranoid	46%	43%	10%	1%
	Vomited	90%	9%	1%	0%

Source: Adapted from Vandrey et al, 2012

In summary, the present case report survey indicates that Spice product use is similar to that of other abused drugs. The frequency, manner, and consequences of use vary widely, and range from those who engage in sporadic use without negative consequence to those who experience acute adverse reactions to the drug and those who develop significant problems related to chronic use.

Reference Number: 80423

ROSE, D.Z., W.R. GUERNO, M.V. MOKIN, C.L. GOOCH, A.C. BOZEMAN, J.M. PEARSON, AND W.S. BURGIN. "Hemorrhagic Stroke Following Use of the Synthetic Marijuana Spice." *American Academy of Neurology*, 85: 1177–79, 2015 (2 figures, 10 references)

Abstract: A 31-year-old man and a 25-year-old woman presented at hospital with a subarachnoid hemorrhage (SAH) after inhaling Spice (K2 or herbal incense). Both were previously healthy.

Physicians, nurses, emergency medical technicians, hospitals, public health officials, educators, and law enforcement see dangers of inhaled synthetic compounds firsthand. Collectively, we should address this growing public health threat aggressively.

Reference Number: 80424

SAMAAN, J., G.F. FERRER, B. AKINYEMI, P. JUNQUERA, J. OMS, AND R. DUMENIGO. "Synthetic Cannabis Overdose and Withdrawal in a Young Adult: A Case Report, Commentary on Regulation, and Review of the Literature." *Case Reports in Psychiatry,* 7 pp, 2016 (1 table, 31 references)

Abstract: An 18-year-old man was brought to the ED after five days of acute auditory hallucinations, paranoid delusions, and panic attacks. The patient had a history of cannabis abuse and used synthetic cannabis.

The urine test was negative for cannabinoids. The patient was released under the care of a psychiatrist and recovered.

> This case, as many others nationwide, exemplifies the impact of synthetic cannabinoid use and abuse in adolescents. Side effects and adverse health consequences of synthetic cannabinoid use warrant stricter regulations and policies in order to decrease psychiatric hospital admissions and associated health care costs.

Reference Number: 80425

SPRINGER, Y.P., R. GERONA, E. SCHEUNEMANN, S.L. SHAFER, T. LIN, S.D. BANISTER, M.P. COOPER, L.J. CASTRODALE, M. LEVY, J.C. BUTLER, AND J.B. MCLAUGHLIN. "Increase in Adverse Reactions Associated with Use of Synthetic Cannabinoids – Anchorage, Alaska, 2015–2016." *Morbidity and Mortality Weekly Report,* 65: 1108–11, 2016 (2 tables, 9 references)

Abstract: Synthetic cannabinoids (SC) are a chemically diverse class of designer drugs that bind to the same cannabinoid receptors as THC. Between July 2015 and March 2016, a total of 1,351 ambulance transports to ER occurred in Anchorage due to adverse SC reactions. Eleven different SCs were identified. Some SCs were clear viscous liquids labelled as car air fresheners and could easily be vaped using e-cigarettes. Forty percent of patients were homeless, 7 percent required endotracheal intubation, and 10 percent required intensive care. Lethargy, confusion, agitation, and aggressiveness were common reactions. The percent of SC-related ambulance transports were 0.9 percent pre-outbreak, 7.1 percent pre-ordinance, and 4.0 percent post-ordinance. Judicial and law enforcement actions limited the SC manufacturing and distribution and educational outreach was also conducted to limit the outbreak.

Table: Percentage of Clinical Signs for 167 ED Visits Due to Use of Synthetic Cannabinoids

Clinical Signs	% of ED visits
Lethargy (confusion, somnolence, sleep, unresponsiveness)	68.9%
Agitation (distress, anxiety, aggressiveness, violence)	32.9%
Both lethargy and agitation	22.2%
Tachypnea (respiratory rate > 16 breaths/minute)	45.5%
Tachycardia (heart rate > 100 bpm)	31.1%
Required physical restraint en route to hospital	15.6%
Intubation	6.6%

Reference Number: 80425

Clinical Signs	% of ED visits
Admission to ICU	0.2%

Source: Adapted from Springer et al, 2016

Educational outreach campaigns focused on the considerable health risks of SC use need to complement judicial and law enforcement actions to reduce SC use, particularly among groups at high risk, such as homeless populations.

Reference Number: 80426

USTUNDAG, M.F., E.O. IBIS, A. YUCEL, AND H. OZCAN. "Synthetic Cannabis-Induced Mania." *Case Reports in Psychiatry,* 3 pp, 2015 (11 references)

Abstract: Synthetic cannabinoids (SC) are psychoactive substances that are CB1 and CB2 agonists. SC is known as chronic and K2. An 18-year-old male developed mania after using SC for six months (several times per week) before presenting to the clinic with mystical and grandiose delusions. He was treated with anti-psychotic drugs.

The use of SC is now a serious health problem. SC is also being sprayed on different herbal mixtures and similar to cannabis smoking as mixtures of herbal cigarettes are released. SC is a more powerful stimulant than natural cannabinoids. SC is easy to obtain and undetermined in routine tests. SC is also easily accessible.

Reference Number: 80427

ALTINTAS, M., L. INANC, G.A. ORUC, S. ARPACIOGLU, AND H. GULEC. "Clinical Characteristics of Synthetic Cannabinoid-Induced Psychosis in Relation to Schizophrenia: A Single-Center Cross-Sectional Analysis of Concurrently Hospitalized Patients." *Neuropsychiatric Disease and Treatment*, 12: 1893–1900, 2016 (4 tables, 47 references)

Abstract: Fifty male patients (mean age 25.9 years), who were diagnosed with a psychotic disorder related to synthetic cannabis use, and thirty-one patients with schizophrenia (mean age 42.9 years) were compared. The mean age of psychosis onset was 22.3 years for SC users. Suicidal ideation occurred in 26 percent of the SC-induced psychosis patients and 58.4 percent were hospitalized involuntarily. Cannabis was the most common first used substance (72 percent). SC-induced psychosis is considered an acute onset psychosis that typically lasts from one to five weeks with an average hospital stay of 8.5 days.

> Paranoia, disorganized behaviour, visual and auditory hallucinations, and suicidal thoughts are considered among the psychotic-like symptoms that can be triggered by SCs, not only in vulnerable individuals but also in subjects with no previous history of psychosis. Indeed, the rarity of negative symptoms in SC-induced psychosis has been reported; the term "spiceophrenia" is used to refer to the involvement of hallucinations, delusions, and increased positive psychotic symptoms in SC-induced psychosis. Therefore, our findings are in line with the publications describing SC psychosis and support that SCs may trigger new-onset psychosis in otherwise healthy young men with no previous history of psychosis. This seems notable, given that exposure to cannabis in adolescence is thought to contribute to an increased risk of psychosis later in life.

Reference Number: 80428

CASTANETO, M.S., K.B. SCHEIDWEILER, A. GANDHI, A. WOHLFARTH, K.L. KLETTE, T.M. MARTIN, AND M.A. HUESTIS. "Quantitative Urine Confirmatory Testing for Synthetic Cannabinoids in Randomly Collected Urine Specimens." *Drug Testing and Analysis,* 7: 483–93, 2015 (4 tables, 2 figures, 58 references)

Abstract: Twenty thousand and seventeen randomly selected US military urine samples were screened using synthetic cannabinoid immunoassay between 2011 and 2012. There were 1,432 presumptive positive samples, of which LC/MS/MS confirmed 290 positive samples that contained 22 metabolites from 11 parent SCs. The most common metabolites detected were from JWH-018, AM2201, and JWH-073.

> Synthetic cannabinoids and their metabolites do not cross-react with routine cannabinoid immunoassays, making them desirable for circumventing drug detection efforts. Urine drug testing programs typically employ immunoassay screening for identifying presumptive positive specimens and confirmation by GC-MS or LC-MS/MS. Immunoassay screening for synthetic cannabinoids is challenging due to the time required to raise antibodies to metabolites of constantly varying new drugs on the market and to develop, validate, and commercialize new

assays. Therefore, many laboratories are developing mass spectrometric screening methods for synthetic cannabinoids.

Reference Number: 80429

GIERON, J., AND P. ADAMOWICZ. "Fatal Poisoning with the Synthetic Cannabinoid AB-CHMINACA and Ethyl Alcohol: A Case Study and Literature Review." *Problems of Forensic Science*, 106: 482–95, 2016 (2 tables, 2 figures, 13 references)

Abstract: The synthetic cannabinoid AB-CHMINACA is considered to be much more potent compared to other SCs, but is also described by users as having the most similar effects to marijuana. Animal studies show that it is eleven to fifty-eight times more potent than THC. A male alcoholic in his thirties smoked a pipe with the herbal mixture "Strongman." After two puffs he collapsed and became unconscious. One hour later he was dead. The postmortem blood, urine, and vitreous humor alcohol concentrations were 0.180 g/100 mL, 0.278 g/100mL, and 0.226 g/100mL respectively. The postmortem blood and urine AB-CHMINACA concentrations were 1.5 ng/mL and 0.1 ng/mL respectively.

This case is the first in which the simultaneous presence of AB-CHMINACA and ethyl alcohol was demonstrated, which may indicate a dangerous depressive effect of both these substances on the central nervous system.

Reference Number: 80430

SHANKS, K.G., W. CLARK, AND G. BEHONICK. "Death Associated with the Use of the Synthetic Cannabinoid ADB-FUBINACA." *Journal of Analytical Toxicology*, 40: 236–39, 2016 (3 tables, 1 figure, 23 references)

Abstract: Synthetic cannabinoids are man-made substances that bind to the cannabinoid receptors CB1 and CB2. A new SC was detected by GC-MS/MS called ADB-FUBINACA. A 41-year-old woman smoked an SC known as Mojo. Shortly after consumption, she became violent and aggressive toward the family. She was restrained by family members and became non-responsive. She was declared dead by emergency responders. The postmortem blood contained 7.3 ng/mL ADB-FUBINACA, 1.1 ng/mL THC, and 4.7 ng/mL THCCOOH.

The decedent's cause of death was certified as coronary arterial thrombosis in combination with synthetic cannabinoid use. Manner of death was accidental.

Reference Number: 80431

SHEIKH, I.A., M. LUKSIC, R. FERSTENBERG, AND J.A. CULPEPER-MORGAN. "SPICE/K2 Synthetic Marijuana-Induced Toxic Hepatitis Treated with N-Acetylcysteine." *American Journal of Case Reports*, 15: 584–88, 2014 (1 table, 1 figure, 22 references)

Abstract: A 45-year-old drug abuser was admitted to hospital due to somnolence, fatigue, and lethargy. It was determined that he had hepatocellular necrosis and worsening liver failure. He tested negative for acetaminophen or alcohol. His treatment included N-acetylcysteine and he eventually recovered. He admitted to smoking Spice/K2 prior to hospital admission.

Health care providers should suspect Spice/K2 as a possible cause of unexplained liver injury and failure, especially when caring for individuals with a history of substance abuse.

Reference Number: 80432

SCHNEIR, A.B., AND T. BAUMBACHER. "Convulsions Associated with the Use of a Synthetic Cannabinoid Product." *Journal of Medical Toxicology*, 8: 62–64, 2012 (24 references)

Abstract: A 19-year-old male had a witnessed, generalized one to two minute convulsion while smoking a synthetic cannabinoid product called "Happy Tiger Incense." During his transportation to hospital, the patient vomited and had a second generalized seizure, which was treated with 5 mg of midazolam. The remains of the "incense" he smoked was analyzed and found to contain four synthetic cannabinoids, JW-018, JWH-250, JWH-081, and MA2201.

Convulsions have only rarely been associated with marijuana exposures. Recreational use of synthetic cannabinoids is a very recent phenomenon and there is a very limited, albeit burgeoning, literature detailing the associated complications, including the convulsions we have reported here. The absence of anti-convulsant phytocannabinoids in Spice products could potentially be one of multiple unknown mechanisms contributing to convulsions.

Reference Number: 80433

ZARIFFI, C., AND S. VYAS. "Spice-y Kidney Failure: A Case Report and Systematic Review of Acute Kidney Injury Attributable to the Use of Synthetic Cannabis." *The Permanente Journal*, 21: 16–160, 2017 (1 table, 1 figure, 15 references)

Abstract: A 21-year-old man presented to hospital with new onset seizures after using the synthetic cannabinoid Spice during the previous month. Over the next two days, the patient developed uncontrolled hypotension, agitation, respiratory failure (requiring intubation), and acute kidney injury (AKI). He recovered with supportive therapy. It is proposed that Spice and its metabolites are toxic to the kidney because they bind to cannabinoid 2 receptors in the kidney. Spice abuse is an ongoing issue that has affected many people in the US, especially in Southern California.

Spice, a synthetic cannabinoid, is an increasingly popular new street drug that often is perceived as harmless by young adults because it is easily accessible and sold in smoke shops, convenience stores, and online as an herbal blend, incense, or air freshener. Spice is also a popular drug because it is not detectable on conventional urine drug screens. A 2012 study revealed that 11 percent of high school seniors admitted to Spice use during the previous twelve months. The first case of acute kidney injury (AKI) related to synthetic cannabinoid use was described in 2012, even though synthetic cannabinoids have been on the market since the 2000s. A new Spice metabolite, likely introduced in 2012, is associated with AKI.

Reference Number: 80434

KATZ, K.D., A.L. LEONETTI, B.C. BAILEY, R.M. SURMAITIS, E.R. EUSTICE, S. KACINKO, AND S.M. WHEATLEY. "Case Series of Synthetic Cannabinoid Intoxication from One Toxicology Center." *Western Journal of Emergency Medicine*, 17: 290–94, 2016 (1 table, 12 references)

Abstract: Eleven patients (ages 13 to 50 years of age) presented at an ED in Pennsylvania between April and June 2015 as a result of exposure to the synthetic cannabinoid MAB-CHMINACA. All patients required sedation for agitation, nine required intubation, three had seizures, one developed hyperthermia, and one developed anoxic brain injury and died. Urine drug testing by LC/MS confirmed SC use.

Table: Summary of Cases Involving Eleven Patients Presenting to the Emergency Department after Use of Synthetic Cannabinoids.

Case (Number, age, gender)	Clinical Presentation	Intubated	Outcome
#1 (18yo male)	Altered mental status, combative, agitated	No	Discharged same day
#2 (28yo male)	Combative and hallucinating	Yes	Developed aspiration pneumonia, discharged after 6 days
#3 (17yo female)	Agitated and delirious	No	Discharged following day
#4 (14yo male)	Intermittent unresponsiveness, followed by agitation	Yes	Discharged following day
#5 (13yo female)	Altered mental status with unresponsiveness	Yes	Discharged after 2 days
#6 (13yo male)	Found unresponsive	Yes	Developed aspiration pneumonia, discharged after 3 days
#7 (50yo male)	Found unresponsive	Yes	Discharged to inpatient drug rehabilitation facility
#8 (40yo female)	Combative, delirious, seizures	Yes	Discharged after 2 days
#9 (19yo female)	Found unresponsive, seizure-like activity	Yes	Treated for infected forearm wound secondary to IV drug use. Discharged after 4 days.
#10 (14yo male)	Agitated and combative	Yes	Discharged following day
#11 (20yo male)	Found unresponsive and posturing; approximate down-time was 24 to 36 hours	Yes	Expired. Anoxic brain injury. Family withdrew care after 7 days.

Limitations in real-time detection by routine toxicologic immunoassay screening appear to be a factor in SC use. The reasons for the abrupt, recent increase in exposures, however, remain unclear. The celebration of 4/20 (a counterculture holiday celebrating cannabis) correlated with this surge and might have influenced users. Management of the SC-intoxicated patient centres on meticulous supportive care, as no specific antidote currently exists. Decontamination is of little value. Given their beneficial pharmacokinetic profile, administration of benzodiazepines titrated to clinical effect can control agitation, delirium, hyperthermia, and seizures. Cooling measures without antipyretic administration can also be implemented for hyperthermic patients. Administration of intravenous fluids is helpful for associated rhabdomyolysis. Endotracheal intubation may be required for the severely intoxicated patient. SCs pose a substantial and dangerous public health risk. Emergency physicians must be aware of their clinical presentation, difficulties in identification, and treatment. Further studies are required to elucidate the exact mechanisms of SCs and, more specifically, MAB-CHMINACA toxicity.

Reference Number: 80435

LANK, P.M., E. PINES, AND M.B MYCK. "Emergency Physicians' Knowledge of Cannabinoid Designer Drugs." *Western Journal of Emergency Medicine,* 14: 467–70, 2013 (2 tables, 1 figure, 13 references)

Abstract: A survey was conducted of seventy-three emergency physicians (EPs) at a large academic urban ED about synthetic cannabinoids. Two-thirds of EPs had never heard of Spice and 51 percent had never heard of K2. Twenty-five percent of EPs familiar with SCs were not aware that they are synthetic drugs.

This study showed unfamiliarity and inexperience with SC among EPs during a time when their use was growing in popularity. Even among those familiar with SC, there were many misconceptions about SC and their clinical effects, with most physicians obtaining their information from non-medical sources. This study brings to light the problems physicians face when treating patients who are using new drugs of abuse. Specifically, it became clear that there is an inherent difficulty in treating patients using a new drug of abuse because of a lack of available medical literature on the substance. Further confounding the issue, the medical literature that is available constantly changes with reports of novel side effects and complications.

Reference Number: 80436

LERNER, A.G., C. GOODMAN, O. BAR, AND S.L. RAN. "Synthetic Cannabis Substances (SCS) Use and Hallucinogen Persisting Perception Disorder (HPPD): Two Case Reports." *Israeli Journal of Psychiatry and Related Science*, 51: 277–80, 2014 (25 references)

Abstract: Two male cannabis users (ages 26 and 24 years) who used botanical cannabis for years developed a Hallucinogen Persisting Perception Disorder (HPPD) after heavy use of synthetic cannabinoids (e.g., Spice, Nice Guy). Both men had visual disturbances when smoking SCs and both discontinued use after suffering panic attacks, but they continued to experience visual disturbances despite abstention. Both were treated with clonazepam and reported substantial improvement in symptoms.

The use of Natural Cannabis Substances (NCS), which are CB1 receptor partial agonists, has been associated with the appearance of perceptual disturbances during use and after total cessation. Thus, it is plausible to expect that the intake of Synthetic Cannabis Substances (SCS) like JWH-018, JWH-073, and HU-210 that are generally CB1 full receptor agonists and were also associated with the appearance of perceptual disturbances during use might affect some predisposed and susceptible users, provoking a partial or total recapitulation of the previous perceptual experience in the absence of SCS use. We present the cases of two SCS users with prior history of NCS use who reported the presence of Hallucination Perception Persisting Disorder (HPPD) after stopping SCS consumption. To the best of our knowledge, this is the first report of SCS-associated HPPD in the professional literature.

Reference Number: 80437

SOLIMINI, R., F.P. BUSCARDO, M.C. ROTOLO, S. RICCI, L. MASTROBATTISTA, C. MORTALI, S. GRANZIANO, M. PELLEGRINI, N.M. DI LUCA, AND I. PALMI. "Hepatotoxicity Associated to Synthetic Cannabinoids Use." *European Review for Medical and Pharmacological Sciences*, 21 (1 Suppl): 1–6, 2017 (25 references)

Abstract: Synthetic cannabinoids (SCs) were first developed in the 1960s to better understand the endocannabinoid system and receptors. SCs are of at least thirteen different types and have receptor affinities 2 to

800 times that of THC. Some of the numerous SCs are given initials for where they were synthesized, e.g., HU-Hebrew University, CP- Charles Pfizer and Company, and JWH for the researcher John W. Huffman. Two young males who had SC-related liver failure had positive 5F-PB-22 serum concentrations of 1.3 and 1.5 ng/mL respectively.

Table: The Main Synthetic Cannabinoid Chemical Families and Their Principal Compounds

Synthetic Cannabinoid Chemical Family	Principal Compounds
Benzoylindole	AM-694, AM-2233, AM-679, RCS-4, RCS-8
Naphthoylindole	JWH-018, JWH-022, JWH-073, JWH-081, JWH-122, JWH-210
Phenylacetylindole	JWH-167, JWH- 250, JWH-315
Indazolecarboxamide	ADB-PINACA, ADB-FUBINACA, AB-PINACA, CP-55
Cyclohexylphenyl	CP-55, CP-47
Naphthylmethylindole	JWH-175
Naphthylpyrrole	JWH-145, JWH-307, JWH-370
Naphthylmethylindene	JWH-176, JWH-220
Aminoalkylindole	WIN-55, 212-2
Adamantoylindoles	AB-001
Tetramethylcyclopropylketone indole	UR-144, XLR-11
Quinolinyl ester indole	5F-PB-22, PB-22
Dibenzopyram	HU-210, JWH-133

SCs consumption is dangerously widespread worldwide and cases of severe health effects, including overdoses and deaths, are alarmingly growing. Young people use SCs as an apparently legal alternative to cannabis and are also being tricked by the external aspect of the product made of herbs marked as harmless, but actually added with potent synthetic compounds. Unexplained liver injuries can be suspected to be Spice/K2-related, particularly in substance abusers. An increasing use of SCs in adolescents and young adults is a matter of great concern, especially for physicians and pediatricians who have to deal with toxic health effects (cardiovascular, psychoactive, neurological, metabolic, gastrointestinal, renal, pulmonary, ophthalmologic) more severe than those caused by cannabis and difficult to clinically identify.

Reference Number: 80438

SHANKS, K.G., T. DAHN, AND A.R. TERRELL. "Detection of JHW-018 and JWH-073 by UPLC-MS-MS in Postmortem Whole Blood Casework." *Journal of Analytical Toxicology*, 36: 145–52, 2012 (5 tables, 5 figures, 19 references)

Abstract: Many of the synthetic cannabinoids were synthesized at Dr. John W. Huffman's research laboratory at Clemson University in the 1980s and 1990s. During the approximately twenty years of research, about 450 SCs were synthesized. Hence, the name for many SCs have the initials "JHW." A method is described to determine the postmortem blood JHW-018 and JHW-073 concentrations by ultra-high-performance liquid chromatography tandem mass spectrometry (UPLC-MS-MS) using a liquid/liquid extraction technique. Serum is not a typical sample encountered in postmortem toxicology, as it is very improbable (or impossible) to separate hemolyzed blood into serum. In eighteen postmortem cases, the blood JWH-018 concentration ranged from 0.1 to 199 ng/mL and JWH-073 from 0.1 to 88.3 ng/mL. JWH-073 was detected about one-half the times as JWH-018.

Table: Postmortem Blood JWH-018 and JWH-073 Concentrations in Three Case Reports

Case Number	Case Report	JWH-018 Concentration (ng/mL)	JWH-073 Concentration (ng/mL)	Other Drugs Detected
1	A 57-year-old man was found unresponsive by emergency medical services and later died at hospital. He was known as a SC user and JHW-018 was found at the scene.	199 ng/mL	Not detected	Clonazepam, Methadone, Morphine, Naloxone
2	A 52-year-old man was found nude and unresponsive at his parent's residence. He was an avid SC user. A K2 herbal package was found at the scene.	19.6 ng/mL	68.3 ng/mL	None detected

Case Number	Case Report	JWH-018 Concentration (ng/mL)	JWH-073 Concentration (ng/mL)	Other Drugs Detected
3	A 29-year-old man committed suicide following smoking a K2 blend.	83.3 ng/mL	Not detected	None detected

Source: Adapted from Shanks, Dahn, and Terrell, 2012

JWH-018 and JWH-073 are members of the naphthoylindole group of synthetic cannabinoids, which have been detected in various herbal incense smoking blends that can be readily purchased via convenience stores, gas stations, and the internet. The DEA has temporarily placed JWH-018 and JWH-073 into schedule I of the Controlled Substances Act. These compounds are agonists at the cannabinoid receptors in the body and can produce some severe side effects. For these reasons, these compounds are of forensic significance and the modern forensic toxicology laboratory must be able to detect them in the typical biological matrices, including whole blood.

Reference Number: 80439

DE HAVENON, C., A.B. CHIN, K.C. THOMAS, AND P. AFRA. "The Secret Spice: An Undetectable Toxic Cause of Seizure." *The Neurohospitalist,* 1: 182–86, 2011 (2 figures, 21 references)

Abstract: A 24-year-old man and 36-year-old woman, both with polydrug abuse, attended ED for generalized clonic-tonic seizures after smoking Spice, a synthetic cannabinoid (SC). Synthetic cannabinoids will not cross-react or be detected with traditional cannabinoid immunoassay methods.

Spice is an umbrella term for a variety of synthetic cannabinoid products whose inhalation has been associated with an increasing number of toxic side effects, resulting in emergency department visits. These side effects (including psychosis, tachyarrhythmia, and seizures) are not typically seen with marijuana (cannabis sativa) use. We report two patients with no prior history of neurological disease that experienced their first generalized tonic-clonic seizure after smoking Spice. The mechanisms behind the possible pro-convulsant effect of synthetic cannabinoids is not known but it may be due to their effects at the cannabinoid receptor (CB1). Although the US Drug Enforcement Administration placed five synthetic cannabinoids into schedule 1 for a twelve-month period beginning March 2011, new Spice products containing different synthetic cannabinoids continue to emerge. Because synthetic cannabinoids are not detectable on commercial drug screens, it is important that neurologists and emergency department physicians consider Spice inhalation in their differential diagnosis of a first generalized seizure.

Reference Number: 80440

SARSU, S.B. "Unusual Side Effect of Cannabis Use: Acute Abdomen due to Duodenal Perforation." *International Journal of Emergency Medicine*, 9: 18–22, 2016 (2 figures, 11 references)

Abstract: A 16-year-old boy who had been regularly using the synthetic cannabinoid bonsai for the past three years was admitted to hospital for abdominal pain, abnormal distension, and bilious vomiting. He was diagnosed with peptic ulcer disease (PUC), which is rarely seen in adolescents. Surgical intervention with an omental patch and primary closure (Graham patch) was successful. Chronic use of cannabinoids can result in harmful gastric effects, such as a delay in gastric emptying and hyperemesis.

> Development of duodenal perforation due to the chronic use of SC is an unusual condition. There, patients can consult to the emergency service with recurrent abdominal pain. Since their use is forbidden by law, the patients do not tell they are using SC in their anamnesis. In order to determine etiology, it is important to investigate the use of addictive substances that are increasingly popular among adolescent cases admitted to the emergency services with PUD or its complications.

8.05 OTHER CANNABINOIDS

THCV illustrates the problem of relying on NIAD-grown standard cannabis for research and may not reflect what cannabis is used for in the field (80501). Cannabinol (CBN) is a decomposition product of THC during storage and has about 10 percent the psychoactivity of THC (80504).

THCA (tetrahydrocannabolic acid) is the non-psychoactive precursor of THC found in fresh cannabis plants. It converts to THC upon drying and especially upon heating, vaporizing, or smoking. The extraction of butane hash oil from cannabis does not produce much THC and so it must be smoked rather than consumed orally (80503).

Reference Number: 80501

LEVIN, F.R., J.J. MARIANI., D.J. BROOKS, S. XIE, AND K.A. MURRAY. "Delta-9-Tetrahydrocannabivarin Testing May Not Have the Sensitivity to Detect Marijuana Use among Individuals Ingesting Dronabinol." *Drug and Alcohol Dependence,* 106: 65 (8 pp), 2010 (33 references)

Abstract: Delta 9-THCV (tetrahydrocannabivarin) is a naturally occurring cannabinoid in marijuana but does not occur in orally administered medicinal cannabis such as dronabinol. A urine sample was collected from 117 patients enrolled in a clinical trial and who reported using cannabis at least five times in the past week. Urinary THCCOOH and THCVCOOH concentrations were determined by GC-MS with a limit of quantitation of 1 ng/mL. All 117 urine samples were positive for THCCOOH (mean 1,724 ng/mL) but only 50 percent of the samples had a positive THCVCOOH concentration detected (mean 4.4 ng/mL).

> Since all published laboratory studies of THCV testing have used NIDA-grown marijuana and since all published data using NIDA marijuana have affirmed the presence of THCV, it is unquestionable that THCV is present in this strain. However, as suggested by the results of the present study, there may be substantial variability in the THCV content in cannabis cultivated and sold in the community and some domestically grown cannabis may contain minimal or no THCV at all. At present, it does not appear that THCV can be used as a reliable detection method of recent marijuana use. Nor can it be used as a reliable discriminatory method between illicitly smoked cannabis and therapeutic dronabinol ingestion. A corollary to this finding is that since there may be variability between NIDA-grown marijuana and marijuana available in the community, generalizing the results of laboratory research findings using NIAD-grown marijuana to the general population may have limitations.

Reference Number: 80502

ILAN, A.B., A. GEVINS, M. COLEMAN, M.A. ELSOHLY, AND H. DE WIT. "Neurophysiological and Subjective Profile of Marijuana with Varying Concentrations of Cannabinoids." *Behavioral Pharmacology*, 16: 487–96, 2006 (4 tables, 4 figures, 54 references)

Abstract: Eleven female and twelve male cannabis users (ages 21 to 45 years) were divided into a low (1.8 percent THC) and high (3.5 percent THC) group. The cannabis cigarettes contained either high or low cannabichromere (0.1 percent vs 0.5 percent) and low or high cannabidiol (0.2 percent vs 1 percent CBD). The subjects also smoked a placebo. Subjective measures of anxiety and feeling high as well as HR and neurophysiological tests, such as word recognition (episodic memory), EEG, and ERP were conducted. Word recognition of new words decreased substantially but recognition of old words did not change after cannabis use.

> Taken together, these results advance our understanding of the factors that influence responses to marijuana. They show the systematic variations in constituents other than THC that may have little effect on the behavioural or neurophysiological responses to the drug. However, the possibility remains that even higher concentrations of CBD or other cannabinoids appearing in natural marijuana may affect responses to the drug or that the constituents affect other measures that were not measured here (e.g., emesis or analgesia).

Reference Number: 80503

MEEHAN-ATRASH, J., W. LUO, AND R.M. STRONGIN. "Toxicant Formation in Dabbing: The Terpene Story." *American Chemical Society, Omega*, 2: 6112–17, 2017 (1 table, 2 figures, 42 references)

Abstract: Butane hash oil (BHO) is a resinous, non-water-soluble extract of cannabis, made using butane as a solvent and with ranges in THC concentration of between 50 and 90 percent. Since the process does not involve heating sufficient to convert (or decarboxylate) the native form of THC-THCA (delta 9-tetrahydrocannabinolic acid) into THC, BHO is not orally active and must be vaporized or smoked to achieve the psychoactive effect. THC is an oil at room temperature and THCA is a solid. A dab of concentrate is placed on a small heated surface (the nail) that is connected to a water pipe. The main reasons for dabbing is that less material is required to get high and it allegedly produces a cleaner high that is safer for the lungs than smoking. The formation of mycrene and other terpene degradation products during dabbing was measured using NMR (nuclear magnetic resonance).

> The results of these studies clearly indicate that dabbing, although considered a form of vaporization, may in fact deliver significant amounts of toxic degradation products. The difficulty users find in controlling the nail temperature put users at risk of exposing themselves to not only methacrolein but also benzene. Additionally, the heavy focus on terpenes as additives seen of late in the cannabis industry is of great concern due to oxidative liability of these compounds when heated. This research also has significant implications for flavoured e-cigarette products, due to the extensive use of terpenes as flavourings. Future research will also be directed toward assessing the contribution of terpenoids to the existing toxicant formation in e-cigarettes. Additionally, the methods discussed herein will also be used to further study the degradation of cannabis extracts used in dabbing and cannabis e-cigarettes.

Reference Number: 80504

PERTWEE, R.G. "Cannabinoid Pharmacology: The First 66 Years." *British Journal of Pharmacology*, 147: S163–S171, 2006 (1 table, 3 figures, 40 references)

Abstract: A scientific history of cannabinoid research is presented. Cannabinol (CBN), which forms from THC during storage, was the first cannabinoid isolated from a red oil extract of cannabis at the end of the nineteenth century. CBD was first isolated in 1940. The endogenous cannabinoid receptors (CB1 and CB2) were discovered in the 1980s. The endogenous cannabinoid, anandamide (from "anada," which means "bliss" in Sanskrit), was isolated from pig brains in Jerusalem by Raphael Mechoulam's research group in the 1990s. The review discusses various animal studies as well.

Table: Plant-Derived or Botanical Cannabinoids (Phytocannabinoids): Types and Number in Each Group

Phytocannabinoid Group	Number in Each Group
Delta 9-THC type	9
Delta 8-THC type	2
Cannabidiol type	7
Cannabigerol type	6

Phytocannabinoid Group	Number in Each Group
Cannabichromene type	5
Cannabicyclol type	3
Cannabielsoin type	5
Cannabitiol type	9
Miscellaneous type	11
Cannabinol and cannabinodioltypes (air oxidation artefacts)	n/a

Adapted from Pertwee, 2006

Results from experiments conducted during the 1970s indicated that tolerance can develop to many of the effects of cannabis and delta 9-THC, that this is induced more readily and rapidly to some effects than to others, and that it is essentially pharmacodynamic in nature and does not depend to any significant extent on changes in cannabinoid disposition or metabolism. When psychoactive cannabinoids other than delta 9-THC were developed, it became clear that these too can induce tolerance. However, a fuller elucidation of the mechanisms that underlie the development of this tolerance had to await the discovery of cannabinoid receptors. It then became possible to establish, at least for effects mediated by cannabinoid CB1 receptors, that internalization of these receptors with or without their subsequent degradation decreases in CB1 receptor protein synthesis and reductions in the efficiency of CB1 receptor signaling (desensitization) can all contribute to the development of tolerance to agonists for these receptors.

Appendix: Cannabis Timeline

6000 BCE	Cannabis seeds are first used for food in China.
4000 BCE	Hemp textiles are made in China.
2723 BCE	First recorded use of cannabis as medicine is made in China.
200CE	It is recorded in Imperial Rome that cannabis was sometimes given to promote hilarity and enjoyment.
1155	The Sufi mystic Haydar allegedly invents hashish and becomes talkative.
1400s	Venice controls hemp production as a basis of naval power.
1533	King Henry VIII fines farmers who do not raise hemp.
1753	Cannabis sativa is described and classified by Carolus Linnaeus.
1784	Cannabis indica is described and classified by Jean-Baptiste Lamarck.
1793	Eli Whitney invents cotton gin, which separates cotton fibre from seeds and makes cotton cheaper for sails, rope, and cloth than hemp.
1798	Napoleon invades Egypt and his troops start to use cannabis and bring it back to France, despite Napoleon's ban on it.
1842	Irish physician William O'Shaughnessy publishes his cannabis research in medical journals.
1850	Cannabis is added to the US Pharmacopeia.

1894–96	The 3,000-page Indian Hemp Drugs Report concludes that regular and moderate use of ganja or bhang produces the same effects as regular or moderate doses of whiskey.
1920	Soviet botanist Nicolai Vavilov first describes and classifies Cannabis ruderalis.
1923	Marijuana is criminalized in Canada. No arrests are made until 1937, when four arrests were made. The number of annual arrests remained stable until 1958, when fourteen charges were laid.
1924	Cannabis is outlawed by the Geneva Convention on Opium.
1925	The Panama Canal Zone Report investigated the use of cannabis by US troops and concluded that there is no evidence that it is habit-forming or deleterious and recommends its use or sale should not be banned.
1936	The propaganda movie "Reefer Madness" is produced in the US.
1937	Marijuana is outlawed in the US by the *Marijuana Tax Act*.
1941	Cannabis removed from US Pharmacopeia.
1961	The Single Convention on Narcotic Drugs standardizes legal controls on cannabis among UN member countries.
1964	Israeli scientist Raphael Mechoulam (the father of cannabis research) and his team first synthesize THC. Dr. Mechoulam has never smoked weed.
1967	Dr. James L. Goodard, the head of the US Food and Drug Administration, states he is unsure that cannabis is more dangerous than alcohol.
1969	The Wootton Report in the UK concludes that cannabis is no more harmful than tobacco or alcohol and recommends that penalties for all cannabis offences be minimized.
	On May 19, the Supreme Court of the US declared the thirty-two-year-old *Marijuana Tax Act* to be unconstitutional.
1970	In Canada, the Le Dain Report recommends the legalization of the possession of marijuana.

1971–73 President Nixon ignores the Shaffer Commission and declares a "War on Drugs." The Drug Enforcement Agency (DEA) is formed. Its mission is to destroy all marijuana cultivated in the US.

1976 The Dutch legalize the sale of cannabis in cafes, "front door legal, backdoor illegal."

1980 US President Reagan declares marijuana is the "most dangerous drug in the world."

1988 US Federal DEA Judge Francis Young states that "Marijuana in its natural form is one of the safest therapeutically active substances known to man."

1992 W.A. Devane and Lumir Hanus first describe the endogenous cannabinoid-anandamide ("ananda" is a Sanskrit word meaning "joy" or "bliss").

1996 California and Arizona legalize medical marijuana use.

2001 Canada becomes the first country in the world to legalize cannabis for medical use. This was the result of a Supreme Court of Canada ruling.

2005 Sativex, a cannabinoid spray consisting of equal amounts of THC and CBD, is approved as a medical drug in Canada.

2012 Colorado and Washington state legalize recreational use of cannabis.

2018 Canada becomes the first G7 country to legalize cannabis.

Abbreviations and Chemical Symbols

°C	degree Celsius
=	equal to
>	greater than
<	less than
%	percent
2D-GC-MS	two-dimensional gas chromatography mass spectrometry
11-OH-THC	11-hydroxy-THC (psychoactive metabolite of THC)
AM	alcohol and marijuana use
AMI	acute myocardial infarction
AO	alcohol use only
APA	American Psychiatric Association
ARD	acute respiratory distress
ARR	adjusted relative risk
AUC	area under the curve of a drug concentration versus time graph
BAC	blood alcohol concentration
BrAC	breath alcohol concentration
BOLD	blood oxygen level dependent
BP	blood pressure
bpm	beats (of the heart) per minute
BZE	benzoylecgonine
C_2H_5OH	ethanol, alcohol
$C_{21}H_{30}O_2$	tetrahydrocannabinol
CBD	cannabidiol
CBF	cerebral blood flow

CBN	cannabinol
CC	THCCOOH: creatinine ratio
CFS	Centre of Forensic Sciences
Cmax	the extrapolated maximum drug concentration
CMV	capillary micro-extraction of volatiles
CNS	central nervous system
COAD	Committee on Alcohol and other Drugs
COHb	carboxyhemoglobin
COPD	chronic obstructive pulmonary disease
CTT	critical tracking task
CUD	cannabis use disorder
CWS	cannabis withdrawal syndrome
DAT	divided attention test
DEC	drug recognition and classification
DFSA	drug facilitated sexual assault
DDT	Drager drug test
DMTS	delayed match to sample
DPX	disposable pipette extraction
DRC	drug recognition and classification
DRE	drug recognition expert
DRUID	driving under the influence of drugs, alcohol, and medicines
DSM-V	Diagnostic and Statistical Manual of Mental Disorders, Fifth Edition by the American Psychiatric Association
DSST	digit symbol substitution test
DUI	driving under the influence (of alcohol)
DUIC	driving under the influence of cannabis
DUID	driving under the influence of drugs
DVA	dynamic visual acuity
DWI	driving while impaired
ECG	electrocardiogram
ED	emergency department
EEG	electroencephalogram
EI	electron ionization
EIA	enzymatic immunoassay
ELISA	enzyme-linked immunosorbent assay
EM	episodic memory
EMIT	enzyme multiplied immunoassay technique
ERN	error related negativity
EtOH	ethanol

ER	emergency room
ESI	electrospray ionization
EWDTS	European Workplace Drug Testing Society
FA	fractional anisotropy
FARS	Fatality Analysis Reporting System
FEV	forced expiratory volume
FEV_1	forced expiratory volume in one second
FMPV	female to male partner violence
fMRI	functional magnetic resonance imaging
FMVC	fatal motor vehicle collision
FPIA	fluorescence polarization immunoassay
FVC	forced vital capacity
g/kg	grams per kilogram
g/100mL	grams (usually of alcohol) in 100 millilitres of blood
GC	gas chromatography
GC/MS	gas chromatography/mass spectroscopy
GCS	Glasgow coma scale
GERD	gastro-esophageal reflux disease
GHB	gamma hydroxybutyric acid
GLC	gas liquid chromatography
-glu	glucuronide
h	hour
HGN	horizontal gaze nystagmus
HMJ	head movement jerks
HPLC	high pressure liquid chromatography
HR	heart rate
HSA	human serum albumin
HS-SPDE	headspace solid-phase dynamic extraction
HS-SPME	headspace solid phase micro-extraction
IA	immunoassay
ICU	intensive care unit
IOP	intraocular pressure
IV	intravenous
KG	Kerala Ganja
L	litre
LC/MS/MS	liquid chromatography/mass spectrometry/mass spectrometry
LLE	liquid-liquid extraction
LOD	limit of detection
LOQ	limit of quantification

MDMA	methylenedioxymethamphetamine (ecstasy)
MALDI-MS	matrix-assisted laser desorptive ionization mass spectrometry
MFPV	male to female partner violence
mg	milligram
mg/g	milligram per gram
mg/kg	milligram per kilogram
mg/m^2	milligrams per square metre
mg/min	milligram per minute
MI	myocardial infarction
MJ	marijuana
mmol/L	millimoles per litre
MMP	medical marijuana programs
MOE	margin of exposure
MRI	magnetic resonance imaging
MRS	magnetic resonance spectroscopy
MS	multiple sclerosis
MSLT	multiple sleep latency tests
MVC	motor vehicle collision
ND	not detected
ng	nanogram
ng/mL	nanogram per millilitre
NIDA	National Institute of Drug Abuse
NMR	nuclear magnetic resonance
NPS	novel psychoactive substance
NPV	non-partner violence
NS	not significant
NSC	National Safety Council
NZ	New Zealand
OAA	odour activity analysis
OADP	Oregon Adolescent Depression Project
OF	oral fluid
OLS	one leg stand
OR	odds ratio
P	picogram
PCP	phencyclidine
PET	positron emission tomography
p/mg	picogram per milligram
pH	measure of acidity of a solution, pH of 7.0 is neutral, pH > 7.0 is basic (alkaline), and pH < 7.0 is acidic

PM	postmortem
PMR	postmortem redistribution
PSD	partial sleep deprivation
PSP	pleasant sensory perception
PVC	premature ventricular contraction
RAPWT	radial arterial pulse wave tonometry
RBC	red blood cell
REA	radiative energy attenuation
RML	recreational marijuana legalization
ROSITA	EU roadside testing assessment
RR	relative risk
RT	reaction time
SAC	serum alcohol concentration
SAMHSA	Substance Abuse and Mental Health Services Administration
SC	synthetic cannabinoids
SCI	spinal cord injury
SFST	standardized field sobriety test
SG	specific gravity
SI	suicidal ideation
SMI	serious mental illness
SMOS	semiconductor metal oxide sensors
SMVA	single motor vehicle accident
SMVC	single motor vehicle collision
SPE	solid-phase extraction
SPST	simulated public speaking test
SST	stop signal task
STEMI	ST-segment elevation myocardial infarction
SWM	spatial working memory
T1/2	half-life
TBW	total body water
THC	delta-9-tetrahydrocannabinol
THCA	tetrahydrocannabolic acid
THCCOOH	11-nor-9-carboxy-THC (inactive metabolite of THC)
THCV	tetrahydrocannabivarin
TIA	transient ischemic attack
TSRP	traffic safety resource prosecutors
UAC	urine alcohol concentration
UDA	unsafe driving action

UHPLC/MS/MS	ultra-high-performance liquid chromatography and tandem mass spectrometry
UV	ultraviolet
VAS	visual analog scale
VCC	vaporizable cannabis concentrates
Vd	volume of distribution
VGN	vertical gaze nystagmus
VOC	volatile organic compounds
v/v	volume of solute per volume of solvent
WADA	World Anti-Doping Agency
WAT	walk and turn
WLS	weight loss surgery
WM	working memory
w/w	weight/weight
XPS	x-ray photoelectron spectroscopy
y	year
yo	year old

Abstracted Studies

Alphabetical by First Author (reference number in bold brackets)

A

ABRAMS, D.I., J.F. HILTON, R.J. LEISER, S.B. SHADE, T.A. ELBEIK, F.T. AWEEKA, N.L. BENOWITZ, B.M. BREDT, B. KOSEL, J.A. ABERG, S.G. DEEKS, T.F. MITCHELL, K. MULLIGAN, P. BACCHETT, J.M. MCCUNE, AND M. SCHAMBELAN. "Short-Term Effects of Cannabinoids in Patients with HIV-1 Infection." *Annals Internal Medicine*, 139: 258–266, 2003 **(10501)**

ADAMS, A.J., B. BROWN, G. HAEGERSTROM-PORTNOY, M.C. FLOM, AND R.T. JONES. "Marijuana, Alcohol and Combined Drug Effects on the Time Course of Glare Recovery." *Psychopharmacology*, 56: 81–86, 1978 **(50101)**

ADEAGBO, B.A., C. CLARK, AND K.A. COLLINS. "Homicides Committed by Youth Assailants. A Retrospective Study." *American Journal of Forensic Medicine and Pathology*, 29: 219–223, 2008 **(60901)**

AGIUS, R., AND P. KINTZ. "Guidelines for European Workplace Drug and Alcohol Testing in Hair." *Drug Testing and Analysis*, 2: 367–376, 2010 **(40303)**

AGUIRRE-VELAZQUEZ, C.G. "Report for a Survey of Parents Regarding the Use of Cannabidiol (Medicinal Cannabis) in Mexican Children with Refractory Epilepsy." *Neurology Research International*, 2017, Article ID 2985729, 5 pp **(80312)**

AHMED, A.I.A., G.A.H. VAN DEN ELSEN, A. COLBERS, C. KRAMERS, D.M. BURGER, M.A. VAN DER MARCK, AND M.G.M.O. RIKKERT. "Safety, Pharmacodynamics and Pharmacokinetics of Multiple Oral Doses of Delta-9 Tetrahydrocannabinol in Older Persons with Dementia." *Psychopharmacology,* 232: 2587–95, 2015 **(10401)**

AKUTSU, M., K-I. SUGIE, AND K. SAITO. "Analysis of 62 Synthetic Cannabinoids by Gas Chromatography-Mass Spectrometry with Photoionization." *Forensic Toxicology,* 35: 94–103, 2017 **(80403)**

ALADAG-CIFTDEMIR, N., I. YUCEL, R. DURAN, U. VATANSEVER-OZBEK, AND B. ACUANS. "A New Emerging Problem in Pediatric Emergency Units: Synthetic Cannabinoids." *The Turkish Journal of Pediatrics,* 58: 492–97, 2016 **(80415)**

ALDINGTON, S., M. HARWOOD, B. COX, M. WEATHERALL, L. BECKERT, A. HANSELL, A. PRITCHARD, G. ROBINSON., AND R. BEASLEY. "Cannabis Use and Risk of Lung Cancer: A Case-Control Study." *European Respiratory Journal,* 31: 280–286, 2008 **(61611)**

ALLEN, J.H., G.M. DE MOORE, R. HEDDLE, AND J.C. TWARTZ. "Cannabinoid Hyperemesis: Cyclical Hyperemesis in Association with Chronic Cannabis Abuse." *Gut,* 53: 1566–70, 2004 (**60301)**

ALLSOP, C., J. COPELAND, M.M. NORBERG, S. FU, A. MOLNAR. J. LEWIS, AND A.J. BUDNEY. "Quantifying the Clinical Significance of Cannabis Withdrawal." *PLOS ONE,* 7: e44864, 12 pp, 2012 **(62102)**

AL-SHIDHANI, T.A., AND V. ARORA. "Cannabis Exposure in an Omani Child. First Case Report from Oman." *Sultan Qaboos University Medical Journal,* 1: 511–14, 2011 **(60602)**

ALTINTAS, M., L. INANC, G.A. ORUC, S. ARPACIOGLU, AND H. GULEC. "Clinical Characteristics of Synthetic Cannabinoid-Induced Psychosis in Relation to Schizophrenia: A Single-Center Cross-Sectional Analysis of Concurrently Hospitalized Patients." *Neuropsychiatric Disease and Treatment,* 12: 1893–1900, 2016 **(80427)**

ALVAREZ, F.J., AND I.F.M.C. DEL RIO. "Cannabis and Driving: Results from a General Population Survey." *Forensic Science International,* 170: 111–16, 2007 **(50502)**

AMARO, H., L.E. FRIED, H. CABRAL, AND B. ZUCKERMAN. "Violence During Pregnancy and Substance Use." *American Journal of Public Health,* 80: 575–79, 1990 **(60213**)

ANDERSEN, S.R., F. BIERING-SORENSEN, E.M. HAGEN, J.F. NIELSEN, F.W. BACH, AND N.B. FINNERUP. "Cannabis Use in Persons with Traumatic Spinal Cord Injury in Denmark." *Journal of Rehabilitative Medicine* 49: 152–60, 2017 **(62001)**

ANDERSON, B.M., M. RIZZO, R.I. BLOCK, G.D. PEARLSON, AND D.S. O'LEARY. "Sex Differences in the Effects of Marijuana on Simulated Driving Performance." *Journal of Psychoactive Drugs*, 42: 19–30, 2010 **(50207)**

ANDERSON, B.M., M. RIZZO, R.I. BLOCK, G.D. PEARLSON, AND D.S. O'LEARY. "Sex, Drugs and Cognition: Effects of Marijuana." *Journal of Psychoactive Drugs*, 42: 413–24, 2010 **(50110)**

ANDREWS, R., K.G. MURPHY, L. NAHAR, AND S. PATERSON. "Cannabinoid Concentrations Detected in Fatal Road Traffic Collision Victims Compared with a Population of Other Postmortem Cases." *Clinical Chemistry*, 61: 1256–64, 2015 **(50503)**

ANSELL, E.B., H.B. LAW, M.J. ROCHE, AND R. SINHA. "Effects of Marijuana Use on Impulsivity and Hostility in Daily Life." *Drug and Alcohol Dependence,* 136–42, March 2015 **(60205)**

ARNOLDI, S., G. RODA, E. CASAGNI, L. DELL'ACQUA, M.D. CAS, F. FARE, C. RUSCONI, G.L. VISCONTI, AND V. GAMBARO. "Characterization of the Volatile Components of Cannabis Preparations by Solid-Phase Micro-Extraction Coupled to Headspace-Gas-Chromatography with Mass Detector (SPME-HSGC/MS)." *Journal of Chromatography, Separation Techniques*, 8: 6 pp, 2017 **(80112)**

ASBRIDGE, M., J.A. HAYDEN, AND J.L. CARTWRIGHT. "Acute Cannabis Consumption and Motor Vehicle Collision Risk: Systematic Review of Observational Studies and Meta-Analysis." *British Medical Journal*, 344: e536, 2012 **(50504)**

ASBRIDGE, M., C. POULIN, AND A. DONATO. "Motor Vehicle Collision Risk and Driving Under the Influence of Cannabis: Evidence from Adolescents in Atlantic Canada." *Accident Analysis and Prevention*, 32: 1025–34, 2005 **(50505)**

ATTWOOD, D.A., R.D. WILLIAMS, L.J. MCBURNEY, AND R.C. FRECKER. "Cannabis, Alcohol, and Driving: Effects on Selected Closed Course Tasks." *Alcohol, Drugs, and Traffic Safety*, Vol. III, L. Goldberg (editor), T80, Almqvist and Wiksell International, Sweden, 938–53, 1980 **(50302)**

AUGSBURGER, M., N. DONZE, A. MENETREY, C. BROSSARD, F. SPORKET, C. GIROUD, AND D. MANGIN. "Concentration of Drugs in Blood of Suspected Impaired Drivers." *Forensic Science International* 153: 11–15, 2005 **(50506)**

AUJAVEB, A., C. DONALD, AND S. DOE. "Breath Holding in a Marijuana Smoker." *Respiratory Medicine Case Reports*, 5: 69–72, 2012 **(61612)**

AZORLOSA, J.L., S.J. HEISHMAN, M.L. STITZER, AND J.M. MAHAFFEY. "Marijuana Smoking: Effect of Varying delta 9 Tetrahydrocannabinol Content and Number of Puffs." *Journal of Pharmacology and Experimental Therapeutics*, 261: 114–22, 1992 **(10402)**

B

BACHS, L., AND H. MORLAND. "Acute Cardiovascular Fatalities Following Cannabis Use." *Forensic Science International*, 124: 200–3, 2001 **(60407)**

BALLARD, M.E., AND H. DE WIT, "Combined Effects of Acute, Very-Low-Dose Ethanol and Delta 9-Tetrahydrocannabinol in Healthy Human Volunteers." *Pharmacology and Biochemistry of Behavior,* 97: 627–31, 2011 **(10504)**

BARANCHUK, A., A.M. JOHRI, C.S. SIMPSON, M. METHOT, AND D.P. REDFEARN. "Ventricular Fibrillation Triggered by Marijuana Use in a Patient with Ischemic Cardiomyopathy: A Case Report." *Cases Journal*, 1: 373 (4 pp), 2008 **(60423)**

BARBER, P.A., H.M. PRIDMORE, V. KRISHNAMURTHY, S. ROBERTS, D.A. SPRIGGS, K.N. CARTER, AND N.E. ANDERSON. "Cannabis, Ischemic Stroke and Transient Ischemic Attack. A Case Control Study." *Stroke,* 44: 2327–29, 2013 **(60408)**

BARIS, Y.I., E. TAN, F. KALYONCU, M. ARTVINLI, AND A.A. SAHIN. "Digital Clubbing in Hashish Addicts." *Chest*, 98: 1545b–46, 1990 **(61101)**

BARNES, A.J., K.B. SCHEIDWEILER, AND M.A. HUESTIS. "Quantification of 11-Nor-9-Carboxy-delta 9 Tetrahydrocannabinol in Human Oral Fluid by Gas Chromatography-Tandem Mass Spectrometry." *Therapeutic Drug Monitoring*, 36: 225–33, 2014 **(30103)**

BARROWCLOUGH, C., L. GREGG., F. LOBBAN, S. BUCCI, AND R. EMSLEY. "The Impact of Cannabis Use on Clinical Outcomes in Recent Onset Psychosis." *Schizophrenia Bulletin*, 41: 382–90, 2015 **(61401)**

BARRY, R.A., AND S. GLANTZ. "A Public Health Framework for Legalized Retail Marijuana Based on the US Experience: Avoiding a New Tobacco Industry." *PLOS Medicine* 13: e1002131, 2016 **(50710)**

BARTHOLOMEW, J., S. HOLROYD, AND T.M. HEFFERNAN. "Does Cannabis Use Affect Prospective Memory in Young Adults?" *Journal of Psychopharmacology*, 24: 241–46, 2010 **(61001)**

BATTISTELLA, G., E. FORNARI, A. THOMAS, J-F. MALL, H. CHTIOUI, M. APPENZELLER, J-M. ANNONI, B. FAVRAT, P. MASEDER, AND C. GIROUD "Weed or Wheel! fMRI, Behavioural, and Toxicological Investigations of How Cannabis Smoking Affects Skills Necessary for Driving." *PLOS ONE* 8: e52545, 2013 **(50102)**

BEASLEY, E., S. FRANCESE, AND T. BASSINDALE. "Detection for Mapping of Cannabinoids in Single Hair Samples through Rapid Derivatization and Matrix-Assisted Laser Desorption Ionization Mass Spectrometry." *Analytical Chemistry,* 88: 10328–34, 2016 **(40301)**

BEDARD, M., S. DUBOIS, AND B. WEAVER. "The Impact of Cannabis on Driving." *Canadian Journal of Public Health*, 98: 6–11, 2007 **(50507)**

BEDI, G., Z.D. COOPER, AND M. HANEY. "Subjective, Cognitive, and Cardiovascular Dose-Effect Profile of Nabilone and Dronabinol in Marijuana Smokers." *Addictive Biology*, 18: 872–81, 2013 **(80204)**

BEIRNESS, D.J., AND E.E. BEASLEY. "A Roadside Survey of Alcohol and Drug Use among Drivers in British Columbia." *Traffic Injury Prevention*, 11: 215–221, 2010 **(50508)**

BEIRNESS, D.J., E. BEASLEY, AND J. LECAVALIER. "The Accuracy of Evaluations by Drug Recognition Experts in Canada."_*Canadian Society Forensic Science Journal*, 42: 75–79, 2009 **(50603)**

BEIRNESS, D.J., AND D.R. SMITH. "An Assessment of Oral Fluid Drug Screening Devices." *Canadian Society of Forensic Science Journal*, 9 pp, December 2016 **(30201)**

BELL, C., J. SLIM, H.K. FLATEN, G. LINDBERG, AND W. AREK. "Butane Hash Oil Burns Associated with Marijuana Liberalization in Colorado." *Journal of Medical Toxicology*, 11: 422–25, 2015 **(60702)**

BELLIS, M.A., K. HUGHES, A. CALAFAT, M. JUAN, A. RAMON, J.A. RODRIGUEZ, F. MENDES, S. SCHNITZER, AND P. PHILLIPS-HOWARD. "Sexual Uses of Alcohol and Drugs and the Associated Health Risks: A Cross Sectional Study of Young People in Nine European Cities." *BMC Public Health*, 8: 155 (11 pp), 2008 **(61713)**

BENJAMIN, D.M., AND M.J. FOSSLER. "Edible Cannabis Products: It Is Time for FDA Oversight." *The Journal of Clinical Pharmacology,* 56: 1045–47, 2016 **(60601)**

BERGAMASCHI, M.M., AND J.A.S. CRIPPA. "Why Should Cannabis be Considered Doping in Sports?" *Frontiers in Psychiatry,* 4, Article 32, 2 pp, May 2013 **(61805)**

BERGAMASCHI, M.M., E.L. KARSCHNER, R.S. GOODWIN, K.B. SCHEIDWEILER, J. HIRVONEN, R.H.C. QUEIROZ, AND M.A. HUESTIS. "Impact of Prolonged Cannabinoid Excretion in Chronic Daily Cannabis Smokers Blood on Per Se Drugged Driving Laws." *Clinical Chemistry*, 59: 519–26, 2013 **(10307)**

BERGAMASCHI, M.M., R.H.C. QUEIROZ, M.H.N. CHAGAS, D.C.G. DE OLIVEIRA, B.S. DE MARTINIS, F. KAPCZINSKI, J. QUEVEDO, R. ROESLER, N. SCHRODER, A.E. NARDI, R. MARTIN-SANTOS, J.E.C. HALLAK, A.W. ZUARDI, AND J.A.S. CRIPPA. "Cannabidiol Reduces the Anxiety Induced by Simulated Public Speaking in Treatment-Naive Social Phobia Patients." *Neuropsychopharmacology*, 36: 1219–26, 2011 **(80310)**

BHATTACHARYYA, S., P.D. MORRISON, P. FUSAR-POLI, R. MARTIN-SANTOS, S. BORGWARDT, T. WINTON-BROWN, C. NOSARTI, C.M. O'CARROLL, M. SEAL, P. ALLEN, M.A. MEHTA, J.M. STONE, N. TUNSTALL, V. GIAMPIETRO, S. KAPUR, R.M. MURRAY, A. ZUARDI, J.A. CRIPPA, Z. ATAKAN, AND P.K. MCGUIRE. "Opposite Effects of delta 9-Tetrahydrocannabinol and Cannabidiol on Human Brain Function and Psychopathology." *Neuropsychopharmacology*, 35: 764–74, 2010 **(80311)**

BIECHELER, M.-B., J-F. PEYTAVIN, THE SAM GROUP, F. FACY, AND H. MARTINEAU. "SAM Survey on Drugs and Fatal Accidents: Search of Substances Consumed and Comparison Between Drivers Involved Under the Influence of Alcohol or Cannabis." *Traffic Injury Prevention*, 9: 11–21, 2008 **(50509)**

BIEHL, J.R., AND E.L. BURNHAM. "Cannabis Smoking in 2015. A Concern for Lung Health?" *Chest*, 148: 596–606, 2015 **(10115)**

BLOWS, S., R.Q. IVERS, J. CONNOR, S. AMERATUNGA, M. WOODWARD, AND R. NORTON. "Marijuana Use and Car Crash Injury." *Addiction*, 100: 605–11, 2005 **(50510)**

BOCKER K.B.E., J. GERRITSEN, C.C. HUNAULT, M. KRUIDENIER, T.T. MENSINGA, AND J.L. KENEMANS. "Cannabis with High delta 9 THC Affects Perception and Visual Selective Attention Acutely: An Event-Related Potential Study." *Pharmacology, Biochemistry and Behavior*, 96: 67–74, 2010 **(50104)**

BOGSTRAND, S.T., M. LARSSON, A. HOLTAN, T. STAFF, V. VINDENES, AND H. GJERDE. "Associations Between Driving Under the Influence of Alcohol or Drugs, Speeding and Seatbelt Use Among Fatally Injured Car Drivers in Norway." *Accident Analysis and Prevention*, 78: 14–19, 2015 **(50805)**

BONNETT, U., AND U.W. PREUSS. "The Cannabis Withdrawal Syndrome: Current Insights." *Substance Abuse and Rehabilitation*, 8: 9–37, 2017 **(62101)**

BOORMAN, M., AND K. PAPAFOTIOU. "The Victorian Legislative Framework for Testing Drivers for Impairment Caused by Drugs Other than Alcohol: An Evaluation of the Characteristics of Drivers Detected From 2000 to 2005." *Traffic Injury Prevention,* 8: 217–23, 2007 **(50604)**

BOSKER, W.M., K.P.C. KUYPERS, E.L. THEUNISSEN, A. SURINX, R.J. BLANKESPOOR, G. SKOPP, W.K. JEFFREY, C. WALLS, C.J. VAN LEEUWEN, AND J.G. RAMAEKERS. "Medicinal Delta 9-Tetrahydrocannabinol (Dronabinol) Impairs On-the-Road Performance of Occasional and Heavy Cannabis Users but Is Not Detected in Standardized Field Sobriety Tests." *Addictions,* 107: 1837–44, 2012 **(50404)**

BOSKER, W.M., E.I. THEUNISSEN, S. CONEN, K.P.C. KUYPERS, W.K. JEFFREY, H.C. WALLS, G.F. KAUERT, S.W. TOENNES, M.R. MOELLER, AND J.G. RAMAEKERS. "A Placebo-Controlled Study to Assess Standardized Field Sobriety Tests Performance During Alcohol and Cannabis Intoxication in Heavy Cannabis Users and Accuracy of Point of Collection Testing Devices for Detecting THC in Oral Fluid." *Psychopharmacology*, 223: 439–46, 2012 **(50605)**

BRAMNESS, J.G., H.Z. KHIABANI, AND J. MORLAND. "Impairment due to Cannabis and Ethanol: Clinical Signs and Additive Effects." *Addiction,* 105: 1080–87, 2010 **(50606)**

BRAND E.J., AND Z. ZHAO. "Cannabis in Chinese Medicine: Are Some Traditional Indications References in Ancient Literature Related to Cannabinoids?" *Frontiers in Pharmacology*, 8: Article 108, 11 pp, 2017 **(80313)**

BRIERE, F.N., J.S. FALLU, A. DESCHENEAUX, AND M. JANOSZ. "Predictors and Consequences of Simultaneous Alcohol and Cannabis." *Addictive Behaviors*, 36: 785–88, 2011 **(60122)**

BROOK, J.S., J.Y. LEE, S.J. FINCH, J. KOPPEL, AND D.W. BROOK. "Psychosocial Factors Related to Cannabis Use Disorders." *Substance Abuse*, 32: 242–51, 2011 **(60503)**

BROOK, J.S., J.Y. LEE., S.J. FINCH, AND D.W. BROOK. "Developmental Trajectories of Marijuana Use from Adolescence to Adulthood: Relationship with Using Weapons Including Guns." *Aggressive Behaviors*, 40: 229–237, 2014 **(60211)**

BROOKOFF, D., C.S. COOK, C. WILLIAMS, AND C.S. MANN. "Testing Reckless Drivers for Cocaine and Marijuana." *The New England Journal of Medicine*, 331: 518–22, 1994 **(50607)**

BROWN, B., A.J. ADAMS, G. HAEGERSTROM-PORTNOY, R.T. JONES, AND M.C. FLOM. "Effects of Alcohol and Marihuana on Dynamic Visual Acuity I. Threshold Measurements." *Perception and Psychophysics*, 18: 441–46, 1975 **(50105)**

BRUBACHER, J.R., H. CHAN, W. MARTZ, W. SCHREIBER, M. ASBRIDGE, J. EPPLER, A. LUND, S. MACDONALD, O. DRUMMER, R. PURSSELL, G. ANDOLFATTO, R. MANN, AND R. BRANT. "Prevalence of Alcohol and Drug Use in Injured British Columbia Drivers." *British Medical Journal Open*, 6: 9 pp, March 10, 2016 **(50511)**

BUCHOWSKI, M.S., N.N. MEADE, E. CHARBONEAU, S. PARK, M.S. DIETRICH, R.L. COWAN, AND P.R. MARTIN. "Aerobic Exercise Training Reduces Cannabis Craving and Use in Non-Treatment Seeking Cannabis-Dependent Adults." *PLOS ONE*, 6: e17465 (6 pp), 2011 **(60508)**

BUCKMAN, J.F., D.A. YUSKO, S.G. FARRIS, H.R. WHITE, AND R.J. PANDINA. "Risk of Marijuana Use in Male and Female College Student Athletes and Nonathletes." *Journal of Studies on Alcohol and Drugs* 72: 586–91, 2011 **(61803)**

BUI, Q.M., S. SIMPSON, AND K. NORDSTROM. "Psychiatric and Medical Management of Marijuana Intoxication in the Emergency Department." *Western Journal of Emergency Medicine*, 16: 414–17, 2015 **(60605)**

BURGDORF, J.R., B. KILMER, AND R.L. PACULA. "Heterogeneity in the Composition of Marijuana Seized in California." *Drug and Alcohol Dependence*, 117: 59–61, 2011 **(80111)**

BURNS, M., AND H. MOSKOWITZ. "Alcohol, Marihuana and Skills Performance." *Alcohol, Drugs and Traffic Safety*, Vol III, L. Goldberg (editor) Stockholm, T80, 954–68, 1980 **(50106)**

BUSSE, F., L. OMIDI, K. TIMPER, A. LECHTLE, M. WINDGASSEN, E. KLUGE, AND M. STUMVOLL. "Lead Poisoning Due to Adulterated Marijuana [Letter]." *New England Journal of Medicine*, 385: 1641–42, 2008 **(61116)**

BUTTERS, J.E., R.G. SMART, R.E. MANN, AND M. ASBRIDGE. "Illicit Drug Use, Alcohol Use and Problem Drinking Among Infrequent and Frequent Road Ragers." *Drug and Alcohol Dependence*, 80: 169–75, 2005 **(60208)**

C

CAMPOS, D.R., M. YONSMINE, AND R. DE MORALES MOREAU "Marijuana as Doping in Sports." *Sports and Medicine,* 33: 395–99, 2003 **(61801)**

CANGA, Y., D. OSMONOV, M.B. KARATAS, G. DURMUS, E. ILHAN, AND V. KURBAS. "Cannabis: A Rare Trigger of Premature Myocardial Infarction." *Anadolu Kardiyol Derg*, 11: 271–75, 2011 **(60404)**

CAO, D., S. SRISUMA, A.C. BRONSTEIN, AND C.O. HOYLE. "Characterization of Edible Marijuana Product Exposures Reported to United States Poison Centers." *Clinical Toxicology*, 7 pp, 2016 **(60606)**

CARLINI, B.H., S.B. GARRETT, AND R.M. HARWICK. "Beyond Joints and Brownies: Marijuana Concentrates in the Legal Landscape of WA State." *International Journal of Drug Policy*, 42: 26–29, 2017 **(61106)**

CASOLIN, A. "Comparison of Urine and Oral Fluid for Workplace Drug Testing." *Journal of Analytical Toxicology*, 40: 479–85, 2016 **(30305)**

CASSWELL, S. "Cannabis and Alcohol: Effects on Closed-Course Driving Behavior." 7th International Conference on Alcohol, Drugs and Traffic Safety, I.R. Johnston (editor), 238–46, 1977 **(50301)**

CASTANETO, M.S., K.B. SCHEIDWEILER, A. GANDHI, A. WOHLFARTH, K.L. KLETTE, T.M. MARTIN, AND M.A. HUESTIS. "Quantitative Urine Confirmatory Testing for Synthetic Cannabinoids in Randomly Collected Urine Specimens." *Drug Testing and Analysis,* 7: 483–93, 2015 **(80428)**

CHACHAMOVICH, E., L.J. KIRMAYER., M. HAGGARTY, M. CARGO, R. MCCORMICK, AND G. TURECKI. "Suicide among Inuit: Results from a Large Epidemiologically Representative Follow-Back Study in Nunavut." *Canadian Journal of Psychiatry*, 60: 268–75, 2015 **(61902)**

CHAIT, L.D., AND J.L. PERRY. "Acute and Residual Effect of Alcohol and Marijuana, Alone and in Combination on Mood and Performance." *Psychopharmacology,* 115: 340–49, 1994 **(50107)**

CHANG, Y.H., AND D.M. WINDISH. "Cannabinoid Hyperemesis Relieved by Compulsive Bathing." *Mayo Clinic Proceedings*. 84: 76–78, 2009 **(60313)**

CHASE, P.B., J. HAWKINS, J. MOSIER, F. JIMENEZ, K. BOESEN, B.K. LOGAN, AND F.G. WALTER. "Differential Physiological and Behavioral Cues Observed in Individuals Smoking Botanical Marijuana versus Synthetic Cannabinoid Drugs." *Clinical Toxicology*, 54: 14–19, 2016 **(80402)**

CHEUNG, E., C. NG, AND J. FOOTE. "A Hot Mess: A Case of Hyperemesis." *Canadian Family Physician*, 60: 633–37, 2014 **(60310)**

CHIHURI, S., G. LI, AND Q. CHEN. "Interaction of Marijuana and Alcohol on Fatal Motor Vehicle Crash Risk: A Case Control Study." *Injury Epidemiology*, 4:8 2017 **(50804)**

CHIPMAN, M.I., S. MACDONALD, AND R.E. MANN. "Being at Fault in Traffic Crashes: Does Alcohol, Cannabis, Cocaine or Polydrug Abuse Make a Difference?" *Injury Prevention*, 9: 343–48, 2003 **(50512)**

CHUN, T.H., A. SPIRITO, L. HERNANDEZ, A.M. FAIRLIE, H. SINDELAR-MANNING, C.A. EATON, AND W. LEWANDER. "The Significance of Marijuana Use among Alcohol Using Adolescent ED Patients." *Academic Emergency Medicine*, 17: 63–71, 2010 **(60114)**

CIMBURA, G., D.M. LUCAS, R.C. BENNETT, AND A.C. DONELSON. "Incidence and Toxicological Aspects of Cannabis and Ethanol Detected in 1,394 Fatally Injured Drivers and Pedestrians in Ontario (1982–1984)." *Journal of Forensic Sciences,* 35: 1035–41, 1990 **(50513)**

CIPRIANI, F., A. MANCINO, S.M. PULITANO, M. PIASTRA, AND G.A. CONTI. "A Cannabinoid Intoxicated Child Treated with Dexmedetomidine: A Case Report." *Journal of Medical Case Reports*, 9: 152 (4 pp), 2015 **(60607)**

CLAUDET, I., S. MOUVIER, M. LABADIE, C. MANIN., A-P. MICHARD-LENOIR, D. EYER, AND D. DUFOUR, "Unintentional Cannabis Intoxication in Toddlers." *Pediatrics,* 140: e2017017, 10 pp, 2017 **(60604)**

CLAYTON, H.B., R. LOWRY, C. ASHLEY, A. WOLKIN, AND A.M. GRANT. "Health Risk Behaviors with Synthetic Cannabinoids versus Marijuana." *Pediatrics*, 138: 10 pp, 2017 **(80404)**

COHEN, N.L., A.J. HEINZ, M. ILGEN, AND M.O. BONN-MILLER. "Pain, Cannabis Species and Cannabis Use Disorders." *Journal of Studies on Alcohol and Drugs*, 77: 515–20, 2016 **(60506)**

COLES, R., T.T. CLEMENTS, G.J. NELSON, G.A. MCMILLIN, AND F.M. URY "Simultaneous Analysis of the delta 9-THC Metabolites 11-nor-9-Caroxy-delta 9-THC and 11-Hydroxy-delta 9-THC in Meconium by GC-MS." *Journal of Analytical Toxicology*, 29: 522–27, 2005 **(40507)**

CONE, E.J., G.E. BIGELOW, E.S. HERMANN, J.M. MITCHELL, C. LODICO, R. FLEGEL, AND R. VANDREY. "Non-Smoker Exposure to Secondhand Smoke. I Urine Screening and Confirmation Results." *Journal of Analytical Toxicology*, 39: 1–12, 2015 **(10101)**

CONE, E.J., G.E. BIGELOW, E.S. HERMANN, J.M. MITCHELL, C. LODICO, R. FLEGEL, AND R. VANDREY. "Nonsmoker Exposure to Secondhand Cannabis Smoke. III Oral Fluid and Blood Drug Concentrations and Corresponding Subjective Effects." *Journal of Analytical Toxicology*, 39: 497–509, 2015 **(10102)**

COOPER, Z.D., AND M. HANEY. "Comparison of Subjective, Pharmacokinetic and Physiological Effects of Marijuana Smoked as Joints and Blunts." *Drug and Alcohol Dependence*, 103: 107–13, 2009 **(10502)**

CORNELIUS, J.R., T. CHUNG, C. MARTIN, D.S. WOOD, AND D.B. CLARK. "Cannabis Withdrawal is Common Among Treatment-Seeking Adolescents with Cannabis Dependence and Major Depression and is Associated with Rapid Relapse to Dependence." *Addictive Behavior*, 33: 1500–05, 2008 **(62107)**

COTHEN, G.C., AND R. SHAMBERGER. "Substance Abuse Countermeasures for the Railroad Industry." *Alcohol, Drugs and Driving*, 8: 241–63, 1992 **(61501)**

CRIPPA, J.A.S., A.C.S. CRIPPA, J.E.C. HALLAK, R. MARTIN-SANTOS, AND A.W. ZUARDI. "Delta-9-THC Intoxication by Cannabis-Enriched Cannabis Extract in Two Children with Refractory Epilepsy: Full Remission after Switching to Purified Cannabidiol." *Frontiers in Pharmacology*, 7: Article 359, 6 pp, 2016 **(80307)**

CROUCH, D.J. "Oral Fluid Collection: The Neglected Variable in Oral Fluid Testing." *Forensic Science International*, 150: 165–73, 2005 **(30401)**

CROUCH, D.J., R.K. HERSCH, R.F. COOK, J.F. FRANK, AND J.M. WALSH "A Field Evaluation of Five On-Site Drug Testing Devices." *Journal of Analytical Toxicology*, 26: 493–499, 2002 **(40205)**

CUNNINGHAM. J.A., J. BLOMQVIST, A. KOSKI-JANNES, AND C. RAITASALO. "Societal Images of Cannabis Use: Comparing Three Countries." *Harm Reduction Journal*, 9: 21 (3 pp), 2012 **(50708)**

CUNNINGHAM, R.M., R. MURRAY, M.A. WALTON, S.T. CHERMACK, M. WOJNAR, P. WOZNIAK, B.M. BOOTH, AND F.C. BLOW. "Prevalence of Past Year Assault among Inner-City ED Patients." *Annals of Emergency Medicine*, 53: 814–23, 2009 **(60210)**

CUNRADI, C.B., M. TODD, AND C. MAIR. "Discrepant Patterns of Heavy Drinking, Marijuana Use, and Smoking and Intimate Partner Violence: Results of the California Community Health Safety Study of Couples." *Journal of Drug Education* 45: 73–95, 2015 **(60201)**

CURRAN, H.V., C. BRIGNELL, S. FLETCHER, P. MIDDLETON, AND J. HENRY "Cognitive and Subjective Dose-Response Effects of Acute Oral Delta 9 Tetrahydrocannabinol (THC) in Infrequent Cannabis Users." *Psychopharmacology*, 164: 61–70, 2002 **(61002)**

D

DARKE, S., AND J. DUFLOU, "Toxicology and Circumstances of Death of Homicide Victims in New South Wales, Australia 1996–2005." *Journal of Forensic Sciences*, 53: 447–51, 2008 **(60902)**

DARKE, S., J. DUFLOU, AND M. TOROK. "Drugs and Violent Death: Comparative Toxicology of Homicide and Non-Substance Toxicity Suicide Victims." *Addiction,* 104: 1000–1005, 2009 **(60903)**

DARKE, A.C., J. DUFLOU, AND M. TOROK. "Toxicology and Circumstances of Completed Suicide by Means Other than Overdose." *Journal of Forensic Sciences*, 54: 490–94, 2009 **(61903)**

DAVIES, B.B., C. BAYARD, S.J. LARSON, L.W. ZARWELL, AND R.A. MITCHELL. "Retrospective Analysis of Synthetic Cannabinoid Metabolites in Urine of Individuals Suspected of Driving Impaired." *Journal of Analytical Toxicology*, 40: 89–95, 2016 **(80405)**

DAVIS, J.M., B. MENDELSON, J.J. BERKES, K. SULETA, K.F. CORSI, AND R.E. BOOTH. "Public Health Effects of Medical Marijuana Legalization in Colorado." *American Journal of Preventative Medicine*, 50: 373–379, 2016 **(60609)**

DE BONI, R., M.C. BOZZETTI, J. HILGERT, T. SOUSA, L. VON DIEMEN, D. BENZANO, G. MENEGON, B. HOLMER., P. DUARTE, AND F. PECHANSKY. "Factors Associated with Alcohol and Drug Use among Traffic Crash Victims in Southern Brazil." *Accident Analysis and Prevention*, 43: 1408–13, 2011 **(50514)**

DECLUES, K., S. PEREZ, AND A.A. FIGUEROA. "A 2-Year Study of delta 9-Tetrahydrocannabinol Concentrations in Drivers: Examining Driving and Field Sobriety Test Performance." *Journal of Forensic Sciences*, 61: 1664–70, 2016 **(50608)**

DEGENHARDT, L., C. COFFEY, J.B. CARLIN, W. SWIFT, E. MOORE, AND G.C. PATTON. "Outcomes of Occasional Cannabis Use in Adolescence: 10-Year Follow-up Study in Victoria, Australia." *The British Journal of Psychiatry*, 196: 290–95, 2010 **(60113)**

DE HAVENON, C., A.B. CHIN, K.C. THOMAS, AND P. AFRA. "The Secret Spice: An Undetectable Toxic Cause of Seizure." *The Neurohospitalist,* 1: 182–86, 2011 **(80439)**

DELFORTERIE, M.J., M. LYNSKEY, A.C. HUIZINK, H.E. CREEMERS, J.D. GRANT, L.R. FEW, A.L. GLOWINSKI, D.J. STATHAM, T.J. TRULL, K.K. BUCHOLZ, P.A.F. MADDEN, N.G. MARTIN, A.C. HEATH, AND A. AGRAWAL. "The Relationship between Cannabis Involvement and Suicidal Thoughts and Behaviors." *Drug and Alcohol Dependence*, 150: 98–104, 2015 **(61911)**

DE SOUZA FERNANDES PERNA, E.B., E.L. THEUNISSEN, K.P.C. KUYPERS, S.W. TOENNES, AND J.G. RAMAEKERS. "Subjective Aggression During Alcohol and Cannabis Intoxication Before and After Aggression Exposure." *Psychopharmacology*, 233: 331–40, 2016 **(60202)**

DESROSIER, N.A., S.K. HIMES, K.B. SCHEIDWEILER, M. CONCHEIRO-GUISAN, D.A. GORELICK, AND M.A. HUESTIS. "Phase I and II Cannabinoid Disposition in Blood and Plasma of Occasional and Frequent Smokers Following Controlled Smoked Cannabis." *Clinical Chemistry*, 60: 631–43, 2014 **(10403)**

DESROSIERS, N.A., D. LEE, M. CONCHEIRO-GUISAN, K.B. SCHEIDWEILER, D.A. GORELICK, AND M.A. HUESTIS. "Urinary Cannabinoid Disposition in Occasional and Frequent Smokers: Is THC-Glucuronide in Sequential Urine Samples a Marker of Recent Use in Frequent Smokers?" *Clinical Chemistry*, 60: 361–72, 2014 **(40207)**

DESROSIERS, N.A., D. LEE, K.B. SCHEIDWEILER, M. CONCHEIRO-GUSAN, D.A. GORELICK, AND M.A. HUESTIS. "In Vitro Stability of Free and Glucuronidated Cannabinoids in Urine Following Controlled Smoked Cannabis." *Analytical Bioanalytical Chemistry*, 406: 785–92, 2014 **(40216)**

DESROSIERS, N.A., D. LEE, D.M. SCHWOPE, G. MILMAN, A.J. BARNES, D.A. GORELICK, AND M.A. HUESTIS. "On-Site Test for Cannabinoids in Oral Fluid." *Clinical Chemistry*, 58: 1418–25, 2012 **(30104)**

DESROSIERS, N.A., J.G. RAMAEKERS, E. CHAUCHARD, D.A. GORELICK, AND M.A. HUESTIS. "Smoked Cannabis, Psychomotor and Neurocognitive Effects in Occasional and Frequent Smokers." *Journal of Analytical Toxicology*, 39: 251–61, 2015 **(50122)**

DHOSSCHE, D.M., C.L. RICH, AND G. ISACSSON. "Psychoactive Substances in Suicides. Comparison of Toxicologic Findings in Two Samples." *American Journal of Forensic Medicine and Pathology*, 22: 239–43, 2001 **(61904)**

DI FORTI, M., A. MARCONI, E. CARRA, S. FRAIETTA, A. TROTTA, M. BONOMO, F. BIANCONI, P. GARDNER-SOOD, J. O'CONNOR, M. RUSSO, S.A. STILO, T.R. MARQUES, V. MONDELLI, P. DAZZAN, C. PARIANTE, A.S. DAVID, F. GAUGHAN, Z. ATAKAN, C. IYEGBE, J. POWELL, C. MORGAN, M. LYNSKEY, AND R.M. MURRAY. "Proportion of Patients in South London with First-Episode Psychosis Attributable to Use of High Potency Cannabis: A Case-Control Study." *Lancet Psychiatry*, 2: 233–38, 2015 **(61403)**

DI FORTI, M., C. MORGAN, P. DAZZAN, C. PARIANTE, V. MONDELLI, T.R. MARQUES, R. HANDLEY, S. LUZI, M. RUSSO, A. PAPARELLI, A. BUTT, S.A.

STILO, B. WIFFEN, J. POWELL, AND R.M. MURRAY. "High-Potency Cannabis and the Risk of Psychosis." *The British Journal of Psychiatry*, 195: 488–91, 2009 **(61416)**

DI FORTI, M., H. SALLIS, F. ALLEGRI, A. TROTTA, L. FERRARO, S.A. STILO, A. MARCONI, C. LA CASCIA, T.R. MARQUES, C. PARIANTE, P. DAZZAN, V. MONDELLI, A. PAPARELLI, A. KOLLIAKOU, D. PRATA, F. GAUGHRAN., A.S. DAVID, C. MORGAN, S.D. STAHL, M. KHONDOKER, J.H. MACCABE, AND R.M. MURRAY. "Daily Use, Especially of High-Potency Cannabis, Drives the Earlier Onset of Psychosis in Cannabis Users." *Schizophrenia Bulletin*, 40: 1509–17, 2014 **(61402)**

DINES, A.M., D.M. WOOD, M. GALICIA, C.M. YATES, F. HEYERDAHL, K.E. HOVDA, I. GIRAUDON, R. SEDEFOVE, EURO-DEN RESEARCH GROUP, AND P.I. DARGAN. "Presentations to the Emergency Department Following Cannabis Use: A Multi-Centre Case Series from Ten European Countries" *Journal Medical Toxicology*, 11: 415–21, 2015 **(60610)**

DIPLOCK, J., D. PLECAS, AND L. GARIS. "Targeting Marijuana Growing Operations in British Columbia." *University of the Fraser Valley, Centre for Public Safety and Criminal Justice Research, Report*, 22 pp, August 2013 **(60701)**

DOGAN, S., C. AKMAN, A. YILMAZ, U.M. KALAFAT, AND T. OCAK. "A Hypothermic Case with Giant Osborn Waves and Atrial Fibrillation after Using Synthetic Cannabinoid." *Anatolian Journal of Cardiology*, 16: 150–52, 2016 **(80406)**

DOS SANTOS, N.A., L.M. SOUZA, E. DOMINGOS, H.S. FRANCA, V. LACERDA JR., A. BEATRIZ, B.G. VAZ, R.T. RODRIGUES, V.V. CARVALHO, B.B. MERLO, R.M. KUSTER AND W. ROMAO. "Evaluating the Selectivity of Colorimetric Test (Fast Blue BB salt) for the Cannabinoids Identification in Marijuana Street Samples by UV-Vis, TLC, ESI (+) FT-ICR MS and ESI (+) MS/MS." *Forensic Chemistry*, 1: 13–21, 2016 **(80103)**

DOWNEY, L.A., R. KING, K. PAPAFOTIOU, P. SWANN, E. OGDEN, M. BOORMAN, AND C. STOUGH. "Detecting Impairment Associated With Cannabis With and Without Alcohol on the Standardized Field Sobriety Tests." *Psychopharmacology*, 224: 581–89, 2012 **(50610)**

DOWNEY, L.A., R. KING, K. PAPAFOTIOU, P. SWANN, E. OGDEN, M. BOORMAN, AND C. STOUGH. "The Effects of Cannabis and Alcohol on Simulated Driving: Influences of Dose and Experience." *Accident Analysis and Prevention*, 50: 879–86, 2013 **(50201)**

DREWE, M., J. DREWE., AND A. RIECHLER-ROSSLER. "Cannabis and Risk of Psychosis." *Swiss Medical Weekly*, 134: 659–62, 2004 **(61404)**

DRUMMER, O.H., J. GEROSTAMOULOS, H. BATZIRIS, M. CHU, J. CAPLEHORN, M.D. ROBERTSON, AND P. SWANN. "The Involvement of Drugs in Drivers of Motor Vehicle Killed in Australian Road Traffic Crashes." *Accident Analysis and Prevention,* 36: 239–48, 2004 **(50515)**

DRUMMER, O.H., AND S. YAP. "The Involvement of Prescribed Drugs in Road Trauma." *Forensic Science International*, 265: 17–21, 2016 **(61201)**

D'SOUZA, D.C., M. RANGANATHAN, G. BRALEY, R. GUEORGUIEVA, Z. ZIMOLO, T. COOPER, K. PERRY, AND J. KRYSTAL. "Blunted Psychotomimetic and Amnestic Effects of Delta-9-Tetrahydrocannabinol in Frequent Users of Cannabis." *Neuropsychopharmacology*, 33: 2505–16, 2008 **(50114)**

DUBOIS, S., N. MULLEN, B. WEAVER, AND M. BEDARD. "The Combined Effects of Alcohol and Cannabis on Driving: Impact on Crash Risk." *Forensic Science International*, 248: 94–100, 2015 **(50803)**

DU MONT, J., AND M.J. MCGREGOR. "Sexual Assault in the Lives of Urban Sex Workers: A Descriptive and Comparative Analysis." *Women and Health*, 39: 79–95, 2004 **(61701)**

DUPONT, R.L., R.B. VOAS, J.M. WALSH, C. SHEA, S.K. TALPINS, AND M.M. NEIL. "The Need for Drugged Driving Per Se Laws: A Commentary." *Traffic Injury Prevention*, 13: 31–42, 2013 **(50701)**

DZODZOMENYO, S., A. STOLFI, D. SPLAINGARD, E. EARLEY, O. ONADEKO, AND M. SPLAINGARD. "Urine Toxicology Screen in Multiple Sleep Latency Test: The Correlation of Positive Tetrahydrocannabinol, Drug Negative Patients and Narcolepsy." *Journal of Clinical Sleep Medicine*, 11: 93–99, 2015 **(40218)**

E

EARLEYWINE, M., AND N.T. VAN DAM. "Case Studies in Cannabis Vaporization." *Addiction Research and Theory*, 18: 243–49, 2010 **(10109)**

F

FABER, M., A. VAN GASSE, V. SABATO, M.M. HAGENDORENS, C.H. BRIDTS, L.S. DE CLERCK, AND D.G. EBO. "Marijuana Allergy: Beyond the Joint." *Journal of Investigative Allergology and Clinical Immunology*, 25: 70–72, 2015 **(61104)**

FABRITIUS, M., B. FAVRAT, H. CHTIOUI, G. BATTISTELLA, J-M. ANNONI, M. APPENZELLER, K. DAO., E. FORNARI, E. LAUER, J-F. MALL, P. MAEDER, P. MANGIN, C. STAUB, AND C. GIROUD. "THCCOOH Concentrations in Whole Blood: Are They Useful in Discriminating Occasional from Heavy Smokers?" *Drug Testing and Analysis*, 6: 155–63, 2014 **(10409)**

FANALI, G., Y. CAO, P. ASCENZI, V. TREZZA, T. RUBINO, D. PAROLARO, AND M. FASANO. "Binding of delta-9-Tetrahydrocannabinol and Diazepam to Human Serum Albumin." *International Union of Biochemistry and Molecular Biology Life*, 63: 446–51, 2011 **(10202)**

FARMER, R.F., D.B. KOSTY, J.R. SEELEY, S.C. DUNCAN, M.T. LYNSKEY, P. ROHDE, D.N. KLEIN, AND P.M. LEWINSOHN. "Natural Course of Cannabis Use Disorders." *Psychological Medicine*, 45: 63–72, 2015 **(60507)**

FATTORE, L., AND W. FRATTA. "How Important are Sex Differences in Cannabinoid Action?" *British Journal of Pharmacology*, 160: 544–48, 2010 **(10404)**

FAVRAT, B., A. MENETREY, M. AUGSBURGER, L.E. ROTHUIZEN, M. APPENZELLER., T. BUCLIN, M. PIN, P. MANGIN, AND C. GIROUD. "Two Cases of Cannabis Acute Psychosis Following the Administration of Oral Cannabis." *BMC Psychiatry*, 5: 17, 6 pp, 2005 **(61417)**

FERGUSSON, D.M., L.J. HORWOOD, AND J.M. BODEN. "Is Driving Under the Influence of Cannabis Becoming a Greater Risk to Driver Safety Than Drink Driving? Findings from a Longitudinal Study." *Accident Analysis and Prevention*, 40: 1345–50, 2008 **(50516)**

FERGUSSON, D.M., L.J. HORWOOD, AND N. SWAIN-CAMPBELL. "Cannabis Use and Psychosocial Adjustment in Adolescence and Young Adulthood." *Addiction*, 97: 1123–35, 2002 **(60109)**

FIERRO, I., J.C. GONZALEZ-LUQUE, AND F.J. ALVAREZ. "The Relationship between Observed Signs of Impairment and THC Concentration of Oral Fluid." *Drug and Alcohol Dependence*, 144: 231–38, 2014 **(50611)**

FISCHER, B., S. IMTIAZ, K. RUDZINSKI, AND J. REHM "Crude Estimates of Cannabis-Attributable Mortality and Morbidity in Canada: Implications for Public Health Focused Intervention Priorities." *Journal of Public Health*, 38: 183–88, 2015 **(60511)**

FISCHER, B., Y. MURPHY, P. KURDYAK, E. GOLDNER AND J. REHM. "Medical Marijuana Programs: Why Might They Matter for Public Health and Why We Should Better Understand Their Impacts?" *Preventive Medicine Reports*, 2: 53–56, 2015 **(61105)**

FISHER, B.A.C., A. GHURAN, V. VADAMALAI, T.F. ANTONIOS. "Cardiovascular Complications Induced by Cannabis Smoking: A Case Report and Review of the Literature." *Emergency Medicine Journal*, 22: 679–80, 2005 **(60406)**

FOGELMAN, S., C. RANGAN, J. KENNEDY, M. SANTOS, M. KIM, R. REPORTER, S.M. TEUTSCH, J.E. FIELDING, AND D. DIAMOND. "Inadvertent Ingestion of Marijuana–Los Angeles, California, 2009." *Morbidity and Mortality Weekly Report*, 58: 947–50, 2009 **(60608)**

FREEMAN, T.P., AND A.R. WINSTOCK. "Examining the Profile of High-Potency Cannabis and Its Association with the Severity of Cannabis Dependence." *Psychological Medicine*, 45: 3181–89, 2015 **(60504)**

FREISTHLER, B., AND P.J. GRUENEWALD. "Examining the Relationship between the Physical Availability of Medical Marijuana and Marijuana Use across Fifty California Cities." *Drug and Alcohol Dependence,* 143: 244–50, 2014 **(61108)**

FRIESE, B., M.D. SLATER, R. ANNECHINO, AND R.S. BATTLES. "Teen Use of Marijuana Edibles: A Focus Group Study of an Emerging Issue." *Journal of Primary Prevention*, 37: 303–9, 2016 **(61710)**

G

GALEA, S., J. AHERN, K. TARDIFF, A.C. LEON, AND D. VLAHOV. "Drugs and Firearm Deaths in New York City, 1990–1998." *Journal of Urban Health: Bulletin New York Academy of Science,* 79: 70–86, 2002 **(60904)**

GALLI, J.A., R.A. SAWAYA, AND F.K. FRIENDENBERG. "Cannabinoid Hyperemesis Syndrome." *Current Drug Abuse Review*, 4: 241–49, 2011 **(60317)**

GAO, Z., R. WOOD-BAKER, R. HARLE, K. MULLER, J. HAUSER, AND D.W. REID. "Bong Lung in Cystic Fibrosis: A Case Report." *Journal of Medical Case Reports*, 4: 371, 2010 **(61616)**

GARGANI, Y., P. BISHOP, AND D.W. DENNING. "Too Many Moldy Joints: Marijuana and Chronic Pulmonary Aspergillosis." *Mediterranean Journal of Hematology and Infectious Diseases*, 3: 6 pp, 2011 **(61613)**

GARRY A., V. RIGOURD, A. AMIROUCHE, V. FAUROUX, S. AUBURY, AND R. SERREAU. "Cannabis and Breastfeeding." *Journal of Toxicology*, ID 596149, 5 pp, 2009 **(40506)**

GENTILI, S., R. SOLIMINI, R. TITTARELLI, G. MANNOCCHI, AND P. BUSCARDO. "A Study on the Reliability of an On-Site Oral Fluid Drug Test in a

Recreational Context." *Journal of Analytical Methods in Chemistry*, 1234581, 10 pp, 2016 **(30404)**

GIERON, J., AND P. ADAMOWICZ. "Fatal Poisoning with the Synthetic Cannabinoid AB-CHMINACA and Ethyl Alcohol: A Case Study and Literature Review." *Problems of Forensic Science*, 106: 482–95, 2016 **(80429)**

GIESE, M.W., M.A. LEWIS, L. GIESE, AND K.M. SMITH. "Development and Validation of a Reliable and Robust Method for the Analysis of Cannabinoids and Terpenes in Cannabis." *Journal of the Association of Official Agricultural Chemists International*, 98: 1503–22, 2015 **(80102)**

GILBERT, C.R., M. BARAM, AND N.C. CAVAROCCHI. "Smoking Wet. Respiratory Failure Related to Smoking Tainted Marijuana Cigarettes." *Texas Heart Institute Journal*, 40: 64–67, 2013 **(61606)**

GINSBURG, B.C., L.R. MCMAHON, J.J. SANCHEZ, AND M.A. JAVORS. "Purity of Synthetic Cannabinoids Sold Online for Recreational Use." *Journal of Analytical Toxicology*, 56: 666–68, 2012 **(80407)**

GIROUD, C., M. DE CESARE, A. BERTHET, V. VARLET, N. CONCHA-LOZANO, AND B. FAVRAT. "E-Cigarettes: A Review of New Trends in Cannabis Use." *International Journal of Environmental Research and Public Health*, 12: 9988–10008, 2015 **(60611)**

GIROTTO, E., A.E. MESAS, S.M. DE ANDRADE, AND M.M. BIROLIM. "Psychoactive Substance Use by Truck Drivers: A Systematic Review." *Occupational and Environmental Medicine*, 71: 71–76, 2014 **(61502)**

GJERDE, H., J. MORDAL., A.S. CHRISTOPHERSEN, J.G. BRAMNESS, AND J. MORLAND. "Comparison of Drug Concentrations in Blood and Oral Fluids Collected with Intercept Sampling Device." *Journal of Analytical Toxicology*, 34: 204–9, 2010 **(30304)**

GJERDE, H., P.T. NORMANN, AND A.S. CHRISTOPHERSEN. "The Prevalence of Alcohol and Drugs in Sampled Oral Fluid is Related to Sample Volume." *Journal of Analytical Toxicology*, 34: 416–18, 2010 **(30402)**

GMEL, G., J. GAUME, C. WILLI, P-A. MICHAUD, J. CORNUZ, AND J-B. DAEPPEN. "Challenging the "Inoffensiveness" of Regular Cannabis Use by Its Associations with Other Current Risky Substance Use: A Census of 20-Year-Old Swiss Men." *International Journal of Environmental Research and Public Health*, 7: 46–59, 2010 **(60501)**

GONZALEZ-PINTO, A., S. ALBERICH, S. BARBEITO, M. GUTIERREZ, P. VAGA, B. IBANEZ, M.K. HAIDAR, E. VIETA, AND C. ARANGO. "Cannabis and First-Episode Psychosis: Different Long-Term Outcomes Depending on

Continued or Discontinued Use." *Schizophrenia Bulletin,* 37: 631–39, 2011 **(61419)**

GOODWIN, R.S., W.D. DARWIN, C.N. CHIANG, M. SHIH, S-H. LI, AND M.A. HUESTIS. "Urinary Elimination of 11 Nor-9-Carboxy-9-tetrahydrocannabinol in Cannabis Users during Continuously Monitored Abstinence." *Journal of Analytical Toxicology,* 32: 562–69, 2008 **(40217)**

GOODYEAR K., D. LAWS, AND J. TURNER. "Bilateral Spontaneous Pneumothorax in a Cannabis Smoker." *Journal of the Royal Society of Medicine,* 97: 435–36, 2004 **(61610)**

GORELICK, D.A., R.S. GOODWIN, E. SCHWILKE, D.M. SCHWOPE, W.D. DARWIN, D.I. KELLY, R.P. MCMAHON, F. LUI, C. ORTEMANN-RENON, D. BONNET, AND M.A. HUESTIS. "Tolerance to Effects of High-Dose Oral delta 9-Tetrahydrocannabinol and Plasma Cannabinoid Concentrations in Male Daily Cannabis Smokers." *Journal of Analytical Toxicology,* 37: 11–16, 2013 **(80205)**

GRANT, P., AND P.A. GANDHI. "A Case of Cannabis-Induced Pancreatitis." *Journal of the Pancreas,* 5: 41–43, 2004 **(60619)**

GRAY, T.R., A.J. BARNES, AND M.A. HUESTIS "Effect of Hydrolysis on Identifying Prenatal Cannabis Exposure." *Analytical Bioanalytical Chemistry,* 397: 2335–47, 2010 **(40501)**

GRAY, T.R., R.D. EIDEN, K.E. LEONARD, G.J. CONNORS, S. SHISLER, AND M. HUESTIS. "Identifying Prenatal Cannabis Exposure and Effects of Concurrent Tobacco Exposure and Neonatal Growth." *Clinical Chemistry,* 56: 1442–50, 2010 **(40508)**

GREEN, K.M., R.J. MUSCI, R.M. JOHNSON, P.A. MATSON, B.A. REBOUSSIN, AND N.S. IALONGON. "Outcomes Associated with Adolescent Marijuana and Alcohol Use among Urban Young Adults: A Prospective Study." *Addictive Behaviors,* 53: 155–60, 2016 **(60116)**

GREENBERG, H.S., S.A.S. WERNESS, J.E. PUGH, R.O. ANDRUS, D.J. ANDERSON, AND E.F. DOMINO. "Short-Term Effects of Smoking Marijuana on Balance in Patients with Multiple Sclerosis and Normal Volunteers." *Clinical Pharmacology and Therapeutics,* 55: 324–28, 1994 **(50103)**

GRONEWOLD, A., AND G.A. SKOPP. "A Preliminary Investigation on the Distribution of Cannabinoids in Man." *Forensic Science International,* 210: e7–e11, 2011 **(70101)**

GROTENHERMEN, F. "Pharmacokinetics and Pharmacodynamics of Cannabinoids." *Clinical Pharmacokinetics,* 42: 327–360, 2003 **(10405)**

GROTENHERMEN, F., G. LESON, G. BERGHAUS., O.H. DRUMMER, H-P. KRUGER, M. LONGO, H. MOSKOWITZ, B. PERRINE, J.G. RAMAEKERS, A. SMILEY, AND R. TUNBRIDGE. "Developing Limits for Driving Under Cannabis." *Addiction*, 102: 1910–17, 2007 **(50702)**

GRUBER, S.A., M.K. DAHLGREN, K.A. SAGAR, A. GONENC, AND S.E. LUKAS. "Worth the Wait: Effects of Age of Onset of Marijuana Use on White Matter and Impulsivity." *Psychopharmacology*, 231: 1455–65, 2014 **(60105)**

GUNAWARDENA, M.D.V.M., S. RAJAPKSE, J. HERATH, AND N. AMARASENA. "Myocardial Infarction Following Cannabis Induced Coronary Vasospasm." *British Medical Journal Case Report* Nov 12: 3 pp, 2014 **(60421)**

GUNN, J.K.L., C.B. ROSALES, K.E. CENTER, A. NUNEZ, S.J. GIBSON, C. CHRIST, AND J.E. EHIRI. "Prenatal Exposure to Cannabis and Maternal and Child Health Outcomes: A Systematic Review and Meta-Analysis." *British Medical Journal Open*, 6: 8 pp, 2016 **(40509)**

H

HACKAM, D.G. "Cannabis and Stroke. Systematic Appraisal of Case Reports." *Stroke*, 46: 852–56, 2015 **(60420)**

HAGGARD-GRANN, U., J. HALLQVIST, N. LANGSTROM, AND J. MOLLER. "The Role of Alcohol and Drugs in Triggering Criminal Violence: A Case-Crossover Study." *Addiction*, 101: 100–8, 2006 **(60203)**

HANCOCK-ALLEN, J.B., L. BARKER, M. VANDYKE, AND D.B. HOLMES. "Death Following Ingestion of an Edible Marijuana Product, Colorado, March 2014." *Morbidity and Mortality Weekly Report*, 64: 771–72, 2015 **(61905)**

HANEY, M., G. BEDI, Z.D. COOPER, A. GLASS, S.K. VOSBURG, S.D. COMER, AND R.W. FOLTIN. "Predictors of Marijuana Relapse in the Human Laboratory: Robust Impact of Tobacco Cigarette Smoking Status." *Biological Psychiatry*, 73: 242–48, 2013 **(62110)**

HANEY, M., Z.D. COOPER, G. BEDI, S.K. VOSBURG, S.D. COMER, AND R.W. FOLTIN. "Nabilone Decreases Marijuana Withdrawal and a Laboratory Measure of Marijuana Relapse." *Neuropsychopharmacology*, 38: 1557–65, 2013 **(62106)**

HANCOX R.J., H.H. SHIN, A.R. GRAY, R. POULTON, AND M.R. SEARS. "Effects of Quitting Cannabis on Respiratory Symptoms." *European Respiratory Journal*, 46: 80–87, 2015 **(61604)**

HARCOURT, P.R., H. UNGLIK, AND J.L. COOK. "A Strategy to Reduce Illicit Drug Use Effective in Elite Australian Football." *British Journal of Sports Medicine*, 46: 943–45, 2012 **(61806)**

HARTMAN, R.L., T.L. BROWN, G. MILAVETZ, A. SPURGIN, D.A. GORELICK, G. GAFFNEY, AND M.A. HUESTIS. "Controlled Cannabis Vaporizer Administration: Blood and Plasma Cannabinoids with and without Alcohol." *Clinical Chemistry*, 61: 850–59, 2015 **(10506)**

HARTMAN, R.L., T.L. BROWN, G. MILAVETZ, A. SPURGIN, D.A. GORELICK, G.R. GAFFNEY, AND M.A. HUESTIS. "Effect of Blood Collection Time on Measured delta 9-Tetrahydrocannabinol Concentrations: Implications for Driving Interpretation and Drug Policy." *Clinical Chemistry,* 62: 367–77, 2016 **(20103)**

HARTMAN, R.L., T.L. BROWN, G. MILAVETZ, A. SPURGIN, R.S. PIERCE, D.A. GORELICK, G. GAFFNEY, AND M.A. HUESTIS. "Cannabis Effects on Driving Lateral Control with and without Alcohol." *Drug and Alcohol Dependence*, 154: 25–37, 2015 **(50202)**

HARTUNG, B., S. KAUFERSTEIN, S. RITZ-TIMME, AND T. DALRUP. "Sudden Unexpected Death under Acute Influence of Cannabis." *Forensic Science International*, 237: e11–e13, 2014 **(60409)**

HASIN, D.S., T.D. SAHA, B.T. KERRIDGE, R.B. GOLDSTEIN, S.P. CHOU, H. ZHANG, J. JUNG, R.P. PICKERING, W.J. RUAN, S.M. SMITH, B. HUANG, AND B.F. GRANT. "Prevalence of Marijuana Use Disorder in the United States between 2001 and 2002 and 2012 and 2013." *Journal of the American Medical Association Psychiatry*, 72: 19 pp, December 2015 **(60505)**

HAVIG, S.M., G. HOISETH, M.C. STRAND, R.A. KARINEN, G-W. BROCHMANN, D.H. STRAND, L. BACHS, AND V. VINDENES. "THC and CBD in Blood Samples and Seizures in Norway: Does CBD Affect THC-Induced Impairment in Apprehended Subjects?" *Forensic Science International*, 276: 12–17, 2017 **(50533)**

HAYDEN, J.W. "Passive Inhalation of Marijuana Smoke: A Critical Review." *Journal of Substance Abuse*, 3: 85–90, 1991 **(10105)**

HEISHMAN, S.J., K. ARASTEH, AND M.L. STITZER. "Comparative Effects of Alcohol and Marijuana on Mood, Memory and Performance." *Pharmacology Biochemistry and Behavior*, 58: 93–101. 1997 **(50111)**

HEISHMAN, S.J., E.G. SINGLETON, AND D.J. COUCH. "Laboratory Validation Study of Drug Evaluation and Classification Program: Ethanol, Cocaine, and Marijuana." *Journal of Analytical Toxicology*, 20: 468–483, 1996 **(50612)**

HERMANN, E.S., E.J. CONE, J.M. MITCHELL, G.E. BIGELOW, C. LODICO, R. FLEGEL, AND R. VANDREY. "Non-Smoker Exposure to Secondhand Cannabis Smoke II: Effect of Room Ventilation on the Psychological, Subjective, and Behavioral/Cognitive Effects." *Drug and Alcohol Dependence*, 151: 194–202, 2015 **(10106)**

HERMES-LAUFER, J., L.D. PUPPO, I. INAN, F-X. TROILLET, AND C. KHERAD. "Cannabinoid Hyperemesis Syndrome: A Case Report of Cyclic Severe Hyperemesis and Abdominal Pain with Long-Term Cannabis Use." *Case Reports in Gastrointestinal Medicine*, 2016, 4 pp **(60302)**

HICKMAN, M., P. VICKERMAN, J. MACLEOD, G. LEWIS, S. ZAMMIT, J. KIRKBRIDE, AND P. JONES. "If Cannabis Use Causes Schizophrenia, How Many Cannabis Users May Need to be Prevented in Order to Prevent One Case of Schizophrenia? England and Wales Calculations." *Addiction*, 104: 1856–61, 2009 (3 figures, 24 references)

HILL, K.P. "Medical Marijuana for Treatment of Chronic Pain and Other Medical and Psychiatric Problems. A Clinical Review." *Journal of the American Medical Association*, 313: 2474–83, 2015 **(80301)**

HIMES, S.K., K.B. SCHEIDWEILER, O. BECK, D.A. GORELICK, N.A. DESROSIERS, AND M.A. HUESTIS. "Cannabinoids in Exhaled Breath following Controlled Administration of Smoked Cannabis." *Clinical Chemistry*, 59: 1780–89, 2013 **(40103)**

HINDOCHA, C., T.P. FREEMAN, G. SCHAFER C. GARDNER, R.K. DAS, C.J.A. MORGAN, AND H.V. CURRAN. "Acute Effects of Delta-9-Tetrahydrocannabinol, Cannabidiol, and Their Combination on Facial Emotion Recognition: A Randomized Double-Blind, Placebo-Controlled Study in Cannabis Users." *European Neuropsychopharmacology*, 25: 325–34, 2015 **(80302)**

HOCH, E., U. BONNET, R. THOMASIUS, F. GANZER, U. HAVEMANN-REINECKE, AND U.W. PREUSS. "Risks Associated with the Non-Medicinal Use of Cannabis." *Deutsches Arzteblatt International*, 112: 271–78, 2015 **(80303)**

HOLLAND, M.G., D.M. SCHWOPE, R. STOPPACHER, S.B. GILLEN, AND M.A. HUESTIS. "Postmortem Redistribution of Delta 9-Tetrahydrocannabinol (THC), 11-Hydroxy-THC (11-OH-THC) and 11 nor-9-Carboxy THC (THCCOOH)." *Forensic Science International*, 212: 247–51, 2011 **(70102)**

HOLLER, J.M., T.Z. BOSY, C.S. DUNKLEY, B. LEVINE, M.R. PAST, AND A. JACOBS. "Delta 9 Tetrahydrocannabinol Content of Commercially Available

Hemp Products." *Journal of Analytical Toxicology*, 32: 428–32, 2008 **(80304)**

HOLLISTER, L.E., AND H.K. GILLESPIE. "Marihuana, Ethanol and Dextro-amphetamine. Mood and Mental Function Alterations." *Archives of General Psychiatry,* 23: 199–203, 1970 **(50112)**

HOLMGREN, P., H. DRUID, A. HOLMGREN, AND J. AHNER. "Stability of Drugs in Stored Postmortem Femoral Blood and Vitreous Humor." *Journal of Forensic Sciences*, 49: 820–25, 2004 **(70103)**

HOUWING, S., B.E. SMINK, S-A. LEGRAND, R.P.M. MATHIJSSEN, A.G. VERSTRAETE, AND K.A. BROOKHUIS. "Repeatability of Oral Fluid Collection Methods for THC Measurement." *Forensic Science International*, 223: 266–72, 2012 **(30403)**

HUAS, C., C. HASSLER, AND M. CHOQUET. "Has Occasional Cannabis Use among Adolescents Also to be considered as a Risk Marker?" *European Journal of Public Health,* 18: 626–29, 2008 **(60101)**

HUESTIS, M.A. "Cannabis (Marijuana)–Effects on Human Behavior and Performance." *Forensic Science Review,* 14: 16–60, 2002 **(50517)**

HUESTIS, M.A. "Deterring Driving Under the Influence of Cannabis [Editorial]." *Addiction,* 110: 1697–98, 2015 **(50703)**

HUESTIS, M.A., A. BARNES, AND M.L. SMITH. "Estimating the Time of Last Cannabis Use from Plasma delta9-Tetrahydrocannabinol and 11-nor-9-Carboxy-delta9 Tetrahydrocannabinol Concentrations." *Clinical Chemistry,* 51: 2289–95, 2005 **(10107)**

HUESTIS, M.A., AND E.J. CONE. "Relationship of delta 9 Tetrahydrocannabinol Concentrations in Oral Fluid and Plasma after Controlled Administration of Smoked Cannabis." *Journal of Analytical Toxicology,* 28: 394–99, 2004 **(30202)**

HUESTIS, M.A., R.A. GUSTAFSON, E.T. MOOLCHAN, A. BARNES, J.A. BOURLAND, S.A. SWEENEY, E.F. HAYES, P.M. CARPENTER., AND M.L. SMITH. "Cannabinoid Concentrations in Hair from Documented Cannabis Users." *Forensic Science International,* 169: 129–36, 2007 **(40304)**

HUESTIS, M.A., I. MAZZONI, AND O. RABIN. "Cannabis in Sport: Anti-Doping Perspective." *Sports Medicine,* 41: 949–66, 2011 **(61802)**

HUESTIS, M.A., H. SAMPSON, B.J. HOLICKY, J.E. HENNINGFIELD, AND E.J. CONE. "Characterization of the Absorption Phase of Marijuana Smoking." *Clinical Pharmacology and Therapeutics,* 52: 31–43, 1992 **(10108)**

HUESTIS, M.A., K.B. SCHEIDWEILER, T. SAITO, N. FORTNER, T. ABRAHAM, R.A. GUSTAFSON, AND M.L. SMITH. "Excretion of delta 9 Tetrahydrocannabinol in Sweat." *Forensic Science International*, 174: 173–77, 2008 **(40402)**

HUGHES, J.R., S. NAUD, A.J. BUDNEY, J.R. FINGAR, AND P.W. CALLAS. "Attempts to Stop or Reduce Daily Cannabis Use: An Intensive Natural History Study." *Psychology Addictive Behavior* 30: 389–97, 2016 **(62109)**

HUNAULT, C.C., T.T. MENSINGA, K.B.E. BUCKER, C.M.A. SHIPPER, M. KRUDENIER, E.C. LEENDERS, I. DE VRIES, AND J. MEULENBELT. "Cognitive and Psychomotor Effects in Males after Smoking a Combination of Tobacco and Cannabis Containing Up to 69 mg delta-9-tetrahydrocannabinol (THC)." *Psychopharmacology*, 204: 85–94, 2009 **(50802)**

HUNAULT, C.C., J.C.H. VAN EIJKEREN, T.T. MENSINGA, I. DE VRIES, M.E.C. LEENDERS, AND J. MEULENBELT. "Disposition of Smoked Cannabis with High delta 9-Tetrahydrocannabinol Content: A Kinetic Model." *Toxicology and Applied Pharmacology*, 246: 148–53, 2010 **(10503)**

I

IACOPETTI, C.L., AND C.D. PARKER. "Cannabinoid Hyperemesis Syndrome: A Case Report and Review of Pathophysiology." *Clinical Medicine and Research*, 12: 65–67, 2014 **(60304)**

ILAN, A.B., A. GEVINS, M. COLEMAN, M.A. ELSOHLY, AND H. DE WIT. "Neurophysiological and Subjective Profile of Marijuana with Varying Concentrations of Cannabinoids." *Behavioral Pharmacology*, 16: 487–96, 2006 **(80502)**

ILAN, A.B., M.E. SMITH, AND A. GEVINS. "Effects of Marijuana on Neurophysiological Signals of Working and Episodic Memory." *Psychopharmacology*, 176: 214–22, 2004 **(61010)**

ILGEN, M.A., M.A. WALTON, R.M. CUNNINGHAM, K.L. BARRY, S.T. CHERMACK, P. DE CHAVEZ, AND F.C. BLOW. "Recent Suicidal Ideation among Patients in an Inner-City Emergency Department." *Suicide and Life-Threatening Behavior*, 39: 508–17, 2009 **(61914)**

J

JACOBUS, J., S. BAVA, M. COHEN-ZION, O. MAHMOOD, AND S.F. TAPERT. "Functional Consequences of Marijuana Use in Adolescents." *Pharmacology and Biochemistry of Behavior*, 92: 559–65, 2009 **(60115)**

JAMERSON, M.H., J.J. MCCUE, AND K.L. KLETTE. "Urine pH, Container Composition, and Exposure Time Influence Adsorptive Loss of 11 nor delta 9 tetrahydrocanninol-9 Carboxylic Acid." *Journal of Analytical Toxicology*, 29: 627–31, 2005 **(40208)**

JEHANGIR, W., M. STANTON, R. KHAN, P. SAHGAL, AND A. YOUSIF. "Did Cannabis Precipitate an STEMI in a Young Woman?" *Cardiology Research*, 6: 283–85, 2015 **(60424)**

JOHNSON, M.B., T. KELLY-BAKER, R.B. VOAS, AND J.H. LACEY. "The Prevalence of Cannabis-Involved Driving in California." *Drug and Alcohol Dependence*, 123: 13 pp, 2012 **(50704)**

JOHNSON, M.K., R.P. SMITH, D. MORRISON, G. LASZLO, AND R.J. WHITE. "Large Lung Bullae in Marijuana Smokers." *Thorax*, 55: 340–42, 2000 **(61608)**

JOHNSON, S., AND E.F. DOMINO. "Some Cardiovascular Effects of Marihuana Smoking in Normal Volunteers." *Clinical Pharmacology and Therapeutics*, 12: 762–68, 1971 **(60401)**

JONES, A.W., A. HOLMGREN, AND F.C. KUGELBERG, "Driving Under the Influence of Cannabis: A 10-Year Study of Age and Gender Differences in the Concentrations of Tetrahydrocannabinol in Blood." *Addiction*, 101: 452–61, 2008 **(50519)**

JONES, A.W., F.C. KUGELBERG, A. HOLMGREN, AND J. AHLNER. "Five-Year Update on the Occurrence of Alcohol and Other Drugs in Blood Samples from Drivers Killed in Road Traffic Crashes in Sweden." *Forensic Science International*, 186: 56–62, 2009 **(50518)**

JONES, A.W., F.C. KUGELBERG, A.H. HOLMGREN, AND J. AHLNER. "Occurrence of Ethanol and Other Drugs in Blood and Urine Specimens from Female Victims of Alleged Sexual Assault." *Forensic Science International*, 181: 40–46, 2008 **(61702)**

JONES, C.G.A., W. SWIFT, N.J. DONNELLY, AND D.J. WEATHERBURN. "Correlates of Driving Under the Influence of Cannabis." *Drug and Alcohol Dependence*, 88: 83–86, 2007 **(50520)**

JONES, J.L., AND K.E. ABERNATHY. "Successful Treatment of Suspected Cannabinoid Hyperemesis Syndrome Using Haloperidol in the Outpatient Setting." *Case Reports in Psychiatry*, Article ID 3614053, 3 pp, 2016 **(60303)**

JOUANJUS, E., M. LAPEYRE-MESTRE, J. MICALLEF, J., ET AL. "Cannabis Use: Signal of Increasing Risk of Serious Cardiovascular Disorders." *Journal of the American Heart Association*, 3: 7 pp, 2014 **(60419)**

JOUANJUS, E., F. LEYMARIE, M. TUBERY AND M. LAPEYRE-MESTRE. "Cannabis-Related Hospitalizations: Unexpected Serious Events Identified Through Hospital Databases." *British Journal of Clinical Pharmacology*, 71: 758–65, 2011 **(60620)**

JUHASCIK, M.P., A. NEGRUS, D. FAUGNO, L. LEDRAY, P. GREENE, A. LINDER, B. HANER, AND R.E. GAENSSLEN. "An Estimate of the Proportion of Drug-Facilitation of Sexual Assault in Four US Localities." *Journal of Forensic Sciences*, 52: 1396–1400, 2007 **(61703)**

K

KARSCHNER, E.L., A.J. BARNES, R.H. LOWE, K.B. SCHEIDWEILER, AND M.A. HUESTIS. "Validation of a Two-Dimensional Gas Chromatography Mass Spectrometry Method for the Simultaneous Quantification of Cannabindiol, delta-9-Tetrahydrocannabinol (THC), 11-Hydroxy-THC and 11-nor-9-carboxy-THC in Plasma." *Analytical Bioanalytical Chemistry* 397: 603–11, 2010 **(40206)**

KARSCHNER, E.L., W.D. DARWIN, R.S. GOODWIN, S. WRIGHT, AND M.A. HUESTIS. "Plasma Cannabinoid Pharmacokinetics following Controlled Oral delta Tetrahydrocannabinol and Oromucosal Cannabis Extraction Administration." *Clinical Chemistry*, 57: 66–75, 2011 **(10110)**

KARSCHNER, E.L., E.W. SCHWILKE, R.H. LOWE, W.D. DARWIN, R.L. HERNING, J.L. CADET, AND M.A. HUESTIS. "Implications of Plasma Delta 9-Tetrahydrocannabinol, 11-Hydroxy-THC and 11-nor-9-Carboxy-THC Concentrations in Chronic Cannabis Smokers." *Journal of Analytical Toxicology*, 33: 469–77, 2009 **(10301)**

KARSCHNER, E.L., E.W. SCHWILKE, R.H. LOWE, W.D. DARWIN, H.G. POPE JR., R. HERNING, J.L. CADET, AND M.A. HUESTIS. "Do delta 9-Tetrahydrocannabinol Concentrations Indicate Recent Use in Chronic Cannabis Users?" *Addiction*, 104: 2041–48, 2009 **(10302)**

KARSCHNER, E.L., D.M. SCHWOPE, E.W. SCHWILKE, R.S. GOODWIN, D.L. KELLY, D.A. GORELICK, AND M.A. HUESTIS. "Predictive Model Accuracy in Estimating Last delta-9-Tetrahydrocannabinol (THC) Intake from Plasma and Whole Blood Cannabinoid Concentrations in Chronic, Daily Cannabis Smokers Administered Subchronic Oral THC." *Drug and Alcohol Dependence*, 125: 313–19, 2012 **(10111)**

KATZ, K.D., A.L. LEONETTI, B.C. BAILEY, R.M. SURMAITIS, E.R. EUSTICE, S. KACINKO, AND S.M. WHEATLEY. "Case Series of Synthetic Cannabinoid

Intoxication from One Toxicology Center." *Western Journal of Emergency Medicine*, 17: 290–94, 2016 **(80434)**

KAUERT, G.J., J.G. RAMAEKERS, E. SCHNEIDER, M.R. MOELLER, AND S.W. TOENNES. "Pharmacokinetic Properties of delta 9-Tetrahydrocannabinol in Serum and Oral Fluid." *Journal of Analytical Toxicology*, 31: 288–93, 2007 **(30203)**

KELLER, T., A. KELLER, E. TUTSCH-BAUER, AND F. MONTICELLI. "Driving Under the Influence of Drugs and Alcohol in Salzburg and Upper Austria during the Years 2003–2007." *Legal Medicine*, 11: S98–S99, 2009 **(50613)**

KELLEY, M.E., C.R. WAN, B. BROUSSARD, A. CRISAFIO, S. CRISTOFARO, S. JOHNSON, T.A. REED, P. AMAR., N.J. KASLOW, E.F. WALKER, AND M.T. COMPTON. "Marijuana Use in the Immediate 5-Year Premorbid Period is Associated with Increased Risk of Onset of Schizophrenia and Related Psychotic Disorders." *Schizophrenia Research*, 171: 62–67, 2016 **(61415)**

KEMP, A.M., M.S. CLARK, T. DOBBS, R. GALLI, J. SHERMAN, AND R. COX. "Top 10 Facts You Need to Know About Synthetic Cannabinoids: Not So Nice Spice." *American Journal of Medicine*, 129: 240–44, 2016 **(80409)**

KEMP, P.M., P.S. CARDONA, A.K. CHATURVEDI, AND J.W. SOPER. "Distribution of delta 9-Tetrahydrocannabinol and 11-Nor-9-Carboxy-delta 9 Tetrahydrocannabinol Acid in Postmortem Biological Fluids and Tissues from Pilots Fatally Injured in Aviation Accidents." *Journal of Forensic Sciences*, 60: 942–49, 2015 **(70107)**

KHAN, M.A., AND S. AKELLA. "Cannabis-Induced Bipolar Disorder with Psychotic Features: A Case Report." *Psychiatry*, 6: 44–48, 2009 **(61421)**

KHIABANI, H.Z., J.G. BRAMNESS, A. BIOURNEBOE, AND J. MORLAND. "Relationship between THC Concentration in Blood and Impairment in Apprehended Drivers." *Traffic Injury Prevention*, 7: 111–16, 2006 **(50614)**

KIBBY, T., AND S.E. HALCOMB. "Toxicology Observation: Nystagmus after Marijuana Use." *Journal of Forensic and Legal Medicine,* 20: 345–46, 2013 **(50615)**

KIM, H.S., J.D. ANDERSON, O. SAGHAFI, K.J. HEARD, AND A.A. MONTE "Cyclic Vomiting Presentations Following Marijuana Liberalization in Colorado." *Academic Emergency Medicine*. 22: 694–99, 2015 **(60305)**

KIM, H.S., K.E. HALL, E.K. GENCO, M. VAN DYKE, E. BARKER, AND A.A. MONTE. "Marijuana Tourism and Emergency Department Visits in Colorado." *New England Medical Journal*, 374: 797–98, 2016 **(60613)**

KIM, H.S., AND A.A. MONTE. "Colorado Cannabis Legalization and Its Effect on Emergency Care." *Annals of Emergency Medicine*, 68: 71–75, 2016 **(60612)**

KLONOFF, H. "Marijuana and Driving in Real-Life Situations." *Science*, 186: 317–24, 1974 **(50401)**

KOH, H.C., W-Y. LEE, L.Z. EH, N.J. ISMAIL, P.S. TEE, A. OTHMAN, AND T. MURGAYA. "Efavirenz Does Not Cause False-Positive Urine Cannabis Test in HIV-Infected Patients on Highly Active Anti-Retroviral Therapy." *Medical Journal of Malaysia*, 68: 249–52, 2013 **(40215)**

KONG, G., N. SINGH, D. CAMENGA, D. CAVALLO, AND S. KRISHNAN-SARIN. "Menthol Cigarette and Marijuana Use among Adolescents." *Nicotine and Tobacco Research*, 15: 2094–99, 2013 **(60111)**

KOSIOR, D.A., K.J. FILLIPIAK, P. STOLARZ., AND G. OPOLSKI. "Paroxysmal Atrial Fibrillation in a Young Female Patient Following Marijuana Intoxication: A Case Report of Possible Association." *Medical Science Monitoring*. 6: 386–89, 2000 **(60411)**

KOWAL, M.A., A. HAZEKAMP, L.S. COLZATO, H. VAN STEENBERGEN, N.J.A. VAN DER WEE, J. DURIEUX, M. MANAI, AND B. HOMMEL. "Cannabis and Creativity: Highly Potent Cannabis Impairs Divergent Thinking in Regular Cannabis Users." *Psychopharmacology*, 232: 1123–34, 2015 **(61114)**

KRAEMER, R.R., R.M. LA HOZ, AND J.H. WILLIG. "Some Like It Hot: Erythema Ab Igne due to Cannabinoid Hyperemesis." *Journal of General Internal Medicine*, 28: 1522, 2013 **(60311)**

KUMAR, S., Y.S. BANSAL, D. SINGH, AND B. MEDHI. "Alcohol and Drug Use in Injured Drivers: An Emergency Room Study in a Regional Tertiary Care Centre of North West India." *Journal of Clinical and Diagnostic Research*, 9: HC01–HC04, 2015 **(50521)**

L

LABAY, L.M., J.L. CARUSO, T.P. GILSON, R.J. PHIPPS, L.D. KNIGHT, N.P. LEMOS, I.M. MCINTYRE, R. STOPPACHER, L.M. TORMOS, A.L. WIENS, AND B.K. LOGAN. "Synthetic Cannabinoids Drug Use as a Cause or Contributory Cause of Death." *Forensic Science International*, 260: 31–39, 2016 **(80410)**

LACHENMEIER, D.W., AND J. REHM. "Comparative Risk Assessment of Alcohol, Tobacco, Cannabis and Other Illicit Drugs Using the Margin of Exposure Approach." *Scientific Reports*, 5: 8126, 7 pp, 2015 **(61109)**

LALOUP, M., M.D.M.R. FERNANDEZ, M. WOOD, G. DE BOECK, V. MAES, AND N. SAMYN. "Correlation of delta 9-tetrahydrocannabinol Concentrations Determined by LC-MS-MS in Oral Fluid and Plasma from Impaired Drivers and Evaluation of the On-Site Drager DrugTest." *Forensic Science International*, 161: 175–79, 2006 **(30101)**

LAMERS, C.T., AND J.G. RAMAEKERS. "Visual Search and Urban City Driving Under the Influence of Marijuana and Alcohol." *Human Psychopharmacology. Clinical and Experimental,* 16: 393–401, 2001 **(50402)**

LANE, S.D., D.R. CHEREK, L.M. LIEVING, AND O.V. TCHEREMISSINE. "Marijuana Effects on Human Forgetting Functions." *Journal of the Experimental Analysis of Behavior*, 83: 67–83, 2005 **(61005)**

LANE, S.D., D.R. CHEREK, O.V. TCHEREMISSINE, L.M. LIEVING, AND C.J. PIETRAS. "Acute Marijuana Effects on Human Risk Taking." *Neuropsychopharmacology*, 30: 800–9, 2005 **(61704)**

LANGEL, K., H. GJERDE, D. FAVRETTO, P. LILLSUNDE, K.L. OIESTAD, S.D. FERRARA, AND A.G. VERSTRAETE. "Comparison of Drug Concentrations between Whole Blood and Oral Fluid." *Drug Testing Analysis*; 6: 461–71, 2014 **(30303)**

LANK, P.M., E. PINES, AND M.B. MYCK. "Emergency Physicians' Knowledge of Cannabinoid Designer Drugs." *Western Journal of Emergency Medicine,* 14: 467–70, 2013 (**80435**)

LASEBIKAN, V., AND O.O. AREMU. "Cannabis Use and Associated Harms among Schizophrenia Patients in a Nigerian Clinical Setting: A Case Control Study." *Frontiers in Psychiatry*, 7, Article 136, 9 pp, 2016 **(61418)**

LAUMON, B., B. GADEGBEKU, J.L. MARTIN, M-B. BIECHLER, AND THE SAM GROUP. "Cannabis Intoxication and Fatal Road Crashes in France: Population Based Case-Control Study." *British Medical Journal*, 331: 1371, Dec. 10, 2005 **(50522)**

LAUNIAINEN, T., AND I. OJANPERA. "Drug Concentrations in Post-Mortem Femoral Blood Compared with Therapeutic Concentrations in Plasma." *Drug Testing and Analysis*, 6: 308–16, 2014 **(70110)**

LAURE, P., AND C. BINSINGER. "Doping Prevalence among Preadolescent Athletes: A 4 Year Follow-Up." *British Journal of Sports Medicine,* 41: 660–63, 2007 **(61804)**

LAURITSEN, K.J., AND H. ROSENBERG. "Comparison of Outcome Expectancies for Synthetic Cannabinoids and Botanical Marijuana." *American Journal of Drug and Alcohol Abuse*, 42: 377–84, 2016 **(80411)**

LAZARO, I.J.S., L.A. BONET, M.J. SANCHO-TELLO, AND L. MARTINEZ-DOLZ. "Ventricular Tachycardia Due to Marijuana Use in a Heart Transplant Patient." *Revista Espanola Cardiologia*, 62: 459–61, 2009 **(60412)**

LEE, C.M., C. NEIGHBORS, AND B.A. WOODS. "Marijuana Motives: Young Adults' Reasons for Using Marijuana." *Addictive Behaviors*, 32: 1384–94, 2007 **(60103)**

LEE, D., M.M. BERGAMASCHI, G. MILMAN, A.J. BARNES, R.H.C. QUEIROZ, R. VANDREY, AND M.A. HUESTIS. "Plasma Cannabinoid Pharmacokinetics After Controlled Smoking and *Ad libitum* Cannabis Smoking in Chronic Frequent Users." *Journal of Analytical Toxicology*, 39: 580–87, 2015 **(10304)**

LEE, D., AND M.A. HUESTIS. "Current Knowledge on Cannabinoids in Oral Fluid." *Drug Testing and Analysis*, 6: 88–111, 2014 **(30601)**

LEE, D., E.L. KARSCHNER, G. MILMAN, A.J. BARNES, R.S. GOODWIN, AND M.A. HUESTIS. "Can Oral Fluid Cannabinoid Testing Monitor Medication Compliance and/or Cannabis Smoking During Oral THC and Oromucosal Sativex Administration?" *Drug and Alcohol Dependence*, 130: 68–76, 2013 **(30604)**

LEE, D., G. MILMAN, A.J. BARNES, R.S. GOODWIN, J. HIRVONEN, AND M.A. HUESTIS. "Oral Fluid Cannabinoids in Chronic Daily Cannabis Smokers during Sustained Monitored Abstinence." *Clinical Chemistry* 57: 1127–37, 2011 **(30206)**

LEE, D., G. MILMAN, D.M. SCHWOPE, A.J. BARNES, D.A. GORELICK, AND M. HUESTIS. "Cannabinoid Stability in Authentic Oral Fluid after Controlled Cannabis Smoking." *Clinical Chemistry*, 58: 1101–9, 2012 **(30406)**

LEE, D., D.M. SCHWOPE, G. MILMAN, A.J. BARNES, D.A. GORELICK, AND M.A. HUESTIS. "Cannabinoid Disposition in Oral Fluid after Controlled Smoked Cannabis." *Clinical Chemistry*, 58: 748–56, 2012 **(30204)**

LEE, D., R. VANDREY, G. MILMAN, M. BERGAMASCHI, D.R. MENDU, J.A. MURRAY, A.J. BARNES, AND M.A. HUESTIS. "Oral Fluid/Plasma Cannabinoid Ratios Following Controlled Oral THC and Smoked Cannabis Administration." *Analytical and Bioanalytical Chemistry* 405: 7269–79, 2013 **(30205)**

LEHRMANN, E., Z.R. AFANADOR, A. DEEP-SOBOSLAY, G. GALLEGOS, W.D. DARWIN, R.H. LOWE, A.J. BARNES, M.A. HUESTIS, J.L. CADET, M.M. HERMAN, T.M. HYDE, J.E. KLEINMAN, AND W.J. FREED. "Postmortem Diagnosis and Toxicological Validation of Illicit Substance Use." *Addiction Biology*, 13: 105–17, 2008 **(70111)**

LEMBERGER, L., R. MARTZ, B. RODDA, R. FORNEY, AND H. ROWE. "Comparative Pharmacology of delta-9-Tetrahydrocannabinol and its Metabolite 11-OH-delta-9-Tetrahydrocannabinol." *The Journal of Clinical Investigation*, 52: 2411–17, 1973 **(10305)**

LEMOS, N.P., AND E.A. INGLE. "Cannabinoids in Postmortem Toxicology." *Journal of Analytical Toxicology*, 35: 394–401, 2011 **(70104)**

LENGUERRAND, E., J-L. MARTIN, A. MOSKAL, R. GADEGBEKU, B. LAUMON, AND THE SAM GROUP. "Limits of the Quasi-Induced Exposure Method When Compared with the Standard Case-Control Design. Application to the Estimation of Risks Associated with Driving Under the Influence of Cannabis or Alcohol." *Accident Analysis and Prevention,* 40: 861–68, 2008 **(50523)**

LENNE, M.G., P.M. DIETZE, T.J. TRIGGS, S. WALMSLEY, B. MURPHY, AND J.R. REDMAN. "The Effects of Cannabis and Alcohol on Simulated Arterial Driving: Influences of Driving Experience and Task Demand." *Accident Analysis and Prevention,* 42: 859–66, 2010 **(50203)**

LERNER, A.G., C. GOODMAN, O. BAR, AND S.L. RAN. "Synthetic Cannabis Substances (SCS) Use and Hallucinogen Persisting Perception Disorder (HPPD): Two Case Reports." *Israeli Journal of Psychiatry and Related Science*, 51: 277–80, 2014 **(80436)**

LERNER, A.G., C. GOODMAN, D. RUDINSKI, AND A. BLEICH "Benign and Time-Limited Visual Disturbances (Flashbacks) in Recent Abstinent High-Potency Heavy Cannabis Smokers: A Case Series Study." *Israeli Journal of Psychiatry Related Science*, 48: 25–29, 2011 **(62108)**

LESON, G., P. PLESS, F. GROTENHERMEN, H. KALANT, AND M.A. ELSOHLY. "Evaluating the Impact of Hemp Food Consumption on Workplace Drug Tests." *Journal of Analytical Toxicology*, 25: 691–98, 2001 **(80305)**

LEVIN, F.R., J.J. MARIANI., D.J. BROOKS, S. XIE, AND K.A. MURRAY. "Delta-9-Tetrahydrocannabivarin Testing May Not Have the Sensitivity to Detect Marijuana Use among Individuals Ingesting Dronabinol." *Drug and Alcohol Dependence,* 106: 65 (8 pp), 2010 **(80501)**

LEVIN, K.H., M.L. COPERSINO, S.J. HEISHMAN, F. LIU, D.L. KELLY, D.L. BOGGS, AND D.A. GORELICK. "Cannabis Withdrawal Symptoms in Non-Treatment Seeking Adult Cannabis Smokers." *Drug and Alcohol Dependence*, 111: 120–27, 2010 **(62103)**

LEVY, R.S., C.K. HERBERT, B.G. MUNN, AND R.L. BARACK. "Drug and Alcohol Use in Orthopedic Trauma Patients: A Prospective Study." *Journal of Orthopedic Trauma*, 10: 21–27, 1996 **(62002)**

LI, A.M., AND R. RASSEKH. "Hypotension Associated with Ingestion of Cannabinoids in Two Children with Cancer." *Canadian Medical Association Journal*, 188: 596–97, 2016 **(60410)**

LI, G., S.P. BAKER, Q. ZHAO, J.E. BRADY, B.H. LANG, G.W. REBOK, AND C. DIMAGGIO. "Drug Violations and Aviation Accidents: Findings from the U.S. Mandatory Drug Testing Programs." *Addiction,* 106: 1287–92, 2011 **(60803)**

LI, G., A. CHANMUGAM, R. ROTHMAN, C. DISCALA, C.N. PAIDAS, AND G.D. KELEN. "Alcohol and Other Psychoactive Drugs in Trauma Patients Aged 10–14 Years." *Injury Prevention*, 5: 94–97, 1999 **(62006)**

LIAKONI, D., P.C. DOLDER, K. RENTSCH, AND M.E. LIECHTI. "Acute Health Problems due to Recreational Drug Use in Patients Presenting to an Urban Emergency Department in Switzerland." *Swiss Medical Weekly,* 145: 7 pp, 2015 **(60616)**

LIAKONI, D., P.C. DOLDER, K. RENTSCH, AND M.E. LIECHTI. "Presentations Due to Acute Toxicity of Psychoactive Substances in an Urban Emergency Department in Switzerland: A Case Series." *BMC Pharmacology and Toxicology,* 17: 25, 2016 **(60614)**

LIGUORI, A., C.P. GATTO, D.B. JARRETT, W.V. MCCALL, AND T.W. BROWN. "Behavioral and Subjective Effects of Marijuana Following Partial Sleep Deprivation." *Drug and Alcohol Dependence*, 70: 233–40, 2003 **(50204)**

LILE, J.A., T.H. KELLY, R.J. CHARNIGO, A.L. STINCHCOMBE, AND L.R. HAYS "Pharmacokinetic and Pharmacodynamic Profile of Supratherapeutic Oral Doses of delta 9-THC in Cannabis Users." *Journal Clinical Pharmacology,* 53: 680–90, 2013 **(80206)**

LIN, D.-L., AND R.-L. LIN. "Distribution of 11-Nor-9-Carboxy-delata 9 Tetrahydrocannabinol in Traffic Fatality Cases." *Journal of Analytical Toxicology,* 29: 58–61, 2005 **(70105)**

LINDGREN, J.-E., A. OHLSSON., S. AGURELL, L. HOLLISTER, AND H. GILLEPSIE "Clinical Effects and Plasma Levels of delta 9-Tetrahydrocannabinol (THC) in Heavy and Light Users of Cannabis." *Psychopharmacology,* 74: 208–12, 1981 **(50113)**

LINDHOLST, C. "Long Term Stability of Cannabis Resin and Cannabis Extracts." *Australian Journal of Forensic Sciences*, 42: 181–90, 2010 **(80104)**

LIU, C., Y. HUANG, AND J.C. PRESSLEY. "Restraint Use and Risky Driving Behaviors Across Drug Types and Drug and Alcohol Combinations for Drivers Involved in a Fatal Motor Vehicle Collision on U.S. Roadways." *Injury Epidemiology*, 3: 9, 2016 **(50524)**

LJUNGKVIST, G., S. ULLAH, A. TINGLEY, K. STEIN, B. BAKE, P. LARSSON, A-C. ALMSTRAND, E. VIKLUNG, O. HAMMAR, S. SANDQVIST, O. BECK, AND A-C. OLIN. "Two Techniques to Sample Non-Volatiles in Breath-Exemplified by Methadone." *Journal of Breath Research,* 12: 9 pp, 2017 **(40104)**

LOGAN, B.K., A.L.A. MOHR, AND S.K. TALPINS. "Detection and Prevalence of Drug Use in Arrested Drivers Using the Drager Drug Test 5000 and Affiniton DrugWipe Oral Fluid Drug Screening Devices." *Journal of Analytical Toxicology,* 38: 444–50, 2014 **(30302)**

LOGAN, B.K., L.E. REINHOLD, A. XU, AND F.X. DIAMOND. "Identification of Synthetic Cannabinoids in Herbal Incense Blends in the United States." *Journal of Forensic Sciences*, 57: 1168–80, 2012 **(80412)**

LUKAS, S.E., AND S. OROZCO. "Ethanol Increases Plasma delta 9 Tetrahydrocannabinol (THC) Levels and Subjective Effects after Marihuana Smoking in Human Volunteers." *Drug and Alcohol Dependence*, 64: 143–49, 2001 **(10505)**

LUND, A.K., D.F. PREUSSER, R.D. BLOMBERG, AND A.F. WILLIAMS. "Drug Use by Tractor-Trailer Drivers." *Journal of Forensic Sciences*, 33: 648–61, 1988 **(61503)**

LUNDHOLM, L., I. THIBLIN, B. RUNESON, A. LEIFMAN, AND A. FUGELSTAD. "Acute Influence of Alcohol, THC or Central Stimulants on Violent Suicide: A Swedish Population Study." *Journal of Forensic Sciences,* 59: 436–40, 2014 **(61901)**

M

MACCOUN, R.J., AND M.M. MELLO. "Half-Baked: The Retail Promotion of Marijuana Edibles (Perspective)." *The New England Journal of Medicine,* 372: 989–91, 2015 **(60603)**

MACDONALD, S., R. MANN, M. CHIPMAN, B. PAKULA, P. ERICKSON, A. HATHAWAY, AND P. MACINTYRE. "Driving Behavior under the Influence of Cannabis or Cocaine." *Traffic Injury and Prevention*, 9: 190–94, 2008 **(50525)**

MACINNES, D.C., AND K.M. MILLER. "Fatal Coronary Artery Thrombosis Associated with Cannabis Smoking." *Journal of the Royal College of General Practitioners*, 34: 575–76, 1984 **(60403)**

MADEA, B., AND F. MUSSHOFF. "Knock-Out Drugs: Their Prevalence, Modes of Action, Means of Detection." *Dtsch. Arztebl. Int.* 106: 341–47, 2009 **(61705)**

MAGGS, J.L., J. STAFF, D.D. KLOSKA, M.E. PATRICK, P.M. O'MALLEY, J. SCHULENBERG. "Predicting Young Adult Degree Attainment by Late Adolescent Marijuana Use." *Journal of Adolescent Health*, 57: 205–11, 2015 **(60104)**

MALHOTRA, C., N. SHARMA, R. SAXENA, AND G.K. INGLE. "Drug Use among Juveniles in Conflict with the Law." *Indian Journal of Pediatrics* 74: 353–56, 2007 **(60119)**

MAQUIRRIAN, J. "Epidemiological Analysis of Doping Offences in the Professional Tennis Circuit." *Journal of Occupational Medicine and Toxicology*, 5: 30 (6pp), 2010 **(61808)**

MARCHEI, E., D. ESCUDER, C.R. PALLAS, O. GARCIA-ALGAR, A. GOMEZ, B. FRIGULS, M. PELLEGRINI, AND S. PICHINI. "Simultaneous Analysis of Frequently Used Licit and Illicit Psychoactive Drugs in Breast Milk by Liquid Chromatography Tandem Mass Spectrometry." *Journal of Pharmaceutical and Biomedical Analysis* 55: 309–16, 2011 **(40503)**

MARTIN, J.-L., B. GADEGBEKU, D. WU, V. VIALLON, AND B. LAUMON. "Cannabis, Alcohol and Fatal Road Accidents." *PLOS ONE*, 12: e0187320, 16 pp, 2017 **(50534)**

MARSOT, A., C. AUDEBERT, L. ATTOLINI, B. LACARELLE, J. MICALLEF, AND O. BLIN. "Comparison of Cannabinoid Concentrations in Plasma, Oral Fluid and Urine in Occasional Cannabis Smokers after Smoking Cannabis Cigarette." *Journal of Pharmacy and Pharmaceutical Sciences*, 19: 411–22, 2016 **(40209)**

MATEO, I., A. PINEDO, M. GOMEZ-BELDARRAIN, J.M. BASTERRETEXA, AND J.C. GARCIA-MANCO. "Recurrent Stroke Associated with Cannabis Use." *Journal Neural Neurosurgery Psychiatry*, 76: 435–37, 2005 **(60415)**

MATHEW, R.J., W.H. WILSON, T.G. TURKINGTON, AND R.E. COLEMAN. "Cerebellar Activity and Disturbed Time Sense after THC." *Brain Research*, 797: 183–89, 1998 **(60802)**

MAY, M.B., AND A.E. GLODE. "Dronabinol for Chemotherapy-Induced Nausea and Vomiting Unresponsive to Antiemetics." *Cancer Management and Research*, 8: 49–55, 2016 **(80207)**

MCCALLUM, R.W., I. SOYKAN, K.R. SRIDHAR, D.A. RICCI, R.C. LANGE, AND M.W. PLANKEY. "Delta-9-Tetrahydrocannabinol Delays Gastric Emptying of Solid Food in Humans: A Double-Blind Randomized Study." *Aliment Pharmacology and Therapeutics*, 13: 77–80, 1999 **(10508)**

MCCLURE, E.A., J.B. LYDIARD, S.D. GODDARD, AND K.M. GRAY. "Objective and Subjective Memory Ratings in Cannabis-Dependent Adolescents." *American Journal of Addictions*, 24: 47–52, 2015 **(61007)**

MCDONALD, A., N.D. DUNCAN, AND D.I.G. MITCHELL. "Alcohol, Cannabis and Cocaine Usage in Patients with Trauma Injuries." *Western Indian Medical Journal*, 48: 200–2, 1999 **(62003)**

MCDONALD, J., L. SCHLEIFER, J.B. RICHARDS, H. DE WIT. "Effects of THC on Behavioral Measures of Impulsivity in Humans." *Neuropsychopharmacology,* 28: 1356–65, 2003 **(60204)**

MCDONNELL, M.G., F. ANGELO, A. SUGAR, C. RAINEY, D. SREBNIK, J. ROLL., R. SHORT, AND R.K. RIES. "A Pilot Study of the Accuracy of Onsite Immunoassay Urinalysis of Illicit Drug Use in Seriously Mentally Ill Outpatients." *American Journal of Drug and Alcohol Abuse,* 37: 137–40, 2011 **(40204)**

MCILROY, G., L. FORD, AND J.M. KHAN. "Acute Myocardial Infarction, Associated with the Use of a Synthetic Adamantyl-Cannabinoid: A Case Report." *BMC Pharmacology and Toxicology*, 17:2, 2016 **(80413)**

MCKEEVER, R.G., D. VEARRIER, D. JACOBS, G. LASALA, J. OKANEKU, AND M.I. GREENBERG. "K2–Not the Spice of Life; Synthetic Cannabinoids and ST Elevation Myocardial Infarction: A Case Report." *Journal of Medical Toxicology* 11: 129–31, 2015 **(80414)**

MCLEOD, A.L., C.J. MCKENNA, AND D.B. NORTHBRIDGE. "Myocardial Infarction Following the Combined Recreational Use of Viagra and Cannabis." *Clinical Cardiology*, 25: 133–34, 2002 **(10507)**

MEEHAN-ATRASH, J., W. LUO, AND R.M. STRONGIN. "Toxicant Formation in Dabbing: The Terpene Story." *American Chemical Society, Omega*, 2: 6112–17, 2017 **(80503)**

MEHMEDIC, Z., S. CHANDRA, D. SLADE, H. DENHAM, S. FOSTER, A.S. PATEL, S.A. ROSS, I.A. KHAN, AND M.A. ELSOHLY. "Potency Trends of delta 9-THC and Other Cannabinoids in Confiscated Cannabis Preparations from 1993 to 2008." *Journal of Forensic Sciences*, 55: 1209–17, 2010 **(80105)**

MEIER, M.H., M.L. HILL, P.J. SMALL, AND S.S. LUTHAR. "Associations of Adolescent Cannabis Use with Academic Performance and Mental Health: A Longitudinal Study of Upper Middle-Class Youth." *Drug and Alcohol Dependence*, 156: 207–12, 2015 **(60112)**

MEIER, S.I., S.C. KOELZER, M. SCHUBERT-ZSILAVECZ, AND S.W. TOENNES. "Analysis of Drugs of Abuse in Cerumen: Correlation of Postmortem Analysis Results with Those for Blood, Urine and Hair." *Drug Testing and Analysis*, 9: 1572–85, 2017 **(70109)**

MENETREY, A., M. AUGSBURGER, B. FAVRAT, M.A. PIN, L.E. ROTHUIZEN, M. APPENZELLER, T. BUCLIN, P. MANGIN, AND C. GIROUD. "Assessment of Driving Capability Through the Use of Clinical and Psychomotor Tests in Relation to Blood Cannabinoids Levels Following Oral Administration of 20 mg Dronabinol or of a Cannabis Decoction Made with 20 or 60 mg delta 9 THC." *Journal of Analytical Toxicology*, 29: 327–38, 2005 **(50205)**

MERRICK, J., B. LANE, T. SEBREE, T. YAKSH, C. O'NEILL, AND S.L. BANKS. "Identification of Psychoactive Degradants of Cannabidiol in Simulated Gastric and Physiological Fluid." *Cannabis and Cannabinoid Research*, 1: 102–12, 2016 **(80306)**

MILLER, A.M., R. ROSENMAN, AND B.W. COWAN. "Recreational Marijuana Legalization and College Student Use: Early Evidence." *SSM Population Health*, 3: 649–57, 2017 **(60117)**

MILLER, S.M., J.T. SIEGEL, Z. HOHMAN, AND W.D. CRANO. "Factors Mediating the Association of the Recency of Parent's Marijuana Use and their Adolescent Children's Subsequent Initiation." *Psychology of Addictive Behaviors*, 27: 848–53, 2012 **(60110)**

MILMAN, G., A.J. BARNES, D.M. SCHWOPE, E.W. SCHWILKE, W.D. DARWIN, R.S. GOODWIN.D.L. KELLY, D.A. GORELICK, AND M.A. HUESTIS. "Disposition of Cannabinoids in Oral Fluid after Controlled Around-the-Clock Oral THC Administration." *Clinical Chemistry*, 56: 1261–69, 2010 **(30603)**

MILMAN G., M.M. BERGAMASCHI, D. LEE, D.R. MENDU, A.J. BARNES, R. VANDREY, AND M.A. HUESTIS. "Plasma Cannabinoid Concentrations during Dronabinol Pharmacotherapy for Cannabis Dependence." *Therapeutic Drug Monitoring*, 36: 218–34, 2014 **(80208)**

MILMAN, G., D.M. SCHWOPE, D.A. GORELICK, AND M.A. HUESTIS. "Cannabinoids and Metabolites in Expectorated Oral Fluid Following Controlled Smoked Cannabis." *Clinica Chimica Acta,* 413: 765–70, 2012 **(30405)**

MILMAN, G., D.M. SCHWOPE, E.W. SCHWILKE, W.D. DARWIN, D.L. KELLY, R.S. GOODWIN, D.A. GORELICK, AND M.A. HUESTIS. "Oral Fluid and Plasma Cannabinoid Ratios after Round-the-Clock Controlled Oral delta-9-Tetrahydrocannabinol Administration." *Clinical Chemistry*, 57: 1597–606, 2011 **(30208)**

MIR, A., A. OBAFEMI, A. YOUNG, AND C. KANE. "Myocardial Infarction Associated with Use of the Synthetic Cannabinoid K2." *Pediatrics,* 128: e6, 2011 **(80416)**

MISHRA, R., R. PATEL, AND M. KHAJA. "Cannabis-Induced Bullous Lung Disease Leading to Pneumothorax." *Medicine,* 96: 19, 4 pp, 2017 **(61609)**

MITTLEMAN, M.A., R.A. LEWIS, M. MACLURE, J.B. SHERWOOD, AND J.E. MULLER. "Triggering Myocardial Infarction by Marijuana." *Circulation*, 103: 2805–09, 2001 **(60405)**

MOHAMMED, F., K. PANCHOO, M. BARTHOLEMEW, AND D. MAHARAJ. "Compulsive Showering and Marijuana Use: The Cannabis Hyperemesis Syndrome." *American Journal of Case Reports,* 14: 326–28, 2013 **(60316)**

MOKRYZ, C., T.P. FREEMAN, S. KORKKI, K. GRIFFITHS, AND H.V. CURRAN. "Are Adolescents More Vulnerable to the Harmful Effects of Cannabis than Adults? A Placebo-Controlled Study in Human Males." *Translational Psychiatry*, 6: e961, 2016 **(60106)**

MONSHOUWER, K., S. VAN DORSSELAER, J. VERDURMEN, T. TER BOGT, R. DE GRAFF, AND W. VOLLENBERGH. "Cannabis Use and Mental Health in Secondary School Children. Findings from a Dutch Survey." *British Journal of Psychiatry* 188: 148–53, 2006 **(60102)**

MONTANARI, L., B. GUARITA, J. MOUNTENEY, AND N. ZIPFEL. "Cannabis Use among People Entering Drug Treatment in Europe: A Growing Phenomenon?" *European Addiction Research*, 23: 113–21, 2017 **(60513)**

MOORE, C., C. COULTER, S. RANA, M. VINCENT, AND J. SOARES. "Analytical Procedure for the Determination of the Marijuana Metabolite 11-nor-delta 9-Tetrahydrocannabinol-9-Carboxylic Acid in Oral Fluid Specimens." *Journal of Analytical Toxicology*, 30: 409–12, 2006 **(30102)**

MOORE, C., C. COULTER, D. UGES, J. TUYAY, S. VAN DER LINDE., A. VAN LEEUWEN, M. GARNIER, AND J. ORBITA JR. "Cannabinoids in Oral Fluid Following Passive Exposure to Marijuana Smoke." *Forensic Science International*, 212: 227–30, 2011 **(30501)**

MOORE, C., F. GUZALDO, AND T. DONAHUE. "The Determination of 11-nor-delta 9-Tetrahydrocannabinol-9-Carboxylic Acid (THC-COOH) in Hair Using Negative Ion Gas Chromatography-Mass Spectrometry and High-Volume Injection." *Journal of Analytical Toxicology*, 25: 555–58, 2001 **(40309)**

MOORE, C., M. VINCENT, S. RANA, C. COULTER, A. AGRAWAL, AND J. SOARES. "Stability of delta 9-tetrahydrocannabinol (THC) in Oral Fluid Using the Quantisal Collection Device." *Forensic Science International*, 164: 126–30, 2006 **(30407)**

MOOSMANN, B., N. ROTH, AND V. AUWATER. "Finding Cannabinoids in Hair Does Not Prove Cannabis Consumption." *Scientific Reports*, 5: 14906, 6 pp, 2015 **(40305)**

MOOSMANN, B., N. ROTH, AND V. AUWATER. "Hair Analysis for delta 9-Tetrahydrocannabinol Acid A (THCA-A) and delta 9 Tetrahydrocannabinol (THC) after Handling Cannabis Plant Material." *Drug Test Analysis*, 8: 128–32, 2016 **(40307)**

MORGAN, C.J.A., AND H.V. CURRAN. "Effects of Cannabidiol on Schizophrenia-Like Symptoms in People Who Use Cannabis." *The British Journal of Psychiatry*, 192: 306–7, 2008 **(61420)**

MORGAN, C.J.A., T.P. FREEMAN, G.L. SCHAFER, AND H.V. CURRAN. "Cannabidiol Attenuates the Appetitive Effects of delta 9-Tetrahydrocannabinol in Humans Smoking Their Chosen Cannabis." *Neuropsychopharmacology*, 35: 1879–85, 2010 **(80106)**

MORGAN, E., B. SKAATHUN, S. MICHAELS, L. YOUNG, A. KHANNA, S.R. FRIEDMAN, B. DAVIS, D. PITRAK, AND J. SCHNEIDER. "Marijuana Use as a Sex-Drug Is Associated with HIV Risk among Black MSM and Their Network." *AIDS Behavior*, 20: 600–7, 2016 **(61706)**

MORLAND, J., A. BUGGE, B. SKUTERUD, A. STEEN, G.H. WETHE, AND T.C. KJELDSEN. "Cannabinoids in Blood and Urine after Passive Inhalation of Cannabis Smoke." *Journal of Forensic Sciences*, 30: 997–1002, 1985 **(10103)**

MORRISON, P.D., V. ZOIS, D.A. MCKEOWN, T.D. LEE, D.W. HOLT, J.F. POWELL, S. KAPUR, AND R.M. MURRAY. "The Acute Effects of Synthetic Intravenous delta 9-tetrahydrocannabinol on Psychosis, Mood and Cognitive Functioning." *Psychological Medicine*, 39: 1607–16, 2009 **(61422)**

MULLINS, M.E. "Laboratory Confirmation of Flunitrazepam in Alleged Cases of Date Rape." *Academic Emergency Medicine* 6: 966–68, 1999 **(61707)**

MURA, P., P. KINTZ, V. DUMESTRE, S. RAUL, AND T. HAUET. "THC Can Be Detected in Brain While Absent in Blood." *Journal of Analytical Toxicology*, 29: 2005 **(70106)**

MURA, P., P. KINTZ, B. LUDES, J.M. GAULIER, P. MARQUET, S. MARTIN-DUPONT, F. VINCENT, A. KADDOUR, J.P. GOULLE, J. NOUVEAU, M. MOULSMA, S. TILHET-COARTET, AND O. POURRAT. "Comparison of the Prevalence of Alcohol, Cannabis and Other Drugs between 900 Injured Drivers and 900 Control Subjects: Results of a French Collaborative Study." *Forensic Science International* 133: 79–85, 2003 **(50526)**

MURRAY, R.M., H. QUIGLEY, D. QUATTRONE, A. ENGLUND, AND M. DI FORTI. "Traditional Marijuana, High Potency Cannabis and Synthetic Cannabinoids: Increasing Risk for Psychosis." *World Psychiatry*, 15: 195–204, 2016 **(61423)**

MUSSHOFF, F., D.W. LACHENMEIER, L. KROENER, AND B. MADEA. "Automated Headspace Solid-Phase Dynamic Extraction for the Determination of Cannabinoids in Hair Samples." *Forensic Science International*, 133: 32–38, 2003 **(40302)**

MUSHOFF, F., B. MADEA, G. KERNBACH-WIGHTON, W. BUCKER, S. KNEISEL, M. HUTTER, AND V. AUWATER. "Driving Under the Influence of Synthetic Cannabinoids (Spice): A Case Series." *International Journal of Legal Medicine*, 128: 59-64, 2014 **(80417)**

N

NADULSKI, T., F. SPORKERT, M. SCHNELLE, A.M. STADELMANN, P. ROSER, T. SCHEFTER, AND F. PRAGST. "Simultaneous and Sensitive Analysis of THC, 11-OH-THC, THC-COOH, CBD and CBN by GC-MS in Plasma after Oral Application of Small Doses of THC and Cannabis Extract." *Journal of Analytical Toxicology*, 29: 2005 **(10113)**

NAHAS, G.G. "The Pharmacokinetics of THC in Fat and Brain: Resulting Functional Responses to Marijuana Smoking." *Human Psychopharmacology Clinical and Experimental*, 16: 247–55, 2001 **(10201)**

NEWMEYER, M.N., N.A. DESROSIER, D. LEE, D.R. MENDU, A.J. BARNES, D.A. GORELICK, AND M.A. HUESTIS. "Cannabinoid Disposition in Oral Fluid after Controlled Cannabis Smoking in Frequent and Occasional Smokers." *Drug Test Analysis*, 6: 1002–10, 2014 **(30502)**

NIEDBALA, R.S., K.W. KARDOS, D.F. FRITCH, S. KARDOS, T. FRIES, AND J. WAGA. "Detection of Marijuana Use by Oral Fluid and Urine Analysis Following Single-Dose Administration of Smoked and Oral Marijuana." *Journal of Analytical Toxicology*, 25: 289–303, 2001 **(30207)**

NIEDBALA, R.S., K.W. KARDOS, D.F. FRITCH, K.P. KUNSMAN, K.A. BLUM, G.A. NEWLAND, J. WAGA, L. KURTZ, M. BRONSGEEST, AND E.J. CONE. "Passive Cannabis Smoke Exposure and Oral Fluid Testing II. Two Studies of Extreme Cannabis Smoke Exposure in a Motor Vehicle." *Journal of Analytical Toxicology*, 29: 607–15, 2005 **(30503)**

NIEDBALA, R.S., K. KARDOS, S. SLAMONE, D. FRITCH, M. BRONSGEEST, AND E.J. CONE. "Passive Cannabis Smoke Exposure and Oral Fluid Testing." *Journal of Analytical Toxicology*, 28: 546–52, 2004 **(30504)**

NIESINK, R.J.M., AND M.W. VAN LAAR. "Does Cannabidiol Protect against Adverse Psychological effects of THC?" *Frontiers in Psychiatry*, 4: article 150, 8 pp, 2013 **(61414)**

NSC COMMITTEE ON ALCOHOL AND OTHER DRUGS. "Position of the Use of Cannabis (Marijuana) and Driving." *Journal of Analytical Toxicology*, 37: 47–49, 2013 **(50501)**

NUSSBAUM, A.M., J.A. BOYER, AND E.C. KONDRAD. "'But my Doctor Recommended Pot': Medical Marijuana and the Patient-Physician Relationship." *Journal of General and Internal Medicine*, 26: 1364–67, 2011 **(61117)**

NUSSBAUM, A., C. THURSTONE, AND I. BINSWANGER. "Medical Marijuana Use and Suicide Attempt in a Patient with Major Depressive Disorder." *American Journal of Psychiatry*, 168: 778–81, 2011 **(61912)**

O

OBAFEMI, A.I., K. KLEINSCHMIDT, C. GOTO, AND D. FOUT. "Cluster of Acute Toxicity for Ingestion of Synthetic Cannabinoid-Laced Brownies." *Journal of Medical Toxicology*, 11: 426–29, 2015 **(80418)**

ODELL, M.S., M.Y. FREI, D. GEROSTAMOULOS, M. CHU, AND D.I. LUBMAN. "Residual Cannabis Levels in Blood, Urine and Oral Fluid Following Heavy Cannabis Use." *Forensic Science International*, 249: 173–80, 2015 **(40210)**

OELTMANN, J.E., E. OREN, M.B. HADDAD, L.K. LAKE, T.A. HARRINGTON, K. IJAZ, AND M. NARITA. "Tuberculosis Outbreak in Marijuana Users, Seattle, Washington, 2004." *Emerging Infectious Diseases*, 12: 1156–59, 2006 **(61601)**

OHLSSON, A., J-E. LINDGREN, A. WAHLEN, S. AGURELL, L.E. HOLLISTER, AND H.K. GILEPSIE. "Plasma delta-9-tetrahydrocannabinol Concentrations and Clinical Effects after Oral and Intravenous Administration and Smoking." *Clinical Pharmacology and Therapeutics,* 28: 409–16, 1980 **(50601)**

OKANEKU J., D. VEARRIER, R.G. MCKEEVER, G.S. LASALA, AND M.I. GREENBERG. "Change in Perceived Risk Associated with Marijuana Use in the United States from 2002 to 2012." *Clinical Toxicology*, 53: 151–55, 2015 **(61110)**

ORSINI, J., C. BLAAK, S. RAJAYER, V. GURUNG, E. TAM, J. MORANTE, B. SHAMIAN, AND R. MALIK. "Prolonged Cardiac Arrest Complicating a Massive ST-

Segment Elevation Myocardial Infarction Associated with Marijuana Consumption." *Journal of Community Hospital Internal Medicine Perspectives*, 6 pp, Sept. 7, 2016 **(60413)**

ORSINI, J., C. BLAAK, E. TAM, S. RAJAYER, J. MORANTE, A. YEH, AND A. BUTALA. "The Wide and Unpredictable Scope of Synthetic Cannabinoids Toxicity." *Case Reports in Critical Care*, 2015, 5 pp **(80419)**

OSUCH, E. "Marijuana Use in Youth from Bench to Bedside to Longitudinal Outlook." *The Canadian Journal of Psychiatry,* 61: 316–17, 2016 **(61103)**

OYEFESO A., F. SCHIFANO, H. GHODSE, K. COBAIN, R. DRYDEN, AND J. CORKERY. "Fatal Injuries under the Influence of Psychoactive Drugs: A Cross-Sectional Exploratory Study in England." *BMC Public Health*, 6: 148, 2006 **(62007)**

P

PACEK, L.R., AND VANDREY, R. "Cannabis Use History and Characteristics of Quit Attempts: A Comparison Study of Treatment-Seeking and Non-Treatment-Seeking Cannabis Users." *Experimental and Clinical Psychopharmacology*, 22: 517–23, 2014 **(60512)**

PACULA, R., L.B. KILMER, A.C. WAGENAAR, F.J. CHALOUPKA, AND J.P. CAULKINS. "Developing Public Health Regulations for Marijuana: Lessons from Alcohol and Tobacco." *American Journal of Public Health,* 104: 1021–28, 2014 **(50706)**

PALAMAR, J.J., M. FENSTERMAKER, D. KAMBOUKOS, D.C. OMPAD, C.M. CLELAND, AND M. WEITZMAN. "Adverse Psychosocial Outcomes Associated with Drug Use Among US High School Seniors: A Comparison of Alcohol and Marijuana." *American Journal of Drug and Alcohol Abuse*, 40: 438–46, 2014 **(60121)**

PAPA, P., L. ROCCHI, L.M. ROLANDI, M. DI TUCCIO, M. BIFFI, AND A. VALLI. "Illicit Drugs in Emergency Department Patients Injured in Road Traffic Accidents." *Annali delllstituto Superiore di Sanita*, 53: 35–39, 2015 **(40214)**

PAPAFORTIOU, K., J.D. CARTER, AND C. STOUGH. "An Evaluation of the Sensitivity of the Standardized Field Sobriety Tests (SFSTs) to Detect Impairment due to Marijuana Intoxication." *Psychopharmacology* 180: 107–14, 2005 **(50617)**

PAPAFORTIOU, K., J.D. CARTER, AND C. STOUGH. "The Relationship between Performance on the Standardized Field Sobriety Tests, Driving Performance, and the Level of Tetrahydrocannabinol (THC) in Blood." *Forensic Science International* 155: 172–78, 2005 **(50616)**

PAPE, H., I. ROSSOW, AND E.E. STORVOLL. "Under Double Influence: Assessment of Simultaneous Alcohol and Cannabis Use in General Youth Populations." *Drug and Alcohol Dependence* 101: 69–73, 2009 **(50806)**

PARKS, K.A., R.L. COLLINS, AND J.L. DERRICK. "The Influence of Marijuana and Alcohol Use on Condom Use Behavior: Findings from a Sample of Young Adult Female Bar Drinkers." *Psychology and Addictive Behavior*, 26: 888–94, 2012 **(61712)**

PATEL, R., R. WILSON, R. JACKSON, M. BALL, H. SHETTY, M. BROADBENT, R. STEWART, P. MCGUIRE, AND S. BHATTACHARYYA. "Association of Cannabis Use with Hospital Admission and Antipsychotic Treatment Failure in First Episode Psychosis: An Observational Study." *British Medical Journal, Open*, 6: 2016 **(61406)**

PATTERSON, D.A., E.L. SMITH, M. MONAHAN, A. MEDVECZ., B. HAGERTY, L. KRIJGER, A. CHAUHAN, AND M. WALSH. "Cannabinoid Hyperemesis and Compulsive Bathing: A Case Series and Paradoxical Pathophysiological Explanation." *Journal of the American Board of Family Medicine*, 23: 790–93, 2010 **(60312)**

PATTON, A.L., K.C. CHIMALAKONDA, C.L. MORAN, K.R. MCCAIN, A. RADOMINSKA-PANDYA, L.P. JAMES, C. KOKES, AND J.H. MORAN. "K2 Toxicity: Fatal Case of Psychiatric Complications Following AM2201 Exposure." *Journal of Forensic Sciences*, 58: 1676–80, 2013 **(80420)**

PATTON, G.C., C. COFFEY, J.B. CARLIN, L. DEGENHARDT, M. LYNSKEY, AND W. HALL. "Cannabis Use and Mental Health in Young People: Cohort Study." *British Medical Journal*, 325: 195–98, 2002 **(61906)**

PEACE, M.R., K.E. BUTLER, C.E. WOLF, J.L. POKLIS, AND A. POLKIS. "Evaluation of Two Commercially Available Cannabidiol Formulations for Use in Electronic Cigarettes." *Frontiers in Pharmacology*, 7: Article 279, 6 pp, 2016 **(80308)**

PEDERSEN, W. "Does Cannabis Use Lead to Depression and Suicidal Behaviors? A Population-Based Longitudinal Study." *Acta Psychiatrica Scandinavica*, 18: 395–403, 2008 **(61907)**

PEREZ-REYES, M., R.E. HICKS, J. BUMBERRY, A.R. JEFFCOAT, AND C.E. COOK. "Interaction between Marihuana and Ethanol: Effects on Psychomotor Performance." *Alcoholism: Clinical and Experimental Research*, 12: 268–76, 1988 **(50807)**

PERRET, G., A. ABUDUREHEMAN, M. PERRET-CATIPOVIC, M. FLOMENBAUM, AND R. LA HARPE. "Suicides in the Young People of Geneva, Switzerland from 1993 to 2002." *Journal of Forensic Sciences*, 51: 1169–73, 2006 **(61909)**

PERRET, G., M. FLOMENBAUM, AND R. LA HARPE. "Suicides by Fall from Height in Geneva, Switzerland, from 1991 to 2000." *Journal of Forensic Sciences*, 48: 821-826, 2003 **(61908)**

PERTWEE, R.G. "Cannabinoid Pharmacology: The First 66 Years." *British Journal of Pharmacology*, 147: S163–S171, 2006 **(80504)**

PETERS, E.N., R.F. LEEMAN, L.M. FUCITO, B.A. TOLL, W.R. CORBIN, AND S.S. O'MALLEY. "Co-Occurring Marijuana Use Is Associated with Medication Nonadherence and Non-Planning Impulsivity in Young Adult Heavy Drinkers." *Addictive Behaviors,* 37: 420–26, 2012 **(60212)**

PETERSON, B.L., AND F.J. COUPER. "Concentrations of AB-CHMINACA and AB-PINACA and Driving Behavior in Suspected Impaired Driving Cases." *Journal of Analytical Toxicology*, 39: 642–746, 2015 **(50620)**

PIPER, T.M., M. TRACY, A. BUCCIARELLI, K. TARDIFF, AND S. GALEA. "Firearm Suicide in New York City in the 1990s." *Injury Prevention,* 12: 41–45, 2006 **(61910)**

PLASSE, T.F., R.W. GORTER, S.H. KRASNOW, M. LANE, K.V. SHEPARD, AND R.G. WADLEIGH. "Recent Clinical Experience with Dronabinol." *Pharmacology, Biochemistry and Behavior,* 40: 695–700, 1991 **(80209)**

PLETCHER, M.J., E. VITTINGHOFF, R. KALHAN, J. RICHMAN, M. SAFFORD, S. SIDNEY, F. LIN, AND S. KERTSZ. "Association between Marijuana Exposure and Pulmonary Function Over 20 Years. The Coronary Artery Risk Development in Young Adults (CARDIA) Study." *Journal of the American Medical Association*, 307: 173–81, 2011 **(61605)**

POLEN, M.R., S. SIDNEY, I.S. TEKAWA, M. SADLER, AND G.D. FRIEDMAN, "Health Care Use by Frequent Marijuana Smokers Who Do Not Smoke Tobacco." *Western Journal of Medicine*, 158: 596–601, 1993 **(61602)**

POLLIO, A. "The Name of Cannabis: A Short Guide for Non-Botanists." *Cannabis and Cannabinoid Research* 1: 234–38, 2016 **(80107)**

POPE JR., H.G., A.J. GRUBER, J.I. HUDSON, G. COHANE, M.A. HUESTIS, D. YURGELUN-TODD. "Early Onset Cannabis Use and Cognitive Deficits: What Is the Nature of the Association?" *Drug and Alcohol Dependence* 69: 303–10, 2003 **(60118)**

PORATH-WALLER, A.J., AND D.J. BEIRNESS. "An Examination of the Validity of the Standardized Field Sobriety Test in Detecting Drug Impairment

Using Data from the Drug Evaluation and Classification Program." *Traffic Injury Prevention*, 15: 125–31, 2014 **(50618)**

PORATH-WALLER, A.J., D.J. BEIRNESS, AND E.E. BEASLEY. "Toward a More Parsimonious Approach to Drug Recognition Expert Evaluations." *Traffic Injury Prevention*, 10: 513–18, 2009 **(50609)**

POULSEN, H., R. MOAR, AND C. TRONCOSO. "The Incidence of Alcohol and Drugs in Drivers Killed in New Zealand Road Crashes 2004–2009." *Forensic Science International*, 223: 364–70, 2012 **(50527)**

PRICE, S.L., C. FISHER, R. KUMAR, AND A. HILGERSON. "Cannabinoid Hyperemesis Syndrome as the Underlying Cause of Intractable Nausea and Vomiting." *Journal of the American Osteopathic Association*, 111: 166–69, 2011 **(60314)**

PURSCHKE, K., S. HEINL, O. LERCH, F. ERDMANN, AND F. VEIT. "Development and Validation of an Automated Liquid-Liquid Extraction GC/MS Method for the Determination of THC, 11-OH-THC and Free THC-Carboxylic Acid (THC-COOH) from Blood Serum." *Analytical Bicanalytical Chemistry*, 408: 4379–88, 2016 **(20106)**

R

RAJA, M., AND A. AZZONI. "Suicidal Ideation Induced by Episodic Cannabis Use." *Case Reports in Medicine*, 2 pp, 2009 **(61915)**

RAMAEKERS, J.G., G. BERGHAUS, M. VAN LAR, AND O.H. DRUMMER. "Dose Related Risk of Motor Vehicle Crashes after Cannabis Use." *Drugs and Alcohol Dependence*, 73: 109–19, 2004 **(50809)**

RAMAEKERS, J.G., G. KAUERT, E.L. THEUNISSEN, S.W. TOENNES, AND M.R. MOELLER. "Neurocognitive Performance during Acute THC Intoxication in Heavy and Occasional Cannabis Users." *Journal of Psychopharmacology*, 23: 266–77, 2009 **(50117)**

RAMAEKERS, J.G., G. KAUERT, P. VAN RUITENBEEK, E.L. THEUNISSEN, E. SCHNEIDER, AND M. MOELLER. "High-Potency Marijuana Impairs Executive Function and Inhibitory Motor Control." *Neuropsychopharmacology*, 31: 2296–303, 2006 **(50116)**

RAMAEKERS, J.G., M.R. MOELLER, P. VAN RUITENBEEK, E.L. THEUNISSEN, E. SCHNEIDER, AND G. KAUERT. "Cognition and Motor Control as a Function of Delta 9-THC Concentration in Serum and Oral Fluid. Limits of Impairment." *Drug and Alcohol Dependence*, 85: 114–22, 2006 **(50115)**

RAMAEKERS, J.G., H.W.J. ROBBE., AND J.F. O'HALON. "Marijuana, Alcohol and Actual Driving Performance." *Human Psychopharmacology*, 15: 551–58, 2000 **(50808)**

RAMAEKERS, J.G., J.H. VAN WEL, D.B. SPRONK., S.W. TOENNES, K.P.C. KUYPERS, E.L. THEUNISSEN, AND R.J. VERKES. "Cannabis and Tolerance: Acute Drug Impairment as a Function of Cannabis Use History." *Scientific Reports*, www.nature/scientific reports, srep26843, 8 pp, 2016 **(50118)**

RAMESH, D., J.E. SCHLOSBURG, J.M. WIEBELHAUS, AND A.H. LICHTMAN. "Marijuana Dependence: Not Just Smoke and Mirrors." *Institute for Laboratory Animal Research Journal*, 52: 295–308, 2011 **(60502)**

RANGANATHAN, M., AND D.C. D'SOUZA. "The Acute Effects of Cannabinoids on Memory in Humans." *Psychopharmacology*, 188: 425–44, 2006 **(61003)**

REAM, G.L., E. BENOIT, B.D. JOHNSON, AND E. DUNLAP. "Smoking Tobacco Along with Marijuana Increases Symptoms of Cannabis Dependence." *Drug and Alcohol Dependence*, 95: 199–208, 2008 **(60515)**

REECE, A.S. "Severe Multisystem Dysfunction in a Case of High Level Exposure to Smoked Cannabis." *British Medical Journal Case Reports*, 10 pp, 2009 **(61615)**

REECE, A.S., A. NORMAN, AND G.K. HULSE "Cannabis Exposure as an Interactive Cardiovascular Risk Factor and Accelerant of Organismal Ageing: A Longitudinal Study." *British Medical Journal Open*, 2016, 6 pp **(60414)**

REEVE, V.C., J.D. GRANT, W. ROBERTSON., H.K. GILLESPIE., AND L.E. HOLLISTER. "Plasma Concentrations of delta 9-Tetrahydrocannabinol and Impaired Motor Function." *Drug and Alcohol Dependence*, 11: 167–75, 1983 **(10203)**

REINGLE, J.M., S.A.S. STARAS, W.G. JENNINGS, J. BRANCHINI, AND M.M. MALDONADO-MOLINA. "The Relationship between Marijuana Use and Intimate Partner Violence in a Nationally Representative, Longitudinal Sample." *Journal of Interpersonal Violence,* 27: 1562–78, 2012 **(60209)**

REITER, A., J. HAKE, C. MEISSNER, J. ROHWER, H.J. FRIEDRICH, AND M. OEHMICHEN. "Time of Drug Elimination in Chronic Drug Abusers Case Study of 52 Patients in a Low Step Detoxification Ward." *Forensic Science International*, 119: 248–53, 2001 **(10303)**

RIBA, J., M. VALLE, F. SAMPEDRO, A. RODRIGUEZ-PUJADAS, S. MARTINEZ-HORAT, J. KULISEVSKY, AND A. RODRIGUEZ-FORNELLS. "Telling True from False:

Cannabis Users Show Increased Susceptibility to False Memories." *Molecular Psychiatry*, 20: 772–77, 2015 **(61004)**

RICE, S., AND J.A. KOZIEL. "Characterizing the Smell of Marijuana by Odor Impact of Volatile Compounds: An Application of Simultaneous Chemical and Sensory Analysis." *PLOS ONE* 10: 17 pp, December 10th, 2015 **(80108)**

RICHARDS, J.R., V. SCHANDERA, AND W. ELDER. "Treatment of Acute Cannabinoid Overdose with Naloxone Infusion." *Toxicology Communications*, 1: 29–33, 2017 **(60621)**

RICHER, I., AND J. BERGERON. "Driving Under the Influence of Cannabis: Links with Dangerous Driving, Psychological Predictors and Accident Involvement." *Accident Analysis and Prevention*, 41: 299–307, 2009 **(60206)**

RIEDERER, A.M., S.L. CAMPLEMAN, R.G. CARLSON, E.W. BOYER, A.F. MANANI, P.M. WAX, AND J.A. BRENT. "Acute Poisonings from Synthetic Cannabinoids: 50 US Toxicology Investigators Consortium Registry Sites, 2010–2015." *Morbidity and Mortality Weekly Report*, 65: 692–95, 2015 **(80421)**

ROBBE, H. "Marijuana's Impairing Effects on Driving Are Moderate When Taken Alone but Severe When Combined with Alcohol." *Human Psychopharmacology*, 13: S70–S78, 1998 **(50810)**

ROBERSON, E.K., W.K. PATRICK, AND E.L. HURWITZ. "Marijuana Use and Maternal Experiences of Severe Nausea during Pregnancy in Hawai'i." *Hawai'i Journal of Medicine and Public Health*, 73: 283–87, 2014 **(40505)**

ROBSON, P. "Abuse Potential and Psychoactive Effects of delta 9-tetrahydrocannabinol and Cannabidiol Oromucosal Spray (Sativex), A New Cannabinoid Medicine." *Expert Opinion Drug Safety*, 10: 675–85, 2011 **(80202)**

RODRIGUEZ-CASTRO, C.E., H. ALKHATEEB, A. ELFAR, F. SAIFUDDIN, A. ABBAS, AND T. SIDDIQUI. "Recurrent Myopericarditis as a Complication of Marijuana Use." *American Journal of Case Reports*, 15: 60–62, 2014 **(60615)**

ROHRICHM, J., I. SCHIMMEL, S. ZORNTLEIN, J. BECKER, S. DROBNIK, T. KAUFMAN, V. KUNTZ, AND R. URBAN. "Concentrations of Delta 9 Tetrahydrocannabinol and 11-Nor-9-Carboxytetrahydrocannabinol in Blood and Urine after Passive Exposure to Cannabis Smoke in a Coffee Shop." *Journal of Analytical Toxicology*, 34: 196–203, 2010 **(10104)**

ROMERO-SANDOVAL, E.A., S. ASBILL, C.A. PAIGE, AND K. BYRD-GLOVER. "Peripherally Restricted Cannabinoids for the Treatment of Pain." *Pharmacotherapy*, 35: 917–25, 2015 **(10112)**

RONEN, A., H.S. CHASSIDIM, P. GERSHON, Y. PARMET, A. RABINOVICH, R. BAR-HAMBURGER, Y. CASSUTO, AND D. SHINAR. "The Effect of Alcohol, THC and Their Combination on Perceived Effects, Willingness to Drive and Performance of Driving and Non-Driving Tasks." *Accident Analysis and Prevention*, 42: 1855–65, 2010 **(50811)**

RONEN, A., P. GERSHON, H. DROBINER, A. RABINOVICH, R. BAR-HAMBURGER, R. MECHOULAM, Y. CASSUTO, AND D. SHINAR. "Effects of THC on Driving Performance, Physiological State and Subjective Feelings Relative to Alcohol." *Accident Analysis and Prevention*, 40: 926–34, 2008 **(50206)**

ROOKE, S.E., M.M. NORBERG, AND J. COPELAND. "Successful and Unsuccessful Cannabis Quitters: Comparing Group Characteristics and Quitting Strategies." *Substance Abuse Treatment, Prevention and Policy*, 6: 30, 9 pp, 2011 **(62111)**

ROSE, D.Z., W.R. GUERNO, M.V. MOKIN, C.L. GOOCH, A.C. BOZEMAN, J.M. PEARSON, AND W.S. BURGIN. "Hemorrhagic Stroke Following Use of the Synthetic Marijuana Spice." *American Academy of Neurology*, 85: 1177–79, 2015 **(80423)**

ROSER, P., J. GALLINAT, G. WEINBERG, G. JUCKEL, I. GORYNIA, AND A.M. STADELMANN. "Psychomotor Performance in Relation to Acute Oral Administration of delta 9-Tetrahydrocannabinol and Standardized Cannabis Extract in Healthy Human Subjects." *European Archives for Psychiatry and Clinical Neuroscience*, 259: 284–92, 2009 **(80309)**

ROTH, K.D.W., N.A. SIEGEL, R.W. JOHNSON JR., L. LITAUSZKI, L. SALVATI JR., C.A. HARRINGTON, AND L.K. WRAY. "Investigation of the Effects of Solution Composition and Container Material Type on the Loss of 11 nor-delta 9 THC-9-Carboxylic Acid." *Journal of Analytical Toxicology*, 20: 291–300, 1996 **(40211)**

RUSSO, M., R. DE LUCA, M. TORRISI, C. RIFICI, E. SESSA, P. BRAMANTI, A. NARO, AND R.S. CALABRO. "Should We Care About Sativex-Induced Neurobehavioral Effects? A 6-Month Follow-Up Study." *European Review for Medical and Pharmacological Sciences*, 20: 3127–33, 2016 **(80203)**

RUSSO, E.B., G.W. GUY, AND P.J. ROBSON. "Cannabis, Pain and Sleep: Lessons from Therapeutic Clinical Trials of Sativex, a Cannabis Based Medicine." *Chemistry and Biodiversity*, 4: 1729–43, 2007 **(80201)**

S

SAITO, J., A. WTSADIK, K.B. SCHEIDWEILER., N. FORTNER, S. TAKEICHI, AND M.A. HUESTIS. "Validated Gas Chromatographic-Negative Ion Chemical Ionization Mass Spectrometric Method for delta 9-Tetrahydrocannabinol in Sweat Patches." *Clinical Chemistry*, 50: 2083–90, 2004 **(40401)**

SAMAAN, J., G.F. FERRER, B. AKINYEMI, P. JUNQUERA, J. OMS, AND R. DUMENIGO. "Synthetic Cannabis Overdose and Withdrawal in a Young Adult: A Case Report, Commentary on Regulation, and Review of the Literature." *Case Reports in Psychiatry*, 7 pp, 2016 **(80424)**

SANSONE, R.A., AND L.A. SANSONE. "Marijuana and Body Weight." *Innovations in Clinical Neuroscience*, 11: 50–54, 2014 **(61115)**

SARSU, S.B. "Unusual Side Effect of Cannabis Use: Acute Abdomen due to Duodenal Perforation." *International Journal of Emergency Medicine*, 9: 18–22, 2016 **(80440)**

SATTOUT, A.H., AND M.F. NICOL. "Cardiac Arrest Following Cannabis Use: A Case Report." *Cases Journal*, 2: 208 3 pp, 2009 **(60417)**

SCHEEL, A.H., D. KRAUSE, H. HAARS, I. SCHMITZ, AND K. JUNKER. "Talcum Induced Pneumoconiosis Following Inhalation of Adulterated Marijuana, A Case Report." *Diagnostic Pathology*, 7: 26–30, 2012 **(61607)**

SCHEIDWEILER, K.B., M. ANDERSSON, M.J. SWORTWOOD, C. SEMPIO, AND M.A. HUESTIS "Long-Term Stability of Cannabinoids in Oral Fluid after Controlled Cannabis Administration." *Drug Testing and Analysis*, 9: 143–47, 2017 **(30409)**

SCHEIDWEILER, K.B., N.A. DESROSIERS, AND M.A. HUESTIS. "Simultaneous Quantification of Free and Glucuronidated Cannabinoids in Human Urine by Liquid Chromatography-Tandem Mass Spectrometry." *Clinica Chimica Acta*, 413: 1839–47, 2012 **(40203)**

SCHEIDWEILER, K.B., S.K. HIMES, N.A. DESROSIERS, AND M.A. HUESTIS. "In Vitro Stability of Free and Glucuronidated Cannabinoids in Blood and Plasma Collected in Plastic Gray-Top Sodium Fluoride Tubes Following Controlled Smoked Cannabis." *Forensic Toxicology*, 34: 179–85, 2016 **(20303)**

SCHERER, M., R.B. VOAS, AND D. FURR-HOLDEN. "Marijuana as a Predictor of Concurrent Substance Use among Motor Vehicle Operators." *Journal of Psychoactive Drugs*, 45: 211–17, 2013 **(50812)**

SCHNEIR, A.B., AND T. BAUMBACHER. "Convulsions Associated with the Use of a Synthetic Cannabinoid Product." *Journal of Medical Toxicology*, 8: 62–64, 2012 **(80432)**

SCHOELER, T., N. PETROS, M. DI FORTI, E. KLAMERUS, E. FOGLIA, O. AIJNAKINA, C. GAYER-ANDERSON, M. COLIZZI, D. QUATTRONE, I. BEHLKE, S. SHETTY, P. MCGUIRE, A.S. DAVID, R. MURRAY, AND S. BHATTACHARYYA. "Effects of Continuation, Frequency, and Type of Cannabis Use on Relapse in the First 2 Years after Onset of Psychosis: An Observational Study." *Lancet Psychiatry*, 3: 947–53, 2016 **(61407)**

SCHROEDER, J.L., L.J. MARINETTI., R.K. SMITH, W.E. BREWER, B.L. CLELLAND, AND S.L. MORGAN. "The Analysis of Delta 9-Tetrahydrocannabinol and Metabolite in Whole Blood and 11-Nor- delta 9-Tetrahydrocannabinol-9 Carboxylic Acid in Urine using Disposable Pipette Extraction with Confirmation and Quantification by Gas Chromatography-Mass Spectrometry." *Journal of Analytical Toxicology*, 32: 659–66, 2008 **(70108)**

SCHUBART, C.D., I.E.C. SOMMER, W.A. VAN GASTEL, R.L. GOETGEBUER, R.S. KHAN, AND M.P.M. BOKS. "Cannabis with High Cannabidiol Content Is Associated with Fewer Psychotic Experiences." *Schizophrenia Research*, 130: 216–21, 2011 **(61409)**

SCHULLER, A., V. COTTIN, A. HOT, AND J-F. CORDIER. "Finger Clubbing and Altered Carbon Monoxide Transfer Capacity in Cannabis Smokers." *European Respiratory Journal*, 31: 473–81, 2008 **(61102)**

SCHUSTER, R.M., N.A. CRANE, R. MERMELSTEIN, AND R. GONZALEZ. "The Influence of Inhibitory Control and Episodic Memory on the Risky Sexual Behavior of Young Adult Cannabis Users." *Journal of International Neuropsychology*, 18: 827–33, 2012 **(61708)**

SCHUSTER, R.M., N.A. CRANE, R. MERMELSTEIN, AND R. GONZALEZ. "Tobacco May Mask Poorer Episodic Memory Among Young Adult Cannabis Users." *Neuropsychology*, 29: 759–66, 2015 **(61008)**

SCHWEINSBURG, A.D., B.C. SCHWEINSBURG, K.L. MEDINA, T. MCQUEENY, S.A. BROWN, AND S.F. TAPERT. "The Influence of Recency of Use on fMRI Response during Spatial Working Memory in Adolescent Marijuana Users." *Journal of Psychoactive Drugs*, 42: 401–12, 2010 **(61011)**

SCHWILKE, E.W., R.G. GULLBERG. W.D. DARWIN, C.N. CHIANG, J.L. CADET, D.A. GORELICK, H.G. POPE, AND M.A. HUESTIS. "Differentiating New Cannabis Use from Residual Urinary Cannabinoid Excretion in Chronic, Daily Cannabis Users." *Addiction*, 106: 499–506, 2010 **(40212)**

SCHWILKE, E.W., E.L. KARSCHNER, R.H. LOWE, A.M. GORDON, J.L. CADET, R.I. HERNING, AND M.A. HUESTIS. "Intra- and Inter-Subject Whole Blood/Plasma Cannabinoid Ratios Determined by 2-Dimensional Electron Impact GC-MS with Cyrofocusing." *Clinical Chemistry,* 55: 1188–95, 2009 **(20201)**

SCHWOPE, D.M., W.M. BOSKER, J.G. RAMAEKERS, D.A. GORELICK, AND M.A. HUESTIS, "Psychomotor Performance, Subjective and Physiological Effects and Whole Blood Delta 9-Tetrahydrocannabinol Concentrations in Heavy, Chronic Cannabis Smokers Following Acute Smoked Cannabis." *Journal of Analytical Toxicology,* 36: 405–12, 2012 **(50119)**

SCHWOPE, D.M., E.L. KARSCHNER, D.A. GORELICK, AND M.A. HUESTIS. "Identification of Recent Cannabis Use: Whole-Blood and Plasma Free and Glucuronidated Cannabinoid Pharmacokinetics Following Controlled Smoked Cannabis Administration." *Clinical Chemistry,* 57: 1406–14, 2011 **(20202)**

SCHWOPE, D.M., K.B. SCHEIDWEILER, AND M.A. HUESTIS. "Direct Quantification of Cannabinoids and Cannabinoid Glucuronides in Whole Blood by Liquid Chromatography Tandem Mass Spectrometry." *Analytical Bioanalytical Chemistry,* 401: 1273–83, 2011 **(20104)**

SCOTT-HAM, M., AND F.C. BURTON. "Toxicological Findings in Cases of Alleged Drug-Facilitated Sexual Assault in the United Kingdom over a 3-Year Period." *Journal of Clinical and Forensic Medicine,* 12: 175–86, 2005 **(61709)**

SCURLOCK, R.D., G.B. OHLSON, AND D.K. WORTHEN. "The Detection of delta 9 Tetrahydrocannabinol (THC) and 11-nor-9-Carboxy-delta 9-Tetrahydrocannabinol (THCA) in Whole Blood Using Two-Dimensional Gas Chromatography and EI Mass Spectrometry." *Journal of Analytical Toxicology,* 30: 262–66, 2006 **(20102)**

SEWELL, R.A., A. SCHNAKENBERG, J. ELANDER, R. RADHAKRISHNAN, A. WILLIAMS, P.D. SKOSNIK, B. PITTMAN, M. RANGANATHAN, AND D.C. D'SOUZA. "Acute Effects of THC on Time Perception in Frequent and Infrequent Cannabis Users." *Psychopharmacology,* 226: 401–13, 2013 **(50121)**

SHANKS, K.G., W. CLARK, AND G. BEHONICK. "Death Associated with the Use of the Synthetic Cannabinoid ADB-FUBINACA." *Journal of Analytical Toxicology,* 40: 236–39, 2016 **(80430)**

SHANKS, K.G., T. DAHN, AND A.R. TERRELL. "Detection of JHW-018 and JWH-073 by UPLC-MS-MS in Postmortem Whole Blood Casework." *Journal of Analytical Toxicology,* 36: 145–52, 2012 **(80438)**

SHEEHAN, C.M., R.G. ROGERS, G.W. WILLIAMS IV, AND J.D. BOARDMAN. "Gender Differences in the Presence of Drugs in Violent Deaths." *Addiction,* 108: 547–55, 2013 **(60905)**

SHEIKH, I.A., M. LUKSIC, R. FERSTENBERG, AND J.A. CULPEPER-MORGAN. "SPICE/K2 Synthetic Marijuana-Induced Toxic Hepatitis Treated with N-Acetylcysteine." *American Journal of Case Reports*, 15: 584–88, 2014 **(80431)**

SHI, Y., M. LENZI, AND R. AN. "Cannabis Liberalization and Adolescent Cannabis Use: A Cross-National Study in 38 Countries." *PLOS ONE*, November 25, 2015, 15 pp **(60107)**

SHINAR, D., E. SCHECHTMAN, AND R.P. COMPTON. "Drug Identification Performance on the Basis of Observable Signs and Symptoms." *Accident Analysis and Prevention*, 37: 843–51, 2005 **(50619)**

SHIPLO, S., M. ASBRIDGE, S.T. LEATHERDALE, AND D. HAMMOND. "Medical Cannabis Use in Canada: Vapourization and Modes of Delivery." *Harm Reduction Journal*, 13: 30 (10 pp), 2016 **(10114)**

SILINS, E., L.J. HOWARD, G.C. PATTON, D.M. FERGUSSON, C.A. OLSSON., D.M. HUTCHINSON, E. SPRY, J.W. TROUMBOUROU, L.D. DEGENHARDT, W. SWIFT, C. COFFEEY, R.J. TAIT, P. LETCHER, J. COPELAND, AND R.P. MATTICK. "Young Adult Sequelae of Adolescent Cannabis Use: An Integrative Analysis." *Lancet Psychiatry*, 1: 286–93, 2014. **(60108)**

SIMOES, S.S., A.C. AIENJO, AND M.J. DIAS. "Qualitative and Quantitative Analysis of THC, 11-hydroxy-THC and 11-nor-9-carboxy THC in Whole Blood by Ultra-Performance Liquid Chromatography/Tandem Mass Spectrometry." *Rapid Communications in Mass Spectrometry,* 25: 2603–10, 2011 **(20105)**

SIMONETTO, D.A., A.S. OXENTENKO, M.L. HERMAN, AND J.H. SZOSTEK. "Cannabinoid Hyperemesis: A Case Series of 98 Patients." *Mayo Clinic Proceedings*, 87: 114–19, 2012 **(60306)**

SKOPP, G., AND L. POTSCH. "Stability of 11-Nor delta 9 carboxy-tetrahydrocannabinol Glucuronide in Plasma and Urine Assessed by Liquid Chromatography-Tandem Mass Spectrometry." *Clinical Chemistry,* 48: 301–6, 2002 **(20301)**

SKOPP, G., AND L. POTSCH. "An Investigation of the Stability of Free and Glucuronidated 11-Nor-delta 9-Tetrahydrocannabinol-9-caboxylic Acid in Authentic Urine Samples." *Journal of Analytical Toxicology*, 28: 35–40, 2004 **(40213)**

SKOPP, G., AND L. POTSCH. "Cannabinoid Concentrations in Spot Serum Samples 24–48 Hours after Discontinuation of Cannabis Smoking." *Journal of Analytical Toxicology*, 32: 160–64, 2008 **(10306)**

SKOPP, G., P. STROHBECK-KUEHNER, K. MANN, AND D. HERMANN. "Deposition of Cannabinoids in Hair: After Long-Term Use of Cannabis." *Forensic Science International*, 170: 46–50, 2007 **(40308)**

SLAUGHTER, L. "Involvement of Drugs in Sexual Assault." *Journal of Reproductive Medicine*, 45: 425–430, 2000 **(61711)**

SMITH, P.H., G.G. HOMISH, K.E. LEONARD, AND R.L. COLLINS. "Marijuana Withdrawal and Aggression among a Representative Sample of U.S. Marijuana Users." *Drug and Alcohol Dependence*, 132: 63–68, 2013 **(60207)**

SODERSTROM, C.A., P.C. DISCHINGER, T.J. KERNS, AND A.L. TRIFILLIS. "Marijuana and Other Drug Use Among Automobile and Motorcycle Drivers Treated at a Trauma Center." *Accident Analysis and Prevention* 27: 131–35, 1995 **(61202)**

SOLIMINI, R., F.P. BUSCARDO, M.C. ROTOLO, S. RICCI, L. MASTROBATTISTA, C. MORTALI, S. GRANZIANO, M. PELLEGRINI, N.M. DI LUCA, AND I. PALMI. "Hepatotoxicity Associated to Synthetic Cannabinoids Use." *European Review for Medical and Pharmacological Sciences*, 21 (1 Suppl): 1–6, 2017 **(80437)**

SOLOMONS, K., V.M. NEPPE, AND J.M. KUYL. "Toxic Cannabis Psychosis Is a Valid Entity." *South African Medical Journal*, 78: 476–81, 1990 **(61408)**

SOLOWIJ, N., AND R. BATTISTI. "The Chronic Effects of Cannabis on Memory in Humans: A Review." *Current Drug Abuse Reviews*, 1: 81–98, 2008 **(61006)**

SONTINENI, S., S. CHAUDHARY, V. SONTINENI, AND S.J. LANSPA. "Cannabinoid Hyperemesis Syndrome: Clinical Diagnosis of an Under Recognized Manifestation of Chronic Cannabis Abuse." *World Journal of Gastroenterology*, 15: 1264–66, 2009 **(60307)**

SOULEMAN, A.M.A., A.E-D.A. GAAFAR, O.M. ABDEL-SALAM, S.A. ELSHEBINEY. "Determination of delta-9-tetrahydrocannabinol Content of Cannabis Seizures in Egypt." *Asian Pacific Journal of Tropical Medicine*, 10: 311–14, 2017 **(80114)**

SPRINGER, Y.P., R. GERONA, E. SCHEUNEMANN, S.L. SHAFER, T. LIN, S.D. BANISTER, M.P. COOPER, L.J. CASTRODALE, M. LEVY, J.C. BUTLER, AND J.B. MCLAUGHLIN. "Increase in Adverse Reactions Associated with Use of

Synthetic Cannabinoids – Anchorage, Alaska, 2015–2016." *Morbidity and Mortality Weekly Report,* 65: 1108–11, 2016 **(80425)**

SPRONK, D., G.J.H. DUMONT, R.J. VERKES, AND E.R.A. DE BRUIJN. "Acute Effects of Delta-9-Tetrahydrocannabinol on Performance Monitoring in Healthy Volunteers." *Frontiers in Behavioral Neuroscience,* 5, Article 59, 1–11, 2011 **(50108)**

STARK, M.M., K. ENGLEHART, B.F. SEXTON, R. TUNBRIDGE, AND P. JACKSON. "Use of a Pupillometer to Assess Change in Pupillary Size Post-Cannabis." *Journal of Clinical Forensic Medicine*, 10: 9–11, 2003 **(50602)**

STEFANIS, N.C., M. DRAGOVIC, B.D. POWER, A. JABLENSKY, D. CASTLE, AND V.A. MORGAN. "Age at Initiation of Cannabis Use Predicts Age at Onset of Psychosis: The 7- to 8-Year Trend." *Schizophrenia Bulletin*, 39: 251–54, 2013 **(61413)**

STEPHANSON, N., M. JOSEFSSON, R. KRONSTRAND, AND O. BECK. "Accurate Identification and Quantification of 11 nor-delta 9 tetrahydrocannabinol-9-carboxylic Acid in Urine Drug Testing: Evaluation of a Direct High Efficiency Liquid Chromatographic-Mass Spectrometric Method." *Journal of Chromatography B,* 871: 101–8, 2008 **(40201)**

STEPHANSON, N., S. SANDQVIST, M.S. LAMBERT, O. BECK. "Method Validation and Application of a Liquid Chromatography-Tandem Mass Spectrometry Method for Drugs of Abuse Testing in Exhaled Breath." *Journal of Chromatography B,* 985: 189–96, 2015 **(40101)**

STOGNER, J.M., AND B.L. MILLER. "Assessing the Dangers of Dabbing: Mere Marijuana or Harmful New Trend?" *Pediatrics,* 136: 3 pp, 2015 **(60703)**

STRASHNY, A. "Marijuana Admissions to Substance Abuse Treatment Aged 18 to 30: Early vs. Adult Initiation." *Substance Abuse and Mental Health Services Administration, The CBHSQ Report*, August 13, 2013, 7 pp **(60510)**

STROUGO, A., L. ZUURMAN, C. ROY, J.L. PINQUIER, J.M.A. VAN GERVEN, A.F. COHEN, AND R.C. SCHOEMAKER. "Modelling of the Concentration-Effect Relationship of THC on Central Nervous System Parameters and Heart Rate–Insight into its Mechanisms of Action and a Tool for Clinical Research and Development of Cannabinoids." *Journal of Psychopharmacology*, 22: 717–26, 2008 **(10204)**

SULLIVAN, N., S. ELZINGA, AND J.C. RABER. "Determination of Pesticide Residues in Cannabis Smoke." *Journal of Toxicology,* 6 pp, 2013 **(80110)**

SULLIVAN, S. "Cannabinoid Hyperemesis." *Canadian Journal of Gastroenterology*, 24: 284–85, 2010 **(60308)**

SUN, S., AND A.E. ZIMMERMANN. "Cannabinoid Hyperemesis Syndrome." *Hospital Pharmacy* 48: 650–55, 2013 **(60309)**

SUN, X., C.S. XU, N. CHADA, A. CHEN, AND J. LIU. "Marijuana for Glaucoma: A Recipe for Treatment or Disaster?" *Yale Journal of Biology and Medicine*, 88: 265–69, 2015 **(61111)**

SWIFT, W., A. WONG, K.M. LI, J.C. ARNOLD, AND I.S. MCGREGOR. "Analysis of Cannabis Seizures in NSW, Australia: Cannabis Potency and Cannabinoid Profile." *PLOS ONE,* 8: 9 pp, July 2013 **(80112)**

T

TALPINS, S.K., E. HOLMES, T. KELLEY-BAKER, H.C. WALLS, AND T. KIMBAL. "Breath Testing for Cannabis. An Emerging Tool with Great Potential for Law Enforcement." *Between the Lines*, 25: 1–3, 2017 **(40102)**

TAYLOR D.R., D.M. FERGUSSON, B.J. MILNE, L.J. HORWOOD, T.E. MOFFITT, M.R. SEARS, AND R. POULTON. "A Longitudinal Study of the Effects of Tobacco and Cannabis Exposure on Lung Function in Young Adults." *Addiction*, 97: 1055–61, 2002 **(61603)**

TAYLOR, M., R. LEES, G. HENDERSON, A. LINGFORD-HUGHES, J. MACLEOD, J. SULLIVAN, AND M. HICKMAN. "Comparison of Cannabinoids in Hair with Self-Reported Cannabis Consumption in Heavy, Light and Non-Cannabis Users." *Drug and Alcohol Review*, 36: 220–26, 2017 **(40306)**

THEUNISSEN, E.L., P. HECKMAN, E.B. DE SOUSA FERNANDES PERNA, K.P.C. KUYPERS, A. SAMBETH, A. BLOKLAND, J. PRICKAERTS, S.W. TOENNES, AND J.G. RAMAEKERS. "Rivastigmine but Not Vardenafil Reverses Cannabis-Induced Impairment of Verbal Memory in Healthy Humans." *Psychopharmacology*, 232: 343–53, 2015 **(61009)**

THEUNISSEN, E.L., G.F. KAUERT, S.W. TOENNES, M.R. MOELLER, A. SAMBETH, M.M. BLANCHARD, AND J.G. RAMAEKERS. "Neurophysiological Functioning of Occasional and Heavy Cannabis Users during THC Intoxication." *Psychopharmacology*, 220: 341–50, 2012 **(50120)**

THORSPECKEN, J., G. SKOPP, AND L. POTSCH. "In Vitro Contamination of Hair by Marijuana Smoke." *Clinical Chemistry*, 50: 596–602, 2004 **(40310)**

TOENNES, S.W., AND G.F. KAUERT. "Importance of Vacutainer Selection in Forensic Toxicological Analysis of Drugs of Abuse." *Journal of Analytical Toxicology*, 25: 339–43, 2001 **(20302)**

TOENNES, S.W., G.F. KAUERT, S. STEINMEYER, AND M.R. MOELLER. "Driving Under the Influence of Drugs–Evaluation of Analytical Data of Drugs in Oral Fluid, Serum, and Urine and Correlation with Impairment Symptoms." *Forensic Science International,* 152: 149–55, 2005 **(30308)**

TOENNES, S.W., J.G. RAMAEKERS, E.L. THEUNISSEN, M.R. MOELLER, AND G.F. KAUERT. "Comparisons of Cannabinoid Pharmacokinetic Properties in Occasional and Heavy Users Smoking a Marijuana or Placebo Joint." *Journal of Analytical Toxicology,* 32: 470–77, 2008 **(10408)**

TOENNES, S.W., K. SCHNEIDER. C. WUNDER, G.F. KAUERT, M.R. MOELLER, E.L. THEUNISSEN, AND J.G. RAMAEKERS. "Influence of Ethanol on the Pharmacological Properties on Delta-9 Tetrahydrocannabinol in Oral Fluid." *Journal of Analytical Toxicology,* 37: 152–58, 2013 **(30602)**

TROJAK, B., S. LECLERQ, V. MEILLE, C. KHOUMRI, J-C. CHAUVET-GELINIER, M. GIROUD, B. BONIN, AND A. GISSELMANN. "Stroke with Neuropsychiatric Sequelae after Cannabis Use in Man: A Case Report." *Journal of Medical Case Reports,* 5: 264, 4 pp, 2011 **(60416)**

TURFUS, S.C., M. CHU, D. GEROSTAMOULOS, AND O. DRUMMER. "An Assessment of the Stability of MDMA, Methamphetamine and THC in Oral Fluid." *Australian Journal of Forensic Sciences,* 46: 397–410, 2014 **(30408)**

TYNDALL, J.A., R. GERONA, G. DE PORTU, J. TRECKI, M-C. ELIE, J. LUCAS, J. SLISH, K. RAND, L. BAZYDLO, M. HOLDER, M.F. RYAN, P. MYERS, N. IOVINE, M. PLOURDE, E. WEEKS, J.R. HANLEY, G. ENDRES, D. ST. GERMAINE, P.J. DOBROWOLSKI, AND M. SCHWARTZ. "An Outbreak of Acute Delirium from Exposure to the Synthetic Cannabinoid AB-CHMINACA." *Clinical Toxicology,* 53: 950–56, 2015 **(80408)**

U

URFER, S., J. MORTON, V. BEALL, J. FELDMANN, AND J. GUNESCH. "Analysis of delta-9 Tetrahydrocannabinol Driving under the Influence of Drugs Cases in Colorado from January 2011 to February 2014." *Journal of Analytical Toxicology,* 38: 575–81, 2014 **(50801)**

USTUNDAG, M.F., E.O. IBIS, A. YUCEL, AND H. OZCAN. "Synthetic Cannabis-Induced Mania." *Case Reports in Psychiatry,* 3 pp, 2015 **(80426)**

V

VALLERSNES, O.M., A.M. DINES, D.M. WOOD, C. YATES, F. HEYERDAHL, K.E. HOVDA, I. GIRAUDON, AND EURO-DEN RESEARCH GROUP. "Psychosis

Associated with Acute Recreational Drug Toxicity: A European Case Series." *BMC Psychiatry*, 16: 293 (8 pp), 2016 **(61410)**

VAN DER LINDEN, T., P. SILVERANS, AND A.G. VERSTRAETE. "Comparison between Self-Report of Cannabis Use and Toxicological Detection of THC/THCCOOH in Blood and THC in Oral Fluid in Drivers in a Roadside Survey." *Drug Testing and Analysis*, 6: 137–42, 2014 **(30307)**

VAN DER POL, P., N. LIEBREGTS, T. BRUNT, J. VAN AMSTERDAM., R. DE GRAFF, D.J. KORF, W. VAN DEN BRINK, AND M. VAN LAAR. "Cross-Sectional and Prospective Relation of Cannabis Potency, Dosing and Smoking Behavior with Cannabis Dependence: An Ecological Study." *Addiction*, 9 pp, 2014 **(60514)**

VAN DER POL, P., N. LIEBREGTS, R. DE GRAAF., D.J. KORF, W. VAN DEN BRINK, AND M. VAN LAAR. "Predicting the Transition from Frequent Cannabis Use to Cannabis Dependence: A Three-Year Prospective Study." *Drug and Alcohol Dependence*, 133: 352–59, 2013 **(60509)**

VANDREY, B., A.J. BUDNEY, J.R. HUGHES, AND A. LIGUORI. "A within Subject Comparison of Withdrawal Symptoms during Abstinence from Cannabis, Tobacco and Both Substances." *Drug and Alcohol Dependence*, 92: 48–54, 2008 **(62104)**

VANDREY, R., K.E. DUNN, J.A. FRY, AND E.R. GIRLING. "A Survey Study to Characterize Use of Spice Products (Synthetic Cannabinoids)." *Drug and Alcohol Dependence*, 120: 238–41, 2012 **(80422)**

VANDREY, R., H.E.S. HERMANN, J.M. MITCHELL, G.E. BIGELOW, R. FLEGEL, C. LODICO, AND E.J. CONE. "Pharmacokinetic Profile of Oral Cannabis in Humans: Blood and Oral Fluid Disposition and Relation to Pharmacodynamic Outcomes." *Journal of Analytical Toxicology*, 41: 83–99, 2017 **(10406)**

VANDREY, R., A. UMBRICHT, AND E.C. STRAIN. "Increased Blood Pressure Following Abrupt Cessation of Daily Cannabis Use." *Journal of Addiction Medicine*. 5: 16–20, 2011 **(62105)**

VELDSTRA, J.L., W.M. BOSKER, D. DE WAARD, J.G. RAMAEKERS, AND K.A. BROOKHUIS. "Comparing Treatment Effects of Oral THC on Simulated and On-the-Road Driving Performance: Testing the Validity of Driving Simulator Research." *Psychopharmacology*, 232: 2911–19, 2015 **(50403)**

VELIZ, P.T., C.J. BOYD, AND S.E. MCCABE. "Competitive Sport Involvement and Substance Use among Adolescents: A Nationwide Study." *Substance Use and Misuse*, 50: 156–65, 2015 **(61807)**

VIDOT, D.C., G. PRADO, N. DE LA CRUZ-MONOZ, C. SPADOLA, M. CUESTA, AND S.E. MESSIAH. "Post-Operative Marijuana Use and Disordered Eating Among Bariatric Surgery Patients." *Surgery for Obesity and Related Diseases*, 12: 171–78, 2016 **(61107)**

VINDENES, V., D.H. STRAND, L. KRISTOFFERSEN, F. BOIX, AND J. MORLAND. "Has the Intake of THC by Cannabis Users Changed Over the Last Decade? Evidence of Increased Exposure by Analysis of Blood THC Concentrations in Impaired Drivers." *Forensic Science International*, 226: 197–201, 2013 **(50531)**

VOAS, R.B., J.H. LACEY, K. JONES, M. SCHERER, AND R. COMPTON. "Drinking Drivers and Drug Use on Weekend Nights in the United States." *Drug and Alcohol Dependence*, 130: 215–21, 2013 **(50705)**

VOGEL, I., P.M. VAN DE LOOIJ-JANSEN, C.L. MIELOO, A. BURDORF, AND F. DE WAART. "Risky Music Listening Behaviors and Associated Health Risk Behaviors." *Pediatrics*, 129: 1097–103, 2012 **(61112)**

VOSS, A., K. WITT, T. KASCHOWITZ, W. POITZ, A. EBERT, P. ROSER, AND K-J. BAR. "Detecting Cannabis Use on the Human Skin Surface via an Electronic Nose System." *Sensors*, 14: 13256–72, 2014 **(40403)**

W

WADSWORTH, E.J.K., S.C. MOSS, S.A. SIMPSON, AND A.P. SMITH. "A Community Based Investigation of the Association between Cannabis Use, Injuries and Accidents." *Journal of Psychopharmacology*, 20: 5–13, 2006 **(62005)**

WALSH, G.W., AND R.E. MANN. "On the High Road: Driving Under the Influence of Cannabis in Ontario." *Canadian Journal of Public Health*, 90: 260–63, 1999 **(50528)**

WALSH J.M., R. FLEGEL, R. ATKINS, L.A. CANGIANELLI, C. COOPER, C. WELSH, AND T.J. KERNS. "Drug and Alcohol Use Among Drivers Admitted to a Level-1 Trauma Center." *Accident Analysis and Prevention*, 37: 894–901, 2005 **(61301)**

WANG, G.S., G. ROOSEVELT, M-C. LE LAIT, E.M. MARTINEZ, B. BUCHER-BARTELSOM, A.C. BRONSTEIN, AND K. HEARD. "Association of Unintentional Pediatric Exposures with Decriminalization of Marijuana in the United States." *Annals of Emergency Medicine*, 63: 1450–55, 2014 **(60617)**

WARE, M.A., AND E. ST ARNAUD-TREMPE. "The Abuse Potential of the Synthetic Cannabinoid Nabilone." *Addiction*, 105: 494–503, 2010 **(80210)**

WARNER, M.L., I. ALFORD, D.M. LAWRENCE, A.C. KOHL, S.J. WILLIAMS, AND D.T. YEATMAN. "Comparative Analysis of Freshly Harvested Cannabis Plant Weight and Dried Cannabis Plant Weight." *Forensic Chemistry,* 3: 52–57, 2017 **(80109)**

WARNER, T.D., D. ROUSSOS-ROSS, AND M. BEHNKE. "It's Not Your Mother's Marijuana: Effects on Maternal-Fetal Health and the Developing Child." *Clinical Perinatology*, 41: 877–94, 2014 **(40502)**

WEI, B., L. WANG, AND B.C. BLOUNT. "Analysis of Cannabinoids and Their Metabolites in Human Urine." *Analytical Chemistry,* 87: 10183–87, 2015 **(40202)**

WEINSTEIN, A., O. BRICKNER, H. LERMAN, M. GREEMLAND, M. BLOCH, H. LESTER, R. CHISIN, Y. SARNE, R. MECHOULAM, R. BAR-HAMBURGER, N. FREEDMAN, AND E. EVEN-SAPIR. "A Study Investigating the Acute Dose-Response Effects of 13 mg and 17 mg delta 9-Tetrahydrocannabinol on Cognitive-Motor Skills, Subjective and Autonomic Measures in Regular Users of Marijuana." *Journal of Psychopharmacology*, 22: 441–51, 2008 **(50109)**

WESTIN A.A., G. MJONES, O. BUCHARDT, O.M. FUSKEVAG, AND L. SLORDAL. "Can Physical Exercise or Food Deprivation Cause Release of Fat-Stored Cannabinoids?" *Basic and Clinical Pharmacology and Toxicology*, 115: 467–71, 2014 **(10205)**

WESTIN, A.A., M.A. HUESTIS, K. AARSTAD, AND O. SPIGSET, "Urinary Excretion of 11-Nor-9-Carboxy-delta 9-Tetrahydrocannabinol in a Pregnant Woman Following Heavy Chronic Cannabis Use." *Journal of Analytical Toxicology*, 33: 610–14, 2009 **(10206)**

WETTLAUFER, A., R.O. FLORICA, M. ASBRIDGE, D. BEIRNESS, J. BRUBACHER, R. CALLAGHAN, B. FISCHER, G. GMEL, S. IMTIAZ, R.E. MANN, A. MCKIERNAN, AND J. REHM. "Estimating the Harms and Costs of Cannabis-Attributable Collision in the Canadian Provinces." *Drug and Alcohol Dependence*, 173: 185–90, 2017 **(50529)**

WHITEHILL, J.M., F.P. RIVARA, AND M.A. MORENO. "Marihuana-Using Drivers, Alcohol-Using Drivers and Their Passengers: Prevalence and Risk Factors among Underage College Students." *Journal of the American Medical Association Pediatrics,* 168: 618–24, 2014 **(50530)**

WIEBELHAUS, N., D. HAMBLIN, N.M. KREITALS, AND J.R. ALMIRALL. "Differentiation of Marijuana Headspace Volatiles from Other Plants and Hemp Products Using Capillary Micro-Extraction of Volatiles (CMV)

Coupled to Gas-Chromatography-Mass Spectrometry (GC-MS)." *Forensic Chemistry*, 2: 1–8, 2016 **(80101)**

WILD, K., AND H. WILSON. "Cannabinoid Hyperemesis." *British Medical Journal Case Reports*, 3 pp, 2010 **(60315)**

WILEY, J.L., J.A. MARUSICH, J.W. HUFFMAN, R.L. BAISTER, AND B.F. THOMAS. "Hijacking of Basic Research: The Case of Synthetic Cannabinoids." *Methods Rep RTI Press*, November 2011, 11 pp **(80401)**

WILKINSON, S.T., R. RADHAKRISHNAN, AND D.C. D'SOUZA, "Impact of Cannabis Use on the Development of Psychotic Disorders." *Current Addiction Reports*, 1: 115–28, 2015 **(61412)**

WILLE, S.M.R., E. RAES, P. LILLSUNDE, T. GUNNAR, M. LALOUP, N. SAMYN., A.S. CHRISTOPHERSEN, M.R. MOELLER, K.P. HAMMER, AND A.G. VERSTRAETE. "Relationship Between Oral Fluid and Blood Concentrations of Drugs of Abuse in Drivers Suspected of Driving Under the Influence of Drugs." *Therapeutic Drug Monitor*, 31: 511–19, 2009 **(30306)**

WILLIAMSON, S., L. JACKSON, C. SKEOCH, G. AZZIM, AND R. ANDERSON. "Determination of the Prevalence of Drug Misuse by Meconium Analysis." *Archive of Diseases in Childhood. Fetal and Neonatal Edition*, 91: F291–F292, 2006 **(40504)**

WILSON F.A., J.P. STIMPSON, AND J.A. PAGAN. "Fatal Crashes from Drivers Testing Positive for Drugs in the US, 1993–2010." *Public Health Reports*, 129: 342–50, 2014 **(50707)**

WINTON-BROWN, T.T., P. ALLEN, S. BHATTACHARRYA, S.J. BORGWARDT, P. FUSAR-POLI, J.A. CRIPPA, M.L. SEAL, R. MARTIN-SANTOS, D. FLYTCHE, A.W. ZUARDI, Z. ATAKAN, AND P.K. MCGUIRE. "Modulation of Auditory and Visual Processing by Delta-9-Tetrahydrocannabinol and Cannabidiol: An fMRI Study." *Neuropsychopharmacology*, 36: 1340–48, 2011 **(80314)**

WOLFF, V., V. LAUER., O. ROUYER, F. SELLAL., N. MEYER, J.S. RAUL, C. SABOURDY, F. BOUJAN., C. JAHN, R. BEAUJEUX, AND C. MARESCAUX. "Cannabis Use, Ischemic Stroke, and Multifocal Intracranial Vasoconstriction. A Prospective Study in 48 Consecutive Young Patients." *Stroke*, 42: 1778–80, 2011 **(60418)**

WONG, A., M.E. MONTEBELLO, M.M. NORBERG, K. ROONEY, N. LINTZERIS, R. BRUNO, J. BOOTH, J.C. ARNOLD, AND I.S. MCGREGOR. "Exercise Increases Plasma THC Concentrations in Regular Cannabis Users." *Drug and Alcohol Dependence*, 133: 763–67, 2013 **(10207)**

WONG, K., J.E. BRADY, AND G. LI. "Establishing Legal Limits for Driving Under the Influence of Marijuana." *Injury Epidemiology*, 1: 26, 2014 **(50709)**

WOODALL, K.L., B.L.C. CHOW, A. LAUWERS, AND D. CASS. "Toxicological Findings in Fatal Motor Vehicle Collisions in Ontario, Canada." *Journal of Forensic Sciences*, 60: 669–74, 2015 **(50532)**

WOODHOUSE, E.J. "Confirmation of the Presence of 11-Hydroxy delta-9-Tetrahydrocannabinol in the Urine of Marijuana Smokers." *American Journal of Public Health,* 62: 1394–96, 1972 **(10407)**

WOODRUFF, S.I., C.T. MCCABE, M. HOHMAN, J.D. CLAPP, A.M. SHILLINGTON, K. EISENBERG, C.B. SISE, E.M. CASTILLO, T.C. CHAN, AND M.J. SISE. "Characteristics of Cannabis-Only and Other Drug Users Who Visit the Emergency Department." *Cannabis and Cannabinoid Research,* 1.1: 149–53, 2016 **(60618)**

WOOLARD, R., J. BAIRD, M.J. MELLO, C. LEE, M. HARRINGTON, T. NIRENBERG, B. BECKER, L. STEIN, AND R. LONGABAUGH. "Injuries, Negative Consequences and Risk Behaviors among Both Injured and Uninjured Emergency Patients Who Report Using Alcohol and Marijuana." *Journal of Emergencies, Trauma and Shock*, 2: 23–28, 2009 **(62004)**

WRIGHT, N.E., D. SCERPELLA, AND K.M. LISDAHL. "Marijuana Use Is Associated with Behavioral Approach and Depressive Symptoms in Adolescents and Emerging Adults." *PLOS ONE*, 11: 17 pp, 2016 **(61913)**

Y

YACOUBIAN JR., G.S., AND E.J. CONE. "A Comparison between the Intercept Oral Fluid Collection Device and Urinalysis among Baltimore City Probationers." *Journal of Criminal Justice*, 34: 413–24, 2006 **(30301)**

YESAVAGE, J.A., V.O. LEIRER, M. DENARI, AND L.E. HOLLISTER. "Carry-Over Effects of Marijuana Intoxication on Aircraft Pilot Performance: A Preliminary Report." *American Journal of Psychiatry*, 142: 1325–29, 1985 **(60801)**

YONKERS, K.A., H.B. HOWELL, N. GOTMAN, AND B.J. ROUNSAVILLE. "Self-Report of Illicit Substance Use Versus Urine Toxicology Results from at-risk Pregnant Women." *Journal of Substance Abuse*, 16: 372–89, 2011 **(40219)**

YURTDAS, M., AND M.K. AYDIN. "Acute Myocardial Infarction in a Young Man; Fatal Blow of the Marijuana: A Case Report." *Korean Circulation Journal*, 5 pp, 2012 **(60422)**

Z

ZACHARIAH, S.B. "Stroke after Heavy Marijuana Smoking." *Stroke*, 22: 406–9, 1991 **(60402)**

ZAKI, N.N., AND M.A. IBRAHEIM "Effect of Alcohol and Cannabis Sativa Consumption on Handwriting." *Neurobehavioral Toxicology and Teratology*, 5: 225–27, 1983 **(61113)**

ZARIFFI, C., AND S. VYAS. "Spice-y Kidney Failure: A Case Report and Systematic Review of Acute Kidney Injury Attributable to the Use of Synthetic Cannabis." *The Permanente Journal*, 21: 16–160, 2017 **(80433)**

ZHANG, C., J.S. BROOK, C.G. LEUKEFELD, AND D.W. BROOK. "Trajectories of Marijuana Use from Adolescence to Adulthood as Predictors of Unemployment Status in the Early Forties." *American Journal of Addictions*, 25: 203–9, 2016 **(60120)**

ZIMMERMAN, E.G., E.P. YEAGER, J.R. SOARES, L.E. HOLLISTER, AND V.C. REEVE. "Measurement of delta-9-Tetrahydrocannabinol (THC) in Whole Blood Samples from Impaired Motorists." *Journal of Forensic Sciences*, 28: 957–62, 1983 **(20101)**

ZVOLENSKY, M.J., J.R. COUGLE, K.A. JOHNSON, M.O. BONN-MILLER, AND A. BERNSTEIN. "Marijuana Use and Panic Psychopathology among a Representative Sample of Adults." *Experimental and Clinical Psychopharmacology*, 18: 129–34, 2010 **(61411)**

ZWENGER, S.R. "Bogarting that Joint Might Decrease Oral HPV among Cannabis Users." *Current Oncology*, 16: 5–7, 2009 **(61614)**

Author Index

Reference number of first author is bold

Publication Year Index

Subject Index

(unless otherwise stated, the cannabinoid indexed is tetrahydrocannabinol (THC))

About the Author

James G. Wigmore worked as a forensic toxicologist for over twenty-nine years at one of the foremost forensic laboratories in North America — the Centre of Forensic Sciences in Toronto, Ontario. He has testified in over 700 criminal cases throughout Canada and in numerous personal injury civil cases and coroner's inquests. He has published over seventy scientific articles in forensic toxicology, which have been cited by the Supreme Court of Canada (*R v St Onge-Lamoreux*, 2012) and the High Court in Cape Town, South Africa (*S vs Hendricks*, 2013). In 2005, he was awarded the prestigious Derome Award from the Canadian Society of Forensic Science in recognition of outstanding contributions in the field of forensic sciences. From 2004 to 2012, he taught at the Robert F. Borkenstein Course at Indiana University in Bloomington. *Wigmore on Cannabis* is his third book published with Irwin Law.

Printed and bound by CPI Group (UK) Ltd, Croydon, CR0 4YY

17/09/2026

14964160-0001